The
Communist Experience
in the Twentieth Century

A Global History through Sources

GLENNYS YOUNG

New York   Oxford

OXFORD UNIVERSITY PRESS

Oxford University Press, Inc., publishes works that further Oxford University's
objective of excellence in research, scholarship, and education.

Oxford   New York
Auckland   Cape Town   Dar es Salaam   Hong Kong   Karachi
Kuala Lumpur   Madrid   Melbourne   Mexico City   Nairobi
New Delhi   Shanghai   Taipei   Toronto

With offices in
Argentina   Austria   Brazil   Chile   Czech Republic   France   Greece
Guatemala   Hungary   Italy   Japan   Poland   Portugal   Singapore
South Korea   Switzerland   Thailand   Turkey   Ukraine   Vietnam

For titles covered by Section 112 of the US Higher Education
Opportunity Act, please visit www.oup.com/us/he for the latest
information about pricing and alternate formats.

Published by Oxford University Press, Inc.
198 Madison Avenue, New York, New York 10016
http://www.oup.com

Library of Congress Cataloging-in-Publication Data
Young, Glennys.
The communist experience in the twentieth century : a global history through sources / Glennys Young.
    p. cm.
ISBN 978-0-19-536690-7
1. Communism—History—20th century. I. Title.
HX40.Y59 2011
335.4309'04—dc22   2011016414

Printing number: 9 8 7 6 5 4 3 2 1

Printed in the United States of America
on acid-free paper

The
Communist Experience
in the Twentieth Century

To the memory of
Reggie Zelnik (1936–2004),
and for Elaine Zelnik

CONTENTS

————★————

PREFACE

———————★———————

How did people from many walks of life relate to Communist ideology, programs, and political tactics? How did they subjectively experience, resist, and, in some cases, help to refashion the Communist polities and societies in which they lived, or the Communist political movements to which they belonged? These were questions that were very much on my mind as I prepared to teach, for the first time, a lecture course, the "History of Communism" at the University of Washington early in 2007. These were questions that I wanted my students to be able to explore, discuss, and debate. But as I looked for readings for the course, I ran into a problem.

The only anthology of primary documents concerning the history of communism throughout the world incorporated only the voices of elite political leaders. It was an excellent anthology of Communist Party programs, decrees, and policy statements of Communist regimes, and documents from the organizations of international Communism (Comintern and Cominform). To allow students to hear other voices, I had to piece together a very inadequate and limited selection of primary documents.

Amazingly enough, nearly twenty years after the fall of the Berlin Wall, there was still no collection of primary documents (diaries, letters, autobiographies, memoirs) produced by citizens living in Communist polities or involved in Communist movements around the globe—the very kinds of documents that had been unearthed and published with the fall of Communism. Existing collections of documents that did include such voices have tended to be restricted in their scope, usually focusing on a very specific group (for example, diaries written in the Stalin era, or interviews with the "Sputnik Generation") within only *one* Communist polity. I also found that the few that did treat more than one case had restricted themes (such as political violence and repression). As a result, Communism as a way of life—a way of life that necessitated difficult and sometimes painful choices about how to live, what kind of person to be, and how to present oneself to the state, as well as to coworkers, friends, and family—had remained an abstraction, a vessel to be filled.

This volume—*The Communist Experience*—is designed to help students, their instructors, and general readers get beyond the abstractions and stereotypes of Communism as a way of life. It is meant to provide an inside, and intimate, look at the complexity of what it meant to be—sometimes simultaneously so—victim, perpetrator, enthusiast, agent, resister, reshaper, and tolerator of an ideological project and way of life that was (and, for some, still is) both humanity's darkest nightmare and its brightest hope.

And so my work on *The Communist Experience* began. A book project that began in a seemingly accidental way—as I responded in an *ad hoc* way to the request to teach a new course—had become, to my surprise, something that consumed my intellectual passion.

But even if there was something serendipitous about how I developed the project, the more I worked on it, the more it made sense, both in the context of my own life and in the history of the (largely) post-Communist present. I probably grew up with more of an awareness of the Cold War, and the existence of Communist regimes, than the average person born in the late 1950s or early 1960s. One reason derived from where I grew up—in rural Pennsylvania, in a town (Nazareth) founded by Protestant missionaries—the Moravians, in 1740. Growing up in rural Pennsylvania might seem to reduce the odds of developing an awareness of, and interest in, Communism. But this was not just anywhere in rural Pennsylvania, or rural America, for that matter. In fact, Nazareth had been founded as a religious *commune* (by some of my ancestors)—and remained so well into the nineteenth century. Growing up there, I was puzzled by the relationship between Nazareth as a "commune" and the Communist "enemy" that we were fighting in the Cold War. Why was one celebrated (at least locally), and the other vilified? And what was life like under the Communism that was so vilified? What were people like?

I made my first trip "behind the Iron Curtain," to invoke the rhetoric of the Cold War, in August 1983. After completing a summer language course at a Goethe Institute in southern Germany, in the picturesque town of Schwäbisch Hall, I took the train with a classmate through East Germany to Berlin. Touring East Berlin by bus with other people from the United States and Western Europe, I was introduced, if only briefly, to elements of Communist everyday life: to unremitting drabness, Communist slogans on the tops of buildings, to Communist rituals and monuments, and the black market (when I tried to buy a postcard at a lunch stop). But the most memorable part of the trip was the train ride itself. Over most of the day, I listened to a woman (probably in her sixties) from West Germany, whose husband was an executive for Mercedes-Benz in Stuttgart, and a woman from East Berlin, a pensioner of seemingly very modest means who was returning from visiting relatives, compare their lives in the "other" Germany. In subsequent trips to West Germany during the 1980s, as I took train trips that brought me within view of the highly fortified border, I often thought about their conversation and its comparisons.

Less than three years after I traveled through East Germany to Berlin with these German women, I made my first trip to the Soviet Union for a summer language program in Leningrad. That stay—as well as a much longer one over the academic year 1987–88 on an official government exchange between the United States and the USSR—allowed me to meet many Soviet citizens, and get a sense of what Communism meant to them. But it also gave me the chance to compare the choices *they* made—about how to live, how to deal with the "system," how many risks to take, how to present themselves—to those that *I* had to make about the same issues.

Retrospectively, all of these trips were as much about exploring the subjective experience of Communism in comparative perspective—on a day-to-day, first-hand basis—as they were about tourism and language practice (in the case of East Germany) or scholarly research (in the case of the Soviet Union). And this was certainly not just true for me. It was also the case, I would suggest, for the considerable number of other scholars and visitors from the "West" who ventured behind the "Iron Curtain" during the Cold War, especially in the 1980s, as it became easier for those from the "West" to travel to, and live in, East Germany, other countries of the Warsaw Pact, the USSR, and other Communist societies around the world. As borders became, even if in fits and starts, more porous, so too did the boundary between who was, and who was not, a person living in a Communist polity.

Since the collapse of Communist regimes that began in 1989, such questions of how people subjectively experienced and shaped Communism—as well as the question of the choices they made about who they were—have not lost their political significance. In fact, quite the contrary is the case. For one thing, the opening of many formerly closed Communist archives has given scholars the opportunity to research the political significance that the construction of the self had across Communist regimes, polities, and movements. A good many of the documents in this book—previously unavailable diaries and letters, for example—are the product of this archival revolution, so to speak.

But there is another dimension of political significance that is no less important. With the collapse of Communism and the de-legitimization of Communism as a way of life, with the revelations of violence, repression, surveillance, deceit, and environmental degradation, has come the question of who was responsible and why. As scholars, truth commissions, and contemporaries have wrestled with these questions, not only Communism's leaders but also its peoples have not been able to hide. They have not been able to evade issues of guilt, responsibility, and complicity. And because of this, how one now portrays who one was under Communism has great political significance. Hence, the memoirs and autobiographies that have been born of the ashes of Communism are almost always texts in which individuals seek to portray themselves in certain ways and not others, so as to avoid the stigma of being complicit in Communism's crimes, and so as to take credit for having played a role in its demise. Readers of the documents in this book will find examples of this latter type of politicization of the self in the post-Communist present. They should also keep in mind that because of this politicization, we can only see the people who lived within Communist polities and participated in Communist movements through a glass darkly, so to speak.

ACKNOWLEDGMENTS

By their very nature, all scholarly books are collective enterprises even though they have a single author. As I have worked on this book, I have been especially struck by my debts to others, and by their generosity.

Without the help of other scholars, I would not have been able to include some of the documents in this book. I am especially grateful to Carlos Aguirre, who took time away from his own research in Lima to obtain documents relating to Peru's Shining Path (Sendero Luminoso) at the Centro de Información para la Memoria Colectiva y los Derechos Humanos in Lima, Peru. Elizabeth McGuire was also very generous in sharing materials from her own research. Other scholars who provided documents from their own research are Scott Brown, Igal Halfin, Steven Harris, Dan Healey, Ali Igmen, Dalia Leinarte, and Mary Neuburger. Those who gave advice on selecting documents are Adeeb Khalid, David Bachman, Madeleine Yue Dong, Christoph Giebel, Dan Healey, Clark Sorensen, Padraic Kenney, Christina Manetti, Guntis Schmidchens, Amanda Swain, Catherine Wanner, and Adam Warren.

Thanks to funds provided by the Hanauer and Keller Funds of the University of Washington's Department of History, I was able to employ translators of documents from Chinese (Yuting Li), Bulgarian (Peter Gruen), Croatian (Aleksandra Petrovic), Polish (Christina Manetti), and Slovak (Scott Brown). Lydia Gold and Jennifer Weiss of the History Department worked wonders with the paperwork involved. Mark Haslam solved computer problems galore. Other individuals with native or near-native language skills gave me the benefit of their counsel on my translations from French (Tip Ragan), German (Christoph Giebel, Sabine Lang, Wolfram Latsch, Uta Poiger, Dorothea Trottenberg, and Helma Young), Russian (Elena Campbell, Galya Diment, and Dorothea Trottenberg), and Spanish (Tony Geist, Maria Elena Garcia, Tony Lucero, Olga Novikova Monterde, Ileana Rodríguez-Silva, and Adam Warren). Jipar Duishembieva translated a document from Kyrgyz. Dan Healey translated the letter from Harry White to Stalin, and Elizabeth McGuire translated a document written by a Chinese student in the USSR. Mary R. O'Neil translated a document from Italian. Clark Sorensen translated a document from Korean. Those who read parts of the text and gave me invaluable suggestions for improvement or responded to my questions are David Bachman, Scott Brown, Galya Diment, Katarzyna Dziwirek, Madeleine Yue Dong, James Felak (who read an earlier draft with great care), Vsevolod Gakkel', Maria Elena Garcia, Kent Guy, Igal Halfin, Susan Hanley, Padraic Kenney, Richard Kirkendall, Wolfram Latsch, Tony Lucero, Peter Newman, Vjeran Pavlakovic, Uta Poiger, Scott Radnitz, Florian Schwarz, Lewis Siegelbaum, Clark Sorensen, Sarah Stein, Quintard Taylor, Gregor Thum, John Toews, Julie Van Pelt, Martha Walsh, Susan Whiting, and Kozo Yamamura. I would also like to thank my colleagues who evaluated the project at various stages of its development: Bradley Abrams, Columbia University; Maxim Kupovykh, University of Pennsylvania; Dennis Laumann, The University of Memphis; Irina Livezeanu, University of Pittsburgh; James Mark, University of Exeter; Maxim Matusevich, Seton Hall University; Alan McDougall, University of Guelph; Robert Strayer, California State University, Monterey Bay and Cabrillo College.

I am also indebted to those who helped me obtain photographs. Ali Igmen provided the photo of Sabira Kumushalieva that he took in Kyrgyzstan in 2002. Peter Newman excavated his slides from his trip to the Soviet Union (including Samarkand) in 1970, and converted them to digital form.

Thanks to the Harry M. Bridges Labor Studies Center at the University of Washington, directed by Jim Gregory, I had a research assistant at a crucial stage in the process. Lilia Putintsev could not have been more effective in bringing sources to my attention, corresponding with copyright holders, translating a document from French, and completing other essential tasks as well.

In a formal sense, I began working on this book in 2007. But it was brewing, so to speak, well before then. A senior fellowship from the Rutgers Center for Historical Analysis in 2000–2001 gave me the luxury of thinking broadly. The University of Washington's Simpson Center for the Humanities, directed by Kathleen Woodward, provided a quarter's release from teaching in the spring of 2009. My chairs—John Findlay (whose request that I teach the History of Communism in winter 2007 inadvertently led to the book), Kent Guy, and Anand Yang—supported my requests for research quarters.

For assistance in obtaining access to documents, I am grateful to librarians and archivists at the following institutions: the Bancroft Library at the University of California, Berkeley; the Bundesarchiv in Berlin; the Centro de Información para la Memoria Colectiva y los Derechos Humanos in Lima; the International Institute for Social History in Amsterdam; the Kansas City Public Library; Princeton University; the Library of Congress; the University of Miami; the New York Public Library; and the Tamiment Library at New York University. Closer to home, the University of Washington's interlibrary loan service was indispensable.

I am exceedingly fortunate to have worked with Oxford University Press on this project. Brian Wheel, my first editor, was keen on the book from the start, and acquired it. It has been a joy to work with Charles Cavaliere, my second editor. His enthusiasm and support helped me immeasurably in seeing the book to completion. Thanks also to Marianne Paul, Lauren Aylward and, early in the process, Danniel Schoonebeek, Laura Lancaster, as well as the rest of production team at the press.

Many friends cheered me on as I wrote this book, and I will not be able to mention all of them here, despite my gratitude to them. Among those whose interest in the history of Communism convinced me of the importance of this book were Tony Geist, Susan Glenn, Lisa Jackson-Schebetta, and Mark Jenkins, with whom I co-organized a film and lecture series when I wrote most of the text.

Always reminding me to keep at it were Edith Hipp, Doris Koehler, and Irene Reinish. Others whose support made a difference to me were Nancy Bristow, Karen Eikenberry, Dick Frace, Cathy Kudlick, Tip Ragan, Bill Rosenberg, Elaine Zelnik, Pam Zelnik, my family in Pennsylvania, Kozo Yamamura, the late Nick Z. Young, and the late Nadezhda K. Gilman. Susan Hanley was the consummate cheerleader. She somehow always knew when to urge me to push on and when to tell me to take a break. May all authors be so blessed.

While I was going over the proofs of this book, another great teacher and wonderful human being, Nicholas V. Riasanovsky, left us. His influence, too, can be seen, I hope, on these pages.

I am extraordinarily grateful to Meri Gilman, who provided constant support on a daily basis as I struggled with the book's challenges. My debt to her is beyond words. I hope that the opportunity to travel to interesting research venues made up, even if partially, for my preoccupation with the book over several years.

Not at all needless to say, I am responsible for all the book's errors and shortcomings. Please do not hesitate to bring them to my attention by writing to me at glennys@uw.edu, or Box 353650, Henry M. Jackson School of International Studies, University of Washington, Seattle, WA 98195.

NOTE ON TRANSLITERATION

As I have transliterated Russian words, I have, in the main, used the Library of Congress transliteration system. Exceptions are names and words that tend to be used in English with a different spelling. I have, for the most part, used the *pinyin* system of transliteration for Chinese. The exceptions are names of major historical figures that are usually rendered either according to the Wade–Giles or an alternative system of transliteration. Thus, for example, I have used Chiang Kai-shek rather than the pinyin form, Jiang Jieshi. Korean words have been rendered in the McCune–Reischauer transcription system.

INTRODUCTION

———★———

The twentieth century was the Communist century. It is impossible to understand our world today without basic knowledge of the history of Communism. This is because its history and the history of the world have been deeply intertwined—not only in the twentieth century, but, in fact, from the nineteenth through the twenty-first centuries. The Bolshevik revolution in 1917 was but the first of many attempts to build a polity and society based on Communist doctrine. No part of the world was untouched, either by the quest to install a Communist regime or by the reality of such a regime. For some, Communism was the scourge of humanity. For others it was humanity's greatest hope. For some, the nature and legacy of Communism can be defined by its misguided ideology, its authoritarian regimes, and the human casualties and suffering it necessarily caused. For others, Communism was not only a noble ideal; it generated major achievements. Even if Communist ideology never produced the truly just and equal society, Communist regimes had their triumphs. They included modernization, literacy, opportunity for personal advancement, and a society in which values such as sociability and the welfare of the community were important.

Whatever position one takes on these issues, one central question remains: How did people in Communist polities around the world subjectively experience, resist, and in some cases help to refashion the polities and societies in which they lived? This book gives readers an unprecedented chance to grapple with this question. It does so by providing the first collection of primary documents (diaries, letters, autobiographies, memoirs) produced by citizens living in Communist polities or involved in Communist movements around the globe. It seeks to offer its readers an inside, and intimate, look at what it meant to live under Communism. It seeks to explore the choices that people made about their lives and who they were.

The organizing concept of this book—one that readers will find in some chapter titles and (explicitly or implicitly) in introductory essays—is the Communist "subject."[1] This requires some comment. The Communist "subject" is indeed an apt concept for capturing the complexity of people's engagement with the Communist project in very different societies and cultures. It is apt for evoking their reaction to, and transformation of, the ideas and political tactics that Communism entailed. On the one hand, "subject," in its traditional usage, calls to mind the acted-upon subordinate of a political regime. What is being emphasized here, in other words, is the repressive power of a political regime—the power to control people's lives. But "subject" can also have a different meaning. In cultural studies—a field that has recently influenced the study of Communism and post-Communism—"subject" evokes something else. It has come to be associated with the individual's active construction of the self. This process, in which individuals themselves make choices about who they are and want to become, has occurred in multiple and changing contexts, especially in dialogue with Communist ideology and with political practices. Those political practices, as we will see later in this introduction as well as in the chapters of this book, may or may not be specific to Communism (for example, surveillance, writing autobiographies, petitioning the state, etc.).

Communist ideology almost automatically evokes the specter of a revolutionary transformation of *society*, a transformation in which the private property, socioeconomic inequality, and intrinsic oppression of capitalism disappear in the name of the proletariat's salvation of humanity. But Communist ideology also invokes a transformation of the *self*. Karl Marx (1818–1883), the great synthesizer of intellectual currents that would comprise modern Communist ideology, offered a historically lawful—and, in his view, scientific—view of human history and humanity's future in which the suffering self would, without fail, become the thriving self. For Marx, the transformation of the self that the building of a truly Communist society entailed was to occur on several levels. One level was material: socialism's destruction of capitalist (or *bourgeois*) economic relations would bring better living and working conditions for workers. Another level was cultural: socialism would mean, for the hitherto oppressed, educational opportunities, literacy, and an entry into the culture of socialist modernity. But another level—one that is unfortunately often overlooked—was spiritual: socialism promised a transformation of the *self*.

This book aims to offer a concise and powerful (and hence necessarily controversial) interpretation of the relationship between the Communist subject and the global history of the Communist project. It proceeds from the premise that we cannot understand either the nature, or the legacy, of Communism as a global movement without appreciating the complexity of how people subjectively experienced, understood, and sometimes subverted official ideology and practices. What this book offers is *one* selection of documents that seeks to develop this interpretation.

COMMUNISM AND THE TRANSFORMATION
OF THE SELF

This was to be a transformation in which the soul-sickness of industrial capitalism would become a thing of the past. Marx had a special word for this soul-sickness: "alienation." In contemporary colloquial usage, alienation means a feeling of estrangement or separation, perhaps from something or someone to which one has belonged, or wants to belong. But for Marx, it had a specific meaning tied to his critique of capitalism. Operating on four levels, it referred (1) to the separation of the worker from the very act of labor itself, (2) to the separation of the worker from the product of his labor, since that product was appropriated by the capitalist class or bourgeoisie, (3) to the separation of workers from each other, as capitalism made labor a commodity as opposed to a social relationship, and (4) to the separation of workers from their true essence (or "species-being") as human beings, since capitalist labor conditions turned work into drudgery devoid of satisfaction. Because the socialist revolution would eliminate the material base that generated these types of alienation, it would reshape the self. But it was not a transformation that would happen effortlessly. To transcend the habits and ways of thinking tied to capitalism, individuals would need to engage in a laborious and intimate project of self-fashioning, a willful process of helping themselves grow into their true, socialist selves.

As an ideology that promised self-liberation from the soul-sickness of capitalism, Marxism drew upon core ideas in three major currents of European intellectual history: the European Enlightenment, the Hegelian (and post-Hegelian) intellectual tradition, and European Romanticism. The ideas that Marx took from the European Enlightenment of the seventeenth and eighteenth centuries had both a negative and a positive component. As for the negative component, thinkers of the European Enlightenment in France, Germany, England, and Scotland, among other places, rejected superstition, institutionalized religion, and clerical authority. In a positive vein, they championed the belief that human beings can use "reason" (critical thinking, manifest in the capacity to discern the scientific laws through which nature operates) to restructure society to eliminate secular evils—poverty, injustice, and the tyrannical abuse of power. It was especially from central figures of the French enlightenment—from Jean le Rond D'Alembert (1717–1783), Voltaire (or François-Marie Arouet, 1694–1778), Denis Diderot (1713–1784), and the Marquis de Condorcet (1743–1794)—that Marx took the belief that human "reason" could discern the laws of society, and those of human action in a social context.

As for Marx's theory of history, the most important source was the philosophy of Georg W. F. Hegel (1770–1831). For Hegel, human history was an educational process whose deep structure followed a discernible logic. The image that best represents Hegel's understanding of history is a spiral, in which human consciousness ("Geist," which can be translated from German as either "mind" or "spirit") ascends ever higher through ethical action in the world ("Sittlichkeit"), and cultural activities to institutionalize and commemorate such action ("Bildung"). Rejecting Hegel's fundamental notion of historical progress as entailing the development of human consciousness, Marx nonetheless preserved the Hegelian deep structure of history as lawful, cumulative, and progressive. As well, Marx took Hegel's concept of "alienation"—in which human beings were alienated spiritually from themselves—and grounded it in the material world, as seen above.

There is another important intellectual source for Marxism's promise of the redemption and reconstruction of the self through socialism: the European

Romanticism of the first half of the nineteenth century. The "Romantic" genealogy of Marxism is often overlooked.[2] It is from European Romanticism (among other sources)—from thinkers such as Johann Wolfgang von Goethe, among others—that Marx incorporated the idea that human history is a story of the decline, fall, and redemption of the self. The self—the subject of history—is said to have first undergone a trauma (alienation from her true essence or "species-being"), continued suffering, and, finally, a period of striving whose culmination brings redemption in recovery of a higher form of the initially harmonious self. The protagonist of the Marxist story (or philosophy) of history is a self that constantly seeks expression. It is a self whose evolution to an ever higher level of self-realization unfolds from within—not effortlessly, but through application of the will (what Goethe called "striving") in the proper ideological and social context.

To make the promise of self-realization in Communism a reality, the political practices of various Communist polities assumed great importance. (By "political practices," I have in mind the routine or "default" ways of conducting politics or engaging with the political process, as set in an institutional dimension.) Communist polities around the world harnessed a diverse repertoire of practices that people were to use to bring themselves from "darkness" to "light," so to speak. Some practices were specific to certain societies. But others seem to have been universal, or nearly so. One of these ubiquitous practices was that of "self-criticism" (in Russian, *samokritika*; in Chinese, *ziwo piping*; in German, *die Selbstkritik,* to give but a few renderings). This was the ongoing process of comparing the existing self—especially one's political mistakes and lack of Communist consciousness—to the ideal self promised by the self-liberation and self-realization project inherent in Communist ideology. Self-criticism could take many forms. For Party members from the highest echelons of the Communist elite to the grassroots, self-criticism could occur at a meeting of a Party cell (or higher body), during which a Party member was presented with charges entailing political errors, and required not only to repent but to demonstrate that one had understood the political significance of one's mistakes. Mock trials—sometimes a prelude to the real thing—also served the same purpose.

But despite the Communist penchant for organizing social and cultural transformation, it was also the case that the non-party individual was to be self-monitoring even outside formal state and Party institutions, ideally around the clock. Self-reflection in a Communist polity was never a private activity but always a political activity entailing political self-transformation. Not only in the USSR, but also in many Communist polities, it was common for people to write their autobiographies in an official context. For example, it was expected that people would present their autobiographies when they applied for admission to an institution of higher education, during the course of their activities in a Communist youth organization, and especially when they applied for membership (or candidate membership) in a Communist Party organization. Writing an autobiography not only meant elaborating a record of one's achievements according to the project of Communist self-liberation. The very act of writing an autobiography was itself a means of self-fashioning; it involved demonstrating that one had understood the proper Communist conventions for presenting oneself (to give but one example, presenting one's decision to join the Communist movement as bringing unremitting joy and happiness, as well as liberation from the anxiety and terror of bourgeois capitalism.) Some of the selections that appear in this volume have been excerpted from the pan-Communist practice of people writing their autobiographies as a means of simultaneous self-expression and transformation.

COMMUNISMS AND PEOPLE'S LIVES

So far, I have written of Communism in the singular, for simplicity's sake. But it is time to introduce readers to "Communisms," in both ideology and practice, especially to the diverse forms that the global project of Communism took in local contexts. For it is the diversity of Communism—the emergence, transformation, decline, and sometimes fall of *Communisms*—that needs to be kept in mind as we consider how people perceived, experienced, and reshaped the project of self-transformation.

Certainly Karl Marx intended for Communist doctrine to provide not just an authoritative, but a lawful and scientific, way of viewing the totality of the human past, present, and future. But Marx himself seemed to change his mind (or, at a minimum, express himself differently) over time on some of the basic issues that his philosophy of history entailed.[3] His followers—all of whom claimed that they were Marxists—nonetheless amended some of his basic ideas to fit the local circumstances in which they received his ideas and built a revolutionary movement.

To take one example, Marx viewed peasants as a backwards group tied to the feudal period of history. For him, peasants could not be revolutionary actors in the socialist revolution. But Lenin modified this, claiming that urban factory workers could form an alliance with the poorest, most exploited peasants—the proletariat within the peasantry, so to speak. And Mao Tse Tung (1893–1976), the leader of Chinese Communism, went even farther. He believed that peasants alone would make the socialist revolution that would be the prelude to Communism. Mao's revision of Marx had great influence upon subsequent twentieth-century Communists, who searched for a surrogate proletariat or working class in the context of decolonization and national liberation movements, as well as peasant insurgency in the face of global capitalism. And this is just one of the significant variations in ideology over the course of Communism's complicated history.

This brings us to variation in political practices. There was, as has been noted, quite a bit of common ground in terms of genre (such as self-criticism, or writing an autobiography.) But beyond this, there was also significant variation that occurred on several different levels.

Communist regimes varied in the specific practices they used to transform different *groups* of people. Let us take but one example: children, whose subjective experience of Communism is the subject of one of the chapters of this book. For all Communist polities, children were the great hope of the socialist future.

But different Communist regimes used different tactics. For example, in East Germany, in the 1980s, children were offered the chance to play on military vehicles such as tanks and motorcycles, and to meet border soldiers, on the annual 'Day of the Border Troops,' 1 December. In other Communist polities, however, children received different types of military socialization in elementary school and in Communist youth groups.

There was also variation in the kinds of political practices that Communist polities (and Communist movements) used to transform people. In China and Russia, for example, Communist leaders believed that it was important to manage the emotions of their citizens, to get them to feel enthusiastic, particularly about socialist labor, and to prevent them from having a pessimistic and hence ideologically generate mood. Emotions were thereby invested with considerable political significance. But not all Communist regimes, it seems, attached as much importance to emotion management as did China and Russia. Based on existing research, it appears that certain other Communist regimes—among them those in Central Europe—did not invest as much effort in this regard.

And yet another level of variation was the form that Communist political practices—especially those used to involve people in the reconstruction of their selves—took. When people wrote the autobiographies encouraged or required by Communist institutions, they brought to the process different literary models, myths, and styles depending on the local context. For example, for Semën Kanatchikov (1879–1940), a Russian worker turned Bolshevik (an excerpt of whose autobiography appears in the first chapter), literary models included the Lives of the Saints, the Gospels, and the works of his contemporary, the great Russian writer Maxim Gorky (1868–1936).[4] For Xuan Phuong (1929–), a Vietnamese woman whose excerpted autobiography is also included in this book, literary references may have included the French and other European literature she read at an elite boarding school when French colonialism was at its apex in Indonesia. In other documents in the book, readers will find other examples of the variety of tools that people themselves used to shape official political practices.

There was also significant variation in the political practices that people themselves *devised* in response to Communist ideology, practices, and technologies of the self. Across Communist polities, people resisted the implementation of state policies, or at least sought to work the implementation thereof to their advantage. People wrote letters and presented petitions, for example. But their strategies and content varied significantly—for instance, in the extent to which the petitioners drew upon the laws of the socialist polity itself in making their claims (such as for environmental protection). Another significant axis of variation concerned the institutions in which people invented and deployed their own political practices. For example, in Poland, the Catholic Church was an important site of resistance. In East Germany, however, it was a case of using the Protestant Church, somewhat tolerated by the state and the East German Communist Party (SED) but also infiltrated by state security (Stasi) agents, to create a space where people could gather, express unorthodox views, and mobilize around issues such as the peace movement and ecology. In Poland, Solidarity, the first independent trade union in a Communist country, played a significant role in Communist opposition after it was created in 1980. But in many other Communist polities (among them the USSR, East Germany, China, North Korea), trade unions were but a handmaiden of the state.

Why did these Communisms, this tremendous variation in Communist ideology and political practices, exist over space and time? Why, in other words, this tremendous variation in the context in which individuals subjectively experienced Communism, made choices about how to live their lives, and constructed their identities on an ongoing basis? Why—as the documents in this book will show—the tremendous variation in how people themselves contributed to the reshaping of Communist ideology and political practices? These are very complex issues. And the answer to them depends on the particular case one has in mind. Nonetheless, there are some general factors to be considered. These are factors that will come into play regarding the people whose voices readers will hear in this book.

One important factor has to do with the socio-economic context in which Communist movements developed, struggled, and sometimes came to power. Marx envisioned that the revolution of the proletariat, or the working class comprised of urban, literate, and politically conscious factory workers, would be made in an industrially advanced, technological developed, and highly urbanized national setting. Writing in the nineteenth century, he predicted, in fact, that the revolution would occur in Germany (or the German states, since German unification occurred only in 1871). But Germany was not, in fact, where the revolution happened, despite the short-lived experiment of the Bavarian Soviet Republic in 1919. The first revolution led by a socialist political party occurred in the Russian empire, in the midst of World War I, in November of 1917 (according to the Western or Gregorian calendar). Beginning in the last decades of the nineteenth century, Russia had experienced considerable industrialization, technological developments, and urbanization. But in comparison to other countries, especially those in Western Europe as well as the United States, Russia was not highly industrialized, technologically developed, or significantly urbanized. When the Bolsheviks, led by Vladimir Lenin, seized power in 1917, peasants still comprised 80 to 85 percent of the population. In its underdevelopment relative to more "advanced" nations, Russia would prove to be the model, not the exception, for the successful Communist revolutions of the future.

In fact, with partial exceptions, the Communist revolutions of the twentieth century—in China, Vietnam, Korea, to give but a few examples—would all occur in relatively underdeveloped countries. The partial exception is East Europe, where, after World War II, Communism came from abroad, via the Soviet occupation, even though there was some indigenous support for Communism in certain cases. East European countries such as Poland, Hungary, Czechoslovakia, Yugoslavia, and the German Democratic Republic had undergone significant industrialization, technological development, and urbanization, though they had done so later than Western European nations and the United States. Bulgaria, and especially

Romania and Albania, were, even in comparison to these Central European nations, less developed according to the same criteria. It is the *relative* degree of industrial, technological, and urban development that needs to be kept in mind—relative both to the Marxist script for necessary socio-economic preconditions for a socialist revolution, and relative to other countries at a given point in time—as a factor that explains variation in ideological doctrine and political practice. In turn, this variation is part of the context for appreciating the kinds of choices that individuals had to make about how to live and survive, and about what kinds of people they wanted to be, in different Communist polities around the globe.

A second significant factor that contributed to variation in Communism, and to the way in which people engaged with it, was the local *cultural* context. Communist political movements came into being, and sometimes came to power, in countries and regions with different religious traditions, with different literary traditions, with different popular myths, with different levels of literacy, with different architectural, art, and musical traditions. In principle, Communists everywhere condemned these diverse elements of local culture and local tradition as "bourgeois" survivals of the capitalist era of human history. Hence, Communist regimes all embarked on a massive project of cultural transformation from above. The specific goals of this cultural transformation were mass literacy, secularization, modern hygiene, and the diffusion of literature, art, music, and architecture that exemplified Marxist ideology and socialist values. However, as readers will see in this volume, there was tremendous variation—not just from region to region (Asia vs. Europe), and country to country (Russia vs. China vs. Poland), but also *within* countries (for example, different forms of cultural transformation crafted for the different religious and ethnic groups within large land empires such as Russia and China). As Communist regimes sought to create "new" men and women who understood the world in the right (Marxist, Marxist–Leninist, Maoist, etc.) way, as they sought to engineer a "cultural revolution" in diverse local contexts, they generally took into account these local traditions and cultures. An example is that, shortly after the Bolsheviks came to power, they churned out political posters and other images in which a male worker, sometimes depicted as riding a horse, was slaying a monster in the form of a reptile.[5] For many people, this must have brought to mind the Russian allegorical legend of St. George slaying the menacing dragon, who, in the icons of Eastern Orthodoxy, had taken the form of a soldier who represented the sinful desires of Christians themselves, or even the devil.

At the same time, people drew upon different local traditions and cultures as they tolerated, ignored, accommodated, resisted, and opposed Communist ideology and political practices. How they subjectively experienced the significant variation in Communist ideology and political practices also differed, because of the local cultures, religious beliefs and practices, traditions, and social networks that they retained despite the Communist project of cultural transformation. These were, at times, their "weapons of the weak"—that is, their acts of everyday resistance, which, although uncoordinated and seemingly banal, could nonetheless, over time, cripple state power.[6] Readers will find numerous examples of this in the pages that follow. It should be noted that some of these cultural elements were not even indigenous, but seem to have been brought in by dissidents who had contacts with foreigners. To take one of many possible examples, in the peace movement in East Germany in the 1980s, as well as in other oppositional circles such as ecology groups connected to the Protestant Church, there was even a detectable Quaker influence in rhetoric (such as the importance of "having the courage of one's convictions").[7]

Another factor that contributed to the tremendous variation in Communist ideology and political practices, and the way people engaged with them, pertains to the specific juncture—in global history and in the history of Communism as an international movement—in which Communist movements developed, were contested, and sometimes took power. Although the twentieth century was the Communist century, there were very different twentieth-century moments or junctures during which Communist political movements developed and came to power.

When the Bolsheviks seized power in Russia in November 1917, they assumed that the revolution would quickly spread to the West, and elsewhere. But it did not. To be sure, Communist movements led by Marxist political parties developed in the 1920s and 1930s, in the United States, Western Europe, China, and South Africa, among other places. People throughout much of the world were working out for themselves what they thought about Communism, and whether to join a Communist political party. But none of these Communist movements successfully seized power, for reasons that will be discussed in the narrative accompanying the documents.

It was not until the aftermath of World War II that people living in many countries and regions across the globe would find themselves living in a Communist polity. In Europe, the emergence of Communist regimes east of the Elbe River was a cornerstone of the post–World War II order. There, in Eastern Europe—in Poland, East Germany, Czechoslovakia, Hungary, Yugoslavia, Bulgaria, Romania, and Albania—Communist regimes were established in the Soviet sphere of influence. And it was East Europe that proved to be one of the major fronts of the Cold War, and where, as Gail Stokes has put it, "the politics of superpower rivalry received its initial rehearsal."[8]

In Asia, too, World War II marked a crucial juncture for Communist seizures of power—in Vietnam (1945) and China (1949), for example. The post–World War II decolonization movements elsewhere, as well (especially in Africa), would prove favorable to Communist revolutions. For many people, Communism would be seen as a path to national and racial—and of course personal—liberation. The aspiration for national liberation in the context of decolonization would also be among the factors making Communism attractive to people in Latin America, such as in Cuba. There, Fidel Castro's 26th of July movement seized power in 1959, though Castro himself was not yet a Communist. Castro became a Communist in 1961, and led the transformation of the Cuban polity, as well as its economy and society, along Marxist–Leninist lines. One such person who lived through part of this transformation was Carlos Eire,[9] a brief excerpt of whose autobiography is included later in this introduction. As a little boy, he struggled to make sense of what Communism meant for Cuba, for his family, and for him.

For citizens of Communist polities, it would prove to be of tremendous consequence how "their" Communist regime came into being. Readers will find numerous examples of this in the analysis that accompanies the documents. For example, it mattered whether or not a Communist polity came into being as a home-grown phenomenon (as in Russia, in 1917, despite the influence of World War I), or whether Communism was instituted to a significant degree because of military occupation (East Germany and Eastern Europe more generally). Depending on which of these was the case, people not only perceived Communism differently, but were also inclined to see resistance to Communism in different ways (as national liberation from the Russian/Soviet yoke in the case of Poland, Ukraine, Lithuania, Estonia, Latvia, East Germany, among other places, but not in others, such as in China and in the Russian Soviet Federated Socialist Republic within the USSR[10]).

ORGANIZATION AND SCOPE OF THE BOOK

This book consists of ten chapters. They treat different kinds of Communist subjects, the way in which people understood Communist ideology as well as its political violence, different facets of everyday life, and different historical moments in the history of the Communist subject around the world. Within each chapter, documents are arranged chronologically. When chronological development is not pertinent, the principle that I have used in deciding the order of the documents is to place documents in succession in order to raise important issues of comparative analysis.

The first eight chapters are thematic. Chapter 1, "Becoming a Communist," includes documents that show how people themselves perceived, constructed, and represented the process of becoming a Communist. It is designed to introduce readers to the *variety* of meanings (among them religious conversion, personal liberation, joining a new political family, or all of the preceding) that people ascribed to the process. Chapter 2, "Children of the Revolutions," includes documents that evoke how children understood Communism and reacted to its demands—at times suffering in, and at others benefiting from, Communist polities and movements. Chapter 3, "Varieties of Communist Subjects: Beyond the Ordinary," continues this focus on the subjective experience of Communism by seeking to give voice to types of Communist subjects who are often overlooked or forgotten in studies of Communism as a global movement. This chapter includes documents written by foreigners, by gay people, and one by the mother of a disabled child.

Chapter 4, "Ideology and Self-Fashioning," offers autobiographies and memoirs (among other sources) that suggest how citizens engaged with official ideology. The documents in this chapter seek to introduce readers to how people did, and did not, transform official Communist ideology in the process of reception—that is, as they sought to understand it, and ascribed their own meanings to it. The documents in this chapter also speak to another theme: the *range* of relationships that Communist subjects forged to official ideology, and how those relationships have changed over time. In the Soviet field, for example, a scholar has recently shown that the vast majority of Soviet citizens born after 1956 were neither true believers nor dissenters.[11] Rather, their relationship to Soviet ideology, and the official values of the regime, was neither intensely critical nor wholly approving. The documents explore the degree to which people in other Communist polities constructed political identities beyond the true believer, on the one hand, and the dissenter or dissident, on the other.

In the ongoing debates about the nature and significance of Communism, no issue is more controversial than the relationship of Communist polities to political violence and repression. For some, political violence and repression come from the very essence of Communist ideology; for others, they are incidental to that ideology, and are a product of circumstance and/or the nature of the modern state. Chapter 5, "Contesting the Meaning of State Violence and Repression," focuses on a theme to which less attention has been given: How did people in Communist polities understand the violence inflicted on them or other people? How did they perceive and interpret political violence, for example, in Stalinist Russia during the 1930s, during the Hungarian Revolution of 1956, or in the prelude to, and aftermath of, the massacre on Tiananmen Square that halted China's 1989 protest movement—to give but a few cases from which examples will be drawn?

The next three thematic chapters explore different aspects of people's everyday lives under Communism. The first of these chapters, "Everyday Life, I: Work" (chapter 6), focuses on labor. "He/she who does not work, shall not eat": This official Soviet slogan, which appeared in the 1918 Constitution of the Russian Socialist Federated Soviet Republic (RSFSR), is well known—indeed, it is from the Bible (2 Thess. 3:10). Also obvious is the preeminent value that all Communist regimes placed on labor of all kinds. But how did people perceive labor, in all its varieties, over the life spans of various Communist polities? The selection of documents provides examples of types of labor that have not usually been featured in historical narratives about the history of Communism. Including but also going beyond the standard focus on the urban factory worker in such narratives, the documents will allow readers to hear the voices of Chinese students studying to be good Communists in the Soviet Union in the late 1920s, a rural Communist Party cadre during China's "Great Leap Forward" of 1957–1961, and Soviet rock musicians of the late 1970s and early 1980s seeking *underemployment* working in boiler rooms, or as yard sweepers and night watchers, among other examples.

The next chapter, "Everyday Life, II: Space" (chapter 7), proceeds from the following assumption: Communism not only produced a civilization of shared values, rules, and discourse; it also produced a material culture, or material *cultures*, that varied across space and time. The most basic dimension of these material cultures was where people lived. Among the themes to which the documents in this chapter seek to introduce readers is that of the struggles that people engaged in to secure adequate living space. Some documents also suggest the meanings that they ascribed to such struggles (as well as to small successes and victories) and, even more fundamentally, to different concepts of what adequate and/or desirable living space was, and was not. A related yet separate theme that the documents speak to is what the "good life" came to mean to people across the life spans of different Communist polities.

The third chapter in this trio, "Everyday Life, III: Are We Having Fun Yet? Leisure, Entertainment, Sports, and Travel" (chapter 8), proceeds from the fact that leisure—travel, sports, entertainment, and general sociability—was a central, and politically significant, part of Communism as a way of life. Documents in this chapter explore the subjective meanings that people gave to sports, music, and travel. They also suggest, if to a limited degree, how these meanings did and did not vary across time and space.

The last two chapters of the book are thematic, but they pertain to a specific chronological moment in the history of Communism. They speak to the construction of the self during and after the fall of Communist polities. Chapter 9, "Search for the Self and the Fall of Communism," presents documents that allow readers to explore the following question: What was similar, and what was not, about the way that people around the world experienced the dismantling of Communist regimes, and the way of life that went along with them? Chapter 10, "Taking Stock: Reckoning with Communism's Pasts," presents documents designed to introduce readers to the broad *range* of self-understandings—and presentations of the self—that people have constructed in the post-Communist present, as they have reflected on what Communism has meant for them and their societies.

In the selection of documents and narrative about them, it is impossible to avoid highly charged political issues raised by our confrontation with the Communist past. Indeed, this volume aims to clarify what those issues are with respect to how people subjectively experienced, and themselves shaped, the Communist project.

I have sought to avoid evoking the familiar and perhaps comforting verdicts of the Cold War and the post-Cold War triumphalist rhetoric of the "West." This volume does not seek to pay homage to the triumph of peoples' resistance against Communist authoritarianism. It does not aim to present people as heroes whose resistance brought down Communist regimes. Resistance there was, to be sure. It is certainly a distortion, as recent research has shown, to regard citizens of Communist polities as merely the passive victims of evil Communist dictators and the repressive apparatuses of Communist regimes. But to cast people living under Communism as *only* heroic resisters or brainwashed accomplices is much too simplistic. The subjective experience of people under Communism cannot be captured by these categories alone. For across Communist polities, people not only resisted and submitted. They did much that fell in between, too. It was common for people to resist, submit, dissent, reform, retreat—and much else—in a single lifetime, or sometimes even in the course of a day, month, or year.

SELECTION OF DOCUMENTS: CHALLENGES AND OPPORTUNITIES

Choosing documents would appear to be a daunting task with considerable risks, such as overgeneralization and premature comparison. There is also the danger that, in the themes to be explored, what we will have is a "scattershot" selection of documents.

Such risks can be minimized, however, when the goals of this or any anthology of documents are carefully formulated. For one thing, this book does not seek to be comprehensive. It does not aim for a thorough and/or systematic treatment of the general topic of people under Communism; nor do any of its chapters claim to be comprehensive.

What the book *does* aim to do is provide a selection of documents that introduces readers to the themes indicated in each of the chapters, as well as to the debates and issues encompassed by each theme. It also aims to convey a method, namely guidance concerning how to study Communist subjects as a global phenomenon. For example, the book seeks to demonstrate how studying Communism in comparative perspective, especially people's subjective experience, can generate new questions about particular cases (national, regional, imperial) of Communism.

A few words are in order about the conventions I have followed in publishing the documents in this book. Many have been condensed, sometimes from much larger works, such as book-length autobiographies, memoirs, or unpublished archival documents. For those interested in reading the entire document, full citations to the originals are provided. To indicate where cuts have been made, I have not eliminated ellipses. This will enable those who are curious to go back, when possible, to the original document and have a sense of what they wish to read. Except when it would detract from the reader's appreciation of the text's meaning, I have standardized spelling, punctuation, and capitalization, and have corrected typographical and grammatical errors. I have retained the diacritical and other orthographical symbols of the original texts.

This book offers additional resources beyond the documents and the narrative that accompanies them. It includes visual material (photos, posters, etc.) which themselves are an important historical source for understanding a person's construction of the self under Communism. Another resource is a bibliography of general works and monographs for students, instructors, scholars, and other readers to explore. The bibliography also includes additional primary sources produced by citizens of Communist polities and members of Communist movements.

Who was the Communist subject around the world, and why does it matter? Not only are these questions that cannot be answered by a single volume of documents, no matter how aptly chosen. Almost necessarily, these are questions that will be revisited in an ongoing way, as each post-Communist generation rewrites its own history. But this volume allows readers to explore, discuss, and debate such questions. It does so by giving them an unprecedented chance to hear voices that have been ignored, suppressed, and forgotten.

NOTES

1. To vary the usage in the text, I sometimes use "subject" interchangeably with "people," and "citizens."
2. A point made by Igal Halfin and Jochen Hellbeck in "Rethinking the Stalinist Subject: Stephen Kotkin's 'Magnetic Mountain' and the State of Soviet Historical Studies," *Jahrbücher für Geschichte Osteuropas* 44 (1996), 463.
3. Such was the case, for example, regarding the "motor" of history. In Marx's *Communist Manifesto* (1848), the motor of history was class struggle. But in his 1859 *Preface to a Critique of Political Economy*, it was the conflict between the material productive forces and the relations of production. However, the 1859 text is thought to refer to how Marx was thinking in the early 1840s.
4. See Reginald E. Zelnik, ed. and trans., *A Radical Worker in Tsarist Russia: The Autobiography of Semën Kanatchikov* (Stanford, CA: Stanford University Press, 1986). Moreover, as Richard L. Hernandez has persuasively argued, the "social contexts depicted in Kanatchikov's autobiography resembled those of Augustine's *Confessions.*" See his "The Confessions of Semën Kanatchikov: A Bolshevik Memoir as Spiritual Autobiography," *The Russian Review* 60, no. 1 (2001): 14.
5. In one iteration—a political poster from the era of the Russian Civil War (1918–1921), in which the Bolsheviks fought their political opponents for the right to decide Russia's political future—Leon Trotsky, then the Commander of the Bolsheviks' Red Army, is depicted as the St. George figure slaying the counterrevolutionary dragon.
6. The reference here is to James Scott, *Weapons of the Weak: Everyday Forms of Resistance* (New Haven, CT: Yale University Press, 1985).
7. On contacts between East German political activists and Western Quakers, see Mary Fulbrook, *Anatomy of a Dictatorship: Inside the GDR* (New York: Oxford University Press, 1998), 284.
8. Gail Stokes, *From Stalinism to Pluralism: A Documentary History of Eastern Europe Since 1945* (New York: Oxford University Press), 3.
9. He is now a professor in Yale University's Department of History.
10. The Russian Soviet Federated Socialist Republic (often abbreviated as RSFSR), whose constitution came into being in 1918, was territorially the largest as well as the most populous of the fifteen Soviet republics in the USSR.
11. Alexei Yurchak, *Everything Was Forever, Until It Was No More: The Last Soviet Generation* (Princeton, NJ: Princeton University Press, 2006).

CHAPTER 1

————★————

Becoming a Communist

How and why did people across the globe become Communists? Marxist–Leninist thought provided one answer to this question. According to official ideology, the individual's prospects for becoming a Communist could be easily and objectively discerned. What mattered was the individual's relationship to what for Marxists was the "relations of production," most basically, the property relations that existed in a given society. During the capitalist or "bourgeois" phase of human history, society was increasingly polarized into the capitalists (or the *bourgeoisie*) that owned the means of production (capital, factories, machinery, banking systems, etc.) and the workers (or the proletariat) that did not. It was the proletariat's labor that the capitalist bourgeoisie exploited to generate profit and, thereby, to perpetuate its economic (and hence political) dominance. Marxist theory thus held the following to be a scientific law of history: as workers experienced greater oppression by capitalists, they would, without fail, embrace the Marxist worldview. They would, therefore, join the political movements and parties led by Marxists.

Yet Marxist categories do not, as the following documents suggest, explain who was won over by Communism and who was not. How and why individuals became Communists—a process that was never uncomplicated or without doubts and hesitation, and even "backsliding"—is, of course, a huge subject. But the documents herein remind us of the importance of personal connections: of, in the case of a Russian worker in late nineteenth-century Russia, meeting other workers whose personal commitment to Marxism was compelling, or, in the case of a young Vietnamese woman, of members of her family. For others, historical watersheds and the meaning ascribed to them were enormously important. This was the case, for example, for Eastern Europeans *after* World War II, such as Jacek Kuroń, who saw Communism as deliverance from the old order that had culminated in the Holocaust. For others, such as Henri Alleg, Communism held the promise of national liberation from colonial domination, as in that of Algeria from France. Self-interest, combined with economic betterment and the desire for a society where wealth and power were distributed according to different rules, also came into play. Poor villagers in Peru, as the last

1

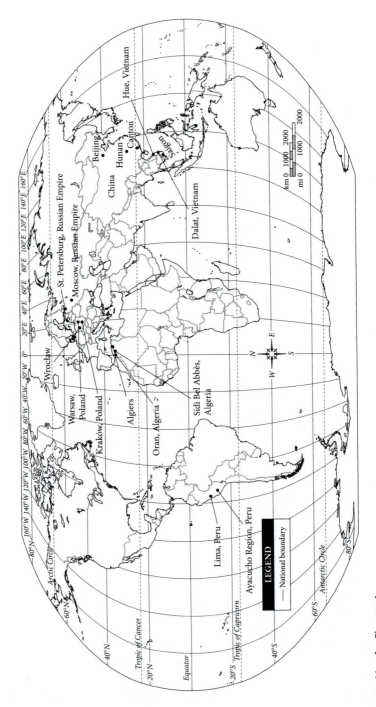

Locator Map for Chapter 1

documents suggest, not only joined the Maoist organization Shining Path (Sendero Luminoso) because they feared reprisal, but also because it promised social justice.

A separate but related issue is how people subjectively experienced, and narrated, the process through which they became Communists. As the excerpt from the autobiography by Angelo Herndon, an African-American Communist attests, some people likened Communism's emotional appeal to that of religion. Part of that emotional appeal, as the selection from an interview with the Chinese Communist Xiao Ke reminds us, was that Communist Party comrades came to seem like new family members. It seemed as though they replaced the old ones of one's biological family, a family whose internal dynamics reproduced the oppression of the feudal or bourgeois order.

Upakovochnoe otdelenie, Borzhom (Packing Department, Borzhom). This photograph depicts workers in the packing department of a mineral water warehouse in Borzhom, Georgia, in the Russian Empire. (Borzhom is the Russian name; Borjomi is the Georgian name that is used today.) Borzhom was a resort town, and it produced, through Soviet times, some of the best mineral water available in the Soviet Union. Although St. Petersburg and Moscow were major industrial centers of the Russian Empire, factories of various kinds were located elsewhere. The Transcaucsus region (where Borzhom was located), for example, was known for its industrial supply of manganese and coal.

The end of the ten-year range (1905–1915) in which this picture was taken was a period in which an increasingly militant workers' movement was emerging in St. Petersburg and elsewhere. Following the massacre of striking miners by Tsarist troops in the Lena goldfields in March 1912, the number of strikes and demonstrations soared. The Bolsheviks drew support away from the Mensheviks, the more moderate Marxists in the Russian Social Democratic Labor Party. The split between the two factions had become permanent in 1912. Photograph by Sergei Mikhailovich Prokudin-Gorskii (1863–1944). Courtesy of the Library of Congress.

Russia

Semën Kanatchikov (1879–1940) on His
Circuitous Road to Marxism

The importance of personal connections in an individual's path to Communism can be seen in this selection from the autobiography of the Russian worker Semën Kanatchikov. Kanatchikov, who was born to a peasant family in 1879 in the Moscow hinterlands of Central Russia, was taken in 1895 by his father to work in a Moscow factory. Like many young peasant lads (including, in the following excerpt, Korovin, another peasant from the same village) who worked in Russia's factories during the great industrial take-off of the 1890s, he was to earn money to help out his family back in the village. It was expected, moreover, that he would eventually marry and return to village life. But Kanatchikov, like countless other peasant in-migrants to Moscow, St. Petersburg, and other cities, encountered people who introduced him to the different currents of the Russian revolutionary movement, including Marxism.

In the passage that follows, Kanatchikov is in dialogue with one such interlocutor, a certain Savinov. Nearly fresh from the village, to whose cultural and emotional world he is still deeply connected, Kanatchikov is only beginning his circuitous road to Marxism and, eventually, to Bolshevism.[1] In fact, at the time that Kanatchikov and Savinov were first getting to know each other in Moscow, the Russian Social Democratic Labor Party (Russia's first Marxist political party, founded in 1898) had not yet been established, and Russian Populists (whose socialism was based on the Russian peasant commune and the general belief that peasants, not workers, were Russia's revolutionary class) were at the helm of Russia's revolutionary movement.

Not all peasant in-migrants to Russia's urban factories would embrace Marxism, let alone Bolshevism. But when they did, such a journey inevitably meant redefining one's spiritual, intellectual, and emotional relationship to Russian Orthodoxy and village religiosity. Kanatchikov's profound ambivalence toward religion during his first years as an urban dweller can be seen in the following dialogue. Kanatchikov would eventually sever ties with the religious

From Semën Kanatchikov, "The Beginning of My Apostasy," in *A Radical Worker in Tsarist Russia*, trans. and ed. Reginald E. Zelnik (Stanford, CA: Stanford University Press, 1986), 27–36. Reprinted with permission of Stanford University Press.

world of the village and embrace Russian Marxism's (and later Bolshevism's) secular worldview. This was an emotionally traumatic process in which what mattered decisively were the personal characteristics (the appeal to young Semën, for example, of Savinov's "comradely, jocular" style) displayed by those who scared yet attracted him with radical ideas, books, and actions. It was also a complicated, tortuous process in which Kanatchikov's simultaneous straddling of peasant past and urban present demonstrates the inadequacy of the very "Marxist analytical scheme that Kanatchikov himself would eventually adopt (capitalist, petty bourgeois, proletarian)."[2]

"THE BEGINNING OF MY APOSTASY"

The Gustav List machine-building factory never held a ranking position in the struggle of the working class for its emancipation....

In those days, however, it was the Gopper factory that was considered really advanced. Even in those early years strikes had already taken place there.[3] The leading role in that factory was played by the pattern shop, some of whose pattern-makers had already spent time in exile or under police surveillance. The workers in the pattern shop at my factory used to call the Gopper pattern-makers "students"*—that is, people who are against the tsar and do not believe in God— and they were somewhat afraid of them.[4]

My own conception of these "students" was extremely confused. My only encounters with them were on the streets, and my feeling toward them was always one of great admiration mingled with fear and terror. I feared them because they didn't believe in God and might be able to shake my faith as well, which could have resulted in eternal hellish torments in the next world—"not for a hundred years, not for a thousand years, but for eternity without end," where there will be "weeping and the gnashing of teeth"—I often recalled the words of some divine revelation. But I admired them because they were so free, so independent, so well-informed about everything, and because there was nobody and nothing on earth that they feared....

How great were my surprise and curiosity when I learned one fine day that a pattern-maker from the Gopper factory had joined our workshop.

Just three benches away from mine a thin, sinewy man of medium height, with curly, light-colored hair and huge blue eyes, was fidgeting about. His shirt was tucked in and he wore his trousers outside his boots. In short, his outward appearance was no different from that of most of our pattern-makers. But he struck me as being particularly impetuous and fidgety.

My acquaintance with him began on the very first day.

"Well, my boy, how about giving me a hand with this cabinet," he said, beckoning me with his finger. "What's your name?"

"Semën."

---

* In those days the word "student" meant the same thing as "revolutionary." (Author's note.) [This was written by the author of the autobiography, Semën Kanatchikov.]

"Have you been working here long?"

"This is my second year."

"I guess you already chase the girls, right?"

I grinned and, to cover my embarrassment, began to lift the heavy cabinet filled with tools.

"Hey, wait a second, watch out or you'll break your back! I have so many tools
    in there that even two of us can't lift it."...

This person was definitely beginning to appeal to me. I was won over by his comradely, jocular tone, a tone that other adult workers assumed with me only rarely.

"What if he has approached me in this roundabout manner in order to con-
    vert me to his godless faith?" I cautioned myself....

Merry, sociable, and thoroughly skilled in our trade, he quickly over-came the normal workshop hostility with which the old-timers always treat the newcomer....

Not infrequently, fierce and bitter political or theological arguments would be launched....Savinov (that was the newcomer's name) was particularly fond of making sport of the sacred things of Moscow. He would refer to the Iversky icon of the Mother of God, which at the time was being carried about in a carriage harnessed to a team of six horses, as "a priest's tool for gaining money"; he'd refer to monks as "parasites," to priests as a "breed of horses," to Ioann of Kronstadt as "Vaniukha," and so forth.[5]

"Well all right, let's say that the priests really are greedy, dissolute parasites; there's still no point in your sneering at miracles and the relics of saints, Savinov," the venerable and respectable-looking old worker Smirnov, a dogmatist and churchgoer, would say, losing his patience....

After arguments like that were over the older workers would sigh sorrowfully as they dispersed, shake their heads, and whisper to each other: "What a hopeless man: he doesn't believe in God, he's against the tsar, he stirs up the Orthodox faithful, the people. He'll never escape the prison wagon, that's for sure!"

"When I lived in St. Petersburg lots of troublemakers like that got caught," old Smirnov would say....

The younger workers, on the other hand, listened to Savinov's talk with enthusiasm and interest. Often they would turn to him with questions and requests for clarifications. Nevertheless, it wasn't easy for him to overcome their suspicion—rooted in them from early childhood—of everything that was new, hard to grasp, or unfamiliar.

There were times when I was deeply angered and pained by Savinov's words. Questions that I had long since resolved, so I thought, and which had raised no doubts in my mind, would suddenly begin to drill themselves slowly and steadily into my brain, as if a piece of thin cold steel was being thrust into it. My beliefs, my views of the surrounding world, the moral foundations with which I had lived and grown up so nicely, peacefully, comfortably—suddenly began to shake....Shivers ran up my spine—I became cold and terrified, as if I were preparing to leap across some abyss. But at the same time I felt light and free when I remembered that together with the old principles would also disappear that terrible nightmare that threatened me with the tortures of hell "not for a hundred years, not for a thousand years, but for eternity without end."

Having mastered my rage and indignation over his insulting remarks about "sacred" things, I timidly, cautiously began to get into arguments with Savinov....

"You say there is no hell, there is no heaven, no holy relics, no saints; then are you also saying there is no God?" I inquired, my heart already sinking in anticipation of his answer.

"No God? Of course there's a God, only not the kind that's conjured up by the priests," Savinov answered evasively, alerted by my passion....

My talks with Savinov became more frequent, more prolonged and detailed. His confidence in me was apparently increasing....

One evening, as I was approaching my workbench, Savinov stealthily and cautiously thrust some kind of disheveled, grease-stained little book under my bench.

"Read it, Semën, and don't show it to anyone else," he whispered to me.

Tormented by curiosity and fear, I could barely wait for the bell. I finished the book in two sittings. It was Hauptmann's *The Weavers*.[6] At the time it was still an illegal publication. The book made a rather strong impression on me. I soon learned the "song of the weavers" by heart and would recite it to the other apprentices of my age group in the workshop. The words kept echoing again and again in my ears:

So merciful and upright, the court in our land:
To the worker it shows scorn, honor to the gentleman!
    Our workers are tormented, as in a torture cell,
They plunder, starve, oppress us, but you are silent, silent!...[7]

The book had a very disturbing effect on me, stirring up my animosity toward the rich and my pity for the oppressed and awakening many new, previously unknown emotions, yet it did not really satisfy me. It failed to answer the questions that were tormenting me: how should I live and what should I do? It had nothing to contribute to the formulation of my world outlook.

That task was to be accomplished by yet another little book that I read, also passed on to me by Savinov: *What Should Every Worker Know and Remember?* I don't remember the author's name.[8] Clearly written, in a popular but passionate style, this book produced a total transformation in my ideas. A complete revelation for me was the elegant exposition of its views of the socialist society of the future. Factories, workshops, the land, the forests, the mines—everything would become the common property of the toilers! The organized struggle of the working class against the capitalists, the landowners, and the tsar—that was the meaning of life and work for every conscious worker.

For an entire week I was in a state of virtual ecstasy....My past life seemed completely boring, dull, uninteresting. Every day had been identical, just like clockwork—late to bed and early to rise, again and again, day after day. That was "eternity without end"!

The next book I read was G. Plekhanov's *The Russian Worker in the Revolutionary Movement,* after which many aspects of my father's old stories about the "nahilists" became clear and comprehensible to me.[9] Now my emancipation from my old prejudices moved forward at an accelerated tempo.

I now withdrew from my artel and settled in a separate room with one of my comrades. I stopped going to the priest for "confession," no longer attended church, and began to eat "forbidden" food during Lenten fast days. However, for a long time to come I didn't abandon the habit of crossing myself, especially when I returned to the village for holidays.

Noticing my blatant "apostasy," Korovin made several attempts to lecture me on morality:

"Don't you listen to that heretic Savinov, Senka," he would say. "He's not going to do you any good. They'll kick you out of the factory, and you haven't even learned to do the work properly yet....I think I'll write to your father; let him burn your back with twenty-five strokes!"

"But I'm not doing anything illegal, am I?" I replied in self-justification.

"I know just what you've been doing! They're going to put a necktie made of hemp around your neck—you'll hang there with your feet jerking."

However, these admonitions failed to impress me.

Then Korovin would write letters about my apostasy to my father. Alarmed, Father would insist on each occasion that I return to the village for the holidays to hear his parental admonitions. In the intervals between holidays he would write me edifying letters, in which he advised me to say my prayers, attend church, and call on the reigning Mother of God and St. Nicholas for assistance, that they might guard me from atheism and every other horror.[10]

During my visits to the village on holidays, Father and I would quickly get entangled in theological arguments. Because I was already quite well versed in these questions by then I almost always emerged the victor from these arguments with my father. To be sure, not wishing to cause him great pain, I wouldn't pose the question of the "non-existence" of God very sharply and I gladly agreed to grant His existence as a possibility.

Father would then calm down somewhat and would even be proud of me. But this never lasted very long. As soon as I left for Moscow Father was on his own once more and, when he began to receive disturbing letters from Korovin, Father's edifying letters to me would resume.

But none of this was considered by Father to be all that terrible. There was only one thing he was unable to come to terms with—the fact that I was so indifferent to our home and to our peasant farmstead. Once during one of my visits Father summoned me to the barn, where, three years earlier, he had already prepared himself a good hollow coffin, which in the meantime was used to store oats, cabbages, firewood for the winter, and so on.

"I would like to have a serious talk with you," said my father.

"Fine, let's talk."

"As you know," he began in a sad voice, "I'm already growing old and might die quite soon. I've made myself a coffin and there's really nothing more I need, just seven feet of earth. But for me to die in peace I would like to see you settled down."

"But I am already settled down. I'm working at a factory and I'll soon be earning a good wage," I replied, pretending not to understand what Father was getting at.

"No, that's not what I'm talking about.... As you know, I don't get along well with your brother. I want to give him a separate property settlement and to have you get married while I'm still alive, so that the house will mean more to you and you'll be better off while you're still young, since if you wait until you're older you won't even marry."

"No, I don't want to marry until I've done my military service; when I'm a civilian again, then I'll get married," I answered fairly decisively.

"But I'll be dead by then."

"Well, I will get married on my own," I declared firmly.

Father, understanding that there was no chance of persuading me, gave up the fight and said with sadness:

"Well, God be with you! Live according to your own lights!"

1–2

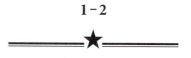

China

Xiao Ke (1909–????) Writes His Life into the Marxist Understanding of History

The founding of the Chinese Communist Party in 1921 expanded political choices for people during a period of political, social, cultural, and military turmoil following the collapse of the last dynasty of Imperial China (the Qing or Manchu dynasty) in 1911. It was not until 1949, when the Communists under Mao Zedong established the People's Republic of China, that the nearly four-decade period of civil war and war against imperial aggressors, especially

Japan, came to an end. Up until 1927, the numerically small Chinese Communist Party and much larger Nationalist Party (and government), the Guomindang (founded in 1912 and reestablished in 1919), joined forces to fight the warlords and establish a nationally unified China, a policy endorsed by the Soviet-led Comintern.

But in 1927 an open split occurred in China's revolutionary movement between the Guomindang and the Chinese Communist Party. Chiang Kai-shek, who had assumed leadership of the Guomindang in 1925 after the death of its former leader, Sun Yat-sen, formed an anti-Communist government in Nanjing in April 1927. Failed urban and rural uprisings further contributed to the seemingly irreversible decline of the Chinese Communist Party. Indeed, by 1937, the Guomindang had consolidated its rule and had succeeded in unifying most of China under a nationalist government. But the Communists gained ground during the 1930s, drawing support from the Nationalist (Guomindang) government's weaknesses (especially its failure to enact social reform and its ineffectiveness in combating Japanese military aggression after 1937 because of preoccupation with fighting the Communists) and the Communist Party's strengths (its pro-peasant social reforms, Mao's successful leadership of the Red Army during the "Long March," and its defiance of Japanese aggression). Among those who made signal contributions to the Red Army's military success was Xiao Ke (in the original text, Wade-Giles transliteration: Hsaio K'ê), the son of a minor Chinese bureaucrat and the author of the excerpt that follows. Xiao went on to become the youngest of the Communist Party's chief military commanders.

Xiao's life exemplified, to some degree, the struggles that people went through as they decided what the "revolution" did and did not mean to them during the Republican period (1911–1949). In 1926, the year after Sun Yat-sen's death, Xiao joined the Guomindang, fighting with its forces until after its open split with the Chinese Communist Party in 1927. By that point, he became convinced that the Guomindang was betraying the revolution, whose future lay with the CCP. Five years later, he assumed command on the 6th Red Army. In 1937, he was appointed to command of the 31st Red Army and was instrumental in reorganizing it. During the war with Japan, he held high military posts.

Just as for Semën Kanatchikov decades earlier, for Xiao Ke, joining the revolutionary movement obliged him to make choices large and small about who he was. Among the decisions he would face would be how he would tell, whether to himself or others, his life story once he had advanced in the ranks of the Communist Party. (The autobiography was told in an interview to Nym Wales in Yenan in the 1940s.) Like Communists around the world, Xiao came to understand that Communism entailed writing his life into its revolutionary

From Helen Foster Snow, *The Chinese Communists: Sketches and Autobiographies of the Old Guard. Book I; Red Dust. Book II: Autobiographical Profiles and Biographical Sketches* (Westport, CT: Greenwood Publishing Company, 1972), 132–140. Reprinted by permission of Greenwood Publishing.

(specifically Marxist) understanding of history. Like other Communist auto-biographers around the world, some of whom readers will meet in this volume, Xiao endeavored to show that the Marxist (and Maoist) understanding of history as an inevitable, if torturous, progression from darkness to light was repeated in his own development as an individual.[11] Having made the journey from a necessarily naïve ideological starting point to a mature, ideologically conscious one, he was for the first time able to understand the true sources of his own oppression in a conservative family that, in its "absolute dictatorship," was a microcosm of the feudalism to be destroyed by Communist revolution.

My father was a *xiucai** Confucian scholar, ranking in the lowest official class of the Qing dynasty[†]. Before 1921 he lived the life of the disintegrating *xian*[‡] gentry of China. In that year he became bankrupt. There were eight or nine persons in my home—including my two elder brothers, whose careers ran no more smoothly than my own. The eldest was executed in April 1923 after being accused of having relations with bandits. The other, Xiao Keyong, with whom I was on friendly terms, entered the Communist Party[§] in 1925 and later joined the Red Army and was killed in battle.

Our home was in Jiahe *xian*, Hunan, in the village of Xiaoketian, named after my family. I was born there in August 1909, but like most Communists I dropped the unnecessary ending.

At the age of six I went to a tutorial school and studied all the old books of Confucius[¶] and Mencius**—the Four Books and the Five Classics[††], which I hated....

---

* The first, or lowest official degree in the traditional examination system that ended in 1905. In contemporary China, it means highly educated, or having exceptional talent.

[†] The Qing dynasty (1644–1911), also called the Manchu dynasty, was the last of the Chinese imperial dynasties. During the Qing period, the size of the empire tripled in relation to that of the Ming dynasty (1368–1644).

[‡] County. Wade–Giles in original: *hsien*.

[§] The Chinese Communist Party was founded in 1921.

[¶] Confucius (551–479 BC) was a philosopher and official whose thought stressed the importance of values (especially filial piety) supposedly central to an earlier, less tumultuous feudal order. Although the thought of Confucius had little influence on the politics of his day, the teachings of his followers were the basis of state political ideology in subsequent dynasties.

** Mencius, writing after 320 BC, took Confucius's ideas and adjusted them to this later period. He is known for his insistence on the goodness of human nature. Mengzi was one of the "Four Books."

[††] The "Four Books and Five Classics" mentioned in the text constituted the canon of the Confucian tradition. Because of their importance in official political ideology in Imperial China, the Communist Party held that to read them, except for the purposes of ideological critique, was counterrevolutionary.

I stopped my school work when I was about seventeen, and in 1926 went to Canton to join the army. I enlisted with Chiang Kai-shek's* Gendarmes as a common soldier. At that time I thought he was a revolutionary leader and he made a good impression on me. My faith in him did not entirely collapse until after he began the counterrevolution in 1927. I considered him a good follower of Sun Yat-sen† and a leftist....

I wanted to go to Canton because it was the center of the revolution. While I was in normal school, a cousin in Canton University had mailed revolutionary books to me, including those written by Sun Yat-sen....

My native village and family were conservative and feudal-minded. I read these books and advanced in thought by my own initiative....

I was also interested in military science, and while in normal school in 1924 I devoured the old Chinese military books.... I remember, too, being very much interested in the record of the Battle of Verdun‡ in the World War.

Most people think I was a Whampoa§ cadet in Canton. This is a mistake. However, during my four months with the Gendarmes there, I picked up a Whampoa education of my own. Although I was very young, I never forgot anything I heard. It was easy for me to absorb all the knowledge of the Whampoa officers, so that I became as well educated as they were—by keeping my ears open....

In 1927 I joined the famous 24th Divison under Ye Ting¶, the Communist.... I was a company political director.... On our return to Wuhan** I was still nominally

---

* Chiang Kai-shek (1887–1975, pinyin: Jiang Jieshi) became the leader of the Guomindang after Sun Yat-sen died in March 1925. The Guomindang was founded as a political party in 1911. Its political goals were parliamentary democracy and moderate socialism. In 1928, the Guomindang captured Beijing and was able to establish a government in Nanjing. The Guomindang party and government unified and ruled China from 1927 to 1937.

† Sun Yat-sen was the founder of the Chinese Nationalist Party, which was also known as the Guomindang. He died on 12 March 1925.

‡ Lasting from 21 February to 18 December 1916, the Battle of Verdun between France and Germany was the longest battle of World War I. It resulted in French victory. But over a million soldiers died on the battlefield, and over a half million were wounded.

§ Here the author refers to the Whampoa Military Academy, which was established on 6 February 1924 by Sun Yat-sen outside the city of Guangzhou. The Academy sought to train a national revolutionary army that would defeat warlord armies and unify China under a single government. The Academy's officers and faculty were chosen by Chiang Kai-shek. In part because of a lack of proper weapons and equipment, training borrowed from the Japanese model that stressed rigorous discipline and self-sacrifice. See Peter Worthing, "The Road through Whampoa: The Early Career of He Yingqin," *Journal of Military History* 69, no. 4 (October 2005): 953–985.

¶ Ye Ting (1896–1946) was a Chinese military leader, first of nationalist forces and then of the Communist Red Army. After joining the Guomindang, he became, in 1921, battalion commander of the National Revolutionary Army. In 1924 he studied in the USSR, and in December of that year he joined the Communist Party of China. In 1927, among the military posts he held was division commander of the 24th Division of the 11th Army. He, along with Zhou Enlai and others, led a (failed) Communist military uprising in Nanchang, Jiangxi province.

** The author refers here to the nationalist government in Wuhan.

only political director, but during the Nanchang Uprising on August 1, 1927*, I became captain of my company in my own right....

I did not join the Communist Party until June 1927, after the split with the Guomindang began[†]. As early as February a friend had talked with me and declared that Chiang Kai-shek was betraying the revolution and opposing the peasants' and workers' movement. This made me angry, and my suspicions began. Then at the end of February, I returned to Wuhan to see what was happening, and there I received a letter from my Communist brother saying that Chiang Kai-shek had betrayed and was plotting a dictatorship. I thought that if this were true we must overthrow Chiang Kai-shek or the Guomindang revolution would fail. Then, when the whole Guomindang itself turned reactionary, I realized that the Communists had the only solution to the problem of accomplishing the tasks of the revolution and that only the soldiers and peasants and workers would carry on....

It was natural enough for me to change from the Guomindang to the Communist Party. Although my family were gentry, they were steadily becoming declassed and bankrupt, until my father owned only six *mu*[‡] of land. When I went to school, the problem of paying the tutorial fee was a big one for my family; my clothes were ragged and poor; the teacher often beat me, having no respect for my bankrupt family. As soon as I read of Sun Yat-sen's "Three People's Principles"[§] I agreed with them with all my heart, especially the principle of uniting with the peasants and workers and with the Communist Party and the Soviet Union. So deep was my belief in this last principle that when the bourgeoisie betrayed it, I hated the counterrevolutionaries very much and felt that the salvation of the nation depended on the overthrow of Chiang Kai-shek's dictatorship....

From 1925 to 1927 the revolution had two primary meanings for me: the overthrow of imperialism—including not only England but all the foreign powers—in order to achieve the independence and equality of the Chinese nation; and the overthrow of the feudal gentry and landlords, including the feudal militarists.

Four or five years before the revolution, I had read about the Unequal Treaties, the Sino-Japanese War, the Boxer Rebellion, and the like. At that time I was not only a nationalist but also an imperialist—I had the narrow, egotistical hope that China would overthrow the foreign nations, including Japan, and conquer them

---

[*] The day that the Nanchang uprising began—1 August 1927—is commonly regarded as the day on which the Red Army was founded. Four days later, troops led by the Chinese Communist Party were forced to leave the city.

[†] The split emerged following the death of Sun Yat-sen, when General Chiang Kai-shek led the Guomindang's Northern Expedition, whose purpose was to unite China by defeating the northern warlords. The split threatened the military success of the Northern Expedition. But it was temporarily resolved when Stalin ordered the Chinese Communists to obey the Guomindang leadership. This allowed Chiang to resume the expedition. In fact, Communist attacks helped the Guomindang to take Shanghai. Following the victory, however, Chiang in 1927 began to massacre Communists in Shanghai. After the Nationalist government in Wuhan dismissed him, he set up his own government in Nanjing.

[‡] One *mu* is equivalent to 6.666 square meters.

[§] The "three principles" were nationalism, democracy, and people's livelihood.

in turn. Gradually my idea changed to wanting only the independence and liberty of China. I think that my main drive toward revolution was anti-imperialism, or nationalism.

I also hated the landlords, however.... Then, however, I hated only that one landlord,—not landlordism as a system.

Then, too, I hated the big yamen officials and the userers. When my eldest brother was put into prison, the family borrowed five or six hundred dollars to try to secure his release, and tis debt was a constant burden. The family could never pay it back....

It was only after I became a Communist that I learned not to be personal in my revenge and hatred, but to see the general social problems of a corrupt semi-feudal society as a whole and understand that the degeneration of my own family and clan was only a part of this phenomenon.

One of the main reasons for my revolutionary tendency was my resentment against the old Chinese family system, which I experienced in its most disintegrating phase. As a child I received a bad impression of family life and I was glad to escape from it. Since I left it, I have never written a letter to my home. I suppose my parents are dead now—they were old then and would now be over seventy. When I went away, my mother thought the family could not find means to exist five years more. The house itself, she said, was in such poor repair that it must collapse within ten years.

Even as I talk I feel bitter toward my feudal family. But I loved very much my young sister and my brother who became a Communist. I never saw this brother again after the failure of the South Hunan Revolt in April 1928*. He wandered around for a while after that, doing secret Party work. He was arrested in Changde, Hunan, but escaped and joined the 85th Guomindang Division to do further secret Party work. He was discovered and again barely escaped with his life. Then he joined the Red Army in Tahuang *xian*, Hupeh. He first taught military training, later became chief of staff in the 3rd Independent Division, and finally was killed in battle at the beginning of 1933.

I also had two elder sisters. The husband of one was betrayed by a corrupt relative and was executed for "having relations with bandits," just as my eldest brother had been. The husband of the older sister was killed in 1927 as a member of a peasant union.

I hate intensely the feudal concept of the family. My father was very authoritarian and dominated his family. It was under an absolute dictatorship, and so was I. I obeyed my father without hesitation on every point. He ordered me not to

---

*The South Hunan revolt was one of the autumn "harvest revolts" led by Mao Zedong. These "harvest revolts" were peasant uprisings whose goals were, as Clarence Martin Wilbur puts it on p. 151 of *The Nationalist Revolution in China, 1923–1928* (1983), to carry out a "land revolution, overthrow the Wuhan government and Tang Shengzhi's regime" and create a "people's government." Peasants were to be the driving force of the revolts, but they were aided by military units. Mao was in conflict with the Politburo in Wuhan over military strategy.

People—many of them African-Americans—at a Communist rally against unemployment in Kansas City, Missouri, most likely in 1931. Sherry Lamb Schirmer's scholarship has shown that the Communist demonstrations protesting unemployment in Kansas City, such as the one depicted here, attracted a high percentage of unemployed African-Americans. Among the Communist Party organizers who spoke in Kansas City's African-American community were Angelo Herndon, part of whose autobiography is reproduced in selection 1–3, "United States of America: Angelo Herndon (1913–1997) on His First Exposure to Communism." In Kansas City, the Communist Party did not attract a large number of followers. But Schirmer has suggested that the anti-unemployment protests, such as the one depicted here, "may at least have encouraged working-class blacks to think about radical changes that the system of partisan politics dared not address." See her *A City Divided: The Racial Landscape of Kansas City, 1900–1960* (2002), 174. Courtesy of the Kansas City Public Library.

gamble, smoke, or play chess, and I did not. At the same time, however, he tried to destroy my spirit with a conservative education. I was not a rebellious child at home, but when I was released from the family yoke for a little while, I was always carefree and daring. I remember, too, how I loved the village theatre where there was noise and freedom. What a relief it was from the stern teachings of my father and his dull rules from Confucius and Mencius!

It was natural that I should want to run away from home. When I was in normal school, just before examinations I borrowed seven dollars in local currency from an old teacher, a Sun Yat-sen sympathizer, and deserted the school without letting my family know. I put on seven layers of clothing—all I had in the world—and set out. Before I left, I wrote a letter to my family and gave it to an illiterate girl-cousin to deliver after I had left. By the time they got it, I was already in Kwangtung.

I walked in the snow all the way to Shaokuan* on the Guangdong border. My only possessions were in a carryall made of my favorite sister's jacket.... My idea then was to find adventure and to join the revolution to overthrow the imperialists and feudal militarists. I had discussed this trip with my schoolmates, but of all forty-eight not one agreed with my purpose and wanted to join me....

I was interested in military more than political matters and wanted to go to Whampoa Academy, but I was two months too late for the 1926 term and couldn't enter the Academy.

1 – 3

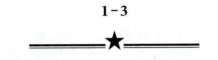

United States of America

Angelo Herndon (1913–1997) on His First Exposure to Communism

In the late 1920s and 1930s, the Communist movement in the United States gained strength, though for different reasons than in the China of Xiao Ke. The Communist Party of the USA, founded in 1919, increased its membership and swelled the ranks of non-Party supporters as the Great Depression wreaked havoc with the American economy and unemployment soared. Not only poor white people, but African-Americans—even in the South—found hope in the Communist message. In 1929, the Communist Party established its "District 17," a region that included Alabama, Georgia, Louisiana, Florida, Tennessee, and Mississippi. Membership in the district grew as a number of Southern blacks joined the Party.[12]

One African-American who joined the Communist Party of the USA during the Great Depression was Angelo Herndon. Herndon, who was born in Ohio, would go on to become a leader among African-American Communists.

From Angelo Herndon, *Let Me Live* (New York: Random House, 1937).

---

* In 1924, Sun Yat-sen moved his military headquarters to Shaokuan.

He organized protests of both blacks and whites in the South. In 1932, he was arrested in Atlanta, Georgia, for "attempting to incite insurrection" after he was found to have Communist writings in his possession. Another reason for his arrest was that he had led unemployed African-Americans and whites in protesting reductions in relief measures. Upon a conviction that was based on an anti-slavery insurrection law of 1861, he was sentenced to eighteen to twenty years' hard labor. Leftist and civil rights organizations made his case a national cause célèbre. Thanks to the efforts of these organizations, especially the International Labor Defense, as well as individuals such as Langston Hughes and Ralph Ellison, he was released in 1934. Herndon's sentence was overturned by the Supreme Court, which ruled that Georgia's anti-insurrection law was unconstitutional.

In the passage that follows, an excerpt from the autobiography he published in 1937, Herndon retrospectively recounts his first exposure to Communist ideas. On 22 May 1930, two years before his arrest, he attended a meeting of the Unemployment Council in Birmingham, Alabama. Run under the auspices of the Communist Party, the Unemployment Council(s) sought to help starving black and white workers in a city that President Franklin Roosevelt deemed "the worst hit town in the country."[13]

The passage is notable in several respects. The meeting, Herndon says, convinced him that poor African-Americans and whites suffered at the hands of the same oppressive force: capitalism. It was through this meeting and other activities of the CP-led Unemployment Council that he embraced Marxist Communism's "rational plan of scientific socialism." Yet he portrays his conversion to Communism as anything but a rational process. Not only does he emphasize Communism's emotional appeal. He draws a parallel between the emotional magnetism of Communism and of religion, of the preaching of his Uncle Jeremiah's first sermon, a sermon that Angelo heard when he was nine years old.

It was on a sultry evening in June, 1930*. I was coming home from work with a friend when some soiled handbills, upon which people had trampled, caught my eye. I was startled by its headline, which read: "Would you rather fight or starve?" My friend and I sat down on a house step and began reading it. We read it over and over again, not believing our own eyes, as if we had been living in an evil dream all the time and suddenly awoke to reality with a bang. The writing on the handbill discussed unemployment, hunger and suffering of both Negro and white workers in Birmingham and throughout the whole country. It called upon all Birmingham workers to attend a meeting under the auspices of the Unemployment Council[14] that afternoon.

Conditions were so bad that many people believed that the only way they could ever get better was to start a new war. As I read the handbill I very naively was under the impression that the Unemployed Council was calling all Negro and

---

* Herndon remembers the meeting as having occurred in June 1930. But its actual date was 22 May 1930. Kelley, "A New War," 370 n. 7.

white workers to a new war. I said to my friend, my eyes suddenly dazzled by the blinding truth: "It's war, all right—war is the only thing that will make times better...."

My friend looked puzzled and hesitated, but out of friendship for me he agreed to accompany me to the meeting....

It was three o'clock that afternoon when I walked into the meeting hall.[15] It was a large and stuffy room, full of cigarette smoke and that indefinable electricity which radiates from a large body of tense and excited men. Outside were gathered hundreds of policemen, looking grim and ready for action.... I was puzzled to understand the presence of police officers in such large numbers. But I began to have an inkling of understanding when I looked at the audience. It was composed of both white and Negro workers. A feeling of astonishment and incredulity came over me when I looked at them.... Suddenly I recalled that prophecy which most Negroes cherish: "And the day shall come when the bottom rail shall be on top and the top rail on the bottom. The Ethiopians will stretch forth their arms and find their place under the sun."

A white worker came over to me and said: "Won't you have a seat?" I was touched by his courtesy, which I had never experienced before from a white man.

Finally the speaker of the evening was introduced. He was Frank Williams,[16] the organizer of the Unemployment Council in Birmingham, a white man possessing a dynamic personality and great strength of character. The following is a transcript of his speech that night: "Friends and fellow-workers: It is estimated that throughout the country there are 17,000,000 unemployed workers.... Through no fault of their own, they have been thrown out of the steel mills, textile factories, coal mines and other industries to lead a wretched and tragic existence.... And particularly here in the South, conditions are even more deplorable.... Negroes are discriminated against. They are given the worst and dirtiest jobs and are paid less for the same work done by a white worker. They are segregated into such disease-infested neighborhoods as Tittersville, East Birmingham, the South Side and others. They are denied the rights of citizenship; they are lynched and terrorized in open violation of the United States Constitution.

"Why must this be? The bosses tell the white workers that they are superior to Negroes, but can't you see that your conditions are the same as those of the Negro people? Thousands of white workers are today unemployed and suffering just as the Negro. Can't you see that those who teach you about white superiority are not only the exploiters of the Negroes, but they play one worker against the other and rob you and starve your children?... If you want to maintain your human dignity instead of being looked upon as vagabonds and paupers, there is only one way to do it, and that is to establish unity among all workers, Negro and white.... That's why we Reds fight for political, economic and social equality for Negroes, not because we must express hypocritically our love for anyone, but because the bosses have our backs against the wall and all of us alike will be threatened with the same danger of pestilence, hunger and untold misery. Remember the slogan of our forefathers in the fight for independence, 'Either we hang together or we hang separately!'"

I said to my friend with the greatest excitement:

"He's right! He does nothing but tell the truth. He's the first honest white man I've seen. Have you heard of another white man who has the courage to publicly tell the truth about the conditions of Negroes?"...

At the end of the meeting I went up to the platform and said to the white organizer.

"I'm with you with all my heart and I would like you to put me down as a member."

Strange, only once before had I walked up to a speaker who had moved me so deeply and been converted. That was the time when my Uncle Jeremiah preached his first sermon and I had gone up to him, extended my hand and piped in my nine-year-old voice: "I know religion is in me, Uncle Jeremiah." The emotional motivation in both cases was identical, but what a difference in their nature and in their aim!...

That night when I went to bed, I couldn't fall asleep.... Something very important had happened to me, I knew, and I lay with wide open eyes staring into the darkness of my room and thinking that it was at last necessary for me to revise my attitude toward white people. I had discovered at last the truth that not all white people were enemies and exploiters of the Negro people. In fact, the same vicious interests that were oppressing Negro workers were doing the same thing to white workers, that both black and white workers could solve their problems only by a united effort against the common enemy: the rich white people, they who owned the mines, the mills, the factories, the banks. I began to reason in the following way:...

The Negro leaders tell us that the poor white workers are responsible for our sufferings. But who controls the powerful weapons with which to spread anti-Negro propaganda, with which to vilify us and spit venom upon us? Decidedly, it could not be the poor white workers who had all they could do to keep themselves alive. Therefore, it could only be the rich white people who were our oppressors, for they controlled the churches and the schools and the newspapers and the radio.... And the real reason for this was that in order that the exploiters might secure their profits from human sweat and brawn they fall back upon these wicked methods of "divide and rule," divide the white workers from their Negro brothers.

Wherever I went I bubbled over with my enthusiasm and discovery of the Unemployment Council. I talked to my relatives about the meeting and told them what the speakers said about Negroes and whites fighting together against their bosses so that they might live like human beings. They looked aghast and warned me very solemnly that I had better stay away from those Reds who were wicked people blaspheming against God.

I began to attend all of the meetings of the Unemployment Council regularly. Never was my mind stimulated to such an extent before!...

One white worker gave me the *Communist Manifesto** to read.... It took me at least a month before I could understand what it was all about. For my own

---

* Karl Marx's *Communist Manifesto*, first published in February 1848.

edification I analyzed it paragraph by paragraph, reading passages over and over many times. I wrote a simple account of it in my own words for my own private use. Marx and Engels' statement "The history of all hitherto existing society is the history of class struggles" impressed me as a very profound truth. Life and history approached in this light assumed a new and startling significance. It dazzled me beyond words with its truth....

Every meeting of the Unemployment Council became a classroom for me. I never left one of them without bearing away with me the discovery of a new idea....

Much water had run under the bridges since I walked up to my Uncle Jeremiah at the end of his first sermon in church and shook his hand, saying: "I've got religion in me, Uncle Jeremiah."

Come to think of it, only eight years had passed. I had travelled much during that period. Life had robbed me of my innocence and illusions, but I had found something more satisfying, a realistic recognition of the world and the rational plan of scientific socialism with which to create order and harmony out of the human chaos.

Now, as if by a miracle, a new world had unfolded itself before my eyes. It, too, was a part of the white man's world, but it did not leave us Negroes standing like beggars outside in the cold. Welcoming brotherly hands were outstretched to us. We were called "comrades" without condescension or patronage.... The bitterness and hatred which I had formerly felt toward all white people was now transformed into love and understanding. Like a man who had gone through some terrible sickness of the soul I miraculously became whole again....

Up to the time I had met the Communists I did not know how to fight the lynching of Negroes* and Jim Crowism†. I was bewildered, grief-stricken and helpless. All of a sudden I found myself in an organization which fought selflessly and tirelessly to undo all the wrongs perpetrated upon my race. Here was no dilly-dallying, no pussyfooting on the question of full equality for the Negro people. The Communist position on this question was clear-cut and definite. Early in the history of the Communist Party its white leaders had been advised that if they would abandon their demand for social, political and economic equality for the Negroes, thousands more of white people would join the movement. But the Communist leaders, true to their cause and to their class, refused to compromise....

---

* It was in 1889–1918 that lynchings of African-Americans were most frequent. Of the 3,224 individuals known to have been lynched, 2,522 were black. Yet lynchings continued through the late 1960s. Lynching tragically took the form of whites burning African-Americans to death as crowds of spectators watched, with some taking parts of the dead bodies as souvenirs. See Richard M. Perloff, "The Press and Lynchings of African-Americans," *Journal of Black Studies* 30, no. 3 (2000): 315–330.

† Jim Crowism refers to state and local laws in the United States from 1876 to 1965, laws requiring separate public facilities for African-Americans and whites.

My bosses and the Negro Uncle Toms*...had warned us to keep clear of the Reds because they were foreigners and trouble makers and that the Communist program could never work in the South. But as I got to know them, the leaders of the Communist Party and the Unemployment Council seemed like the people I had always wished to know. They were workers and spoke to us in direct and heartfelt words; they spoke to us in a language we understood, the language of men who toil and seek a better life.

My new Communist friends carried on their activities under the most trying conditions. We could not work in the open, for, as I have already recounted, our headquarters were raided and closed by the police and our leaders thrown into jail.... Did we feel like conspirators or criminals? Quite the opposite. We knew we were carrying on in the spirit of the truest American patriots and Revolutionary Fathers, who, too, had to fight against the same reactionary forces in their day. I saw Frank Williams, Earl Browder and William Z. Foster[†] as the spiritual descendants of Thomas Jefferson, Thomas Paine, Patrick Henry, Frederick Douglas and John Brown. I felt it a privilege to be working with them toward the same noble goal.

1−4

Vietnam

Xuan Phuong (1929−) on Her Attraction to Vietnamese Communism

We have seen that as Semën Kanatchikov began the process of becoming a Bolshevik, he broke with his biological family. Elsewhere in his autobiography, in fact, he referred to fellow factory workers as "my near ones, my family."[17] But in other times and places, an individual was drawn into the revolutionary orbit by members of one's biological family.

---

* "Uncle Tom" was the name of the hero in Harriet B. Stowe's novel *Uncle Tom's Cabin* (1851–1852). But its most widespread usage, reflected here, was as a derogatory term regarding relationships between whites and African-Africans in which whites treat blacks in a paternalistic yet condescending way, and blacks relate to whites with deference and willing submission to racial oppression.

† As mentioned in note 16, Frank Williams is the pseudonym that Herndon used for Frank Burns. Earl Browder (1891–1973) was the Stalin-appointed leader of the Communist Party of the United States from 1930 until 1945. William Z. Foster (1881–1961) was another leader of the American Communist Party. He ran for president in 1924, 1928, and 1932 and was elected chair of the Communist Party in 1945.

We see how important family members were in this respect in Xuan Phuong's retrospective account of her life in the Vietnamese revolutionary movement. At first glance, the odds against Xuan Phuong joining that movement would seem to have been great. Xuan Phuong was born in 1929 in Eo Bau, near Hue, which had been the capital of Annam, and was raised in Dalat. She came from a family of aristocrats and had a privileged upbringing. For example, she attended the elite French boarding school, Le Couvent des Oiseaux (The Convent of the Birds), when French colonialism was at its height in Indonesia and French colonial power permeated everyday life. Yet in 1946, she joined the Viet Minh.

Indeed, in Vietnam, as in many places around the world, the Communist movement gained its strength from nationalist rejection of colonial domination. The French colonial presence in Vietnam dated in certain respects from the seventeenth century when a French Jesuit priest and Catholic missionary, Alexandre de Rhodes (b. probably 1593, d. 1660), landed at Faifo (now Danang). The Vietnamese had mounted violent though intermittent resistance against France's colonial domination in the seventeenth and eighteenth centuries. But it was not until the early twentieth century that this resistance took an organized political form. In 1920, nine years before Xuan Phuong entered the world, a young man named Nguyen Ai Quoc (Nguyen the Patriot) openly condemned French imperialism when he attended a congress of French socialists. (He would later become known as Ho Chi Minh, or "Bringer of Light.") In 1921, he became a founding member of the French Communist Party and, in the 1920s, lived in Moscow, where he was employed by the Comintern and participated in the Fifth Comintern Congress in 1924, and in China. In 1930, when Xuan Phuong was only one year old, Nguyen Ai Quoc/Ho Chi Minh (1890–1969) founded the Indochinese Communist Party, which combined Marxism–Leninism with Vietnamese nationalism and anti-colonialism.

The struggle thereby launched resulted in the "August Revolution" of 1945, led by Ho Chi Minh's Viet Minh. After Ho became chairman of the Provisional Government (premier of the Democratic Republic of Vietnam), he issued a Proclamation of Independence of the Democratic Republic of Vietnam, a document that was in part based on the French and American declarations. The Emperor, Bao Dai, abdicated. But neither the United States nor any other country recognized the new government. The Democratic Republic of Vietnam would fight against the French until 1954. When Viet Minh paratroopers defeated the French at the Battle of Dien Bien Phu, French colonial domination of Indochina came to an end.

The following is an excerpt from Xuan Phuong's autobiographical account, *Ao Dai*. Here she tells us about an important moment in her life: the day— 10 March 1946—when she left her beloved family to join the guerilla movement. She also tells us about what joining the guerilla movement meant in the days thereafter. We learn about her misgivings (especially concerning, as a Buddhist,

---

From Xuan Phuong and Danièle Mazingarbe, *Ao Dai: My War, My Country, My Vietnam* (Great Neck, NY: EMQUAD International, 2004), 49–62, 63–71.

killing another human being), about her lack of theoretical knowledge concerning Ho Chi Minh's Communism, and about the way in which her clothes, her personal appearance, and her general sense of herself underwent a profound transformation.

Xuan Phuong, who has worked as a chemist, a physician, and a filmmaker, opened an art gallery in Ho Chi Minh City (formerly Saigon). She lives there to this day.

From the earliest days of 1945 I began to hear my aunts' interminable discussions about the struggle of the populace against the Franco-Japanese rice requisitions*. From my grandmother's house, I could hear the rumbling of the drums echoing one another over the countryside. My grandmother lit incense sticks and prayed that Buddha spare us in these troubled times. Every evening at dinnertime, my uncle brought up the problem of that terrible famine that was taking a heavy toll all across the north of the country. At the time, I no longer had any news of my parents, or of the rest of my family in Phan Thiet.

It was then that my uncle began to have me actively participate in illegal actions. "Every day to get to work I have to cross a bridge," he told me. "Two Japanese soldiers armed with bayoneted rifles stand guard over this bridge and check everybody. I would like you to carry a package to someone at the market on the other side." …

Then, my uncle taught me how to make propaganda leaflets. …

In the middle of the night of March 9th, 1945, we were awakened by the sound of gunfire everywhere. The sky was glowing with pale strips of light. My uncle burst into the house: "The Japanese have just disarmed the French!" he cried out at us. …

My uncle failed to come back home one evening, so I realized that he had joined the Resistance. I then went to live with my grandmother, whose house stood in the middle of an immense orchard on the outskirts of Hue. But I didn't stay there for long.

From that moment on, things started to happen in very quick succession. In May, my uncle's organization sent me off to Hanoi to study medicine in the company of four other female students from Hue. Here on in, as Quang said, we shouldn't be satisfied with merely studying out of books. It was better to master a useful trade in order to participate in the fight for independence. … It was only later that evening when I had returned to my grandmother's house that the impact of it all finally hit me. It meant leaving everyone once again—saying good-bye to my family and friends in Hue, and going off to live alone in Hanoi. …

In August of 1945, the situation in Hanoi became very critical. In the *rue des Vermicelles,* two kilometers from the center of town, French soldiers had

---

* Since 1944, rice had been confiscated from the populace and left to rot in Japanese-guarded warehouses. [This is an original gloss by the book's author, Xuan Phuong.]

killed some Vietnamese. Showing up suddenly, Quang gave us orders to go back home: "There is going to be fighting. You must return to Hue." Two days later, the School for Midwives closed. We then left, terrified at the idea of crossing paths with some of those fearsome red-beret legionnaires who had fired on the *rue des Vermicelles*....

When I arrived back in Hue, I found my aunt and her three children living in a small house in my grandmother's garden. Ever since her husband had joined the Resistance, my aunt was living in fear.

On August 25th I witnessed the abdication of Emperor Bao Dai at the Citadel. The evening before the event, the red and gold Vietminh flag was hoisted throughout the city. There were huge demonstrations and the entire population was in the streets....

The Royal Family was grouped on the left-hand side of the courtyard. The crowd was thronging on the right. Suddenly a man's voice cried out: "From this day on, royalty is abolished in Vietnam. Emperor Bao Dai is from here on in the simple citizen Vinh Thuy. And now, citizen Vinh Thuy has permission to speak." Next, Emperor Bao Dai who looked very young stepped forward. He addressed the crowd: "Citizens, let me be understood. I prefer to be a free citizen than an enslaved king." ...

That same evening, our leaders informed us of the Japanese capitulation following the atomic bombings of Hiroshima and Nagasaki. Then, on September 2nd, the day of the official Japanese surrender in Tokyo Bay on board the USS Missouri, President Ho Chi Minh, addressing a crowd from Ba-Dinh Square in Hanoi, declared our country independent....

In my Resistance group, there were three other girls and eight boys from the same social background who came to the meetings. Sung, our new group-leader whom we called "brother," was a short, kindly, but extremely convincing man. It was thanks to him that we finally got to understand the reason why we had to reconquer our country. One evening, he called for a meeting and said: "Since you all speak French, you are going to go on a counter-propaganda mission, to explain to the French that they must not continue the war because they are going to lose it anyway." In other words, time had come for us really to join the Resistance.

Back home at my grandmother's, I hastened to go to bed but did not feel at all like sleeping. Should we obey? Should I leave my family, renounce every single thing that had been part of my life up to that point? The next morning I still hadn't managed to make a decision and when Sung arrived we remained in the garden to avoid being overheard. "You have to go," he repeated, "if we don't become independent, all of this is going to disappear." He was pointing to the house with its magnificent orchard. "Without independence, there won't be anything left of your family."

The next morning my decision was made. All around me, the young people of my generation were going away to participate in the revolutionary movement. I could no longer postpone my decision. I told my mother that I needed to have a talk with her....

Towards five in the evening, I started down the track that led to the river. I boarded the Eo Bau ferry with my heart in my throat and when I turned around there was my younger sister, Yen, who was sobbing. I would then have liked to turn back, but it was already too late.

On the other bank, I met with three people of my group. That was the rule. We only moved in small groups of three at most, to avoid attracting attention. The leader immediately took us to a straw hut, deep into a very destitute area, where the only furnishing consisted in a large bamboo bed-frame. "From now on, you are part of the revolution," he said. . . .

In the morning, as soon as we opened our eyes, each one of us was given two fist-size balls of rice and sesame seeds, to be directly eaten out of our hands. That was to be the entire food ration for the day. Our first mission consisted in preparing propaganda leaflets to be handed out to the French soldiers who came to the market every day. The girls had to be dressed as vegetable hawkers and the boys as bootblacks or cigarette dealers. "French soldiers, why are you staying here? You only know too well that we, the Vietnamese, are fighting for our independence." We all wrote our own leaflets in French, then proceeded to print them. In mine, which were approved by our leader, I explained that we came from well-to-do families, that we had relinquished everything to fight for our independence, and that we would struggle to the bitter end. . . .

It was at that point that I gave up my *ao dai** and started wearing black pants and a brown shirt. White, by then, was forbidden, as it was too conspicuous and too easily dirtied under our living conditions. . . .

One evening, as I was already lying down exhausted on the bed, someone called: "Phuong, your mother is here." Outside, I saw my mother standing by a rickshaw and I ran to her and hugged her. She returned my kisses, crying. "You must come back," she implored. "The entire family is suffering without you. Grandma wants to die. I beg of you, come home."

"Mommy, try to understand me. If no one gets involved in the fight, we shall never become independent. I had to leave. I had no other choice in the matter."

"And your father, how am I to tell him?" she went on.

"You must explain to him that leaving was my decision, and mine alone."

I talked to my mother the whole night long and, at dawn, she left without once turning around. When I got back into the house, Sung was waiting there. He just gazed at me without saying anything because he knew that I had made up my mind.

We stayed in that house until December 19th, 1946. On that day, we had returned so exhausted from the market that we did not even feel like eating. All of a sudden, rifle and machine gun fire burst out in the distance. "There we are. It has begun!" Sung cried out. He then signaled for us to gather around him and he declared solemnly "Up to this point, you have been actors in an unarmed struggle,

---

*An *ao dai* is the Vietnamese national costume for women. Its form has undergone several changes since the eighteenth century. In the 1930s, it was a long, somewhat tight-fitting dress that was often made of silk. (*Dai* means "long" in Vietnamese.)

a propaganda struggle. From now on, you are to be engaged in an armed conflict." In view of the fact that the agreements reached between the French and the Vietnamese had not been respected and Ho Chi Minh's call to President Léon Blum had remained unanswered, Sung explained to us that Ho had just launched an appeal for the reconquest of national independence. He then gave each of us a grenade—the first that I had ever seen. "If the French arrive, pull out the pin and throw it in their direction." As a Buddhist, I realized for the first time what was expected of us. "But I'll kill them!" I cried out. He had a stinging answer: "If they don't die first, then it is you who will die!"...

The second day, the soldiers led us to another straw hut in a district near Hue. It resembled a lot the one we had just left: "Here are your new headquarters. From now on, your mission consists in explaining to those Vietnamese who do not want war why we, on the contrary, do; and to the French that they must surrender." From that point on, we infiltrated the entire area every day in order to explain to the people the reason for our personal engagement....

Within several weeks, we were caught up in a swirl of events. Every day, the bombings followed one another and the number of casualties multiplied. Every day we had another mission to accomplish.... All we knew was that Ho Chi Minh was at the head of the fight, but he seemed very remote to us, like some kind of religious image.... We simply went about fulfilling the tasks that were assigned to us, with our typical enthusiasm and determination....

In January 1947, just after the defeat of the Vietminh in Hue, we left the city. Traveling by night, along with the heavy brigade unit from the Hue front, we went to Nghe An Province, three hundred thirty kilometers away, in the Fourth Zone. It was a forced march through forests, almost always by night, along Route No. 1, which was dotted with French outposts. Some of our comrades had already preferred to return to their families, which was something that we were still free to do.

From here on in, there were only twenty or so of us left in Group C from the district of Phu Cam. The trip seemed endless and, little by little, due to our fatigue, we lightened our loads of food and clothing. When we came across sand dunes, those of us who had preserved some little family mementos, preferred to bury them there. "Here is the tomb of our past," one of us uttered....

The hardest of all was having to take off again with our entire load, and never really being able to stay in the same place for long. When I was in the depths of despair, I would recall my former life, the happy moments with my family, and it was these recollections that helped me to go on.... In these already very poor villages, life was to become still more difficult. The population not only had to till the land to feed itself, but also to "cooperate." In other terms, it had to provide rice for the soldiers and furnish manpower for the army, for Ho Chi Minh had given an order to destroy everything in order to stop the advancing French....

We knew that Ho Chi Minh was a communist. In order to save the homeland, he had been able to mobilize the forces of a whole people, so being a communist, then, was something admirable. But our theoretical knowledge stopped there and I recognize the fact that we didn't really look any further.

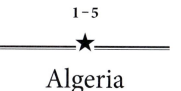

Algeria

Henri Alleg (1921–) on Clandestine Communist Activities during World War II

I
n Algeria, just as in Vietnam, the creation of a Party organization based on the participation and support of the masses was tied up with the question of national liberation from the colonial domination of the French. But in Algeria, the Comintern's 1924 policy of "Bolshevization"—the creation of a party of the masses in which the representation of ethnic groups matched the demographic profile of the entire population—encountered significant obstacles. The most obvious was the absence, until 1936, of a specifically "Algerian" Communist Party.[18] Beginning in 1924, there had been but an Algerian section of the French Communist Party, created in 1920. But other factors, too, caused "indigenization"—the incorporation of native peoples in colonial or settler societies—to proceed slowly in Algeria. Throughout the 1920s–1930s, the Communist Party of Algeria remained predominantly composed of Europeans, some of whom rejected national liberation, and, moreover, believed that social revolution in Algeria was predicated on social revolution having been successful in France.

Nonetheless, despite repression and a small urban working class (located in cities such as Algiers, Oran, and Sidi Bel Abbès), native Algerians did join the Party in increasing—though still very small—numbers in the 1920s, 1930s, and 1940s. Most, but not all, of them believed that national liberation was a necessary precondition of Communism in Algeria. In 1952, the Algerian Communist Party (PCA) had come out formally in favor of Algerian national liberation, and in 1956, during the French-Algerian war that would end with Algerian independence in 1962, the PCA was incorporated into the FLN (Front de Libération Nationale or National Liberation Front).

Among the French Communists living in Algeria who championed the cause of its independence was Henri Alleg. In 1939, when he was eighteen years old, Alleg headed by himself to Algeria, where he soon launched a deep involvement with the Algerian Communist Party. One important dimension thereof was his service as editor in chief of the *Alger Républicaine,* a newspaper that the French authorities would ban in 1955 because of its pro-Communist and pro-

From Henri Alleg, *Mémoire Algérienne: Souvenirs de luttes et d'espérances* (*Algerian Memoir: Recollections of Struggles and Hopes)* (Paris: Editions Stock, 2005). Translated (and partially annotated) by Lilia Putintsev.

independence stance. In June 1957, Alleg was arrested in Algiers by the members of a French Parachutist regiment. Detained on grounds that he had endangered the security of the French state, he was tortured (including being subjected to waterboarding) by French officers. He escaped in 1961, having in the meantime smuggled out *The Question* (*La Question*, 1958), an account of his horrific ordeal.

But in the passage that follows, excerpted from the memoirs he published in 2005, he offers retrospective glimpses of involvement in clandestine Communist activities during World War II. It gives us a sense of the repression faced there by rank-and-file Communists, whether native or French, and their resulting isolation from the formal structures of the Algerian Communist Party. It also shows us the decisions that they made in devising strategies to carry on their activities in the face of both obstacles.

I had not found in Oran* the warmth of the friendships struck up in Algiers† nor the joyous and passionate discussions, followed late into the evening at the M'Guellati Café, beneath the arches perfumed with the exaltation of mint tea. From time to time, Isabelle Vial, the Communist teacher I had met in Marseilles, gathered in her house some thirty young men and women, laborers and office workers who had belonged to the Youth Hostel movement‡. Under her supervision, they often went on weekend excursions. Even if, between her and the majority of the members of the group, there existed a certain political complicity, the Pétainist§ climate that had developed in the country compelled her to a new prudence when questions of current events came up. As if—and this was the case—she was not very certain of who surrounded her. In these meetings and hikes, there were no Muslims. Not because Isabelle did not strongly wish to recruit them, but simply because, at that time, segregation was even stronger and more difficult to transgress in Oran than in Algiers. Under such conditions, meetings and discussions could hardly be appealing and did not capture my interest. Excluded from the school and without real attachment to this city, I decided to go back to Algiers where I returned with the feeling of coming home.

---

* Algerian city on the Mediterranean.

† Capital of Algeria.

‡ This movement began in 1909 when Richard Schirrmann, a German teacher, and Wilhelm Münker, an ecologist, realized that school groups needed lodgings for the night when visiting the countryside. The first *Jugendherberge* (inn of German youth) was opened in Altena, Westphalia, in Schirrmann's own school. In 1912, it was replaced by a permanent inn at the Altena Castle, which is still open today. The movement quickly spread around the world. The International Youth Hostel Federation (IYHF) was founded in Amsterdam in 1932 by representatives of associations in Switzerland, Czechoslovakia, Germany, Poland, the Netherlands, Norway, Denmark, the United Kingdom, Ireland, France, and Belgium. North Africa and New Zealand also took part. Richard Schirrmann became its head in 1933. The Nazis forced him to resign in 1936.

§ Marshal Pétain was the head of Vichy France, a regime centered in the French city of Vichy and one that collaborated with the Nazi occupation from 1940 to 1944. The Vichy regime emphasized conservative values, repressed dissent, deported Jews to concentration camps, and actively stamped out Communists and other antifascists.

Several of my friends whom I had left several months earlier were still there, but not our great conversations at the youth hostel between the Algerians and the refugees who had come from France, Belgium or elsewhere or moreover already belonged to another age. When the hostel closed, each one of us, in order to find housing, dealt with the situation as well as he could. The more monied had rented a room in the hotel or in the home of a resident.... For my part, I should have often had to change housing, but I did not have too much difficulty in finding some work to allow me to survive....

By the intervention of an engineer refugee from Belgium whose acquaintance I had made in the youth hostel, I was able to find a position in a business where he himself worked. This was a factory which produced paint, putty and various building materials, located in Bab el Oued. Other than the boss, M. Legendre, his deputy who took on the role of overseer, the accountant and the engineer, there were some fifteen workers, including myself who was recently hired. The boss and those who assisted him were all European and the workers (with the exception of myself) all Algerian, but the common word to designate them, in the mouths of those who managed, was "indigenous." In the workshop—a great shed which was dominated by the windowed office of the management—great cylindrical vats were installed which turned on central pivots to soften the products. From the first day, they appointed me to the putty making....

At noon, work stopped and all the workers evacuated the workshop for an hour, waiting to begin again. They placed themselves on the sidewalk, backs along the wall of the factory, to eat their snacks—often some grilled peppers, a tomato, a portion of dates or cluster of grapes with a bit of bread. I did as they did and it was an opportunity to join their conversation. The first days, even though no one demonstrated open hostility toward me, I felt a certain mistrust that was not difficult for me to understand. Why would this red-headed, glasses-wearing guy do the "work of an Arab" when he was a European and knew how to read and write?...But, that which worried them above all—and I did not notice it—was my work rhythm. When a truck brought sacks of plaster or chemical products which entered into the making of paint and putty to the factory, the overseer asked several of them to leave their posts for enough time to help with the unloading of the sacks of about thirty kilos each. A tiring job, but I did it willingly for it liberated me from the vat and its emissions. I worked very quickly because I had never been able to do things slowly and, most of all, because I had not learned, as those who are used to manual labor in a factory, that one has to conserve his energy and respect the movement which does not oblige others—the overseer looking on—to accelerate their tempo. When one of the laborers had taken a sack on his back, brought it to the far end of the workshop where the material was accumulating and came back to the truck to take another one, I had already dispatched two sacks. This no longer worked. One day one of the members of the team, one of the older ones, a gnarled and mustached man, gave me a sign to stop behind a column of piled sacks, sheltered from the gaze of the bosses who stood before the windows of their office. His face close to mine and his eyes in mine, he said to me, almost menacingly:

"What do you want?"

I did not understand anything.

"But I don't want anything...."

"Then, listen. You and me, each one the same thing. I take a sack, you take a sack. I place a sack, you place a sack. Nothing more."

This was my first lesson in class struggle and later, when I discovered the theoretical foundations of it and I discovered the mechanism of surplus*, I could not stop myself from thinking gratefully of my first "teacher," an illiterate worker from Bab el Oued, who was, more than I, conscious of what was exploitation and also knew, in detail, how to make sure not to aggravate it by his own conduct....

The Legionnaires† were not simply there for decorum. It was also the time of intense and permanent ratting out in which the "messengers of sepia"—the most motivated being grouped into the SOL, the Service of the Order of the Legion, which was to be mistrusted—played a particularly active role. From time to time, the press talked of the incarceration of Communist and nationalist activists. The concentration camps of the Algerian South, Djenien Bou Rezg, Mecheria, Bossuet, and Gerryville, were filling up with new arrivals, "anti-national elements" interned without legal justification, but, according to the wise principle formulated by those at the top of the Oran Police, that it was better to imprison the "traitors" than to lose time in watching them....

The more cynical and brutal the regime got, the more I felt the need for effective engagement, and I had searched and finally made contact with several Communist activists. One of them, a French worker from France who worked in a workshop in Amiraute, had abruptly broken off contact, no doubt recalled to France. The other was a postal worker. I found out, sometime after our first and very quick meetings, that he had been arrested. The third one was a railway worker, Jacques Bentolila, soon apprehended himself and condemned to forced labor in perpetuity in a trial which made a lot of noise at the time. Sixty-one Communists (including six women) were summoned to appear in court and people ended up calling it "The Trial of the Sixty-One."‡

---

* In Marxist economics, a surplus refers to surplus value, surplus product, and surplus labor.

† A unit in the French Army established in 1831, which served primarily overseas in the colonies.

‡ **Author's [Henri Alleg's] Note:** The trial opened on 9 February 1942, before the special selection of the Permanent Military Tribunal of Algiers, a special jurisdiction created by Pétain against the Resistance to the Occupation and for the policy of collaboration. In Algiers, the defendants were accused of having participated in the reconstitution of the dissolved Algerian Communist Party. The verdict was rendered on 21 March 1942: six death sentences—Lisette Vincent, Thomas Ibañez, Georges Raffini, Danelius Dietmar (an antifascist German who had joined the underground of the ACP), Emile Touati, and Ahmed Smaili (in absentia)—six to forced labor in perpetuity. For the others, two hundred twenty-eight years of forced labor and prison in total. Eight of the accused missed the call. They had died from typhus in the Barberousse prison where an epidemic had left two hundred victims, among them Kaddour Belkhaim, the secretary of the Algerian Communist Party.

Since the Nazi attack of June 1941 against the Soviet Union, all the questions which could have been posed on the nature of the conflict and which, for months, during the "*drôle de guerre*"* and after the defeat, had slowed enrollment into the ranks of the Communists, disappeared before a major obligation: that of fighting against a Nazi Germany and preventing the victory of fascism and its racist and slave thesis. The entire future, that of occupied France, that of Algeria and the colonial peoples under the yoke, the hope of a new and free world, depended on it.

Francis† was in the same state of mind as I. He did not want to stay with his hands in his pockets and wait following events, and thought that another voice was needed to counter the booming Vichy propaganda. Even if our very feeble means only permitted us to reach a very small circle, we knew that in Algiers everyone was not aligned with the policy of submission to the Nazis. It would be like a sign that, despite the repression, the antifascist forces, those on the European side as well as the Muslim, who had expressed themselves in the time of the Popular Front‡, the youth in particular, had not abandoned the struggle. We had lost all contact with the Algerian Communist Party, and its clandestine literature did not reach us. We would speak in the name of the organization of the Algerian Communist Youth, of which we did not know that some groups still existed, despite the arrests and the repression that continued. With sticky labels bought in business and with the help of rubber letters, provided by a game of *Little Printer* sold in toy stores, we had manufactured "butterflies" denouncing fascism and glorifying the struggle of the Resistance in France and in Europe. Come the night, we would go stick them on the walls of the most frequented streets of the city. The printing of the tracts posed problems that, without technical means, we were not able to resolve. We had at our disposal only a plaque of duplicate paste, some greasy flasks of ink and some feathers reserved for this very use....

The few members of the Communist Youth—we called it "Jice," "a Jice," "the Jice"§—who were active in Algiers got wind of this activity carried out without them, texts and sheets signed "Communist Youth," and worried about their origins, asking themselves if there was not a police provocation in it all. But Algiers is a small city and, despite the extreme vigilance with which it is necessary to surround oneself, they ended up discovering the thread that led to us, and we were soon regularly organized in a clandestine group of three, a troika, a word that had until then only evoked for me a sleigh pulled by a team of three horses sliding in the snow of the Russian forest.

Our contact with the higher rank was carried out via the intermediary of a young European with the appearance of a high schooler, a girl from the colonial

---

* "Phoney War," or period of the months leading up to the German invasion of Poland in September 1939, when European armies were on edge but did not launch attacks.

† Francis Reyne was the son of Isabelle Vial, whom Alleg had known since Marseille and the time of the *drôle de guerre*.

‡ An alliance of French leftwing forces (Socialist, Communist, other) that won the 1936 legislative elections, leading to the formation of a government headed by Leon Blum.

§ J/C for Jeunesse Communiste, or Communist Youth.

bourgeoisie. She was not more than fifteen years old and seemed to me very—too—young for such a task, and I worried about it a bit....

Georgette Cottin, that was the name of our liaison, despite her young age, was very mature, very motivated, very efficient, and at the same time, very prudent and discrete. She must have been that way all the time because neither her father nor her mother were Communists and she had to be undercover even in her own family. Her deep feelings of revolt against the misery, racism, and injustice had been perhaps transmitted to her—skipping some generations—by a maternal ancestor, an officer in the French Army toward the middle of the preceding century, who had been condemned and deported to Algeria for refusing to participate in operations of repression against striking workers.

1-6

Poland

Jacek Kuroń (1934–2004) on the Appeal of Communism after World War II

A fter World War II, as Communist-led national liberation movements changed people's lives in countries such as Vietnam and Algeria, Soviet troops occupied much of Eastern Europe, including Poland. Yet the incorporation of Eastern Europe into the Soviet sphere of influence was by no means accomplished only by Soviet military power. In Poland, as in other Eastern European countries, the immediate postwar years constituted a period of political transition in which Moscow gradually established Communist control—and the power monopoly of the various national Communist parties—by rigging elections and by using repressive tactics to deny political power to competitors, such as parties representing socialists, peasants, and national resistance movements. In Poland, for example, it took two years for Poland's Communist Party—the Polish United Workers' Party (PZPR)—to consolidate its power. During this period of political flux, Polish people—even children—grappled with choices about their political identities.

One child caught up in the political confusion of the early postwar years was Jacek Kuroń. Kuroń would go on to become a national (and world) political

From Jacek Kuroń, *Wiara i wina: Do i od komunizmu (Faith and Blame: To and from Communism)* (London: Aneks Publishers, 1989), 28–30. Translation: Christina Manetti.

figure. He did so first as a Warsaw University lecturer whose coauthored "Open Letter to the Party" (1964) condemned the Party as being estranged from the working class, then as the architect of the intelligentsia's partnership with workers in the Committee to Assist Workers (KOR, founded in 1976), and eventually as a member of the Polish Parliament (Sejm) and minister of labor and social policy. He would play a significant role in demolishing the Communist order that, as a fourth-grader, he was beginning to support, and in constructing the new order that would replace it. But here, in the following passage, he recalls a time when he was but another son of an engineer, a child dragged into the world of postwar political conflict by a father seeking to build a new Poland.

For the young Kuroń, just as for certain other Poles, Communism's appeal had to be understood as a response to the horrors of World War II. The logical culmination of the old order was the Holocaust, which resulted in the destruction of Polish Jewry. Only Communism—opposed even to socialism—promised the destruction of the old order and the creation of a new one, in which social justice would reign.

The passage also foreshadows the theme of the next chapter: children's subjective experience of Communism during the ideological (and real!) wars of the twentieth century.

Just after the Soviet army entered, we moved to Kraków. It was there, already, that a choice had to be made. That sounds funny—I was in fourth grade at the time. But the times were like that. At school people talked about politics, the Soviets, Anders' army. People used to sing songs like this one:

> They arrived from Moscow with a ruckus
> With Soviet [automatic] pistols, and propaganda
> They ate and drank up everything
> And instead of paying—punched you in the face.

> Shit whistled in the grass*
> And thought to itself, as it lay there straight,
> "Finally I have lived to see it:
> 'Cause every piece of shit is important today."

I sang along with everyone else, too. But increasingly in discussions I was taking the side of the new order—as the only one in my class, completely alone. Why did I do it? Of course the simplest answer would be: because my father was for it. But of course it wasn't that simple.

My father started supporting the new order because he was hopeful that it was an opportunity for Poland at that time. In 1945, in Kraków, my father's boss in the Office of Information and Propaganda of the Main Headquarters of the Union

---

* From an expression "to be in the know"—*wiedzieć co się w trawie piszczy.*

of Armed Struggle—of the Home Army* and Home Army counterintelligence, Śledziński, proposed that he continue working for him—and he turned him down. I would overhear him explaining how the country and its people were completely devastated, that we didn't have the energy to continue fighting. I think, however, that this was an argument for Śledziński. My father's attitude towards the new order was much more complex.

My grandfather and father both joined the new PPS right away, despite the fact that the London leadership was calling on people to boycott it. For the PPS workers, like my grandfather, it was the same party and name, and people. My father, by the way, was still upset about having been thrown out of the old PPS. Not long before, when Antoni Pajdak was at our house, he was shouting:

"You threw me out of the party!"
"What for?" asked Pajdak.
"For collaborating with the Communists."
"Well, then we were right."

And this seemed to flummox him.

My father organized the first congress of engineers in Wrocław, in the Recovered Territories, in 1946, was in the leadership of the Polish Federation of Engineering Associations (NOT†) and used to write economic texts for *The Worker‡*. He was a true child of his profession. For him, the vision of a new Poland designed and built like a machine was appealing.

My father's colleagues would participate in quite a lot of discussions at our house. Among them were Communists from the PPR, but also socialists who after the war didn't join the PPS. I listened to all of that, especially later in Warsaw, when we were living alone with father on Lwowska [Street]. I would go with him to various meetings as well, where I used to be given real, bitter coffee, which at first I couldn't stand, but it was probably then that I learned to drink it. I would call what my father used to say there faith in the mechanism of nationalization. He was convinced that when the means of production had been nationalized—and he understood this to mean simply the nationalization of industry—the rest of the wonderful system of social justice would come of its own accord, since the source of all evil is private property. This is how it could be said in simplified form.

In the arguments with various "reactionaries," he was decidedly on the side of the new order—but what kinds of things he would tell me! Because on the one hand there was his tie to the Communists, and on the other—his patriotism and what happened in 1920. To me, it all seemed inconsistent. My father was not able to reckon with any phase of his life, he wasn't able to say: "Yes, here I made a mistake." In my youthful way, I tried to understand the world in clear and simple

---

* In the Polish text, Kurón uses the acronym BiP, short for BIP KG ZWZ–AK, or Biuro Informacji i Propagandy Komendy Głównej Związku Walki Zbrojnej–Armii Krajowej.
† NOT: Naczelna Organizacja Techniczna—Main Technical Organization.
‡ *Robotnik*.

categories, hence my rebellion against my father, though even today he is my great love.

A person, as he is growing up, must rebel against authorities—in order to stand on his own two legs, so he doesn't become a cripple for the rest of his life. I saw many people who did not rebel and they have a deep psychological problem: the inability to take responsibility for their own decisions. If I hadn't liked my father, I would have probably gone to the right, but he fascinated me so much that I went to the left, and opposed him only in the sense that I wanted to straighten his life out, to eliminate its contradictions. I didn't know that in doing this I was choosing such a complicated biography for myself.

A person, who is growing up, should rebel against the existing world order. Because that order always betrays the ideals in which children are raised. The alternative to any youth rebellion is adaptation—i.e., obedience and imitation, while every person, particularly a young person, wants after all to be the subject of his own life.

For me, rejecting the old order was the obvious consequence of my experiences in life up to that point, which above all were those of the occupation. The Jewish Holocaust, my most personal, most horrific experience, seemed to me to be the direct result and most complete expression of the era of class rule, exploitation and oppression. The loneliness that I have talked about here meant that I lived through literature—literature truly participated in my life. And thus all that I read—Dickens, Balzac, Zola, Żeromski, Brzozowski, Kaden-Bandrowski... seemed to me to be one great act of deception of the old world. As proof that the Nazi genocide comprised its logical and moral consequence. I was not alone in this conviction, or perhaps independent either. An integral part of my experiences was my witnessing of the Holocaust through literature. This meant works by Borowski, Nałkowska and Andrzejewski, as I recall, who depicted the crematoria, the burning ghettos, and—worse than death—the debasement of people, as a sentence meted out to itself by the old world.

In my eyes, the fact that these shameful times were not yet over was confirmed by the crowd that killed Holocaust survivors in Kielce, Radom and Kraków, and also by the bishops who hesistated to condemn these killings unequivocally.

My father was to thank for my faith—in the name of which I condemned these acts, and which was a source of hope for me. This was why I was all the more unhappy with him for not having condemned such things more vigorously, for not having enough hope—that is, for having a faith that was too weak. I thought to myself—it is impossible to live in this world if you doubt that you can be liberated from the shame that is not yet completely behind us. Can it be so surprising, then, that the new order, the one that was supposed to eliminate this threat once and for all, became my life's sense—its sacrum?

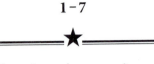

Latin America

Testimonies from Members of Peru's Shining Path (Sendero Luminoso)

The origins of the Shining Path, a Maoist revolutionary movement, date from late 1960s. Abimael Guzmán (b. 1934), a philosophy professor, organized a small revolutionary group at the National University of San Cristóbal of Huamanga, located in the rural region of Ayacucho. But it was in the 1980s and early 1990s that the Shining Path operated most vigorously, launching its terrorist war against the Peruvian government when members burned ballot boxes in a village during Peru's first democratic elections since 1964. Although Guzmán's capture in Lima in 1992 dealt a severe blow to the movement, it has recently been resurgent in Peru's mountainous regions. It regards itself as the sole "true" Communist revolutionary movement remaining in the world.

Whom did the Shining Path draw into its ranks, and why? Its base of social support was somewhat diverse. Among its adherents were young people from rural Peru, such as students at the National University of San Cristóbal of Huamanga, and at Lima's San Marcos University. At these and other institutions, students were exposed to a curriculum that included a dogmatically Marxist schema of history designed to demonstrate the need for collective violence. In the early years, the senderistas (Spanish for members of the Shining Path) also gained the support of many peasants. They believed that the movement would create a rural world in which justice prevailed. But the senderistas failed to demonstrate respect for rural customs and traditions. Their guerilla army, moreover, committed horrific violence, even against their own ranks, as well as terrorist acts designed to overthrow the Peruvian government and create a Communist regime. Eventually, the very peasants whose oppression the Shining Path sought, at least nominally, to alleviate turned against the organization.

The following selections, although brief, are designed to give readers a sense of the different tactics that the Shining Path used to gain members and the different motivations—the quest for social justice, but also the fear of violence and reprisal—that attracted supporters. The interviews excerpted here were conducted by Peru's Truth and Reconciliation Commission (Comisión de la

Published with the permission of the Centro de Información para la Memoria Colectiva y los Derechos Humanos de la Defensoría del Pueblo, Lima, Peru, and the witness himself. Translation: Glennys Young.

Verdad y Reconciliación, www.cverdad.org), established in 2001 by the Peruvian government to investigate the atrocities and human rights violations committed in the 1980s and 1990s by the Shining Path, the Peruvian Army, and another organization, the Cuban-leaning Marxist revolutionary group known as the Túpac Amaru Revolutionary Movement (MRTA). The commission delivered its final report on 28 August 2003.

FROM: TESTIMONY NO 720036. INTERVIEWEE: ANDRÉS OSCOCO ASPUR

The interview took place on 28 October 2002, in the Penal de YANAMILLA, district of AYACUCHO, province of HUAMANGA, department of AYACUCHO. The interviewers were Ulises Mayhuire Córdova and Néstor Vásquez Ayala.

In approximately the year 1983, according to the deponent, "the subversives arrived and began to organize in my village," explaining to them the goals and objectives of their actions in the different districts of national territory, and invited the whole population to leave their homes, to abandon the village and to take refuge in the mountains and streams, arguing that the repression would come for them and would kill them.

Indeed, the village, seeing itself put under pressure by the "senderistas" (militants of Sendero Luminoso) to leave and believing that the police or the military would come to kill them, went to the mountains and streams taking with them their small children, their food supplies, electric blankets and sheets of plastic to make tents and spend the night.

The witness remembers that his mother, Aurora Aspur Orihuela, also did the same thing in order to protect the health and life of their children, having left their home, their farms, went to the mountains, where they lived in huts, made a base from the foliage of the trees or plastic tents, suffering many difficulties, fleeing the persecution of the military, police, and voluntary watchmen of (PALLCAS), district of (CHUNGUI), that many times, they arrived in an unexpected way in (TASTABAMA) and to the places where they had taken refuge, there they burned their houses, stole their possessions, carried off their animals, murdered or detained their fellow countrymen, according to the deponent, without the most minimal respect for life.

FROM: TESTIMONY NO. 202001. TESTIMONY OF CESAR ORIHUELA GUTIÉRREZ

Cesar Orihuela Gutiérrez was born in the community of Orronco, district of (CHUNGUI), province of (LA MAR), department of AYACUCHO. He is relating that when he was twenty-three years old, that during the first half of the decade of the 1980s, the population of the community of ORONCCOY were forced to submit to the Sendero Luminoso organization: "I was young, I didn't know how life was. I had practically just opened my eyes, thought that it was the truth, that I understood clearly that the comrades of Sendero Luminoso were looking after us. They taught us from age five through ten, we were pioneers and carried out the assignment of surveillance and espionage, from age eleven to fifteen they were soldiers of the local force which had as its assignment looking after the population at the senderista base and from age sixteen to twenty they were soldiers of the main force, they went to other communities to carry out actions against the police forces," he recounts.

FROM: TESTIMONY NO. 70054

The interview took place on 9 August 2002, in the Establecimiento Penitenciario de Máxima Seguridad de Mujeres, Chorrillos, Lima, Peru. The interviewer was Alissa Vanessa Tejada Fernández. Date prepared: 15 August 2002.

From the section of the testimony entitled "Context and Antecedents."

Between 1973 and 1974 she, her parents, and four brothers arrived from the interior of the country to live in the district of VILLA EL SALVADOR, province and department of LIMA. The deponent reported that when they arrived at this district, the whole place was an area of sandy ground, it was a very populated zone, generally populated by people who migrated from the provinces.

The residents united to ask for the services of water and light, they were settlers who had a lot of enterprise and tenacity; and, according to what the deponent related this made her enthusiastic.

NOTES

Notes 3–10 were originally published in Reginald E. Zelnik., ed., trans., *A Radical Worker in Tsarist Russia: The Autobiography of Semën Ivanovich Kanatchikov* (Stanford: Stanford University Press, 1986), 402–404.

1. The initial split within Russia's Marxist political party, the Russian Social Democratic Labor Party, occurred in 1903 at what was more or less the Party's founding congress. Lenin and another Russian Marxist, Julius Martov, differed in the definition of a party member. While Lenin demanded that a Party member must demonstrate "personal participation in one of the party's organizations," Martov advocated a more flexible and elastic notion of participation ("regular personal support under the guidance of one of the party's organizations").

2. Reginald E. Zelnik, "Introduction: Kanatchikov's *Story of My Life* as Document and Literature," in Reginald E. Zelnik, ed., trans., *A Radical Worker in Tsarist Russia: The Autobiography of Semën Ivanovich Kanatchikov* (Stanford, CA: Stanford University Press, 1986), xviii.

3. The Gopper factory was a fairly large metalworks (600 workers in 1905, according to Laura Engelstein, *Moscow, 1905: Working Class Organization and Political Conflict*, Stanford: Stanford University Press, 1982, 85) located in Moscow's Serpukhov district in the southernmost part of the city.

4. The equation of "student" with "revolutionary" stemmed from the 1870s, when the revolutionary populist movement first caught on among students in Russia's major university centers. Students remained a prominent element in the revolutionary movement in the decades that followed.

5. The jewel-studded Iversky (Iberian) icon of the Mother of God, located in a chapel at the entrance to Moscow's Red Square, was deeply venerated by the people of Moscow. "Not a day passed but it was taken in a [horsedrawn] carriage, at a high fee, to the bedside of a sick person, or to a newly installed apartment, or to a family feast.... All along the road the passers-by uncovered and crossed themselves, and when the carriage stopped in front of a 'client's' house, a crowd formed to witness the 'descent' of the image. The faithful followed it to the door, while others devotedly kissed the seat on which the ikon had rested...." Henri Troyat, *Daily Life in Russia under the Last Tsar* (New York: Macmillan, 1962), 65–66. Ioann (or John) of Kronstadt (1829–1908) was a renowned Orthodox spiritual leader widely revered for his healing powers. Calling him by the diminutive name of "Vaniukha" was like calling him "Johnny," and was intended to show disrespect.

6. *Die Weber*, a play in five acts by the German writer Gerhart Hauptmann (1862–1946), was completed in 1892, but its performance was repeatedly prohibited by the Berlin police and Prussian judicial authorities. Nevertheless, it had been performed in several German cities by 1894, thanks in part to successful litigation. The play depicts the exploitation of Silesian linen weavers and the bloody uprising that resulted in 1844. Two illegal Russian translations appeared under the title *Tkachi* in 1895, and they soon enjoyed enormous success in radical circles. The translation printed by the "People's Will Group" (*Gruppa narodnovol'tsev*) frequently appeared among the brochures confiscated from workers' groups during police raids in 1895 and the years that followed. See, for example, *Rabochie dvizhenie v Rossii v XIX veke* (*The Workers' Movement in Russia in the Nineteenth Century*), vol. 4, part 1, 33, 35, 75, 319, 321, 680, 715.

7. The "song of the weavers," repeated in various sections of Hauptmann's play, was considered particularly provocative by the German authorities because of its open call for vengeance against employers. The passage cited here appears in Acts 25 and 5 of the original play. (I have translated directly from the Russian, which has only a loose resemblance to the German.) For the full text of the German folksong from which Hauptmann borrowed the song of the weavers, see Hans Schwab-Felisch, *Gerhart Hauptmann: Die Weber: Vollständiger Text des Schauspiels. Dokumentation* (*Gerhart Hauptmann, The Weavers: A Complete Text of the Play. Documentation*)(Ullstein, Frankfurt am Main, 1973), 115–118.

8. The original Russian translation of this Polish pamphlet, *Chto nuzhno znat' i pomnit' kazhdomu rabochemu?* (*What Every Worker Should Know and Remember*), was hectographed in 1895, but was printed for the first time (by the Union of Russian Social Democrats in Geneva) only in 1895. (There were slight variations in the Russian title.) Like *The Weavers*, it was widely used to propagandize workers and was frequently confiscated by the police. (See *Rabochie dvizhenie v Rossii v XIX veke*, vol. 4, part 1, 130, 284, 319–321, 324, 443, 492, 708, 724, for examples from the years 1895–1897.) The original author was the Polish anarcho-Marxist Edward Abramowski (1868–1918).

9. Georgy V. Plekhanov (1857–1918), the most prominent representative of the Russian Marxist intelligentsia from the mid-1980s to the turn of the century, published the partially autobiographical *Russkii rabochii v revoliutsionnom dvizhenii* (*The Russian*

Worker in the Revolutionary Movement)first in his Geneva periodical, *Sotsial-Demokrat* (1890–1892), and then as a separate pamphlet (1892). One of his purposes was to inspire working-class militants by demonstrating that they had had heroic predecessors in the 1870s, when Plekhanov had been active in propagandizing St. Petersburg workers. It is not at all clear in what way Plekhanov's booklet would have shed any light on the biases of Kanatchkov's father or the distortions in his stories.

10. The cult of St. Nicholas (Nikolay-ugodnik), originally a Greek saint, was brought to Russia from Constantinople by merchants and soldiers, and the much-revered saint entered the spiritual world of the Eastern Slavs at least a century before Kiev's official conversion to Christianity in 988. With time, in the popular imagination Saint Nicholas became the spiritual protector of the Orthodox Christian population against marauding infidels such as the Tatars. For a brief summary, see Konrad Onasch, *Icons* (London: Barnes, 1963), 347. The militant revolutionary and student of peasant life Sergey Kravchinsky (1851–1895) wrote: "Of all the saints, St. Nicholas is perhaps the most popular with the Russians." Stepniak (Kravchinsky's pseudonym), *The Russian Peasantry, Their Agrarian Condition, Social Life, and Religion* (Westport, CT: Hyperion Press, 1977), 360. The author recounts some of the popular tales about St. Nicholas on 365–368.

11. I draw here upon Igal Halfin's pioneering work on early Soviet autobiographers. See in particular his *Red Autobiographies: Initiating the Bolshevik Self* (Seattle: Herbert J. Ellison Center for Russian, East European, and Central Asian Studies, University of Washington, 2011), 4–5.

12. Rodney D. Coates, *Race and Ethnicity: Across Time, Space, and Discipline* (Boston: Brill, 2004), 208.

13. Robin D. G. Kelley, "A New War in Dixie: Communists and the Unemployed in Birmingham, Alabama," *Labor History* 30, no. 3 (1989): 367.

14. The Unemployment Council was under the auspices of the Communist Party, whose regional headquarters were in Birmingham because of its leading role in industry in the South; plant closures had made unemployment and the need for relief measures burning issues. The Party's growth in Birmingham derived from its unemployment campaign. See Kelley, "A New War," 383.

15. This meeting, which drew a "sympathetic and predominantly black crowd of 200," was the first one in a series devoted to the skyrocketing rate of unemployment. Kelly, "A New War," 369.

16. Herndon uses Frank Williams as a pseudonym for Frank Burns. At this time Herndon himself went by the name of Eugene Braxton. His given name was Eugene Angelo Braxton Herndon. See Kelley, "A New War," 370. 7.

17. Zelnik, *A Radical Worker*, 51.

18. John Douglas Ruedy, *Modern Algeria: The Origins and Development of a Nation* (Bloomington: Indiana University Press, 2005), 138–139.

CHAPTER 2

Children of the Revolutions

For revolutions in the name of Communism, children were the bright hope of the future. Children, the revolutionaries believed, could be remade in the revolution's image because they did not bear the imprint of the past, or at least their ties were much weaker than those of adults. For Communist revolutionaries across the globe, children were anything but forgotten. They were the objects of education and socialization designed to make them true believers in Communism.

But in histories of Communism, the subjective experience of children is all but forgotten. Almost completely overlooked is how children in different times and places *understood* Communism or socialism, and what it meant to make a revolution. So, too, has little attention been given to the resources—intellectual, cultural, and personal (family, friends, neighbors)—they used to forge such understandings. These understandings were not mere "child's play." They mattered. They mattered because they shaped, in small (and sometimes bigger) ways, the course of the revolution itself, the different forms that the revolutionary process took around the globe—a point exemplified by the writings of Jacek Kuroń in the previous chapter. The documents of this chapter—documents in which readers will be able to hear the voices of children of the Russian, Chinese, Cambodian, Korean, Cuban, and Peruvian (Shining Path) revolutions—will shed even more light on this phenomenon. They show the decisions—large, small, and everything in between—that children made as they decided what Communism and the revolution did and did not mean to them and how they would act on those understandings.

Even if children were not passive victims, they nonetheless suffered wrenching trauma as revolutions unfolded. Children were acutely vulnerable during revolutions because such uprisings were frequently accompanied by war, refugee movements, displacement, and famine. Children of the revolution often became orphans of the revolution. Even if not, the children who grew up during revolutions often realized that their childhoods, as they had previously understood them, had been stolen from them. How did children deal with such trauma—that is, with the separation from parents, siblings, and the past—that revolution and its social cataclysms often brought? This, too, is a hugely important question that deserves much more attention than it has so far been given.

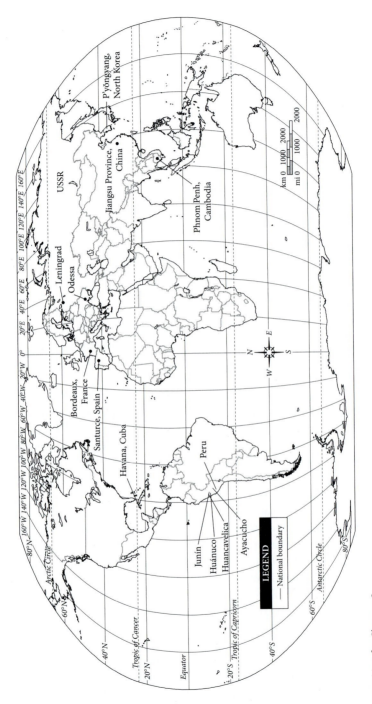

Pyŏngyang, North Korea

Jiangsu Province, China

USSR

Phnom Penh, Cambodia

Leningrad
Odessa

Bordeaux, France

Santurce, Spain

Havana, Cuba

Peru

Junín
Huánuco
Huancavelica
Ayacucho

LEGEND
—— National boundary

km 0 1000 2000
mi 0 1000 2000

N
W E
S

80°N
60°N
40°N
20°N
Tropic of Cancer
Equator
20°S Tropic of Capricorn
40°S
60°S Antarctic Circle
80°S

Arctic Circle

160°W 140°W 120°W 100°W 80°W 60°W 40°W 20°W 0° 20°E 40°E 60°E 80°E 100°E 120°E 140°E 160°E

Locator Map for Chapter 2

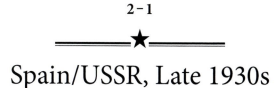

2–1

Spain/USSR, Late 1930s

Letters by Spanish Children Evacuated from Spain to the USSR* during the Spanish Civil War (1936–1939). (Letters are addressed to family and friends in Spain, 1938.)

The ideological wars of the twentieth century—between fascism, liberal democracy, and Communism—had profound implications for how children lived and what childhood meant. When these ideological wars became real wars, children were especially vulnerable to being orphaned or abandoned. And, at times, even caring parents gave up their children to state authorities in order to keep them out of harm's way and give them a better life. Such was the case, for example, during the Spanish Civil War (1936–1939), when the Republican military forces of Spain's democratically elected government and Franco's fascist troops battled for Spain's future.

The Spanish Civil War produced a serious refugee crisis, as Republican Spaniards became exiles. A good many of the refugees were children, who were accommodated by countries such as England, France, Belgium, Mexico, and even the USSR. In 1937–1938, nearly three thousand Spanish children were evacuated to the Soviet Union during the Spanish Civil War. Many of these children, evacuated by ship over stormy and dangerous seas in five voyages, were from the Basque region bombed by Hitler's forces in April 1937. The *New York Times*, in an unsigned column on the editorial page on 26 May 1937, decried that exiled children from the Basque region brought to countries all over the world

Letters are published with the permission of España. Ministerio de Cultura, Centro Documental de la Memoria Histórica (Spanish Ministry of Culture, Document Center for Historical Memory). Letter from Arsenio Uralde. (Carta de Arsenio Uralde) *España. Ministerio de Cultura, CDMH, PS-Santander "O," Caja 51, Expediente 7, Documento 103–104*. Emiliano Aza, letter from Odessa of 31 January 1938. (carta de 31 de enero desde Odessa). *España, Ministerio de Cultura, CDMH, PS-Santander "O," Caja 51, Expediente 7, Documento 6*. Serafín Gonzáles, letter of 10 February 1938 from Odessa (carta de 10 febrero de 1938 desde Odessa), *España. Ministerio de Cultura, CDMH, PS-Santander "0," Caja 51, Expediente 7, Documento 29*. Pilar Uraco, letter of 13 January 1938 from Khar'kov carta desde Khar'kov, 13 de enero de 1938) *España. Ministerio de Cultura, CDMH, PS-Santander "0," Caja 51, Expediente 7, Documento 114–115*. José López, letter of 13 December 1937 carta de 13 de diciembre de 1937), *España. Ministerio de Cultura, CDMH, PS-Santander "O," Caja 51, Expediente 7, Documento 45–46*. Translation: Glennys Young. Punctuation is left as it was in the original of all the letters.

* These children became known in Spain as the *niños de Rusia*.

"the tragedy of their country"—the most horrific of "modern tragedies," when a "people should slaughter its own children, or allow them to be mowed down by foreign mercenaries."[1]

All of the letters now available in Spanish archives—including the ones excerpted herein—were written by the children from the Basque region who were evacuated on the second voyage, which left Santurce (Bilbao) on 13 June 1937 and, after a stop in France to change boats, arrived in Leningrad on 22 June 1937, an expedition in which the Basque Communist Party (El Partido Comunista de Euskadi) played a central organizational role.[2] The letters, having never reached their destinations even though they were hurried by the Soviet authorities to Spain, fell into the hands of the Republican and then the Francoist governments. Certainly, the letters from other children that did reach their addressees—letters that expressed their delight with the care provided by their Soviet hosts—probably enhanced the reputation that the USSR had in the shrinking Republican territory of Spain.[3] Indeed, although there is no way to know exactly how much direction the Soviet caretakers imposed on the children as they wrote the letters, given the May 1937 Politburo's policy directive to make the Spanish children "energetic builders of socialist society," it is safe to assume that the Party's highest leadership (and perhaps some of its representatives on the ground) saw the letters not just as a propaganda tool back in Spain, or as serving the humanitarian purpose of allowing traumatized children to communicate with their anxious, war-torn, family members, but perhaps most importantly as part of the Party's efforts to provide the children with a Communist education. These letters were one of the ubiquitous modes of writing in which Soviet subjects were "to consciously identify with the revolution" and the "drama of its history."[4]

In the following letters, Spanish children grappled with the traumatic rupture from their parents, their families, and their pasts. They—like the other children whose voices we will hear later (Lu Chi Fa, Loung Ung)—also struggled to decide what Communism meant to them and what they thought of their lives amid the turmoil and opportunity of revolution.

EXCERPTS FROM LETTER OF EMILIANO AZA, FROM ODESSA, 1 JANUARY 1938

Dear father and brothers,

... The present letter is to let you know that I am in one of the best sanatoria of Odessa.

When we arrived in the Soviet Union they received us as if we were heroes. ...

They received us in Leningrad with floodlights and with submarines war ships and a big celebration.

Father, the first thing I ask of you is that you send me a photo of you and of the whole family and above all of Martin and Julio since I think of you often and everyone and especially the two [of them]. ...

Here* we are eating very well and we are sleeping better since we get four meals that they give to us in most abundant quantities. . . . So that you can see that I am very content in this nation which is the homeland of all the workers of the whole world. Father, this nation is the first which rose up and conquered the cruel tyranny and the beast of fascism will be conquered by Red Spain and in this way little by little the beast of fascism will fall worldwide it will fall for all time and equality will reign in the entire world and all the workers will work and eat and peace and happiness will reign in the whole world.

Father in the Soviet Union everyone is equal engineers as much as carpenters as well as mechanics and railway workers. Everybody eats the same and works equally whatever their nationality may be whether they are Russian or Italian it is the same.

Your son who loves you very much and does not forget you says goodbye to you.

Emiliano

My address is in Russian and in Spanish and I have to divide it into two parts.
Odessa
Proletarskii bul'var No. 77
Casa de niños No. 3.

LETTER FROM SERAFÍN GONZÁLEZ TO HIS PARENTS

Odessa, 10 February 1938

Dear parents: I am writing you these few words to tell you that I am fine I am in Russia we are very well because it is a country of the proletariat we go to the theaters, movies, circuses, to the opera which is the second most important in Europe and the third in the world it is very pretty it has statues of gold. And the best thing which is going on with us [is that] two comrades are going around with us a Russian woman and another Spanish woman they are very good people also we go to school in which we study Russian and Spanish we already know how to read a little Russian we also know how to write a little bit and we also know how to speak a little bit. If I have a picture I will send it to you in the second letter that I write you without more to say your son who loves you says goodbye and wants [you] to have a big hug and kiss from your son

Serafín González

My address is this
Proletarsky Bulvar Casa de los niños españoles No. 3
Odessa
U.R.S.S.

---

* In Odessa, the sanatorium to which he and other Spanish children were transferred after their arrival in Leningrad.

LETTER FROM JOSÉ LÓPEZ TO HIS PARENTS, BROTHERS AND SISTERS, AND FRIENDS

Russia Khar'kov 13 December 1937

Dear parents, brothers and sisters, and friends

I hope that when you receive this letter you are fine

I have written many letters to you I do not know if you have received any letter from me I have never received any letter from you.

I am very content because they give us all the best for us winter has already come to Russia and it is cold. They have given us good shoes good clothes good winter caps we have things to amuse ourselves....

When we are older we will all go together to defend Spain and our parents and brothers and sisters those cowardly fascists they shall not pass* and we shall pass pushing back fascism until we win red Spain. There are many Communists in Germany in Russia there is not a single fascist. Russia is preparing itself very well and all of the nations of the red army.

We imagine that you are under fascist bombings causing many dead and wounded. We have news from Spain and movies of the bombings and from the front....

Amos and I are wanting to know Something about you I do not know which career Amos will pick.

We also have russian men who know how to speak in Spanish and in russian.

In the first letter that you write me send me some pictures of the whole family above all of Rafael and of uncle,... who will be fighting against the fascist coward they shall not pass we shall pass in Russian it is†....

José Luís López
LONG LIVE RED SPAIN
LONG LIVE RUSSIA AND ALL THE NATIONS OF THE RED ARMY

LETTER FROM ARSENIO URALDE‡

Dear parents and brothers

I will be happy if you are well we are very well....

here in the USSR all of the people have to know two languages russian and that of whatever nation that they like everybody works but they have

---

* "No pasarán" was first used by Dolores Ibárruri, the Republican leader and Communist politician (La Pasionaria, or "Passion Flower") in a speech on 19 July 1936, the day after the Nationalist uprising against the democratically elected Republican government in Spain. The meaning of the phrase is "they will not win."

† Not legible.

‡ Not dated, but probably early 1938, especially given the reference in the letter to Lenin's death having been fourteen years earlier.

still not been able to clean up all of this riff raff a few days ago the 21st it was fourteen years ago that Lenin our dear father died not as the fascists said god that is a lie but his death will never be forgotten and his orders with his written books will be followed until the last drop of blood in the communist world without [saying] more your sons who love you very much say goodbye.

Arsenio Uraldo his two brothers Edilberto and Luís

LETTER FROM PILAR URACO TO HER MOTHER

Khar'kov 12 January 1938

Dear mama my greatest desire [is] that when you receive this you find yourself well at home in the company of other family members we are well in the company of all the children and Spaniards.

    Mama I tell you that Ricardo and the cousins are in another sanatorium but I am in this one and very well what would make me happy is for all of us to be together they have told me that they will unite all the brothers and sisters and cousins.

    Mother I say to you that here I study a lot*.... we eat very well so that we do not want for anything because the soviet people love us a lot and we have spanish comrades with us....

Pilar Uraco
1938

2-2

China, Late 1940s

An Orphan of China's War with Japan Tries to Make Sense of Communism

In the shadows of China's eight-year war with Japan (1937–1945)—the war in which the last chapter's Xiao Ke held high military posts—another battle was being fought: that over the fate of China's war orphans, who numbered at least two million.[5] This battle had several dimensions. One, of course, was the

---

* The next few words are not legible.

struggle to provide for the children's basic needs—food, clothing, shelter, and human affection. But, less obviously yet no less importantly, the Chinese war orphans were the object of an ideological (and cultural) battle between the Nationalists (Guomindang) and the Communists. The Nationalist government, for example, created wartime children's homes that sought not only to provide for their basic needs but to put them on the correct ideological rails, thereby making them into modern citizens.[6] Yet the Communists, too, sought ideological influence over the war orphans. On paper and in practice, war orphans became pawns in a larger military, ideological, and cultural conflict.

One of China's war orphans was Lu Chi Fa*, the author of the following excerpt, taken from his memoirs. Born in 1941, Lu was orphaned in 1944, when he was three years old, that is, just before the civil war between the Nationalists and the Communists that broke out with the Japanese surrender in 1945. He had a significantly older sister, whom he loved dearly. But, at her husband's insistence, she nonetheless abandoned him, and passed him off to another sibling. He was subsequently sold to strangers, including a Communist chief, who purchased him for five hundred pounds of rice. Middle-aged and newly married to a woman who had a twenty-year-old son, the man he would call his "Communist Father" wanted to make him obedient and to instill in him unwavering loyalty to the Communist Revolution. He subjected Lu to serious emotional and physical abuse. Eventually, Lu escaped from this man and from Communist China altogether.

Like other Chinese children, whether orphans or not, Lu was struggling to understand what Communism was and what he thought about it. For him, as for other children around the globe who lived in Communist polities or where Communist regimes were consolidating power, this struggle entailed asking questions. These were pointed questions—sometimes posed to oneself, sometimes asked of others—about things that did not make sense.

…As the weather grew colder, so did my Communist parents. Communist Father said that because I was getting older, I needed harsher punishment. Almost daily there was a beating. On the nights when he went to Communist meetings, he left me home alone with Communist Mother. She didn't beat me; instead, she played tricks on me.…It made my heart sick to know that they had grown to hate me so.

At the time, I didn't understand the things happening in the adult world. I was rarely taken out, and I couldn't read. I didn't know that China was weak from an eight-year war with Japan or that the Chinese Communist Party was taking over large parts of our country. I had my own personal struggles: getting enough to eat, staying warm in the winter, and keeping out of harm's way.

* In Chinese names, the last name comes first, and the first name last. In this case, the first name is Chi Fa, and the last name is Lu. Chi Fa means "new beginning."

Toward the end of the year, Communist Father told Mother, "It is time Double Luck became a man. Tonight I will take him with me to the Communist meeting. We may have the makings of a great Communist here."

I didn't know what being a Communist meant, but as I marched along, like a soldier, I tried to stand tall. I held my shoulders square. It felt good to know I was going to become a man. With all my heart, I wanted to please Communist Father. *If I please him,* I reasoned, *he won't beat me so often.*

When we arrived at the community building, there must have been a hundred people there. Men, women field workers, and a few children were assembled in the basement. Father, the Communist chief of the village, stood in front of them all. I slipped in between two men in the front row where I could see Father standing under a huge picture of Mao Tse-tung. He began, "Comrades, the Chinese Communist Party is well established in the north and northeast."

As I watched him addressing the crowd, for the very first time, I realized I was part of something bigger than myself. I belonged to a race of people called Chinese. As simple as that thought is, at the time, to a young peasant boy, it seemed a great revelation. I lifted my chin and proudly gazed up at the big flag.

"The Nationalists have an advantage in numbers of men and weapons. They control a much larger area of land and have more people than we Communists, but they are exhausted by the long war with Japan. All of China is in turmoil."

A toothless man sitting next to me began stomping his feet. Then everyone cheered. *Why are they glad that China is in turmoil?* I wondered. I watched Communist Father's face closely.

"Our party membership has increased to many millions." As Communist Father spoke, he seemed to grow taller. He puffed out his chest and beat on the table with his fist. His face flushed red. "In the coming months, with minimal resistance, major cities will pass into Communist control."

Again everyone cheered and stomped their feet.

Communist Father lifted both his arms into the air and shouted, "Those who do not join the Chinese Communist Party will be shot. If you do not already belong, join tonight. Don't wait until it is too late. Teachers will be lined up and shot first."

"Teachers will be shot?" I asked out loud. But no one heard me. "Favorite Uncle is a teacher!" I yelled. Still no one listened to a little boy. Suddenly, somewhere outside, someone lit a string of firecrackers. I jumped. I thought it was gunfire and I was going to be shot right there in the basement.

Communist Father went on shaking his fists, his face sweating deeper shades of red. "The Chinese Communist Party will rule China without a fight. Because of this season's floods, millions of Chinese are homeless. Every day thousands of Chinese starve to death."

While the Communists stomped their feet and cheered wildly, those words burned like bamboo in my brain. If thousands of people are starving, I thought, we have to help them. We have to get rice and take it to them. We cannot let our people starve to death.

I was just a boy, but I knew how it felt to have an empty belly. I was not educated in matters of war, and I couldn't understand how people could cheer because others were starving and suffering. Were my family members who lived on the river homeless? I closed my eyes. I imagined Sister holding a crying baby over her head and wading through waist-deep water. Maybe that is why Sister hasn't come after Chi Fa, I thought.

Tears streamed down my face. I felt sick. I stumbled from the crowded room and ran breathlessly up the stairs. I heard Communist Father shout, "Soon all of China will be one—the Chinese Communist Party."

Everyone in the room applauded loudly.

Once outside, I gasped fresh air. Blinking tears from my eyes, I leaned up against the cold brick building to steady my weak knees. I could still hear his voice, but I could not make out his words—nor did I want to. I had heard enough. Realizing that terrible things were happening to the Chinese people, I felt overwhelmed with helplessness.

I crouched on the ground against the building. There was no moon to shed its light, and Heaven's net had pulled in all the stars except one. Gazing upward, I felt as alone as the single star that shone through the blackness. I wondered if Sister could see that same star. I wondered if she often thought about me. I tried to picture her face. I did not want to forget how she looked. Someday I would see Sister again, and I needed to be able to recognize her.

It had been more than a year since my uprooting, and for a young boy that is a very long time. The absence of my family was an ache that I lived with daily, but never had I felt the pain so sharply as I did at that very moment. I was confused about Communism and many other things, too, but one thing I knew for certain—I was lonely.

When the meeting was over, Communist Father found me and scolded me. "Double Luck, you are such a baby. I am ashamed to be seen with you."

He said I disgraced him by running out like a crybaby. "Woo waa," he mocked. "I don't want anyone to think you are my son. Don't walk beside me. Stay back." And he stalked off.

I stayed as far back as I could without losing sight of him, and like an obedient dog, I followed him home. I didn't want to, but I had nowhere else to go. I longed to be part of something good and strong. I wanted to go home to my own village—to my own family....

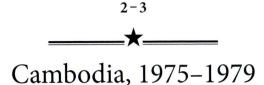

Cambodia, 1975–1979

Childhood under the Khmer Rouge

The Communist regime of Cambodia's Khmer Rouge (1975–1979) brought violent, even genocidal, remaking of Cambodian society, politics, and culture. Driven by a lethal combination of Communist ideology, the quest for total power, and racism, the Khmer Rouge under Pol Pot shut down schools, monasteries, libraries, and even factories, and eliminated money. Fueled with hatred of cities, which they believed to be populated by classes contaminated by foreign influences, they emptied Cambodia's urban spaces. Phnom Penh, a city of approximately 2.5 million people, was almost completely evacuated. The roads leading out of the city were jammed with the wealthy, educated urban residents whom the Khmer Rouge viewed with deep ideological contempt. Even the seriously ill had to flee the city's hospitals.

One of these deportees was Loung Ung, who was five years old in 1975. She and her family had lived a comfortable life in Phnom Penh prior to the Khmer Rouge's seizure of power. But the Khmer Rouge's victory changed all that. As a middle-class bureaucrat, her father exemplified what the Khmer Rouge called the "new people," people who were politically suspect because of their wealth, their connections to foreigners, or the fact that they lived in cities. Forced to flee Phnom Penh, the family was deported to a series of work camps and eventually split apart. Her father was killed, and her sister, Keav, died of food poisoning in one of the work camps. Eventually, Loung and one of her brothers (along with his wife), escaped to Vietnam, and finally made it to the United States.

The following passage conveys what it was like to be a child in the Cambodia of the Khmer Rouge. Like other children in Communist polities across the globe, Loung was obliged to figure out for herself what "Communism" meant. But her plight—and that of Cambodian children more generally—had a distinctive element in the context of global Communism. For, as one scholar has noted, for almost four years, everyday family life disappeared.[7] In no other Communist country was family life so profoundly transformed—distorted, really—as in Cambodia. As the country was turned into a prison camp, the fabric of human relationships in the family was torn apart. The routines of everyday family life disappeared. Communication between family members lucky enough to stay together was

From Loung Ung, *First They Killed My Father: A Daughter of Cambodia Remembers* (New York: HarperCollins, 2000), 21–49. Reprinted by permission of HarperCollins Publishers.

reduced to admonitions about how to behave to avoid repression by the Khmer Rouge. Even the rhythms and forms of affection—such as Loung Ung's nightly ritual of sitting on her father's lap—were casualties of the Khmer Rouge's terror state.

… We are not the only family leaving the city. People pour out of their homes and into the streets, moving very slowly out of Phnom Penh. Like us, some are lucky and ride away in some kind of vehicle; however, many leave on foot, their sandals flapping against the soles of their feet with every step.

Our truck inches on in the streets, allowing us a safe view of the scene. Everywhere, people scream their good-byes to those who choose to stay behind; tears pour from their eyes. Little children cry for their mothers, snot dripping from their noses into their open mouths. Farmers harshly whip their cows and oxen to pull the wagons faster. Women and men carry their belongings in cloth bags on their backs and their heads. They walk with short, brisk steps, yelling for their kids to stay together, to hold each other's hands, to not get left behind. I squeeze my body closer to Keav as the world moves in hurried confusion from the city.

The soldiers are everywhere. There are so many of them around, yelling into their bullhorns, no longer smiling as I saw them before. Now they shout loud, angry words at us while cradling rifles in their arms. They holler for the people to close their shops, to gather all guns and weapons, to surrender the weapons to them. They scream at families to move faster, to get out of the way, to not talk back. I bury my face into Keav's chest, my arms tight around her waist, stifling a cry. Chou sits silently on the other side of Keav, her eyes shut. Beside us, Kim and Meng sit stone-faced, watching the commotion below.

"Keav, why are the soldiers so mean to us?" I ask, clinging even more tightly to her.

"Shhh. They are called Khmer Rouge. They are the Communists." "What is a Communist?"

"Well, it means.… It's hard to explain. Ask Pa later," she whispers.…
Our fourth day on the road starts the same as the all the other days. "Are we there yet?" I keep asking Kim. When I receive no attention, I proceed to sniff and cry.

"Nobody cares about me!" I moan and keep walking anyway.

By noontime we have reached the Khmer Rouge's military checkpoint in the town of Kom Baul. The checkpoint consists of no more than a few small makeshift tents with trucks parked beside them. There are many soldiers at this base.… They move quickly from place to place with fingers on the triggers of their weapons, pacing back and forth in front of the crowd, yelling instructions into a bullhorn.

"This is Kom Baul base! You are not allowed to pass until we have cleared you! Stand with your family in a line! Our comrade soldiers will come and ask a few simple questions! You are to answer them truthfully and not lie to the Angkar! If you lie to the Angkar, we will find out! The Angkar is all-knowing and has eyes and ears everywhere." This is the first time I hear the word "Angkar," which means "the organization." Pa says the Angkar is the new government of Cambodia. He tells us that in the past, Prince Sihanouk ruled Cambodia as a monarch. Then in 1970, unhappy with the Prince's government, General Lon Nol deposed him in a military coup. The Lon Nol democratic government has been fighting a civil war with the Communist Khmer Rouge ever since. Now the Khmer Rouge has won the war and its government is called "the Angkar."

"To your right, you see a table where your comrade brothers sit waiting to help you. Anyone who has worked for the deposed government, ex-soldiers or politicians, step up to the table to register for work. The Angkar needs you right away." Anxiety spreads through my body at the sight of the Khmer Rouge soldiers. I feel like I have to vomit.

Pa quickly gathers our family and stands us in line with other peasant families. "Remember, we are a family of peasants. Give them whatever they want and don't argue. Don't say anything, let me do all the talking, don't go anywhere, and don't make any moves unless I tell you to do so," Pa instructs us firmly....

I soon realize how early everyone gets up when they are already busy about the farm before the sun rises and long before I awake the next morning. Life on the farm is boring and dull, but at least there is enough to eat. Unlike my life in Phnom Penh, I do not have any friends outside the family. It is hard to make friends because I am afraid to speak, afraid I will blurt out secrets about our family. Pa says the Angkar has abolished markets, schools, and universities, and has banned money, watches, clocks, eight-track players, and televisions.

...No matter, I have many cousins to play with. On the days I don't spend watching other people watch us, I help my older cousins bring their cows to the field to graze. I gradually adjust to life on the farm and let go of my dream of returning home....

Even the new experience of riding on a cow becomes dull when you do it everyday. Yet despite the monotony of farm life, the longer we live in Krang Truop, the more fearful and anxious I become. Everywhere I venture I cannot shake the feeling that someone is watching, following, me. Though I have nowhere to go, each morning I hurriedly dress myself so I can catch a glimpse of Pa before he goes off to work. On most days, by the time I am awake, Pa and my brothers are already gone and Ma is busy sewing clothes for the family or working in the garden....

Pa returns late at night looking dirty and tired. Sometimes, after a quick meal, Pa sits quietly outside by himself and stares at the sky. When he comes back into the hut, he falls quickly asleep. I hardly ever sit on his lap anymore. I miss his hugs and how he used to make me laugh at old Chinese stories. Pa's tales were often about the Buddhist gods and their dragons coming down to Earth to fight evil and protect people. I wonder if the gods and dragons will come help us now....

Kim tells me that from now on I have to watch out for myself. Not only am I never to talk to anyone about our former lives, but I'm never to trust anyone either. It is best if I just stop talking completely so I won't unintentionally disclose information about our family. To talk is to bring danger to the family. At five years old,

I am beginning to know what loneliness feels like, silent and alone and suspecting that everyone wants to hurt me.

"I am going to go look around," I tell Kim, bored.

"Don't go far and don't talk to anyone. We might have to leave very soon and I don't want to have to go looking for you."

I want to obey my brother's warnings not to go far, but I'm curious. When my family is looking elsewhere I sneak away from under their watchful eyes to explore the "waiting station." The farther I walk, the more I see of the hundreds of people at the camp. They talk, sit, or sleep anywhere they can. Many tents have wet clothes hanging all over their lines, piles of wood by the crackling fire, and homemade wooden benches. Looking as if they have been waiting for a long time, some lie so motionless I wonder if they are alive. I stop to look at one old woman. Dressed in a brown shirt and maroon sarong, she lies on the ground with her arms at her side and her head propped up by a small bundle. Her eyes are half closed, white hair strewn in all directions, and skin yellow and wrinkled. The young woman next to her spoon-feeds the old woman rice gruel.

"She looks dead to me," I say to the young woman. "What's wrong with her?"

"Gram's half dead, can't you tell?" she says to me in annoyance....

"Are there any doctors or anyone who can help her?"

"There are no doctors anywhere. Go away! Aren't your parents looking for you?"

She is right, of course. I hear Ma calling my name and beckoning me to return. Luckily, my family is too busy boarding yet another truck to be angry with me. As Pa lifts me onto the truck, I notice two very thin middle-aged men in loose-fitting black pajama pants and shirts standing next to us. While one writes something on small brown pads of paper with his black pen, the other points at our heads and counts as we climb onto the truck. I find myself a seat where I can watch the countryside. Quickly, four other families clamber onto the truck and fill up the empty space in the middle. Once all the families are on board, the two men take their notes and count again, without smiling or greeting us. After they are finished, they get into the front seats with the truck driver and we begin to move.

The truck rolls away from the waiting area and onto a bumpy narrow road crossing the mountains. The families are quiet and somber, the only sounds come from the branches brushing against the side of the truck and the slush of mud sticking to the tires. After what seems like forever, I become bored with the scenery and climb onto Pa's lap.

"Pa," I say quietly, so the others cannot hear us, "the people at the place we just left, why were they there?"

"They are waiting for the base people to come and take them."

"Take them like they've taken us?"

"Yes. The men wearing black clothes are representatives from rural villages. At the waiting area, these representatives are given a list of names and people they are to take back to their villages," Pa says quietly.

"Those two men, are they our village representatives?"

"Yes."

"Who are the base people?"

"Shhh....I will tell you later."

"How come we left there so fast while all the others waited?"

"I bribed someone with one of your Ma's gold necklaces to put our names on a list so we could leave." Pa lets out a sigh and is once again quiet. I rest my head on his chest and think how lucky I am to have such a father. I know Pa loves me.

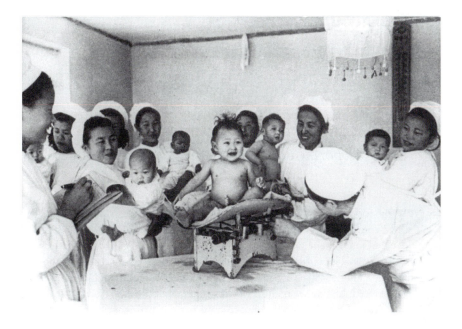

Babies being weighed in a Hamnam Nursery in South Hamgyŏng Province in North Korea, 1955. The scene pictured here seems to be a boy's first birthday (called *tol* in Korean). Taking pictures of naked babies for the occasion is a popular practice in both North and South Korea. (In South Korea, however, the boy would wear a traditional aristocratic child's headdress.) The fat babies in this picture represent an ideal that would have been attained only by a few, since food shortages have been a constant feature of Korean life. Throughout the history of North Korea, food for the people has been scarce. The abundance suggested in this picture, however, is representative of state propaganda that North Korea was a "paradise for children." Due to population loss from refugee movements and the Korean War, North Korea had a pronatal policy up through the 1980s.

This picture dates from the period just after the Korean War when North Korea was still recovering from the effects of bombing and fighting. North Korea had, however, already made a commitment to a comprehensive, free health system focused on preventative care. By the 1980s, P'yŏngyang's maternity hospital was a source of great pride. Clean and well-equipped, and available only to the families of high-level cadres, it was a staple on the itinerary of tours for foreigners.   Courtesy of the Library of Congress.

Back in Phnom Penh, in the movie theater, I would always demand the seat next to Pa. When a movie got scary, I would grab onto his arm, signaling to him that I was ready to hop on his lap. Pa would then lift me from my chair and plop me on his lap so that his body became my chair, his arms my armrest. It seems so long ago now. He seems so serious and sad, and I wonder if I will ever see my fun Pa again.

2-4

North Korea

A Child and His Aquarium during
Deportation to a Concentration Camp

The form that everyday Communism took in North Korea stemmed from a combination of factors. These included the Soviet occupation, the fact that the Korean Communist Revolution of 15 August 1945 was portrayed as Korea's "liberation" from thirty-five years of Japanese colonialism, and the influence of pre-1945 society and culture, including Confucian tradition. Given that the North Korean Communists who rose to the apex of power (such as Kim Il Sung,[8] or the "Great Leader") had fought in the partisan war against the colonial occupation of the Japanese, it makes sense that the North Korean Communist Party remade the North Korean party-state (the DPRK, or Democratic People's Republic of Korea) as a "guerilla-band state."

One dimension of this process was that Kim and his guerilla comrades from Manchuria in the late 1920s and early 1930s eliminated other cohorts of Communist rivals. In 1953–1958 they took power away from other factional rivals, such as the "domestic Communists," mostly of southern origin, who had operated in Korea in the 1930s and 1940s, and the Yanan faction (those Koreans who had fought with the Chinese Communists in the 1930s). North Korea became, even more so than other Marxist–Leninist polities (with the possible exception of Cambodia), a society "on a continuous war footing."[9]

The entire population had to be mobilized—in the militaristic sense of the word—in the creation of a new civilization, one that was to be distinctly Korean, Communist, anti-capitalist, anti-imperialist, and nationalist. This entailed getting

From Kang Chol-Hwan and Pierre Rigoulot, *The Aquariums of Pyongyang: Ten Years in the North Korean Gulag* (New York: Basic Books, 2001), 35–46. Reprinted by permission of Basic Books, a member of the Perseus Group.

North Koreans to imagine themselves in terms of categories such as worker, poor peasants, women, and youth, yet at the same time to identify with the unified whole of the nation. In the creation of the new society, poor peasants indeed lent support to the nominally antihierarchical, egalitarian values of the Communists. To be a poor peasant meant to have opportunity and privilege. But to be identified as an oppressor—to be a landlord, wealthy farmer, or perceived collaborator with the Japanese colonial regime—meant severe hardship and discrimination and having one's wealth and property confiscated.[10] Even as late as the 1970s, so-called "enemies of the state" were also sent to concentration camps, such as the dreaded Yodŏk, located in a mountainous region in the north between the coastal ranges and the Baitou Mountains on the North Korean border. This was a region that, with a rather dry and cold growing season, had very little agriculture: there, the kitchen gardens that sustained people in North Korea and other Communist societies were unproductive. Hence the region's underpopulation, a characteristic that made it suitable for isolating "undesirable" elements from the rest of society. Yodŏk—a camp that exists to this day—looms as a symbol of one of the distinctive features of North Korean Communism: the fact that Stalinism survived there well after Stalin's death in 1953.

Among those imprisoned in the Yodŏk camp was Kang Chol-Hwan, the author of the following passage. From the party-state's perspective, his family was politically suspect. The time period that Kang recalls—the 1970s—was that of the last major purges in North Korea. Associated with the rise of Kim Jong Il, these purges involved the elimination of "undesirables" from P'yŏngyang, the capital of North Korea and home of Kang's family. One reason was that the family—including his grandfather and Communist grandmother—had originally lived in Japan.[11] They only returned to Korea at the grandmother's insistence. But return was fraught with danger. Kang's grandfather was imprisoned for suspected anti-state activity when the author was only nine years old. Because state policy was to send all family members of political prisoners to concentration camps, most of Kang's family was incarcerated at the infamous Yodŏk camp. For ten years, they endured tremendous suffering, some of which entailed witnessing the abuse (starvation, torture, lack of medical treatment) of other prisoners' human rights.

The excerpt here deals not with the camp experience itself but with the moment when Kang and most of his family are being taken from their home in P'yŏngyang. It is a retrospective account of his subjective experience of the deportation. Even though he was but a nine-year-old child, he was able to influence, if in very limited ways, what that experience would be like. Against all odds, he succeeded in taking his aquarium and beloved fish with him. Whether this was an act of "resistance" against the Communist state, a child's attempt to get his way and comfort himself, or a combination thereof is for readers to decide.

Though even more anxious and withdrawn, Grandfather remained the central character of the family. His pronounced eyebrows, round, sparkling eyes, and stentorian voice always enthralled me. So, too, did the respect shown him by

Pyongyang's Party cadres. And yet this never got in the way of our intimacy. Our Sunday walks, in tones of high secrecy, he would tell me stories about his former days in Kyoto: about the jewelry shop where he stayed up all night filling his first orders, the rice warehouses he guarded against envious competitors, the stunning success of his gaming rooms; and the fortunes that grew and fell there in a matter of minutes. These stories were a source of constant enchantment for me. I listened, mesmerized, to their architect and hero, my grandfather. I loved him, and never could I have imagined that our conversations and Sunday walks might one day come to an end.

Yet he disappeared. It was in July of 1977. One night he didn't come home from work. The police said they knew nothing. The heads of my grandfather's department, whom my grandmother anxiously queried, finally told us he had left on a business trip, an urgent matter, they said. The order had come from the Party, and he had to decide right away. "But come back next week and you'll have some news," they assured her. "There's no need to worry."

My grandmother had her doubts about this business trip. Her husband was not the type to leave without warning....

My parents suspected that the Security Force was behind the mysterious disappearance, but they dared not admit this even to themselves. In the preceding months a number of their acquaintances had vanished in similar ways. Yet the family preferred to believe—my grandmother more than anyone—that there was no comparison between my grandfather and those others, who must have plotted against the state or committed some other grave offense. None of us was willing to face the possibility that the police had taken him away from us. We knew that Grandfather was never at a loss for words and that he often criticized Party bureaucrats and their management methods rather too sharply. We also knew that he rarely showed up at Party meetings and rallies, but then again, Grandmother attended enough for two! And had he not always been an honest citizen, entrusting his all to the Party? Had he not handed over his immense fortune upon arriving from Japan? Had he not given the Party everything, down to his Volvo?

A few weeks after Grandfather's disappearance, I was playing on the riverbank when several of my friends came to tell me that a group of people were at my house. Puzzled, I got up and ran to our apartment.

Traditionally, people take their shoes off on entering a Korean home. Not doing so is a sign of disrespect to your host. To my astonishment, I noticed that though the living room was full of people, the entrance hall had only the usual number of shoes. What did this mean? I wanted to move forward, but there were so many people in the room it was hard to maneuver. Apart from my father, mother, grandmother, and sister, there were a number of other people whom I had never seen before. The only one missing was my uncle, who lived with us but was away for a few days at a professional conference in south Hamkyung Province. Who were these other people? I greeted my parents with a big wave, but they, who were ordinarily so happy to see me, responded strangely, remaining distant, like condescending adults who hadn't time for such trifles. My mother sighed and kept on repeating (as though someone would answer!), "But what is happening to us? But what is happening to us?" I pushed forward, determined to see what was going on: three uniformed men were rifling through our things as a fourth took notes. What extraordinary event was this? And how could they keep their shoes on? That was what shocked me the most, but when I tried to tell my mother, she didn't even answer me.

Our apartment consisted of four bedrooms and a living room. The smallest bedroom stored wrapped gifts my grandparents had requested from friends and family who had visited from Japan over the years. The cache of jewelry, clothes, and watches was to be presented at the wedding of my third uncle—whenever that was going to be. (It is customary for Korean families to begin preparing for their children's wedding far—often years—in advance.) The room also contained several cameras and various darkroom materials that my father used in his work. These treasures greatly excited the security agents—for these were who our four visitors were....

They pressed on through the rest of the apartment, three searching, while the fourth continued to take notes. The inventory progressed slowly, and I soon grew bored of a situation that didn't really involve me, since the gentlemen seemed not the least interested in my aquariums. I went and got my sister, Mi-ho, and we started to play, indifferent to what might come next. We were soon running around, romping in the shambles left by the search. I started to jump up and down on my parents' big Japanese bed and encouraged my sister to do the same.... I don't know what my sister thought of that paternal abdication, but it left me feeling very strange. The order of things had changed. I was not yet worried, but I began to feel a certain malaise, the shape and cause of which I could not altogether comprehend. Perhaps this is why a hole persists there in my memory.

Yet I remember perfectly the moment I first heard pronounced the name of "Yodok." One of the agents had begun rifling through my mother's lingerie, and seeing her private things tossed across the room, my mother allowed her voice to rise. Outraged, the man with the notebook jumped to his feet, ordering her to shut up, then pulled out a paper from which he read out loud. According to the document, my grandfather had committed "a crime of high treason," the consequence of which was that his family—all of us there gathered, that is—was "immediately" to present itself at the secure zone in Yodok, a canton of which I had never heard. Everyone around me seemed to go dead. There was a long silence, then tears, and hands taking hold of one another....

There is one moment that particularly stands out in my memory of that night. My grandmother was having a face-off with the agents. They were trying to force her to sign a document, but she objected, pointing insistently at certain passages. The agents offered some perfunctory explanations, their tone alternating between calm restraint and outbursts of angry shouting. Suddenly I saw her reach for the pen holder and sign the paper. The next thing that happened surprised me even more: she had hardly finished signing when the men grabbed her and locked her up in one of the rooms!

When sunrise came and I learned we'd soon be leaving for that unknown place whose mention had so jolted my parents, I was not overly upset. I thought of it as a move to the country, an adventure, something to bring a little excitement to our lives. Truth be told, the idea actually pleased me. My one real concern was finding a way to bring my fish collection along. In some respects, our departure for Yodok resembled a move. We weren't being sent to the camps as criminals but as relatives of a criminal, which meant we were treated with a little more clemency. My grandfather had been picked up from work and taken away to a hard-labor camp without even the chance to pack a bag. His fate was like that of many people arrested in the USSR and Nazi Germany, whose history I was later able to read. We, at least, were allowed to bring a minimum of furniture, clothes, and even food.

From a certain perspective, our case could be seen as one of simple banishment, but as we would soon discover, the barbed wire, the huts, the malnutrition, and the mind-quashing work left little doubt that it really was a concentration camp. The camp's policy of maintaining the cohesion of the family unit merely testifies to the resilience—even in a supposedly Communist country—of the Confucian tradition. This policy does not, however, alter the basic nature of the camp. The stated purpose of sending us away as a family was to reeducate us through work and study. As noncriminals who were contaminated by the reactionary ideology of the criminal in our midst, we were ordered to a place built specifically for the "redeemable" cases. But I'm getting ahead of myself.

The search completed, my parents began packing with the help of several employees from my grandfather's office. They had arrived early in the morning, conscripted, perhaps, by the security agents looking to hasten our departure. My grandfather's former colleagues might have been pleased to lend my family a helping hand, but it is unlikely that the gesture was a spontaneous one. Showing solidarity with a criminal family was dangerous....

As our bundles were being loaded into the five large crates allotted us, I saw my sister take hold of her favorite doll. This gave me an idea: I hurriedly grabbed one of my aquariums and stocked it with a selection of my most beautiful fish. I then hugged the aquarium fast against me, just as I saw my sister do with her doll. One of the agents noticed me and said that taking "that"—gesturing to the aquarium with his chin—was out of the question. The brutality of the order, handed down by someone I didn't even know, threw me into a raging fit. I ranted and raved, yelled and bawled so much the agent finally relented. My swell of tears gradually abated, but the fate of the fish left behind still worried me. When I was first told of the strange goings-on at my house, several of my more treacherous friends said I would probably be sent to "a nasty place" and so would do well to give my fish away to my pals. At the time I hadn't taken their offer seriously, but now, on the cusp of my departure, I regretted it.

A truck was stationed in front our building. The men began loading the crates and the few small furnishings the agents didn't want for themselves: a low table, some kitchen utensils, and a 125-pound bag of rice, the maximum the camp would allow. The rattle of the engine, the lamentations of some, and the orders of others began waking the neighbors.... A minor panic ensued when my father bolted back to the apartment to fetch a few last-minute things. That reminded me of my favorite comic books. Like all the kids, I loved the story about the battle of the hedgehog army, in which the hedgehogs and squirrels join forces to defeat the wolves, rats, foxes, and eagles, all representative of the horrible world of capitalism. I begged the security agent—I think he was the same one who had given way to my earlier temper tantrum—to let me go get it. But by now he'd had enough of my antics and screamed for me to get in the truck. This time I was scared and obeyed without protest. So much for the hedgehog army. At least I had my favorite fish.

My family climbed one by one into the back of the truck, except for my mother, who, to my great surprise, remained standing on the sidewalk. I still remember the immense sadness in her face, streaming with tears. "You're not coming?*" I asked. "No, not right away, my love. I'll join you soon." In a hurry to wrap things up, the agents brusquely confirmed my mother's words and kept everyone going about their business. Reassured, I squeezed myself up against my aquarium, which I topped with a plank of wood to keep the water from sloshing out. After a final good-bye, my attention turned to the novelty of riding in an automobile, a rare event in the life of a private North Korean citizen.

My poor mother! It must have been terrible for her. Much as she tried, she couldn't hide her sadness. Yet her little nine-year-old son had understood almost nothing. He had climbed into the truck quite happily, his fish pressed to his chest. His mother didn't know so many years would pass before she would see her son again. The daughter of a "heroic family," she was spared a trip to the camp where her children and husband spent the next ten years. Shortly after our imprisonment, the Security Force made her get a divorce and terminate all ties with our family of "traitors." She was never asked her opinion, never even gave her signature. She suffered greatly and longed for her lost family throughout the long years of our imprisonment. I later learned she had repeatedly appealed to the Security Force for permission to join us in the camp, but her requests were seen as aberrant and never granted.

We started out just as the day was breaking. The truck was a Tsir, the powerful Soviet-built machine that was standard equipment for hauling away prisoners. The Koreans called it "the crow," a symbol of death, for though white remains the traditional color of mourning in Korea, black is the color of funerals. It was a covered truck, and during the first leg of the trip, my sister and I were not allowed to peek outside. Once we were out in the country, however, the agents let us watch at the passing scenery as much as we wanted. The ride was bumpy, traversing rutted, packed-earth roads. I was holding up fine myself—my one real concern was keeping the water from sloshing out of the aquarium—but Mi-ho started vomiting. Grandmother found her a plastic bag, then spread blankets on the truck floor for her to lie on. Our crates and furnishings were in the forward part of the bed. Two armed security agents stood guarding the back.

At one point my grandmother asked the agents what they intended to do with her youngest son, the one absent member of the household. She said he was innocent

---

* As the daughter of a revolutionary martyr, Kang's mother was herself untouchable.

and that they had no reason to arrest him. The agents agreed.... Yet when our questions turned to the place we were being taken to, the guards claimed ignorance. They did try to cheer us up, though, and even showed a little benevolence, but they swore up and down they didn't even know what a camp looked like. "All I know," said one of them, "is that it's not too bad a place. Nothing's going to happen to you."

Keeping us calm was apparently the guards' main responsibility. It was common knowledge that people in our situation often preferred to take their own lives. The guards wanted none of that. Suicide was a manner of disobeying, of showing that one had lost faith in the future traced out by the Party. The soldiers' good cheer was intended to preserve the utopian myth long enough to get us to our destination....

He was sitting in front of me, hollow-eyed, lost in thought. A little farther on, the truck came to a stop and one of the agents jumped out. A minute later he was back, escorting an elderly woman around my grandmother's age. She was well dressed, all in black, without luggage. We all figured she was an acquaintance or relative of the guard, hitching a ride. She was silent at first, but after about fifteen minutes she started talking and then never stopped. It turned out she, too, was on her way to Yodok, her story running parallel to our own—from her decision to emigrate from Kyoto to the precursory disappearance of her husband, accused of espionage. She had no children and was now entirely on her own, unable to understand why she was being taken away. When she started criticizing the Party, the two agents, who had been standing silently by, ordered her to shut up. But she continued, only less loudly, and the guards, whose only concern was avoiding problems, pretended not to hear.

"How will I survive there without children or a husband?" she kept asking.

2–5

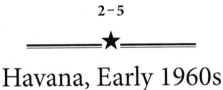

Havana, Early 1960s

Childhood in Castro's Cuba

Following two years of guerrilla warfare against the corrupt Cuban government of Fulgencio Batista, Fidel Castro's revolutionary 26th of July Movement seized power in an armed revolt that culminated on 1 January 1959. At this point, Castro was not yet formally a Communist, and he did not identify himself as a Marxist–Leninist until December 1961. It was not until 1963 that the Soviet Union and, more generally, the international Communist movement officially recognized Cuba as "socialist" (that is, Communist). Nonetheless, the revolutionary remaking of Cuban society began with Castro's seizure of power. Property and wealth were nationalized, a drive for literacy was instituted, and a system of national health care was implemented. But even more basic to Castro's revolutionary remaking of Cuban society—and just as consequential for the people's lives—was the attempt to create a new "socialist" person. At the core of this new identity was an emphasis on the citizen's ethical obligation to society, as opposed to material incentives. Even though Castro's revolutionary vision had significant social support, including from the urban middle classes, a significant number of Cubans opposed his programs from the outset and fled to the United States (and elsewhere). One was Carlos Eire, the author of the following passage.

Eire, who is now Riggs Professor of History and Religious Studies at Yale University, was born in 1950 in Havana, Cuba. His father was a municipal judge in Havana. In 1962, when Carlos was eleven years old, he was airlifted out of Cuba as one of the fourteen thousand Cuban children transported to the United States under Operation Peter Pan. He never saw his father again.

In this passage, Eire, like other children whose voices readers have heard in this chapter, is struggling to understand what "Communism" is and what "revolution" means. And he is grappling with the implications of both for his childhood and identity. He learns how much anxiety his decisions—such as to mouth an irreverent counter slogan to that of the official youth organization, the Pioneers—can cause for his parents in the new world of a "Communist" childhood.

One day, at recess, I couldn't hold it in any longer. It just sort of jumped out of my mouth, like a toad.

"You know, Ciro, I think I'm in love with my right-hand neighbor. You know who." ...

All I can remember is that within four weeks she was gone. Gone forever, just like all the other kids. One by one they disappeared.

It was early 1961. March, to be exact. About one half of my classmates had vanished without saying a word. One day they'd be there, and the next day they'd be gone. Teachers vanished too. Off to the United States or some other country. ...

By April the school had to close because there were too few students and teachers, and because so much had changed for the worse.

We children of the Revolution had much to learn when I was in fifth grade. Everything changed. I will tell you all about that soon enough. And as bombs fell from the sky, and bullets flew, and money evaporated, and Fidel laid claim to our souls, and everyone I knew and cared about vanished quietly, and I began to face the prospect of my own vanishing, what do I remember most vividly?

Her beautiful brown hair brushing against her neck. It was cut in such a straight, straight line....

They say when you die your entire life passes before your eyes in a split second. But even if it's more like an ocean of time than a split second, I'm willing to bet that when my turn comes, I'll see one whole section that is nothing but fragmentary images.

Sometimes, when I least expect it, they'll pop out, these fragments of a world turned upside down. Like flashbacks from a bad trip.

Bummer, man....

There are Pioneers* marching down our street. Kids our age, all dressed alike, wearing red berets and red neckerchiefs, marching like little soldiers.

"Uno, dos, tres, cuatro...."

Soldiers in the making. Militiamen and women of the future. Spies. Informers. Obedient servants of the Revolution.

The marching is relentless. Every single day, and always at the same time....

How I long for the pesticide Jeep to show up and spray them all. Maybe they'll all get tripped up in the fog and march into one another. A heap of Pioneers left behind, all coughing. We all know they probably couldn't take the poison the way we can.

Stupid red berets and red neckerchiefs. Stupid marching slogans.

"Uno, dos, tres, cuatro. Cuba si, Yanquis no, Cuba sí, Yanquis no...."

*"Fidel, seguro, a los Yanquis dale duro....*Fidel, undaunted, hit those Yankees hard....

But there's no more pesticide Jeep. No pesticide to spray. Like everything else, none to be had.

Tony and I had been Cub Scouts for a while, a couple of years earlier, but had given up in disgust....

And now those creeps next door want us to be Pioneers. They badger our parents about it, those creeps who run the Committee for the Defense of the Revolution†. They want us to be just like all those kids marching in lockstep down our street, and all around the neighborhood.

They moved into Chachi's house, these neighborhood spies and busybodies. Chachi's family had moved to that gorgeous house by the seaside, only to leave it

---

*In revolutionary Cuba, the authorities created youth associations modeled on those that existed in the USSR. One of them was the Pioneers, the same name used in the USSR. All schoolchildren were automatically enrolled in the Pioneers.

†Committees for the Defense of the Revolution (hereafter, CDR or CDRs), were one of the three major organizational structures (along with People's Power or Poder Popular and the Communist Party of Cuba) that were to extend into the lives of all Cubans. Their function was to link the central political leadership with Cuban citizens. The CDRs were to offer social services, maintaining ideological enthusiasm, and provide a forum for people to register complaints and demands. It has been estimated that 84 percent of the population over age fourteen belongs to a CDR. Local CDRs had responsibility for the population of a few city blocks, or, in rural communities, a somewhat larger area. See Wilber A. Chaffee Jr., "Poder Popular and the Buro Político: Political Control in Cuba," in Wilber A. Chaffee Jr. and Gary Prevost, eds., *Cuba: A Different America* (Totowa, NJ: Rowman and Littlefield, 1989), 20–22.

behind a few months later. Off to the United States, their new house left for someone else. Their old house left behind for spies and meddlers.

Every block in Havana has one of these houses. They're everywhere. Watching.
Listening. Prodding. Intruding. Threatening. Controlling. We're unlucky enough
to have them next door, and to live in a climate that forces us to keep the windows
open all the time.

Manuel comes up with the perfect counter-slogan for the pioneers:

"*Uno, dos, tres, cuatro, comiendo mierda y gastando zapatos....*" One, two,
three, four, eating shit and wasting shoes....

I must explain: for Cubans, anything that's dumb or a waste of time can be
called "eating shit." A chump or a fool is a *comemierda*, or shit eater.

Anyway, after our resident genius Manuel comes up with his counter-slogan,
we can't refrain from using it. We hide on the porches, or up in the trees, or behind
the shrubs, and shout out as they walk by:

"*Uno, dos, tres, cuatro, comiendo mierda y gastando zapatos....*"

They're all so busy marching in lockstep and shouting out their stupid slogans
that they don't hear us.

Or can they hear us? Maybe they can. Every now and then we see a head or
two turn and look around, at their own peril. Looking in any direction but forward is wrong. For a Pioneer, that is. Che Guevara* has a slogan they also chant,
ad nauseam:

"*Marcha atrás nunca, ni para coger impulso.*" Not one step back, not even to
gain momentum.

It's dangerous for us to call the Pioneers shit eaters and to accuse them of
wasting shoes, especially since shoes are scarce and rationed nowadays....

And I yell at Pioneers from my hiding place and call them shoe wasters. I
wonder how different my life would have been if my mother hadn't caught us
doing it.

It frightens her to the core. She has visions, the kind mothers get. Flash-
forwards rather than flashbacks. Ugly, tormenting visions of my brother and me
being hauled away by militiamen, never to be seen again. Visions of our Defense
Committee neighbors overhearing us. Visions of us in some juvenile prison camp
way out in the provinces, where all we'd do for the rest of our lives is cut sugarcane.

---

* Ernesto "Ché" Guevara (1928–1967) was a close comrade of Fidel Castro's during the
Cuban Revolution. Guevara was a doctor from Argentina who became a Marxist revolutionary in
the 1950s, well before he and Castro first met in Mexico in June 1955. Ché would go on to have
significant influence on Castro's thinking. He also held important administrative posts in Cuba's
Communist government, including implementing agrarian reform as minister of industries,
serving as instructional director for Cuba's armed forces, reviewing appeals of those convicted as
war criminals by revolutionary tribunals, acting as a diplomat on behalf of Cuban socialism, and
functioning as director of the National Bank of Cuba (Banco Nacional de Cuba). He died under
mysterious circumstances—most likely, he was killed by Bolivian forces aided by the CIA—in
Bolivia in 1967 at age thirty-nine.

Or even worse, visions of us being packed off to Russia or East Germany or Czechoslovakia, of us disappearing to some foreign land and never returning.

Someday I'll lose count of how many times she's told me about how much we frightened her that day she caught us yelling at the Pioneers, and how much that awful moment weighed in her decision to get us out of the country as soon as possible, in any way possible....

And the rumor begins to circulate. The rumor of all rumors.

The Revolution is going to take all the children away from their parents, and soon. Something in the new Cuban constitution allows for it: *Patria Potestad*[*]. My mother is now convinced that the state is going to herd us into trucks and ship us off to parts unknown. Maybe even to Russia. After all, it happened during the Spanish Civil War in the 1930s, in some areas controlled by the Communists, and everyone knew someone who had known someone who had known someone whose kid had been sent to Russia, never to be seen again[†].

There are so many Spaniards in Havana, and so many children of Spaniards. The memories are fresh. My mom and many others know it's possible.

Communists? I am hearing the word for the first time. Batista is still president. I am about five years old, and I'm in our car on the way to my grandparents' house, just as we pass what will become the Plaza of the Revolution. It's still under construction. Tony and I are in the back seat, as always, and I hear my parents talking about Communists in the front seat.

"Hey, those Communists must be good guys," I chime in.

"Why do you say that?" asks Louis XVI[‡], with a tone that can only mean I've made a mistake.

"Because they must help people communicate...."

Prolonged laughter from the front seat. "How cute," says my mom.

"What's so funny?"

"Oh, never mind, you're too young to understand. But Communists aren't good. Not at all. They're very bad."

Now I am a few years older, passing the same spot, staring at a hammer and sickle on a billboard from the backseat of the car, and we're all supposed to become Communists.

Fidel has declared himself a Marxist–Leninist and proclaimed the Revolution and the country Communist. No more private property. No more mine and thine. No more exploitation of the masses by capitalists. Share and share equally. And if

---

[*] Eire refers here to the article of Cuba's Family Code stipulating that parental rights or parental authority (*la patria potestad*) could be suspended in the absence of parents or in cases of their incompetence.

[†] This is a reference to the nearly 3,000 Spanish Republican children evacuated to the USSR during the Spanish Civil War (1936–1939), excerpts of whose letters back to family in Spain are included in this chapter. A significant number of them succumbed to tuberculosis and other illnesses, especially during World War II.

[‡] The author refers here to his father, who believed that he was Louis XVI in a past life and that his wife was Marie Antoinette.

anyone fails to work, then he or she will have nothing to eat. And you can't work just for yourself or for your family. Everyone has to work for everyone else. And everyone owns everything, all together.

So he says.

The Chinese hot dog man has lost his hot dog stand. The Revolution won't tolerate anyone claiming a business for himself. Not even a hot dog stand. The hot dogs have vanished along with a lot of other stuff. Like Coke and Pepsi.

My uncle Mario has lost his two businesses to the Revolution. The last thing he did at his furniture store was to burn all the accounting records so those who still owed money on their furniture wouldn't have to pay the state. The Revolution wanted to keep collecting the money they owed. The money they owed to themselves, I guess, according to the logic of the Revolution.

My uncle is almost sent to prison for that subversive act. . . .

Everyone has lost whatever real estate they owned.

The state has compensated them, but with such paltry sums as to make the whole deal stink.

Besides, one fine morning, recently, Che came up with the great idea of doing away with money altogether. I've had it a few times myself, especially when short on cash. No money at all. Let everyone share and share alike. To each according to his or her needs. So all the banks have been seized. This is the first step. Everyone who had a bank account can keep some arbitrary low sum—a few hundred pesos, I think. . . .

My grandfather cries for a while about that.

The second step is to change all the currency so that the bills and coins that people have will be worthless and all Cubans can start on a completely level playing field. Each person is allowed to change a set amount of money, maybe fifty pesos.

It's a fine Sunday morning and everyone in the country has lined up at appointed places to change whatever money they can. If you haven't changed your money by the end of of the day, tough luck. From that day forward, all the old currency will be worthless.

The lines are very long, but they move fast because you are allowed to change so very little. I'm standing in line, and so is my brother Tony, and everyone else I know. . . . When you finally make it to the coins in your hand, they take them from you and give you new colorful bills with pictures of Fidel and Che and other heroes of the Revolution. The new coins are so flimsy that we take turns trying to blow them off one another's hands.

No one panics, but it's still nothing more than controlled chaos. Very quickly, people discover that they can go to more than one changing center. So everyone is trying to hit as many lines as possible. . . .

I think of my relative Pepito Abeillé, who helped me see the futility of saving money. He was one of those who hired himself out as a changer that Sunday morning. He hustled that day as he had never hustled in his entire life. His problem and his salvation were one and the same. He had never worked a day in his life. . . .

On that Sunday, Pepito made more money than he had in his entire life, changing currency for the family that had supported him for so long. He was doing everyone a favor, and everyone felt obliged to let him take his percentage.

I am back in that line again, getting close to the money changers. I see Pepito coming towards us, walking briskly. I've never seen him move so fast. He's walking all over Havana in his white suit, changing bills and coins for everyone he knows—for a fee, of course....

My hero, Pepito....

Almost everything is rationed now. Every now and then the stores get a huge shipment of rice, or black beans, or beef, or whatever, and the word spreads like wildfire. Everyone rushes down to the store and stands in line forever. Sometimes if the line is too long, by the time your turn is near, they run out of the beans, or the garbanzos, or the chickens, or whatever.

But the greatest scam of all is the black market. People sell you their rations for more than they paid for them, or trade them for whatever they need more....

I've been standing in line a lot these past few months.... You have to show up in person, with your card, and stand in line, or you don't get your food.

Everyone has to stand in line, except the leaders of the Revolution. No one ever sees them or their servants standing in line. Yes, they have servants.

Medicines are disappearing too. And clothing. And appliances. And cars. And hardware. And toys. Everything is disappearing.

No more comic books. No more American films. No more American television programs. No more ice-cream man. No more shaved-ice man. No more fruit man. No more vegetable man. No more coal man. No more *guarapo* man. No more Jamaican pastry man, and no pastry man song.

"*Pasteles ... pastelitos ... Pasteeeles, paaasteliitos ... Frecos, fresquitos ....Dulces ... buenitos.*" Pastries, little pastries, fresh and sweet and good....

I love the chocolate eclairs that are the same color as his arms. And I love the way he speaks Spanish.

But now there is no more pastry man.

No more avocado man either.

I can hear him still. The avocado man has one of the prettiest chants I've ever heard.

Aguacate maduro, aguacate. Aguaaacate maaaduuuuro, aaaaguuuuuaaacaaateee! Avocados, ripe avocados.

We have some good counter-jingles for that guy.

"*Aguacate maduro, peo seguro.*" Ripe avocados, fart for sure....

"*Aguacate verdoso, peo apestoso.*" Greenish avocados, stinky farts....

And so on. We have dozens of them. Even my dad has pitched in with a few counter-jingles of his own....

And there are those damn Pioneers marching again, droning on with their stupid slogans.... Stupid Pioneers, reminding us that it is all gone, gone, gone.

A lifetime of memories gone in less than a year. An entire culture pulled up by the roots. It is a Revolution, after all.

The priests have vanished too, along with the monks and the nuns. All religious orders have been banished from Cuba. Gone are the Jesuits who had educated Fidel and my father and grandfather and great-grandfather. Gone are the Dominicans, and the Franciscans, and the Carmelites, and the Christian Brothers, and the Ursulines. Gone are the Italian priests who lived across the street from us....

I am standing in the front parlor of the priests' house. It is a dark room, the windows shrouded in dark velvet curtains. A confessional booth looms large at the foot of the stairs. These priests are pretty nice, for priests. My mom has sent me to have a chat with the older one because I'm starting to worry about death too much, like everyone in my father's family. He tells me I have nothing to fear, that death is the doorway to something much better, and that, anyway, it is so, so far away for me....

But they are crying, those priests, on the day they say good-bye to us.

Bang, bang, bang, bang, bang, bang, bang, bang, bang....

It seems to go on all day long, for all time. It's the sound of sledge hammers pounding on sacred symbols at the former convent and school of the Ursulines, one block away from us. The school where Tony had attended preschool and kindergarten. Sledgehammers demolishing crosses. Sledgehammers pulverizing images of Jesus and Mary and the angels and other saints....

Bang, bang, bang, bang, bang, bang, bang, bang, bang....

There is nothing else in the world like the sound of sacred symbols being pulverized, little by little....

As we ride our bikes to Che Guevara's palace, we can hear the pounding getting louder and louder....

We also like to keep an eye out for Che. Sometimes we can see him pulling in and out of the giant mansion in his Mercedes-Benz. He's always dressed in his military uniform with the beret, the man who wants to do away with money. So is his chauffeur.

Such a beautiful house. So huge. Such beautiful grounds. Such great palm trees. Such a fabulous set of wrought-iron gates. Such a nice Mercedes. It looks bulletproof.

Bang, bang, bang, bang, bang, bang, bang, bang, bang....

And they are crying, those priests, as they say good-bye to us. And my grandfather is crying, as he stands in line to change his currency. And the Jamaican pastry guy is crying for his pastries. He loves them so. And Pepito Abeillé is counting the bills in the pocket of his white slacks.

Whatever. There's always a whatever in Revolutions.

And I wonder if the chauffeur, a good Revolutionary, has dirty magazines....

Bang, bang, bang, bang, bang, bang, bang, bang, bang....

But wait, where are the lizards? Can Fidel and Che make them disappear too? So long as everything else evaporates into memories, why not them, too?

A Peruvian youth—part of one of the peasant self-defense forces (*rondas campesinas*)—holds a sawed-off shotgun. The Law of Rondas Campesinas (Ley de Rondas Campesinas) was approved by the Peruvian Parliament in October 1986. The law recognized the "peaceful, democratic, and autonomous peasant self-defense forces that contribute to development and to social peace, without partisan political goals" in the struggle against the Sendero Luminoso. Peasant self-defense forces had emerged beginning in 1977 in the northern mountains of Peru. They recruited and trained youth. Javier Gamboa Quispe, part of whose testimony before the Truth and Reconciliation Commission is reproduced in document 2-6, served in a peasant self-defense patrol. He was wounded in a clash between the patrol and the forces of the Sendero Luminoso. Quote is from René Kuppe and Richard Potz, eds., *Law and Anthropology: International Yearbook for Legal Anthropology* (The Hague: Martinus Nijhoff Publishers, 1999), 161. Photo by Abilio Arroyo. Source of photo: Enrique Chávez, ed., *La Verdad sobre El Espanto: El Perú en tiempos del terror* (Lima: Caretas, 2003), 73.

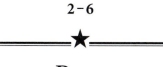

Peru

Testimony from a Child Conscripted by the Shining Path (Sendero Luminoso)

The Sendero Luminoso (PCP-SL) terrorized the lives of Peru's children, especially those who lived in its rural highlands. The *senderistas* targeted young people, even and especially children, for recruitment because they believed that they could more easily infuse young people than adults with their ideology. Children, moreover, represented the Party's future given the inevitable losses in combat during a protracted war. As one of the *senderistas* own documents put it, their goal was to "make the children actively participate in the people's war; they can undertake a number of tasks through which they can begin to understand the need to transform the world, change their ideology and adopt the ideology of the proletariat."[12] Children recruited by the *senderistas* were enrolled in their "pioneer children" or "red pioneers" organization. They were forced to conduct surveillance, transmit messages, engage in espionage, furnish food and supplies, transport flags and ammunition, and work on the farm. The *senderistas* did exempt children who were not yet eleven years old from participating in attacks.[13]

To "recruit" children and young people, the *senderistas* frequently employed coercion, violence, and threatened violence. Some recruitments, to be sure, were not forced. There were children who joined the *senderistas* of their own accord. Among their reasons for doing so were to seek revenge for the murder of a family member or relative, to belong to a larger group, and to pursue the movement's ideals and goals. But in the majority of cases, as testimonies indicate, the *senderistas* conducted their coerced recruitment in schools or forced communities to provide a quota of young recruits. Parents who refused to give up their children were murdered. Records of the Truth and Reconciliation Commission indicate that 20.5% of kidnappings and conscriptions (in cases when the age was recorded) were of children. Moreover, 42 percent of all of the PCP-SL actions against children were kidnappings and conscriptions. One of the children whom the *senderistas* took by force was Javier Gamboa Quispe, the author of the following text.

Testimony Number 332054. Written up by Patricia Olivera Pardes. Drafted 20 December 2002. Published with permission of the Centro de Información para la Memoria Colectiva y los Derechos Humanos and the witnesses themselves. Translation: Glennys Young. Some annotations by Adam Warren.

That Quispe came from the region of Junín is not surprising. That is because 80 percent of all of the kidnappings and conscriptions against children took place in the regions of Ayacucho, Huancavelica, Huánuco, and Junín.[14] (In addition, 76 percent of those kidnapped and conscripted were boys.) The fact that his family (and those of others in his community) was seized by the Sendero Luminoso in 1988 is also not surprising. He was captured by the Sendero Luminoso in one of the two periods, 1983–1985 and 1987–1990, during which the armed conflict intensified—when their kidnapping of children was especially widespread.

Quispe's account gives a sense of what life was like for children forcibly recruited by the *senderistas*. It confronts readers with the unmediated horror of children being forced to kill, having to witness violence and death, learning of the deaths of their parents, and of feeling trapped by the threat of death. Yet Quispe, like some other children forcibly taken by the *senderistas* did decide that he would try to escape. And, perhaps against all odds, he succeeded.

TESTIMONY OF JAVIER GAMBOA QUISPE

This is the testimony of Javier Gamboa Quispe. He tells of the forced use of approximately twenty families by alleged members of the Sendero Luminoso on 3 April 1988, in the Native Community of Puerto Nuevo Asháninka, district of Río Tambo, province of Satipo, department of Junín. He also tells of the murder of his grandparents, seventy-year-old Zacarias Ñaco and seventy-year-old Martha (whose surname he does not know) by alleged members of Sendero Luminoso in 1992 in the Community Center of Puerto Unión, district of Perené, province of Chanchamayo, department of Junín. Moreover, he refers to the confrontation between Sendero Luminoso members and soldiers from the Peruvian Army and the death of six children who were members of the Sendero Luminoso: three boys and three women in 1992.

Note: The person testifying reports that for reasons of personal safety his original name was changed to Gamboa Quispe, and that for this reason he does not bear the last name of his father, Camayteri, nor that of his mother, Ñatos*.

What happened to my mother (Maria Ñatos Zacarias) when [I] was a little boy, when I was eight years old. At that time the subversives arrived in Puerto Nuevo Asháninka. There were like six people and they came at about 10 PM, and then the subversives came placing demands on my father, saying that they came to organize a political base for the party. My father, Jorge Andrés Camayteri Jocari, did not want to agree to this and they were threatening to kill him. And my father kept shaking [out of fear], so then they accepted him and the subversives said: let's go fight all the millionaires.

On 3 April 1988 Sendero arrives (at the Native Community of Puerto Nuevo Asháninka) and takes around twenty families, including my family as

---

*The full names of his parents were Maria Ñatos Zacarias and Jorge Andres Camayteri Jocari. It seems that he was twenty-two at the time he gave the testimony.

2-6 • Peru   73

well. Afterwards, when I was eleven years old, they (the Senderistas) took me until eventually I was [placed] in the Local Force (special group of the Sendero Luminoso that carries out raids) to organize all the masses and forced me in this way to take others. After eleven years and I could not find my father or my mother. They took me (the Senderistas) to (the province of) Ayacucho, and from there I returned by the route they took to get there and my father was no longer there. He was at another site, they sent him to another site, it is a river which is called the Community of Chikireni. There he was working as a farmer planting crops for food for the people, so he was planting manioc, corn, potato.

When they sent me to Ayacucho, I went to (the province of Huanta) as far as the Uchupucria zone.... They made us make a tunnel and low wall, which was to protect us when the enemy arrived. We made a hole in the ground.

It's not very cold in Ayacucho but on the other hand it's cold in Huanta, so much so that I could not take it. I suffered enough [and] certainly could not take it anymore.

The organization I was in had a boss, José, he was an older* person.

My organization (Sendero Luminoso) was called the Main Force†. They integrated young people between the ages of twelve and thirty [into the organization], women and children consisting of people from the mountains, native people from all places joined.

Then they (the senderistas) told me: we are going to fulfill an assignment. So I thought what sort of thing would be an assignment; then I went to a community, Huamanguia, where we had to steal what they had—clothing, supplies. When they killed they killed everyone.

...And also I didn't want to be under the control of the Senderistas, and if I were to escape they would kill me‡.

When these people [the senderistas] were going to kill people, they would show up acting normal, happy, as if they were reclaiming something that had been stolen from them, and getting it back would be cause for a big celebration.

You show up there as if you're meeting with them. We have fulfilled the assignment already because we have killed the whole little population. Now we have to keep fighting§. The party never dies. Although the bird flies away, the seed stays behind¶, they say.

I felt sad about my parents, whom I still could not find. It was apparent to others, and they asked me: Why? Are you sad because you are a wretch? I said, no,

---

* Most likely this means he was in his forties or older.

† In Spanish, the Fuerza Principal.

‡ The author implies that he came to the chilling realization that the senderistas went about killing people as if they were pigs, chickens, or other farm animals. Once he understood that the senderistas would hunt him down and kill him in this fashion were he to try to escape, he began to feel trapped.

§ In other words, at the time, he thought he had to go in, trick villagers, massacre them, and keep going.

¶ Here the author likens the senderistas to birds that travel and move seeds about. The senderistas are planting the seeds of Revolution just as birds leave behind seeds that grow to be trees.

comrade, I am just a bit unwell. If you are unwell leave and rest; and I rested and another one would come by and tell me: you are not sick, you are lying. And so when I was sick they made me work carrying rocks, piling them up....

We returned from the district of Andahuaylas (province of Andahuaylas), department of Apurímac, we returned to the attached area* of Vizcatán, district of Ayahuanco, province of Huanta, department of Ayacucho. Having recently arrived there I worked all day, they made us work in the rain. We planted what grows in the jungle during the daytime until you finish your field, and then they send you to another site. And also there wasn't anything to eat, just an herb, nettles. We ate nettle soup and there wasn't manioc or anything, so that was what we ate.

Then I arrived here in the area of Cutivireni, the district of Río Tambo, the province of Satipo, department of Junín, where I met all the masses, people recruited by Sendero Luminoso, everybody had anemia† and, on top of that, [Sendero Luminoso] comrade Arturo, he who organizes everything, was killing people, he was killing everybody there who was anemic, and they piled them up rather a lot in the cemetery, I have seen that they buried the people at the Base of Kindamito, this is what the Senderistas called this area, located in the Sendero district of Río Tambo, this is in the community of Boca Anapati (located in the district of Pangoa), province of Satipo, department of Junín, their base was in the highlands there, they buried lots of anemic people, there must have been about fifty people.

I remember the place where they had supposedly buried these people. From Boca Anapati I can get to another that was there, Río Tingabeni. It was like an encampment for Sendero near Centro Tingabeni in the highlands, this base is here on the mountainside. I have seen when they made that grave site, here one finds all the dead people.

Throughout this area of Centro Tingabeni there are various common graves where people were buried who were found physically sick with anemia.... They didn't want to treat these people.

With a rope, they killed a [boy] child who didn't want to obey his mother, they hanged him and they sliced him open with a knife that cut into his heart. There he died, and they buried him.

When they killed the people they said: "Hurray!" They raised their hands; when the mothers of these children saw that they were killing their children they started to cry and the subversives said to them: "you shut up or do you also want to die too."

The subversives said: "We don't want idle people here, a petty thief because otherwise the party will kill him."

---

* The Spanish here is *anexo*, which probably means a community or base.

† Unclear is whether he is speaking about anemia in particular or more generally about malnutrition and/or illness. The speaker is not fluent in formal Spanish.

They had ordered me to kill people and told me to go walk about [and] conduct surveillance, to keep patrol at about a distance of two blocks away*....

When I arrived there (in Puerto Ocopa), my mother was already dead. They told me she had died just like that†. Others told me that my father killed my mother, they say my mother was ill, my grandparents as well and my brother told me that my father hadn't killed her, that she had died just like that, afflicted by her colic so that she died with chills, that's what my father told me. They met each other in Río Chikereni in the highlands, my parents, my grandparents and siblings.

I returned to Puerto Ocopa when I was thirteen years old, and I found myself with my brothers, already without our parents, they left six children.

The subversives killed my grandparents with a knife, both of them were killed, my grandfather was seventy years old, my grandmother was seventy years old.

When I arrived at Puerto Ocopa it was already controlled by a Sendero and when I was in the community they told me: "Now we don't want the young people to come here. They have to return to the highlands." When I returned to the highlands I arrived at Vizcatán I wanted to hand myself over, to escape, because I already didn't like it when, being thirteen years old, I walked at night and we slept in by day in Río San Gabeni. We always had training, we didn't use any light or candles; grasping our stick we walked along.

When I had been in the Sendero [Luminoso] for two years, I organized all the masses, [which were] formed of pure old people, youths, women and children, and all of them had their names changed.

They said to me: Combatiente Laureano. The subversives gave me this name.

The subversives had their [own] law, they had eight warnings:

Speak politely, do not speak strongly, pay for honestly what you buy; do not repair damaged objects; do not touch the crops; do not mistreat the prisoners; do not touch the women; do not bother the people, we were not disturbing our neighbor, when you seize someone to forcibly rape them the party will kill you; but it can pardon [you] three times that you find yourself committing rape. If you were to commit rape they would criticize you because you are doing these things and the party doesn't like it and second [on the second occasion]: you had to tell about your life; if you were obeying your parents and all the people in the vicinity would be there listening to you, on the fourth time [you commit rape] they don't pardon you.

We were allowed to rape a woman three times, but the fourth time they didn't pardon you they buried you.

I did commit a third rape, I had to tell publicly what my life was like from when I was little up until the present, I did that in front of everyone. I sat down in the center and I began to tell....

---

* After this, he is sent back to Puerto Ocopa to watch over the masses and make them do work.
† Presumably of her own health problems.

When you didn't fulfill your assignment, when they sent you to another place and you arrived late, you had to say: "I arrived late, I did not keep my word of the party and I surely do not want to become this again on another day."

One had to fulfill one's obligations, if they told you to go kill you had to carry through if you don't carry through they let you off the hook, but on the third time they kill you already.

I was in Puerto Ocopa, then they sent me to Vizcatán but from there I returned another time to the forest as I already could not bear it I escaped, I left my brothers [not mentioning names] who remained in the subversion.

In the year 1994, I left for another community of Valle Esmeralda, when I escaped, I was thinking, when you escape the patrol is going to kill you for this, I didn't want to escape but I had already left, I faced up, and I said what happens doesn't matter.

At this time (1992) there were four [military] clashes with the army in the Sierra. Six children died there, three boys, three girls, since the older ones escaped from Sendero*, and no one died as far as the army was concerned.

I also have had to escape, the bullet also almost reached me but it but it only grazed me on top. I was very scared.

Then when we got here they killed four more from Sendero and of them only one soldier died.

Sendero said: although others will die, we will still get there in ten more years.

At some moment I identified the first time with the thought of Sendero Luminoso. I liked the food that they gave us, later on each day they ordered us you are going to do your assignment, [if] you arrive late you are going to carry water, you fell asleep at one in the morning then they woke you up at 3 AM (you only slept two hours), already I began not to like this. . . .

Until the present time I continue to feel bad, asking myself why all this happened to me.

When I was a child Sendero showed up, and [from that point on] I no longer lived calmly at home. Sendero did not teach us school, they only taught us physical training, they taught us how to use weapons.

I escaped from the Sendero base which is called: the heart of it [of the base] is located inside Boca Anapati, I deceived them saying: I'm going to go conduct surveillance. I went on ahead, there were fourteen [of them] and I was the fifteenth, when I got ahead I escaped and carried a shotgun. I headed to the community of Natalia, there I had an uncle, I arrive and he said to me: who are you, to his face I answered I have escaped from the subversion, is it just you?, he asked me; I answered here yes only me, he said to me sit down and tell me, but before that he admitted to me that earlier he had also been in the subversion and that those from

---

* In other words, the fact that the older senderistas abandoned the child soldiers there caused them to be killed.

the Ronda Campesina* rescued him. They do not kill you, on the contrary they welcome you. The solider is never going to kill you, either, even better will ask you where the Sendero is and you have to guide them, at this moment I was happy.

The community Natalia took me to the army base, Valle Esmeralda, where an official interviewed me and asked me, where did you escape from. I answered him, I have escaped from the subversives. The official said to me, where is comrade Feliciano; I answered him; I don't know him. The official interviewed me for an hour and said to me: "You are a fourteen-year old child, don't worry, nothing is going to happen to you...."

The gentleman Arturo Barriento Quispe asked me if I wanted to live with him and I answered yes. He fetched me to live in his house. He made me study and I finished my primary and secondary [education]. I remained there working on his cocoa farm, every so often he gave me pocket money. I felt free.

The man Raúl Aguiles formed part of the Ronda patrol, he forced me to go out to keep patrol, then there was a clash in Sandoveli on the 25th of September, 1995, between the subversives and the Ronda patrol; it is there that a bullet hit me, I already took myself for dead; thanks to a woman who took me to Satipo so they could treat me, I had the help of the International Red Cross.

From this accident I had I remain an invalid, I could not walk anymore.

I returned to Valle Esmeralda. There I heard, you brothers are free, and we have found each other again; but I do not bear my father's name, now my surname is Gamboa Quispe. My brothers are named Francisco Kauri Zacarias, Hector Kauri Zacarias, Alicia Kauri Zacarias and the last of my brothers is named Rogelio Kauri Brayan, he too has another surname. We are two sons who have the surnames of another person, at this time all our brothers are living in different places but we visit one another, some neighbors said to me: "Your parents died in Puerto Asháninka; there in Río Tairiari they died on their farm itself. The people from Sendero attacked them at about five in the afternoon. They shot them in the mouth and they died there. But before this tragedy occurred, my father had already left Sendero, had changed his mind, and was on the farm together with my brothers.

My brother, Francisco Kauri Zacarias, died from grief about my father because he said: "our father died, the subversives have killed him, why have they killed him, One day I will find the people from the subversion and I will kill them." Then my brother took the decision to end his life by suicide, five days later his body was found thrown in the Río Alberta.

Psychologically I find myself so-so, I want to recover, perhaps I am forgetting everything that happened to my parents and my brother Francisco; in these times I love my brothers more than ever. One of my brothers is in the Hospital, they operated on his legs, and they have cut off two fingers, since he has suffered for four years from a skin disease. He has suffered, no one has seen him since he is a fifteen-year-old orphan.

---

* Peasant civil defense patrol.

At present he is in the hospital being looked after by the Seguro Escolar*, the CART (Central Asháninka of Río Tambo)† is also helping him; I would also like to have other help as well.

Before the arrival of the Sendero in the community of Unión Puerto Asháninka, violence did not exist, we all lived happily. We organized meetings in a group of members of an indigenous community to carry out the jobs; but when the Sendero arrived, everything was different, one didn't live peacefully, one lived with different politics‡.

RECOMMENDATIONS

I want help, recently I am recovering my health, given that I have already been in the hospital for seven years.

I need them to help me in the situation I am in (an invalid), I can't work anymore, I can't expect to have a profession.

We don't want the Sendero to return with their violence, we want to live in peace.

We should learn that among Peruvians ourselves we have done harm to each other.

NOTES

1. *New York Times*, 26 May 1937, 24. Quote is from *Pravda*, 15 September 1936, 2. For discussion of the evacuation of the children in the Soviet press, see Daniel Kowalsky, *Stalin and the Spanish Civil War* (New York: Gutenberg e-book, 2004), chap. 5, 2.
2. On its role in the expedition, and on the expedition's organizational infrastructure more generally, see Alicia Alted Vigil, Encarna Nicolás Marín, and Róger Gonzales Martell, *Los niños de la guerra de España en la Unión Soviética: De la evacuación al retorno (1937–1999)* (*The Spanish "Children of War" in the Soviet Union: From Evacuation to Return (1937–1999)*). (Madrid: Fundación Francisco Largo Caballero, 1999), 49.
3. Kowalsky, *Stalin and the Spanish Civil War*, chap. 5, 13.
4. For details of the wording of the Politburo directive, see Kowalsky, *Stalin and the Spanish Civil War*, chap. 5, 8. Quotes regarding Soviet subjects are from Jochen Hellbeck, *Revolution on My Mind: Writing a Diary under Stalin* (Cambridge, MA: Harvard University Press, 2006), 6.
5. See M. Colette Plum, "Unlikely Heirs: War Orphans during the Second Sino–Japanese War, 1937–1945." (PhD dissertation, Stanford University, 2006), 11.
6. Funding for the homes was provided by the Nationalist government and private donors. The homes, which existed throughout China from October 1938 until December 1944, were under the control of China's National Relief Commission. Most of the homes were in the interior, but some were in Occupied China and in

---

* This is likely insurance for school children.

† The Asháninka are indigenous people of Peru's rainforests. CART is a grassroots community organization that was attacked by the Shining Path, which had tried to infiltrate it.

‡ It is possible that this means they lived under different rules.

Communist base areas. Approximately 200,000 war orphans lived in the homes during the war. See Plum, "Unlikely Heirs," 11.

7. Ben Kiernan, *The Pol Pot Regime: Race, Power and Genocide in Cambodia under the Khmer Rouge* (New Haven, CT: Yale University Press, 2008), 8.

8. Although Kim was in the Soviet Union in the late 1930s, his training in Communism was as a member of the Chinese Communist Party. He went to a Chinese middle school, became fluent in Chinese, and joined the Chinese Communist Party in 1931, when he moved to the mountains of Manchuria. (It was in 1931 that Japan occupied Manchuria, which it subsequently renamed Manchukuo.) Kim played an important role concerning the Korean Communist guerillas who, at times in the 1930s, were a majority of the Communists in Manchuria. These Korean Communists were "revolutionary" in the sense of being opposed to Japan. But the Chinese Communists also suspected them of wanting to attach ethnic Korean areas of Manchuria to Japan. In the 1930s, the Chinese Communist Party conducted serious purges of Korean guerrillas owing to these suspicions. Kim had a reputation for deft mediation between the suspicions of the Chinese and the aspirations of Koreans.

9. Quotes from Charles Armstrong, *The North Korean Revolution, 1945–1950* (Ithaca, NY: Cornell University Press, 2003), 241, 243.

10. At the same time, in part because of the deeply hierarchal nature of pre-1945 Korean society, a new hierarchy formed. This was one in which hereditary distinctions continued, as in the Chosŏn period (1392–1910), to play a role in forming social status groups.

11. There are several reasons for the political vulnerability in the 1970s (and earlier) of repatriates from Japan to North Korea. Most ethnic Koreans who had lived in Japan were of southern Korean origin, due to the proximity of southern Korea to Japan. But Communists of southern origin were viewed with suspicion by Kim and his "guerrilla Communists": they were perceived as serious rivals for Communist legitimacy. (People of southern origin were easily identified by their accent.) Those southern Communists who ventured into the political arena were subject to purges from the Korean War through the 1970s. Second, the ethnic Korean repatriates from Japan tended to live in enclaves in P'yŏngyang. They enjoyed rare access to special stores for Party elites and others having privileged status. This was because they had access to hard currency and other goods from relatives—an access to privileges that elicited other cadres' envy. (For further discussion of such stores in the late Soviet context and other socialist polities, see "Shopping in Special Stores" in the photo essay, "Everyday Life and Every Things under Socialism, 1945–1989, and Beyond," which follows chapter 8.) The third reason for the political vulnerability of the repatriates was likely cultural, in that they sustained differences between south and north and were also influenced by Japanese culture.

12. From the document *Linea de mases*, prepared by the magazine *Sol Rojo* (www.solrojo.org). Quoted in Andrea Portugal, "Voices from the War: Exploring the Motivation of Sendero Luminoso Militants," CRISE Working Paper no. 57, October 2008, 60.

13. Ibid., 59.

14. Statistics are taken from ibid., 56.

CHAPTER 3

———★———

Varieties of
Communist Subjects:
Beyond the Ordinary

It is well known that Marxist–Leninist polities and movements sought to make "new people" who had specifically socialist values, modes of speaking, ways of identifying themselves, and goals. As we saw in the last chapter, this explains the fact that Communist polities invested tremendous resources in transforming children, who, as blank slates or nearly so, were thought to be especially receptive to Communist values and ideology. But no matter the age, the gender, the occupation, or other characteristics of people in Communist polities, Communist regimes and parties sought to put them on the correct ideological rails and involve them in a massive project of self-transformation. This was a project whose goal was, when it came to making the new socialist person, homogeneity and standardization—especially in the long run.

But in implementing this project, Communist polities necessarily ran up against the immense diversity in human attributes. And so these polities had to decide just *how* homogenized and standardized the new socialist person had to be. Could a truly "socialist" person retain particularistic aspects of her/his identity (being a foreigner or member of a minority racial group, being gay, being physically disabled and/or living with emotional disabilities) and still be a full-fledged member of the Communist body politic, let alone a member of the Communist Party? Communist Party organizations around the world faced countless questions of this sort, and their answers varied across space and time. Moreover, whatever official policy was, people themselves faced decisions on an everyday basis about how to reconcile their identities with the Communist project.

What did it mean for people to be of an ethnic minority, to be gay, to be disabled, and to live in a Communist polity or belong to a Communist movement?

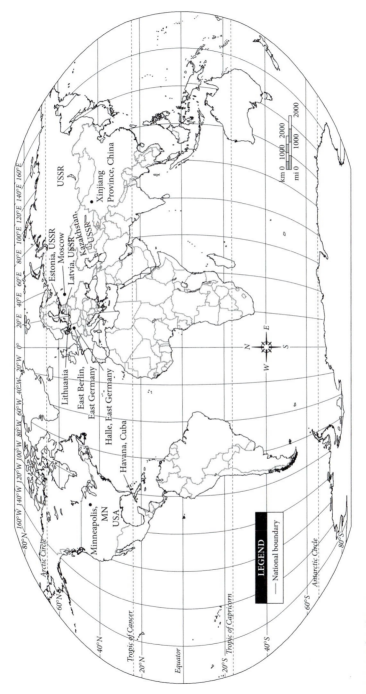

Locator Map for Chapter 3

How might one have combined whatever commitment one had to socialist values and Marxist–Leninist ideology with other aspects of one's identity? These are some of the questions that the selections in this chapter seek to address. They include excerpts written by an African-American man who lived in the USSR in the 1920s and 1930s, by a British Communist who resided in Moscow and in 1934 opposed Soviet legislation on homosexuality, by Chinese students studying in the USSR in the early post-Stalin years, by a mother in Soviet Lithuania with a disabled son, by East Germans seeking permission in 1988 from state authorities to hold a gay dance, and by the authors of the 1994 "Manifesto of the Gay and Lesbian Association of Cuba."

USSR, 1930s–1940s

Homer Smith (1910–1972) on Being an African-American in the Soviet Union

Even before the Bolsheviks seized power in 1917, there were Africans in the Russian Empire. But the number of African-American and Afro-Caribbean migrants to Russia increased during the first two decades of Bolshevik rule. They headed to Soviet Russia for a number of reasons, reasons that no doubt varied for each person. For some, Communist ideology was paramount. But many no doubt sought the racial equality promised by Communist ideology. Additional motivations for their journey included, of course, racial discrimination and violence in the United States and elsewhere and the high levels of unemployment during the Great Depression.

Black migrants to the USSR tended to receive a warm welcome and often found greater opportunities for professional advancement than in the United States and the other countries they came from. The longer they were in the USSR, however, the more likely they were to experience racial discrimination on an everyday basis. Because of that, and because of the heightened political repression during the Great Purges of 1936–1938, these migrants tended to leave the USSR.

One such African-American migrant to the "land of the Soviets" was Homer Smith, the author of the following passage. When Smith headed to the USSR in 1932, he was but twenty-two years old and had graduated from the University of Minnesota's School of Journalism. He would go on to spend fourteen years in the Soviet Union, a period during which he worked as a consultant for the Moscow Post Office and as a journalist. He became the only African-American correspondent stationed in Russia during the Stalin period, and he served as a war correspondent for the Associated Press and African-American newspapers. He managed to leave the USSR for Ethiopia in 1946, partly because he was disillusioned by the racial prejudice that existed in the USSR, but especially because of his fear for himself and others during the arrests of the Great Purges. As he puts it, he experienced "utter disillusionment with the prevailing fear and terror."

From Homer Smith, *Black Man in Red Russia* (Chicago: Johnson Publishing Company, 1964), 1–3, 96–98, 100–101, 103–106.

In the passage that follows, published in 1964, Smith recounts what motivated him to go to the USSR—the desire, as he eloquently puts it, "to be free,
to walk in dignity." His actual experience of being black in the USSR, however,
was more complicated. Ultimately, he had to grapple with whether the com-
paratively greater racial equality in the USSR than elsewhere compensated for
the fear of suffering political repression, a fate to which his *nationality* as an
American made him vulnerable.

What had started me, *a twenty-two year old American* Negro, on the long road
from Minneapolis to Moscow?

To be free, to walk in dignity—for these precious privileges some men will go
anywhere, sacrifice anything. In quest of these rights immigrants have come from
all over the world to America. I yearned to stand taller than I had ever stood to
breathe total freedom in great exhilarating gulps, to avoid all the hurts that were
increasingly becoming the lot of men (and women) of color in the United States.
The solution seemed simple to me: Russia was the only place where I could go and
escape color discrimination entirely. Moscow seemed the answer.

. . . I read avidly the reports of the Soviet experiment, the Five Year Plan, and
the classless Society that was abuilding in Russia. The *Daily Worker* wrote glow-
ingly that Soviet Russia was the one political state which stood for social justice for
all oppressed peoples.

Who, I thought, was more oppressed than the Negro? Who else was being
lynched* with hideous regularity? Twenty Negroes in 1930 alone. Then in 1931
the Scottsboro Case† hit the front pages. Nine Negro boys were sentenced to death,
for allegedly raping two white girls who were riding the same freight train with
them. One day, after some heated words in a restaurant about not getting waited
on, I made my decision.

Naturally, my father and mother were aghast at the idea. My staunchly
Christian mother was particularly upset and tried hard to dissuade me. . . . I began
getting my dollars and clothes together. Being somewhat conservative, though toy-
ing with radical ideas, I had no desire to starve in the streets of Moscow. So I sent
off a letter to the Moscow Post Office, stating my qualifications, and was thrilled

---

* On lynching, see the gloss in document 1-3.

† The basic outline of the infamous Scottsboro case is as follows: In 1931, nine young black
men were falsely accused of raping two white women on a train traveling near Scottsboro, Alabama.
They—Charles Weems, Ozie Powell, Clarence Norris, Olen Montgomery, Willie Roberson, Haywood
Patterson, Eugene Williams, and Andrew and Leroy Wright—were convicted and faced execution.
The injustice of their predicament exemplified the racism of the American legal system and generated
international demonstrations on their behalf. Eventually, the conviction was overturned when the
case reached the Supreme Court in 1937. The case was taken up by the American Communist Party,
whose legal branch, the International Labor Defense, led the national and international campaign to
have the verdict overturned.

to receive a reply almost immediately offering me a position as consultant to the Moscow Post Office at a higher salary than I was then receiving.

The Negro Press had no correspondent in Russia, and the editors of the several papers I approached were agreeable that I represent them under my pen-name of Chatwood Hall, which actually was a pen-name I had coined while a university student.

I had my first contact with Russian officialdom at the border station of Byeloostrov*.... White lettering on a red streamer across the station platform pronounced: "Workers of all lands, Unite!" On important days, when Western trade union delegations or other sympathetic groups of pilgrims to the "Fatherland of the world's toiling masses" arrived, a brass band would unfailingly be on hand blaring out the rousing strains of the *Internationale*[†]. Naturally there was none for me.

...But though nothing had really come of my brush with the MVD[‡], it was for me somehow the end of the beginning. It actually went back farther than this, however, probably to the time when I had left the Postal Service to devote my full time of journalism. Actually, that had not been my sole reason for not renewing my contract. My utter disillusionment with the prevailing fear and terror had begun with the assassination of top-ranking Leningrad party boss, Sergei Kirov[§] in party headquarters. It really hit home, however, when my boss, Postmaster Uvarov, was liquidated[ˢ] along with several other postal officials that I knew personally. Many disappeared without a trace. Postal employees had begun talking in whispers and looking back over their shoulders. Stalin's Secret Police had begun to show a keen interest in the Postal Service.

This jungle of terror was not for me, I decided, so when my contract expired in 1935 I did not renew it. Instead I cast my lot with news reporting. Besides it was

---

[*] Smith refers here to a station on the railroad between St. Petersburg (or, from 1924 to 1991, Leningrad) and Vyborg. Until the Winter War between the USSR and Finland in 1939–1940, Beloostrov—which means "White Island" in Russian—was the last railway station in Finland prior to the Soviet border.

[†] "The Internationale," originally a late nineteenth-century French song, went on to become the most famous song of international socialism and communism. It was translated into countless languages. From 1918 until very late in 1943, it was the official anthem of the USSR. The English words of its last stanza are as follows: "This is the final struggle/let us group together and tomorrow/ The Internationale/Will be the human race." The words were originally written by Eugène Pottier in 1871. Pierre Degeyter wrote the music in 1888.

[‡] Though Smith is referring to the late 1930s, he uses the initials for the Soviet secret police— MVD—that were adopted in March 1946. At that time, the NKVD (People's Commissariat of Internal Affairs) was renamed the USSR's MVD.

[§] On 1 December 1934, Leningrad Party boss Sergei Kirov was murdered by Leonid Nikolaev in the Smolny Institute, Leningrad Party headquarters. The most recent examination of archival material does not find conclusive evidence that Stalin was behind his murder. See Matthew Lenoe, *The Kirov Murder and Soviet History* (New Haven, CT: Yale University Press, 2010).

[ˢ] In other words, arrested, tried, and executed.

in that year that I first met Marie Petrovna, though I was not to see her again until two years later....

It had been on New Year's Eve. Christmas had come and gone; it had meant nothing more to atheistic Russia than just another date on the calendar. But one of the biggest and most festive non-political holidays—if anything can be called non-political in Russia—was and still is the celebration of the arrival of the New Year.

A giant fir tree—just like a Christmas tree anywhere, but without any Yuletide connotations—had been placed in the center of the spacious, lofty, snow-white hall of the former Club of the Nobility, just off Red Square. Thousands of young Russians were gathering here to greet the New Year with a students' ball....

A schoolteacher friend of mine had invited me to accompany her to the celebration. We occupied seats in a loge behind the balustrade on the main floor to watch the students dance and sing around the New Year's tree, holding long colored streamers, rather like a Maypole celebration in America.

One young brunette girl whirled close to our loge, holding her streamer and skipping with youthful abandon....

"Who is that rosy-faced brunette?" I asked.

"Oh, that's Marie Petrovna, one of our Moscow beauties. Isn't she lovely?" My companion replied, "Would you like to meet her?"...

In wintertime, Marie Petrovna and I were regular habitues of the Bolshoi and other theaters in Moscow—excellent places for holding hands. And we were also regular skating partners at the city's numerous rinks....

Our marriage was later to give Marie Petrovna her first opportunity for moving in high bourgeois society....

At another diplomatic party in the National Hotel one autumn night near the end of the war, I was unable to find a taxicab to take us home. Seeing our predicament, the Mexican Ambassador, Señor Luis Quintanilla, who was a good friend of ours, offered his car. He and his American wife went along for the ride to our house.

The war-time blackout and curfew were still in effect, though less rigid than it had been earlier in the war. We headed up Gorky Street, past the Byelorussian Railway Station and continued out Leningrad Chaussee. Suddenly, two policemen stepped out of the darkness onto the roadway. One stood in front of the car, the other beamed his flashlight into the car.

Ambassador Quintanilla and his wife spoke no Russian. The Russian chauffeur and I got out of the car and began remonstrating with the policemen. I told them to be gone, that this was a diplomatic car.

But the looks of the car and its passengers did not support my contention. The war had prevented new cars from reaching Russia, and the Mexican Ambassador had managed to wheedle an old and decrepit Ford car out of the Soviet Government. The policemen were clearly and justifiably in doubt about this old rattle-trap being a diplomatic vehicle. Adding to their doubt were the assorted passengers. The Ambassador looked exactly like an Aztec Indian; I looked like what I was. The night was still—the Mexican flag hung limp from its staff on the front left fender of the car. I moved to the front of the car and held the flag open. One of the policemen turned his flashlight on it—there was the figure of a large eagle in the white center stripe doing battle with a squirming snake. The policemen appeared baffled; they had never seen such a strange flag. But this appeared to convince them that this was in fact some sort of diplomatic vehicle. They relented, saluted and waved us on....

Then our troubles began. The times were inauspicious for a foreigner to become a member of a Russian family. The bloody purges were still on and all foreigners, white or black, were suspected of engaging in espionage. Marie soon lost her job and could not find another. Every application blank that she filled in had to show the name Smith—and that obviously was a foreign name. She and her parents came under Secret Police surveillance because a foreigner was now a member of the family—even though they, and he, were honest people not engaged in any sort of illegal activity. It was not my color, for a change. In Moscow, my nationality was quite enough.

Inwardly, I strengthened my resolve to leave Russia. I had begun to question the intelligence of remaining even before leaving the Postal Service. My disappointment had grown with the passing years. Downright fear of the Secret Police was universal....

As always, I traded in well stocked shops where only valuta (foreign money) was accepted. These shops were out of bounds for the Russian citizen.... I, as a foreign newsman, fared well enough, but other Negroes who had come to Russia seeking a better life had been less successful.

My direct contacts with these expatriates convinced me that they would certainly have been better off materially in the United States. They had all, long since, worn out their good American clothing and now were living, on their subsistence salaries, a step above starvation. They had equality to be sure, but there was also a poverty line which they shared equally with the Russians. I often mulled over the questions posed by this; was the racial equality worth the bare subsistence living in an atmosphere filled with fear and suspicion? I believe that every Negro who lived in Russia was primarily interested in the complete racial equality that existed there, but was this enough compensation for the lack of material amenities and the absence of civil liberties?

I cannot speak for all Negroes, but for me it was not. But after 1938, international events were moving in such a chaotic manner that it was nearly impossible for me to make any definitive plans for leaving Russia with my wife.

Political agreements, as well as economic and trade agreements between Russia and Germany, culminating in the notorious Molotov–Ribbentrop Pact, were signed in Moscow during August of 1939. The political agreements were openly publicized, but attached to the Pact was a secret pact within a pact, dividing Poland and the Baltic States between Russia and Germany and assigning Russia a sphere of influence in the direction of India and the Persian Gulf. Though we didn't know it then, this was the appetizer in the menu labeled World War II.

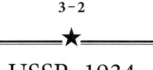

USSR, 1934

Harry Whyte, a British Communist, Challenges Stalin on Homosexuality

An example of how people combined their commitment to Marxist–
Leninist ideology with other aspects of their identity can be seen in the
following letter of 1934. In it, a British Communist living in Moscow reacts
to Stalin's promulgation of the anti sodomy statute in 1934. Reinstating the anti-
sodomy law that had been taken off the books in 1922, the 7 March 1934 legislation, Law on the Penal Culpability for Pederasty, stipulated imprisonment of at
least three years for men who engaged in sexual intercourse with each other.
Soviet archival materials that were declassified and published in 1993 indicate
that the Soviet secret police (or OGPU) had been the initiators of the legislation.
On 15 September 1933, OGPU deputy chief Genrikh G. Iagoda wrote a letter to
Stalin in which he claimed that the needs of state security demanded against
"pederasty." Iagoda delivered to Stalin the text of a draft law on 15 December
1933. In March 1934, anti sodomy legislation that ostensibly applied throughout
the Soviet Union was promulgated. However, the actual timing of the legislation, as well as the content, varied between some republics (for example, from
Ukraine to Turkmenistan). The reasons for the legislation remain, according to
an authority on Soviet policy toward homosexuality, rather unclear.[1] Though
Iagoda caught Stalin's attention when he mentioned an espionage threat in his
September 1933 letter, no subsequent correspondence, nor the draft legislation
itself, contained such an allusion.[2]

The letter is a remarkable document for many reasons. Not only does it give
us a sense, however partial, of how people, especially homosexuals living in the
USSR, reacted to the anti sodomy statute. It is likely that it also influenced the
"spin" placed on the anti sodomy law in subsequent public pronouncements
of the Stalin era. It is also remarkable in giving testimony to the bravery of the
author, who, after all, was writing to Stalin! Last but surely not least, it is remarkable, and deserves to be brought to an Anglophone audience, because its author
drew upon his own interpretation of then-prevailing Marxist stances on homosexuality to challenge Stalin's own Marxist–Leninist position on the issue.

Reprinted in English translation from *Istochnik*, vols. 5–6 (1995): 185–191. The original document
can be found in APRF (Archive of the President of the Russian Federation), f. 3, op. 57, d. 37, ll.
29–45. Translation: Dan Healey.

The author of the letter was Harry Whyte, a British Communist who was living in Moscow and was an editorial employee at the *Moscow Daily News*. He offers the basic elements of his political biography at the end of the letter. What he does not say anywhere, however, is that his lover had been arrested by the Soviet secret police (or OGPU) in the raids on Moscow homosexuals that had occurred between December 1933, and March 1934. No archival evidence has been found concerning what happened to Whyte after he wrote the letter.

LETTER FROM HARRY WHYTE TO
IOSIF STALIN, MAY 1934*

To Comrade Stalin,

To summarize the contents of my letter: the author is a member of the Communist Party of Great Britain, and asks you to give the theoretical basis for the decree of the Central Committee of the USSR of 7 March (1934) on criminal responsibility for sodomy; the author of this letter, attempting to examine this question from a Marxist perspective, considers that the decree contradicts not only the facts of reality but also the principles of Marxism–Leninism....

Dear Comrade Stalin!

Although I am a foreign Communist, not yet having been transferred to membership in the Soviet Communist Party, nevertheless I think that you as the leader of the world proletariat will not think it unnatural, that I am writing to you to ask you to illuminate a question that seems to me to be of great importance for a large number of Communists in the USSR and in other countries as well.

The question is: can a homosexual be considered a person worthy of becoming a member of the Communist Party?

The law just published about criminal responsibility for sodomy, confirmed by the CC of the USSR on 7 March this year, obviously means that a homosexual cannot be considered worthy of bearing the name of Soviet citizen, and still less, consequently, could he be considered worthy of membership in the Soviet Communist Party.

---

* Source: Garri Uait [Harry Whyte]. "'Mozhet li gomoseksualist sostoiat' chlenom kommunisticheskoi partii?'." *Istochnik*, no. 5–6 (1993): 185–191. The precise date of this letter is unknown. For more information on the document and its publication, see Dan Healey, *Homosexual Desire in Revolutionary Russia: The Regulation of Sexual and Gender Dissent* (Chicago: University of Chicago Press, 2001), 188–190.

As I am personally interested in this question, because I am a homosexual, I have put it to a great many comrades from the OGPU* and the People's Commissariat of Justice, and also among psychiatrists; I have also questioned comrade Borodin, the managing editor of the newspaper where I work.

I have heard nothing but contradictory opinions that show that among these comrades there is no clear theoretical understanding that can serve as the basis for the enactment of this law. The first psychiatrist I asked about this confirmed to me twice, after first checking with the Justice Commissariat, that his patients, if they are honest citizens or good Communists, may organize their personal lives as they see fit. Comrade Borodin, saying that he personally disapproves of homosexuality, also told me that he considers me a rather good Communist, says that I can be trusted and that I can lead whatever sort of personal life I wish. Sometime earlier, when the arrests of homosexuals had just started, comrade Borodin was very far from viewing me a criminal and did not consider me a bad Communist; his view of me was such that he promoted me to the position of editorial office director, the most responsible post except for those who sit on the editorial board. A little later, when the 17 December (1933) variant of the law already existed, but before its publication on 7 March (1934), I applied to the OGPU, to ask if there was anything incriminating me, in connection with the arrest of a certain person with whom I was engaged in homosexual relations, and they told me that there was nothing incriminating me[†].

These various inquiries created the impression that the Soviet organs of justice were not pursuing all homosexuals in general, but only certain socially dangerous homosexuals. If that was the case, why have a law against homosexuality in general?

However, on the other hand, after the publication of the law of 7 March, I had a conversation with the OGPU and was told that the law would be strictly applied in every case of homosexuality observed.

As a result of this lack of clarity I am writing to you in the hope that you will find the time to explain this question.

Permit me to explain this question as far as I understand it.

First of all I would like to point out that I regard the position of homosexuals belonging to the working or toiling classes in general, as analogous to the position of women under capitalism, and analogous to the imperialist persecution of colored races; it is very similar in many respects to the persecution of Jews under Hitler's dictatorship, and generally it is not difficult to see

---

* OGPU: Unified State Political Administration, that is, the secret police.

† In December 1933, on the advice of the OGPU, the Soviet Communist Party's Politburo adopted a resolution to enact the anti sodomy law. In March 1934, Soviet government bodies published the corresponding legislation. During this interlude, arrests of circles of homosexuals had already started. See Healey, *Homosexual Desire in Revolutionary Russia*, 182–190.

the similarity with the persecution of any social group subject to exploitation and persecution in conditions of capitalist hegemony.

To analyse the character of the persecution of homosexuals one must take into account that there are two types of homosexuals: first, those who are that way from birth (and if there is disagreement among scientists about what exactly causes this, there is absolutely no disagreement about the existence of profound underlying causes): second, there are homosexuals who have known a normal sex life but later become homosexuals as a result of the influence of vice or sometimes from economic factors.

This second group can be dealt with relatively simply. Persons who become homosexual purely from their own vice belong principally to the bourgeoisie, from which certain individuals become sated by all manner of pleasures and perversions available to them within the limits of sexual intercourse with women. Among those who go down this road for economic reasons we find members of the petty bourgeoisie, lumpenproletariat and—however strange it may seem—from the proletariat itself. As a result of material need, especially in periods of crisis, these people are forced to temporarily turn to this means of satisfying their sexual desires, because the lack of means renders it impossible to marry or even turn to female prostitutes. There are even those who become homosexual not to satisfy their own sexual needs but to earn their daily bread via prostitution (this phenomenon became widespread in modern Germany).

However, science has established that there are also constitutional homosexuals. Research has demonstrated that this type of homosexual exists in equal proportion in all classes of society. It can also be taken as proven that, with some insignificant variation, homosexuals constitute about 2% of the population. If this proportion is applied here, then there are about 2 million homosexuals in the USSR. Among this number there are undoubtedly many who give active support to the construction of socialism, and surely such a large number of people do not merit imprisonment as foreseen in the law of 7 March!

Just as women from the bourgeois class suffer significantly less from the injustices of capitalism (as you of course recall from Lenin's works), inborn homosexuals who are members of the ruling class suffer much less from persecution than homosexuals among the working class. It must be said that even in the USSR conditions exist which complicate the everyday life of homosexuals and often place them in a difficult position (I mean here the difficulty in finding a partner for the sexual act, since homosexuals constitute a minority of the population, to some extent compelled to hide their genuine inclinations).

What is the attitude in bourgeois society to homosexuals? Even taking into account the variety of legislation in various countries on this question, is it possible to speak of a specific bourgeois attitude to this question? Yes, it is! Beyond any consideration of the laws, all the class strivings of capitalism work against homosexuality. This can be confirmed throughout history, but nowadays it is particularly intense with the general crisis of capitalism.

Capitalism, which requires for its flourishing an enormous labor reserve and reserve of cannon fodder, regards homosexuality as a factor threatening to lower the birthrate (as is well known capitalist countries have laws against abortion and contraception).

Of course the bourgeois attitude toward homosexuality is typically hypocritical. The bourgeois homosexual experiences almost no unpleasantness from strict legislation. Anyone who knows anything at all about the internal history of the capitalist class knows about the many scandals on this basis which nevertheless result in little suffering for the ruling class. I can mention a little known fact regarding such affairs. A few years ago one of the sons of Lord and Lady Astor was prosecuted for homosexuality. The press of England and America remained silent about this fact. The only exception was the "Morning Advertiser" newspaper. It was the organ of a beer manufacturer, and it was from these interests that it sought to compromise Lord and Lady Astor, who were campaigning vigorously for a "dry law" [banning alcohol]. The fact became well known because of the internal contradictions within the governing class.

Thanks to their wealth, the bourgeois can avoid the law's punishment, which works its full power only on the worker-homosexual, unless the latter prostitutes himself to members of the governing classes.

I have already said that capitalism fights against homosexuality because it needs labor reserves and cannon fodder. Yet at the very same time by worsening the living conditions of the workers capitalism creates the objective conditions for an increase in the number of homosexuals, who go down this road because of economic need.

This contradiction finds its expression in the fact that fascism, having used the pederast Van der Lubbe as a weapon in its provocation, simultaneously brutally attacked the liberal-intellectual "liberator" of the homosexual movement Dr Magnus Hirschfeld (see the Brown Book, which discusses the Hirschfeld affair as a fact of the anti-cultural barbarism of fascism*).

---

* Here Whyte refers to Marinus van der Lubbe, accused by the Nazis of being a Communist arsonist responsible for the Reichstag fire in 1933 and denounced by the Communists as an anarchist and as a homosexual. The "Brown Book" was written by a collective of Communists to present evidence against the Nazi claims that leftists had destroyed the Reichstag; it characterized van der Lubbe's homosexuality as the result of bourgeois influences in his upbringing. See Harry Oosterhuis, "The 'Jews' of the Antifascist Left: Homosexuality and Socialist Resistance to Nazism, in G. Hekma, H. Oosterhuis, and J. Steakley, eds., *Gay Men and the Sexual History of the Political Left* (Binghamton, NY: Harrington Park Press, 1995). On Hirschfeld as socialist Jewish physician and leader of the world's first movement for the emancipation of homosexuals, see James D. Steakley, "Per scientiam ad justitiam: Magnus Hirschfeld and the Sexual Politics of Innate Homosexuality," in Vernon Rosario, ed., *Science and Homosexualities* (New York: Routledge, 1997).

Another expression of this contradiction is the figure of André Gide, the French homosexual writer, one of the leaders of the antifascist movement and a warm friend of the USSR. Gide's homosexuality is well known to the broad masses in France, for he has written about it in his books. Yet nevertheless his authority is unshakeable as a fellow-traveller of the Communist Party of France. Gide's allegiance to the revolutionary movement has not prevented the growth of that movement and the strengthening of the masses' leadership of the Communist Party. This proves, in my view, that the masses are not intolerant of homosexuals.[3]

Fascism with its slogan of "racial purity" and family principles, is more hostile toward homosexuality than the pre-Hitler government. However, since fascism destroys the worker family and increases poverty, it actually stimulates the growth of homosexuality created by economic need, that is, the second type of homosexuality I mentioned above.

The only resolution of this contradiction is the revolutionary transformation of the existing social structure and the creation of a society, in which the absence of unemployment, the growing well-being of the masses, and the eradication of the economic isolation of the family, will guarantee the establishment of conditions in which no one will be forced into pederasty as a result of want. As for so-called constitutional homosexuals, as an insignificant portion of the population, they cannot present a threat to the birthrate in a socialist state.

"The overall results of the growth of material well-being have led to the fact that if in capitalist countries death increases alongside poverty, then in the USSR mortality is decreasing and the birthrate, increasing. In comparison with pre-war figures the growth of the population in the USSR has risen by one third, while in capitalist Europe it has fallen by 10%. Right now our country, with 165 million inhabitants, has the same increase in population as the 360 million inhabitants of capitalist Europe; as you can see, even in these matters our tempo is a stormy one (laughter)." (Report of comrade Kaganovich* on the work of the CC of the Soviet Communist Party at the conference of the Moscow Party organization. Comrade Kaganovich's emphasis.)

Regardless of the unusually strict laws about marriage in capitalist countries, perversions in the sphere of normal sexual relations are much more widespread in capitalist countries than in the USSR, where marriage legislation is the freest and most rational of any place in the world. It is well known, yes, that in the early years of the revolution some tried to abuse this freedom which Soviet marriage law offered. However this abuse was curtailed not by repressive means, but by wide political-enlightenment and cultural work and by economic development in the direction of socialism. It seems to me that in

---

*Lazar Kaganovich (1893–1991) was one of Stalin's most loyal and important lieutenants. He became a full Politburo member in 1930. Later in the 1930s, he became head of heavy industry, a position he held through the end of the Stalin period. He opposed Khrushchev's de-Stalinization.

relation to the second form of homosexuality such a line would be the most effective.

I have always considered it incorrect to promote a separate slogan about the liberation of working-class homosexuals from capitalist exploitation. I believe that this liberation is indivisible from the general struggle for the liberation of all humanity from the exploitation of private property.

It has not been my intention to make a problem of this, to bring this question to a theoretical level and seek out a specific party line on the issue. However at the present time reality itself has raised the question and I consider it highly important to achieve clarity of principle on this question.

Comrade Borodin has indicated to me that the fact that I am a homosexual in no way diminishes my value as a revolutionary. He has shown great trust in me by naming me editorial office director. At that moment he did not regard me as someone who could be or should be punished by the criminal law. He even said that my personal life was not something that could in anyway harm my position as a member of the party and a worker in the editorial office.

When I asked him about the arrests [of homosexuals], he again, and through him, the OGPU, reassured me that in this instance the reasons were of a political character, and in no way of a public-morals character, although at that time the 17 December 1933 version of the law already existed. When I made inquiries directly to the OGPU they told me, "There is nothing incriminating against you." When I first heard about the version of the law of 17 December, I got similar sorts of answers from a range of persons. True, comrade Degot' of the Commissariat of Justice explained the law by saying that homosexuality was a form of bourgeois degeneration.

A psychiatric specialist with whom I discussed the issue refused to believe in the existence of this law until I showed him a copy of it.

It is absolutely obvious that regardless of the existence of a number of uncertain impressions from some comrades, nevertheless in the time before the publication of this law, social opinion on this issue was in no way hostile toward homosexuals. And this did not surprise me at all.

The arrests of homosexuals I understood as a perfectly logical measure since the grounds were reasons of a political character. All this fully conformed to my analysis of the question as expressed above, and in no way contradicted the officially expressed viewpoint of Soviet society. Comrade Borodin advised me that I should not assign great significance to the article on homosexuality in the Great Soviet Encyclopedia (GSE), because, as he said, the author was himself a homosexual, and the article was published at a time when a great many deviations had not yet been uncovered.[4] I do not think that we should disbelieve a history of the Communist Party if it was written by a Communist; if this article was written by a homosexual, then an objective and scientific approach to homosexuality is what was demanded of him. Second, I know enough about the reality of Soviet political control over publishing to doubt that an article with serious deviations would appear in a publication like the GSE. That might be possible with regard to single articles in insignificant magazines or newspapers, but not in the GSE. In any case I consider it possible to trust in full a publication with editors including such persons as Molotov, Kuibyshev, Pokrovskii (or even Bukharin*, albeit deserving of less trust).

Yet the point of view I am defending bears little relation to the article in the GSE. The views of Soviet society to this question were expressed with sufficient clarity in the law that existed before 7 March. If the law had said nothing about this issue then there could have been doubts about it before. But the law really did express public opinion on this question: it defended the interests of society by forbidding the seduction and corruption of minors. Consequently one concluded that homosexual relations between adults were not forbidden.

Naturally the law is dialectical and it changes with changing circumstances. However it is apparent that when the first law [decriminalizing homosexuality] was confirmed it dealt with the broad question of homosexuality as a whole (or so one must conclude on the basis of this law). With this law it was established that the Soviet government rejected the persecution of homosexuality in general. This principle was a fundamental one, and it is well known that one does not alter fundamental principles to bring them into line with new circumstances. Changing fundamental principles for such reasons is the sign of an opportunist, not a dialectician.

I can comprehend that changing circumstances require some minor legislative changes to enact new measures of social defense, however I cannot understand what changed circumstances have forced us to change one of our fundamental principles.

I have visited two psychiatrists to ask them if it is possible to "cure" homosexuality—you may be surprised by this. I admit that this was opportunism on my part (I could be forgiven on this occasion), but what forced me to try this was to find some way out of this damned dilemma. Least of all did I want to be in contradiction with a decision of the Soviet government. I am prepared to go to any lengths to avoid the necessity of contradicting Soviet law. I sought this out regardless of the fact that I did not know of any recent research that has identified the genuine nature of homosexuality, and has supposedly made it possible to turn homosexuals into heterosexuals, i.e. persons who engage in the sex act only with members of the opposite sex. If such an opportunity was really possible then everything would be much simpler of course.

---

* Viacheslav Molotov and Valerian Kuibyshev were Communist Party leaders closely allied to Stalin; Mikhail Pokrovskii (1868–1932) was a Marxist historian. After the expulsion of Leon Trotsky in 1929 from the USSR, Nikolai Bukharin was Stalin's chief political opponent until his arrest and execution after his show trial in 1938. At the time Whyte writes, Bukharin had been expelled from the highest Party circles, but he remained a prominent figure under a cloud of suspicion.

But speaking openly if this possibility really did exist I would still hesitate over whether it is desirable to change from homosexual to heterosexual. Of course there could be particular political motives making it desirable. It seems to me, though, that the need for such a levelling measure would have to be supported by unusually strong motives.

It is undoubted that the majority of people should be normal in a sexual sense. I fear however that this will never be the case. And I believe that my fears are confirmed in the facts of history. I think that it is possible to say with certainty that the majority of people wish and will wish to live a normal sex life. However I strongly doubt that all people will be absolutely the same in their sexual inclinations.

I remind you that homosexuals make up in all just two percent of the population; I remind you also that among that two percent were such exceptionally gifted people as Socrates, Leonardo da Vinci, Michelangelo, Shakespeare and Tchaikovsky. These were among those known to be homosexuals. How many other talented people who were homosexuals concealed their inclinations? In no way am I trying to defend the absurd theory that homosexuals belong to a race of superhumans, that homosexuality and genius are synonymous, that homosexuals supposedly seek revenge on society for their suffering by conspiring against heterosexuals. That sort of "theory" was condemned with all the contempt it deserves by Engels in his letter to Marx of 22 June 1869.[5] In that letter Engels wrote about the "theory" propounded by a clique of German bourgeois homosexuals who founded their own special organization; Engels characterized all this activity with the epithet "schweinerei"—swinishness.

That it was the political "theory" of this organization, and not the specific sexual inclination of its members that aroused Engels' condemnation, can be seen from his letter to Sorge of 8 February 1890 in which he writes, "Here a tempest in a teacup has erupted again. You will read in the 'Labour Elector' about the uproar started by Pike, the assistant to the editor of the 'Star,' who in a local newspaper openly accused Lord Gaston of sodomy in connection with a scandal about sodomy among the local aristocracy. The article was extraordinary, but only of a personal character; the question was hardly political. Nevertheless it raised a great uproar." (Translation [into Russian] is imprecise; taken from the English text printed in an English Communist magazine.)

"The question is hardly political." The fact that the question of a sodomy scandal in the aristocracy, involving a member of the hostile class, is evaluated by Engels "hardly a political question", as a "tempest in a teacup"; for us this has a great significance as a matter of principle. If homosexuality is regarded as a characteristic feature of bourgeois degeneracy, then it is right to attack individual instances of it, especially in the period when homosexual scandals were so widespread in the aristocratic sphere. However it is evident in this quotation that Engels did not regard homosexuality as a specifically bourgeois form of degeneration. He only attacked it when, for example, in the case of the Germans [in 1869], it took the form of a political organization by specific bourgeois elements. When the affair had no political coloring as in the example just presented, Engels considered it unnecessary to condemn it.[6]

I suggest that certain kinds of talent, in particular talent in the artistic field, is often strikingly combined with homosexuality; it seems to me that this should be kept in mind and we should carefully weigh up the dangers of sexual "levelling" for Soviet culture, so long as we lack a satisfactory scientific explanation for homosexuality.

I permit myself to cite one passage from comrade Stalin's report to the XVII Party Congress:

"...Every Leninist, if he is a genuine Leninist, knows that levelling in the field of needs and personal life is reactionary ignorance, worthy of some kind of primitive sect of ascetics, but not of a socialist state organized in a Marxist fashion, since it is impossible to demand that people all have the same needs and tastes, that all people in their personal lives lived according to a single model....

...To conclude from this that socialism requires levelling, making the needs of all members of society the same, making their tastes and personal lives all the same, that Marxism says that all should wear the same clothing and eat one and the same food in precisely the same quantities—is vulgar and a slander of Marxism." (Stalin. Report to the 17th Party Congress on the Work of the CC of the Soviet Communist Party. Lenpartizdat, 1934 g., str. 54–55. [1934, 54–55] My emphasis. H. W.)

It appears to me that this citation from comrade Stalin's speech has a direct bearing on the question I have raised.

The most important factor is that even if we tried to achieve levelling in this matter at the present time, there is no way that we could do so, not by medical or by legislative means.

When both psychiatrists to whom I put my questions confirmed that cases of incurable homosexuality exist, this led me to my current view of the issue.

One has to admit that there is such a thing as ineradicable homosexuality (I have still not found any evidence to the contrary) and as a result, I think that we must conclude by recognizing the existence of such a minority in society, regardless of whether it is capitalist or socialist. In this case there is no justification for making these people criminals on the basis of their distinguishing features, which they are in no way responsible for creating, which they cannot change, even if they wanted to.

In this fashion, having tried to reason this out using the principles of Marxism–Leninism as I understand them, I have found a contradiction between the law and those conclusions which flow from my line of reasoning. It is just this contradiction that compels me to ask for an authoritative explanation of this question.

With Communist greetings

HARRY WHYTE

INFORMATION ABOUT THE AUTHOR OF THIS LETTER.

Whyte, Harry. 27 years old. Born in Edinburgh, Scotland. Son of a painter with recently acquired property. Secondary education. Profession: journalist. Worked in bourgeois newspapers until 1932. In his free time worked for the magazine of the Society of the Friends of the USSR "Russia Today" in 1931–1932. Joined the Independent Labour Party, 1927; then the Communist Party of Great Britain, in 1931. Worked in party cells and the district organization of Fleet Street, the centre of the British press. In 1932 invited to join the staff of the "Moscow News." In 1933 named editorial office director of this newspaper. Singled out as an outstanding shockworker. Transfer from the English Communist party to the Soviet Communist Party has been deferred until the end of the current party purge.

Note: The arguments expressed in this letter were first formulated by me in a letter addressed to comrade Borodin, the managing editor of the Moscow Daily News, in the hope that he would bring the questions it raises to the attention of comrade Stalin. He found it impossible to do this, however. In addition to the contents of the present letter, the one to comrade Borodin contains personal facts concerning me which have little relevance to the wider questions discussed here, but which I felt were necessary to bring to his attention. A copy of that letter was presented to the OGPU on their request, after I mentioned the letter to a comrade in the OGPU.*

* On the first page of the letter: "To the archives. An idiot and degenerate. I. Stalin."

3–3

Kazakhstan, USSR

A Chinese Student Reflects on His Role in the Soviet Union's Virgin Lands Campaign in 1958

As the beacon of Communist internationalism, the USSR attracted foreign Communists, or at least those sympathetic to the socialist project, from the earliest days of Soviet power through the decades of its existence. Just who came, and why, depended on both the phase of the revolutionary process in the USSR itself (that is, a revolutionary process conceived as a decades-long endeavor lasting from 1917 to 1991) and that of the Communist revolutions outside the USSR. The revolutionary processes in the USSR and elsewhere did not, of course, follow the same chronological timetable: as revolutions in power, they were separated by periods ranging from a few years (Mongolia) to several decades. One of the most politically consequential cases of such chronological disjuncture was that of China, where over three decades separated the launch of its Communist system from that of the USSR.

When the Chinese Communists came to power in 1949, the USSR had already achieved the rapid industrialization and forced collectivization of the late 1920s and 1930s. This achievement was a product—at least as maintained by the Soviets' own rhetoric—of an early period of popular enthusiasm and personal sacrifice for the "building of socialism." But the People's Republic of China still had its great phase of modern industrial and technological development in front of it, not to mention the essential rebuilding of the national economy following civil war and war with Japan. To build the industries that China did not yet have—in aircraft, automobiles, tractors, power and heavy machinery, instrument making, and electrical infrastructure—the country needed engineers, technicians, and skilled workers.

It was the USSR that provided, in good measure, the training of such cadres. Between 1948 and 1963, roughly eight thousand Chinese students came to the Soviet Union to study in Soviet institutes of higher education—almost always those in the scientific and technological fields. In the late 1950s, Chinese students comprised nearly half of all the foreign students in the Soviet Union.[7] As Sino-Soviet relations deteriorated in the late 1950s and early 1960s, the number of Chinese students in the USSR dropped. But it was not until January 1967 that the Chinese Ministries of Education and Foreign Affairs formally ordered all students in the USSR to return to China.

What Chinese students in the USSR experienced varied greatly, depending on when they came, where they lived, and where they traveled. But a constant in their lives was interaction with Soviet students. These interactions were supposed to contribute to the cause of Sino-Soviet friendship, and hence to the amorphous yet all-important world Communist revolution. But Chinese students often found that their encounters with their Soviet counterparts were fraught with tension. Chinese students, the ambassadors of the early, "enthusiastic" phase of China's revolution, were often much more studious than Soviet students, who, as products of a later revolutionary period, were more interested in listening to jazz and making love than in being good students. The tensions between Chinese and Soviet students exemplified the chronological disjuncture between the two revolutions.

But one place the revolutions seemed to converge, as historian Elizabeth McGuire has emphasized, was in Soviet Kazakhstan. Located near the Chinese border, northern Kazakhstan was the site of the Virgin Lands campaign, a massive project of agricultural transformation designed to bring grain cultivation

From Chen Peixian, *The Highest Soviet Honor*. Reprinted by permission of the Russian Returned Students Association and Chen Peixian. Translation: Yuting Li.

(mainly wheat) to vast areas of steppe land. In 1954, the first year of the campaign, nineteen million hectares (forty-seven million acres!) were brought under cultivation. The mass mobilization of Komsomol members, truck and combine drivers, soldiers, and students—some three hundred thousand people in all—evoked the mythologized heroism of the early phase of the Soviet revolution. Hence, the Chinese students who participated in the Virgin Lands project found themselves in a place—geographically and psychologically—that was closer to the ethos of their own revolutionary moment than anywhere else in the USSR. One of these Chinese students was Chen Peixian, the author of the retrospective, even nostalgic, appraisal reproduced herein.

The following passage is not just a recounting of the dry facts of how Chen Peixian and his three Chinese compatriots from the Moscow Railway School participated in the Virgin Lands campaign in 1958. To be sure, it does tell us what everyday life was like for these Chinese students in the Kokchetav state of the Kazakh SSR in a Kazakh village located only one hundred miles or so from Xinjiang. But it also falls into the genre of the "public" autobiography, that is, one in which the author desired to leave a certain impression for posterity.[8] Not only was Chen Peixian concerned to leave the impression that the Chinese students' participation in the Virgin Lands project *did* contribute to Sino-Soviet friendship. He also sought to demonstrate their ideological (and, in a sense, spiritual) *growth* as Chinese youth in the Soviet land. When the Soviet students went on strike because they weren't being paid and because the rotten meat they had to eat was making them sick, the Chinese students faced a dilemma. As volunteers for labor training, they couldn't strike if they wanted to remain in the good graces of Soviet officials. But nor could they endanger Sino-Soviet friendship by failing to show solidarity with their Soviet counterparts. It was in coming up with a solution on their own, without advice from the Chinese embassy—one that entailed the Chinese students doing their own back breaking labor as well as that of the Soviet students—that Chen Peixian and the other Chinese students developed ideologically, thereby attaining a deeper understanding of what "Sino-Soviet friendship" meant.[9]

Such labor brought Chen Peixian and his Chinese compatriots a Virgin Lands gold medal, which he prizes even to this day.

In the summer break of 1958, we heard that the Educational Department of the Moscow city soviet was recruiting college students to participate in the wheat harvest in a remote village farm (about four hundred kilometers away from the Sino–Soviet border in Xinjiang province) located in the virgin lands in the Kokchetav State of the Kazakh S.S.R. (today's Republic of Kazakhstan) far away from Moscow. Upon knowing this news, we believed that it would be a good opportunity for us to get more familiar with our Soviet classmates as well as to enrich our understanding of the Soviet Union. Once we got permission from the Chinese Embassy's Section of Overseas Students through the local party branch, we signed up for the work and received a warm welcome from our school leaders.

There were four Chinese students from our school (Moscow Railway College, Mechanical Engineering Department) who signed up for the wheat harvest in the virgin lands: Yang Chao, Zhang Boru, Gong Desheng, and I. In addition to some necessary clothes, the only medicine we could bring with us was the Essential Palm (*qing liang you* in Chinese). Our major responsibility was to turn over the wheat to dry in the sun at the work base in the farm. Summer time went from July, August, to September. The weather in Kokchetav was extremely hot, and the living and sanitary conditions were really bad. The flock of mosquitoes with an abnormal size was also very annoying.... The most serious problem, however, was the lack of any refrigeration or icebox in such a hot summer. Whenever they killed a pig or a steer, it always took us a few days to eat all the meat. Without refrigeration or icebox, the meat all went bad towards the end. The cafeteria, running on a tight budget, however, still cooked them for sale. For that reason, we constantly had diarrhea ever since we arrived in the virgin lands. We had to use the bathroom many times a day, and sometimes even smeared our underwear when it went out of control.

At this time in the virgin lands, payments were determined in accordance with the principle of distribution according to one's work. Every student was supposed to receive a defined amount of remuneration that would be paid in full after she or he finished all the work. For those Soviet students who didn't take enough money with them, they could eat in the cafeteria on credit but choose their meals only from assigned dishes that were usually cooked with rotten meat and vegetables. This regulation, without doubt, eventually led to significant discontent among student that later on evolved into a formal request from students asking the farm to pay the salaries they were entitled to and allow them to choose any dishes they desired.

Due to the rampant bureaucratism of the village farm leadership, this reasonable request wasn't properly handled in time, and eventually developed into a more intensified conflict. The entire Soviet student body that ate in the work base of the virgin lands finally decided to organize a strike, which put us four Chinese students in an awkward situation. From the Soviet officials' perspective, since we had volunteered to work here to help with the wheat harvest in the border areas, we shouldn't join the strike; on the other hand, as far as the Soviet students were concerned, we couldn't afford to let them misunderstand us and think that we wouldn't sympathize and support their battle against bureaucratism, if we still wanted to stay on their side. We fully understood that this unexpected event had very complicated political implications. If we dealt with it in a proper way, we could enhance the Sino–Soviet friendship; otherwise, it would not only damage our relations with those Soviet classmates, but also undermine the general image of Chinese students. For this kind of big problems, we would consult the Chinese Embassy if we were in Moscow. In Kokchetav, however, we were completely on our own. After many rounds of careful discussion and evaluation, we decided to "keep on participating in the harvest, and in the meantime obtain Soviet students' full understanding of our stance through effective communications." Once decided, we started to make it clear, first to those Soviet students who were relatively close to us, and then to their team leaders that we, as Chinese, were there to voluntarily support Soviet wheat harvest. In the middle of the busy harvest season, we should continue working for the sake of Sino–Soviet friendship. Furthermore, we also explicitly expressed to those Soviet students that we firmly believed that the bureaucratic problem within the village farm leadership would eventually be resolved through their efforts. Two or three weeks later, the whole matter was resolved with the intervention of the local government. The Soviet students returned to their work, and our relations with them weren't harmed in any way.

During these two to three weeks under strike, we four Chinese students had to unload all the wheat that was harvested and transported back from the field, and turn them over to dry in the sun. We often had to stop eating to unload wheat whenever the trucks arrived, and couldn't finish a meal without multiple inter-ruptions like this. To be honest, as a result of diarrhea we sometimes were too exhausted to even stand up, and wanted to lie down on the ground for a rest. Once we thought that we shouldn't embarrass Chinese people in any way in such a difficult time; however, we forced ourselves to endure all the difficulties and well accomplished our tasks through mutual support, mutual encouragement and collective work. In the end, throughout three months of labor work in the village farm, although we suffered a lot of weight loss, fortunately we gained some use-ful agricultural knowledge, better understood the grassroots organizations of the Soviet and the working and living conditions of those agriculture personnel, and furthermore greatly improved our political sense and awareness.

When the work was done, we received a commendation from the local gov-ernment. Based on an order issued by the highest Soviet in the Soviet Union on 20 October 1956, the local government gave us four Chinese students and one Soviet team leader respectively the "The Pioneer in Virgin Lands" gold medal and associated certificate on 9 October 1958.... For us, it was a very special honor to receive such a high award.

Forty years later, my memory is still fresh whenever I look at this highest Soviet medal that is still shining nowadays. It has recorded our growth as Chinese youth in the foreign land, and our commitment to enforce faithfully the teachings of Chairman Mao.

April 1997

Chen Peixian was born in Xinhui, Guangdong Province. He graduated from the Moscow Railway College in 1961 and has worked for the Chinese Ministry of Railway in many positions such as technician, engineer, senior engineer, assistant research fellow, etc.

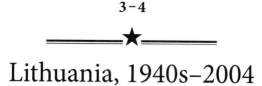

3-4

Lithuania, 1940s–2004

A Lithuanian Mother Reflects on Her Disabled Son's Life

The Soviet occupation of Lithuania, Latvia, and Estonia in 1940 had profound consequences for the everyday life of people in the Baltic states. The standard of living had already declined when Nazi Germany, the second occupier of the Baltic states during the wartime years, occupied the region in 1941, driving out the Soviets and the Red Army. When, in 1944, the Red Army returned to Lithuania and the other Baltic states, the Soviet reoccupation launched anew a slow but steady process of what is often called "Sovietization." Though the particulars of Sovietization differed in each Baltic state, just as they would vary in the Eastern European countries that came under Soviet influence after World War II, there were certain constants everywhere. They included a reorganization of the economy (in the Baltics, the nationalization of large enterprises and reorganization of agriculture, though not the full-fledged collectivization thereof), repressive measures (especially deportation) against perceived enemies of Soviet power, and the ideological refashioning of Baltic people in the service of loyalty to the USSR and Soviet Communism. Nonetheless, both active and passive resistance to Soviet power continued for years after the Soviet reoccupation. In Lithuania, organized resistance took the form of a partisan movement comprised of nationalist guerillas living in the forests and the network of Lithuanians who helped them. One of them was Monika Jonynaitė-Makūnienė, the author of the following passage, who risked NKVD repression to function as an informant for the partisans.

Jonynaitė-Makūnienė was born on 12 April 1920 in a rural Lithuania county to parents who "worked a medium-size farm." She stayed at home until 1931, when she began to attend school at the gymnasium (equivalent to high school) in Alytus, which she finished in June 1939—that is, a little more than a year prior to the Soviet occupation. Later that year, she enrolled in the Dotnuva Academy of Agriculture. The jobs that she held after the war—working as a gardener from November 1945 to March 1946, at the Kauanas dairy from 1946 to 1969, and as a seasonal laborer at sugar factory—brought her into personal contact with the post-war Sovietization of the Lithuanian economy. She married her husband,

From Dalia Leinarte, *Adopting and Remembering Soviet Reality: Life Stories of Lithuanian Women, 1945–1970* (New York: Editions Rodopi B.V., 2010), 75–88. Used by permission of the interviewer and interviewee, and Editions Rodopi B.V.

Kazimieras, in 1951, and in 1952 their son, Eugenijus, whom they called Genutis, was born. Disabled because of a birth trauma caused by inadequate medical care during the delivery, Genutis lived most of his short life with his mother. He died when he was eighteen years old.

Although it is abridged from a single case history, this passage gives insight into the general struggles of Lithuanian women as they juggled the demands of work and family, especially during the first years after the war. Jonynaitė-Makūnienė faced the especially demanding challenge of making difficult, ongoing choices about Genutis's care. Yet her story, while of course unique, also speaks to an important theme in the lives of all Lithuanian women in the postwar years: how they fashioned their own identities, beliefs, and values in response to the ideological and cultural dimensions of Sovietization. Jonynaitė-Makūnienė was among the many Lithuanian women who managed to keep the Soviet ideological project somewhat at a distance, even though they were influenced by Khrushchev-era policy that exhorted women to relinquish "traditional" roles and become educated, socially active, and emancipated. Her narrative also exemplifies another general characteristic of those of Lithuanian women: Whereas the narratives of Russian women suggest an identity as "active subjects of history" and pride in Soviet achievements, those of Lithuanian women lack such "heroic pathos." Rather, Lithuanian women represented themselves as resigned citizens of an occupied, partly Sovietized land, rather than enthusiastic participants in "building socialism" in Lithuania.[10]

INTERVIEW OF MONIKA
JONYNAITĖ-MAKŪNIENĖ (1920–)

It was the summer of 1945. I didn't fit in anywhere; I lived at home and worked on the farm. Partisans dropped by. I fed them. I knew their names and aliases. That year I acted as an informant for the partisans. In the autumn of 1945, some partisans started giving up on their mission; they realized that even though the Americans kept promising, there was in fact no real help. I was wanted by the NKVD agents, too, because I was suspected of being an informant to the partisans. Therefore, it became dangerous for me to live at home and I fled, along with my sister, in the autumn of 1945...

We had relatives in Balbieriškis, so we thought we'd sleep at our cousin's place. But we got caught by the NKVD agents, and they put us in a cell. Fortunately, the town was not in Alytus county, but Marijampolė: Because of military actions the phone connection was still poor, and the agents couldn't check our identities, so they let us go in the morning.

Then we went farther up to the town of Išlaužas, and nearby there was a Soviet farm settlement called *Daukšiagiris**....

I worked as a gardener at *Daukšiagiris* from November 1945 to March 1946, until we changed our Lithuanian passports that had been issued under Smetona, to Soviet

---

* Village in Prienai district. [This is an original gloss by the interviewer.]

ones. When we got them, I had an urge to sneak out of Daukšiagiris....Somehow I managed to reach Kaunas, found someone I used to know at the academy, spent one night in one place, another night somewhere else....

While living in Kaunas, we didn't have enough money to buy food. I had to help my brother and sister, so I started to take home some butter from the storage. Because I was a laboratory employee, I had the right to access all storage areas, so I'd take half a kilo of butter. Otherwise we wouldn't have survived...

I—I probably haven't told this to anyone—but while working at the dairy, I was a heavy drinker, because life seemed so meaningless. There was no future, no hope; we didn't know how to improve things. I didn't see any future: My brothers were murdered, my home was dismantled; we'd lost all our foundation, perhaps even our self-respect and ability to feel shame. Maybe that's why we stopped appreciating life....

...I spent three years working at the Kaunas dairy, until July 1949. They fired me because I was from a repressed family, and I was suspected of being a partisan informant. Later, in the autumn, some acquaintances helped me get a seasonal job at the Kaunas procurement division of a sugar factory in Marijampolė....

I'd been dating a man named Kazimieras for ten years. I'd met him at the academy. I came to Dotnuva in 1939, and he in 1941, when I was in my third year....

I got married in 1951. There was no wedding ceremony—we just registered our marriage and that was all. We bought a can of food, a bottle of booze and went over to the apartment of some acquaintances. That was our wedding. If we hadn't registered our marriage officially, the priest wouldn't have given his blessing. So after a month, we got his blessing and my husband's sisters went to the Carmelite church to check if we really had gotten the priest's blessing, because they were a deeply religious family.

I got to know him quite well during those ten years*; he was like a relative to me: a child of farmers, handsome, calm....

But, in reality, he had this drinking problem. I thought he'd be practical, that when he'd got his own life sorted, he'd stop drinking. And even if he had kept drinking, he would have taken care of the home anyway. As a matter of fact, I was right—he always brought his salary home....

We had a room where we lived with my father. We were only separated by a wardrobe. There was no kitchen at all—we cooked food on a tiny electric stove. First we slept on the floor. Only later I bought two chairs, a table and a sofa...

We got married in the summer of 1951, and our son Eugenijus was born in 1952. We called him Genutis. I was already pregnant when we got married....I was in labour the night between January 6 and 7.

At that time, there was only one medical nurse at the maternity hospital. She left me and went to the wards. When she came back, the child was already suffocating. She noticed that it was bad. When she called the doctor on duty, it was already morning. The doctor laid me on the table and forcefully pressed on me to

---

* During the ten years that they dated.

get the baby out. He also gave me oxygen*. But while he was pressing, a blood-vessel snapped in the child's tiny head—the result was a birth trauma.

...We spent one month at the hospital because the child was paralysed. Nobody explained it to me, they didn't bring the baby for breastfeeding, and I didn't see him the whole month....After a month they gave me the child and let us go home.

Nobody spoke about the aftermath, nobody explained that to me: he seemed like an ordinary child. Then I noticed that he wasn't able to control his hand and showed no reaction. I saw that the child's development was slower than usual; his little hand was clenched all the time. When he was four months old, I realised how bad the situation was....

A doctor in Panevėžys† said that it was a birth trauma and that nothing could be done then. And that was it; I was left on my own. Genutis was able to speak a few words but couldn't control his hand and his leg and was lame. Nobody paid any attention. Doctors said that such cases did happen and that it was normal—a misfortune! When he was about five or six years old, I took him to doctors at the Kaunas Clinic; the answer was the same—he was handicapped, and there was no treatment....

Little Genutis had a strong desire to work. Grandfather used to put a log on a sawhorse, and he'd saw it with one hand. What a joy it was when he managed to saw it off; what a delight that he managed to produce something. In the autumn, I used to bring in some green beans from the garden; so he, with that one hand, would pinch the pod through and would shell some green beans into a bowl. My daughter Nijolė used to bring home her friends, and he would be so happy and jump with excitement; he wanted to show his pleasure at their prettiness. Perhaps he had entered puberty? I'd dress him and take him outside. He went out and hung from the fence all the time. He would have epileptic seizures four or five times a day.

My husband would spend all day away from home to work at the *kolkhoz*, he was rarely ever there, at home....

...My husband never came home after work. I didn't think about getting a divorce. What would happen then?...

...I wanted to give him away‡. At that time, in 1961, he was nine years old. Until that time I'd lived with him and nobody had helped us. Nobody. Absolutely nobody. There was a woman named Fainbliuvienė, she was head of the social welfare division. I asked her to admit Genutis to the childcare center. I begged her with tears in my eyes, and she said, "So what? You want the state to support your child?" She refused, and that was it.

And thus I lived on with three children and two parents, and in 1962 I started thinking about sending him to a nursing home. I thought it would be easier for my

---

* Oxygen was a widely accepted means to make labor more comfortable. [This is an original gloss by the interviewer.]

† Where the couple moved in March of that year.

‡ She is responding here to the interviewer, who asked her whether anyone had suggested that she turn her son over to the care of the state.

family to live; I'd get a job. At that time, my second son, Jonas, was already eight, my daughter Nijolė was three. Because the head of the division refused to speak to me, I used my connections and paid a visit to the chairman of the Executive Committee. He gave me a letter of resolution, and I got a letter of reference to give to the Kaunas nursing home for the handicapped. I gave Genutis a bath, put some clean clothes on him, and took the child there.

Eleven days later, I paid him a visit only to realise he didn't even have his underwear on; he was soiled. Who would look after him when there were 23 children in the group, and only one supervisor? The kids threw cereal in each other's hair. In those days social matters were totally neglected; nobody cared! So those Communists really shouldn't boast....

...That house* was enclosed by a long fence. Genutis saw me coming and ran along the fence shouting, "Mummy, mummy, mummy!" I had some chicken and milk in my bag, so I fed him. God, I felt so sorry for him.

My brother lived in Kaunas at that time, so I took him there and bathed him thoroughly. I thought about taking him back to the nursing home, but my heart didn't let me do that, so I brought him along to Panevėžys. He was overjoyed when we got home....

Nowadays, handicapped child benefits are twice as much as they used to be—or even more—and the mother's work experience is taken into account while she cares for her disabled child. That's really wonderful, but what about me? I received nothing.

In 1968, when Genutis turned 16, I got 16 roubles of social benefits for him. I received them for two years because he passed away at the age of 18. He lived for 18 years and four months. I almost wanted him to die; it may sound cruel, but... I knew he wouldn't be able to live.

It was spring, such cold winds. Genutis was standing in the doorway, a gust of wind blew; I thought he would catch a cold. It started with a sore throat. Then the fits began, over and over. He was almost unable to recover; he came down with fever of over 40 degrees Celsius, and his blood started thickening. And he died. I called for an ambulance a couple of times; they wanted to take him to the hospital, but I knew he wouldn't be better off at the hospital, so I refused. He was already a mature, big man; I knew he wasn't facing a happy life anyway, as a handicapped man. I thought: "When I die there will be no one to care for him anymore, and he will be taken to a nursing home, and he won't survive there, anyway, because the conditions there will be even tougher."

My father had already gone too, and he was the one who loved him so much; he was his most beloved grandson. That handicapped child passed away on May 2, 1970.

...I recovered [from Genutis's death] in 1975 when I started to work at an experimental linseed farm at the Upytė research center. Why did I start working? I knew that I didn't have any work experience. If my husband collapsed

---

* The nursing home where her son was being cared for.

drunk somewhere in a ditch and kicked the bucket, I wouldn't receive any retirement benefits. What would I do then? Work was hard in Upytė, because it was 13 kilometres from Panevėžys. I used to get up, travel to the museum, and walk two more kilometers to the linseed farm.

... But I knew that I had created such a life myself: it was I who proposed marriage. As a result, I had to bear the entire burden.

Later I started making handicrafts. While working in Upytė, I noticed that Soviet farms and research centers kept in touch with each other, that they needed souvenirs to exchange. They'd buy those souvenirs from Dailė, a trust company. So I offered my services and they liked my work. I was allowed to make those souvenirs at home.

DVD cover from the film *Coming Out* (Heiner Carow, East Germany, 1989, DVD produced by ICESTORM Entertainment). The German says, "In the end, you have to follow your heart." The film tells the story of a young man who is dating a woman to "pass" as being straight. But he accidentally—or so it seems—makes his way to a gay bar, meets a man, and falls in love. He comes to accept himself for who he is. This was the first gay film to "come out" of East Germany. But it was not so much the product of the revolutionary rupture of 1989 as, arguably, the official tolerance of homosexuality by the East German regime since 1985. Reproduced with the permission of ICESTORM Entertainment.

Every now and then an accountant visited me, appraised the souvenirs and paid me for that month. I worked until January 4, 1991, when I'd worked enough to receive my own pension—that is, twenty years. I celebrated my 70th birthday making those souvenirs at Upytė....

My husband Kazimieras and I moved to Vilnius on July 16, 2003. Kazelis [her husband] couldn't bear this—the fact that we wouldn't live under our own roof, that we'd be senile under somebody's care. Or maybe he was pursued by death and his spirit gave in and, without any preparation, he left this world. I was left alone—sad. I lost a person with whom I'd spent 62 years of my life's journey.

I say the words, "I'm 85 years old," without thinking, but I can't really fathom it. My eyes are unable to see, I can't do any work anymore, and so what's the purpose of such a life? I remember the words of a Kyrgyz writer, Chingiz Aitmatov: that to a human being, life's biggest hardship is a non-ageing mind and soul—the body ages while the spirit still rambles on about about love, goals, dreams; the body dies off while the soul lives on.

Autumn, 2004

3–5

East Germany

Letter of 1988 from a Working Group on Homosexuality in a Protestant Church in the City of Halle to the East German Ministry of the Interior

The contexts in which gay (and bisexual) people in Communist polities made decisions related to their sexual identity were shaped by factors beyond national Communist parties and Marxist–Leninist ideology. Generational change within Communist societies, combined with global economic and political developments, played a significant role in creating the contexts for such decisions. There is perhaps no more stunning example of such abstract generalizations than the story of the dramatic shift in 1985 in East German state policy toward homosexuals.

Reprinted by permission of the Bundesarhiv, Berlin. From BArch, Abteilung DDR, D0 4/821, Bl. 876–878. Translation: Glennys Young.

It was in that year—as it turned out, four years before the fall of the Berlin Wall—that the Politburo of the East German Communist Party (the SED, Sozialistische Einheitspartei or Socialist Unity Party) recommended that homosexuals be integrated into East German society. (In 1968, East Germany had done away with Section 175 of the German criminal code, which had stipulated that male homosexual acts were illegal. West Germany did the same in 1969.) Though the Politburo recommendation itself was never made public, this launched a series of state-promoted efforts to reduce discrimination against homosexuals and make them full-fledged members of socialist society. Stretching on for several years, this encompassed state-encouraged discussion of homosexuality in the media (including TV), the creation of gay and lesbian clubs within state and party institutions (such as the official network of youth groups, the Freie Deutsche Jugend, or Free German Youth), and university research and conferences. Such tolerant efforts were not only unprecedented among Communist polities. Among *Western* European countries, only Scandinavia had as liberal a policy toward homosexuality.

The reasons for East Germany's policy shift are complex. But one of the dynamics in play was state response to popular social pressure stemming from social and generational change. In the late 1970s, a new generation was coming of age in East Germany. In contrast to the earlier generation that had grown up with postwar economic hardship, Soviet occupation, and Stalinist political repression under SED leader Walter Ulbricht, the new one was formed by material security (easy satisfaction of basic needs and a socialist consumer culture) and the relaxation of severely repressive rule. As in Western Europe, and other advanced industrial societies, the new generation had the luxury to embrace causes centering around individual fulfillment. In East Germany, this took many forms, but a significant one was the grassroots creation of homosexual self-help groups in the state's main institutional competitor, the Protestant Church. In the early 1980s, such groups emerged in cities such as Berlin, Halle, Leipzig and Karl-Marx Stadt. Facing the threat of the church-sponsored gay movement joining forces with other movements (chiefly environment and peace issues) within the church, the state sought to co-opt the gay and other movement to head off a unified political opposition with an institutional base. The 1985 policy shift also had other roots beyond church-state tensions: a positive stance on homosexuality in German Marxism and Communism, the goal of reducing high-risk sexual practices during the AIDS crisis, and the threat of emigration by dissatisfied homosexuals.

Although the East German party-state sent clear signals that homosexuality was to be tolerated, how regional and local officials would implement the policy remained to be seen. It fell to state and party bureaucrats to interpret the Politburo's recommendation. Because gays and lesbians could not be sure how the policy would be implemented, they faced opportunity, uncertainty, and frustration. This is exemplified by the following document, a letter written by the director of the working group on homosexuality in the Evangelical Church in the city of Halle to the Ministry of the Interior. Such groups provided support, held social events, and sought to educate heterosexual church members about homosexuality. When the Halle group's request to hold a dance and river cruise was refused on the local and regional levels, it sought to appeal to the central government and its "official line of reasoning" on homosexuality.

Homosexuality Working Group
At the Evangelical City Mission of Halle
Directorship

Dehnert, Klaus-Dieter
Strasse der Freundschaft*20
Halle 4070

To: The Ministry of the Interior
Major General Helmut Ferner
MdI[†] HA Schutzpolizei
Mauerstr. 29–32
Berlin 1086

Halle, 8 August 1988

In Regard To: Approval of two events

Dear Comrade Generalmajor!

Our Working Group "Homosexuality" has existed since 7 March 1985 at the Evangelical [Lutheran] City Mission in Halle. During this time, a tradition was developed of having a boat cruise on the Saale River once a year. Thus in 1985 and 1986 we were able to have one that had not been approved by the government and in 1987, one that had been approved by the police. This occasion was a delightful and enriching affair for all participants and contractual partners.

Since 27 October 1987, we have had a preliminary contract with the management of the restaurant "Silberhöhe" for a dance event on 15 October[‡] 1988 in the hall of this establishment and a pre-contractual agreement since 26 January 1988 for a boat cruise on 2 October 1988 on the MS *Kosmos* with Department of Waterborne Transportation of the VEB Kraftverkher Halle. This has been the course of preparation up until this point:

On 25 November 1987, a dance event that had been declined on short notice by the local police department[§] in Bitterfeld for 28 November 1987 in the restaurant "Lindenhof" in Bitterfeld was rejected as well by the Regional

---

[*] In English, "Friendship Street."

[†] Ministry of Interior.

[‡] The month is not completely visible.

[§] In the text, VPKA or Volkspolizeikreisamt: District Office of the People's Police.

Police of Halle [BDVP]*, General First Lieutenant Schlösinger. In the verbal explanation given for the decision it was explained, among other things, that we are not an association recognized by the State. However, we represent, according to 92 of the VAVO†, an association of citizens that would like to hold two events that require registration with the police.

At the Permit Department of the District Office of the People's Police, in Halle, where I was summoned on 30.12.87, this explanation was repeated to me. I presented a supporting document from the head of the regional church, Abel, in which it was confirmed to me, as the leader of the Working Group, that I am permitted to conclude all verbal agreements concerning the Working Group "Homosexuality" in Halle at the Lutheran City mission. Nevertheless, I was told that we are not an association recognized by the state and that we had no right to make such applications. This resulted in the petition to the chairperson of the Regional Council, and as a consequence, the first petition to the Head of the State Council of the DDR.

Next began the talks with Mr. Forkel of the Regional Council's Department of Internal Church Questions. In reference to this state of affairs I made an inquiry once again on 25 May 1988 with Ltn. Göhring of the local police department in Halle [VPKA], Permit Department, on account of both events mentioned above. At this point I received permission to submit the applications.

This I did on 31 May 1988. On 15 June 1988 I received a notice to the following effect: According to the present situation and as per the determination neither event is approved. It would not be in the interest of society that homosexuals meet each other on purpose at such events. In response to my question about who had determined this, Lieutenant Göhring answered: "I [did]." A representative of the MfS‡, Mr. Schneider, who was present, said to me, however, that until October of this year sudden changes might be possible. Lieutenant Göhring commented that since everything is off his desk now, that I could apply to the official agencies, with which I have contact.

He meant the Regional Council. A telephone consultation with First Lieutenant Schlösinger, of the District People's Police Authority in Halle, only resulted in that he could also not approve these events, that the MdI would make this determination, that homosexuals should not meet one another on purpose, because it is not in the interest of society. He would not revoke this.

Our contact at the Regional Council is also unable to help us further with the question of getting the events approved right away, even though our

---

* In German, Bezirksbehörde der Deutschen Volkspolizei [der DDR].

† This is the abbreviation for Veranstaltungsverordnung, or the (East German) "Statute for Conducting [Public] Events."

‡ Stasi, or Ministry for State Security. The East German secret police.

requests supposedly were positively discussed between Mr. Forkel and First Lieutenant Schlösinger. First Lieutenant Schlösinger also said further that we would not be able to do something different at the regional level, but for now this determination remains in force. It appears that there has been no progress on the regional level. I point out, that such events, in order to be organized in a legally and technically correct manner, as well as carried out financially, are not possible under artificially caused time pressure. I request a speedy decision, so that the contract costs can be calculated and so that contract fines can be avoided.

My concern now is that we need to expect our members to react unfavorably. Many of them will interpret the "prohibition" of our events as decision made by the state against them as homosexuals. This, however, goes against the official line of reasoning which has been developed in the preceding discussion about homosexuality in our country. It also raises the question why the possibilities for having [such] events are treated with such different standards throughout the Republic. (For example, Berlin-Weissensee-Buschallee, Leipzig, Bayrischer Hof, Dresden, among other places.)

There exists also the danger of isolation and of stalling our common efforts to find another legal carrier, since possibly many participants will be pushed into a conflict of trust towards all that has previously been achieved and expressed, which in turn can lead to isolated, thoughtless applications to exit the country.

We therefore ask that the conditions as to how unified, central decisions should be made in practical management correspond to the current state of scientific knowledge and the broad discussion concerning the phenomenon of "homosexuality" and mutual association.[11] I have the impression that these indecisive or reneging actions of the [East] German Police authorities on the district level originate in a "look towards the superordinate authorities." It can not be that such a State supported and legally binding position of the State's Ministry of the Interior exists—one that, in my opinion, does not correspond to our reality.

Considering that at this point we are a unique institution within our geographical area and that in order to handle jointly the phenomenon "homosexuality," to give active support to the affected individuals and to educate, and considering that we have positive results and experiences, we ask you to support these efforts through a politically correct decision. It would be a shame if negative decisions would cause unnecessary and severe setbacks to the present good standing of things, because we are genuinely committed to find, together with the Regional Council, new ways also for another connection of our working group.

We would like to refer to the Workshop on Homosexuality held in Karl-Marx Stadt on 23 April 1988[12], which was carried out under the responsibility of Prof. Dr. E. Günther,[13] Stud.-R. Dr. K Bach and other leading sexologists and andrologists.

A petition that reads in a similar way is being addressed to Comrade Erich Honecker, the Chair of the State Council of the DDR*.

With optimism for the matter and friendly greetings we remain

Klaus-Diener Dehnert
Director of the Working Group
"Homosexuality" in the
Lutheran City Mission
in the City of Halle

Direct the response to:

Dehnert, Klaus-Dieter
Str. d. Freundschaft 20
Halle—Silberhöhe
4070

Confirmed By:

Dorowksy, Uwa-Holger
Heinrick, Monika
Member of the Directorship
Member of the Directorship

3 - 6

Havana, Cuba, 1994

Manifesto of the Gay and Lesbian Association of Cuba

In Cuba, gay people made choices about their identities and their sexuality in a very different context than did gay people in the GDR (German Democratic Republic, or East Germany). Not only did the Cuban government *not* seek

From "Manifesto of the Gay and Lesbian Association of Cuba" (28 July 1994) in Ian Lumsden, *Machos, Maricones, and Gays: Cuba and Homosexuality* (Philadelphia: Temple University Press, 1996) appendix C, 213–216. Reprinted with permission of Temple University Press.

* In the German text, Vorsitzender des Staatsrates der DDR.

to "tame" or "co-opt" the movement by incorporating it within state and party institutions. Not only has the Cuban Communist regime not sought to end discrimination against sexual minorities. Castro's Cuban government has also been infamous for perpetrating harsh forms of repression against gay people: arrest, discrimination in employment, expulsion from the Party, and forced marriages to persons of the opposite sex. One is mentioned in the following selection: UMAP (Unidades Militares para el Aumento de la Producción), or Military Units to Increase Production. Though the name may sound innocuous, in fact these were labor camps to which the government sent Cubans it believed needed rehabilitation for "delinquent" behaviors—including homosexuality.[14]

The sources of such repression and discrimination are complex and controversial. One is Cuban culture, which, despite its legendary pan sexuality, has historically been intolerant of public displays of homosexuality.

Prior to the 1959 Revolution, when Fidel Castro's 26th of July Movement took power, there were, to be sure, gay bars and tacit knowledge of who was gay. But there was no cultural toehold for public acknowledgment of gay relationships. Gays led closeted lives. Culture, however, only takes us so far in explaining the nature and degree of discrimination against, and persecution of, homosexuality under the Castro regime.

Just as the causes of Cuba's repression of homosexuality were varied and complex, so were the responses of gay people themselves. One was emigration. Shortly after Castro came to power, gay Cubans left the island, generally for Miami, Florida, and its environs. The most well-known case of emigration came in spring 1980, when over a hundred thousand Cubans, some of them gay, left for the United States from Mariel, Cuba. (In accepting gay Cubans as refugees— especially gay males—the U.S. government emphasized anti-Communism over political persecution of homosexuals.[15] Despite emigration, an everyday gay life of clandestine meeting places, parties, and sex persisted due to the efforts of many courageous individuals. Everyday gay life in fact became, over the decades, somewhat less hidden and more public because of such factors as generational change and tourism.

The amazing document reprinted herein—the "Manifesto of the Gay and Lesbian Association of Cuba" (28 July 1994)—testifies to those courageous efforts. In offering such testimony, it is, in a sense, a culmination. But it is more than that. It is a triumphal moment (as the authors of the document put it, 28 July 1994 "is certainly the Cuban gay community's most important day"). It is a call to action ("today is the moment to define the issues necessary to achieve social recognition"). It is a call to action on many levels—seeking "social recognition," leading a political and social struggle for "rights," battling AIDS, and obtaining "anti-discriminatory measures" from the Cuban government. But perhaps the most fundamental of those levels is the ongoing project of self-redefinition—of gay people seeing themselves, and being seen, not as "victims," not as "sick," "pathological," or "antisocial," but as "human beings" having "natural rights to exist in liberty." It marks, in that sense, not just a culmination, but a beginning. After closely reading the text, readers may find their own ways of defining the document and its historical significance—for Cuba, international Communism, and the global gay rights movement.

MANIFESTO OF THE GAY AND LESBIAN
ASSOCIATION OF CUBA

Hello,

Today on Thursday, July 28, 1994, slightly after 5.00 PM, we are meeting here. It is certainly the Cuban gay community's most important day.

Will the Parque Almendares*, at present a space for a formal and disguised meeting, become a place that is remembered? Time will tell. It will be responsible for giving us the answer.

The gay and lesbian population is the part of society that throughout *machista* and homophobic history has been most victimized by discrimination and marginalization; our culture has been denounced from generation to generation. Perhaps five years ago there were far more gays and lesbians who hid their real sexual identity as the only way to find a space among heterosexuals, the majority of society who were considered "normal" and who condemned and obscured the existence of any sexual orientation that was different—condemning with their accusatory finger thousands of human beings who only sought to have their rightful place in society.

Obscurity was the degrading condition to which we were sentenced:

lack of space

lack of meeting places

lack of freedom

lack of means of expression.

Remember for example the homosexual victims of the UMAP who were despotically sent to work camps on the grounds that they were antisocial, the constant raids on gays in public spaces for "disturbing the public peace" when they were only trying to have fun. Remember the gays and lesbians who have had to live part of their lives in jail, accused of transgressions they never committed; the numerous university students expelled from their faculties for having long hair, for not dressing "according to socialist morality," for using earrings, for dressing in an effeminate way, or simply for sexually desiring someone of the same sex, even though it could never be proven. Let us also remember the outrages and discrimination committed against homosexuals in other parts of the world. These facts can serve to make us reflect upon the extent to which we have been humiliated, the extremes to which our natural rights to exist in liberty have been denied by the homophobic and *machista* society in which we live. But today darkness begins to give way to light—light that is necessary to show the way; and light that we alone have the responsibility of ensuring will never again be extinguished.

---

* The Parque Almendares is a park, located in the center of Havana (La Habana), whose acreage is formed by the valley of the Almendares River. It features old-growth trees that make it suitable for the "disguised" meetings mentioned in the text. The park is located but a few kilometers from the ocean.

Today we have not met here in order to say who is responsible for all that has happened to us over time. Today is the moment to define the issues necessary to achieve social recognition; it is the moment to unite ourselves behind one national voice that demands our rights with strength and dignity.

Let us agree that in recent times coercion against gay groups has considerably diminished and that we are already experiencing more acceptance by the heterosexual part of society. The gay and lesbian world already has a small space, "a brief reference" in the means of communication, in cultural institutions (film, theater, literature), in the streets in which we share our love, in Saturday night fiestas. And this is important; it is a step forward for Cuban gays who, as a result of our hardships, begin to be conscious of our situation. That is why we are here, to defy censorship, to defy any distorted information that condemns us.

Our prospects depend upon ourselves and on our own capacity to demand our rights. Society may marginalize us; but we have to offer an image that we are people who have virtues and defects, just as anybody else, that the choice of being gay, lesbian, or heterosexual does not imply anything else; this is and will be our battlefield to believe in ourselves and for society to believe in us.

For how long must we endure being treated as if we are sick or pathological?

Why should we allow them to accuse us of being antisocial?

For how long must we be an object of discrimination, of prejudices, of abuses, of blackmail, of repression, of phobias?

Let us show them that we are not sick, that we are not antisocial, and let us struggle against discrimination, abuses, and blackmail.

For the first time we have consciously gathered here in unity. Being afraid can only help the ideas of our detractors.

Being afraid is absurd if we want to defend our rights.

It is necessary to act proudly, to make a daring gesture; it is necessary to act with courage. We will struggle without rest and will conceive our struggle as one of cultural and personal liberation.

Politics are inevitable in any struggle, but it is not what unites us here; let us leave that to the faithful.

It is more important to search for the freedom of which we have dreamt. Ending homophobia is fundamental; it is essential to destroy sidafobia [the fear of AIDS], to stop this disease, whatever it may cost, and let us show loving solidarity with those who are seropositive, so that they will feel that we are on their side, so that they will know that our struggle is their struggle and on their behalf.

It is necessary to obtain antidiscriminatory measures that will guarantee people who live together the same rights that any couple is entitled to.

The state should not make moral judgments, only juridical and legal rules. Whether or not a couple is heterosexual or homosexual should not affect the standpoint of the state.... that is our belief.

If society can help the lives of individuals, why should it make them more difficult?

The question is personal and intimate, it relates strictly to private life. Organizations connected to the state have to accept that this is a social fact and should create policies that do not discriminate in principle against those who are already subject to considerable discrimination, be it with respect to sexual orientation or anything else.

Every individual's sexual freedom should be respected. The means to enjoy such freedom should be established.

It must be understood that the sexuality of our species has no natural limits.

There is much to say but much more to do. Action is power.

Let us defend the right to sexual freedom.

Let us unite with strength.

This will be our first triumph and the day that we will celebrate.

Let us name the 28th of July "Gay Pride Day of Cuba" and let us celebrate it every year.

On behalf of gay and lesbian rights,

Liberation

The Organizers.

NOTES

1. For these and other details, see Dan Healey, *Homosexual Desire in Revolutionary Russia: The Regulation of Sexual and Gender Dissent* (Chicago: University of Chicago Press, 2001), esp. 185–188.

2. Dan Healey, "Sexual and Gender Dissent," in Lynne Viola, ed., *Contending with Stalinism* (Ithaca, NY: Cornell University Press, 2002), 153.

3. On Gide's troubled relationship with Communism, see Patrick Pollard, "Gide in the USSR: Some Observations on Comradeship," in Gert Hekma, Harry Oosterhuis, and James D. Steakley, eds., *Gay Men and the Sexual History of the Political Left* (New York: Harrington Park Press, 1995).

4. Whyte refers to Mark Sereiskii, "Gomoseksualizm (Homosexuality)," *Bol'shaia sovetskaia entsiklopediia (Great Soviet Encyclopedia),* 1st ed. (Moscow, 1930): 593–596; on the article and its author, see Healey, *Homosexual Desire in Revolutionary Russia,* 170–173, 323. The article is reproduced in Mark Blasius and Shane Phelan, eds., *We Are Everywhere: A Historical Sourcebook of Gay and Lesbian Politics* (New York: Routledge, 1997), 214–215.

5. For the text of this letter in English see: http://www.marxists.org/archive/marx/works/1869/letters/69_06_22.htm (accessed 7 August 2009).

6. For an analysis of Marx and Engel's views on homosexuality that contradicts this interpretation, see Hubert Kennedy, "Johann Baptist von Schweitzer: The Queer Marx Loved to Hate," in Hekma et al., *Gay Men,* 69–96.

7. For these and other pertinent statistics, see Elizabeth McGuire, "Between Revolutions: Chinese Students in Soviet Institutes, 1948–1966," in Thomas Bernstein and Hua-yu Li, eds., *China Learns from the Soviet Union, 1949–Present,* Harvard Cold War Studies, (Lanham, MD, Rowman and Littlefield: 2010), 361.

8. On the distinction between "private" and "public" autobiographical types, see Georges Gusdorf, "Conditions and Limits of Autobiography," in James Olney, ed., *Autobiography, Essays Theoretical and Critical* (Princeton, NJ: Princeton University Press,1980), 33.

9. These comments on the symbolic dimensions of Sino–Soviet friendship, and the Chinese students' awareness thereof, as well as the analytical points made in this framing of the Chen Peixian document more generally, draw upon McGuire, "Between Revolutions," 359–377.

10. A point made by Dalia Leinarte in the introduction to *Adopting and Remembering Soviet Reality: Life Stories of Lithuanian Women, 1945–1970* (New York: Editions Rodopi, b.v., 2010), 2–4. Quotes at 3.

11. Almost certainly, the author had in mind a number of state-led initiatives concerning homosexuality. One was the fact that in 1987, the East German Ministry of Health commissioned a book on homosexuality, which appeared in two very large editions. See Reiner Werner, *Homosexualität: Herausforderung an Wissen und Toleranz (Homosexuality: A Challenge for Knowledge and Tolerance)* (Berlin: Verlag Volk und Gesundheit, 1987). Among his recommendations—which were in part prompted by the AIDS crisis and the attempt to reduce high-risk sexual behavior among homosexual men—were the creation of counseling centers, expedited allocation of apartments for same-sex couples, and legal partnerships for gays and lesbians. See Raelynn J. Hillhouse, "Out of the Closet Behind the Wall: Sexual Politics and Social Change in the GDR," *Slavic Review* 49, no. 4 (1990): 592.

12. The author likely refers here to one of three national conferences on "Psycho-Social Aspects of Homosexuality," held in 1985, 1988, and 1990. These conferences included East German gays and lesbians. See Hillhouse, "Out of the Closet," 588. The conferences followed the establishment of the first university-level gay and lesbian studies committee at Humboldt University (East Berlin) in 1984.

13. Among Erwin Günther's publications of the 1970s and 1980s were articles on adolescent sexuality and homosexuality.

14. See Karin Alejandra Rosenblatt, "State, Gender and Institution Change: Federación de Mujeres Cubanas," in Elizabeth Dore and Maxine Molyneux, eds., *Hidden Histories of Gender and the State in Latin America* (Durham, NC: Duke University Press, 2000), 317.

15. For further details, see B. Ruby Rich and Lurdes Arguelles, "Homosexuality, Homophobia, and Revolution: Notes toward an Understanding of the Cuban Lesbian and Gay Male Experience, Part II," *Signs: Journal of Women and Culture in Society* 11, no. 1 (1985): 120–136 (here 120, 128), and "Homosexuality, Homophobia, and Revolution: Notes toward an Understanding of the Cuban Lesbian and Gay Male Experience, Part I," *Signs: Journal of Women and Culture in Society*, 9, no. 4 (1984): 683–699.

CHAPTER 4

Ideology and Self-Fashioning

Until recently, a person living in a Communist polity was, in scholarly accounts and the popular media alike, either a true believer in Communism or a disaffected dissenter. There was no middle ground. People either bought into Communist ideology completely, sometimes because they were the victims of "brainwashing," or, having triumphantly resisted ideological indoctrination, they regained their capacity for autonomous action and rejected the Communist program completely. The idea that a person might embrace some aspects of the Communist ideological program and not others, or might make up her own version of that program yet not necessarily regard herself as engaging in "dissent," was conceptually impossible.

But things have changed. In imagining what people's relationship to Communist ideology was, historians of Communism have allowed for greater complexity than the simple true believer vs. dissenter/dissident dichotomy. Communist citizens, it has been acknowledged, constructed complicated and messy relationships to Communist ideology and to the Communist political system more generally. There were true believers, dissenters, and dissidents, to be sure. But there were also people who made decisions about Communist ideology and Communist "civilization" that cannot be categorized so simply.

People not only made choices that did not entail a complete acceptance or utter rejection of Communist ideology. They also made decisions that involved transforming elements of Communist ideology—especially as it was presented at any given moment and on any given issue—even though they were not rejecting any fundamental elements of the Communist worldview. For example, people— even Party members—might disagree with the Party's position on a given issue, yet do so by arguing that their position was indeed compatible with Marxist-Leninist (or Maoist) ideology. Or, they might take a specific theme in Communist ideology—such as the belief in the power of the human will to transform a "bourgeois" or capitalist society into a socialist or Communist one—and assign the importance of the will to another domain.

120

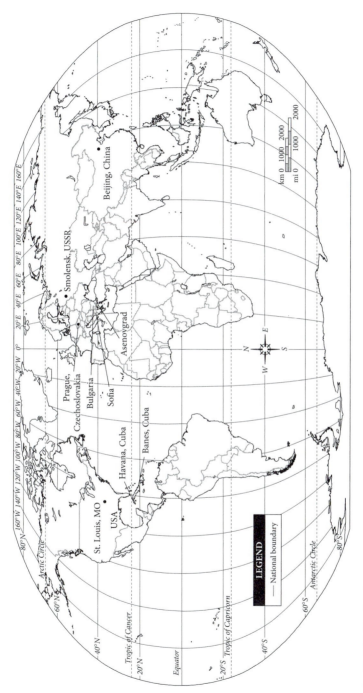

Locator Map for Chapter 4

The documents in this chapter all offer examples of people who demonstrated agency, and even creativity, in creating their complicated relationships to Communist ideology and Communist political systems. They represent different walks of life in Communist polities: the autobiography of a Bolshevik Party member, rank-and file Communists in St. Louis in 1948, a regional Communist Party leader in Bulgaria, a child and his mother in Castro's Cuba, striking students in Czechoslovakia in 1968, and a student during China's Cultural Revolution. They also represent different literary or textual *genres* prominent in Communist polities—autobiographies penned for admission to Party membership, discussions during meetings at Communist Party cells or other kinds of Communist organizations, memoirs, and letters to fellow Communist citizens.

USSR

The Politics of Self-Presentation in the 1921 Autobiography of a Communist Party Member

Self-perfection was at the core of the Bolshevik project and of Communist regimes in power more generally. In the early decades of Soviet power, the Bolsheviks placed great emphasis on creating a new kind of person. To attain this goal, every individual was expected to work on herself or himself, to effect as much a break with the past as was possible and necessary to serve the emancipation of the working class in Soviet society and, eventually, of humanity writ large.

What did working on oneself in the early Bolshevik context mean for Communist citizens? It all depended on what one wanted to attain. If one wanted to join the Communist Party, and remain there, the requirements were stiff indeed. One had to demonstrate not only one's commitment to the revolutionary mission but that one had attained "consciousness." This was not individual self-awareness. Rather, in Marxism it meant the merger of the individual's consciousness with Party doctrine, which, in turn, embodied a "supra-personal proletarian consciousness."[1] The burden of proof was great, requiring one to submit voluminous paperwork, produce recommendations from experienced Party members, and endure searching interrogations by local Party cells. But it was somewhat less so for those individuals who could demonstrate that they came from the working-class or at least from the poorer peasantry. For those whose class origin was more dubious—for those, for example, whose parents had been wealthier peasants or had other connections to the former "capitalist" world of bourgeois Russia (for example, a father who was a priest, an industrialist, or some other type of "exploiter")—the burden was especially great. Though class origins did not *automatically* prevent anyone from entry into the Bolshevik Party, dubious class credentials required that the candidate pay special attention to presenting a credible narrative of conversion to the Bolshevik cause. One had to learn how to represent the blemishes of one's past so that they did not invalidate the claim of having led oneself from "darkness" to "light."

Perhaps the most important way in which one could do this was by mastering the rules of the presentation of self in the autobiography that one submitted

From the Smolensk (Province) Communist Party Archives, "Autobiography of V. Korolev," Smolensk WKP, 326, ll. 172–174. Reprinted by permission. Translation: Glennys Young.

in application to the Party. (Sometimes autobiographies were written by those who had already attained Party membership.) Though such autobiographies varied in length, they were usually several pages long. The genre of the autobiography has, of course, a long history, and the Bolshevik incarnation has antecedents in Christian confessions after the Fourth Lateran Council (AD 1215). But, unlike Christian autobiographers, Bolshevik authors were to be self-reliant agents who achieved self-affirmation through Marxism. They were to write themselves, and their self-development, into the Marxist schema of history.

The autobiography reproduced next was written by V. Korolev, who joined the Bolshevik Party on 16 November 1918. Korolev had some blemishes in his past. Prominent among them was his class origin: though he came from the peasantry, his parents had become village capitalists. Readers will see how Korolev attempted to put the most positive spin on his class origin: not only was he born when his parents lived in the city of Smolensk (in the Bolshevik lexicon, there was a close association between the urban environment and the proletariat), but he emphasized how *unsuccessful* in business his parents were, not to mention how he suffered victimization by the Tsarist regime (such as when his application to go to the *Realschule*—or secondary school—was rejected when the director decided that he was the "unworthy son of the kitchen help (*kukharkin syn*')." Korolev also understood the importance of portraying his conversion to Bolshevism in the proper way. He was not a Bolshevik when the February Revolution brought the Russian autocracy's collapse in 1917. But he was brought from "darkness" to "light"—from dismissing the Bolsheviks as traitors to the Germans to heralding them as humanity's liberators—by interactions with workers and exposure to Bolshevik ideology via the Bolshevik press.

AUTOBIOGRAPHY OF V*. PETROVICH KOROLEV, MEMBER OF THE RUSSIAN COMMUNIST PARTY (BOLSHEVIKS) SINCE 16 NOVEMBER 1918, PARTY CARD NUMBER 7505707

I was born on 7 March 1899 in Smolensk in the kitchen of my grandfather, a peasant whose family had [too] many members for the land they had. He sent out his children, my father included, to tend to the cattle, made his children get to work. When a liberal landowner, Obukhova, offered to pay for Father's education, Grandfather refused, preferring, as he put it, that my son hand over to me a salary of three to five rubles each summer rather than studying God knows what in the city. In this way, my father continued to tend to the cattle and work among the poor peasant laborers. Unsatisfied by the countryside, he headed to the city as a seasonal laborer, where he tried out many jobs—he worked in a factory, then as a janitor, as a shoemaker, a turner, a conductor. My mother, being completely orphaned from age seven to twenty-five, worked as a cook, a water carrier, [and]

---

* The full first name is illegible on the copy of the document.

a laundress. Having saved four hundred rubles by the sweat of their brows, my parents opened a dairy shop. But since the business went bad and the family never became rich, I was sent to a parish school which charged nothing and provided students with books free of charge. High tuition meant that I could not attend high school so I went instead, with great difficulty, to a trade school in Smolensk, which was cheap and required no uniform. When, at age sixteen years and two months, I finished the trade school, I got a temporary job in the Smolensk Province Railway Technical Department, where I was paid twenty-five rubles a month. I worked for the zemstvo* for a year and a half, at a time when it was a relatively liberal institution, when the charms of bureaucracy were displayed to me in all their beauty.

Scared that I'd spend the rest of my life in this sewer of office drudgery, I decided to do what ever it took to continue my education. And so, avoiding spending time on anything that wasn't absolutely necessary, and working eight hours a day at the zemstvo, and hitting the books for six hours a day, I began to prepare myself to matriculate at the Smolensk *Real Schule*†. My body could not tolerate such intensive work (I was sleeping five to six hours a day), and I overslept until right before the exams started, which had the following result: I failed French. Failure didn't stop me, and I began to prepare just as persistently as I had been, expecting to take the [the exam] in the middle of the school year. When I was ready, I quit work in order to take the exam, but had the misfortune to displease somehow the director of the Second *Real Schule* and he, although he had the right and the opportunity to allow me to take the exam, didn't do it—he had apparently decided that I was the unworthy son of the kitchen help and I remained unemployed and not in school. Indignant in the depths of my soul because of my legal and economic situation, I went from Smolensk to Tarnopol' (Austria), where I worked for eight months as a clerk in the 135th roadbuilding detachment. There the February Revolution caught me by surprise. Until 1917 my political virginity was intact: I was not familiar with the program of [any] political parties; why, what the term "socialism" meant to me was "riot-strikes"—that was what the "lords" my mother worked for taught me to think. Being thrifty [and] economical by nature, and seeing how much of the Russian Army's precious property had been lost to the Germans in the Tarnopol' disaster‡—which had been blamed on Bolshevik agitation, I was not, owing to my lack of consciousness, in agreement with Bolshevik

---

*Local organ of self-government created during the reforms undertaken during the reign of Tsar Alexander II (1855–1881). Rural *zemstvos* (Russian plural: *zemstva*) were created in 1864 and urban ones in 1870.

†A secondary school. Though the author uses the German term, there was also a Russian equivalent in common usage at the time: *real'noe uchilishche*.

‡Tarnopol is a city in western Ukraine. The author refers here to the successful counteroffensive, during World War I, of Austro-German forces against Russian forces near Tarnopol. The city fell in two days, during 19–21 July 1917. The author uses the Polish spelling of the city. In Ukrainian, the city's name is Ternopil and, in Russian, Ternopol'.

tactics and I bought into the accusations Kerensky made against the Bolsheviks of treason and spying for the Germans.

Having arrived on leave and having found out about the opening of the Technical School, my passion for science rose to the surface and I decided to do whatever it took to enroll there. I succeeded in doing so. In 1917, before the Smolensk Technical School opened, I was elected by the other students as the chair of the Academic Committee, in which capacity I served the entire year. This was the first elected position I held in my life, so for that reason, naturally, I gave it everything I had. From May 1918 onwards, I worked on summer projects, building two iron-concrete bridges on Dukhovskoi Street in Smolensk. My interactions with workers, and especially the presence of Soviet and Communist literature, led me to abandon my perception of the Bolsheviks as traitors, [as] German agents, and I made the firm decision to familiarize myself thoroughly with the Bolshevik program. Some time later, I handed in my application to our cell, where it was accepted on 16 September 1918. In 1918, my material conditions were hellishly awful and, in spite of my studies, I had to take up work as an office clerk in the Smolensk Province Central Department of Prisoners and Refugees. The Party Committee decided that I should join the [Party] cell of the Central Department for Prisoners and Refugees, staying four to five months in the second cells. Upon my election as a comrade in the [Party] cell of the Department for Prisoners and Refugees, I gave up the position of chair of cell of Technical School. In May, during Kolchak's* attack, following the model of the complete mobilization of the [Party] cell of the Technical School, the cell of the Department of Prisoners and Refugees was, upon my urging and pressure, also fully mobilized. And I, as a Red Army soldier of the First Smolensk Shock Regiment, went to the Eastern Front, where I and my comrades were appointed to the 30th Rifle Unit. There I worked in a number of capacities—as the secretary of a collective of school employees, for the culture committee, in the library, as a member of disciplinary courts, the whole time being also a rank-and-file Red Army solider, that is, with Communist comrades from the school in all these instances. From the front, I was ordered to the Military School of the Eastern Front, where, upon my arrival, I organized a Bolshevik Party group, and I became the secretary. A week later, I became very sick with typhoid fever, which I survived only by a miracle. Halfway back to health, I arrived in Smolensk from Ufa. When my leave was over, I was sent to Automobile Command School. There I worked as an assistant to a chauffeur for the chief clerk of the Military Command....Several times in 1921 I filled in at the Military Command in Smolensk. I turned up at the Smolensk City Soviet† as a member

---

* Admiral A. V. Kolchak (1874–1920) was one of the leaders of the anti-Bolshevik White forces during the Russian Civil War of 1918–1921.

† In Russian, *soviet* means council. The institution after which the Soviet Union was named had its origins in the Revolution of 1905 as a strike committee of workers' deputies. During the Soviet period, city soviets were organs of urban administration. There were also village or rural soviets.

of the Inspection Commission of the SPI cooperative,…and as a student in the second course of the Department of Communications.

V. Korolev

Smolensk, 30 September 1921

I have known Comrade Korolev since he enrolled in the Technical School…and I confirm the veracity of his autobiography.
Member of the Russian Communist Party (Bolsheviks)
since September 1918 and Party Card number 182295*

4–2

St. Louis, 1948

A Communist Party Cell Puts "White Chauvinism" on Trial in a Baptist Church

The struggle against racism was an important cause for American Communists, whether central political leaders or rank-and-file, over the course of the twentieth century. To be sure, the Communist Party of the United States (CPUSA) did not include African-Americans when it was founded in 1919. Nor did the Party concern itself with racism until 1928, when the 6th Comintern Congress (17 July–1 September 1928) was held. At this Congress, the Comintern decried the discrimination (and worse) against African-Americans and insisted on their right to self-determination. Two years later, in 1930, the Comintern issued a resolution evincing not only its concern about the racial oppression of African-Americans—which it decried as "white chauvinism"—but also about discrimination against African-Americans within the CPUSA.

The CPUSA's decades-long campaign against "white chauvinism" had far-reaching consequences for Party life, for its rank-and-file Communists, and for American political culture more generally. As orchestrated by the Central

From Oleta O'Connor Yates Papers, the Bancroft Library, University of California, Berkeley BANC MSS C-B 924. Reprinted by permission of the Bancroft Library, University of California, Berkeley. The wording and punctuation are consistent with the original text.

*The name of the Party member confirming the autobiography's veracity is illegible.

Committee of the CPUSA and carried out to different degrees by local Party cells, this campaign took a variety of forms, some of which assumed prominence in particular periods and not others. One of these forms consisted of trials against white Party members charged with discrimination against their black comrades, trials whose aim was to convince African-Americans that the CPUSA was opposed to racism. These trials, the first of which was held in 1931, sometimes attracted hundreds of people, who watched as a cell made its accusations, heard the responses of the accused, judged the degree to which they not only exemplified "white chauvinism" but also reflected a proper understanding of Party doctrine (not just on race, but on other issues such as the relationship between the personal and the political), and a recommended a course of action with regard to the accused. Such trials continued throughout the 1930s, 1940s, and 1950s. In the early 1950s, when the campaign against "white chauvinism" was at is apogee, the Party sanctioned and even expelled hundreds of members for employing language such as "'whitewash'" or "black sheep," or, even more seriously, for treating black comrades with condescension or ignoring them altogether.[2] Over the decades, the CPUSA's campaign against "white chauvinism," and the trials more specifically, had considerable influence beyond the Party itself, raising awareness about racism in American political culture.[3]

The following document is an excerpt from a transcript the trial of "white chauvinist" CPUSA members in St. Louis in 1948. The accused, who were Jewish, were charged with having failed to invite African-American comrades in the Party to their wedding. Thanks to the fact that the entire transcript of the trial has been preserved, readers can get a firsthand sense of what the trials were like and what they meant for the accused and other participants. It was not just that the accused had to endure public censure in front of their comrades, in an exercise of political theater.[4] As the following excerpt demonstrates, the accused, their accusers, and the other participants all had to make decisions, sometimes on-the-spot, about what the Party's ideological position on "white chauvinism" meant for their identities as Party members.

"THE FIGHT AGAINST WHITE-CHAUVINISM FOR UNITY OF NEGRO AND WHITE TOILERS!"

Summary of Reports and Discussion of the Trial Against White-Chauvinism Held on Sunday

—FEB. 22, 1948

PLEASANT GREEN BAPTIST CHURCH
St. Louis, Mo.

ISSUED BY
STATE EDUCATION—ORGANIZATION DEPARTMENT
COMMUNIST PARTY OF MISSOURI
1041 N. GRAND BLVD.
ST. LOUIS, MO.

RACE PREJUDICE ON TRIAL
AT

Pleasant Green Baptist Church Auditorium

4570 Page Blvd.—(Page and West End Ave.)
Sunday, February 22nd, from 2 PM to 5 PM

Dear Comrade and Friend:

The Communist Party invites and urges you to attend this trial of members of the Communist Party charged with racial prejudice and white chauvinism.

This trial will demonstrate the position of the Communist Party on the fight for Negro rights. It is part of the fight of the Communist Party against white chauvinism.

The preamble of the Constitution of the Communist Party states:

"The Communist Party upholds the achievements of American Democracy and defends the United States Constitution and its Bill of Rights against its reactionary enemies who would destroy democracy and all popular liberties. It uncompromisingly fights against imperialism and colonial oppression, against racial, national and religious discrimination, against Jim Crowism*, anti-Semitism and all forms of chauvinism."

Racial prejudice is a powerful weapon in the hands of the capitalist class to undermine the democratic rights of the people....

This trial will expose the rotten system of Jim Crowism and all it stands for. You owe it to yourself and your people to join your fellow Americans in this all-important event. Please come on time so that the meeting can complete its business and adjourn promptly."

"Labor in a white skin can never emancipate itself as long as labor in a black skin is branded."—Karl Marx.

With comradely regards,
FOR THE STATE BOARD:
Ralph Shaw, Chairman
Al Murphy, Negro Commission

...DISCUSSION AT THE TRIAL.
A number of Negro and white comrades participated in the discussion. The following is brief summary of comments made:

Sam D:—He sharply condemned the conciliatory attitude of some comrades towards white chauvinism. He considers white chauvinism as a cancer, which must be cut out and rooted out of our ranks.

---

* On Jim Crowism, see the gloss on page 20 in document 1-3 (Angelo Herndon).

He pointed out that a Communist cannot shed his principles and program like you do a coat. You can't be a Communist at a party meeting and then go home and be something else. He questioned seriously those who think that personal life can be separated from political life, it is one.

He particularly stressed the reasons why the Jewish Communists, as part of a discriminated minority, must stand in the forefront of struggle for the Rights of the Negro masses."

Rose: (Defendant): "I have tried to follow the program of the Communist Party to the best of my understanding. I am not a chauvinist."

Doty: Discusses her own [Doty's] wedding where no Negro comrades attended, although they were invited. How can this be explained? The only way this absence of Negro comrades can be explained is that they felt the widespread existence of white chauvinism in the Party.

"'Lil's wedding was a chauvinist wedding and there is no doubt about it."

Doty further criticized the leadership, who were present at the wedding but did not do anything about it. The comrades should have boycotted the affair.

Lil (Defendant): " I want to speak for the family and answer some of the questions point by point:

"I want to state that I was brought up in the Party, and I should understand the program of the Party on the Negro question. And what I will say, is not an attempt to absolve myself of responsibility.

"We did commit a white-chauvinist act and it is in that light that I wish to discuss. It is a serious thing when our Party has to spend its energy and time to expose such bourgeois influences in our ranks.

"Our first reaction was too personal and emotional. After discussing it with the Party Committee we finally succeeded to take it out of the personal realm and discuss it politically. Our lives have been devoted to the Party and everything that the Party stands for. How then does it happen that we did not invite the Negro comrades to the wedding.

"We did not think it through. The problem was not on the part of my husband, but with my father's family. We considered the economic position and we capitulated to the family.

"I was asked why did we take a position as if this situation was a personal thing? I want to ask a question? How can we define the difference between personal and political things? I can't understand how you can solve the question of family and society, and how to solve this relationship. Nothing has been said so far on this question.

          ...

SUMMARY OF THE TRIAL AGAINST WHITE-CHAUVINISM
Comrades:

This trial against white-chauvinism reveals much more than has been discussed. It is just a beginning of our struggle against this capitalist poison which is plaguing the life of our Party in Missouri, and particularly in St. Louis.

This trial cannot be considered as being over. It must and will be continued in the form of a vigorous struggle to root out this dangerous disease.

One of the outstanding features of this trial is that it is a revelation. It has revealed to all of us not only how deep white-chauvinism has eaten into our midst, but it also clearly shows that there is a squirming mass of bourgeois concepts, ideas, and the glaring manifestation of bankrupty of the thinking of some of the comrades on the question of white-chauvinism.

It is shocking although not surprising that most of the white comrades who spoke, with the exception of Comrades Ralph, Ray, Bill, Sam, etc., (and some shop comrades), took either a conciliatory or a defensive position at this trial. None of them spoke self critically. All that was said was in the main very good but what the comrades did was to re-enforce the criticism of the Sanders and Lil. They did not feel that their own white-chauvinism too was on trial, instead they appeared as only participating in the trial of "other comrades" guilty of white-chauvinism.

We must recognize that the fact that this trial is far from being satisfactory. We must admit, that this trial was held* again against a background of a series of serious organizational and political weaknesses, that this question of white-chauvinism serves to point up in sharper emphasis the need for further fundamental organizational changes in our Party's structure and for developing a sharp and relentless struggle against all forms of deviations and bourgeois influences within the Party....

Today Comrade Rose states that she is "not a white-chauvinist." The joint statement which Rose and Lil submitted to the sub-committee of the Party does more to express their genuine feeling and thinking than all they have said at this trial today. The sub-committee rejected their original statement because it was non-political and it placed the whole question of their white-chauvinistic act solely on the personal plane. This statement did not deal with the question of white-chauvinism but rather it dealt with the "reason" why they committed the act.

In the discussion here today Comrade Lil contradicts herself when she says that in preparing for her wedding, they had given serious thought to the question of inviting Negro comrades and friends. She states that they decided after careful consideration that it would be best not to invite Negros because of the white-chauvinistic attitude of their business associates who might in some way isolate them and result in jeopardizing their economic security. Then, in the same speech, she blames the "lack of understanding" for their action and attempts to shun the issue. Since when do people without understanding make such carefully thought out and definite decisions? Comrade

---

* The preceding two words are difficult to read in the original.

Lil's remarks show clearly an attempt to cover up a monstrous crime they have committed against the Party and the Negro people.

Comrade Esther (formerly of the Tom Paine Club) openly criticized the trial and proposed that it should be merely an* educational discussion on a club level (privately, that is). This position is white-chauvinistic and hypocritical. Comrade Esther cannot deny the fact that the Tom Paine Club does not even hold meetings. Yet she proposes to hold a discussion in her club on the question of white-chauvinism.

Most of the Negro comrades who spoke contributed to the discussion in a constructive manner. However, the remarks of Comrade Jimmie, who is a very good comrade, did not help the fight against white-chauvinism of which he and his people are the worse suffers and victims. The position of Comrade Jimmie was the same as that taken by Comrades Rose and Lil when he discusses the trial of these comrades on the basis that their "economic well-being should be considered." Comrade Jimmie did not sufficiently "consider" the fact that this trial demonstrates the program of the Communist Party against all forms of chauvinism and for the complete economic, political and social equality for the Negro people. We must realize, however, that the very fact that Comrade Jimmie came to the defense of these comrades poses more sharply the question of white comrades combatting every sign of white chauvinistic expressions and actions.

Comrade Ray raised correctly the question and answered those comrades who relied on the weak sentimentalism that was hauled into the discussions prior to the trial. They asked: 'Why put the comrades on trial? Lil was being married. Why spoil the happiest moment of a young girl's life?" Lil's marriage was never the issue. The issue is the practice of white-chauvinism which came out in its most glaring form at her wedding.

What is involved here is not the wedding, but the problem of waging a struggle against the poisonous virus of the southern slaveowners' idea of white supremacy and Negro inferiority.

When we consider the fact that these comrades are of Jewish extraction, their action toward their Negro comrades calls for further and deeper analysis. These comrades have been members of the Party for a number of years and have had the unusual opportunity to witness the program of the Communist Party in action against anti-Semitism and white-chauvinism.

The white ruling class uses the weapon of racial prejudice, Jim-Crowism, anti-Semitism and many other forms of discrimination to drive a wedge between Negro and white workers, to foment hatred and strife between Jew and Gentile, between Protestant and Catholic, to divide them and exploit them for profits. The constant bestial oppression of the Negro people (and Jewish capitalists are a part of the oppressor class) has engraved upon the hearts and minds of the Negro people an immortal hatred of white ruling

---

* "And" appeared in the original text.

class chauvinism and domination. This hatred is diverted by the ruling class into false channels sometimes....

But we must see clearly that this sort of Negro petty bourgeois nationalism manifesting itself in a form of anti-Semitism on the economic field is the direct result of white-chauvinist oppression of the Negro people by whites....

Comrade Sanders and Lil and all the Jewish comrades should study the history of their own people thoroughly, the role the Jews have played in our country's struggle for its national independence, against chattel slavery and for greater democracy. There should be the closest unity between the Negro people and the Jewish people not only because of their position as oppressed people in this country, but also because historically the role of the Jews and the Negroes in America is a history of struggle against bigotry and for freedom from oppression.

I therefore propose that the Comrades Sanders and Lil be given the opportunity to prove their sincerity to the Party's program of struggle as set forth in the preamble of the Constitution of the Communist Party.

These comrades are expected to accept and to carry out Party assignments and to conform strictly to Party discipline for a specific period of time after which their work will be evaluated and measures taken to assist them to correct their mistake....

4–3

Bulgaria, 1949/1981

*A Regional Communist Party Leader on
Resistance to Collectivization*

For people who lived in Eastern Europe after World War II, the establishment and consolidation of Communist systems brought cataclysmic change to their lives. A central dimension of such consolidation was the nationalization of the economy. In agriculture, this meant collectivization, or the socialization of agriculture, by suppressing the market and by eliminating (or radically curtailing) private property. No uniform chronological timetable

From the Regional State Archive of Plovdiv (Bulgaria), fond 1943, opis 2, archivna edinitsa, list 2. Reprinted by permission of the archive. Transation: Peter Gruen.

existed in Eastern European countries in the Soviet bloc for the long, drawn-out process of collectivization. But some common patterns, deviations granted, can be observed.

It was in the second half of 1948 that East European states (with East Germany not beginning until 1949, and Poland never getting started) began the collectivization process. After some strides were made in the late 1940s and early 1950s (though East Germany remained at an impasse), the process was slowed by the political cataclysms of 1953–1956: Stalin's death, Khrushchev's de-Stalinizing thaw, the repercussions of the 17 June 1953 uprising (see the third document in chapter 6) in East Germany and throughout the Eastern bloc, strikes and protests in Poland in 1956, and the Hungarian Revolution of 1956. After political "normalization" had been reestablished, East European states (with the continuing exception of Poland) resumed what in official rhetoric was called their collectivization "campaigns." Two major exceptions to political unrest's temporary derailing of the collectivization process were Albania (which remained outside the Soviet bloc) and Bulgaria (where there was, to be sure, some slowing down in 1952–1956).[5]

In Bulgaria, where, prior to World War II, 80 percent of the population had worked in the agricultural sector, collectivization began on a voluntary basis in 1944. But it was not until 1945 that the labor cooperative farm (the TKZS, or *trudovo-kooperativno zemedelsko stopanstvo*, the form of agrarian economic organization mentioned in the following document) was officially approved.[6] Though Bulgaria, together with Yugoslavia and Czechoslovakia, were the East European countries to take the first major steps in collectivization, the process nonetheless proceeded slowly there. When, in 1947, Bulgarian Communists won the first postwar elections, they increased pressure on private landhold-ers. Yet by 1949, when the first postwar Bulgarian Communist Party head Georgi Dimitrov (1882–1949) died, the Bulgarian state had control of only 12 percent of arable land, and collectivization was generating resistance from peasants. The 1950 ascendancy of the Stalinist Vulko Chervenkov (1900–1980) to first secre-tary of the Bulgarian Communist Party (BCP), prime minister, and Chairman of the Communist mass organization, called the Fatherland Front brought a major assault on the noncollectivized peasantry. Wielding violence, threats, and vari-ous economic tactics, Chervenkov and company produced, in what would be the last three years of Joseph Stalin's life, the most rapid collectivization anywhere in Eastern Europe. By 1952, when collective farms encompassed 92 percent of all arable land, the Bulgarian Communist Party declared the process complete. Among the Bulgarian Communist Party members who carried out collectiviza-tion was the author of the following document, Kosta Kichukov (1909–), who had joined the BCP in 1929, served jail terms in the 1930s in Macedonia for being a Communist, and fought as a partisan against fascism from 1941 to 1944. On 9 September 1944, he became a member of the Bulgarian Communist Party's district and regional committees in Plovdiv.[7]

Beyond violence and other punitive measures, the collectivization process in Bulgaria (and throughout the Communist orbit more generally) consisted of a number of political practices that the Communist state used to turn peasants into enthusiastic members of the cooperative farms and productive agricultural workers. One was the holding of meetings of the local population, such as the cooperative assembly mentioned in the passage, designed to rally support and prevent defections by explaining the advantages of collectivized agriculture. But peasants, too, had their own political practices that they employed to contest the state's violent transformation of agriculture and of peasant customs. Among these "weapons of the weak"[8]—strategies of everyday resistance—was the decision by peasant women to lie down in front of tractors so the agricultural "revolution" could not begin. In Bulgaria, as in many other peasant societies facing the collectivizing Communists, women were often at the forefront of peasant resistance and even violence.[9]

The other kind of political practice this document speaks to is that of the political memoir or autobiography. Not only are Kichukov's recollections filtered through the passage of time, since he was recounting events that occurred thirty-two years prior, in 1949. Like Chen Peixian's memoir in chapter 3, this document is by no means just the dry facts. It, too, falls into the genre of "public" autobiography, that is, one in which the author desired to leave a certain impression for posterity. Writing himself into the Marxist-Leninist narrative of history, he sought to portray himself as a heroic figure in the building of socialism in Bulgaria, in the overcoming of peasant opposition to collectivization.

"ALONG THE UNBEATEN PATH" [WRITTEN IN 1981]

Seen and experienced before the formation and consolidation of TKZS*

... I was chosen as a member of the regional committee of the BCP and managed the internal-party information. One year later, by the party's decision I was sent to work in the regional cooperative union. There I became the first instructor-organizer of the formation and consolidation of TKZS in the former Asenovgrad region....

As first paid instructor and later, as manager rural division of the regional committee of the party and as acting chairman of N.K.† of O.N.S.‡ responsible for agriculture in the region till 1956, and later, when I accepted the responsibility to work in the first Plovdiv region and surrounding national (people's) council, I had the good fortune to participate in the formation, consolidation and the further development of TKZS.

... I wanted to tell the memories and the events that I saw and experienced. I intend that what I tell will be useful to be known and understood by the young

* The acronym for a cooperative farm.
† *Naroden komitet*: National/people's committee.
‡ Union for National Salvation.

generation that grew up before the conditions of the victory of socialism in our country....

In 1948 there were TKZSs created in the villages of Khristo Milevo, and Popovitsa, and, in 1949, also in the villages [of] Zlatovrah and Izvor....

In a number of places dissatisfaction and unrest arrived before the formation of cooperative blocks* of those farms whose lands fell into cooperative tracts of land and were not maintained....

"My field, my garden, there's nothing in the world I would give to be included in the cooperative block"—cried those, who didn't want to join TKZS. "This is a grab [to seize] ownership of the land," cried, kulaks, the enemies and the opposition.

On this basis...the Soviet military tractor drivers under the direction of the officer...blazed the first tracks of the commune....In the village called Konush, over eighty women laid down in front of the tractors and didn't allow the boundaries to be ploughed up. It was an exciting moment. The ground was blackened with people....The village music was playing revolutionary partisan songs....Others commented among themselves. A third group fell silent. And many cried... [and] judged the action of the women, lying in line on the ground in the tract of land in front of the tractors....Bai† Tocho Gailakiev, the first chairman of TKZS cried: "Comrades, people: this is the village revolution, this is village socialism, for which we have struggled and we have waited to come for so many years! Get up women! I beg of you!...." But none of the women wanted to listen to him. The women lay in front of the tractors and didn't move! The Soviet officer Sasha and the two military tractor drivers Misha and Vanya watched and wondered what to do...they have no idea about power of the local ownership. They watch and can't believe their eyes. They stand in front of the tractors and they wonder what to do!

Then Bai Tocho, furious at the women yelled as long as his voice held. "Women, either get up, or I will order to the tractor drivers to drive over you." But the women lay on the ground in front of the tractors and didn't move!...

"Sasha, Misha, Vanya"—yelled Bai Tocho—"Get on the machines and drive across them! Go ahead....This is revolution!...In a minute the three Soviet tractor drivers were on the machines....The ground began to shake. The music began to play. A powerful cheer split the air....Intimidated, the women instantly jumped straight up and opened a path for the powerful Soviet tractors which immediately began to cleave soil and cut the first furrows of the Bulgarian–Soviet friendship....

On the following day, the joy was darkened by the enemies. During the night the evildoers smashed the door of the office of TKZS and all the declarations, writings and documents of the newly formed farms....

The first years were guided by the work. There was no time for sleep, [or] learning. We didn't have machines, [or] cadres who were prepared. MTS‡ had only fifteen tractors and two trucks at its disposal. The majority of them were worn out....It

---

* A block was a tract of land in the TKZS, or cooperative farm.
† The title of an older, respected man in the village.
‡ MTS: Machine Tractor Station.

became hard to feed and house both workers and productive livestock. This was cleverly used by the enemy. In 1946, B. Bumbarov had come to the countryside—Minister of the opposition of N. Petkov*. He poured gasoline on the fire. The village Konush turned out to be a difficult target in the region. Bumbarov undermined a large segment of the people. They began to support the opposition. In the elections in 1946, over sixty percent of the population voted for the traitorous opposition of N. Petkov.

The government came to the rescue of the TKZS in getting it out of this difficult situation. The Asenovgrad branch of the BZKB[†] granted significant loans. They were used for the people's support and [they] began to purchase fodder for the livestock. Credits were granted also for the building of farm fences, for seeds, chemicals and peat. In general, for the three years, the TKZS had a debt of 18,000,000 Leva[‡] to the BZKB.

This difficult situation was bred from the three-year drought and the devastating hailstorms that fell in 1948, which, I said, was cleverly used by the enemies.... Of 198 households, 156 submitted requests for quitting the collective farm system. There were also many party members in this figure. It also included some members of the party committee. The situation in the neighboring TKZS village Izbeglii wasn't any better. This village, in contrast to the village of Konush, was a fortress of our party at the time of the resistance.... Here, as in Konush, more than sixty percent submitted requests for quitting the collective farm system.

In the regional committee of the party and in the RKS[§], we mulled over what to do. It was decided that I would go to Konush, to stay there for a month or two, more if I had to,... to be strengthened to preserve the collective farm system. I left for the village. I stayed at the home of Dimcho Ivanchev, member of the Party committee, a participant in the resistance from 1941–1944[¶]. Dimcho represented himself with great authority and trust in the village....

His agenda was to surpass Bai Tocho as chairman of agriculture. The rural party committee unanimously welcomed this point of view. It was decided that Dimcho was to be put forward as chairman. The reasons for wanting to get rid of Bai Tocho were that during these three tense years, Bai Tocho had become irritable, became rude with the people, abused, yelled and complained....

---

* Nikola Petkov, the leader of the Agrarians, formed a coalition with the Soviet-supported BCP (Communist Party of Bulgaria). The purpose of this coalition, which was named the Fatherland Front, was to drive out the fascists from Bulgaria during World War II. Petkov was made to endure a sham trial and then was executed, so that Dimitrov could carry out "Sovietization" (on this concept, see the document on Lithuania in chapter 3) under Stalin's direction.

† The acronym for a bank, that is the Bulgarian Agricultural Commercial Bank, or Bulgarksi Zemnodelski Komerchni Bank.

‡ Lev (plural: leva): Bulgarian currency.

§ RKS: Cooperative union for the district. (District here in Bulgarian is raion, which is smaller than another geopolitical term, okolia, which is also translated as "district.")

¶ Reference here is to the partisan resistance movement (both armed and unarmed) to the Nazi occupation of Bulgaria, and to the Axis powers more generally, a resistance movement that was highly sympathetic to Communism and to the USSR in particular.

From this change, Bai Tocho was hit hard, but toward the end of his life he became a believer in the cooperative work of the party. He was not a vengeful guy.... He got sick.... He begged me to tell the comrades [that he wanted] to be buried without a priest, [but] with music. He wished to have played for him the music that he was obligated to play before the boundaries of the first cooperative tract of land were ploughed up. His wish was fulfilled! The whole village mourned the death of Bai Tocho. Everyone came to send him on his final path. Resounding with life, he and the village accomplished yet one more revolution—a revolution in the consciousness of the people—burial without a clergyman [but] with music. For those years, this was, as he himself expressed, a revolution!

We called a general cooperative assembly.... The people unanimously accepted and elected Dimcho as chairman. But even this didn't help us.... Openly in the village bar, in the streets and in the houses, support was being whipped up among the people for quitting the collective farm system....

In this situation we decided to call a general cooperative assembly, at which we would openly speak to the people.... Men, women, old and young had come in large numbers. Everyone knew that the question of who would leave and who would stay in the collective farm system would be decided.

Dimcho opened the assembly and gave me the floor!

I began in a roundabout way.... I spoke of the first apostles of Bulgarian freedom. About Rakovski* and Levski†, about Botev‡ and Karadzha§. I talked about what conditions they were struggling against at the outset: the five centuries of Turkish slavery, as the village lords and *chorbadzhiite*§ and the infidels called them vagabonds, scoundrels and *hayirsizi*". But thanks to them and the hundreds like them, who shed their blood for national freedom, they provoked the intervention of the brother Russians, in the Russo–Turkish war, which brought freedom to our people††.

---

*Georgi Stoykov Rakovski (1821–1867), who was also known by his Greek surname as Georgi Sava Rakovski, was a major figure in nineteenth-century Bulgarian national liberation and in the revolutionary resistance of Bulgarians to Ottoman rule.

†Celebrated as Bulgaria's "Apostle of Freedom," Vasil Levski (1837–1873) was the chief architect of the revolutionary movement to free Bulgaria from Ottoman rule.

‡Hristo (or Khristo) Botev (1848–1876) was a Bulgarian poet and a major figure in the revolutionary movement for Bulgarian liberation from Turkish rule.

§Stefan Karadzha (1840–1868) was another nineteenth-century Bulgarian hero. He was a revolutionary seeking national liberation from Ottoman rule.

§*Chorabadzhiite*: Middle-class village merchant collaborators. This term refers to those Bulgarian local notables who, in Ottoman times, "collaborated" with the Ottomans. Literally, the word means "keeper of the soup."

"This is a Turkish word that literally means "lacking God's grace." More broadly, and in this context, it means rogues or rascals. (It is used in the plural here.)

††As a result of the Russo-Turkish war (1877–1878), the Bulgarian state was reconstructed as the principality of Bulgaria. Romania, Serbia, and Montenegro gained full independence from the Ottoman Empire.

The people were silent and listened with great interest...about the numerous victims, about the first partisans, how the fascists and chorbadzhiite called them. And they shed their blood for the freedom of our people from fascism.

The people listened with attention. This helped me to continue further!...

The people in the room were silent. They waited for what I was about to say. I continued....Only through communal labor, through collectivization of the land, through mechanization, agrotechnology and irrigation, will we be able to lead our collective farm system, and improve the difficult conditions of the rural people in which they now find themselves! Will you think it over yourself? It's no longer possible to make it in this condition, when we are receiving of 80–100 kg of wheat per decare*. With sixty to seventy kg of sunflowers, and with 120–130 kg of corn. What do you say? Our land is rich, but you live poor....

A voice from the audience. "We don't even have water to drink...."—laughter in the room.

"Yes it's like that now, but the national authority will confirm what I said about this condition. We will be energetic and we'll see that not only will you have water to drink but the whole land will be irrigated"—I said.

A voice from the audience: "Oh brother, master Chekalara† has lost it. He doesn't know what he's talking about." General laughter in the room.

I continued further....He who quits the collective farm system will be mistaken. Now the newest history of the countryside is being written....Don't give yourself in to the enemy agitation. Don't quit the collective farm system....

[He was] interrupted by cooperative farm member, Vaklush Iskrov: "Comrades, don't listen to him!...We are still at the beginning and we're drowning ourselves. We're dying! But he is advising us to stay, for us to enter into the sea in order to save ourselves!" Laughter in the room. Everyone clapped for him!...They yelled bravo!

"The salvation is to give us the fields, livestock and equipment. To leave the collective farm system, to swim out of the sea of evil..."—exclaimed Ivan Blagoev, leader of the rural opposition. General applause. They yelled bravo....Then Angel Vasilev came forward to the table and wanted the floor. Without having it, he began: "...Understand (this) people—the TKZS is not to be. While [there is] 'time', [let's] run to save ourselves."

"Bravo Angel, cried out some voices,—only just so. More of this collective farm system I don't need....This is what we want!" This is the desire of all—," began the statement by Georgi Manchev, a member of the cooperative farm.

Without wanting the floor, I stood [up]. Wait, Manchev! Listen everyone! We, established members of TKZS we will stay the course. This is the law of our party and the authority of the Fatherland Front. We will free everyone who decides to

---

* A decare is a metric unit of area that is equal to ten acres, or 0.2471 acres =100 sq. meters = 119.60 sq. yards.

† Chekalara is the author's nickname.

quit the collective farm system. Know this, that nobody will be held onto by force. The three year period has run out. Each person, together with his family, is free to decide. I repeat: we won't hold (on) to anyone but I'm obliged once again to say to you. That each one who quits will be sorry....

Everyone fell silent. The words I said, that nobody would be obliged to be held in the collective farm system, made a very strong impression. Among themselves,

Japanese Election Poster, 16 April 1946. A crowd is gathered outside the Mitsukoshi Department Store in Tokyo to read an election news bulletin of the Japanese Communist Party. The headline says, "What if the Communist Party Governs Japan!"

The fact that the news bulletin was displayed in 1946 is significant. The Japanese Communist Party, which was founded in 1922, was legalized in 1945 when the Americans occupied Japan. The Communist Party gathered votes under Japan's postwar democratic government, but to gain control it would have had to align with another political party, since it was not going to gain a majority of votes on its own. However, to ensure that this did not happen, the American occupying force collaborated with the Japanese to prosecute Communists.

It is ironic that this sign is displayed at Mitsukoshi because this department store, which got its start selling dry goods in the seventeenth century, has long been the crème de la crème of Japanese department stores catering to the well-to-do. Gifts with Mitsukoshi wrapping paper were and still are highly prized. Courtesy of the Library of Congress.

the people began to look at each other. They didn't believe their ears about what they heard.

After that our people began to take the floor and express themselves. . . . They all spoke firmly and clearly that the enemies would not succeed in messing up the collective farm system. The healthy strength of the party and the unity of BZNS*, together with the people who aren't in the party, will nationalize victory. The TKZS will exist and flourish. Each one who quits the farm will be sorry.

The last word at the assembly was taken by Granny Tsena Petkova. Her pronouncement was made toward the women. That made a strong impression and left a mark on the people's consciousness.

"Women—she said,—don't listen to the men! Who has been bearing the work (load) in TKZS, during these three years? . . . We have a greater right to speak and to decide whether there will be a collective farm system or not! And not the men!" "We have set off on a new path. We will go to the end. According to me and many other women, like me—there is no going back. Every beginning is difficult. But not all was bad during these three years in the collective farm system. We alone have verified that communal labor is easier and more enjoyable . . . we stood like sisters and brothers. Should we now split up? What do we have to gain? . . ."

"Their [alternative] arrangement is no better. . . . Although I'm a widow, I am firm in my decision not to quit the collective farm system. . . ."

Women's voices from the room and corridor. "That's right Granny Tsena. Good rebuke, that's the way it is!"

Men's voices: "She told a fairytale because she's a widow! . . ."

After Granny Tsena made her opinion known, the assembly began to shut down. Large numbers of people began to leave in groups. They argued and spoke out in the streets for and against TKZS.

---

* BZNS (Bulgarian Agrarian People's Union, or Balgarski Zemedelski Naroden Sayuz): A peasant political party. It was the successor to the Bulgarian Agrarian National Union (BANU), which was founded at the turn of the twentieth century and remained in power under Alexander Stamboliiski (1918–1923). The BZNS, which had significant rural support, continued to exist throughout the Communist period, though it lacked true power.

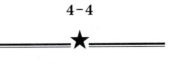

Cuba, 1960s

*Luis M. Garcia (1959–) on Folk and
"Western" Medicine in Castro's Cuba*

When Communists have come to power, people have found themselves torn between the secular, and often stridently anti religious, worldview inherent to Marxist–Leninist ideology, and the religious world(s) in which they had lived prior to revolutions. Communism holds that all religions (and the folk medicine that sometimes went along with them) are a "survival" of the capitalist oppression of the bourgeois era of human history. As socialist forces (economic, cultural, political) gradually suppress those of capitalism, religion and its accompanying cultural practices would slowly, though inevitably, wither away. State efforts in cultural transformation, combined with repression and coercion, would help the process along.

In Marxist–Leninist writings on religion, individuals were imagined as *either* believers *or* nonbelievers. But in practice, many individuals living in Communist polities around the world embraced hybrid mixtures of religion and irreligion, as well as "scientific" and "folk" medicine. To limit ourselves to concepts such as believers, non believers or atheists, and resisters (or dissenters) is to miss the complexity of how people combined and reconciled the seemingly opposed and irreconcilable. Such was the case, as readers will see, in Castro's Cuba during the 1960s and early 1970s.

In Cuba, despite the official insistence on the superiority of modern, "Western" medicine, and the impressive expansion of state medical care, people still turned to folk medicine. That is, they availed themselves of the services of the *curandera* (or healer) as practitioner of rituals essential to Santería, a folk religion closely connected to the Yoruba traditions of West Africa, a religion that enslaved people brought with them and sustained in Cuba, Brazil, and Trinidad.[10] As Luis M. Garcia, who spent his boyhood in Castro's Cuba, implies in the following passage, some Cubans went to both the state polyclinic and to the *curandera*. To avail oneself of the services of a curandera did not necessarily go hand-in-hand with public (or perhaps even private) opposition to Castro or Cuban socialism.

Garcia was born in 1959 in Banes, a small town near the coast in northeastern Cuba. In 1971, when he was twelve years old, his family was allowed to leave

From Luis M. Garcia, *Child of the Revolution: Growing Up in Castro's Cuba* (Crows Nest, Australia: Allen and Unwin, 2006), 55–59. Reprinted by permission of Allen and Unwin.

Cuba. As owners of a small haberdashery, his parents struggled as the state's piecemeal suppression of private enterprise following the revolution caused their business to shrink. Currently a journalist, he lives in Sydney, New South Wales, Australia.

My stomach has been playing up again. I wake up with a stomachache—an *empacho*—feeling queasy, and with what may or may not be a slight fever. In most other places, I now know, you get a stomach-ache, some indigestion and a little nausea and you live with it. Not in Cuba. Here, the first thing your mother does is look you in the eyes, touch your stomach to see if it feels lumpy, check for a fever, and then she takes you to see a *curandera,* a kind of healer who will use her powers to make you feel okay again. There are various *curanderas* around Banes but my mother always goes to the one who lives about half an hour's walk from home because, my mother says, she is the best. I don't know how you compare *curanderas* but if my mother says she is the best, then she is the best.

This *curandera* is not only good at making your stomachaches go away—I hope—but she can do much, much more because she is also a bit of a *santería,* which means she is well above your average healer. I am sure she can communicate with the great gods of Afro-Cuban *santería,* the religion brought over from Africa by the slaves, which means this *curandera* can also help solve marital problems, putting a spell on those who have done something wrong, like husbands who sleep with women who are not their wives. She can take away spells too, and importantly, she can tell mothers how to protect their new babies from *mal de ojo,* the evil eye. But what she does best, or what she does most often, is cure stomachaches. She is an *empacho* expert.

Don't get me wrong. It's not that Cubans don't believe in medicine, or that there is a shortage of doctors. On the contrary, Fidel says Cubans have never been healthier. Thanks to the Revolution, there are now more doctors in Cuba than anywhere else in the entire world, he says, unlike in capitalist countries where there is always a shortage. Still, my mother takes my brother and me to the *curandera* whenever we don't feel well. I don't mind. I know from experience that to see one of those revolutionary doctors Fidel is talking about you have to go to the polyclinic and then queue for hours until one of the doctors is free to see you. On the other hand, I know that when you go to see the *curandera,* you don't have to wait. She is waiting for you.

Now, as my mother and I walk to see the *curandera,* I tell her that my *empacho* appears to be getting better. I feel fine now, I say, but she isn't listening—we are going to see the *curandera* regardless, whether Fidel approves or not. We haven't come all this way for nothing, my mother says. The house where the *curandera* lives is what Cubans would call *humilde pero honrada.* Humble but proud. And sure enough, as we approach the house, there she is, waiting for us. She is standing just inside the doorway, a huge woman with caramel-coloured skin who seems to be, to my eyes at least, really old. At least forty, I think, as she welcomes us with a wide smile and an apology that she cannot offer my mother *un cafecito* because, she says to my mother with knowing eyes, her ration has run out....

This is not the first time I have been in here and it won't be the last, and every time it feels kind of strange. It's too dark, but somehow very peaceful at the same time. Inside the *humilde pero honrada* house time seems to stand still.... And there at the back, as I knew it would be, I can see up on the wall the small altar that this *curandera*, like all *curanderas*, has set up with a foot-high plaster statue of San Lazaro, the *santería* saint that is supposed to heal physical as well as spiritual pain. He looks so skinny you can see his rib cage, and he has bandages on his body and head, open wounds on his side; he supports himself on crutches of some sort, looking in absolute pain but resigned to a life of martyrdom. Next to him is his faithful dog, a skinny mongrel that stands right beside his leg looking up at the totally exhausted face of San Lazaro while licking one of the wounds. It's scary and I suspect I am going to have a nightmare tonight that involves San Lazaro and his mongrel.

On the altar just in front of the statue of San Lazaro there are a couple of lit candles giving out a warm glow, and next to them I can see a small glass which should have some rum in it, a couple of medium sized cigars whose aroma I can smell even from here, and a handful of bananas, stark yellow but quickly turning black.

And then, on the wall just behind the San Lazaro altar, there is a different kind of altar: it's a picture of Fidel wearing his trademark military cap and staring into space, as if challenging the Americans to come and get him, which is after all what he is always doing whenever he is on television or the radio. It's the type of picture you find in almost every house in Cuba, with an inscription underneath that says, *Fidel—esta es tu casa.* Fidel, this is your house. I don't need to tell you that there is no picture of Fidel in our house, and no promise that our house is his either.

By now my mother has finished gossiping with the *curandera*, who comes over to me and asks me to lie down on my back on a kind of canvas folding bed by one of the windows. She then asks me to take my shirt and singlet off and to lower my pants a little, so she can feel my stomach. I do as I am told, thinking that the one thing you must never do is disobey a *curandera*—unless you want to end up like San Lazaro, with wounds and a dog that keeps licking them. Her hands are leathery and I can feel the roughness of her skin as she moves them across and up and down my stomach, all the while mumbling something to my mother that I cannot understand. Truth is, I don't want to know what she is saying.

I look at the San Lazaro altar and at the Fidel photograph high up on the wall and think about something I heard one of my uncles say: that the Revolution doesn't have any time for *curanderas* and *santerías*. My uncle should know, of course, because he is a big shot in the local Communist Party. He says *curanderas* and *santerías* are a leftover from the bad old days, from the days of capitalism and exploitation. Just like Catholicism, *santería* is meant to keep the poor in their place. It will take time, my uncle says, but the Revolution will prove those *santerías* wrong. My mother always listens politely to my uncle because he is so much more educated than she is and because he is important, but when it comes to *curanderas* she ignores him. She is still doing what a lot of other Cubans do—without making a fuss, she visits the *curandera* whenever it's required.

That is why we are inside the house of the *curandera*, who is now feeling my stomach. I can see she is almost done because she goes out and returns with a bunch of *yerba buena,* the Cuban herb used to ward off evil spirits. She is gently moving the bunch across my stomach and then in the air, and as she does, I can smell the pungent aroma of the herbs,[11] and it's almost as if she has gone into a trance, her eyes closed, her smile gone, looking mighty serious as she mumbles something I can't make out.[12] She then raises the herbs into the air one last time, waves them around vigorously, sets them aside and opens her eyes again....

As we walk out of the house I can still smell the *yerba buena* on me but my stomachache is gone and I am not nauseous any more. I tell my mother, who smiles at me knowingly. Then she sends me to school.

4–5

Czechoslovakia, 1968

*Students Explain to Workers and Farmers Why They
Are on Strike, and Why Their Strike Is "Socialist"*

I n Czechoslovakia, the bold political reform program embraced by the Communist Party in 1968 gave people the opportunity to decide what socialism did and did not mean to them. The roots of the "Prague Spring" in internal politics went back at least half a decade and had been laid by Soviet leader Nikita Khrushchev's criticisms of Stalin at Congresses of the CPSU in 1956 and 1961. But it was the appointment, in early 1968, of the Slovak Alexander Dubček

From 1968, 18. listopadu. Praha—Otevrený dopis delníkum a rolníkum v nemž stávkujících studenti vysvetlují smysl a cíl sve akce. (18 November 1968. Prague—Open letter to the workers and peasants in which the striking students explain the purpose and goal of their actions. In Jindrich Pecka and Vilém Precan, eds., *Promeny pražského jara 1968–1969: Sborník studií a dokumentu o nekapitulantských postojích v ceskoslovenské spolecnosti,* (*Transformations of the Prague Spring 1968–1969: Collection of Studies and Documents Concerning the Defiant Stance in Czechoslovak Society*), eds. Jindrich Pecka and Vilém Precan (Brno: Nakladatelství Doplnek, 1993), 259–262. Reprinted by permission of the Institute for Contemporary History, Academy of Sciences of the Czech Republic. Translated and partially annotated by Scott Brown.

as leader of the Communist Party of Czechoslovakia that broke down the barriers preventing reform. Debate percolated throughout the Party at all levels.

A milestone was the reformist document, the Action Program of the Communist Party of Czechoslovakia, published in 1968. The reformist Communist leaders who drafted it were, to the alarm of other East European Communist leaders such as Walter Ulbricht and Wladyslaw Gomulka, following popular sentiment in their articulation of reform. Though it neither advocated political pluralism nor questioned the "leading role" of the Communist Party, the document sent shockwaves through East European Communism with its departure from norms of then-orthodox Communism: the rejection of party organs' monopoly on power, the critique of political slavishness in the preceding decades, the bureaucratization of socialism, the violation of the law and curtailment of political and civil liberties, and the call for an independent judiciary and legislative oversight of the Ministry of the Interior. Economic liberalization was also on the table.

As popular involvement in political reform outstripped the initial boundaries set by the Action Program, and radical elements grew more vocal in subsequent months, Czechoslovakia and the Warsaw Pact allies engaged in negotiations to halt the pace of reform. With the negotiations failing, the Soviet Union and its Warsaw Pact allies invaded Czechoslovakia on 21 August 1968. There was little military resistance. With Dubček gone and replaced by the realist Gustáv Husák, Czechoslovak political life was, to use then-current Soviet language, "normalized." The reversal of Dubček's reforms brought profound disillusionment to many in the Party and in society.

"Normalization" could not, however, stop Communist citizens (including Party members) from discussing and debating what socialism really meant. From the regime's perspective, this might have been "dissent," or "anti-socialist" attitudes and actions. But for people such as the students who wrote the following letter in which they explained why they went on strike, this was not "dissent." Rather, they saw themselves as articulating *their* vision of socialism. As they put it, "this is how we understand socialism."

How, in fact, *did* they understand socialism? In the letter that follows, the striking students drew a clear boundary between what socialism was and was not—in its goals, in general political practices, and in the specific context of Czechoslovakia after the Prague Spring and Soviet crackdown. Socialism was not bureaucrats acting untransparently, in slavish loyalty to Moscow, to advance their own careers. Socialism was not self-censorship. Socialism was not promising the continuation of liberal reforms and reneging on that promise. Socialism was not pretending that the Soviet invasion had not violated Czechoslovak sovereignty when, in fact, it had. Socialism was the practice of politics to help people "achieve a happy, materially and spiritually rich life in peace." It was transparency in state and Party operations and the eradication of self-censorship in those institutions. It was speaking truth to power about the disjunction between assertions about political life and what was really happening. For these students, in Czechoslovakia after the Soviet invasion, socialism also meant going on strike.

Prague, 18 November 1968—An open letter to workers and farmers in which striking students explain the meaning and goal of their action.

Dear comrade workers and farmers,

As a result of incomplete and very limited information, our news media have been disseminating various explanations of the motives and intent of the strike of Prague university students. Therefore, we, the striking students, appeal to you with an open letter in which we want to explain the evolution and the real reason of our strike.

The strike was called under the influence of the situation that has arisen in our political life at present. The strike has a purely local character and is occurring right in the rooms of our universities. It is not destructive in nature and it will not harm the quality of our continued studies. Our teachers are also sympathetic to the strike....

What led us to decide to call a strike? Like the overwhelming majority of our workers, we are deeply dissatisfied that the so-called current reality continues to limit our free socialist and democratic life, which we entered after January* and which was clearly expressed by the KSČ Action Program†. We learned to judge politics not only according to words, resolutions, proclamations, promises, etc., but according to the deeds and actions of our representatives, of government or party organs, of fraternal parties or the governments of friendly countries. Therefore, we still do not regard it as a victory of truth, of democratic and humane socialism, or as a victory of progressive, high-principled and honorable Communists, when, for example, the concluding resolution of the ÚV KSČ plenary session includes statements that raise hopes that the democratic post-January development will continue, that there will not be a return to pre-January conditions‡, etc., when on the other hand, in terms of concrete acts, it does not respect, for example, the spontaneous desire and wish of our people that leading

* At the beginning of January 1968, the KSČ (Komunistická strana Československa, or Communist Party of Czechoslovakia) Central Committee removed Antonín Novotný as first secretary and replaced him with Alexander Dubček, who had been the first secretary of the Communist Party of Slovakia since 1963. Novotný's ouster at the January plenum removed an important obstacle to liberalization and made "January" synonymous in popular discourse with the beginning of the reform movement known as the Prague Spring.

† In April 1968, the KSČ published its Action Program, an ambitious program of reform that promised elements of political pluralism.

‡ This is a reference to the ÚV KSČ November plenum (14–17 November 1968), which raised hopes for maintaining the principles of the Prague Spring. However, the way in which the plenum distanced itself from the "negative elements of post-January politics" produced a foreboding that such hopes were illusory. Almost exactly the same phrasing can also be found in the Proclamation of the Action Committee of České Budějovice Colleges of 21 November, which refers to the results of the November plenum with the description "as if they raise hopes that the democratic post-January development will continue...."

positions are not held by people who lost the trust of the people, whether
for reasons of politics or expertise, of character flaws or biological shortcomings. We all know quite well who these unqualified functionaries are
at the top and the bottom. We do not want to abuse, to do wrong to anyone, we only want to remind them that subjective conclusions or the attitudes of individuals are not decisive, only the objective effect of their deeds
and actions. We judge the quality of the work of leading functionaries and
organs according to this perspective.

The Action Program is an exceptional document that we accepted with
satisfaction. We accepted the Moscow Protocol and the document about the
temporary stationing of foreign armies on our territory as a "hard reality" for
a small nation in the middle of Europe in the divided world of the present*.
But in no case do we want to reach the point where we are described with
the words sovereignty and independence, while in reality there is systematic
external pressure on us....

In no case do we want to resign ourselves to a situation where, for example, the necessity of politics open to the people is acknowledged in words, yet
in reality there is less and less information about the activity and problems
of leading representatives and organs, that even the highest representatives
of our party and state, who have the complete and wholehearted support of
our people, are afraid to speak openly about their own problems and concerns in front of their own people.... We want to live freely, to work peacefully, to have the certainty of our own future, and we want to have it in our
own hands.... The form of our protest, the strike, should draw attention to
the fact that we are able to express our own fears about the subsequent fate
of our country in a dignified way and in accord with the traditions of our
working people, that we refuse to promote our attitudes and opinions through
epithets, hysterical assaults, threats, violent acts or incantations of "loyalty to
the ideas of Marxism–Leninism, proletarian internationalism, loyalty to the
Soviet Union and the international workers movement, loyalty to the people, to our party," etc., just as several people we call Jodases† are doing. These

---

* After the Warsaw Pact invasion of Czechoslovakia began on the night of 20–21 August 1968,
most of the Czechoslovak political leadership was brought to Moscow for tense and often hostile
negotiations that lasted from 23 to 26 August and ended with the signing of the Moscow Protocol. The
text of the protocol included, among other clauses, pledges to protect socialism in Czechoslovakia,
to denounce as illegal the 14th KSČ Congress that had convened in a factory in Prague in the wake of
the invasion, and to rein in the Czechoslovak media. In September 1968, continued discussions led to
the signing of an agreement on the "temporary stationing" of the Warsaw Pact allies on Czechoslovak
territory. Soviet troops remained stationed in Czechoslovakia until 1991.

† This name for the pro-Soviet group, overwhelmingly made up of old KSČ members, was
derived from its spokesman, Josef Jodas (1903–1970), who, in the interwar period, worked for the
Party in proletarian physical education and later held lower Party posts and worked at Czechoslovak
Television. In 1968 he stood definitively against the democratizing spirit of the Prague Spring and in
the post-August period he identified with the military invasion of the Warsaw Pact armies under the
slogan of "proletarian internationalism."

people of powerful words, who assume that the force of weapons and outside pressure stands behind us, must not influence the acts of our representatives and our organs. We appeal, therefore, to the representatives of our party and our state:

"Do not try to convince us that, for example, the news media gave space to antisocialist forces when we all know the truth. Do not try to justify real deeds that are in conflict with the post-January path with the argument that they were forced on you. Our working people are courageous, wise and persistent. They will not panic, they will not give up, they long for peace and friendship with all nations, they have humane goals, they long for justice, democratic socialism, socialism with a human face, they detest coercion and injustice, humiliation, oppression, they love the truth and fair play. Remain loyal to these values of our people, you are a part of them. Until the time comes when you are no longer able to work in your positions, you will start on a democratic path, in front of the eyes of the whole nation, you will create an opportunity for your successors, whom the people will choose according to intellect and sensibility. Do not let cabinet positions at the head of our party and state go to people who will serve foreign powers, who will be slaves to their own ambitions and their own foolishness, to their desire for power and to their own crudely distorted ideas of socialism*."

Dear friends in the factories, in the villages,

This is the true meaning of our strike, which we expressed at its commencement and in ten concrete points. This is the true meaning of the strike of us youth, we who are fighting for our own future. We have our whole lives ahead of us, we want to live, we do not want to be humiliated. We want to create new values, in our own studies now and in our own work later in factories and in research institutes, that will help our people to achieve a happy, materially and spiritually rich life in peace. This is how we understand socialism.

We urge you, inform all the workers in your own firm about our stance. In Prague on the 18th day of November 1968.

The council of striking students of the mechanical college of ČVUT†,

the council of striking students of the electrotechnical college of ČVUT,

the plenum of the all-Prague action committee of university students.

Teachers and employees of ČVUT in Prague expressed agreement with meaning and content at the college ROH‡ meeting held on this day....

---

   * According to the testimony of witnesses, this passage was intended as a specific example of resolutions that workers themselves should draft. However, its phrasing was too cerebral. Hence, workers did not adopt it.

   † ČVUT: České vysoké učení technické (Czech Technical University).

   ‡ ROH: Revoluční odborové hnutí (Revolutionary Union Movement).

Shaming a "capitalist roader" during Mao's Cultural Revolution. Date stamped on verso:
15 February 1967. Central to Mao's Cultural Revolution (1966–1976) were mass criticism
sessions with youth as the bearers of the revolutionary message. Here, in an act of public
shaming, youth (and others) have placed a dunce cap on the individual who is the object
of mass criticism. Using a dunce cap to shame "capitalist roaders" was a common practice
during the Cultural Revolution. (The Chinese writing on the dunce cap says, in fact,
"capitalist roader," and gives his name, which is not completely legible. To the right, on the
building, is "Long live the Communist Party of China.") But in so doing, Cultural Revolution
activists were following in the footsteps of revolutionary peasants in the 1920s. They had
put tall, pointed hats on gentry oppressors and forced them to march through the streets.
This practice was not only designed to shame the oppressors but to engineer specific
emotions, such as anger and solidarity, among the revolutionaries—whether those of the
1920s or of the Cultural Revolution.

For Communist revolutionaries, whether in China or elsewhere, emotions were a key
weapon of mass mobilization. Communist revolutionaries sought not just to harness pre-
existing emotions, such as the anger workers (and other oppressed laborers) were assumed
to feel toward their capitalist oppressors (the "bourgeoisie"). They also employed tactics,
such as the one depicted here, that were designed to *produce* specific emotions in projects
of social engineering on a psychological level. As China scholar Elizabeth J. Perry has shown,
Chinese Communists, unlike their Guomindang (Nationalist) competitors, gave significant
attention to such "emotion work." In fact, there is evidence to suggest this "emotion
work" was a decisive factor—along with, of course, ideology, organization, and social
structure—in the Communists' revolutionary victory. See her article, "Moving the Masses:
Emotion Work in the Chinese Revolution," *Mobilization: An International Quarterly* 7, no. 2
(2002): 111–128. Photo courtesy of the Library of Congress.

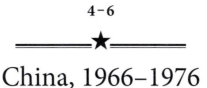

China, 1966–1976

Contesting the Official Meaning of China's Cultural Revolution: Rae Yang (1950–)

Rae Yang, the author of the following passage, was, in a sense, a "child" of China's Cultural Revolution, Mao's multi faceted mobilization campaign (1966–1976) designed to take Chinese culture from "feudalism" or "capitalism" to "socialism." The Cultural Revolution began in 1966, when she was sixteen years old. Prior to that, she had led a sheltered life. She was a daughter of Chinese diplomats stationed in Switzerland. In 1963, she began attending an elite school, Beijing 101 Middle School.

Despite her privileged upbringing, she took to heart the official norms of the Cultural Revolution—especially its egalitarianism and its agenda of bridging the divide between city and countryside. And so, in 1968, she voluntarily left Beijing for China's Great Northern Wilderness. She became one of Mao's Red Guards, the revolutionary storm troopers (initially Beijing high school students, but later professionals from the cities as well) who led the assault on the bourgeois enemy: school teachers, capitalist roaders, (senior to middle-level Communist cadres), followers of "capitalist roaders" such as technical and other professionals, as well as those with ties to foreign countries and/or to the pre-1949 Nationalist (Guomindang) government. Wearing the badge of the Red Guards—a red armband—she joined in their revolutionary crusade to remake everyday life.

But her belief in the official norms and values of the Cultural Revolution turned out to have its limits. In a visit back to Beijing in 1971, her certainty that the Cultural Revolution would remake society in an egalitarian way crashed on the rocks of her observations that army representatives had abused their power by moving their own families into vacated residences (such as that of her parents). The suffering of her grandmother, forced to live in a small, cold, and windowless room in her former home, personified for her the Cultural Revolution's human cost.

The following passage affords readers a sense of her disillusionment with the Cultural Revolution. Yet the question is how to interpret, or conceptualize, that disillusionment. Arguably, it is best thought of as an example of what has

From Rae Yang, *Spider Eaters: A Memoir* (Berkeley: University of California Press, 1997), 262–267. Reprinted by permission of the University of California Press.

been called "personal Bolshevism" (or, moving beyond the Soviet context, "personal Communism"): that is, how people took elements of the "ruling ideology" and redirected and refashioned them.[13] The fundamental ideological principle on which the Cultural Revolution was based was the Marxist-Leninist-Maoist one of "class struggle" between the bourgeoisie and the proletariat, a concept that Yang did not, at the time, question. But she has transformed its meaning from that of a struggle between, as Mao insisted, "capitalists and workers," to one between "Communist Party officials and the ordinary Chinese people."

My favorite activity was our daily walk at dusk. After supper we usually walked on the remains of an ancient city wall, which might date back to the Three Kingdoms period (AD 210–280). At that time Ji was the stronghold of Yuan Shao, the most powerful warlord in China. The city wall must have been tall and thick, the moat around it deep and formidable. But the warlord was defeated by his opponent Cao Cao and died spitting blood. Since then, the city wall had fallen into ruin and the moat was flattened. Now on both sides of the wall winter wheat grew, thin and short because of constant drought.

This place, my parents discovered, was ideal for people to talk. At home they did not dare to. Even with windows closed and doors shut, the walls had ears. That is, they thought the neighbors were eavesdropping on them. Some became my parents' enemies at the beginning of the Cultural Revolution. Espionage was these people's specialty anyway. World-class espionage.

But my parents were no fools. Thus they discovered the city wall, on which they could say things as loud as they liked.... The moment I got there, I poured out what had been on my mind these couple of years.

"You know what? The campaign of educated youths going to the countryside has become a tremendous waste and unprecedented human tragedy! Nevertheless I did learn a few things from it, things the leaders may not have anticipated. For example, now I agree with Chairman Mao that class struggle continues to exist in China under socialist conditions—but not between landlords and poor peasants or capitalists and workers. It goes on between Communist Party officials and the ordinary Chinese people! The officials at all levels abuse their power. The corrupt ones as well as those who are not so corrupt yet. As for the Party, it has been blocking information and creating lies. By doing so, it made us into idiots and clowns! But now I can see it in its true light and I have lost faith in it! Over the years it has been purging those who are honest, intelligent, and dare take responsibility. Those who survive the incessant inner struggles are the mediocre and cowardly ones. As a result, you see nowadays more and more officials curry favors with their superiors and care nothing about the people! They are all hypocrites!..."

"Stop!" Mother said under her breath. "Your thoughts are very dangerous! How come you talk like a counterrevolutionary?"

I shut up. I had anticipated that my parents would be upset or furious. After all, they were both Communist Party members for many years. I wasn't trying to provoke them though. I just wanted to let them know what my reeducation in the countryside had taught me.

Father, on the other hand, remained calm and silent. A trace of smile in his eyes? That could be just my imagination. It was not until several days later when Father and I walked by ourselves on the city wall that he told me he agreed with much of what I had said the other day. In fact, even before 1949 in the liberated areas the Party leaders had already begun to abuse their power and the struggle within the Party was ruthless. If the problem then was like cancer incubating in the body of the Party, now the disease was full-blown....

"So you knew how false and selfish some of the leaders were! You knew it even in the forties, Father! Yet you kept telling me the Party was always right and I must do whatever it asked me to do! Why? Why didn't you tell me what you knew? Instead you let me grope in the dark, bump into walls, be scared to death, and make terrible, terrible mistakes!"

"Because I did not want you to get into trouble! Do you know what the famous artist Zheng Banqiao once said? 'It is a blessing to be dull-witted.' This is especially true today! On the other hand, of course, I did not want you to get me into trouble either. If I had told you I was disillusioned about this revolution a long time ago, and I thought with all our good intentions, relentless efforts, and tremendous sacrifice we only managed to build a gigantic prison as strong as cast-iron, and also I felt maybe I made a mistake by joining the revolution, because the proletarian dictatorship was worse than the corrupt rule of the Nationalist government.... If I had said all this to you back in the sixties when you were a fanatic Red Guard, how would you have responded? Would you have reported me and condemned me? Or if you didn't, on the other hand, how would you have felt? I did not want to put you into such a dilemma!"

He was right. I had to admit it. In 1967, without his confession, my mind was already in a turmoil. If he had told me all this, I might have become another Zhang. In fact, even in 1973 there were things Father and I could talk about, but we would not discuss them in front of Mother. Mother belonged to a generation that came of age in the fifties. For many of them, the Nationalist Party was corrupt to the core and the Communist Party was the savior of China. Many of them were the so-called Three-Door Cadres—they went from home door to school door, then to the doors of government organizations. Thanks to their privileged positions and limited scope, the harsh reality in China did not seem to strike them as hard. Or maybe they thought and felt that way because of fear, which had been driven home by the anti-Rightist campaign and the Cultural Revolution. Thus they not only obeyed authority, they identified themselves with it. There was a big generation gap between them and us.

Between Father and me, for some reason, there was no generation gap. So we could talk rather freely. Sometimes the subjects grew quite personal. Once I was shocked to hear Father say that marrying Mother was a big mistake he made. He realized this soon after he made the proposal. His personality and Mother's were incompatible. But he married her anyway, out of a sense of honor and despair, thinking he'd never be able to find the woman of his dreams. Afterwards, he said, he was quite unhappy and wanted to have a divorce. But he decided against it, mainly for the sake of us. It was also for Mother, he said, for he knew she loved him still and did not want a divorce. In China, divorce always did more harm to women than men....

So I was the result of a mistake Father had made many years ago. Then I became the shackle that held him in a loveless marriage. No wonder he used to get mad at me, beat me with a ruler on the palm, say I was a bad girl.... After thirteen years, he finally apologized and I forgave him. My childhood wasn't so bad after all. Whether my parents loved each other or not, they both loved us. Then there was my dear old Aunty! She was my safe haven when a storm hit home. And there was Nainai too. What else could I ask?

So after I came back from the Great Northern Wilderness, I discovered that Father was quite different from what I had imagined. Our relationship changed. In the past five years I had grown up and Father realized this. So he began to treat me as an adult who was his equal. We became good friends. This was very rare in China. I enjoyed our talk in the evenings, on that dilapidated city wall. Watching the setting sun, I could feel his unspeakable loneliness in my own heart. I realized that he too was vulnerable, while in the past his prestige and authority had oppressed me.

NOTES

1. Quote from Halfin, *Red Autobiographies*, 4. My analytical points on the Bolshevik autobiography and politics on the self draw upon this study and his other work.
2. Kate Weigand, *Red Feminism: American Communism and the Making of Women's Liberation* (Baltimore, MD: Johns Hopkins University Press, 2002), 91. By contrast, Weigand asserts, there is no evidence to suggest that the CPUSA's campaign against "male chauvinism," which was also underway in the late 1940s and early 1950s, resulted in expulsion from the Party. On the CPUSA's campaign against "white chauvinism," see also Amy E. Carreiro, "The 'Art and Protest' in Ralph Ellison's Anticommunist Rhetoric," *Western Journal of Black Studies* 30, no. 1 (2006): 46–53; James A. Miller, Susan D. Pennybacker, and Eve Rosenhaft, "Mother Ada Wright and the International Campaign to Free the Scottsboro Boys," *American Historical Review* 106, no. 2 (2001): 387–430; Gerald Zahavi, "The 'Trial' of Lee Benson: Communism, White Chauvinism, and the Foundation of the 'New Political History' in the United States," *History and Theory* 42, no. 3 (2003): 332–362; Jane Mansbridge and Katherine Flaster, "The Cultural Politics of Everyday Discourse: The Case of 'Male Chauvinist,'" *Critical Sociology* 33, no. 4 (2007): 627–660; for primary documents, see Philip S. Foner and Herbert Shapiro, eds., *American Communism and Black Americans: A Documentary History, 1930–1934* (Philadelphia: Temple University Press, 1991).
3. A point made in Mark I. Solomon, *The Cry Was Unity: Communists and African Americans, 1917–1736* (Jackson: University Press of Mississippi, 1998), 141.
4. This is emphasized by Mark I. Solomon, ibid., 137.

5. This summary draws upon Karl Eugen Wädekin and Everett M. Jacobs, *Agrarian Policies in Communist Europe: A Critical Introduction* (Lanham, MD: Rowman and Littlefield, 1982), 35, 63–64.
6. In the TKZS, a share of the profits was guaranteed to members. In theory, membership was voluntary.
7. Biography at beginning of "Along the Unbeaten Path," the excerpt that begins on 135.
8. James Scott, *Weapons of the Weak: Everyday Forms of Peasant Resistance* (New Haven, CT: Yale University Press, 1985).
9. As Lynne Viola has noted, in the Soviet case this was because women (and men) knew that they were less likely to be punished according to Soviet law. See her "*Bab'i bunty*: Peasant Women's Protests During Collectivization," *Russian Review* 45, no. 1 (1986): 23–42. Hence, men were content to let women "do the talking" (as a peasant man put it in Soviet Russia during the forced collectivization of the late 1920s and early 1930s)—and take physical risks.
10. K. Wirtz, "Enregistered Memory and Afro-Cuban Historicity in Santería's Ritual Speech," *Language and Communication* 27, no. 3 (2007): 247–248. Cuban Santería exemplified a fusion of the orisha worship practices of the Yorubas of southwestern Nigeria with "Spanish folk Catholic traditions of hagiolotry," or the veneration of persons. George Brandon, "The Uses of Plants in Healing in an Afro-Cuban Religion, Santería," *Journal of Black Studies* 22, no. 1 (1991): 55–57. Quote at 55.
11. The use of plants as a medicinal species was an important element of Afro-Cuban Santería. See Brandon, "The Uses of Plants."
12. In Cuban Santería, practitioners "can temporally inflect their ritual speech by deploying two marked registers that contrast with standard Cuban Spanish and each other." The registers are called "Lucumi" and "Bozal." They carry associations with "mythic character-types" and with certain domains of ritual practice. By drawing upon the chronotypes of all three registers, practitioners sustain the "power of ancestors and African deities." For more, see Wirtz, "Enregistered Memory."
13. Jochen Hellbeck, "Fashioning the Stalinist Soul: The Diary of Stepan Podlubnyi," in Sheila Fitzpatrick, ed., *Stalinism: New Directions* (New York: Routledge, 1999), 98.

CHAPTER 5

———————★———————

Contesting the Meaning of State Violence and Repression

The violence of Communist polities throughout the world is undeniable.[1] It took many forms. There was headline-grabbing suppression of strikes, political reforms, and protests. Horrific cases include the deadly repression of the strikes throughout East Germany in June 1953, the invasion of Czechoslovakia by the USSR and its Warsaw Pact allies in 1968, and the massacre of peaceful protesters on Beijing's Tiananmen Square in June 1989. There was the state violence against the revolution's own during Stalin's Great Purges of 1936–1938, the arrests, trials, and executions of alleged "bourgeois nationalists" in the Eastern European Communist parties during the 1950s, and the Chinese Cultural Revolution of 1966–1976. There was the everyday violence of Communist polities, the kind of violence that did not make newspaper headlines around the world yet must not be forgotten: detention and humiliating questioning for seemingly innocuous behavior, the rifling through of apartments and personal property, intimidation (including strip searches) at border crossings. It is chilling to take stock of the state violence that Communist regimes committed against their citizens (as well as, of course, political elites, including those in Communist parties themselves) in the name of *"defending"* the revolution, *protecting* it from "counterrevolution," "*eliminating impurities*" in socialist society, and so forth. Paradoxically, Communist polities often justified their violence, and the millions and millions of deaths and untold psychological suffering it brought, as a necessary measure for the creation of a world in which there would *be* no violence.

The unrelenting violence of Communist states has generated a simple, yet intractable, question: why? How can we explain the number of victims and the forms that state violence took? Who or what was to blame: Marxist-Leninist (or Marxist-Leninist-Maoist) ideology, circumstances such as the objective threat of counterrevolution, or the paranoia (and perhaps psychological imbalance) of

156

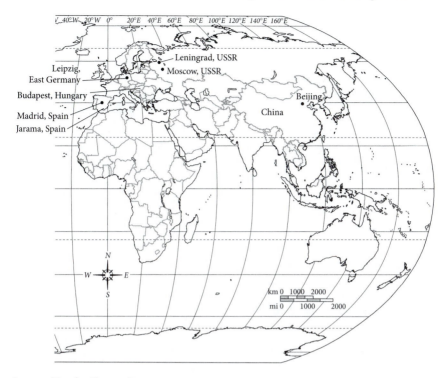

Locator Map for Chapter 5

Communist leaders? Or all of the above? Countless scholarly articles have been written on such questions, and heart-wrenching memoirs of survivors (and sometimes even former perpetrators) of the violence address them, too. But far less attention has been given to other, and no less important, questions: How did Communist citizens perceive and interpret political violence? How did those perceptions and interpretations change over the life span of Communist polities? What consequences did such perceptions and interpretations have?

No collection of documents can do justice to these questions. They are, moreover, issues to which scholars need to devote serious research. But the selection of texts that follows—excerpts from a diary of a Soviet teenager coming to grips with political violence in Stalin's Russia, the diary of an American volunteer with Communist sympathies fighting against Franco's fascism in a Spain riven by civil war, a diary kept by a student who witnessed the Soviet suppression of the Hungarian Revolution in 1956, writings about the deadly violence on China's Tiananmen Square in 1989, and the text of one of the Fall 1989 "Peace Prayers" held in Leipzig during the 1989 Revolution (or *Wende*)—are designed to allow readers to explore these questions, and, hopefully, generate others of their own.

Poland's Solidarity indicts the Polish government for failing to punish victims of state violence in March 1981 in Bydgoszcz. The "Bydgoszcz Crisis," as it came to be called, marked the first time that the Polish government used violence against Solidarity activists. On 19 March 1981, Polish Security Service (SB) officers brutally assaulted two Solidarity leaders and a member of the farmers' union. The violence occurred as the Security Service forces tried to end an occupation strike of a local council building in Bydgoszcz.

Without delay, Poland began to contest the meaning of the violence, with the government and Solidarity activists, of course, taking opposing positions. On 21 March 1981, General Jaruzelski, the head of the Polish government, appointed a committee charged with investigating what happened in Bydgoszcz. The next day—on 22 March 1981—the Politburo of the Polish United Workers' Party claimed that Solidarity itself had created this provocation and had caused "mass neurosis." As this image suggests, Solidarity rejected these claims and accused the government of unjustified violence (deliberate provocation, in fact), as well as failing to punish the perpetrators of the violence; yet there

(*Continued*)

(*Continued*)

was division among Solidarity's leaders about how to respond to the regime's violence. The violence also resulted in strikes that were not under the control of Solidarity's leaders.

As tension soared, both Solidarity and the Catholic Church counseled moderation, helping to avert a national response of protest. Had one occurred, it almost surely would have been the target of violent repression by Security Service forces. Such an action had, by the end of 1980, been finalized by the Polish government and presented to Moscow; it had been in the works since the 1976 workers' uprisings in Radom and Ursus. Though this did not come to pass, the government did, in the wake of the Bydgoszcz Crisis, step up its preparations for future repression. Martial law was declared by Jaruzelski on 13 December 1981.   Quote is from Andrzej Paczkowski and Malcolm Byrne, eds., *From Solidarity to Martial Law: The Polish Crisis of 1980–1981: A Documentary History* (Budapest: Central European University Press, 2008), xxxvii. Photo courtesy of the Hoover Institution on War, Revolution, and Peace, Stanford University.

USSR

A Soviet Teenager (Nina Sergeevna Lugovskaya, 1918–1993) Grapples with the Meaning of Political Violence in 1934 in Stalinist Russia

Nina Lugovskaya was thirteen years old when, in 1934, she wrote the excerpts from the diary reproduced next. Her concerns were, in some ways, those of teenagers the world over: her crushes, her physical attractiveness, her relationship with her family. But her teen years were also specifically Soviet, shaped by the dramatic political events of the early Stalin years.

One such dramatic event was the murder, on 1 December 1934, of Sergei Kirov, Leningrad Party boss, in Leningrad Party headquarters (Smolny), by Leonid Nikolaev, a former member of the Communist Party. (Whether Stalin was behind Kirov's murder is still keenly debated, though recent evidence casts doubt that he was.[2]) The assassination brought a swift and powerful response from Stalin and the Party leadership. Using the event as pretext for expanding the state's powers, Stalin had a decree passed the next day that established the legal and judicial framework of summary justice for "terroristic organizations or acts." Twenty days after Kirov's death, the Stalinist state came up with its official line (and indictment): Kirov's murder had been perpetrated by a "Leningrad opposition center" connected with major Party leaders such as Grigory Zinoviev and Lev Kamenev, in turn organized from abroad by Leon Trotsky.[3] Soviet people like Lugovskaya, too, had to come to terms with the murder, deciding whether they agreed with the Party's line on who did it, and why.

Her diary reveals her to have been as exercised about the Kirov murder—and the meaning of Soviet state violence in general—as about Evgeny, the object of her affection. The fundamental issue that she was working through was the meaning of socialism itself: Could the Soviet state, given its violence, be considered "socialist"? Lugovskaya's answer was a resounding "no." But her response should hardly be considered representative. As other diaries now made available by the (partial) opening of Soviet archives reveal, other Soviet citizens, whatever their age, would have condemned her harsh critique of the Stalinist state and its repressive violence.

From Nina Lugovskaya, *The Diary of a Soviet Schoolgirl, 1932–1937* (Moscow: Glas Publishers, 2003), 129–133, 140–141. Used by permission of Glas Publishers.

In 1937, two days after she penned the last entry, the diary was confiscated by secret police (NKVD) agents when they searched her home. Nina, her mother, and her sisters were all arrested; the passages of her diary that were underlined by the NKVD (see diary entries, following) were used to prosecute her. Yet all four survived their five years in the Kolyma Labor camp. Nina married and lived to age seventy-four, when she died in Vladimir.

2 December 1934

Is this fortune or misfortune? Evgeny was here yesterday. He knocked with the secret knock and I opened the door thinking it was Olga. I said hello but he brushed past me without noticing and went into the girls' room. They started working on a composition. I couldn't do anything. I walked nervously around my room when I wasn't listening to his voice. From Mama's room, drowning out Evgeny's voice, came Zhorka's raspy voice. They'd divided up into pairs again.

I wandered into the girls' room a couple of times, dug around in the bookcase and stole looks at his back. Then I sat in my room for a long time. Having seen Evgeny, I calmed down a little and could even read a page or two. But whenever I heard him laughing, I couldn't bear it and pressed my ear to the cold stone wall. The sound was so magnified that I could even hear certain words. I didn't try to make sense of them; I just enjoyed the sound of his voice....

Nina and Dusya were supposed to come by around eight, but it was already half past and no sign of them. "Will I really have to sit here the whole evening and not see him again?" I wanted to cry. Again I went and listened to their conversation through the wall. And again I couldn't stand it and decided to go into the next room and listen to the radio.

Around eleven they announced that comrade Kirov, a member of the Politburo, had been killed in Leningrad. "O-oh, my God!" Evgeny exclaimed. His voice was full of tears. I felt a little ashamed that nothing inside me shuddered at this report. On the contrary, I felt glad: That means there's still a struggle going on, there are still organizations and real people. Not everyone is gobbling the slops of socialism. I was sorry I hadn't been a witness to that terrible and sensational event. Now they'll raise such a ruckus. The whole rest of the evening that's all anyone talked about.

8 December 1934

The other evening Zhenya asked me: "Well, how do you like Evgeny? Isn't he good-looking?" "Evgeny? Yes, he's a jolly fellow," I said blandly. But later she said: "You know, Nina, you blushed when he was talking to you." "When was that? Oh, now I remember. When he said, 'And how are we today?' I was just surprised." After that I watched myself very carefully, making sure to speak calmly and not blush again. What the hell is a going on? How do they know that I like him? Or have they read my diary? No, they wouldn't do something as low as that. And yet they suspect something. Every evening as soon as Olya sees me looking lonely, she asks: "You aren't in love are you, Nina?"

9 December 1934

Zhenya and Olya came home today so happy and excited and full of life. I don't have any life of my own. The past is back in school, what I dream about is somewhere in the infinitely distant future, and the present is a void. A void! Kolya and Granny think I'm lazy and every day when I go there to eat lunch they make cutting remarks. Soon I'll start believing them. I'm now sure I won't have time to prepare for the rabfak*. And then there's Evgeny! It's awful to love someone who doesn't even notice you, who talks to you the way they do to Betka and looks at you as if you were an inanimate object.

11 December 1934

I was already in bed when the girls came home last night. What made me decide to get up? I was hoping they'd tell me something and at least mention his name in passing, but they didn't. Somehow we got onto the most dangerous subject: Soviet rule, the Bolsheviks and life today. The girls and I have always been at opposite ends of the spectrum. We're like the seeing man who tries to explain colors to a blind man. We can't understand each other.

How could I refute their mindless, mechanical arguments: "If you're not for the Bolsheviks, you're against Soviet rule": "This is all temporary, things will get better"? Were those five million deaths† in the Ukraine temporary? What about the 69 people who were shot‡? Sixty-nine!! What government under what rule could pass such a sentence with such cold cruelty? What nation would agree to all these outrages with such slavish meekness and obedience? We talked for a whole hour but it didn't change anything. How I cursed my stupidity and inability to express myself. How could I with such strong weapons as the facts and the truth, not prove to my sisters the lie of the Bolshevik system? I must be extraordinarily inept.

Still, I went back to bed feeling happy and excited. Zhenya talked about how they'd rearranged the studio and put up new pictures. They're all so inspired and anxious to work. It made me want to work, too. But the next morning I woke up in a horribly pessimistic mood. I imagined myself— shy and fearful, sullen and homely—among crude, semiliterate workers. I imagined the badgering, the sarcasm and the crude jokes. Wouldn't I be better off back at school? Won't my new life be just a new form of torture?

---

* *Rabfak* is short for *rabochii fakul'tet*, or worker's faculty. Worker's faculties were educational institutions designed to give working class and peasant students the functional equivalent of a secondary school education in preparation for higher education.

† [This gloss appeared in original text.] Of famine as a result of collectivization.

‡ [This gloss appeared in original text.] A reference to those arrested and executed without a trial right after Kirov's murder (see note for 30 December 1934).

I'll have to figure this out for myself. Zhenya and Olya are wrapped up in themselves and their art, Mama in her work. No one will advise me, no one understands how afraid I feel. <u>Papa is here today. He brought news from the Printing Institute. He said there's a slight chance I might get in.</u> Suddenly I felt not only fear, but a lack of desire. I realized that all my plans were focused on Evgeny, that the motivating force was simply love. How shocked my parents would be if they knew that their daughter had given herself up to such silly feelings, that for their sake she was ready to ruin her life....

30 December 1934

<u>Many days have gone by since Nikolaev, a member of an underground terrorist group, murdered Kirov at the Smolny*. Many lead articles in the papers have screamed about it, and many parrots and Soviet self-seekers, shaking their fists, have screamed over the heads of the workers: "Get the viper!" "Execute the traitor whose cowardly shot snatched from our ranks," and so on. And many so-called Soviet citizens, who have lost all sense of human dignity, have behaved like beasts and raised their hands in favor of execution.</u>

<u>It's hard to believe that in the 20th century there is a corner of Europe where medieval barbarians have taken up residence; where savage concepts get on so strangely with science, art and culture. Before the investigation began, before they knew of any terrorist group, more than a hundred former White Guards[†] were killed only because they had the misfortune to be on Soviet territory.</u>

<u>Today they shot another fourteen "conspirators" and all for one Bolshevik life. It made me think of the 19th century reign of Alexander II and his assassination by the People's Will[‡]. What a furor people raised over the execution of the six assassins. Why is no one incensed now? Why is this now considered perfectly natural and normal? Why is it that now no one will tell you straight out that the Bolsheviks are scoundrels? And what right do these Bolsheviks have to deal with the country and its people so cruelly and arbitrarily, to so brazenly proclaim outrageous laws in the name of the people, to lie and hide behind big words that have lost their meaning: "socialism" and "Communism"?</u>

<u>To call Nikolaev a coward! He went willingly to his death for what he believed in, he was better than all those so-called leaders of the working class</u>

---

* [This gloss appeared in original text.] Kirov's murder was in fact organized by Stalin who saw in Kirov his main rival. The murder also gave Stalin a pretext for unleashing his campaign against "enemies of the people."

† Reference here is to the military institution of the White movement, a motley array of political movements who combined to fight against the Bolsheviks during the Russian Civil War of 1918–1921. "White Guard" and "White Army" are used interchangeably.

‡ Founded in 1879, the People's Will (in Russian, Narodnaia Volia) was an underground, illegal, conspiratorial party based on socialist ideology. It embraced political terror, and it assassinated Russian tsar Alexander II in St. Petersburg in March 1881.

Gulag prisoners at work in a forest, 1936–1937. Soviet citizens arrested during the Great Purges of 1936–1939 were sometimes sent to labor camps throughout the Soviet Union. But concentration camps had existed since Lenin decreed their opening in 1918. What changed over time—specifically in the late 1920s, as Stalin's "great break" was underway—was the purpose to which forced labor was put. In official decrees and other pronouncements, forced labor of camp inmates was deemed a solution to the Soviet state's labor shortage, especially for back-breaking work in remote and inhospitable regions. In 1930, the "Gulag"—actually a specific department of the Commissariat for Internal Affairs—started to run these forced labor operations. The Gulag directed forced labor into the timber industry, mining (of both metals and coal), and construction work. This image probably depicts forced labor in Karelia, near the coast of the White Sea, where the main Gulag industry was timber. This region was the original nexus of the labor camps. Courtesy of the Slavic and Baltic Division, the New York Public Library, Astor, Lenox, and Tilden Foundations.

put together! What do they think abroad? Can they really be saying there too: "That's how it should be"? Oh, no! My God, when will this all change? When will we be able to truly say that all power belongs to the people, that we have complete equality and freedom? What we have now is not socialism, it's the Inquisition*!

---

* An inquisition was a tribunal of the Roman Catholic Church. Its purpose was to uncover, try, and punish heretics. Questioning and punishment were notoriously severe. The first practice of an inquisition was in Rome, by Pope Innocent III (1198–1216), and it was vigorously applied in the thirteenth century in central and western Europe, with the exceptions of England and Scandinavia. But Lugovskaia probably had in mind the Spanish Inquisition, which started in 1481. Among the targets of the Spanish Inquisition were Jewish converts to Christianity and *conversos* (secret Jews). Victims were arrested, tried, and burned at the stake. On the parallels and differences between the Inquisition and the Great Purges in the USSR, see Stephen Kotkin, *Magnetic Mountain*, 336–337.

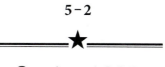

Spain, 1937

Robert Hale Merriman (1908–1938), an American
University Student and Volunteer Commander in the
International Brigades during the Spanish Civil War

R obert Hale Merriman was one of about twenty-eight hundred American
volunteers who fought Franco's fascist forces to defend the democratically
elected Republican government of Spain during the civil war of 1936–
1939. This crisis led forty thousand volunteers from over fifty countries to join
the International Brigades—which, under the USSR's direction, were organized
by Communist parties throughout the world—to fight against Franco, Hitler,
and Mussolini on Spanish battlefields from 1936 to 1939. (From 1936 to 1938,
the USSR sold arms to the Spanish Republic, and was its chief source of weapons
in the face of the League of Nation's military embargo. The USSR also provided
military advisors.) Americans such as Merriman fought in the Abraham Lincoln
Brigade and the George Washington Battalion, which were merged in August
1937 into the Lincoln-Washington Battalion. The relationship of individual members of the brigades to Communism was complex. Some formally belonged to
the CPUSA, but others were not formal members yet were sympathetic to the
Communist agenda. Merriman seems to have been such a fellow traveler.

In 1935, after graduating from the University of Nevada and becoming
a graduate student in economics at the University of California at Berkeley,
Merriman and his wife, Marion, whom he had met while an undergraduate,
moved to Moscow. It was an excursion from Moscow to Vienna that convinced
Robert to join the Abraham Lincoln Brigade and head to Spain in 1937. He rose
through the ranks of the International Brigades, first training American volunteers and eventually attaining the rank of chief of staff of the 15th International
Brigade. After Robert was wounded in March 1937 at the Battle of Jarama, Marion
came to Spain from Moscow to take care of him. She herself contributed mightily
to the brigades as a clerk and hospital worker and attained the rank of corporal
before returning in March 1938 to San Francisco. But Robert stayed on in Spain
to fight and disappeared during an ambush at Corbera (Ebro Valley). Later in
1938, he was presumed dead. A year later, fascist military might defeated Spain's
fledgling democracy, a defeat that proved to be a prelude to the even greater

Published with permission of the Tamiment Library, Robert F. Wagner Labor Archives, New York
University.

savagery of World War II. The excerpts that follow, from the diary that he kept in Spain, though brief, give a sense of what it meant for him to use military force in pursuit of Communist ideals. Merriman wrote these passages on the eve of, and during, his first battle.

From the diary of Robert Hale Merriman

16 February [1937]

Worked all during night and early morning—trenches—just before daylight panic—cubans fired and Irish followed also wounded own men—took up new outline—went to staff meeting... talked to officer—Marion dear I love you! I am willing to die for my ideas—-may I live for them and you!

17 February [1937]

Received order to go into action and now sitting with Cooperman. Calm and hope men are. Afraid of some officers at last moment. The actual fighting with weapons is the highest stage a real Communist can ask for. About to lead first Battalion of Americans in this war. Life has been full because I made it so. May others live the life I have begun and may they carry it still further as I plan to do myself. Long Live Communism! Long live the Soviet Union! Men may die but let them die in a working class cause. Men die and mean to die (if necessary) so that the revolution may live on. They may stop us today but tomorrow we still take up the march.

18 February [1937]

Early in day air raid—bombs just missed us and how close. Edwards killed by bullet thru [sic] head while scouting. Was bawled out for not keeping men down.... Later in day another raid and... Some fight in air, where definitely located. Went to inspect trenches after dark and artillery started on us. Plenty tough and lost one man. [name illegible] killed by shrapnel... and during night cross fire. Harris out.

    ...Harris went to hospital and got back. Steve... cracked up and I recommended him to rest home.... Men ate well....

    I am now writing on the 13th of March after a long period during which we were in the front lines and after which the diary was lost.

    About 20* in the evening we received orders to move forward to support....

---

* Not legible. It is likely this is a symbol that means 20 hours, or 8 PM.

Hungary, 1956

A University Student Reacts to the USSR's Violent Suppression of the Hungarian Revolution

Sergei Khrushchev's de-Stalinizing "thaw," launched with a fierce condemnation of Stalin at the 20th Party Congress in 1956, had an immediate effect on Communist polities in Eastern Europe. Poland and Hungary were the sites of the two "October Revolutions" of that year. In both countries, intellectuals, workers, as well as political leaders and others dissatisfied with Soviet encroachment upon national prerogatives, brought unstoppable pressures for reform and, in the case of Hungary, revolution. While in Poland, Władysław Gomułka proved to be a leader who could both press for reform yet restrain it to prevent Soviet military intervention, there was no analogous figure in Hungary during its revolution of 22 October through 10 November.

Hungary's people, especially students such as Laszlo Beke (whose diary is excerpted herein), played a significant role in the rapidly escalating events. On 23 October, the five thousand students who gathered at Budapest Technological University produced a sixteen-point revolutionary document. It called for, among other things, the immediate withdrawal of Soviet troops. The next day, tens of thousands of Hungarians cheered as a huge statue of Stalin in central Budapest was felled. That day, too, Imre Nagy was appointed prime minister, a move designed to reduce reformist pressures after the ill-advised replacement of the Stalinist Mátyás Rákosi, general secretary of the Hungarian Communist Party, with the equally odious Ernő Gerő. Street demonstrations brought the collapse of the government and its replacement, on 30 October, with a coalition government under Nagy that included non-Communist parties. This represented a heretical break with one of the fundamental principles of Soviet Communist regimes in Eastern Europe, namely the "leading role" of the Communist Party. Following popular pressure, Nagy also demanded withdrawal of Soviet troops and Hungary's exit from the Warsaw Pact. With Hungary having broken with the two fundamental principles of Communist polities in Eastern Europe, the USSR decided on military intervention. (To be sure, one line of argument proposed by historians is that the Soviet intervention *preceded* Hungary's withdrawal from the Warsaw Pact; the withdrawal, it is claimed, was in fact the *result* of the intervention.)

From Laszlo Beke, *A Student's Diary: Budapest, October 16–November 1, 1956* (New York: Viking, 1957), 68–71, 88–89, 105–106, 107–109. Reprinted by permission of Viking Press/Penguin Group.

Most, though not all (as the following passage attests), of the twenty-five hundred Hungarian deaths came between 4 and 7 November. Twenty thousand Hungarians were wounded seriously enough to be taken to the hospital. On the Soviet side, there were 700 deaths and 1,050 wounded. Nagy himself was tried, sentenced to death, and hung by the neck in 1958. The Soviets justified this violence (and the arrests, imprisonments, and execution that followed the new Prime Minister János Kádár's reimposition of Communist control) as a necessary defense against "counterrevolution."

How Hungarians understood the violence was, of course, another matter. There were, to be sure, Hungarians, some of them highly placed, who believed that the Soviet military intervention was necessary. But most, condemning the violence as illegitimate, supported the resistance to Soviet violence. Laszlo Beke, the student whose diary is excerpted next, had a single, yet powerful, word for the deaths resulting from Soviet violence. It was murder. Murder, that is, not just of human beings, but of the Hungarian nation.

October 25, 1956

... I dropped in on Eva again after this. She was sleeping in her bloodstained dress, but she woke up as soon as I closed the door. Each time she saw me now, she began to cry with relief. She saw so many corpses in our district that she began to imagine I was among them when I was away from her.

"The little boy with the wounded lung died," she told me. "There wasn't anything I could do for him."

She had a message from the boy to pass along to his mother. But we never did see the mother.

The radio was reporting that the Communist Party newspaper *Szabad Nep (Free People)* had been captured by the revolutionaries. They set the whole plant afire and burned every Communist book in the plant's bookstore.

I stretched myself out on the bed for a short rest. I suddenly felt so tired I couldn't stand up any longer. If I could only relax for a few minutes, I thought. Only a few minutes' rest, and I'll be all right again.... The voice on the radio was saying, "The Politburo of the Central Committee of the Communist party has relieved Ernő Gerő of his post as First Secretary of the Central Committee, and appointed Janos Kadar to his place.... Imre Nagy and Janos Kadar have issued a joint communique: 'Hungarians, put out the national flag. Raise the tricolor....'"

The next thing I remember is the sound of loud sobs, and the rattle of machine-gun fire outside. The room was bright with sunlight, and I realized I had been sleeping well into the day. Eva was sprawled across the bed, crying as if in great pain.

"Oh, Laszlo!" she said, sobbing. "You should have seen it. It was the most ghastly sight I have ever seen. Our whole nation is being massacred!"

"Eva! Where were you?" I cried out. "What happened? How long have I been sleeping?"

A crowd of twelve thousand people had been gathering at Liberty Square while I slept, she told me. The students at the hostel told Eva it was to be a peaceful demonstration in the light of the Nagy–Kadar announcement.

"I thought I would go down to the Parliament to watch," she told me.

"When I got there I saw that the square was already filling up with people, mostly women, children, and older people who weren't in the fight. The purpose of the meeting was to protest against the inhumanity of the secret police and the Russian troops toward the Hungarian people. Everyone wanted the killings to stop.

"Some of the people stood in front of the British and United States Embassy buildings and shouted, 'Why don't you help us? Please help us!'

"Laszlo, it was the most terrible thing you could imagine!" My wife shivered with shock as she spoke. There were beads of perspiration on her brow, and she was almost hysterical.

"A small group of Soviet tanks stopped at the edge of the square, bearing Hungarian flags that young boys had draped over the gun barrels. The Russians looked out from the tank turrets and waved to the crowd. The people cheered and waved back. They thought the Russians were on their side.

"Then three of the tanks turned into the crowd of people that was making its way to the center of the square, and women climbed aboard and waved. Everyone was singing national songs and hymns. There were a few more Soviet tanks in the middle of the square.

"Suddenly the tanks moving with the people turned around and began heading in the direction of the Rakoczy statue.

"The crowd was still singing when the tanks started firing their guns on the women and children. There was absolutely no warning. And as soon as the tanks started shooting, there was shooting from all over the square. The AVH police* were up on the rooftops, behind windows—everywhere!

"No one could realize what was happening, and even the tankmen themselves didn't know who was on the rooftops, for they started firing up into the AVH roof groups.

"It was cold, cold murder, Laszlo!" my wife said through her tears. "Bits and pieces of people were all over the square.

"They kept it up for fifteen minutes, and there was no place for the people to run to or hide. Everyone just stood there and waited his turn for the bullets.

"A woman standing next to me saw both of her children mowed down. They were, a girl, about nine, and a boy, about eleven.

"Finally we were able to find our way out into the side streets. But an hour after, the Communists blocked off the square. They didn't even let families

---

* AVH refers to the Hungarian State Security Police.

in to look for their loved ones. They brought their trucks in, instead, and started piling bodies into them like so much firewood." (We learned later the Communists had dumped the bodies into the Danube River's tributary streams.)

I put my arm around Eva to comfort her, and swore I wouldn't believe a word of what the radio told us from then on. Lies! I thought. All lies!

I calmed Eva down, and scolded her for going out of the house. "You're not like the rest of the girls now," I told her. "You have to watch your health—for your sake, for mine, and for the three of us!" But I didn't get too angry with her, because I didn't want her to get too excited.

She finally fell asleep. It was just past noon....

October 27, 1956

...Army units had taken matters into their own hands and had blasted open jails at Marko Street and Fo Street, while others freed inmates of the Vac political prison, thirty miles out of the capital.

About fifteen thousand Hungarians came back to life today, a little less than the number lost in the Budapest battle so far. Many foreign prisoners were also freed, among them British, French, and German citizens.

Fog was setting in so heavily today there wasn't much street fighting to be heard. Artillery rumbled in the distance. It was the life-and-death battle at Kilian Barracks. One of the students who was there told us the whole area around Ulloi Street and Jozsef Boulevard was a mass of debris, with more Soviet reinforcements pouring in by the hour to crush the Army contingent. He saw Soviet tanks attacking the barricades there and grinding their own wounded into the dust. The Soviet troops who fell screamed for help, but their own tanks drove over them without a shred of mercy. About 45 young soldiers isolated in one part of the barracks surrendered and hoisted a white flag. The Russians accepted the surrender, took away their arms, then lined them up against the wall and shot them down to the last man.

It was rumored that the postmen had resumed their duties, but we received information that this move was just another piece of treachery on the part of the Communists. They were using the postmen as informers. Word got around, and everyone started to slam doors in the faces of mailmen.

Today Stalin Square, Stalin Bridge, and Stalin Boulevard were being renamed. One thing was quite certain. We wouldn't keep any Communist names.

On my way home I saw a little girl propped up against the doorway of a building with a machine gun clutched in her hands. When I tried to move her, I saw she was dead. She couldn't have been more than eleven or twelve years old. There was a neatly folded note in her pocket she had evidently meant to pass on through someone to her parents. In childish scrawl it read: "Dear Mama, Brother is dead. He asked me to take care of his gun. I am all right, and I'm going with friends now. I kiss you. Kati."

I placed the slip of paper in her pocket, moved her farther back from the street into the doorway, and covered her with my scarf.

Tomorrow is Sunday, and I was looking forward to a night of rest. I told Eva a little later that there were virtually no more AVH men in Budapest. Most of the pockets had been wiped out, and stragglers of the AVH gendarmerie hid in sewers and burned-out areas of the capital. She looked forward to her first night without fear in many years....

October 30, 1956

...But at the same time that Moscow reported in news broadcasts that the Soviets were ready to discuss withdrawal of troops from Hungary, we saw Russian tank columns digging in around the capital.

We began to realize the terrible truth. The Russians were *not* leaving.

This truth became more obvious as Soviet jets made several passes at the city.

We sat by our radio the whole night, listening to latest bulletins from free radio transmitters and Radio Budapest. From Miskolc, a stronghold in the north, we heard the report that 750 of the heaviest Soviet tanks, the Joseph Stalin class, had been sighted in the Diosgyor heavy industry district. From my military training I knew this could mean only attack. These monsters were used only in major attacks, while smaller tanks were used to restore order and quell disturbances.

"The Joseph Stalin tank," I kept repeating to myself. "Something terrible is in the wind!" I couldn't get the picture of the lumbering giants out of my mind....

October 31, 1956

By 5 AM I couldn't stand it any longer and got out of bed. I hadn't slept a wink. I headed for the radio transmitter.

Outside I looked at the moon, and the moon looked as sad as the fate of our Hungarian nation seemed to be. I began to imagine I saw gallows silhouetted against the moon. I sat down on a bench in the early-morning stillness and put my head in my hands. As I sat in the quiet of Moszkva* Square I heard footsteps. Why hadn't I taken my machine gun? Then something warm brushed against my leg. I looked down to see a small hungry dog nuzzling against me. Then I looked up and saw that the dog's master was an old man with a white beard. The minute he greeted me, I knew he must be an educated man.

"Greetings in the Lord!" he intoned. He asked me what I was doing, and I started telling him about my doubts and fears—I, who had learned not to trust anyone or talk to strangers. Yet he seemed to be a person who would

---

* That is, Moscow Square.

listen and understand. As I talked, my head began to clear up and the fierce headache I had began to disappear. After I told him my story, he talked a bit about himself.

As it turned out, he was a Catholic priest. At least, he had been a priest until the Communists took away his little church where he had served for thirty years.

That happened in 1949, but he had been spared imprisonment because a parishioner brought a warning to him. He was spirited away to Budapest and has lived here since, under an assumed name, and practicing his former hobby as a profession—training dogs.

"But today I feel I am a priest again. I have been walking about for the past few days, administering last rites to the dying, and I want to believe my country will let me be a priest again now."

He told me Cardinal Mindszenty* was coming home to Budapest today. "Don't you want to come with me and see him come in, my son?"

I am a Protestant, but I felt I should go to see this great man come home.

On my return home, I found an important message waiting for me. The Students' Council wanted me to represent them at a meeting of the newly formed Hungarian Revolutionary Youth Committee, comprising every youth committee in Hungary.

"What's the use of going to any more meetings?" I asked Bertalan after I reached him by phone. "I'm sick and tired of meetings. What can this one hope to accomplish?"

"But we want to place an ultimatum before Premier Nagy," Bertalan said. "Unless Soviet forces leave Hungary by December 31, the youth of Hungary will take up arms again and fight until we do get freedom. But if you would rather do something else, I can send someone else in your place."

There was something else I had in mind, and I asked Bertalan to relieve me for this one meeting.

I went to get the boys at the students' hostel. "Let's go see the Cardinal," I said. "He's coming back today."

I didn't need to use too much persuasion, for the Cardinal was one of the great leaders of Hungary—probably the only man in Hungary whom all factions and all the people could respect and trust in this hour of suspicion and tragedy.

---

* When the Hungarian Revolution began, Hungarian cardinal József Mindszenty was serving a sentence of life imprisonment, handed down in a show trial of June 1949. He was released during the revolutionary events of October 1956 and gave a speech broadcast on 3 November 1956. Though Beke portrays Mindszenty as having unified the nation, it could also be argued that the cardinal was a divisive figure and a reactionary who supported the monarchy. Mindszenty's role in fanning the flames in 1956 is in contrast to Cardinal Wyszyński's actions in 1956 in Poland. Released from detention, Wyszyński called on Poles to unite and support Gomułka, then the first secretary of the Central Committee of the Polish United Workers' Party, Poland's Communist Party.

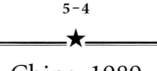

5–4

China, 1989

Chinese Writers on State Violence before and after the Massacre on Tiananmen Square

I n 1989, China was the site of political conflict among Communist party elites, intellectuals, workers, and students that culminated in the Tiananmen Square massacre of 3–4 June.[4] The protests at Tiananmen—and, indeed, in every city in China—had long- and short-term causes. Among the former were Deng Xiaoping's economic reforms of the 1980s and the recovery of higher education from the Cultural Revolution's destruction. When, in 1986, General Secretary Hu Yaobang and Deng himself extended the limits on discussion of political reform, university students not only advanced critiques that went further than the political leadership wanted but also engaged in protests in late 1986 and early 1987. Hence, the student demonstrations that had begun in mid-April of 1989, following the popular Hu's death, had been years in coming. In late April, students at Beijing University and other universities in Beijing did the seemingly impossible, breaching police barriers to enter Tiananmen Square, where Mao's portrait loomed. The students' bold action confronted an already politically divided elite, one torn between repression and liberalization: while Li Peng wanted to use violence to restore order, Zhao Ziyang wanted dialogue with the students.

Adding to the internal Party conflict and the students' courageous determination was the upcoming visit of Mikhail Gorbachev. To be sure, Deng had approved Gorbachev's visit. But the fact that the Soviet Communist Party leader had publicly rejected the use of violence to sustain socialism brought into high relief a central issue in the history of Communist polities: what place should state violence have in the maintenance of Communist systems? Gorbachev's anticipated visit, moreover (the first to China of a Soviet leader since that of Nikita Khrushchev in 1959), lent symbolic legitimacy, for those who wanted it, to the possibility of a full-blown Chinese *perestroika* and *glasnost'*.*

---

* Perestroika and *glasnost'* were the two watchwords of the reforms that Soviet leader Mikhail Gorbachev launched beginning in 1986. *Glasnost',* which means "openness," initially meant the party-state's increasing tolerance for public acknowledgment of corruption as well as social and economic problems. *Perestroika* (literally, "restructuring"), which initially meant the reforms sponsored by the Party to improve economic efficiency and production, came to be the mantra of Gorbachev's increasingly radical reforms as a whole.

173

While Deng and the Chinese leadership fretted about how to restore order on Tiananmen when the world media would be focusing on Gorbachev's visit, students, intellectuals, and workers voiced their discontent—and their alternative political vision (not so much liberal democracy but reformist socialism à la Gorbachev's *perestroika*)—more and more loudly. With Gorbachev gone from Beijing, so was the reformist Zhao, who was forced to resign as general secretary on 19 May. Yet the ranks of demonstrators in the capital kept swelling, despite (and because) martial law was imposed on 20 May. Demonstrating their inventiveness in marshalling the power of symbols against the symbols of power,[5] in late May, students from the Central Academy of Fine Arts began constructing a thirty-foot statue, the "Goddess of Democracy," whose evocation of the Statue of Liberty challenged Mao's visual hegemony on the square. That symbolic breach, coupled with Party members' defection to the rebels, seems to have pushed Deng to use force. The military crackdown of 3–4 June brought an estimated six hundred to one thousand killed, six thousand to ten thousand injured, and thousands of arrests.

Yet the official justification for the violence had been articulated by the conservative Li Peng more than two weeks earlier. On 19 May he had spoken to this issue on national television. In the words of the prime minister, "To fulfill our responsibilities to our sacred motherland and to the entire people, we must take firm, decisive measures to put a swift end to the turmoil, protect the leadership of the Party, and protect the socialist system."[6] And so the "Goddess of Democracy" was crushed, and lives were brutally cut short.

Despite the severe state repression that followed, dissident Chinese intellectuals wrote about the Tiananmen massacre. Following are two reflections on the meaning of the violence, especially in relationship to Chinese socialism, both before and after the massacre of 3–4 June. The first piece, a letter to Deng, was written on 25 April by Wang Ruowang, whose basic biographical details precede the excerpt. The second piece is a meditation by an anonymous poet from China's provinces, with a comment by the poet Yang Lian*, who lived in New Zealand when the massacre occurred.

STILL OUT OF CONTROL [INTRODUCTION IS FROM ORIGINAL PUBLICATION]

Wang Ruowang, a writer who had been expelled from the party in 1987 after Deng Xiaoping declared he was "absolutely out of control there in Shanghai," wrote an

---

From *New Ghosts, Old Dreams: Chinese Rebel Voices*, ed. Geremie Barmé and Linda Jaivin (New York: Times Books, 1992), 50–53, 100–105. Reprinted by permission of Times Books.

---

* [The following is from the original text.] Yang Lian, a poet from Peking who was in New Zealand at the time of the massacre and is now living in exile, wrote this comment on "The Howl" in October 1989 in Auckland. For samples of Yang Lian's poetry, see Geremie Barmé and John Minford, *Seeds of Fire* (New York: Hill & Wang, 1988), 36, 135, 246–249, 398–399, 434–437.

open letter to Deng shortly after the state funeral for Hu Yaobang*, excerpts from which are produced below. It was finished on the evening of April 25, the same day Deng first ordered the crushing of the students and after a People's Daily *editorial was broadcast nationwide (before being published on April 26) declaring that the student disturbances were being manipulated by a small group plotting to overthrow the party.*

The letter is written like a memorial to the throne, and Wang even avails himself of the traditional language of the outspoken loyal minister. As he was unable to publish anything in Mainland China, Wang was forced to have the letter issued in Hong Kong and Taiwan. He knew that both this act as well as the contents of the letter could lead to his arrest.

Like Liu Xiaobo†, Wang was detained after the massacre and vilified in the national press. He was finally released from custody in late 1990. It was not his first stint in jail: He'd been a political prisoner at various times under both the Nationalists and the Communists, and had once said he preferred the jails of the former.

Comrade Xiaoping:

…It seems inappropriate for a true Marxist to view a mass movement of students demonstrating for democracy and freedom as "floodwaters and wild beasts." Rather, it should be seen as a force that can help further the progress of history. Mao Zedong warned us all that "anyone who crushes a popular movement will come to no good end." But your comments on and policies toward the 1986 Student Movement contravened this principle. In early 1987, you launched a nationwide Anti-Bourgelib‡ Movement and were unconcerned about forcing General Secretary Hu Yaobang, a man devoted to Reform, from office. You did not hesitate to punish severely the most forward-thinking intellectuals in the party§, availing yourself instead of experts in political purges and extreme "leftist" plotters. All of this is proof that the direction you chose was incorrect, and as a result every concrete policy decision was wrong and perverse. The year 1987 was a historical turning point. Once more the heinous methods of the Maoist era and the sense of personal insecurity of the past reappeared. The prestige of the party suffered a disastrous decline among the people.

---

* His funeral had occurred on 22 April 1989.

† Liu Xiaobo (born 1955), a literary critic known for his iconoclasm, played a significant role in the Tiananmen protest movement. When, on 4 June 1989, the People's Liberation Army surrounded Tiananmen Square, Liu stopped soldiers and workers from using weapons against the army. Under his leadership, students took a voice vote and concurred on evacuating the square. Liu, who was not a victim of the massacre, was, however, taken into custody on 6 June. The Chinese press then undertook a campaign of vilification against him, part of which involved publishing his writings so that they could be the target of criticism. Convicted in late June 1991 of "counterrevolutionary agitation," he was nonetheless not punished, and was released from custody, for his role in preventing protesters from using weapons. This note is from Barmé and Jaivin, *New Ghosts, Old Voices*, 72–73.

‡ In other words, "bourgeois liberalization."

§ Including, in fact, Wang himself.

You have been the object of great veneration and respect both at home and abroad. Internationally, you were even dubbed Man of the Year*. During the National Day parade [of 1984, when Deng turned eighty], university students held up a placard that read "How are you, Xiaoping!" and so on. But from 1987 your reputation has suffered badly.... You have become divorced from reality and divorced from the masses. You have issued incorrect directives that have had the most serious and disastrous consequences. In the early 1980s†, you returned from your visit to the United States deeply impressed by our industrial backwardness and were willing to admit that there were problems with our party's leadership. You proposed emphasizing knowledge and respect for talented people. But how is it that within a few years of taking the throne Mao had occupied for so many years you became so totally unrecognizable?

I have reflected on this long and hard, and the conclusion I have reached is virtually the same as your own: Our political system is a hotbed of bureaucratism. But I'll add something: If the political system and the party in power are not reformed, it doesn't matter how many good people there are, the moment any of them get into power, they will become autocratic, arrogant, and corrupt. And the monopoly control of the print media only encourages the protection of evil people, nefarious activities, and the abuse of power. For this reason I say that not only has this anti-democratic dictatorship failed to mobilize the creativity of the people, it also makes difficult the continuation of economic Reform itself. It harms not only the party, but also our most dearly beloved Comrade Xiaoping.

The student movement calling for democracy and freedom inspired by the unfortunate passing of Comrade Yaobang this April is the sequela of the inappropriate fashion in which the students were dealt with two years ago. Forgive my boldness, but it is punishment for your own policy errors....

I wish to give you a few words of sincere advice:

When Chun Doo-hwan in South Korea did repentance in front of the Buddha for using the army during his rule to mercilessly crush the mass protests at Kwangju and Wonsan, he shed tears of sorrow, deeply regretful of his actions. When you meet Gorbachev [in mid-May] you can learn from his experience in dealing with the demonstrations in the minority republics of the Soviet Union that are demanding autonomy...that these are incidents which have occurred in neighboring parts of Asia in the past year. I advise our policy makers, who have already revealed their bloodlust, to learn from them and, above all, not to act impetuously.

If you feel that the experience of the Soviet Union and South Korea do not conform to our national characteristics, then perhaps you could learn

---

* In fact, this honor was bestowed upon him twice.
† Actually, it was in 1979.

something from President Chiang Ching-kuo* in Taiwan. In the last year of his life he made a series of farsighted political decisions that are widely admired. The Taiwanese are of the same race and language as we are†; and like us they have a one-party dictatorship.

You are in a unique position, and I hope you will use your unparalleled prestige to do some real good for the Chinese nation while you still have the time. Do something for which you will be remembered by history and future generations. You are at the crossroads of history; will you be remembered as a good official or as a tyrant? I pray you will consider this very, very carefully. Whatever you do, don't compound your past mistakes!

As I write this I am overcome by emotion and my tears prevent me from continuing.

Wang Ruowang,
a writer and citizen of Shanghai

"THE HOWL" (ANONYMOUS)

Following are the last two sections of a lengthy prose poem by a young poet from the provinces, completed just after the June massacre and smuggled out of China. In the poet's own recording of it, smuggled out with the words, he at times screams, weeps, and repeats phrases again and again, conveying a mood of hysteria. Writers connected with this poem and its distribution in a number of provincial cities were reportedly arrested in May and June of 1990.

> *But another sort of slaughter takes place at Utopia's core*
>
> *The prime minister catches cold, the people cough, martial law is declared again and again*
>
> *The toothless old machinery of the state rolls on toward those with the courage to resist the sickness*
>
> *Unarmed hooligans fall by the thousands, ironclad professional killers swim in a sea of blood, set fires beneath tightly closed windows, wipe their army regulation boots on the skirts of dead maidens. They're incapable of trembling*
>
> *These heartless robots are incapable of trembling!*
>
> *Their electronic brains possess only one program, an official document full of holes*
>
> *In the name of the motherland slaughter the Constitution! Replace the Constitution and slaughter righteousness! In the name of*

---

* Chiang Ching-kuo (18 March 1910–13 January 1988) had permitted the democratization process in Taiwan to go forward.

† This is a claim that many people in Taiwan strongly dispute.

mothers throttle children! In the name of children sodomize
fathers! In the name of wives murder husbands! In the name of the
citizens blow up cities! OPEN FIRE! FIRE!FIRE!FIRE! Upon the
elderly! Upon the children! OPEN FIRE on women! On students!
Workers! Teachers! OPEN FIRE on peddlers! OPEN FIRE!
BLAST AWAY! Take aim at those angry faces. Horrified faces.
Convulsing faces. Empty all barrels at despairing and peaceful
faces! FIRE AWAY to your heart's content! These faces that come
on like a tide and in the next moment are dead are so beautiful!
These faces that will be going up to heaven and down to hell are so
beautiful! Beautiful. A beauty that turns men into beasts! A beauty
that lures men on to ravage, vilify, possess, despoil! Do away with
all beauty! Do away with flowers! Forests. Campuses. Love.
Guitars and pure clean air! Do away with flights of folly! OPEN
FIRE! BLAST AWAY! IT FEELS SO GOOD! SO000 GOOD!
Just like smoking dope. Taking a crap. Back on base giving the old
lady a good fuck! OPEN FIRE! ALL BARRELS! BLAST AWAY!
FEELS GOOD! SO00 GOOD! Smash open a skull! Fry his
scalp! Spill the brains out. Spill the soul out. Splatter on the
overpass. Gatehouse. Railings. Splatter on the road! Splatter
toward the sky where the drops of blood become stars! Stars on the
run! Stars with legs! Sky and earth have changed places. Mankind
wears bright shining hats. Bright shining metal helmets. A troop of
soldiers comes charging out of the moon. OPEN FIRE! ALL
BARRELS! BLAST AWAY! SUCH A HIGH! Mankind and the
stars fall together. Flee together. Can't make out one from the
other. Chase them up to the clouds! Chase them into the cracks of
the earth and into their flesh and WASTE THEM! Blow another
hole in the soul! Blow another hole in the stars! Souls in red skirts!
Souls with white belts! Souls in running shoes doing exercises to the
radio! Where can you run? We will dig you out of the mud. Tear
you out of the flesh. Scoop you out of the air and water. OPEN
FIRE! BLAST AWAY! IT FEELS GOOD! SO00 GOOD! The
slaughter takes place in three worlds. On the wings of birds. In the
stomachs of fish. In the fine dust. In countless species of living
things. LEAP! HOWL! FLY! RUN! You can't pass over wall after
wall of fire. Can't swim across pool after pool of blood. IT FEELS
SO GOOD! Freedom feels SO GOOD! Snuffing out freedom feels
SO GOOD! Power will always triumph. Will be passed down
forever from generation to generation. Freedom will also be
resurrected. Generation after generation. Like that dim light just
before the dawn. No. There's no light. At Utopia's core there can
never be light. Our hearts are pitch black. Black. Scalding. Like a
crematorium. Phantoms of the burnt dead. We will survive. The

*government that dominates us will survive. Daylight comes
quickly. IT FEELS SO GOOD! S0000 GOOD! The butchers
are still howling! Children. Children with cold bodies. Children
whose hands grasp stones. Let's go home. Girls, your lips drawn
and pale. Let's go home. Brothers and sisters, your shattered bodies
littering the earth. Let's go home. We walk noiselessly. Walk three
feet above the ground. Forward, on and on, there must be a place
to rest. There must be a place where sounds of gunfire and
explosions can't be heard. We yearn to hide within a stalk of grass.
A leaf. Uncle. Auntie. Grandpa. Granny. Daddy. Mommy. How
much farther till we're home? We have no home. Everyone knows.
The Chinese have no home. Home is a gentle desire. Let us die in
this desire! OPEN FIRE! BLAST AWAY! FIRE! Let us die in
freedom. Righteousness. Equality. Universal love. Peace. In these
vague desires. Let us become these desires. Stand on the horizon.
Attract more of the living to death! It rains. Don't know which is
falling, raindrops or transparent ashes. Run quickly, mommy! Run
quickly, son! Run quickly, elder brother! Run quickly, little
brother! The butchers will not let up. An even more terrifying day
approaches.*

*OPEN FIRE! BLAST AWAY! FIRE! IT FEELS GOOD! FEELS
S000 GOOD!*

Cry Cry Cry Cry Crycrycrycrycrycrycrycry

*Before you've been surrounded and annihilated, while you still
have the strength left to suckle, crycrycry*

*Let your sobs cast you off, fuse into radio, television, radar, testify
to the slaughter again and again*

*Let your sobs cast you off, fuse into plant life, semivegetable life
and microorganisms, blossom into flower after flower, year after
year mourning the dead, mourning yourself*

*Let your sobs be distorted, twisted, annihilated by the tumult of the
sacred battle*

*The butchers come from the east of the city, from the west, from
the south, from the north*

Metal helmets glint in the light. They're singing—

*The sun rises in the east, the sun rises in the west, the sun rises in
the south and north*

Putrid, sweltering summer, people and ghosts sing—

*Don't go to the east, don't go to the west, don't go to the south and
north*

*In the midst of brilliance we stand blind
On a great road but we cannot walk
In the midst of a cacophony all are mute
In the midst of heat and thirst all refuse to drink*

*People who misunderstand the times, people who think they're
surrounded, people who plot to shoot down the sun*

*You can only cry, you're still crying, crycrycrycrycrycrycry! CRY!
CRY! CRY!*

*You've been smothered to death, baked to death, your whole body
is on fire! And yet you're crying*

*You get up on the stage and act out a farce, you're paraded before
the crowds in the streets, and yet you're crying*

*Your eyeballs explode, scald the surrounding crowd, and yet you're
crying*

*You offer a bounty on yourself, track yourself down, frame yourself, you
say you were mistaken, this accursed epoch is all wrong! And yet you're
crying*

You are trampled, you cry

You are pulverized, you cry

A dog licks up the paste, inside a dog's belly you cry! CRYCRYCRY!

In this historically unprecedented slaughter only the sons of bitches can survive.

COMMENT BY YANG LIAN

We forget all too quickly. The Cultural Revolution, Wei Jingsheng*, "eliminating
Spiritual Pollution," the "Four Basic Principles"—the crystal-clear executioner's

---

* Born in 1950 in Beijing, Wei Jingsheng is an internationally known human rights activist and
dissident opposing Chinese Communism. He has spent more than eighteen years in jail. One of his
two imprisonments was the result of his 1978 essay, "The Fifth Modernization." In the 1990s, he was
essentially forced into exile in the United States.

manifesto of Deng Xiaoping. Has the slaughter ever stopped? What difference does it make if the blood is shed on Tiananmen Square or in the labor camps of Qinghai? If the shock of the Peking Massacre comes as something totally new and disturbing, it is proof that people forget their past all too easily.

How can I trust the repeated cries of the mourners? In the cycles of farce there are always those who shed tears in silence. The dead cannot weep; nor can those who remember the past. That young lives were lost is tragic, for they believed that their sacrifice was a novel thing. But no, everyone has gone through the motions of dying many times before. They are worn out, like the cries themselves.

Cry we must, but let us hope that memory is not washed away in the flood of tears.

—Yang Lian

Pictured are several victims of the Chinese army crackdown of 3–4 June. As noted in the text accompanying document 5-4, it is estimated that 600–1,000 were killed, 6,000–10,000 were injured, and thousands were arrested. But the exact figures will probably never be known. As army forces fired at random on unarmed protesters, student protesters are reported to have yelled "Fascists stop killing" and "Down with the government." Among the victims of military violence were city residents who were not part of the protest.
Photo courtesy of First Post Newsgroup IPR limited.

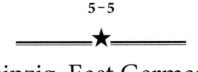

Leipzig, East Germany, September 1989

*A Lutheran Pastor Uses Biblical Passages to Condemn
State Violence and Counsel Nonviolence*

W hat role did East German citizens play in the collapse of an East German police state that was, by 1989, much more repressive than the USSR itself? To be sure, the SED leadership had, by that year, discredited itself through its enormous debt to the West, its inability to deliver—for all its borrowing—the consumer goods enjoyed by West German citizens, and its own incapacity for reform from above.[7] But while the fissures in the seemingly unshakeable East German edifice began at the top, its citizens played a remarkable role in causing its walls to come tumbling down.[8]

One of the spaces from which they challenged the regime, and set in motion a spontaneous revolution of collective action without a centrally organized leadership, was the Protestant Church. Building upon a 1978 agreement between the East German state and the Union of Evangelical Lutheran Churches (BEK), in which the church promised to abjure political opposition in exchange for limited toleration of its activities, East German citizens of a dissenting mindset became active in church groups supporting issues such as "demilitarization, democratization, decentralization, and self-determination."[9] By the middle of the 1980s, oppositional groups within the church had gained strength, in part because there were an increasing number of clergymen who supported such political activism. Though activist church groups existed throughout the GDR, and though there was even, by 1986, an activist organization independent from the church (the Institute for Peace and Human Rights, or Institut für Frieden und Menschenrechte), a singularly important locus of church opposition

---

From *Freunde und Feinde: Friedensgebete in Leipzig zwischen 1981 und dem 9 Oktober 1989,
Dokumentation*, Herausgeben von Christian Dietrich und Uwe Schwabe im Auftrag des "Archiv
Bürgerbewegung e. V," Leipzig (*Of Friend and Enemy: The Peace Prayers in Leipzig between 1981
and 9 October 1989, Documentation*, published by Christian Dietrich and Uwe Schwabe for
the "Civic Movement Archive," (Leipzig. Leipzig: Evangelische Verlaganstalt, 1994).
Reprinted with permission of Evangelische Verlagsanstalt, Leipzig. Translation:
Glennys Young.[16]

had emerged by 1988–1989: the St. Nikolai Church in Leipzig, a compact city of 550,000 located about an hour by train from Berlin.

The Peace Prayer services at St. Nikolai, which had begun as far back as 1981, had metamorphosed by 1988–1989 into something new: a kind of "speaker's corner."[10] Held on Monday evenings, the Peace Prayers were, on the surface, a vigil in which worshippers expressed solidarity with the nominally pacifist orientation of the East German state itself. But under Pastor Wonneberger, who in 1987 was given responsibility for the prayers after being transferred from Dresden to Leipzig but two years earlier, activists were given more say in deciding the content of the services. In May 1989, for example, activists involved in the Peace Prayers were vocal critics of the fraud in that month's common elections. When, after the usual summer recess, the prayers resumed in the fall, each service drew increasing numbers, and, at the service on 4 September, protests (with ensuing arrests) followed the service for the first time.[11]

The Peace Prayer of 25 September, part of whose service is reproduced next, marked a crucial stage in the opposition's development. By this point, it had become common knowledge that the Monday services had developed into a locus of political opposition, and anyone interested knew where to go. But at the 25 September service, with a Tiananmen outcome hanging in the balance, Pastor Wonneberger went even further than his colleague, Pastor Führer, had gone at the previous service in calling for nonviolent yet courageous protest and in denouncing the state's violence with inspiring preaching based on biblical passages.[12] After the service itself, demonstrators, as one scholar has put it, "burst the boundaries local authorities had been able to impose so far." About four thousand people,[13] most of them first-time protesters, joined the demonstrations outside of St. Nikolai after the services. Singing the Latin hymn "Dona nobis pacem" ("Give Us Peace"), they chanted new slogans such as "Freedom, Equality, Fraternity," and, in counterpoint to the regime's press campaign, "We are not rowdies." Finally, the peaceful demonstrators went further beyond the immediate area around St. Nikolai than any previous crowd, heading north to Karl Marx Square, the city's administrative and transportation center.[14] They demanded the recognition of the independent reform group, New Forum (Neues Forum), as well as, more generally, human rights, freedom of expression and association, and release of those arrested in demonstrations following prior Peace Prayers. The demonstration of 25 September marked the crystallization of a common knowledge and a common tactical repertoire about how, when, and where to protest. Only fifty people were arrested.[15]

Pastor Führer [Greeting]: [... Reference to the fact that the Church had to be closed on account of overflow and there are more people standing in front of the Church.] ... I am making known the wording of a letter concerning the events of last Monday [last Monday's Peace Prayers], [a letter] signed by Pastor Wugk*, who was on vacation at the time of the signing, and who is

---

* Pastor Wugk, as mentioned later, was the deputy superintendent.

filling in for the superintendent*, and from me, the chairman of the parish council at St. Nikolai Church.

[...Reading of the Letter from the Deputy Superintendent Wugk and Pastor Führer to the authorities responsible for the police actions that had been carried out on 20 September....]

I would further like to offer thanks for last Monday's offering. It was requested, like today's offering, for the external renovation and the internal work of St. Nikolai Church. The silent prayer worships for those detained on 11 September are taking place at the following times: at 6 PM [...] So, then I would again like to offer heartfelt greetings to all female and male Pastors, church staff members and members of the parish councils from congregations in Leipzig....

The Biblical slogan for the week[†]: 1 John 4 [Verse 21]" We have this commandment from him, that, [he] who loves God, that he is also to love his brother and his sister. Amen.

Chr. Miehm [Canon]: "Alone you are small, but together...."

Chr. Wonneberger [Homily]:

"With *force!*"—said the barber's assistant, his razor at my throat—"man cannot be changed."

My nodding proves to him that the opposite is true[‡]. (Laughter, Applause). A human being is, by all means, to be changed with force. With force a whole person can be made into a broken person (applause), from a free person into a prisoner, from a living person into a dead one. There is plenty of evidence of this, throughout history. But I would not advise you to test this proposition. You could expect a criminal indictment for coercion pursuant to paragraph 129 of the Criminal Code, (Applause) since you will be sentenced to no less that two years imprisonment for illegally coercing someone using violence or the threat of adverse consequences,... (Laughter, Applause)....

Even trying to coerce someone is punishable—at least if it is attempted by an *individual citizen* (Laughter, Applause).

It is a different situation if the state's behavior itself meets the definition of coercion. If the state itself uses violence, or the threat of violence, or attempts to use violence, or encourages others to do so. If the state itself uses,

---

* In the Evangelical Lutheran Church, the position of superintendent is equivalent to that of a bishop.

† In the first half of the twentieth century, the German Protestant Church (Evangelische Kirche in Germany or EKD) introduced into its liturgy a short weekly "slogan" from the Bible to open the Sunday service at every Protestant church in Germany. See the list at http://www.ekd.de/liutrgische_konferenz/download/TB-2=Wochensprueche.pdf.

‡ This is a literary quote from the East German poet Kurt Bartsch (1937–2010), from his collection *zugluft: gedichte, sprüche, parodien* (Berlin, 1968), 63. The German is as follows:

'Mit Gewalt', sagt der Friseurgehilfe

Das Rasiermesser an meiner Kehle

'Ist der Mensch nicht zu ändern.'

Mein Kopfnicken beweist ihm das Gegenteil."

or threatens to use, violence, it does not have to face prosecution (laughter, applause), but it does have to face the consequences: (Laughter, Applause): whoever practices violence, or threatens or uses violence, will themselves be the victim of violence.

He who takes up the sword will perish by the sword. He who takes up the Kalashnikov will have to anticipate a shot to the head. (Lengthy applause). . . . He who throws a hand grenade, should expect to have their arm severed. He who flies a fighter plane will find themselves in the crosshairs. He who swings a billy club, should better wear a hard hat. He who blinds another, will themselves be blinded. He who arbitrarily deprives another person of their freedom will soon find themselves without a way out. (Laughter, Applause). He who takes up the sword, will perish by the sword.

This, to me, is not about questioning the powers of the state. I endorse the state's monopoly on violence. I do not see any sensible alternative to it.

But. . . 2. The powers of the state have to be limited in a sensible way. Our country (for example) is not so rich, that it can afford such a gigantic state security apparatus. (Twenty seconds of Applause)

"A country's constitution should not destroy the constitution of its citizens," so wrote Stanislaw Jercy Lec twenty years ago. Then the constitution will (have to be changed). . . . (Applause)

Fear? (We are all afraid, I think. And not only when we are alone. As we heard in the first Canon.

But:) "Fear not! To Me [to God] is given all the power in Heaven and on Earth."—as Jesus once said.

That was not a threat. This was not coercion and is not coercion. There is no organized force behind it.

"To me is given all the power . . . ," that means inner strength *and* external credibility and that means for me: *true legitimacy*: full authority (is what the elders would have called it.) And you will receive this authority if you think responsibly, speak credibly, and act transparently. And, today, I invite you to do all these things. In the face of this authority, the Stasi machinery and the hundreds of police and the battalions of guard dogs will prove to be paper tigers (Applause).

So: Fear not! We can refuse violence.

Frau Richter: [Reports about experiences of violence:] When we speak today about violence, of course we do so thinking of that violence that is repeated every Monday after the peace prayer—and against which we are powerless and helpless. I will say right away that I am concerned in the following only with the violence emanating from this state.

Structural state violence rarely appears openly and immediately visible to everyone. (Perhaps) we have gotten too used to the censorship of the press and to seeking permission to publish. But it represents the practice of power as much as the travel bans and the ban on public assemblies.

Who can really imagine the pressure that weighs upon young men who refuse their military service because of their conscience? But [at the same time] those who perform [military] service in the NVA* also suffer oppression on a daily basis. . . . They were faced with in-depth searches of their rooms and lockers. Letters, notes, and diaries were confiscated.

Bans on the employment of critical and engaged citizens, as well as for people who apply for an exit visa, are just another instance of state violence. (Applause)

Finally, [here are] two more examples:

There has been long and intensive reporting about the first: the obvious election fraud of 7 May. (Applause)

The other is the reporting about the wave of escape and emigration in the media of the GDR. (Applause) Not only are West German and foreign journalists being defamed, this country's media are even using the vocabulary of National Socialism [the Nazis]. (Lengthy applause.)

Before they write their next articles these journalists should be made to read Viktor Klemperer's book *Lingua Tertii Imperii* [*The Language of the Third Reich*†]. [Applause]

The growing physical violence of the state against peaceful citizens is also becoming more serious. Renditions, arrests, prosecutions and even injuries are everyday occurrences. According to the Working Group on Human Rights, Jens Uwe Drescher and Kai Kuhlmann are sentenced to, respectively, ten and eighteen months in jail for [distributing] leaflets calling for an electoral boycott and for a demonstration on 7 May.

On 13 August, in Dresden-Gittersee, the police bludgeoned participants in a church service as they were attempting to go to a silicon purification plant. Neither the disabled nor mothers with small children were spared.

A brutal police operation took place in Berlin, where people gathered in protest against the municipal elections on 7 August [in the manuscript: wanted to gather]. The result here: a broken arm and for many, including women, bruises.

I don't need to say much about the inhumane action of the so-called state security forces in Leipzig. Most of you experience that [in the manuscript: it each Monday] personally.

In addition to the arrests and sentences of Udo Hartmann [in the manuscript: (birthday)], Carola Bornschlegel, Ramona Ziegner and Jörg Müller (they were all sentenced to four months in prison as summary punishment—they are still imprisoned): Katrin Hattenhauer, Alex Gebhart, [in the manuscript: Jutta Gätzel,] Gundula Walter, Mirko Kätzel, Günther Müller, Frank Elsner, Jens Michalke, Peer Matzeit, Holger König, Udo Suppa, Silvia Ulbricht

---

* East German armed forces.

† Viktor Klemperer, *Lingua Tertii Imperii: Notizbuch eines Phililogen* (*The Language of the Third Reich: Notebook of a Phililogen*) (Berlin: Aufbau Verlag, 1947).

and Andreas Gay and the punitive fines for hundreds of people in the case where a minor found himself overnight in police custody, although he pointed out that his parents were expecting him at home. The father, who began to search for him, was not admitted to the police station and was given no information about his son.

I am particularly struck by the way in which civilian and uniformed police are carrying out renditions.

For many people, this violence and abuse of power came unexpectedly. They thought that it [this kind of thing] could not possibly happen in our country and most of us were not prepared for this. And here I see the great danger! Experiencing this state violence, we build up anger and aggression. But can we deal with this properly? A week ago, one of those present [at this service, that is, the Peace Prayer service] learned, through the reading of the names, that a friend or an acquaintance, whom he had not seen for a while, was among those who had been taken into custody. From their reactions, one can see clearly during the Peace Prayer how difficult it was for him to deal with his anger (his [feeling of] disappointment and his powerlessness).

But one thing is clear: the first injured policeman will lead without fail to an unimaginable escalation of violence.

Therefore those of us assembled here have to act strictly in accordance with the principle of non-violence. That holds also ... (lengthy applause) with regards to the provocateurs who are among us. (Applause)

We will later give you some suggestions for non-violent conduct. (Applause)

Joh. Fischer, Fr. Richter, Chr. [alternating; intercessions]:

God, we pray for ... [the names of those who, on 25 September 1989, were prosecuted or arrested]. (They all were detained after last week's Peace Prayer, arrested and, in some cases, have already been sentenced. I am thinking especially of Udo Hartmann, whose 27th birthday is today.)

Congregation and Organ: Kyrie Eleison....

(God we pray for) Stanislaw Devaty, Petr Cibulka, Ina Vojtkova, and Frantizek Starek, who were sentenced to imprisonment in Czechoslovakia on account of their advocacy for Peace and Human Rights.

Congregation and Organ: Kyrie Eleison....

(God, we pray for) Sven Kulow, who has been in custody pending trial ever since the end of June.

Congregation and Organ: Kyrie Eleison....

(God, we pray for) Jens-Uwe Drescher and Kai Kuhlmann as well as for all those who have been unjustly arrested (and who remain unknown to us)....

(God, we pray) for all, who have become victims of violence, (in this situation we are thinking of), for example, those people who are fighting for their rights in South Africa and the victims of the IRA terror attacks of the last weeks.

Congregation and Organ: Kyrie Eleison....

"Swords into Ploughshares." Pictured is one of the original signs used to inform people about the Peace Prayers held at the St. Nikolai Church in Leipzig from 1982 through what has become known as the Leipzig Fall (Leipziger Herbst)—that is, the "peaceful revolution" of 1989 in which people took to the streets of the city to demand political change. Written inside the circle, surrounding the male figure, is "Swords into Ploughshares," a slogan that St. Nikolai's pastor, Christian Führer, had suggested in the early 1980s, when the diplomatic crisis regarding NATO cruise missiles was underway. Around the lower edge of the circle is "Peace Prayer in St. Nikolai [Church]." The rectangle on the right gives the day and time—Mondays at 5 PM—that the Peace Prayers were held. The photo was taken inside the St. Nikolai Church in Leipzig, Germany, in June 2009. Photo by Glennys Young.

(God, we pray to you) for all those fulfilling their military service in the riot police, who are here in action every Monday against their wills.
Congregation and Organ: Kyrie Eleison....

J. Fischer, Fr. Richter, Chr. Wonneberger, Chr. Motzer [alternating; beautitudes]:
Blessed are the meek: for they will inherit the earth*....
J. Fischer [Suggestions for non violent conduct]:
(Now I would like to provide some suggestions for nonviolent conduct. I ask:)
—that you restrain yourselves and help your neighbors in this regard.
—that you seek dialogue, with your neighbor and with any other person.

---

* Matthew 5:5, King James Version of the Bible.

—be polite and appropriate, do not use any swear words; a chorus of cat-calls does not signal your willingness to engage in dialogue.

—singing songs together helps to reduce one's fears, and to demonstrate non-violence to the opponent.

For this reason you do not have to return your song sheets when you leave. (Applause)

—If they attempt to arrest anyone, sit down and link arms with one's neighbors. (Strong applause)

—If you are arrested, call out your name to those you leave behind.

—From inside the police vehicle, call out how many have been arrested with you.

—(during and after the interrogation) refuse to sign anything.

—during the interrogation, do not make any statements that go beyond the information provided on your identity card. (Pause, Applause)

Chr. Wonneberger: (... We would like to close the Prayer with a common song.)

Chr. Miehm: ["We Shall Overcome" with German lyrics.

For this, the attendees arose from the pews and joined hands.]

Chr. Wonneberger: [Our father ... and blessing.]

[After that, many of the approximately twenty-five thousand visitors sang the Peace Prayer "We Shall Overcome" even as they were leaving the church.]

NOTES

1. For exhaustive documentation, see Stéphane Courtois, Mark Kramer et al., *The Black Book of Communism: Crimes, Terror, Repression* (Cambridge, MA: Harvard University Press, 1999).

2. See Matthew E. Lenoe, *The Kirov Murder and Soviet History* (New Haven, CT: Yale University Press, 2010).

3. Zinoviev, Kamenev, and seventeen others were tried in January 1935. The defendants accepted responsibility for Kirov's murder, even in the absence of convincing evidence tying them to the act.

4. The best source on Tiananmen is Dingxin Zhao, *The Power of Tiananmen: State-Society Relations and the 1989 Beijing Student Movement* (Chicago: University of Chicago Press, 2001).

5. I adapt here the title of Jan Kubik's study of Polish Solidarity's use of symbols. See *The Power of Symbols against the Symbols of Power: The Rise of Solidarity and the Fall of State Socialism in Poland* (University Park: Pennsylvania State University Press, 1994).

6. Quoted in Archie Brown, *The Rise and Fall of Communism* (New York: Ecco, 2009), 446.

7. This line of argument has been advanced most recently in Stephen Kotkin (with a contribution by Jan T. Gross), *Uncivil Society: 1989 and the Implosion of the Communist Establishment* (New York: Random House, 2009).

8. Here I adapt the title of Gail Stokes's *The Walls Came Tumbling Down: The Collapse of Communism in Eastern Europe* (New York: Oxford University Press, 1993).

9. Steven Pfaff, *Exit-Voice Dynamics and the Collapse of East Germany: The Crisis of Leninism and the Revolution of 1989* (Durham, NC: Duke University Press, 2006), 88.

10. Quoted in ibid., 95.

11. After the Peace Prayer, people gathered outside of St. Nikolai in the small square located in Leipzig's compact city center. They held up a banner that read "For an Open Land with Free People" ("*Für ein offenes Land mit freien Menschen*").

12. These were by no means the first critiques of East German state violence in oppositionist circles. In the summer of 1989, the *Environmental Newsletter* (*Umweltsblätter*) of East Berlin's Zion Church had drawn upon Gorbachev's "New Thinking" to condemn the regime's violence as "'bloodily and permanently betraying socialist goals.'" Quoted in Pfaff, *Exit-Voice Dynamics*, 99.

13. A figure of eight thousand people is given elsewhere. See, for example, Dirk Philipsen, *We Were the People: Voices From East Germany's Revolutionary Autumn of 1989* (Durham, NC: Duke University Press, 1993), 394.

14. This summary is drawn from Pfaff, *Exit-Voice Dynamics*, 104–105. Quotes at 104.

15. This is the figure given in Jörg Schönbohm, *Two Armies and One Fatherland: The End of the Nationale Volksarmee*, trans. Peter Johnson (Providence, RI: Berghahn Books, 1996), 13. On the demonstrators' political goals, see Philipsen, *We Were the People*, 394, and Schönbohm, *Two Armies*, 13.

16. I am grateful to Sabine Lang, Dorothea Trottenberg, Helma Young, and, especially, Wolfram Latsch for consulting with me about the nuances of this translation. The German text begins with the following note by the editors of the volume in which it originally appeared: "This reconstruction of the Peace Prayer on 25 September 1989, which was held by the Working Group of Human Rights under the responsibility of Pastor Wonneberg, was based on the manuscript and a tape recording." For details, see *Freunde und Feinde,: Friedensgebete in Leipzig zwischen 1981 und dem 9. Oktober 1989. Documentation* (Leipzig, 1994), 417 n. 646.

CHAPTER 6

Everyday Life, I: Work

"H e who does not work, neither shall he eat." Such was Lenin's famous pronouncement on the importance of labor in a Communist polity.[1] In
fact, this phrase is often called the fundamental "commandment" of socialism.
Marxism privileged the proletariat, or working class, as the class that, by virtue
of the specific *nature* of its suffering under capitalism, was to be the redeemer
of humanity. When Communist parties came to power and embarked on state-
building projects that stretched on for decades, they enacted policy after policy
that sustained the importance of worker identity in membership in the Communist
party, in securing educational opportunities, and in the allocation of other scarce
resources such as pay, housing, and vacations. As we saw in chapter 4, individuals
in Communist polities learned how to play the identity game, that is, how to invoke
the poetics of self-representation to show that, no matter one's class origins, one
was really, truly, now a "worker" and had attained working-class consciousness.

Yet the kinds of labor that Communist polities valorized, and the ways in
which they delivered messages about the importance of labor, varied greatly across
time and space. In general, as Communist polities proliferated around the world,
they proved to be increasingly flexible on the issue of who was a "worker." While
Lenin had already assigned poor peasants to the proletariat prior to the Bolshevik
Revolution, Mao and other Chinese Communists made peasants the center of the
"proletarian" revolution. Soviet political posters of the late Stalin era and beyond
moved beyond the iconic heroism of industrial laborers and collective farm workers in the political posters of the 1930s to praising "heroes of labor" in white-collar,
even technocratic, positions.[2] The same shift can be seen in political posters in
other Communist polities.[3]

Not only was there significant change in who could be "labor heroes" on the
socialist front. Beyond a shift in the message, there was also transformation in the
medium, or *media,* through which it was delivered. The technological revolutions
of the post–World War II period—the emergence of television, home music entertainment systems, the expansion of radio, and so on—seeped into Communist

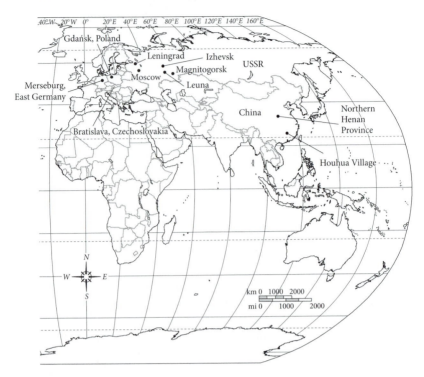

Locator Map for Chapter 6

polities. The new media provided additional ways to transmit changing messages about the valorization of labor to the population. To the extent that the state could not control access to unofficial sources, people in Communist polities were able to view and hear nonsocialist messages about labor and its rewards. For example, East Germans could watch West German television,[4] and people living in the "Estonian Soviet Socialist Republic" could watch Finnish TV.[5] Some Soviet citizens were exposed to alternative views about labor through underground music performances.

Hence, what also varied was the meaning, or meanings, that people living in Communist societies ascribed to the work they did (and didn't do!) over the life-course of Communist polities. The comparative study (over both time and space) of attitudes to labor within and across Communist polities is in its infancy. But what we do know is that in some cases, highly educated individuals sought, during the USSR's "late socialism," to be underemployed—to take jobs in which they would have a lot of free time—such as working in boiler rooms—so that they could pursue other kinds of "labor" that had more meaning to them (writing music, fiction, poetry, etc.).

The selections in this chapter provide readers with glimpses into how people's understandings of labor, and attitudes toward it, varied across time and space in Communist polities. Readers will encounter Chinese students studying to be good

Communist cadres in Moscow in the late 1920s, people involved in the labor crusades of the heroic building of heavy industry in the USSR during the "building of socialism" (roughly 1929–1934), East German workers who mounted the first major uprising in Communist Eastern Europe in the post–World War II period, Chinese cadres (and, though obliquely, Chinese peasants) during Mao's utopian bid to have China surpass the West in industrialization during the "Great Leap Forward" of 1957–1961, working people in Slovakia calling for improvements in working and living conditions in the early 1960s, underground Solidarity activists in Poland who, in the early 1980s, counseled workers on creating a culture of everyday resistance at their workplaces, and a late Brezhnev-era Soviet rock musician on the kinds of jobs that worked well with his creative pursuits.

6-1

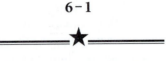

Moscow, 1928

A Chinese Student in the USSR Grapples with Love,
Sex, Labor, and the Building of Socialism

ould a good Communist cadre have a love life and enjoy sex? And if so, what was the appropriate balance between love and work for the Party? How much, and in what ways, did one have to "love" the Party? These were questions that ran through the lives of Communist Party members throughout the world. They were also questions debated by Party leaderships around the world. Even in the PRC of the 1950s, the Party transmitted the clear message that pursuing love for purely personal reasons was a bourgeois idea, and that love had to be subordinated to the socialist liberation of humanity.[6] In the document that follows, a Chinese student in Moscow in the late 1920s grapples with the choices about one's personal life that being a good Communist entailed.

This Chinese student was attending the Communist University of the Toilers of the East (KUTV)*, an important institution in the history of Communism as an international movement. Established by the Comintern on 21 April 1921, in Moscow, the KUTV opened its doors six months later.[7] A sort of preparatory school for young Communists from East Asia and the colonial world, it offered training in Marxist theory, Party organization, and trade union organization. The KUTV would become the *alma mater* of a long list of Communist luminaries: Ho Chi Minh (1890–1969), President of Vietnam; Nazim Hikmet (1902–1963), a Turkish poet; Khasan Israilov (1910–1944), a Chechen revolutionary; Khalid Bakdash (1912–1995), the Syrian Communist Party's secretary from 1936–1995; Fahd (1901–1949), secretary of the Iraqi Communist Party, 1941–1949; Manabendra Nath Roy (1887–1954), who was instrumental in establishing Communist parties in India and Mexico; Sen Katayama (1859–1933), a figure in the American and Japanese Communist parties;[8] Tan Malaka (1894–1949), a member of the Indonesian Communist Party; and Mirza Sultan-Galiev (1892–1940), a Bolshevik who championed "Muslim National Communism." Among the major figures in Chinese Communism who attended KUTV were Liu Shaoqi (1898–1969),

---

From RGASPI (Russian State Archive of Socio-Political History), fond 532, op. 1, d. 401, ll. 122, 122 ob., 123, 123 ob. Reprinted with permission of RGASPI. Translation: Elizabeth McGuire.

---

*In Russian, the Kommunisticheskii universitet trudiashchikhsia Vostoka. The KUTV had regional branches in Azerbaijan (Baku), in Siberia (Irkutsk), and in Uzbekistan (Tashkent).

President of the People's Republic of China from 1959–1968. Its alumni also included lower-profile Communists from around the world.

Among the debates that consumed students within the KUTV's Chinese community was that concerning the proper relationship between love, litera-ture, and revolution.[9] The pretext for the article reproduced next, which was published in the KUTV's Chinese student newspaper on 5 July 1928, was another Chinese student's criticism of those young Chinese who were devoting too much time to reading novels about romance. The title of the essay, "No More Young Werthers," is a reference to Johann Wolfgang von Goethe's *The Sorrows of Young Werther* (1774)*, a literary work about a star-crossed lover, Werther, whose unre-quited love for a married woman, Lotte, ends with his suicide. In response to the worry about the danger of the Werther phenomenon for the Communist move-ment, the author not only asserts that good Communists can and should spend their time reading literature—if it is of the right type, that is. Also advanced is the argument that one can be a good Communist and still fall in love—as long as one does so in the appropriate way!

STUDY, REVOLUTION, LITERATURE, AND LOVE—AFTER READING "DO NOT BECOME YOUNG WERTHER"

One has only to remember our purpose in coming to the Red Capital, considering our mission upon our future return to our country, especially in the context of vigorous attacks by international imperialists on the working class, at a time when white terror in China is continually increasing to ever higher levels, to know just how we should intensify our studies! The success of our future work is directly proportional to the amount of our studies: if we can study more revolutionary theory, methods, and tactics, then our subsequent work will yield a greater result....

In the second place, the results of study are quite related to the quality of each comrade's physical condition and everyday self-cultivation; we don't hope and can't hope that every comrade will become a universal genius, we can only hope that each comrade can develop his strong points as best he can, preparing to sacrifice his everything for the revolution. Leninism and Marxism are things we should study carefully, but why is it not acceptable, if some comrades who are sensitive and like literature use the time they have left over after studying Leninism and Marxism to read some writings that only describe the conditions of society and individual feelings, even though the writings can't "research the causes of social phenomena and point out the way out for people"? Of course, we should suppose that what they are reading isn't the type of literature like *Dream of the Red Chamber* about

---

* The novel, whose German title is *Die Leiden des jungen Werthers*, was then revised and republished in 1787. The novel, in which Goethe drew upon incidents from his own life, became a piece of cult literature and, tragically, inspired numerous deaths similar to Werther's.

[the love of] Brother Bao and Sister Lin*, nor the literature on historic figures from ancient times such as the story about Xiang Yu and Liu Bei—because this is the literature of feudal times with an ideology of individual heroism and full of plots in families of gentry class. Even though they also have their literary value, they aren't working class literature, not the literature that we need to study. However, if they are going to read working class literature, why can't they? Moreover the usefulness of literature "describing social conditions and personal emotion" is something we should not overlook: literature that describes the oppressive lives of the proletariat can strengthen readers' feelings of sympathy and increase revolutionary spirit; descriptions of the happiness of future society can awaken optimistic sentiment and can imbue them with limitless hope; Gorky's *Mother*†, even though I can't read it in the original, still the magical greatness expressed in the movie has already had unexpected effects. So even if literature can't "research social phenomena and people's lives," it actually can illustrate the inner evils of society, and inspire people to find their way forward. . . .

Finally, about the question of "Young Werther type" "introspective worry" love. Now people, unless they no longer have their private parts, all have sexual desires and excitement as well as the painful hopes and desires of love. So love is an uncontrollable element in the lives of people; and unhappiness in sex, although we can use all kinds of methods to lessen it, will only turn out to be paper flowers, unable to yield any fruit! . . . Actually, love doesn't jeopardize our studies in any serious way, but can increase our interest in studying. On the contrary, if appropriate concessions aren't made to youthful sexual desire, and if unstable passion has no outlet, if there is no way to smooth and steady such urges, only then will we "worry" and then will love harm our studies!

Unfortunately, the average person's ways and process of loving have hardly been entirely revolutionized! Marx, before he succeeded in love, could not achieve his true candor. What we so actively oppose is placing the basis of love on money; we also strike against the official-type of love, that is, taking advantage of the importance of one's job to attract one's lover. But seeing lovers as formidable enemies, exhausting every kind of hypocritical method to make them fall into my trap, can you see yourself here? Like pickpockets, using all sorts of low and vulgar methods to steal the treasures of another, is this what we find so admirable?

I don't understand psychology, and I also don't think we can resolve such psychic conflicts based on the natural laws of the psyche. The reality of the conflict is this:

---

* Brother Bao is a reference to Jia Boayu, and Sister Lin is a reference to Lin Daiyu, the main characters in *Dream of the Red Chamber*, one of the most famous novels in classical Chinese literature. Mao once offered a class analysis of love in the novel. I thank Madeleine Yue Dong for this point.

† Regarded as the great Russian writer Maxim Gorky's (1868–1936) signature work, his 1907 novel *Mother* (in Russian, *Mat'*) tells the story of a Russian working woman whose oppression under capitalism transforms her into the revolutionary leader of a strike.

"He doesn't really love me. If he really loves me, when I refused his first letter why doesn't he write a second, a third letter declaring his love?" This is what one student at Sun Yat-sen University* said, and I got to know this from someone who heard her words in person. If she really doesn't love him, doesn't care about his [higher] status, then why does she want him to write a second and third letter? If she already loved him, why did she refuse the first letter? What do such conflicts mean?

There are many reasons for such conflicts. We can often hear this kind of situation: "She loved his beautiful white face, but when he wrote her a love letter, he was refused by her!" It's just these kinds of conflicts that produce "worry," this "worry" really isn't a person's fault! Werther's "worry" bore the evil influence of feudalism! If Lotte and Werther didn't harbour illusions of monogamy, and her husband didn't have some petty jealous feelings, then why would Werther resort to killing himself!

If people's love—especially Communist Party people's love—can nakedly and without an iota of hypocrisy, on the basis of their common understanding of the political line, through ties of sincere love, realize their beautiful dreams, what's the "worry," and how can it harm our studies…?

7.5.1928 Dreamed up at Communist University

6–2

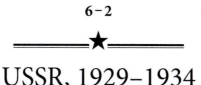

USSR, 1929–1934

Labor and Its Meaning During Stalin's "Great Break"

For people living in the USSR at the end of the 1920s and beginning of the 1930s, Stalin's "great break" (*velikii perelom*)—industrialization of heavy industry and forced collectivization—brought massive change to their lives. The "great break" meant the building of huge steel plants for making

---

* In 1925, following the death of Sun Yat-sen on 12 March 1925, Sun Yat-sen University was founded in Moscow for Chinese revolutionaries of the Guomindang and the Communist Party of China. Run by the Comintern, it was completely separate from KUTV. In 1928, Sun Yat-sen University (SYSU) was renamed the Communist University for the Toilers of China (KUTK). Most Chinese then attended SYSU/KUTK, but some attended KUTV. (Deng Xiaoping himself attended SYSU/KUTK.) SYSU/KUTK closed in the mid-1930s. For more details, see Min-ling L. Yu, "Sun Yat-sen University in Moscow: 1925–1930," PhD Dissertation, New York University, 1995.

machinery, the expansion of existing metropolises (such as Moscow) as peasants flocked to the cities to work in new factories, the building of new cities (such as Magnitogorsk, located on the Russian steppe at the base of the Ural mountains), and, for the swelling ranks of factory workers, new work habits, a new sense of time (one oriented toward the rhythm of factory life rather than that of agricultural productions), and new values. These peasant in-migrants turned factory workers, for example, had to attain the proper political understanding of work in the "building of socialism"—the creation of the world's first socialist society.

Work, official discourse made clear, was not something one did to survive, or for personal fulfillment. One had a civic, indeed political, obligation to work. This was true for everyone in Soviet society, but industrial workers had a special mission. Each moment that one worked in a factory, whether smelting steel, making machine tools, or building the factory itself, one helped humanity transcend capitalism and move toward socialism.[10] Labor, and especially the labor of the industrial proletariat, had paramount significance in the epic battle between socialism and capitalism, between good and evil, between light and darkness, a battle being fought every moment, every hour, every day in the international arena. To be the best soldier in this battle, the industrial worker had not only to know how to work, but to be "politically literate"—that is, to understand and believe that the Communist Party was deputized by history to lead the USSR to socialism, and that its decisions were always correct.

Beyond understanding, of course, one had to *act*. Acting meant, in the realm of industrial labor, not only striving to be the most productive worker in socialist work competitions, in which a given labor unit, whether an individual, a brigade, a shop, or a factory, strived to produce more than the others. Acting also meant, as the "Letter to Marfa" published hereafter attests, exhorting one's spouse—especially one's husband—to work harder, and to shame and scold when he/she did not. One learned to speak as if one understood the proper meaning of work in a socialist society.

The official discourse of the Soviet state (and Communist Party) valorized worker enthusiasm, of course, above all. Among the almost countless documents from Stalin's "great break" that attest to such enthusiasm are the first two documents presented next. In the first text, the wife (Anna Kovaleva) of the best locomotive driver in the transportation network within the factory does her part to enlist the wife of the *worst* such worker (Marfa Gudzia) to get her husband to work harder.[11] But workers could also complain, provided that they did not challenge the Bolshevik program and the Party's justification for ruling. One could not question the mission of building socialism. In the second document, workers complain—appropriately, of course—that they are going hungry. (And indeed, during the "great break," there were strikes, riots, and other cases of collective action generated by worker discontent.[12])

"LETTER TO MARFA"

Dear Marfa!

We are both wives of locomotive drivers of the rail transport of Magnitka*. You probably know that the rail transport workers of the MMK [Magnitogorsk Metallurgical Complex] are not fulfilling the plan, that they are disrupting the supply of the blast furnaces, open hearths, and rolling shops.... All the workers of Magnitka accuse our husbands, saying that the rail workers hinder the fulfillment of the [overall] industrial plan. It is offensive, painful, and annoying to hear this. And moreover, it is doubly painful, because all of it is the plain truth. Every day there were stoppages and breakdowns in rail transport. Yet our internal factory transport has everything it needs in order to fulfill the plan. For that, it is necessary to work like the best workers of our country work. Among such shock workers is my husband, Aleksandr Panteleevich Kovalev. He always works like a shock worker, exceeding his norms, while economizing on fuel and lubricating oil. His engine is on profit and loss accounting.... My husband trains locomotive drivers' helpers out of unskilled laborers. He takes other locomotive drivers under his wing.... My husband receives prizes virtually every month.... And I too have won awards....

My husband's locomotive is always clean and well taken care of. You, Marfa, are always complaining that it is difficult for your family to live. And why is that so? Because your husband, Iakov Stepanovich, does not fulfill the plan. He has frequent breakdowns on his locomotive, his locomotive is dirty, and he always overconsumes fuel. Indeed, all the locomotive drivers laugh at him. *All the rail workers of Magnitka know him—for the wrong reasons, as the worst driver. By contrast, my husband is known as a shock worker* [original translator's italics]. He is written up and praised in the newspapers.... He and I are honored everywhere as shock workers. At the store we get everything without having to wait in queues. We moved to the building for shock workers [*dom udarnika*]. We will get an apartment with rugs, a gramophone, a radio, and other comforts. Now we are being assigned to a new store for shock workers and will receive double rations.

...Soon the Seventeenth Party Congress of our Bolshevik Party will take place. All rail workers are obliged to work so that Magnitka greets the Congress of Victors† at full production capacity.

Reprinted from Stephen Koktin, *Magnetic Mountain: Stalinism as a Civilization* (Berkeley, CA: University of California Press, 1995), 218–219. Published with permission of the University of California Press. The original document can be found in GARF (State Archive of the Russian Federation), f. 7952, op. 5, d. 303, ll. 3–5. Translation: Stephen Kotkin.

---

* "Magnitka" was (and still is) the popular name for both the city of Magnitogorsk and its Metallurgical Complex.

† "Congress of the Victors": the shorthand for the Seventeenth Congress of the Communist Party of the Soviet Union, held from 26 January to 10 February 1934. The victory that Stalin and the Party celebrated was the building of socialism.

Therefore, I ask you, Marfa, to talk to your husband heart to heart, read him my letter. You, Marfa, explain to Iakov Stepanovich that he just can't go on working the way he has. Persuade him that he must work honorably, conscientiously, like a shock worker. Teach him to understand the words of comrade Stalin, that work is a matter of honor, glory, valor, and heroism.

You tell him that if he does not correct himself and continues to work poorly, he will be fired and lose his supplies. I will ask my Aleksandr Panteleevich to take your husband in tow, help him improve himself and become a shock worker, earn more. I want you, Marfa, and Iakov Stepanovich to be honored and respected, so that you live as well as we do.

I know that many women, yourself included, will say: "What business is it of a wife to interfere in her husband's work. You live well, so hold your tongue." But it is not like that.... We all must help our husbands to fight for the uninterrupted work of transport in the winter. Ok, enough. You catch my drift. This letter is already long. In conclusion, I'd like to say one thing. It's pretty good to be a wife of a shock worker. It's within our power. Let's get down to the task, amicably. I await your answer.

Anna Kovaleva

LETTER RECEIVED BY COMRADE ALEXEI RYKOV, THE PRIME MINISTER OF THE USSR*, ON 17 AUGUST 1930

Comrade Rykov:

We beg you, in the name of the fifty thousand workers of the Izhevsk factory[†], to save us from hunger. The cafeterias are shutting down, they give out water with oatmeal and a little bread. In the stores, they give out a half pound of black bread or meal per person, they haven't given out more than that for a month already. We are swelling up from hunger, [we] don't have the strength to work. Before they gave the sponger-soldiers three pounds of black bread

---

From *Golos naroda: Pis'ma i otkliki riadovykh sovetskikh grazhdan o sobytiiakh 1918–1932 gg.*, (*Voice of the People: Letters and Comments by Ordinary Soviet Citizens about the Events of 1918–1932*), 320–321. Reprinted by permission of ROSSPEN (Rossiiskaia politicheskaia entsiklopediia). The original document can be found in RGAE (Russian State Archive of the Economy), f. 8043, op. 11, d. 26, II. 13–13 (ob).

---

* But even at the time the letter was written, Alexei Rykov's political future in the Communist Party of the Soviet Union was in peril. He was a prominent leader of the "Right Opposition" to Stalin's industrialization and forced collectivization. Just slightly over four months after he received this letter—on 19 December, 1930—Vyacheslav Molotov would replace Rykov as Prime Minister (the exact title was Chairman of the Council of People's Commissars of the USSR).

† Izhevsk, a city in the Ural Mountains, was the site of what was at the time one of the largest factories in the USSR. The factory in question specialized in metalworking.

and a quarter pound of meat and a half pound of groats for dinner, but they weren't doing anything. But we are doing difficult work, especially in the [factory's] foundry shop. Workers are running from production, they are selling everything they have just so they can feed their children. Those children are innocent victims of the fact that you didn't know how to provide us with anything, such is what your heavy industry is to us, when there is no small industry at all, you will not be satisfied with heavy industry [with the way heavy industry is going], you should have provided yourselves with goods that are supremely essential, and then think about heavy industry, or everybody will go to rack and ruin from hunger.

Comrad Rykov, what we are suggesting to you—listen to us—is that you not persist further. Stop it now, it is enough—they were having a good time, you see, nothing is coming of it, it's possible to switch over to another path. The first thing that's necessary is to open private factories, mills, and private trade. The private trader who isn't driven into a corner by taxes will find everything, then create model economies, that is, you'll be able to do so...and [let] the middle peasants have three to four horses, a group of ten cows, half a hundred cows and chickens, and geese*... When you [once again] have private trade, the peasant will do his best to get more agricultural products from his labor and, to this end, will sell bread and wool cheaply, and flour and meat. And when a peasant isn't interested in buying, he won't sell anything, this means there will be few agricultural products, but it means...they will be expensive, but agricultural products will be expensive, urban products will be expensive, too....

We beg you, don't make us take drastic measures, we are approaching you in a comradely fashion, there are many Communists among us, and everybody arrived at a unanimous decision. The situation is catastrophic, it's impossible to stand it any longer.

Of course, there is still a way to save [our] country from destitution, it's to get everything from abroad, don't fritter way the time getting this kind of support, save us from hunger...at the first opportunity.

The signatures of the representatives of the shop follow.

Signatures:
Skvortsov and Tatarnikov

---

* There is a gap in the original.

6 – 3

East Germany, 17 June 1953

Workers (and Others!) Against the "Workers' State"

Uprisings, or demonstrations, constituted another context in which people developed political practices to contest economic conditions and political regimes in Communist polities. The first major uprising in the Communist satellite states of Eastern Europe occurred in June 1953, in East Germany—only months, in other words, after Joseph Stalin's death in early March 1953. An economic crisis had been brewing in East Germany for some time. It had been caused by the implementation of policies linked to the GDR's "Expanding Socialism According to Plan," which entailed state expropriations of private farms to create gigantic state farming collectives, as well as the breakneck construction of heavy industry. The GDR's economy was already stressed by reparations payments from World War II. But the catalyst for the uprising, or proverbial last straw, was the imposition of economic policies in May 1953. The anger of East Germans was stoked by the raising of workers' production norms (which translated into a sharp increase in working hours), coupled with a simultaneous increase in food prices. (This was a dangerous combination that the Soviet regime also put into place in 1962, setting off a major workers' uprising in Novocherkassk, a city in the Caucasus Mountains of southern Russia.)

During the last days of May, and the first days of June 1953, some workers went on strike in East Berlin. But the first major wave of mass protest did not occur until 16 June when, in East Berlin, thousands of construction workers took to the streets in protest of wage cuts. On 17 June, events came to a head. More than a million people went on strike in seven hundred cities and towns throughout the GDR, even though East Berlin remained the epicenter of the action. Although the uprising began with economic demands, workers and other East Germans soon began to air political grievances. Assembling in public on city and town squares throughout East Germany (including in the provincial city of Merseburg, featured in the following document), they demanded free elections, the release of political prisoners, political transparency, the end of Communism, and German reunification.

Excerpted from Karl Wilhelm Fricke, *Der Arbeiteraufstand: Zeitzeugen und Zeitdokumente zum 17. Juni 1953. Gesendet im Deutschlandfunk am 17. Juni 1983* (*The Workers' Uprising: Witnesses and Documents Concerning 17 June 1953. Broadcast on German Radio on 17 June 1983.*) Köln: Deutschlandfunk, Abteilung Presse und Öffentlichkeit, 32, 1984. Reprinted by permission of Karl Wilhelm Fricke. Translation: Glennys Young.

Not only the legitimacy, but also the very existence, of the East German regime was on the line. In the event, East German Party leader Walter Ulbricht had to turn to the USSR and its military power so that order could be restored. Soviet tanks rolled into East Berlin and other locales, and Soviet forces inflicted violence. To this day it is a matter of dispute how many people were shot and wounded. (Officially, the East Germans claimed that twenty-one people were shot and 187 sustained wounds.) At least fourteen hundred people were tried and sentenced by the regime. Although Ulbricht's fate hung in the balance, he managed to stay in power, convincing the Soviet leadership that East Germany needed a "Stalinist" leader. Yet the courageous actions of East Germans had demonstrated the limits of Stalinization to their country's leaders, and caused Communist leaders elsewhere in Eastern Europe to fear similar demonstrations and strikes.

In the text that follows, readers can hear the voices of participants and observers of the events that occurred on 17 June 1953—a date henceforth ignored in East Germany and observed as a national holiday in West Germany. This document takes us out of Berlin, to provincial cities of East Germany, namely Leuna and Merseburg. There are excerpts from eyewitness accounts by Friedrich Schorn, head of a strike committee at the Leuna Chemical Plant, Wilhelm Grothaus, an older, experienced SPD member who had been persecuted by the Nazis for joining with the Communist party in an antifascist protest, a nineteen-year-old student (*Abiturient*) from Görlitz, and a journalist from the provincial city of Halle. The excerpts give a sense of the remarkable resourcefulness that people displayed when they organized strike committees, spread word of the protests, and even, in one remarkable incident, demanded that Soviet troops leave the factory grounds. They also give us a sense of the rollercoaster of emotions—from caution to hopefulness to despair—that people claimed they felt as more and more joined demonstrations for fundamental political change and then were violently suppressed.

AN EYEWITNESS ACCOUNT FROM A WORKER IN LEUNA, A PROVINCIAL CITY IN THE GDR

On Tuesday evening [16 June 1953] we heard the reports from the Stalinallee and heard that the construction workers were striking. This naturally spurred us on in a certain way, and we resolved to do the same thing on another morning, and to support the workers in Berlin. Things remained quiet in Leuna until breakfast, and then it began, in building 15 it was, that the workers mutinied. We found out [what was going on] through people on bicycles, thus, through workers, who were now driving around on the factory grounds, and the entire workforce was ordered by these workers and bicyclists [to go] from the shop floor of the Leuna factory to the administration building. And then things also started to gear up, and as we got to the administration building, there were maybe at least already twenty thousand people gathered there. The Leuna Factory Workers has a twenty-eight thousand person workforce. Then speakers appeared, [one] was present, who had been in Buchenwald after '45, who now formulated the workers' demands.

FRIEDRICH SCHORN (AT THE TIME AN AUDITOR AT THE LEUNA FACTORY COMPLEX, SCHORN HAD BEEN, AFTER 1945, A PRISONER IN THE BUCHENWALD INTERNMENT CAMP*.)

I now asked the personnel to elect men or women from the separate departments, who would also be appointed to the strike committee of the Leuna Factory Complex. As this was happening, I delivered a short address and elaborated once more on the events in East Berlin. I also demanded the rescinding of the ten percent increase in work norms and refused a voluntary ten percent increase in target output. In the same breath I demanded the complete "release of political prisoners"; especially the release of our fifteen co-workers who were being detained pending trial in Halle. I demanded "free elections"; but I also warned about possible acts of violence. I said emphatically, no threats, no acts of violence against the Soviet occupying powers. I stressed that we wanted to leave the Soviets out of these matters, this is a purely German matter....

We assembled in an orderly fashion and marched to Merseburg. On the way there, I would say thousands of residents of [the towns/cities of] Leuna, Bad Dürenberg and the surrounding towns had already joined our demonstration march. We were met by quite a few police patrols, who were disarmed by us and joined [us]. In the beginning, I had not counted on the support of our youth, but I was so pleasantly surprised....Because the youth were among the most active! As we arrived in Merseburg and marched to Nuland Square, laborers and white collar employees came onto the square from the other side. Within a half an hour the square was so overcrowded with more and more commercial vehicles, tractors with men, people from the surrounding farm areas and the surrounding coal mines coming to join in, that between one and one thirty approximately one hundred thousand people were congregated on Nuland Square.

HANS LÜTZENDORF (A PARTICIPANT IN THE AFOREMENTIONED RALLY, HE WAS WORKING AT THE TIME AS A JOURNALIST IN HALLE.)

Protest marches naturally formed from the protest gatherings in Leuna and Buna. People marched to Merseburg and joined with the buddies from the brown coal factories. The police, who were completely surprised, professed themselves to be in solidarity with the striking workers and marched shoulder to shoulder with the striking workers. Farmers left their tractors, business people, their shops

---

* Buchenwald was used by the Soviets as an internment camp ("Internierungslager") from 1945 to 1950, as opposed to the Nazi concentration camp in the same location and with the same name.

and employees, their offices, to demonstrate with the workers from the chemical factory who wearing leather aprons, clogs, and welders' glasses. Posters with party slogans, SED logos, and the hated red flags, which had been torn up and shredded, bordered the procession, which had quickly swelled to more than ten thousand people. Everybody gathered on the square in the center of the city, what had previously been Nuland Square, in order to form a joint strike committee. A euphoric mood had taken hold of everybody. The German national anthem* was heard and, this time, nobody heard any overbearing nationalism in its text. Most thought of unity, justice and freedom as they were singing, even if they did not have the text in their memory. It was an intoxication that had gripped the crowd, in which complete strangers embraced, women cried and Party comrades furtively disposed of their badges. The demands that were transmitted to the crowd over a commandeered car with a loud speaker mounted on the roof to roaring applause: "Dissolve the government," "free elections," "reduction of production quotas," "lower prices in the state-H0 stores," and—most importantly—"Free all political prisoners."

WILHELM GROTHAUS (AN EXPERIENCED, OLDER SOCIAL DEMOCRAT PERSECUTED BY THE NAZI REGIME FOR ANTIFASCIST RESISTANCE THAT HE MOUNTED WITH OTHER COMRADES FROM THE KPD. HE DIRECTED THE STRIKE COMMITTEE OF HIS FACTORY, THE VEB ABUS.)

We then found ourselves in the big assembly hall. Here the representatives of the central Party management, the regional management [of the Party] tried to speak, [and] were shouted down. Then the factory shop steward† tried to speak, but he also wasn't able to get a word in. Then I got up onto a big lathe and I spoke to those gathered, about sixteen hundred workers, and then things quieted down. The workers all knew me and also knew what I wanted, more or less. Then I told all the workers that the cause of the struggle in Berlin, the question of the production quotas having been raised, was not so decisive, but that we had to reshape the struggle, that, in Berlin, still had the appearance of a union struggle, into a political fight, and that our demands could not lead to redressing [the issue of] the raising of production quotas, but rather that the decisive demands, the basic, decisive demands, should be: "Elimination of the Regime," "Overthrow of the Communist system," "Release of all political prisoners," "free and secret elections," and then the "restoration of German unity."

---

* It should be emphasized that they were singing the *West* ("Einigkeit und Recht und Freiheit"), not the *East*, German anthem.

† In other words, union boss.

INGO HAVENSTEINS (A NINETEEN-YEAR-OLD, WHO, AT THE TIME, WAS A HIGH SCHOOL GRADUATE IN GÖRLITZ.)

I was nineteen years old on 17 June 1953. I lived in Görlitz. I estimate that almost all the plants in Görlitz had gone on strike, because when I came at this point in time from the upper market to the square, where at other times the big demonstrations [led by the] SED took place, there was a crowd of approximately fifteen to twenty-five thousand people. The square was full. More kept on coming. And then someone showed up at the podium. Then I heard someone speaking over the loudspeaker: "Is then there nobody here who can speak?' Everybody was silent. Then the same voice said: "But we really want to sing the national anthem." For us, the *Nationalhymne* was the third verse of the West German national anthem "Unity and Justice and Freedom!"

WILHELM GROTHAUS

I was really hopeful for a short time, as I saw that the Russians did not move. They also did not stir themselves; they observed that some of the police officers were joining in, they marched along, not all of them, but however a large number of policemen joined the march. And as I watched, things went on like this.... Then the people came thither, tens of thousands of them stood along the streets. You could have collected basketfuls of SED party badges and party membership books into a trash can. The people threw all of that away. We passed a school where all the children had torn up their Russian textbooks, had thrown them out of the window into the school courtyard. The Party bigwigs had all fled. Besides, no one was there any more. I was thinking that things are really going swimmingly, thus without any preparation, without any weapons whatsoever, only carried out from the will of the people. Consequently I was really hopeful, I must say.

FRIEDRICH SCHORN (SCHORN, FROM WHOM A FIRST-HAND ACCOUNT APPEARED EARLIER IN THIS CHAPTER, BECAME A LEADER OF THE STRIKE AND SOUGHT TO NEGOTIATE WITH THE DIRECTOR OF THE LEUNA PLANT.)

Between four and four thirty I suddenly heard great screaming and shouting and calls for protests in front of the administration building. I stood up, went to the window; there I saw the first Russian trucks and panzers pulling up outside. Ten minutes passed in this way, the doors opened and a Soviet Major General with his staff came into the directors' room. I knew very well that it was crunch time. Meanwhile I had remained completely alone as the representative of the strike leadership, and we chatted. I told the Soviet officers our wishes and then I said to him: "I demand: withdraw the troops, withdraw the troops from the Leuna

Works. You can position your troops in the vicinity of the Works, but leave the plant. I know," I said, "if you don't leave the plant, the factory will be blown up. I know that I will die, but so will all of you." After thinking it over for a short while, the Russian officer ordered that the troops be withdrawn from the plant. That happened then, too. I further struck an agreement with him that the strike committee should and could meet on the 18th [of June] at 7 AM*.

KURT UNBEHAUEN (HE WAS AMONG THE FOURTEEN HUNDRED PEOPLE SENTENCED BY THE DDR COURTS IN CONNECTION WITH 17 JUNE 1953. AT LEAST EIGHTEEN DEATH SENTENCES WERE HANDED DOWN. HERE, HE TELLS OF HIS TRIAL BEFORE THE REGIONAL COURT.)

The [defense] lawyer appeared five minutes before the trial. I had not seen one earlier before he introduced himself; he also did not trust himself to say anything at the trial, because he was scared that something would "happen to him." Witnesses were not admitted, only the Communist domestic and foreign press. The proceedings did not last all that long; they lasted about three hours, including the presentation of evidence. As I stated the reasons, I was told that on the basis of my utterances I was to be given an especially harsh sentence. Then sentences were read: life imprisonment. I then submitted an appeal. My wife, who was not admitted to this trial, hired a defense lawyer because of this. This person collected signatures in my hometown. It was a very large number. Almost the whole population had protested against my sentence, for I was very much appreciated in my hometown. And because of this the attorney had to flee to the West. The state security service from East Berlin, from the highest place, appeared in my hometown, in order to intimidate the people so that they would not stand up for me.

---

* The Soviets occupied the Leuna Plant on the morning of 18 June 1953. Schorn realized he had to flee to West Berlin. Other strike leaders who did not flee were charged as "ringleaders," "provocateurs," and "fascists." They were subjected to court-martial by the Soviets, and soon thereafter tried in GDR courts.

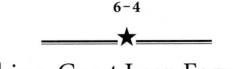

China, Great Leap Forward (1957–1961)

Recollections of a Local Cadre (Wang Fucheng, 1923–)
and His Wife (Wang Xianghua)

For the 542 million (or so) people living in China in 1949, the establishment of the PRC in that year began a complex revolutionary process
that changed the fabric of their lives. Though the process of revolutionary transformation would stretch on for decades, the changes that the
Party leadership effected from 1949 to 1956 created a socialist state, at least
in name.

Among the profound changes for China's people was land reform, which
had entailed dividing up the land, breaking the power of the traditional elite,
and collectivization—a process more or less complete by 1956. Another state-
driven change with profound consequences for people's lives was the suppression of the market. By 1956, the Chinese state had succeeded in eliminating most
of the private market and imposing state regulation on what remained. This
meant that peasants could only sell their grain to the state, and only at prices
that the state set. The state had also either nationalized, or had taken ownership of, industry and handicrafts. As the state reorganized the economy along
socialist lines, it also attacked "counterrevolutionaries," and suppressed political
opposition to the PRC.

During the same period, there were three other revolutionary processes
that profoundly affected, and were shaped by, China's people: China's emergence as a formidable power in the international system, industrialization and
economic modernization, and a revolution in the way that the Chinese were
governed—and governed themselves. Not only did such projects as the national
census of 1953, the classification and identification of ethnic groups, and the
creation of class categories and work groups mean that Chinese people were
counted and sifted into ascribed categories as never before. Not only were the
patterns of social mobility and physical mobility of Chinese people undergoing
major shifts. People in China found themselves under the state's watch as never

Reprinted from Peter J. Seybolt, *Throwing the Emperor From His Horse: Portrait of a Village Leader in
China, 1923–1995* (Boulder, CO: Westview Press, 1996), 52–58. Reprinted by permission of Westview
Press.

before, as government expanded with the creation of government structures below the county level, and bureaucracies, modeled on Soviet practices, ballooned. Topping off this decade or so of multilevel revolutionary transformation was the "Great Leap Forward," Mao's campaign to make China an industrial power, one that, he announced, would surpass Britain in producing steel and other products in fifteen years![13]

A campaign whose goals were even more utopian than Stalin's "Great Break," the "Great Leap Forward" sought to harness China's most plentiful resource—peasant labor—to finance industrialization and carry out its projects. In contrast to typical patterns of industrialization in both Communist and non-Communist polities, the Chinese version during the Great Leap Forward was to be a rural, not an urban, phenomenon. Mobilized for heroic labor in militias led by local party activists, peasants were to undertake both agricultural projects (for example, constructing irrigation systems) and industrial ones (the famous/infamous backyard furnaces for making iron and steel). The scale on which human beings were mobilized is daunting: In the winter of 1957–1958, for example, more than one hundred million peasants were involved in building large-scale water-conservation works.[14]

For both local leaders and peasants, the Great Leap Forward brought chaos, agonizing choices, unbearable demands, and, in the ensuing family, death in a tragic number of cases. Pitted against one another in revolutionary competition, local leaders were under enormous pressure to inflate the results of their harvests to the authorities in Beijing—a pressure that the author of the following document, Wang Fucheng, an illiterate peasant who became a battalion political instructor in charge of Party matters, resisted. But many local leaders succumbed to such pressures, and what was thought to be surplus grain was sold abroad. By 1959, the rural mess halls that had been set up to provide free food had little or nothing to offer. As famine set in, peasants struggled to survive. Some left their homes in quest of food. Others—probably a third of all Chinese peasants—left the rural communes and embarked on private farming. In time, such decisions would bring an improvement in agricultural production. But in the short term, the chaos, hunger, and starvation ruled lives. Rural militias went on the hunt for food, robbing people of grain, beating them, and sometimes raping women. The famine, which is estimated to have taken between 17 and 40 million lives, was the worst of the twentieth century, and perhaps of human history altogether.

The following document gives but tantalizing glimpses into an important subject about which we still know too little: How did Chinese people experience the Great Leap Forward, which in some ways was the culmination of the Party-state's increasing claims upon them during the revolutionary transformations of the 1950s? How did the chaos, devastation, starvation, and death that ran through so many lives affect what the survivors thought of the Party,[15] and of Chinese socialism? These are questions that deserve serious research.

Born in 1923, Wang Fucheng rose from abject poverty to village leader in rural Communist China. For thirty years (1954–1984), he held the highest position in his village (Houhua Village in northern Henan province): Communist Party branch secretary. He knew next to nothing about the world beyond his village, and was only known in his village and its hinterlands. From 1987 to 1994, he engaged in conversations with the American historian of China, Peter Seybolt.

WANG FUCHENG, I

In mid-1958 cadres from the county and township came to the village and took over all farming decisions. This was the beginning of the Great Leap Forward. We worked three shifts a day. We got up at 5 AM and worked until breakfast at 8 AM, then we worked until supper in the evening, and after that we worked at night. We were urged to do two days' work in one day. In the beginning we all supported the cadres and constantly shouted slogans. At times I was so busy I didn't have time to eat. We were afraid of wasting time, so we moved our cooking stoves and pots to the field. Thirty or forty people shared the same pot. Sometimes we slept in the fields at night. We were organized into a military system. The village was a battalion with companies, platoons, and squads under it. I was the battalion political instructor in charge of all Party matters. The village leader was the battalion commander in charge of farming affairs. We used loudspeakers to criticize those who made mistakes and to praise those with merit. I remember a man named Wang Dehui who slept in the field instead of working after we moved our cooking materials there. I severely criticized him at a meeting, saying, "Your thought is not correct. If all are like you, how can we have a happy life?" Wang Dehui had criticized the Great Leap Forward as unreasonable....

Village leaders had no right at that time to decide what to plant and what not to plant. The county and township government planned everything. They said to plant corn, sorghum, and especially sweet potatoes. We planted one thousand mu* of sweet potatoes that year, and they grew very well. About twenty-two villages in this area ate sweet potatoes from our fields. But we didn't even have time to harvest them all because the outside cadres were in such a rush to plant the next crop. They paid little attention to the harvest but mainly concentrated on planting winter wheat. Then they reported to the township and county government how fast they had done their job. If they planted wheat fast, the government would praise them. Otherwise they were criticized. A nearby village, Weihuang, had been told to plant peanuts. At harvest, in their rush to plant the next crop, they just pulled up the stems and leaves and left most of the peanuts in the ground. Then they plowed the land and planted other crops so the cadres could report that their work had been done very fast. Some of our sweet potatoes rotted in the ground for the same reason. What we did dig up, we dried in pieces. To keep them during the winter we buried them in the ground, but they rotted after two months. We distributed them to the villagers, but they didn't want rotten potatoes. They were hungry and dissatisfied.

---

* 6.666 square meters.

When we planted the winter wheat we were told to dig deep, one or two chi [1 chi = 1/3 meter]. An animal pulling a plow couldn't dig that deep, so we had to do it with spades. A cadre from outside the village said, "An ox can't dig as much as a human." We all listened to this cadre's words, but we knew that they were nonsense. We were also told to sow forty to fifty jin* of wheat seed per mu instead of the usual eighteen jin. In Dongjiang Village next to us they were told to use one hundred twenty jin. We had to spread the seed with our spades because the planting box couldn't sow it in that quantity.

I still didn't have any doubts about the Party's general policy, but I knew in my heart that that was not the way to plant crops. Is it right to waste so much seed? Is it right to cut crops at night? I did not argue with the township and county cadres, but sometimes I said what was true: "That is not the way to do farm work."

We worked in the fields day and night, but often we were forced to waste time. For instance, when visiting groups came from different places, sometimes two or three times a day, we had to greet them, shouting slogans and saying, "Welcome! Welcome!" Sometimes when we were working in the east field, we had to go welcome them in the west. Sometimes when we were working in the west, we had to go welcome them in the east. I was the leader of the village, and I showed my dissatisfaction to the outside cadres. They criticized me for rightist tendencies and said I was lagging behind the developing situation. . . .

At harvest time we were under a lot of pressure to exaggerate the amount of grain production. Many cadres made mistakes on this issue. Many villages gave a "Great Leap Forward report" when they reported their harvest. If they harvested four hundred jin, of grain, they would say five hundred or seven hundred jin. The higher the report, the more praise from the commune cadres. If the report was low, they were criticized. We had meetings almost every day to report output. I was honest—I didn't exaggerate—so I was severely criticized. A cadre said to me, "Why is production in your village so low compared to others? You are the leader. There is a problem with your thought. If the villages don't give grain, how can the country run? We must think first of the nation, then of the village." I replied that I was reporting true figures; I didn't exaggerate.

Did I ever lie? Did I ever report false figures? Yes. I had to tell lies. We all did. When cadres from outside the village held a meeting to struggle against a village cadre, I had to protect him. They wanted us to estimate the production amount for the next harvest. When that harvest came, we reported the real figure. They kept asking us to give a higher figure until they were satisfied. . . .

After we had reported the grain amount to the outside cadres, each village had to decide how much grain to give to the government. I'll give you an example that is an approximation, not the real figures. If we had a grain output of thirty thousand jin, we might keep twenty thousand to eat, save five thousand for various uses in the brigade, and give five thousand to the government. The government didn't pay us for that amount. We called it "patriotic grain." Villages that reported very

---

* A measure of weight that is equivalent to about half a kilogram.

high grain production figures had to give a greater amount to the government. Because of false production reports, there was not enough to eat....

It wasn't the weather that caused this shortage, as some officials said later. It was humans who made the disaster. I remember that there was a flood that affected this village at that time, but it wasn't too serious. Only some fields were flooded. Bad management was the cause of the disaster.

The Great Leap was supposed to be a leap in making steel and digging ditches as well as in agriculture. In late 1958 my wife went to Anyang City to work for a steel plant during a national campaign to make iron and steel. Thirty-four men and sixteen women from our village went to Anyang....

WANG FUCHENG, II

I had a lot of difficulties at that time. I was working too hard and coughed up a lot of blood. We had a two-year-old son. When my wife went to Anyang, we had to send him to live with his maternal grandmother who lives about one hundred meters from here. Grandmother was also a Party member and had to go to meetings. She once locked the house and left the child sleeping on the bed. She was gone three hours, and when she came back she couldn't find him. She finally found him naked in a basket that had some cotton in it....

I was very displeased and in low spirits when this happened. There were two provincial-level cadres here at the time. One asked why I was so dejected. I told him the truth, and he immediately sent a letter ordering that my wife be sent back to take care of the baby. The next day a cadre went to Anyang to bring her back. The provincial cadre also asked about my attitude toward village work. I said no matter how hard the work, I would put the affairs of the village first.

In late 1958 we established a commune in this area. Liucun Township (which had political jurisdiction over twenty-two natural villages) became the commune headquarters. The twenty-two villages each became production brigades. We had six production teams under the brigade in this village. I was the top leader in the brigade.

We built a large building in the field as a big eating hall and also for holding meetings and sleeping. Actually, it was a very simple structure made of corn and sorghum stalks. We also had a "happiness home," sometimes called a courtyard, for nurturing the old; a children's courtyard; and a maternity-courtyard....

WANG XIANGHUA [WANG FUCHENG'S WIFE]

I was the head of the children's courtyard. I also worked in the maternity courtyard. We gave women twenty jin of white flour and three jin of sugar if they came there to have their babies. If they didn't come, they got nothing. We did away with all of those things when the Great Leap Forward ended. The people didn't like them. Actually, for the most part, they were all just forms. At that time, the form was more important than the reality. People talked a lot and shouted a lot of slogans, but they didn't do so much work.

WANG FUCHENG

We had to talk and shout a lot because there were so many struggles against those who didn't. The cadres judged people by their attitudes. If they talked and shouted, the cadres would say their attitude was good.

When the commune was set up, we also trained a militia. This is an old base area-with a long tradition of citizen soldiers. They existed long before liberation and even before the War of Resistance. In those earlier times only some of the villagers were in the militia, but during the Great Leap Forward, almost all labor hands joined. We still have a militia today, but there is no training. After the Cultural Revolution, the weapons of the militia were taken away by the county government. We don't allow people to own guns.

After the first year of the Great Leap Forward, outside cadres no longer had control of farming. The brigade and team leaders could decide what to plant and where to plant it. Also at that time, the work-point system was restored and we added extra workpoints for extra work. When the Great Leap Forward began, we did not count work points, we just counted family members and distributed the harvest on the basis of need, not on the basis of work.

After we were in charge of farming decisions again, I asked the people here to plant a lot of turnips because turnips were not taxed. That is one of the main reasons that people here did not starve during the Great Leap Forward famine. The government only wanted wheat after the summer harvest and corn and dried sweet potatoes in the fall. They didn't want our turnips, so we got by on those. I still didn't exaggerate grain output. If I had, most people in my village would have had the swelling disease, and some would have died from hunger because we would have had to give more grain to the government. I could do things that other people dared not do because of my uncle's influence. The situation in this village was better than other villages, so many people wanted to marry their daughters into this village.

The Great Leap Forward lasted for over two years. It stopped in 1960. No one in this village died of hunger or cold at that time, but a lot of people from other villages did. Three died in Zhonghua Village next to us, and in Caopo Village Bocheng Commune, several li from here, an average of one person a day died of hunger for a period of time. We must analyze concretely why they died. Generally it was because the local cadres did not pay enough attention to people's problems. I took care of the health of the villagers: I knew of three people who almost died of starvation. Their legs began to swell, and medicine had no effect. I knew the swelling was because of hunger. One was a young man of twenty-five. The other two were old people. I sent them all to the courtyard for nurturing the old and let them rest there for a month. I gave them 1.5 jin of grain per day rather than the usual one jin. They gradually recovered....

A government inspection team came to this village three times to see why our production figures were so low. A secretary of my uncle Wang Congwu came twice. Wang Congwu was then Secretary of the Central Government Inspection Bureau. His secretary lived in the commune headquarters for one or two days and spent one night in my house. The ordinary masses didn't know he was my uncle's secretary. He checked the production figures in our village account book. I was not struggled against because my uncle was Wang Congwu. It was not because he protected me purposely, but everyone knew of his influence and our relationship, so I was only asked to pay attention to my words....

After the secretary reported the real situation in this and other villages to the central government, they realized that the living standard was poor in the

Cuban Poster. "Let's do our job!" for campaign for literacy, ca. 1961. Designer unkown. Publisher: Comisión Nacional de Alfabetización (National Commission for Literacy). Mobilizing labor was a constant priority of Communist polities. For example, in 1961, Cuban schools closed for several months as students went to the countryside in a crusade to bring literacy to rural Cuba. The students comprised "literacy brigades," whose purpose was to teach rural people how to read and write. (The bottom of the poster says "Let's All Salute the Victorious Brigades!") In Cuba, as in other communist polities, teaching literacy had a Marxist–Leninist content. Marxist–Leninist principles were applied to past, present, and future. In Cuba in the early 1960s, for example, the exercise books for teaching literacy had as their first words "Organization of American States," "Agrarian Reform," and "Cooperation." Courtesy of the International Institute of Social History, Amsterdam.

countryside. Beijing ordered Henan Province to stop what it had been doing. Finally the central government sent aid—wheat, sweet potatoes, sugar, and fish. The people were joyful. Other villages also got aid, as did other counties, for instance, Hua and Xun counties nearby. There had been a lot of suffering in this area during the Great Leap Forward, and we had a great feeling of relief when it was finally over.

6–5

Bratislava, June 1963

The "Working People of Slovakia" Express Their Grievances to the President of Czechoslovakia and the First Secretary of the Communist Party of Czechoslovakia, Antonin Novotný

From 1963 until the Prague Spring of 1968, people in Czechoslovakia—especially Slovaks—expressed more openly their complaints about the political leadership, about the status of the Slovak nation within Czechoslovakia as a whole, and about economic issues than they had during the years of Czechoslovak Stalinism in the 1950s and early 1960s. There were a number of reasons for this. Khrushchev's de-Stalinizing thaw, as we have already seen, sent shockwaves through the Soviet bloc in Eastern Europe, opening the doors for criticism of Stalinist leaders and political practices such as the "show trials" of alleged Trotskyists, Titoists, Zionists, and Slovak "bourgeois nationalists"* in the Communist Party of Czechoslovakia. Another important

From the Slovak National Archive, Fond Central Committee of the Communist Party of Slovakia, Secretary Dubček, Carton 2393, Bundle XI, Folder 93 (1963). Reprinted with the permission of the Slovak National Archive. Translation: Scott Brown.

* For example, in the early 1950s, when the Stalinist era was at its height in Czechoslovakia, the prominent Slovak Communist Gustáv Husák was attacked for "bourgeois nationalism." Husák, who had been a leader of Slovak resistance during World War II, had argued that Slovaks should have a greater role in self-administration. Other prominent Slovak communists who were politically repressed as "bourgeois nationalists" were Vladimír Clementis, the foreign minister, and Ladislav Novomeský, a Slovak poet and notable Communist figure in the Slovak National Uprising of 1944. (On the Uprising, see the gloss on page 218.)

factor was change in the top leadership of the Communist Party: In April 1963, for example, the previously unknown Alexander Dubček became the first secretary of the Communist Party of Slovakia. The shakeup in the Slovak Party leadership served as an impetus for Slovak intellectuals, journalists, and politicians to press, and even recast, the "Slovak question"—whether, and on what basis (autonomy? federalization? sovereignty?), the Slovak nation should be given "self-rule" within a unified "Czechoslovak" state under the rule of the Communist Party. This they did through debates in historical scholarship, the press, and in public.

In this reexamination of Slovakia's status within the Czechoslovak Socialist Republic, a major issue was the economic situation in Slovakia. Most Slovaks believed that their "half" of the country had performed worse economically than the Czech lands. This was especially the case for the early 1960s, when Czechoslovakia as a whole was in economic crisis. Though the Slovak economy sustained rapid economic growth at the end of the 1950s, and the annual rate of industrial growth was ten percent, all was not well. This rapid growth was only made possible by using more raw materials, even in a wasteful manner, to increase production, a questionable long-run strategy. The quality of consumer goods was shoddy. As industrial growth surged in Slovakia, agriculture struggled to keep up. And despite the economic growth, Slovaks, facing unemployment in their half of the country, had to go to the Czech lands to find work. The *relative* economic backwardness of Slovakia in comparison to the Czech lands led Slovaks to view the country's national woes through an economic prism, and vice versa.

As Slovaks tried to redress their complaints about the status of their national organs*, their economy, and the lack of democracy in the Czechoslovak Socialist Republic, they catalyzed a larger, and growing, opposition to the dogmatic and inflexible Antonín Novotný, the president of Czechoslovakia and first secretary of the Communist Party of Czechoslovakia (KSČ), and his people in the Party leadership. It turned out to be Slovak politicians and intellectuals who, with their demands for de-Stalinization, economic reform, and political liberation, first put Novotný on the defensive in the early and mid-1960s. Slovaks and Czechs alike regarded Slovakia as having, rightly so, a reputation for both political and cultural laxity.[16]

Certainly, the origins of the Prague Spring of 1968 are complex. But the way in which the debate about the "Slovak question" unleashed opposition to Novotný, both in Slovakia and in the Czech lands (since addressing the Slovak question entailed change in Czechoslovakia as a whole), was a major factor.

The following document, a letter from "working people" in Bratislava to Antonín Novotný, exemplifies how Slovaks saw their economic grievances

---

* The then-new Czechoslovak Constitution of 1960 insulted Slovak national pride in its debasement of Slovak national organs. The Constitution, for example, abolished the Board of Commissioners, which, at least on paper, had existed as the executive organ of the Slovak nation.

through a national lens, and vice versa. It also demonstrates their perception that only fundamental political reform—especially de-Stalinization—could redress their complaints about their economy and their nation.

ANONYMOUS LETTER SENT TO THE GENERAL CONSULATE OF THE USSR IN BRATISLAVA

Bratislava, 18 June 1963

Dear General Consulate of the USSR,
Bratislava

Allow us to send you a copy of a letter to CSSR pres. com. Novotný about internal conditions in our state and about the feelings of the overwhelming majority of our working people, mainly concerning the relations of Slovaks and Czechs.

Since we definitely trust you and the fraternal Russian nation is especially close to us, and true Slovaks have always carried their own banner along-side it, especially during the difficult periods of slavery in the distant past and during the fascist occupation, we are sending you this information with the plea that, after translating it into Russian, you will inform the Russian nation about this and in particular Com. Khrushchev, whom the Slovak nation truly regards as the logical political leader of the camp of socialism and peace.

We thank you for your trust and ask that you forgive us for not pro-viding our address—it could cause a bit of trouble for us with the Czech comrades.

For the working people of
Slovakia V.M. and R.K.

ANONYMOUS LETTER SENT TO ANTONÍN NOVOTNÝ FROM "THE WORKING PEOPLE OF SLOVAKIA"

Bratislava, 18 June 1963

Dear Comrade Antonín Novotný,
President of the CSSR,
Prague–Castle

Dear Comrade President!

Allow us to address this open letter to you. Although we are neither journal-ists nor writers, but ordinary working people, though also participants in the

Slovak National Uprising*, we decided to familiarize you with some of the ideas that, based on our beliefs and observations, practically all Slovak people identify with, except perhaps for a few individuals who are not interested in such matters. That is to say, we were inspired by your speech in Eastern Slovakia in Košice on 12 June [1963]†, when you revealed that you do not agree in substance with the unleashing of freedom here, as you emphatically called it in Slovakia. Several articles published in our press, as well as the speeches of our writers and journalists, have become a thorn in your side, even though the general public here accepted them with great sympathy and hopes for a better life.

We got the impression that you came to Slovakia to "extinguish" this free flow of ideas of freedom and that you brought a speech written in Prague to deliver in Slovakia. But we would have welcomed it more if, instead, it approved in full of these ideas recently voiced in Slovakia. Instead, what you brought here was only disillusionment and to a certain measure disappointment and damage to our mutual relationship of Slovaks and Czechs.

For a long time, every citizen here has been shaking her head at how in eliminating the cult of personality, nothing has changed here, aside from the removal of sculptures of Stalin, that is to say, in every sector of our public life, Stalinist methods remain unchanged in the net effect. It gives a simple person the impression that those "above," who are compelled to speak out against the cult of personality under the pressure of the CPSU 20th and 22nd congresses, are all talk. Because they were dyed-in-the-wool Stalinists themselves, they do not know how and do not want to purge thoroughly our party and

---

* The Slovak National Uprising was an anti-fascist military operation that began on 29 August 1944 when the Slovak army mutinied and began to fight the Germans. The Uprising built upon years of preparation by Slovak partisans. During the Uprising, Slovak partisans, both Communist and non-Communist, as well as Czech, fought the Nazis, as well as the formally independent state of Slovakia, then led by President Josef Tiso. (Some Slovaks wanted to reform a united state with the Czechs, with parity for both nations. Other Slovaks, however, wanted to retain independence. There were, in fact, certain Slovak Communists who wanted Slovakia to join the Soviet Union rather than Czechoslovakia after the war.) Germany defeated the uprising, whose fighters lacked support from the outside and heavy weapons. It occupied Banská Bystrica on 27 October 1944. Yet guerilla operations persisted until the USSR occupied Slovakia in 1945. The best-researched book on the Slovak National Uprising available in English is Josef Jablonický and Ján Pivovarči, *The Slovak National Uprising* (Bratislava: Obzor Publishing, 1969).

† Novotný's speech to a group of workers in Košice responded to criticisms raised two weeks earlier at the congress of the Union of Slovak Journalists. One Slovak journalist, Mieroslav Hysko, denounced the persecution of Slovak Communists like Gustáv Husák as "bourgeois nationalists" in the 1950s. Hysko also gained notoriety for his attack on Viliam Široký, the sitting Czechoslovak prime minister and one of Novotný's main Slovak political allies, for his culpability in the crimes of the Stalinist era in Slovakia. Novotný's Košice speech sought to denounce the criticisms of Hysko and other Slovak journalists and writers, but it also gained notoriety in Slovakia for Novotný's insistence on a policy of "convergence" of Slovaks and Czechs, which many Slovaks regarded as an attempt to assimilate them into the Czech nation. I thank Scott Brown for this point.

state apparatus of known Stalinists, because they would fall themselves, thus our state remains the last of the socialist states loyal to Moscow not to have had a radical purge of Stalinists from public life, a situation for which Prague alone is responsible. And thus even this Slovak, who previously had never had anything to hold against the fraternal Czech nation, is slowly beginning to wonder why we are so "cursed" here, why they can't be removed from their positions and why Stalinist methods from the period of the cult of personality still do harm here.

Our ordinary person is always given pause at how the critical [food] supply situation has lasted more than a year here and is not improving at all, and wonders how it reached such a state. Let's acknowledge openly that many were shot here in the past, that under the slogan of "voluntarism" we used unscrupulous methods to force farmers to join cooperatives, that we did not give a single farmer any incentive to work, and that those whom we should have dispossessed compassionately were driven mad. And we have imposed onerous production quotas on the farmers who have been left to farm privately in the mountains, giving no reason for these maltreated, impoverished people to toil more and hand over what they often cannot grow. Yes, it's true, and here the party—or rather, its leadership or Prague—as the bearer of power, has the opportunity to redress this injustice committed on our farmers—to leave them free to farm in the mountains without quotas, and also to provide similar possibilities for private plots in more fertile areas where cooperatives exist, just like, for example, in Hungary, Poland, etc.

The unhealthy policy in education is another of the harsh transgressions against the humanity and dignity of human beings. We use arbitrary means to exclude teachers if they are religious in nature and we banned students completely from secondary and post-secondary schools just because someone happened to see them in church. Even though, as Communists, we should be inclined toward atheism, every reasonable person and comrade must also condemn these abominable methods and what was knowingly done against the constitutional freedom and rights of the individual.

If the current leadership of our party does not identify with this, let them condemn it publicly and "concretely," but we still haven't heard this. Our people listen to everything they can, but when they should hear something from the responsible members of the government and party, they often hear nothing. Specifically, they do not hear how a housewife here will have to wait half a day in line in front of a shop for a kilo of meat or lard. Our working person searches in vain for an explanation for why we must always have such an unhealthy economic policy in foreign trade, etc. (e.g., helping others while leaving our own people to their own devices).

It is a hard truth but one hundred percent true. Therefore, no one should frown on it. Many of us read in the newspapers how criticism is necessary, how it is necessary to criticize things openly, and yet, they get wrongly criticized for doing so. The result of this is the aforementioned speech in Košice. This is one side of things. The second side of things is this, that Slovaks were significantly harmed when the hard-won gains of the Slovak National Uprising and the Košice Program* disappeared and this was caused by Prague, which also made up all sorts of deviationists from among the Slovak comrades who did not go along with it, [who were called] bourgeois nationalists, and even enemies of the state and ridiculed as agents of the imperialists. The aforementioned speech in Košice struck almost a similar tone, even if not as a whole.

Now, just because Slovaks, regardless of political conviction, are first of all Slovaks, it's not necessary to reproach them for this, because even the last Slovak feels that he was not born in order to "serve" someone forever, to be yanked by the nose, but today's Slovak would also be very curious to see how many Slovaks are [Czechoslovak] ambassadors and even how many people on the staff of our foreign embassies are Slovaks, whether Slovaks are being given the same opportunities to travel abroad as brother-Czechs, to investigate what obstacles are put before them in sports, etc.

That said, the feeling remains widespread among Slovaks that our state union is best. This is the only solution that would definitively eliminate the distrust between Slovaks and Czechs. However, if things keep going they way they've gone up to now, if the current conditions and Prague's methods of governing don't change, the anger of our people could simmer to the point that sooner or later it could mean the complete parting of Slovaks with Czechs in one state entity. Just like the comrades, we certainly do not wish this, but Prague, first of all, must understand this.

It is ironic that the backward states of Africa are gaining full freedom yet Slovaks still would not deserve it, when we live in the twentieth century, when inquisitorial methods should no longer apply, while we say more and more that we buried the cult of personality.

Comrade president, rise to the occasion in implementing these principles and the Slovak nation will have nothing but thanks for you and there will be mutual satisfaction between our nations. Otherwise, we could only say, as the folk saying goes, that "a fish rots from the head down," and believe us, we would not want this.

We greet you in the spirit of this letter.

The working people of Slovakia.

---

* This is the what the 1945 document that set up the structure of the new Czechoslovak state came to be called; it bears the name of the city in Eastern Slovakia where the new government was proclaimed. Drawn up the by KSČ (the Communsit Party of Czechoslovakia), the document asserted that Czech lands and Slovakia would henceforth be joined together as equal national partners in a common state, a "people's democracy." It also set forth the rights of Czechoslovak citizens, and defined citizenship as contingent upon the individual's capacity to prove "national and patriotic credentials." For more on this last point, see Melissa Feinberg, *Elusive Equality: Gender, Citizenship, and the Limits of Democracy* (Pittsburgh: University of Pittsburgh Press, 2006), 193.

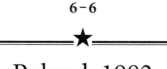

Poland, 1982

Polish Workers Generate a Common Knowledge of How to Resist on an Everyday Basis

In August 1980, Polish workers grabbed world headlines with strikes that would lead to a dramatic development in the history of Communism. Perhaps the best organized strike was staged in Baltic port city of Gdańsk, in the Lenin Shipyards. Adding to the strike's organizational power was the way that workers marshaled symbols. Images, and even festive performances, were everywhere. The strikers, joined by their supporters, placed flowers on one of the shipyard's gates, and also hung pictures of Pope John Paul II (who, of course, was Polish), and the Virgin Mary. One of their most dramatic actions was to erect a wooden cross inside the factory, on the very spot where, in 1970, the regime had killed shipyard workers engaging in protests. No doubt the power of symbols galvanized a strike movement that brought to a standstill a Polish economy already saddled with unsustainable debt to the West.

At the end of the proverbial day, the Communists, led by Stanisław Kania, had to allow trade unions that operated independently of state control. Following negotiations in August 1980 between this new entity—Solidarity— that was independent of party control, and representatives of the Polish Party-Sate, the two sides signed agreements that legalized the former's independent status. The next sixteen months brought mutual suspicion, if not tense hostility, between the regime and Solidarity. Finally, facing a planned strike by Solidarity in December 1981, Poland, under pressure from the USSR, declared martial law. General Wojciech Jaruzelski (born in 1923), who had replaced Stanisław Kania in October 1981, kow-towed to Moscow's pressure for repression. However, street demonstrations continued until the autumn of 1982, as did deaths from state violence, as well as arrests of demonstrators and Solidarity activists.

But what exactly was Solidarity, and how does its symbolic repertoire speak to that question? Countless textbooks and scholarly studies have labeled

"Basic Principles of Resistance," from Bulletin Solidarność [Solidarity Bulletin], no. 2 (March, 1982). (Originally published by Solidarity in Warsaw Solidarity's Information Bulletin, no. 8.) (Bulletin Solidarność was published in New York, jointly by the Committee in Support of Solidarity, the League for Industrial Democracy, and the Polish Workers Task Force.) Reprinted by permission of Eric Chenoweth, Editor, Bulletin Solidarność, and Director, Institute for Democracy in Eastern Europe.

Solidarity a trade union—the first independent trade union anywhere in the Communist world. That it was. But it was also more than that. Solidarity was not just about securing better working conditions, better pay, better goods, or even political rights. As its powerful symbolic dimension suggests, Solidarity was also about using culture to create a new identity, a new way of life. Because of that, it is more accurate to speak, as one scholar has done, of a "Solidarity Culture" of 1976–1981, and, in its underground phrase (1982–1988).[17]

The following passage exemplifies the sense in which, even and especially during its underground phrase, "Solidarity culture" entailed a way of life. In sustaining and elaborating that way of life, the everyday decisions of workers—decisions about how quickly one was going to work, whether one was going to show up at all, what kind of excuse to give for not showing up—were of utmost importance. For Solidarity was about creating a common knowledge (one thinks here of the common knowledge of how to protest generated by the Leipzig Peace Prayers) of how to resist on an everyday basis. Such everyday resistance, by definition,[18] lacked leaders and central organization, but this by no means diminished its power.

SOLIDARITY UNDERGROUND

Basic Principles of Resistance

Despite the harsh penalties that have been imposed for organizing resistance, spreading information, and possessing printing equipment, Solidarity continues to publish underground bulletins, which call for passive resistance on a large scale, disseminate what is known about the resistance and about the brutalities committed by the army and police, and instruct people how to organize Solidarity underground, as well as how to assist prisoners, their families, and those deprived of jobs for continuing union activity.

In Warsaw alone, ten publications have appeared, such as the War Weekly, Current Commentary, *and a Warsaw Solidarity* Information Bulletin. *Reports indicate that in every region, widespread underground publications exist and that the people are organizing resistance to the military junta.*

THE FOLLOWING APPEARED IN WARSAW SOLIDARITY'S INFORMATION BULLETIN NO. 8, DATED IN LATE DECEMBER [1981]

THE COUP D'ETAT PRESENTED SOLIDARITY MEMBERS WITH a dramatic choice: Resist or capitulate? The following is some practical advice for those who choose the courage to resist and who will participate in Solidarity's Union of Resistance. The present oppression is a variant of the total Stalinist terror [before 1956], which our generation has not yet encountered. The new situation imposes new rules, which must be learned as quickly as possible.

These are some principles of resistance:

1. During a strike or other form of protest, stay with your colleagues.
2. Do not establish strike committees. Protect your leaders and organizers. Basic principle of action: the entire crew goes on strike—there are no leaders.
3. In contacts with the police or the military, YOU ARE UNINFORMED, YOU KNOW NOTHING, YOU HAVE HEARD NOTHING.
4. In every work place Solidarity members must be present *physically*—don't risk arrest by foolhardiness—and *morally*—the behavior of a Solidarity member should be a clear signal of reassurance to the factory crew that WE SHALL NOT DESERT YOU, WE ARE WITH YOU.
5. Do not denounce ordinary people. Your enemies are: the *policeman*, the *eager conformist,* the *informer.*
6. Work slowly; complain about the mess and incompetence of your supervisors. Shove all decisions, even the most minor, into the lap of commissars and informers. Flood them with questions and doubts. Don't do their thinking for them. Pretend you are a moron. Do not anticipate the decisions of commissars and informers with a servile attitude. They should do all the dirty work themselves. In this way you create a void around them, and by flooding them with the most trivial matters you will cause the military-police apparatus to come apart at the seams.
8. [Number 7 did not appear in the original text.]. Eagerly carry out even the most idiotic orders. Do not solve problems on your own. Throw that task onto the shoulders of commissars and informers. Ridiculous rules are your allies. Always, remember to help your friends and neighbors regardless of the martial law rules.
9. If you are instructed to follow mutually contradictory rules, demand written orders. Complain. Try to prolong such games as long as possible. Sooner or later the commissar will want to be left in peace. *This will mark the beginning of the end of the dictatorship.*
10. As often as possible take sick leave to care for an "ill" child.
11. Shun the company of informers, sycophants, and their kind.
12. Help the families of the arrested, wounded, and killed.
13. Establish Social Self-Help Funds and collect money.
14. Take an active part in the campaign to counter official propaganda, spreading information about the situation in the country and the examples of resistance.
15. Paint slogans, hang posters on wails, and distribute leaflets. Pass on independent publications—*but be cautious.*
16. In any organizational activity adhere to the old conspiratorial rule: I KNOW ONLY WHAT I NEED TO KNOW. Remember: there is nothing more important than the struggle to free those who were arrested, for the lifting of the state of war, for civil liberties, and for union rights.

WE SHALL WIN! *Solidarity's Union of Resistance*

Leningrad/St. Petersburg, Early 1980s/Early 1990s/Early 2000s

Alexei Rybin (1960–), The Guitarist for the Soviet Rock Band Kino, on the Meaning of Work and Other Things

Alexei Rybin, the author of the next passage, was the guitarist for the Soviet rock band *Kino** from 1981–1983. Like many Soviet rock-and-roll bands that got their starts in the late 1970s and early 1980s, *Kino*, which was formed in the summer of 1981 in Leningrad,[19] first played in the apartments of band members, as well as in quasi-underground clubs. In 1982, when Rybin was still *Kino*'s guitarist, the group made its first album, *45*, as a joint effort with the underground Soviet rock band *Akvarium* (about which there is a document in chapter 8 of this volume.) Distributed through underground channels, the album brought the group some notoriety.

But it was not until 1986, after Gorbachev's *perestroika* was underway and Rybin had left the band, that *Kino* had its first major success with the album *Noch'* (*Night*). The band reached the height of its popularity with its 1988 album *Gruppa krovi* (*Blood Type*) and continued to draw large audiences even after the tragic death in 1990 of its leader, Viktor Tsoi, who wrote the lyrics for all of its songs—including the song "Electrichka," whose composition is mentioned in Rybin's account (following). As the name "Electrichka" (Russian for "suburban commuter train") suggests, Kino's songs tended to focus on everyday life in what turned out to be the twilight years of the USSR. Few songs had an overtly political content.

Though Rybin and his co-musicians in Kino did not know it at the time, they were part of what, in fact, was the "last Soviet generation."[20] This was the generation of Soviet citizens who were entered the world between the 1950s and 1970s, and came of age in it between the 1970s and mid-1980s. Despite the

---

From Aleksei Rybin, *Kino s samogo nachala i do samogo kontsa* (*Kino from the Very Beginning to the Very End*) (Rostov-na-Donu: Feniks, 2001), 107–109. Rybin's 2001 book is a revised and expanded version of his 1992 *Kino s samogo nachala* (Smolensk, 1992). Reprinted by permission of Aleksei Rybin. Translation: Glennys Young.

---

* "Kino" means "cinema" in Russian. The name of the band was often placed in all capital letters: KINO.

important differences in characteristics such as ethnicity, gender, career, and locale that divided them, the approximately ninety million people who were between the ages of eighteen and thirty-four in the mid-1980s had important things in common, too. For one thing, unlike the Soviet generations that preceded and followed it, this one was not defined by any "inaugural event" such as the revolutions of 1917, Stalin's Great Break, the "Great Patriotic War" (World War II), or Khrushchev's de-Stalinizing "thaw."[21] Rather, what was common about their identity stemmed from the regime's official discourse and official institutions during the Brezhnev years. Almost without exception, members of this generation belonged to the Komsomol, where they were exposed to official rhetoric and to the official values of late socialism—concern for the environment, for the welfare of others, for peace. Though shaped by this milieu and its values, they nonetheless interpreted the latter in ways that the Soviet Party-state did not foresee. Usually highly educated and the offspring of professionals, members of this generation often took up cultural pursuits such as the visual arts, literature, theater, and, like Rybin and Kino, music, and rock 'n' roll in particular.

For members of the last Soviet generation committed to such creative pursuits, certain jobs were coveted and others were to be avoided. Many of them, like Rybin, engaged in a deliberate search for what some might call underemployment—for jobs that didn't ask much, and offered free time on the job, and the privilege not to show up without sanction. Among the most coveted positions were those in the boiler rooms of cities such as Leningrad. Such jobs allowed those committed to certain creative pursuits to comply with the Soviet state's law on mandatory employment (thereby, as Rybin points out, avoiding criminal charges), but to use the employment provided and required by the state to create meanings and identities that the state did not anticipate, yet could not control. Individuals like Rybin—in fact, the prevalence of amateur rock musicians who worked in boiler rooms spawned the slang term "boiler-room rockers" (*kochegary-rokery*)—had identities that were both inside and outside the system. Jobs in boiler rooms, as well as the other positions mentioned by Rybin (yard sweepers and night watchpersons), were so coveted in the early 1980s that they became scarce, and one had to have an "in" to get one.[22]

In the passage that follows, Rybin elaborates on his attitudes toward work. He explains why he wanted to work, and why he sought the jobs he did. This passage is valuable as a lens into the social and cultural history of late Soviet socialism and the "last Soviet generation." Yet it should also be kept in mind that Rybin was writing *after* the Soviet collapse in 1991. Thus, readers should take note of how he may have wanted to portray himself, and might take with a proverbial grain of salt that he hated bureaucrats as much as he said he did.

I had to find work—money was necessary, yes and with our way of life in those times, it was rather dangerous not to be counted at any kind of employment more than two or three months. They could easily bring a criminal charge according to the article [of the criminal code] "For Parasitism" or "For Unearned Revenues," I don't exactly know how it was formulated. I also don't know the numbers of these articles. Superfluous information.

In the case of young people playing rock music, they [the Soviet authorities] fought as if [against] a terrible infection, of the sort we also seemed to be for the Soviet way of life and for Soviet ideology. Any purely formal violations of the law that they would write off for others, could be for us, and for many did become, fatal, and the consequences were extremely unpleasant.

Rock musicians for the most part settled into boiler houses, stokers, watchmen and similar establishments (see the song BG "Storohz Sergeev" and others), where it was not required to drive into your head the Soviet manner of production and one had sufficient free time. Some worked one in two days, others—once in three, some got away with going to work once in five days, and my acquaintance Maika Rodion worked one day in seven.

"I get tired," he said "when I work every day. This week—on Monday, the next [week] on Tuesday....

Some, like Gena Zaitsev, for example, worked only in the winter, and resigned in May, travelled for three months, and in September got fixed up in the old job. But when I faced the problem of finding work, all the prestigious boiler room, watchmen, and janitor positions were already taken. Fall was beginning, and the rock musicians, writers, poets, artists, philosophers and journalists of Leningrad had already returned to the city and occupied their work positions. Yes, to speak honestly, the pay for being a watchman didn't work very well for me—I was collecting records, and then, just as now, this is a rather expensive pleasure, and also it was necessary to give some money to the family.... And, moreover, instruments were necessary.

And for almost the entire month of September I walked throughout the city searching for decent work—finding it turned out to be a matter that was not at all easy.

The certificates I got during my internship at the institute for being a metalworker of some sort of category, a lathe operator, and something else as well, which I allegedly studied at the factory, lay about in disorder in a drawer in my desk, and I didn't intend to retrieve them from there in any event*. It is too much of a good thing†. Nor did I want to work in some laboratory in an institute....I would have to interact with the big-wigs, and even more loathsome, with the little bureaucrats, but they make me sick. In general, I physically could not and cannot exist in any bureaucratic structure, be it an office, an institute or something else.

Up until this point, in second place on my personal scale of unpleasant feelings stand departments of cadres, bookkeepers, registration department, and all the rest that is connected [with them] in characteristics and features. In first place

---

* In other words, he did not want to use the certificates to obtain these jobs.

† In other words, having the internships was enough for him. He is being sarcastic here.

are dentists. However with time dentists have become much nicer and closer to me, than any deputies for cadres....

And I roamed the streets, reading the notices, dropping in on acquaintances, and inquiring about the presence of open positions anywhere, when didn't I see a notice saying that the Theater for Young Spectators was looking for a decorator. I went to TIuZ [Theater for Young Spectators] and they hired me in an instant, without any filling out any forms. Owing to the fact that the work turned out to be physically very difficult, it of course became beneficial to me to complain not as a tiresome person and appropriately. Moreover, a huge plus was that I could quietly not show up for work, when I didn't want to. All I was obliged to do was notify the foreman in advance, and they divided my daily earnings among those working as members of the team. This situation suited [me best] of all, and I worked at the TIuZ for more than a year. That was almost a record length of time for me....

I went to work at seven in the morning on the *elektrichka* from Glory Street and somehow shared with Vit'ka* my impressions of these morning commuter trains, about the rumbling platforms that had frozen overnight, about people who had overslept who were trying to wake up with the help of "Belomor†" or "Arrow‡." Vit'ka could understand this—he also went to his school by taking morning commuter trains. It was a very unpleasant moment—the rumbling, cold journey every morning. The impressions were so strong that Vit'ka began to curse everything that was connected with the railroads, and on one of the evenings, anticipating tomorrow's journey, after one hour of work he composed some half-mystical, joking song, "Elektrichka." This was a hypnotizing thing, based in two chords, in which I played solo with minor seconds, an interval which grates upon one's ears. "I went to sleep too late last night, got up early today...."

NOTES

1. For the context, see Vladiimir Ilyich Lenin, *The State and Revolution*, ed., trans., and introduced by Robert Service (New York: Penguin, 1993), 85.
2. For examples from the late Stalin era, see Victoria Bonnell, *Iconography of Power; Soviet Political Posters under Lenin and Stalin* (Berkeley, CA: University of California Press, 1997), Figure 6.2, Viktor Koretskii, "Soiuz nauki i truda—zalog vysokikh uro-zhaev!," [The Union of Science and Labor Is the Guarantee of High Yield Harvests!], 1948, and Figure 6.3., Boris Mukhin, "Aktvinost' i initsiativa—vazhneishii istoch-nik nepobedimykh sil kommunizma! [Active and Initiative Are the Most Important Source of the Invincible Strength of Communism!], 1952.

---

*This is a reference to Viktor Tsoi, the leader of KINO, and its lead singer and guitarist from 1981 until his death on 15 August 1990, in a car accident near Riga, Latvia.

†A popular brand of Soviet cigarettes, named after the White Sea Canal, which was built using forced labor under Stalin's watch.

‡In Russian, the name of this brand was "Strela."

3. See, for example, James Aulich and Marta Sylvestrová, *Political Posters in Central and Eastern Europe 1945–1995: Signs of the Times*, (Manchester, UK: Manchester University Press, 1999), 165 (depiction of women as part of a specialist and scientific elite).

4. See, *inter alia*, Fritz Stern, *Five Germanys I Have Known* (New York: Farrar, Straus, and Giroux, 2007).

5. See, e.g., Andrus Park, "Ethnicity and Independence: The Case of Estonia in Comparative Perspective," *Europe-Asia Studies* Vol. 46, no. 1 (1994): 69–87.

6. For details, see Yihong Pan, *Tempered in the Revolutionary Furnace: China's Youth in the Rustication Movement* (Lanham, MD: Lexington Books, 2003), Chapter 8 ("Love and Marriage"). The author remembers youth who, in the 1950s and 1960s, who said things like: "My first love? It was Mao Zedong" and "In those days we did not pursue love; we pursued political progressiveness." (182)

7. The KUTV shut its doors late in the 1930s.

8. Katayama co-founded the Japanese Communist Party in 1922.

9. For detailed elaboration on this issue, see Elizabeth McGuire, "The Sino-Soviet Romance: How Chinese Communists Fell in Love with Russia, Russians, and the Russian Revolution," Ph.D. Dissertation, University of California at Berkeley, July 2010.

10. For an effective exposition of the political significance of work during Stalin's "Great Break," see especially Stephen Koktin, "Coercion and Identity," in Lewis H. Siegelbaum and Ronald Grigor Suny, eds., *Making Workers Soviet: Power, Class and Identity* (Ithaca, NY: Cornell University Press, 1994), 278–282, and *passim*.

11. In Magnitogorsk, there were reportedly cases in which wives didn't let their husbands come home at night because the latter had performed so poorly at work. There were also wives who visited their husbands on the job, checking up on them, encouraging them, or scolding them. Wives' tribunals shamed husbands, too, and tried to get them to stop drinking. See Stephen Kotkin, *Magnetic Mountain: Stalinism as a Civilization* (Berkeley, CA: University of California Press, 1995), 218.

12. See especially Jeffrey J. Rossman, *Worker Resistance Under Stalin: Class and Revolution on the Shop Floor* (Cambridge, MA: Harvard University Press, 2005).

13. A year after making this proclamation, Mao changed the deadline. All this would happen in one more year, not fifteen. Such fantastical revisions in the timetable of already exaggerated targets (for such products as steel, cotton, and grain) was as characteristic of Mao's Great Leap Forward as it had been of Stalin's "Great Break." On the frequent revision of goals and the schedule for reaching them, see Dali Yang, *Calamity and Reform in China: State, Rural Society, and Institutional Change Since the Great Leap Famine* (Stanford, CA: Stanford University Press, 1996) and http://chronicle.uchicago.edu/960314/china.shtml, accessed on 9 February 2010.

14. Yang interview, University of Chicago website. http://chronicle.uchicago.edu/960314/china.shtml. Accessed on 9 February 2010.

15. The delegitimizing effect of these catastrophes on the Party's authority in one village (Da Fo, in the decimated Henan region) is demonstrated in Ralph Thaxton, *Catastrophe and Contention in Rural China: Mao's Great Leap Forward Famine and the Origins of Righteous Resistance in Da Fo Village* (New York: Cambridge University Press, 2008), esp. 262. Though it remains unclear how typical Da Fo was, it is likely that the Party's authority was significantly weakened throughout most of China. See also David Bachman, "China in the 1950s: Nationalizing the Revolution,

Revolutionizing the Nation," 15, paper presented at Stanford University, January 2010. Cited by permission of the author.

16. For example, Jaroslava Krajčová, a forty-year-old factory clerk living in Prague, said the following in April 1968: "I've been in Slovakia several times on business and it seemed to me that life is freer there than in the Czech Lands." (*Práca*, 6 April 1968.) Quoted in Scott Brown, "Socialism with a Slovak Face: The Slovak Question in the 1960s," (Ph.D. Dissertation, University of Washington, 2010), introduction.

17. On "Solidarity culture," see Jan Kubik, *The Power of Symbols Against the Symbols of Power: The Rise of Solidarity and the Fall of State Socialism in Poland* (University Park, PA: Pennsylvania State University Press, 1994), 2 and *passim*.

18. The pioneer in the conceptualization and investigation of "everyday resistance" in the politics of subordinate groups is James Scott. See his classic book, *Weapons of the Weak: Everyday Forms of Peasant Resistance* (New Haven, CT, 1987). There he shifted scholars' attention to the "prosaic but constant struggle" between peasants and superordinate groups, struggles in which the "relatively powerless" engage in actions that require little planning, mimic self-help, and avoid open symbolic conflict with elites. Examples include "foot dragging, dissimulation, false compliance, pilfering, feigned ignorance, slander, arson, and sabotage." See 29.

19. First founded as a punk-rock band, the group's first name was "Garin i giperboloidy," after Alexei Nikolaevich Tolstoy's novel, *Giperboloid inzhenera Garina* [*Engineer Garin and His Death Ray*], 1926.

20. The already classic work on the "last Soviet generation's" experience of late Soviet socialism is Alexei Yurchak, *Everything Was Forever, Until It Was No More: The Last Soviet Generation* (Princeton, NJ: Princeton University Press, 2006).

21. Ibid., 32.

22. This paragraph draws upon the section entitled "Boiler Rooms" in Yurchak's *Everything Was Forever*, 151–154.

CHAPTER 7

———★———

Everyday Life, II: Space

The space in which one lived, worked, shopped, and traveled had tremendous political significance in Communist polities. In Marxism, Marxism–Leninism, and other strains of Communist thought, the revolutionary process had an essentially spatial dimension, or rather spatial dimensions. As Marx and his followers divided human history into classes, they also divided it into different types of space. Feudal space, for example, was that of the aristocratic estate and the "backward" peasant. The spaces of the bourgeoisie were the offices of high capital, the factories that caused workers to suffer immiseration and alienation, and the battlefields where the colonizers defeated the colonized. In the working class or proletariat's redemption of history and humanity through the particular nature of its suffering, the future promise that human beings could thrive in a socialist society was a promise about, among other things, the transformation of space. To give but one example, factories would be transformed from sites of suffering to palaces of labor.

Marxist–Leninist thought was not, of course, the only major influence on the ways in which Communist polities and movements sought to transform space. Also influential were the cultural values that influenced the decisions that Communist elites and citizens alike made about how space would be used, about the kinds of political significance it would have, and about the meanings that people would themselves assign to different kinds of space (for example, the meaning that Soviet citizens would assign in the late 1960s and beyond to the move from the communal to the separate family apartment). Another major factor that influenced such decisions were constraints in resources: the creation of socialist cities, such as the USSR's Magnitogorsk in the early Stalin period and Poland's Nowa Huta (New Foundry) in years after World War II, was affected by the availability of building materials. War and other man-made calamities—such as the chaos produced during China's Great Leap Forward and its creation of rural industry—were also important causal factors. As architects and city planners made decisions about the construction of socialist spaces—apartment complexes, urban design layouts, and public buildings—they borrowed from the repertoire of "modern" styles.

Locator Map for Chapter 7

Residents of Nanjing, China, for example, lived in an apartment building modeled after public housing projects that Josef Hoffmann had designed in Vienna in the early 1920s.

Another important context for the politics of space in the Communist world was the global economy. It should be kept in mind that in the decades after World War II, whose years are the focus of the documents that follow, the Cold War's contest between socialism and capitalism was fought on the terrain of consumer culture, including the size of apartments and the amenities in them. As Western Europe, the United States, and Japan created dynamic economies that supplied consumers with affordable yet high-quality consumer goods, socialist economies struggled to keep up. Hence, the meaning, or meanings, that people living in post–World War II Communist polities assigned to the spaces in which they lived, worked, and played came to be greatly affected by the comparisons they made between life in the socialist world and life beyond. For many Soviet citizens, for example, the communal apartment symbolized everything that was "abnormal" about their lives, in contrast to the supposedly "normal" life that people lived in the West. Yet access to information about the West throughout the Communist world varied depending on where one lived, what one did for a living, and how old one was.

The following documents are designed to introduce readers to the political meanings of space in Communist societies. In the first selection, a survivor of the Holocaust confronts the housing and food shortage in post–World War II Communist Romania. The second selection concerns Communist Poland's new socialist city, Nowa Huta, and the attempt to provide cultural forms, namely theater, that would turn recent in-migrants from the countryside into civilized workers with a socialist consciousness. From post-war Poland, readers can move to post–World War II Vietnam, where the Viet Minh used natural space—hills, forests, caves—as weapons in their guerilla war against the French during the First Indochina War. The next document takes us back to Poland, to the meanings that a Polish-Jewish novelist (and editor) assigned to the everyday experience of riding on Warsaw trams in the 1950s. Differential access to living space—and awareness of the "hierarchies of consumption"[1] in socialist societies such as the USSR—is one theme of the last selection, the aforementioned documents in which Soviet citizens sought to leave their communal apartments for "rooms of their own."

Timişoara, Romania

University Students, "Living Space," and Everyday Life after World War II

Dora Apsan Sorell, the author of the passage that follows, was born in 1921 in Sighet, Romania, where she lived until World War II.[2] Sighet, which is located the northern part of Romania that shares a border with Czechoslovakia, then had a population of thirty thousand people, comprised of approximately equal numbers of Romanians, Hungarians, and Jews. Her father, who operated a grain store after World War I and worked as an insurance agent for an Austrian company, was part of a Hasidic sect called the Vishnitzer. In her youth, she participated in several Zionist organizations, and her family kept kosher and were religiously observant Jews. In what was a rare achievement for a young woman in Romania of those days, she graduated from high school in 1940.

This achievement was tarnished, however, by the anti-Semitism that pervaded Romanian life, when, several months after her graduation, the Hungarians, now Hitler's allies, occupied and annexed Northern Transylvania, the part of Romania where Sighet was located. They enacted anti-Jewish decrees, such as prohibiting Jews from attending public high school. In 1944, she was one of Sighet's ten thousand Jewish residents who were deported to Auschwitz; after a year, she was among the Jews moved to another Nazi camp, which had the bizarrely euphemistic name Weiswasser (White Water)*.

But she survived the Holocaust.[3] Two days before World War II ended, she was liberated. Upon her return to Romania, she married her high-school sweetheart (Tzali), settled in the city of Timişoara, in Western Romania, and enrolled in medical school.

Sorell was part of Romania's post-war, multi-ethnic population that lived through the establishment of a Communist government. Although this did come to pass in 1947, the result was by no means a given. In fact, in contrast to other Eastern European nations, such as Hungary and especially Czechoslovakia,

From Dora Apsan Soell, *Tell the Children: Letters to Miriam* (San Rafael, CA: Sighet Publishing, 1998), 170–173. Reprinted by permission of Dora Apsan Sorell.

* *Weisswasser* was a labor camp located in Czechoslovakia, which was then under Nazi control. The camp was liberated by Russian soldiers on a morning in early May. See www.holocaustcenter.org (accessed on 14 February 2010).

popular support for the Communists was relatively low. Romania had been allied with Nazi Germany and the other Axis powers during the War, and Romanians, unlike Czechs and Slovaks, felt no linguistic or cultural kinship with their Slavic brethren. Nor had Communists played much of a role in the government that King Michael established when, in 1944, he overthrew the German-allied regime of Ion Antonescu. But the fact that the Soviet Army was occupying Romania, coupled with typical Soviet strategies in claiming victory via electoral fraud and then subsequently squeezing more moderate political parties from power, resulted in the Communists' declaration of the Romanian People's Republic (Republica Populară Romînă) after they had forced King Michael to abdicate at the end of December 1947.

For people such as Dora Apsan Sorell and her family, the years immediately prior to, and after, the establishment of the Romanian People's Republic brought difficulties in everyday life. In addition to the arrests and imprisonments, the growing power of the secret police, the violence (including beatings and deportations) that accompanied collectivization in 1948, inflation, and the shipping of food and other Romanian goods to the Soviet Union, people faced a shortage in housing, as Aspan Sorell relates in the following selection. Eventually, the Communist government in Romania would undertake a number of housing projects, such as, under the Ceauşescu regime that began in 1965, the building of densely populated high-rise neighborhoods outside cities such as Bucharest.

The book from which this text has been excerpted, *Tell the Children: Letters to Miriam,* is an epistolary autobiography. It is a book in which she tells the story of her life through a series of letters to her granddaughter, whose birth brought to life memories from her past, and a desire to educate a new generation about the chamber of horrors in twentieth-century Europe.

STUDENTS WITH A BABY

By the time Silvia came along we had moved from Schiller's to a new place, a nice furnished room in the apartment of Mrs. Deutsch.

Housing in the post-war Timişoara was a huge problem. With new universities opening up the city became very crowded. There were few dormitories for students, mostly at the old, established universities. Office buildings were confiscated from their former owners and hastily furnished for the thousands of students flocking to the city. The girls' dormitory of the medical school, close to the administrative building, looked like a large hospital ward. In each room there were about twenty cots along the walls, no closets, no dressers, only pegs on the walls full of dresses on hangers. Suitcases were on the floor, books piled up on makeshift shelves on stacks of bricks. There were no cooking facilities. The bathrooms were at the end of the corridor, serving several hundred students. The men's dormitory was a similar building on the other side of the plaza, with the same inconveniences. Those who could afford it took better lodgings in private homes. This was also the only choice for the few married couples like us, who couldn't claim space in the cheap campus dormitories.

The Deutsches, an elderly couple who had been well-to-do before the war, owned a large apartment. Under the new regime, they were not entitled to so much "living space" and were required to rent out all rooms that had separate access. A long hallway led from the front door to the kitchen and bathroom. On the right side, facing a busy street, were the Deutsches' living quarters, a living room and a bedroom. On the left, toward the backyard, were the rented rooms. Ours was small and narrow, with two single beds, which allowed us a good night's sleep. There was a wardrobe closet and a desk for study, and later we added a crib for Silvia. The room was not too expensive, and, most importantly, it provided us with the privacy we longed for. We found this arrangement quite satisfactory.

The room next to us was rented by an obstetrician, who became our friend and delivered our first two children. He used the room as a clandestine office where he performed abortions, which were illegal at that time, though fairly common, as contraception was never available in Romania. At night we often heard women moaning and groaning....

At the end of the corridor, between the bathroom and the kitchen, there was a little window. As the Deutsches did not share their kitchen, I was allotted the space under that window for a gas burner, where I could heat water for all the necessities, boil the milk, and make some simple food for the baby.

Cooking dinner at home was out of question. The market and the grocery stores were very poorly stocked. One could usually find the most basic foodstuffs, which were rationed, but there were long lines whenever anything else was available, and we didn't have time to shop. We were grateful to cousin Yankl, who occasionally brought us some hard-to-find produce from the market.

The city had a large number of government subsidized factory cafeterias, where at noontime a pretty substantial dinner was served to the workers. For a small price students could purchase meal tickets at those cafeterias. Very soon it became apparent that important people, students with Communist Party or Student Union affiliations, were assigned to choice factories where meat dishes were served almost daily. But we were pleased to be assigned to a cafeteria which permitted us to take food home in a lunch pail, so I could stay home with Silvia while Tzali bicycled over to get the food. Then the three of us would make a meal from the two portions.

When we had some extra money we subscribed to a boarding house for dinner, where there was more variety, meat was served regularly, the food tasted better, and we even got dessert....

For a few months after Silvia was born we had a helper to take care of her. I was nursing, and was lucky to have enough milk, because formula was not available and preparing baby food was quite a task. In the morning I went to classes. At 11 I got up, left the classroom discreetly (though the teachers knew where I was going), took the trolley, rode the three stations to our home, and returned within an hour. The morning classes ended in time for the next nursing. Life was easier when we had the helper because she also did some cleaning and the laundry, took the baby out, and made a fire in the wood stove in the winter so the room was warm when we came home.

But we didn't always have money for help, and when Silvia grew older, and could sit on the bicycle baby seat that Tzali had built, we took her to a day care center at a nearby factory. She didn't seem to mind. Every day we had to wash baby clothes and diapers. Tzali would warm up the water and carry it to the room, I would wash the diapers, Tzali would rinse and wring them, then we would hang them on three or four clotheslines strung between the window and the door. They would be dry in the morning. Friends coming to see us had to dodge between the drying diapers.

Our scholarships covered only tuition, and the funds we had brought with us from Sighet were soon used up. My brothers sometimes sent us packages, but no money, because getting foreign currency was illegal. Nevertheless we were able to obtain some through clandestine transactions. Occasionally Tzali earned some money tutoring high school students in math and physics. Zionist organizations from abroad also sent clothes and food packages for poor Jewish students, but the Communist Party and the Students' Union ruled that these would be accepted only if all the students could benefit. This was in keeping with Communist ideals of equality, except that the Party officials, who controlled the distribution of these packages, got to pick the choice items for themselves, leaving the rest for the other students. It became rather amusing to see them all dressed alike in fine American shirts and slacks, as if in uniform....

Adding to our financial difficulties was the severe inflation of the post-war years. The economy was in shambles. Merchandise and agricultural products were scarce. Prices soared. Speculation and corruption pushed up inflation even more. In late 1946 and early 1947 prices went up by the hour. All income had to be spent immediately, because the next day prices would be higher. There were times when we needed a pocketful of money, hundreds of lei*, to buy a loaf of bread, and a suitcase of money to buy a pair of shoes. Savings lost all their value. Apartments were rented for the equivalent of two kilos of butter a month and the black market thrived....

My dearest girlfriends, Rolla and Klari, were several years younger than I. They had always lived with their families in Timisoara, and each was an only child. I felt they belonged to a separate and privileged category of Jewish students who had never lost their homes and families, had never been deported. When the quota system was enforced in the public schools in Romania, they were able to attend the prestigious Hebrew High School where my brother Mild had once studied. And now, even the medical school came to their hometown.

Klari's father was a retired businessman, a former jeweler. It was he who sometimes helped us out with a loan when we were in need; he was our "banker."

---

* *Lei* is the plural form for the currency of Romania, whose singular form is the *leu*. The value of the leu declined precipitously after WWII. In 1947, the Communist government revaluated the currency—20,000 old *lei* became the equivalent of one new *leu*—in order to devalue the assets of the pre-war Romanian middle and upper classes.

Rolla lived with her widowed mother, who took care of everything. They were among the few Jews of Sephardic origin and even spoke Ladino*. Rolla and Klan respected our troubled past without ever asking questions about it. They looked up to us for being older, having more life experience, being married and having a child. They were always available if we needed their help, and we often ate in their homes.

February 28, 1988

7–2

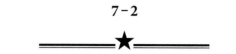

Nowa Huta ("New Steelworks"), Poland

Building Socialism in Poland's New Socialist Town from a Cultural Perspective

Perhaps nowhere in Poland was the Communist government's attention to the politics of space as evident as in Nowa Huta, a self-enclosed, model socialist city built on the outskirts of Kraków, in south-central Poland. Construction of Nowa Huta, whose symbolic core was a giant metallurgical complex, began immediately after World War II ended as the new Communist state sought to consolidate its power. Common wisdom then had it that Poland's new socialist town was located outside of Kraków in particular

---

From Aleksandra Mianowska, *Teatr "Nurt" Nowa Huta: Kartki ze wspomnień (Theater Nurt in Nowa Huta: Pages with Recollections)* (Kraków: Towarzystwo Przyjaciół Książki, 1980), 21–22. Reprinted with the permission of Towarzystwo Przyjaciół Książki. Translation: Christina Manetti.

---

* Ladino, which is also known as Judeo-Spanish, is the language of the descendants of the Jews expelled from Iberia who settled in Ottoman Southeast Europe and Asia Minor beginning in the fifteenth century. Largely based on Medieval Castilian and written in a Hebraic script, the language integrates words of Hebrew and the regional languages that Sephardic Jews encountered in the course of migrations, resettlement, and their five-hundred-year life in the Ottoman lands, including Turkish, Greek, Italian, and Bulgarian. Beginning in the nineteenth century, the language was Gallicized and, by the early twentieth century, was written in the Latin alphabet in Republican Turkey and elsewhere. See Tracy Harris, *Death of a Language: The History of Judeo-Spanish* (Newark, DE: University of Delaware Press, 1994).

because of the city's resistance to the state's agenda in 1946. It was widely believed—though recent archival research has established it to have been a myth—that residents of Kraków had voted "no" on each of the three policies in the nationwide referendum of that year. Yet even if, in the results of that referendum, Kraków had not differed all that much from nationwide patterns, certainly the construction of Nowa Huta was designed to symbolize the triumph of the new, Communist order over the old order, one exemplified by the medieval city of Kraków's architectural splendor that had, unlike its Jewish population, survived the war. Kraków, which had been the former seat of Poland's kings and was Poland's capital from 1038 to 1596, also possessed great historical and political significance.[4]

From its launch in 1949, Nowa Huta embodied the core values and symbols of Polish Communism. The opening of the Vladimir Lenin Steelworks in 1954 was only one example of the emphasis on heavy industrialization in the new Communist economy. With its huge apartment blocks and wide boulevards, its monumentalism evoked, for example, that of Stalin's original "city of steel," Magnitogorsk, documents concerning which were explored in chapter 6. In embodying the architectural style of socialist realism, the buildings of Nowa Huta were designed to transform the consciousness of those who inhabited the city. Statues and other symbols of Communism—such as a famous statue of Vladimir Lenin (torn down in 1989)—added to official efforts to use public space in the service of socialist ideals.

Yet everyday life—and public space, in particular—did not turn out to be only what the Communist government wanted it to be. A major example of how Polish people themselves influenced its evolution was the building of a church. Given the atheistic bent of the Communist government, it is not surprising that there was not a single church in Poland's new socialist city. Some residents of Nowa Huta wanted it to be otherwise. The two-decades-long quest to construct a church began in 1960, when people began the process of receiving the necessary permission from the government to build a church, and street fights broke out when residents constructed a cross. Though some of its residents did, in 1966, build a church, Lord's Ark, Karol Wojtyla, then cardinal archbishop of Kraków and eventually Pope John Paul II, was able to consecrate it only in 1977.

The residents of Nowa Huta who spearheaded the local campaign to build the church were, in their social and cultural profile, quite representative of the kinds of people who populated the new city in the late 1940s and early 1950s. They were, that is, industrial workers[5] who had brought with them rural customs, behaviors, and cultural values. In fact, Nowa Huta was designed, not just architecturally but also culturally, to transform these "backwards" country folk into "modern" workers for socialist industry. To that end, the city offered its new, socialist culture, one important example of which was theater productions designed to transmit Communist values.

In the 1950s, there were several theaters in Nowa Huta, among them the amateur theater, "Teatr Nurt," featured next, in the passage that comes from the

Polish theater director, Aleksandra Mianowska*. The "Nurt" Theater started in June 1952, assumed the status of a factory theater in May 1953, and, operated until February 1954. It was located in one of the "workers' hotels" that provided housing for rural in-migrants. Mianowska emphasizes how successful she was in reaching the worker audiences and transforming their behavior—for example, getting them not to smoke and to respond politely. Yet the passage is also valuable for its glimpses of what was not, in fact, so "model" about Poland's socialist city—the lack of light during a nighttime performance in a building that was more or less a shed.

Yes, I can't complain in the least about our audiences from those workers' hotels. I was even able to get them to abide by the rather unpopular requirement of refraining from smoking during our programs. Of course not by the method of saying that it is "not permitted," but rather by saying: "you [plural] after all know, my dears, that one doesn't smoke in the theater, and we are from that very institution, and we will be organizing a theater piece for your eyes, and the fact that we don't have any stage decorations isn't important—the most important thing is that there is an author, there are actors and there is an audience," etc. "Taken by the ruff of their necks"—not only did they not smoke, but they behaved impeccably. Moreover, having come to like our programs, they would come to our "evenings" not having been herded there, they occupied all the seats, even the standing room. One day, the light "crashed" in the hotel to which we had gone for the planned performance. We could have said in good conscience "not our fault," that we showed up and then have gone home early, especially since these were extra activities for which we didn't receive any money at all.

Being a child of parents who were enthusiasts themselves, however, who had themselves been activities in the field of culture and education, I decided that a lack of light should not scare us off, especially since there was a room filled with a willing audience, and outside the street lamp was already burning and shone some light on our actor silhouettes. Those gathered there assured us that they want to listen to us, even like this, in the dark. My colleagues shared my opinion, and so we stayed. Except that one couldn't count on the help of the prompter at all! Nonetheless, we emerged from the hotel, still unlit—the problem apparently was a serious one—with a pinch of satisfaction, even as actors.

My excellent knowledge of slang helped me enormously in my contact with those audiences—who were to a large extent comprised of fresh arrivals from the countryside. Having been raised in a village near Kraków, I could address them "in their language" in private conversations after the performances, or during them—thanks to which I immediately became "one of them." Maybe some drop of blood inherited from my great-grandfather Gustaw Fiszer also helped make it easy for

---

*In April 1957, Mianowska co-directed, with Jerzy Grotowski, Eugene Ionesco's *The Chairs* in Kraków. Grotowski (1933–1999) was a leading figure in Poland's Expressionist theatre movement in the 1950s, 1960s, and 1970s. For more on Mianowska, see also Kazimierz Braun, *A History of Polish Theater, 1939–1989: Spheres of Captivity and Freedom* (Westport, CT: Greenwood Press, 1996).

me to strike up a rapport with the audiences. He was not only an excellent comedic actor, but in his monologues that he had written himself he travelled the cities and towns of Galicia, adored by the public and eagerly awaited, as legend has it—and not only in our family lore. Regardless of whether or not I inherited this from my great-grandfather, it remains a fact that I liked this difficult job. Sometimes it even seemed to me that my colleagues and I were fulfilling some very important task, and I pushed the idea that came to my mind, and probably not only mine, that no one is doing this work except for us, or even notices it. A certain "evening" in a workers' hotel became etched in my mind. We finished the program, and as the moderator, "the last word" belonged to me. One of the workers stood up at that point, a middle-aged man, and said, I remember exactly: "If my gal talked as purty as you do, ma'am, then I wouldn't be sittin' here, and wouldn't'a come to Huta, or any of us here, ain't that right?" Those present showed their support with energetic bravos for this humorous and essentially polite praise for our efforts.

Yes, those were very grateful and good audiences. In the theater as well. They might have been coming straight from work, in their work clothes, filling up the hall of the wooden shed, a hall that was arranged as an amphitheater, with a good view from every seat and great acoustics. Many of them were undoubtedly in a theater for the first time, and were taking an active part in what was happening on the stage, showed their sympathy or disapproval of the characters, but never in a way that went beyond the norms of good behavior.

7-3

Vietnam, 1946–1949

Organic Space, Human Space, and the Viet Minh's
Guerilla War against the French

Duong van Mai Elliott, the author of the part family-history, part memoir[6] from which the following passage is excerpted, was born in 1941 in the province of Nam Dinh during the Japanese occupation of Vietnam.[7] Like Xuan Phuong, (the author of *Ao Dai*), whom we met in the first chapter, Duong van Mai Elliott came from an educated, urban, and distinctly middle-class

From Duong Van Mai Elliott, *The Sacred Willow: Four Generations in the Life of a Vietnamese Family* (New York: Oxford University Press, 1999), 159–163. Reprinted with the permission of Oxford University Press.

family.[8] Not only had her great-grandfather been a mandarin and a member of the Imperial Court. Her father was a government official when the French ruled Vietnam. He served as the mayor of Haiphong and governor of the Maritime Zone[9] from the beginning of the first Indochina War in 1946 (a year in which the French seized Haiphong) between the guerilla forces of the Viet Minh and the French, until shortly after the Viet Minh's attainment of a truly independent Vietnam in 1954. (In 1949, the Vietnamese Emperor, Bao Dai, returned to Vietnam as Chief of State in a Vietnam nominally independent from the French.)

While her father held these official positions in the city of Haiphong, he cooperated with the French because he saw them as preferable to the Communists. But his ultimate goal, after defeat of the Viet Minh, was a "peaceful transition to independence from France."[10] When the Viet Minh's 1954 defeat of the French in the battle of Dien Bien Phu brought the end of French involvement in Indochina and the division of Vietnam into the Communist North and the anti-Communist South, the Duong family initially supported Ho Chi Minh. To them, his vision of national liberation resonated with their complete rejection of French rule. Though the family became disillusioned with Communism and moved from the North to the South, her sister, Phu, stayed with the Communists.

In the passage presented next, Duong Mai van Elliott makes perceptive observations about the military and political uses of space—especially the landscape—as she relates the story of her oldest sister (Thang) and brother-in-law's (Hau's) life with the Viet Minh during its guerilla war against the French.[11] Especially between 1946, when the Viet Minh began their guerilla war against the French, and 1949, when the Chinese Communists emerged victorious in their own civil war, the Viet Minh lacked for weapons. But then, and throughout First Indochina War, they used the mountainous terrain of Northern Vietnam as a weapon in itself, as a stronghold of resistance to the French. Caves, peaks, and hills became a kind of "organic machine" for waging guerilla warfare.[12] Yet even as the Viet Minh struggled to defeat the French by using natural space, they began the process of using man-made space—the communal dormitories in which Thang and her husband Hau lived—in service of producing people who had a truly "socialist" consciousness.

Before war broke out, the Viet Minh had set up two bases in Tonkin, one in the northeast near the Chinese border and one south of the Red River Delta. The one in the northeast, called the Viet Bac, included six provinces spread over 10,000 square miles. The other one covered the hilly and jungly areas of Thanh Hoa, Nghe An, and Ha Tinh—the provinces bordering on the sea that my ancestors had crossed in their journey to Van Dinh. Other bases also existed in the central and southern parts of the country, but the Viet Bac was the best prepared and the most important. Throughout the war, it would serve as the nerve center of the resistance and as the seat of the Viet Minh government-in-exile. Ho Chi Minh and his key lieutenants would direct the war from here until the final climactic battle of Dien Bien Phu. The Viet Bac, in fact, covered the same ground favored by rebels and bandits over the centuries, because its mountainous terrain, limestone peaks and caves, and forested hills provided good cover and made the base easily defensible.

Beginning in March 1947, as French troops fanned out to pacify the delta, Viet Minh agencies and their employees retreated into the Viet Bac. At the same time, thousands of civilians also moved into the base, choosing to live under the Viet Minh rather than under the French, or simply trying to get as far as possible from the fighting in the delta. Among the refugees was a contingent of intellectuals, writers, singers, musicians, actors, and actresses who had trekked into the Viet Minh zone to support the resistance. In the Viet Bac, government agencies scattered in the forest to avoid detection, and would change locations once in a while to throw the French off their track. The employees lived in huts spread among the various hill tribes that inhabited the area, whose languages, customs, and cultures shared little in common with their own. The Viet Minh had successfully wooed these tribes very early on. In fact, the mountain people provided the initial recruits for the Viet Minh army, and one of their leaders, Chu Van Tan, rose to become a famous general. Tribal support for the Viet Minh, though widespread, was far from being total, however, and the French were also able to recruit allies among these diverse groups.

Knowing that they would be cut off from supplies in the delta for a long time, the Viet Minh had stockpiled rice, salt, and cloth in the base. Before leaving the lowlands for the mountains, they had also dismantled machinery they had taken from shops in the delta and reassembled the equipment in the forest. Small factories sprang up in caves, and using raw materials that had been painstakingly carried into the forest, produced soap, matches, cloth, paper, and a few other basic goods. Medical equipment was also carted into the base, along with a small quantity of weapons and ammunition. Makeshift workshops were set up to repair weapons and produce a few small firearms: But with thirty thousand soldiers now to equip, General Vo Nguyen Giap—the Viet Minh commander—did not have enough weapons for his men. The shortage was so acute that several soldiers had to share a rifle. In some units, the ratio was twelve men to a rifle.

Employees of the government-in-exile settled under the canopy of trees in the forest. They sorely missed things they had taken for granted, such as electricity and running water. Everything was scarce, from cloth to soap to matches. But at the beginning when enthusiasm was at its peak and the hardships had not taken their toll, most of them did not mind. Initially, they found that having their life reduced to the barest necessities actually had its advantages. They felt liberated from the material worries and personal ambitions that used to dog them in the cities. They poked fun at their dramatic transformation from city residents to forest dwellers and laughed at themselves. Their biggest fantasy was to visit Bac Can, the capital of the resistance, to stroll among its modest coffee shops, restaurants, bazaars, and bookstores, and to get light by simply flicking a switch and water by simply turning on a tap. Their only aspiration was to win the war quickly.

Thang and Hau would end up in the same primitive conditions. After a few months, as a French attack appeared imminent, they and the four other families that had settled down at-the plantation retreated into the forest, about twenty kilometers away. The weather was unstable. One moment, the rain would soak them, and then the sun would come out and steam their wet clothes dry....

Thang and Hau and the other four families settled in a forest clearing, where they shared a long house on stilts—similar to those used by the Tho tribe—that had been built for them. A rickety ladder led up into the hut. They cooked their food in a small area located on the porch near the ladder, setting their pots over a fire in a three-by-three-foot bamboo frame with sides that were six inches tall and a bottom covered with a thick layer of packed dirt to insulate the bamboo floor from the flames. Chickens foraged and slept underneath the house. The hut and the narrow strip of land around it formed the only open space. Beyond the fringe was the forbidding forest, where boars, bears, and tigers roamed among the trees. At night, the ladder had to be pulled up to keep tigers from climbing in.... Thang liked the rhythm of life here and enjoyed watching the people go about their business, tending to their animals and trees, or dropping seeds into holes in the soil fertilized with the ashes of the trees they had burned down to clear land for planting.

In that long house, Thang had her first taste of what the Communists, who secretly controlled the Viet Minh, called the collective, or communal, life. In the mountain base, everyone had to set aside their own wants and learn to live in harmony with others. The common good of the collective had priority over everything else. My sister, who never paid much attention to her own needs, found the constant compromises easy to accept. Thang's group of five families lived in a dormitory-like setting and ate together. Each family's living space was confined to a reed mat spread on the bamboo floor. Not even a curtain separated one mat from the ones next to it. In another setting, the close quarters could have created strains, but among these families bound by a common goal, the arrangement seemed to encourage socializing and bantering. There was much laughter, and the good humor that prevailed—as well as the fact that they were sharing the hardships together—made the challenge of their stay in the forest less formidable. Besides, they were then intoxicated with the dream of winning freedom for their country, and this initial enthusiasm allowed them to ignore their privations. It was a bond Thang would remember for the rest of her life.

For bathing and washing, the families went down to the clear stream that flowed nearby. The men had rigged up a series of bamboo tubes to carry water from the stream into the hut for washing food and dishes and for drinking and cooking. Each person had only one change of clothing. All the clothes were dyed either brown or indigo blue, to blend in with the surroundings and make the wearers less visible to French airplanes. Hau's spare outfit was made by Thang, dyed and sewn with the help of the women in the group. Sewing was not one of her skills, so the pants and shirt were lopsided and lumpy. But Hau did not criticize her clumsy work, and instead cherished his brown outfit. He wore it throughout the war. Thang kept it for years after they returned to Hanoi in 1954. Sometimes, in later years, she would take it out of the dresser and examine it with misty eyes.

In that forest clearing, the four cadres and their wives would become like a family to Thang, replacing the one she had left in Van Dinh. She tends to look back on this phase with nostalgia now, and thinks of it as the happiest period of her life in the resistance zone. One of the wives was a graduate from Thang's secondary girl school in Hanoi. Of the five women, only one was involved in Viet Minh activities. Revolution was primarily seen as a man's work, and women tended to do things like sewing flags and writing slogans on banners. A higher level of participation would be working in the Women's Association to encourage women to support the resistance, but "supporting" usually meant standing behind husbands and sons, taking care of their families so the men could focus their attention and energy on the fight against the French, or serving as porters to carry weapons and supplies for the army.

The women who had small children spent all their time taking care of them, and were spared any work except cooking and cleaning up. If they were not summoned away, the men focused their energy on finding food to supplement the rice provided by the government. They cleared some land to grow vegetables and raise chickens for eggs. They also fished for shrimp in the stream, and foraged for wild bamboo shoots and edible leaves in the forest. Hau turned out to have a knack for locating the tender shoots, and was crowned champion bamboo shoot gatherer. The active part of each day was short. By six o'clock each family had to retire to their reed mats and pull down the nets to keep from being bitten by mosquitoes. But no one could be careful enough. In spite of all the precautions, Thang, Hau, and the baby all came down with malaria.

With thousands of displaced civilians, employees, and soldiers to feed, the Viet Minh faced the enormous task of producing enough food for everyone. Supplies from the delta were no longer available, because of the distance and also because this region—Tonkin's traditional food basket—was now under French control. To avert a crisis, the government urgently asked everyone—soldiers, government employees, teachers, students, civilians—to grow food and become self-sufficient. Producing food became part of the fight to liberate the country.

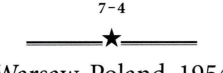

Warsaw, Poland, 1954

*A Polish Writer (Leopold Tyrmand, 1920–1985) on
the "Anti-Civilization" of Warsaw's Trams*

Unremitting drabness and the hunt for goods in short supply: such were some of the features of everyday life in Communist polities around the world. Of course, the quality and texture of everyday life varied enormously, not just between Communist societies, but from region to region, from city to countryside, and even from city to city and village to village. And, to generalize broadly, everyday life in Communist polities was not without its pleasures: delicious ice cream, candy, and pastries (not to mention bountiful bread whose price was kept artificially low) in Brezhnev's and Gorbachev's USSR, for example. But everyday life, as memoirs and novels attest, was something of a Kafkaesque struggle against challenges both expected and unforeseen. Among those challenges was the crowdedness of public transportation.

In the next passage, Leopold Tyrmand, a Polish-Jewish novelist and editor,[13] relates his subjective experience of what it was like to ride on Warsaw trams in the 1950s. Before emigrating to the United States in 1966, he became well-known in Poland for publishing newspapers critical of the regime.

In Tyrmand's account, the tram and its terrors exemplify the inhumanity of Polish Communism writ small, so to speak. They constitute what he condemns as the "anti-civilization" of Polish Communism—an "anti-civilization" defined by feelings, values, and ways of being that bring out the baseness of humanity.

Today I spent my life in trams. The Warsaw trams are still a symbol and reflection of existence. Dirt and neglect are their nature. Their purpose is to release people's instinct to hate each another. The most gracious Christian is transformed in a Warsaw tram into pure biology and evil. The psychological principle of the tram is a mythologized, blind urge to push oneself to the front and a blind fear of not being able to get out in time. Its culture is comprised of an extremely elaborate intolerance of one's neighbor and an inexhaustible lexicon of invectives. The one with the loudest mouth and strongest elbow is its positive hero, the pride of

From Leopold Tyrmand, *Dziennik, 1954* (*Diary, 1954*) (Warsaw: Wydawnictwo Res Publica, 1989), 68. Reprinted with the permission of Wydawnictwo Res Publica. Translation: Christina Manetti.

its folklore. What happened today on the route from Mokotów to Krakowskie Przedmieście between the conductor, passengers, bundled up babies and even a certain dog hidden in a briefcase, demands a literature that is beyond my means.

But who should we blame, and for what? The poverty and discomfort, the bitterness of endless waiting at the stops, the freezing cold, airlessness, and floor awash in mud—these culminate in wild attacks on another similarly underprivileged person, on another poor wretch and victim. The Communists use this to their advantage. In anti-civilization, they can profit amidst fanfares from even the slightest improvement or convenience, which becomes an accomplishment of historic proportions. The cost of one May Day celebration would probably cover that of bringing Warsaw mass transit to the level of rural Sweden at the end of the last century, but there have already been eight May Days in Warsaw. Only a madman however would be able to put forth such a proposition.

A snippet of conversation overheard: "...but after all no one can survive on one salary.... You have to try to get a second job, a third...."

Please consider this: what kind of flexing of the powers of production do the economic stewards of this country achieve by virtue of the fact that no one is able to survive on one job? And what kind of apathy? And what kind of tiredness? And what kind of physiological ruin?

7–5

The USSR, Late 1960s

Soviet Pensioners Try to Leave the Kommunalka (Communal Apartment) for a Room or Rooms of Their Own

In Communist polities, there was, officially, no clear distinction between the "public" and the "private" sphere when it came to space. For Lenin and other Soviet revolutionaries, the distinction between "public" and "private" was a bourgeois convention from the capitalist era, an outdated, and even counter-revolutionary, way of thinking that was to be transcended by the building of socialism. One such space in Soviet everyday life that came to demonstrate the porous, if not nonexistent, boundaries between "public" and "private" was the communal apartment (in Russian, the *kommunalka*).[14]

The Soviet communal apartment got its start in the first years after the Bolshevik seizure of power in October 1917. During these early revolutionary

years, local authorities and citizens alike, who badly needed housing, expropri-
ated the (former capitalist) expropriators, seizing the single-family apartments
that had belonged to the Tsarist-era bourgeoisie and aristocracy. This process
of expropriation, or nationalization of housing, stretched on throughout the
1920s. By the 1930s, it was almost complete: the vast majority of single-family
apartments had been seized by the state (in the name of the "People," of course),
broken up into smaller sub-units in which residents shared a kitchen, a bathroom (and, eventually, if they were lucky, a telephone), and distributed to new
residents. Even into the postwar period—especially in cities such as Leningrad
and Moscow that, unlike new cities such as Magnitogorsk, had a supply of apartments from pre-revolutionary days—the communal apartment continued to be
the main form of housing in Soviet cities. For the Soviet citizens who resided in
them, the communal apartment meant abiding by common rules, fearing (during the Great Purges of the late 1930s, but also beyond) being denounced by
one's fellow apartment mates, and, sometimes, having built-in babysitters for
one's children, especially in the case of single mothers. In émigré memoirs, the
communal apartment symbolizes the absurdness of everyday Soviet life. During
the Cold War, such memoirs, and other sources of information available in the
West, made the communal apartment into a "chief example of the 'abnormal'
condition of the Soviet everyday that made life so difficult."[15]

A perhaps lesser-known story, however, is the decline and fall of the *kommunalka*. In the 1950s and 1960s, the Soviet government began a mass housing
campaign. This involved the building of new apartment buildings—such as five-
to sixteen-story complexes constructed using concrete panels that defined the
new housing settlements or estates (in Russian, *mikroraiony*) of the Khrushchev
era, vast clusters of seemingly soulless skyscrapers clustered on the outskirts of
cities. It also meant the transfer of millions of Soviet families from communal
apartments to rooms of their own, that is, to single-family, separate apartments.
In the post-war period of Soviet history, and especially during the Khrushchev
and Brezhnev eras (and beyond), it was the single-family separate apartment
that would define urban life.[16] Yet, despite this dominance, separate apartments
continued, even in the late 1960s and beyond, to be in short supply, just as did
many consumer product in late Soviet socialism. (And, in fact, the communal
apartment has outlived the dismantlement of the Soviet system!) Getting one
often took years—even for Soviet pensioners whose poor health meant they
did not necessarily have years to wait—and an ongoing struggle with the Soviet
bureaucracy. In this battle, pensioners and other Soviet citizens seeking a separate apartment drew upon some of the political practices we have already seen in
this volume, such as letters to local officials and even to the highest Communist
Party leaders, such as Leonid Brezhnev and Alexei Kosygin.

The letters that follow are two such examples. The first is a letter sent in March
1966, during the early Brezhnev years, by Aleksei Stephanovich Zlobin, a Leningrad
pensioner and a former political prisoner,[17] to the local Leningrad authorities. The
second letter, sent in 1968 by N. I. Portnov, was, in fact, addressed to none other
than Brezhnev and Kosygin themselves! Though Zlobin's and Portnov's life stories
differed, they both drew upon official language (for example, in Portnov's letter,
"With our chest, we saved the Soviet homeland from fascist invaders"). And, like

pensioners and even younger people seeking separate apartments, they both appealed to officially approved social identities that entitled one to separate housing, such as being a veteran of World War II or the Great Patriotic War. These letters also serve as an introduction to the range of meanings that the separate apartment had to those who sought and petitioned for them. More than just shelter and/or comfort, the separate apartment sometimes represented the chance to escape from the stigma of having been a political prisoner (a stigma reinforced by other residents of the communal apartment). But it could also mean the opportunity to gain validation from the state for one's suffering in service of the socialist cause.[18]

LETTER OF 1966 FROM ALEKSEI STEPANOVICH ZLOBIN TO THE CHAIR OF THE LENINGRAD CITY SOVIET, V. IA ISAEV[19]

Text of Letter[*]: (Date: 3 March 1966)

Until the [Great] Patriotic War of 1941[†], I and my family of 5 people had a separate apartment: 42 cubic meters (42 kb m.) [on] Vasilevskii Island, the Seventh Line[‡], building no. 24, apartment 19.

My son and I were mobilized into the army from this apartment, but my wife and her sisters were evacuated to Cheliabinsk oblast[§].

In 1949 they arrested me for what was called at that time the "Leningrad Affair[¶]," but they sent my wife to Siberia, Ust'tarskii[**] district[††].

Document is from TsGA SPb (Central State Archive of St. Petersburg), f. 7384, op. 42, d. 1367, ll. 63–4. Reprinted by permission of TsGA SPb. Translation: Glennys Young.

---

[*] This is not the full text, but excerpts.

[†] In text: "Otechestvennaia voina, 1941 goda" or Patriotic War. The official Soviet name for the war of 1941–1945, in which the USSR fought Germany and its allies, was the "Great Patriotic War," or "Velikaia Otechestvennaia Voina."

[‡] This is the street name. In Russian, "7-aia Linia."

[§] Cheliabinsk oblast' was an administrative district in the Ural mountains. It surrounded the city of Cheliabinsk.

[¶] The "Leningrad Affair" of 1949–1952 was a major purge, following the death in 1948 of Leningrad Party leader Andrei Zhdanov, of the Leningrad Communist Party Organization. Victims of the purge—which in some cases resulted in the first execution of Party leaders since the Great Purges of 1936–1938—included, in addition to the chair of the State Planning Commission, Nikolai Voznesensky, top state and Party officials in Leningrad and the surrounding regions, and their underlings. For recent interpretations of its origins and purpose, see David Brandenberger, "Stalin, the Leningrad Affair, and the Limits of Postwar Russocentrism," *Russian Review* 63, no. 2 (2004): 241–255; Benjamin Tromly, "The Leningrad Affair and Soviet Patronage Politics, 1949–1950," *Europe-Asia Studies* 56, no. 5 (2004): 707–729; and "Contributors Exchange: The Leningrad Affair," in *Russian Review* 64, no. 1 (2005).

[**] Zlobin, the author of the letter, writes "Ust'tarskii" as one word. But according to a 1958 sourcebook on administrative territories of the USSR, the official spelling was Ust'-Tarskii raion in Novosibirsk oblast'. I thank Steve Harris for providing this information.

[††] The Russian word here is "raion."

In 1954 they rehabilitated me and my wife, Zlobina M. F. I arrived in Leningrad from the camps in Bratsk, and my wife from exile to Siberia.

We received an eighteen-square-meter room in a two-room apartment on Frunze Street, building 5, apartment 4.

I am a pensioner according to seniority, but still working. My wife, an industrial invalid, receives a pension of twenty-two rubles. Spending three years living in a Siberian dugout during exile took its toll on her health; she could not work the number of years she needed to in order to qualify for a pension[*].

Well, in this communal apartment we don't get any rest in our old age; rather almost everyday there's a squabble, especially shouts directed at us that we're "jailbirds[†]."

We are both native residents of Leningrad.

Tell us, after what we've been through in the "Beria' period," did my wife and I suffer innocently only to end in an apartment without rest and with only this emotional agitation?

We earnestly ask to exchange our eighteen square-meter communal room for a one-room apartment of thirteen to fifteen meters. By doing that you will give [us] the possibility of living through the few remaining years of our lives and allow us to die quietly.

Aleksei Stepanovich Zlobin
Dated 3 March 1966. Signed by both by hand; letter typed (l. 64)

LETTER OF 1968 FROM N. I. PORTNOV TO COMRADE BREZHNEV AND COMRADE KOSYGIN

..Life in these cities [big cities such as Moscow, where the author lived, and Leningrad], is very tense and restless, and should be compensated with a peaceful and quiet home....

In the past the party solved the problem of industrialization in five years. In the following five-year plan the problem of collectivization was solved, but the housing problem has not been resolved in the fifty-one years of the existence of the Soviet state....

We cannot say that they did little in the area of housing construction, but we cannot confirm that we have already solved this problem. What is

---

Author of Letter[20]: N. I. Portnov. The letter was received by the State Planning Commission on 13 December 1968. Document is from RGAE (Russian State Archive of the Economy), f. 4372, op. 66, d. 2778, II. 110–114. Translation: Glennys Young.

---

[*] In Russian, "do trudovogo pensionnogo stazha," that is, the number of years one needed to work in order to qualify for retirement benefits. Soviet citizens could receive pension benefits either upon reaching a specific age or after they had worked a certain number of years. The length of time one had worked (in Russian, "trudovoi stazh") also determined the amount of money one received.

[†] In Russian, "tiuremshchiki."

fifty-one years???—it's the life of my generation. And what has our generation endured?...

We endured the difficulties of the imperialist war*, the difficulties of the civil war, the difficulties of the restoration period†. On our shoulders, with our hands, we realized the grandiose plans of industrialization and complete‡ collectivization. With our chests we saved the homeland from the fascist invaders. After the war we not only reconstructed the economy of our country, but made our country still more powerful in economic and political relations. No metal could withstand such strains, but we did....

But it did not pass to us as a gift. The majority of us are now sick....

Many became invalids from the war and naturally our nerves give out. As they say, 'the soul and body need peace,' but there isn't any peace in communal apartments....

One shouldn't forget that we want not only the future of our descendants to make us happy, but rather as people we too want to live in normal apartments§....

Many of us still work and conduct large-scale party-educational work among the population and especially among youth for the upbringing of the young generation in the spirit of unlimited devotion to the party and the Motherland....

The slogan of providing each family with a separate apartment will further the political development in the country and give great economic results....

IS IT POSSIBLE TO FULFILL THIS TASK?

Signed, Portnov, N. I.
Received by: GOSPLAN, 13 December 1968

NOTES

1. I borrow this phrase from Sheila Fitzpatrick, "The Good Old Days (Review Essay)," *London Review of Books,* 9 October 2003.
2. The biographical information here is taken from *Letters to Miriam* and interviews undertaken by a number of interviewers in Berkeley, California on 1 May 2007 and 15 January 2008. For the complete text of those interviews, see http://www.tellingstories.org/holocaust/dsorell/index.html.
3. But her parents, two of her seven brothers, and approximately forty members of her extended family did not. See www.letterstomygrandchildren.com, accessed on 14 February 2010.

---

* "Imperialist war" was Lenin's term for World War I.
† The "period of restoration" (in Russian, "vosstanovitel'nyi period") was, in historiography produced in the USSR, the period of 1921–1925, that is, the first four years of "New Economic Policy."
‡ The original Russian word is hard to make out, but it is likely "sploshnaia," or "complete."
§ Literally, according to the text, in "normal apartment conditions."

4. The summary in this paragraph draws upon Peggy Watson, "Nowa Huta: The Politics of Post-Communism and the Past," in June Edmunds and Bryan S. Turner, eds., *Generational Consciousness, Narrative, and Politics* (Lanham, MD: Rowman and Littlefield Publishers, 2003), 165–170.

5. On the role of Nowa Huta's industrial workers in building this and other churches, see Michael Jansen and Günther Saathoff, eds., *"A Mutual Responsibility and a Moral Obligation": The Final Report on Germany's Compensation Programs for Forced Labor and Other Personal Injuries* (New York: Palgrave Macmillan, 2009), 169, for a more detailed profile of one such worker, the electrician Marian Siewiera, who was also a devout Catholic. Siewiera contributed to the construction of "nearly all" of Nowa Huta's churches.

6. Her book is based on different kinds of sources, including interviews with relatives, archival material, research in Vietnam, and a reading of secondary sources. See Duong Van Mai Elliott, *The Sacred Willow: Four Generations in the Life of a Vietnamese Family* (New York: Oxford University Press, 1999), xi.

7. The author attended Georgetown University on a scholarship. She then returned to Vietnam, where she lived from 1963–1968. She worked for the Rand Corporation, for whom she interviewed Viet Cong war prisoners.

8. *The Sacred Willow*, xii.

9. He was formally given these titles, which he had held in practice, after the 1949 treaty in which France recognized Vietnam's independence, and agreed that Cochinchina was part of its territory. These titles suggested, as Duong Van Mai Elliott points out, that her father was an "official of an independent country." But, in fact, because the French still had control of "political, financial and military affairs," they dictated his budget, and two French advisers supervised his work. Ibid., 203.

10. Ibid., 196.

11. Though some members of the author's clan supported the Viet Minh only because of its popularity, Thang and her husband Hau were true believers. See ibid., 124.

12. I adapt here the title of Richard White, *The Organic Machine: The Remaking of the Columbia River* (New York: Hill and Wang, 1996).

13. His books include *Kultura Essays* (New York: The Free Press, 1970); *Explorations in Freedom: Prose, Narrative, and Poetry from Kultura* (New York: The Free Press, 1970); *Notebooks of a Dilettante* (New York, Macmillan, 1970); and *The Seven Long Voyages* (London: M. Joseph, 1959). Among his novels are *The Man with the White Eyes* (New York: Knopf, 1959). After coming to the United States, he published essays in the *New Yorker* and *New York Times Magazine*.

14. A superb resource for information and primary sources concerning the communal apartment or *kommunalka* is the website "Communal Living in Russia: A Virtual Museum of Soviet Everyday Life," by Ilya Utekhin, Alice Nakhimovsky, Slava Paperno, and Nancy Ries. (It also has a Russian-language version: "Kommunal'naia kvartira: Virtual'nyi muzei sovetskogo byta.") See http://kommunalka.colgate.edu/.

15. Quoted in Steven E. Harris, "In Search of 'Ordinary' Russia: Everyday Life in the NEP, the Thaw, and the Communal Apartment," in *Kritika: Explorations in Russian and Eurasian History* 6, no. 3 (2005): 584.

16. The "mass housing campaign" was to a large extent the creation of the Soviet state bureaucracy. A major pillar of the campaign was the July 1957 decree, "On the Development of Housing Construction in the USSR," which laid out a housing vision for the future in which single-family separate apartments predominated,

proclaimed that the USSR would overcome its housing shortage in ten to twelve years, and elaborated state and economic policies for doing so. See "O razvitii zhilishchnogo stroitel'stva v SSSR (On the Development of Housing Construction in the USSR)," 31 July 1957, art. 102, *Sobranie postanovlenii pravitel'stva SSSR* (*Collection of Resolutions of the Government of the USSR*), no. 9 (1957): 332–348. Yet, in the early stages of the campaign, factory managers and workers also played a role in developing housing innovations. For more details, see Harris, "In Search," 597.

17. As Zlobin mentions in his letter, he was charged in the "Leningrad Affair" in 1949, found guilty, and sent to a prison camp. (On the "Leningrad Affair," see the gloss in the text.) See also, for more details, Harris, "'We Too Want to Live in Normal Apartments': Soviet Mass Housing and the Marginalization of the Elderly Under Khrushchev and Brezhnev," *The Soviet and Post-Soviet Review* 32, no. 2–3 (2005): 143–174.

18. On escape from stigma, see Harris, "'We Too Want to Live,'" 162.

19. For a chart of Leningrad City Soviet leaders, see Blair Ruble, *Leningrad: Shaping a Soviet City* (Berkeley, CA: University of California Press, 1990), 223–227. (http://ark.cdlib.org/ark:13030/ft500006ml/, accessed on 10 August 2010.)

20. Excerpts from "Letter Sent to TsKPSS, forwarded to the Deputy Chair of Gosplan (the State Planning Commission) in the Soviet Union, V. Ia. Isaev."

CHAPTER 8

———★———

Everyday Life, III: Are We Having Fun Yet? Leisure, Entertainment, Sports, and Travel

For Communist political leaders around the world, leisure—mass entertainment, sports, travel—was *not* a private, non-political part of everyday life. It was, like physical space and the material world, invested with enormous political significance. The challenge for Communist governments was to get their citizens to ascribe the correct meaning, or meanings, to the different ways in which they could spend their leisure time.

One fundamental problem was that leisure was inherently at odds with a Communist worldview, and philosophy of history, that prioritized *labor*. Another stumbling block was the following: when people went to the movies, theater and musical productions, were spectators or participants in sporting events, or traveled, they became *consumers* in an economic system that privileged not *consumption*—whether of household goods or of forms of leisure and entertainment—but *production*, especially of industrial goods.[1] As consumers, people living in Communist regimes developed and expressed preferences, and could, therefore, register their dissatisfaction, approval, and everything else in between. When Communist governments and economic systems failed to satisfy their citizens' preferences for spending their leisure time, they had to deal with the political consequences thereof. As these governments increasingly transmitted the message, especially in the post–World War II and post-Stalin eras, that the truly Communist society was one in which people enjoyed abundance (including in leisure pursuits), they inadvertently created the possibility for people to indict the socialist system itself when it didn't deliver.

Locator Map for Chapter 8

Thus, to generalize, Communist polities could not, to their dismay, control the *meanings* that leisure had for their citizens. The degree of control—or, putting it more aptly, the extent to which there was convergence between the meanings desired by Communist political leaderships and those constructed by the people—varied tremendously over time and locale space. As, especially in the post-Stalin era (particularly in the USSR and Eastern Europe, or, in the case of China, from the late-1970s onward), there was more cultural interaction between the Communist and capitalist worlds than before, people proved to be even more inventive in the meanings they gave to the films they watched, the music they heard, the sports teams they cheered for, and the places, people, and things they saw when they traveled. Nor could Communist governments, despite state censorship, state funding, and state unions for artists and other cultural figures, control what their citizens did during their leisure time. People took risks. They played banned music (whether jazz or rock) in private apartments, rooted for sports teams that weren't the state's favorite, and produced art that challenged Communist values.

These are vast generalizations, of course. But they are based, fortunately, on an expanding body of original research,[2] some of which has informed the selection and introduction of the documents herein.

The documents open a window into a number of themes. One theme—evoked by excerpts from an interview with a stage and movie star in Soviet Kyrgyzstan, as well as the autobiography of a Chinese Olympic trainer who grew up in the Soviet

Photograph of Sabira Kumushalieva (1917–2007), Kyrgyz stage and film star in the USSR. Selections from an interview with her comprise document 8–1. The photo was taken in her dressing room in the Kyrgyz National Theater in Bishkek, Kyrgyzstan, on 19 July 2002. She is wearing a traditional Kyrgyz coat (a *chapan*) made of thin velvet with hand-stitched embroidery. This is a ceremonial coat for both women and men. In general, only the elderly or esteemed people (such as elders, teachers, professors and *akyns* or bards) in Kyrgyz society wear it. The hat (in Kyrgyz, *elechek*) is worn only by old or married women to show respect, and is considered to be holy. (In fact, in yurts [in Kyrgyz, *bozui*], women place the *elechek* next to the Koran, which, as a holy item, is on a shelf above people's heads.) Kumushalieva wore the *chapan* and the *elechek* on this particular day because a foreign scholar was coming to interview her: she usually dressed like a "Western" woman. The *elechek* is made out of a scull-cap and about twenty meters of fabric wrapped like a turban around the cap.   Photo by Ali Igmen. Used by permission.

Union, and that of a Korean actress who served Korean Communists during the Korean War—has to do with the *official* meanings of entertainment in Communist polities. A second theme pertains to the meanings that people ascribed to the way they spent their leisure time, meanings at odds with what officials desired. Two selections—one relating to jazz in East Germany in the late 1940s and early 1950s, and a compilation on Soviet rock 'n' roll in the 1970s and early 1980s, suggest what musical forms associated with the "evil" world of capitalism came to mean to people who played and listened to them. And another theme—evoked by the selection on travel from Yugoslavia to Western Europe in the 1950s and 1960s—is related to how journeying beyond the borders of socialism influenced people's sense of themselves and of their societies' place(s) in the world.

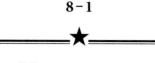

8-1

Kyrgyzstan

Sabira Kumushalieva (1917–2007) On Becoming a Star of the Kyrgyz Stage and Screen

Sabira Kumushalieva was one of the most famous actresses of the Kyrgyz stage and of Kygryz film during the Soviet period. She rose from humble beginnings to become, as an article written in a Kyrgyz newspaper would put it in 2001, a "symbol of the [Kyrgyz] people's fate," a "symbol of Kyrgyz theatre," and a "symbol of Kyrgyz film."[3] The village in which she grew up, Tököldösh, would become famous as the hometown of not only Kumushalieva, but of three other major figures of the performing arts in Soviet Kyrgyzstan: they would become known to other Kyrgyz as the "four daughters of Tököldösh," who, as one scholar has put it, "defined the modern conventions of Kyrgyz stage and film."[4] Kumushalieva was honored with a Kyrgyz postage stamp, released on 5 April 2008, that depicted her as "Hero of the Kyrgyz Republic.[5]"

Kumushalieva and other performers in the Kyrgyz cultural world had careers that were shaped significantly by Soviet cultural policy, and by Soviet policy toward non-Russian nationalities in the USSR as well. The basic premise of Soviet nationality policy in the 1920s and 1930s was one of "nation building"—that is, policies designed to facilitate the preeminence of "titular nationals" (such as, in the case of Kyrgyzstan, the Kyrgyz) in national Party and state institutions, and to encourage the development of national cultural forms that would, of course, be "socialist in content." Hence, as Moscow sought to solidify Soviet power in the non-Russian republics of the USSR, including Kyrgyzstan, it also aimed to provide people with everyday entertainment and cultural programs in local venues, such as the "people's culture houses," mentioned in the following selection. Over the decades, too, Soviet Kyrgyzstan developed theater, film, literature, and music that featured the national cultural traditions of the Kyrgyz. One of the films in which Kumushalieva starred, *Among the People* (*Sredi Liudei*, 1979) was based on a children's story by the celebrated Kyrgyz writer, Chingiz Aitmatov.[6]

In an interview of 2002, excerpted here, Kumushalieva recalls the major junctures in her life and, as she does so, employs official Soviet rhetoric. Even eleven years after the end of the USSR, she speaks of herself as a daughter of a *kulak* (the Russian word for wealthy peasant), the bourgeois class enemy in

The interview was conducted by Ali F. Igmen in Bishkek, Kyrgyzstan, on 19 July 2002. Used by permission of the interviewer and interviewee. Translation: Jipar Dushembieva.

the countryside during the forced collectivization, and violent resistance to it, of 1929–1930.[7] She, like other offspring of kulaks, was expelled from school. Nonetheless, she recalls with pride and gratitude what her career owed to the Kyrgyz State Drama Theatre in Bishkek, which she entered when she was seventeen. Though she does not deny the suffering of the Purges, she claims that witnessing it—and helping to entertain people on collective farms during those years—enhanced her inner strength and even put her more "in touch with her own Soviet Kyrgyz culture."[8]

"ON HOW I BECAME AN ACTRESS"
(INTERVIEW WITH
SABIRA KUMUSHALIEVA)

Sabira: I studied at the pedagogical college. There were only two colleges; one was pedagogical, another one was a women's college. I entered the older group at the college. There were three groups; younger, middle, and older groups. Then, they expelled me as a daughter of a rich man [*kulak*]. My ancestors were very rich people. After I was expelled there was nothing for me to do. I was fourteen years old then. At that time, there was a woman in our village, one of my aunts. She took me to the school #50, she was a teacher herself there, and I became a teacher where I taught the first and the second graders. The school was located in *Kyzyl Asker*, and I worked there for two years. I became a very good teacher. All, children and teachers, all of them liked me....

One day there wasn't anybody at school and the artists came. One of them was Maldybaev*, a great actor, with his wife. Kuttubaeva†, a good actress, and her husband, also an actor and Eshimbekov, another good actor. The reason I am telling you this [is] because they were the founders of the theater. They led the road. It was 1934, a year of starvation. Kazakhs were suffering a lot at this time. Maldybaev came and asked, "Can you gather all your children? We are in a hurry; we will give them a concert and leave." They would give concerts for free at that time. So, they gave their concert. After the concert we fried some corn and served them with some tea. (Now, of course, they have vodka.) After having tea they started singing. Everybody sang. They asked me to sing. I sang one song, and they asked me to sing more. I sang another one. "You have a nice voice, why are you teaching? Come to the theater," they said. I said, "What if they expel me as a daughter of a rich man?'" "No, nobody will expel you," they said. They told me to come on the 1 September, after they get back from their break. On 1 September 1934, I went to the theater. I passed all the

---

* She is referring to Adylas Maldybaev, the Director of the Kyrgyz Theatre.
† She refers here to the acclaimed Kyrgyz actress, Anvar Kuttubaeva.

exams [she is showing how, or doing what] receiving all A's. I was very scared in the beginning that they would expel me as a daughter of a rich man, but they didn't. After three months, Kuttubaeva, a good actress, fell ill. She would play a girl named Karachach in Kasymaly Zhantoshev's play *Karachach*. One day, when I came to the theater, people were quite worried. Kuttubaeva had a surgery and was in a hospital. Now, who would play her part? At that time there weren't any cancellations allowed. Somebody had to play her part. In three months I had already learned all the parts by heart. I used to imitate Kuttubaeva's roles all the time. I became Kuttubaeva myself. I am Sabira, but everything I did was like Kuttubaeva's. They started looking for a person to play Kuttubaeva's part. On the one hand, I wanted to tell them, but was scared of being laughed at. On the other, I really wanted to play that part. When Kuttubaeva was rehearsing her part, I would also practice behind the stage. In short, I was ready. When they looked at the people, all of the actresses were old, only Kuttubaeva was younger, but she was sick. They went through a lot of trouble. Finally, they decided to call our Head, the Head of the Art Institute, Ashyrbaev. He said they could not cancel the play. They came back and didn't know what to do. They never thought of me! Then I got up and said "*Agay* [Esteemed elder], I will play." They started laughing at me which made me angry. They asked if I could play. At that time Zhantoshev said, "No she cannot play, she said it out of her childishness." "No, I can play," I insisted. The director had no choice, so he asked everybody to leave and started practicing my part with me. At the end he said, "Good for you, you are ready." There was a play that night, I played. I didn't forget any of my lines, I played just like Kuttubaeva. The only thing, since I had never played with great actors before, I became very shy. I couldn't look at the men straight up. Ashyrbaev, our head, came that night and saw my acting. Three days later an article about me was published in the newspaper. . . . After the play was over, they gave me a nice red scarf and everybody congratulated me. I was waiting for Kuttubaeva to return, and I thought that they wouldn't let me play after she came back. She returned in seven to eight days. "You are a good girl, you played very well, from now on we will take turns playing this part," she said. I was so happy. At times like this, one's kindness makes you so happy. I was so happy and came to love her, and I never said anything against her till she died. If there was somebody else, she might have said, "Why this young girl?" Little by little, I became an actress by playing Kuttubaeva's parts.

ON CULTURE HOUSES

When we were studying at the pedagogical college, there was a building next to the Russian Drama theater. It was a one-story building, [a] very big one. They would have silent movies there. When there was water coming from the screen, all of us would run out of the theater thinking that we would drown in the water. If there was a fire, we would run out thinking that it might burn us. We would show plays and sometimes, they would have movies in that building. I didn't know that it was a culture house, because we never heard of the name back then. And later on they said that there would be another theater built. Soon after, there was a theater built on the place where the Russian Drama Theater is right now. We worked in that theater, and later they demolished it and built the Russian Drama Theater. However, when they were demolishing the old building, I felt very sad. I thought, why they were demolishing it, it was quite nice. I regretted it a lot.

We didn't have our own house to stay. We used to rent rooms from Uzbeks and Dungans. However, they would drive us out once we had children saying they cried too much. We, then, would put all of our belongings onto a donkey cart and move from one place to another. Then life got better. They started building [a] new opera theater. My younger brother*, Altymysh Usubaliev, was a great painter. He decorated all of the Opera House. One day he called me. He was painting the ceiling of the Opera House. He asked if he could paint my picture on the ceiling, but I was too shy, though I was an actress, and refused. So, we finished building the Opera House and started moving. We separated as Drama Theater. However, they didn't let me go. I used to play in one play [the name is unclear]. I played a part of Kelgi†. People loved watching me play Kelgi. Because of that role, they didn't want me to leave. However, I wanted to be in the Drama Theater and go with other artists, such as Ryskulov [Kumshalieva's husband], Botaliev, and Eshimbekov. Thus, for a year, I worked in two theaters. After a year, they found somebody else to replace me, and I came to this theater. Thank God, this theater became a good theater. For instance, all of the artists such as Ryskulov, Eshimbekov, Botaliev, Kuiukova, etc., all of them were illiterate. They had five to seven years of schooling. As for Ryskulov, he never studied. He came‡ when he was twenty years old, in 1936, to become a teacher. Here, he met Kalyk§. Both of them were from the same village, Zhumgal. When Ryskulov came to the city with his three friends, he couldn't find a job. All of them came to become teachers. They didn't know anything. They couldn't find anything and didn't have anything to eat. One day, when they were working at the theater construction site, they met Kalyk. He asked if Ryskulov was a son of Ryskul. Since they were from one village, they used to see each other quite often. That's how they recognized each other. Ryskulov told him that he came to the city to become a

---

* [Translator's note: He doesn't necessarily have to be her own brother. It could be any younger man from either her village or her tribe.]

† The name here is unclear.

‡ Presumably to Bishkek.

§ Kalyk was a Kyrgyz oral poet.

teacher, but he couldn't find a job. Kalyk took them to the theater. When Kalyk tested Ryskulov, it turned out to be that he didn't have any musical talent. He couldn't repeat what Kalyk asked. But if a person really wants something, he can achieve it. That's why he is a man. Since he didn't have musical talent, the next day they told him to leave. Ryskulov went back to the construction work again. However, he saw Kalyk, and he took him back again for testing. This time, Ryskulov did everything right, probably because he was too ashamed. Thus, he got accepted into the theater and began to study....

I asked Ryskulov if he knew how to read. He said he didn't. So I started teaching him. He learned all of the Kyrgyz letters in fifteen days. He started writing in a month. He was very talented. I had never seen any talented person like him before. The lines of Othello, King Lear, Egor Bulychev lasted for hundreds of pages. He learned all of them by heart and played them very well.... One day, one of the actors fell ill; it was Zhantoshev, I think. He had a part where he had to dance. They gave Ryskulov that part. I was worried; since he didn't have any musical talent, how could he dance? He came out, and I didn't know if he was dancing well or not, but everybody started clapping. So, his first role was a role of Kudake. From that on he started growing and became Ryskulov. Later, he went to England for Shakespeare's four hundredth anniversary to play Othello and King Lear. People in Moscow chose the thirty best actors among all of the actors from Uzbekistan, Kazakhstan, all over the Soviet Union. Ryskulov alone passed the competition, but they took all thirty people to England. They came to the hall, and he went up onto the stage and recited King Lear's lines. People started applauding. He finished his lines and came down to his place. Applause had continued even after he took his seat. A man next to him asked Ryskulov to get up and bow, but applause still continued. He had to go up the stage again and bow. He couldn't leave the stage without saying anything, so he said, "Desdemona, you died, my dear!" and left the stage. The applause started anew.

He would always boast about those things. We do not like when people boast about themselves. However, I would praise him myself. I really cared about Ryskulov. One has to take good care of an artist, and has to try not to hurt his feelings, because if he gets offended, he can give up on art. I knew that he was a good actor, and I cared. He would wake me up at 1 AM in the morning and ask me to look at his lines. I would get up whenever he asked me to. We would put our children to sleep in another room and rehearse. I stopped caring about myself, though I was a good actress.

After Ryskulov died, since I didn't have small children, I decided to serve my people. It has been thirty years already. I have been doing it since then.

Creative work is very hard. One has to be very careful with an artist. If one is angry with him/her all the time, an artist will disappear. One has to praise a person from time to time. People grow only when they are praised....

During the winter times, during the war, the theater wouldn't be heated, but the plays would continue. Theaters were very cold. I would bring a bottle with hot milk in it to theatre, try to keep it warm, and I would give it to Ryskulov after each episode. There wasn't anything warm. Those were really hard times. Our houses were cold as well. We would move from one place to another. We went through the most difficult times, but we didn't cry over it. We didn't cry over difficulties, didn't cry over the war. Friendship between the people was very strong during the war. That was the best thing. People cared for each other. Even if the three of us had little bit of bread, we would be sharing it among us. Now, people are changing. I think of it sometimes; how can we change people today?

Interviewer: We moved away from showing respect to the creative, talented people. We stopped caring about the culture, we forgot our culture.

Sabira: We worked with Stanislavskii, a good director, that is why our theater developed. Kydykeeva had five years of school; I had six years at the Pedagogical College. Ryskulov was completely illiterate. When teachers came to Ryskulov's parents to enroll him to the classes, his father told them, "He doesn't have to study. Just take my cow and my horse and leave my son alone." Thus, he didn't let Muratbek go to school, and he [Muratbek] suffered a lot because of this. And later, teachers and other learned men started coming to his village. He saw them dressed nicely and thought, "That is how I should be dressed and become a teacher." That is how those three young men came to the city.

Now, how can we improve the culture? It is very hard now. Nobody cares about the culture now. How should I say this...Stanislavskii once said, "Deceit is a very bad thing in art. In art, we do not need artists who deceive and do not work hard. The art should be pure. Deceiving is like a knife to the art. One can't do it." I am saying it in my own words. We had a good director, Il'ia Grigor'evich Bolov, he came from Moscow. He made us good actors. There wasn't such a thing as bragging about oneself. The power of a director was strong at that time....Later we put "Father's Fate" on the stage. Both me and Ryskulov played parts in it. A theater critic, Ershova, gave a good response to the play. She said, "Ryskulov's part is an important part. Though Kumushalieva has a small part in the play, she realized her character very well." Once we came from Moscow, they gave me a title of the People's Artist. I was approaching my fifties then. [She shows something.]...

Interviewer: What were the most memorable years in your life?

Sabira: In 1939, after we had our first decade (it was in Moscow), happy years started for me. Although I didn't play myself, I admired my friends; people who worked with me, directors. Till now I remember them dearly. Ryskulov comes to my mind at times like this. He didn't know Russian. And I would ask why he was laughing, to which he replied, "you just have to laugh when everybody else is laughing. Let people think that I know the language." I lived good days; however, bad days prevailed in my life—difficult days, starvation, the war, reconstruction after the war, all of them. There is a Big Chui Channel. Only women dug that channel. Only one comedian, Sharshen Termechikov, was there. Thus, we lived through these kinds of interesting days. They would give us a little bread in the morning and for lunch. At night we would cook corn ourselves. Those were interesting times for me. Despite all the difficulties we would sing. Where there is labor, that place is always interesting, beautiful. That's why I tell to my children, "You have to work." I work hard when I am on stage. When I get up on the stage, I forget myself. The stage becomes my friend, my companion, my life. I received a title of the hero for the small part. I played it in "Kurmanzhan Datka." In the beginning, they didn't give it to me, I was in the hospital. They gave the part to a young actress. After I came out from the hospital, the director refused to give me the part. I asked the young actress if I could practice her part. She allowed me to do so. I came to the stage and did it very well from the beginning. Il'ia Grigor'evich would say, "You have to come out strong from the start. You cannot say that you will play better later." He made a good person out of me. Another thing: I often went to the road trips with the famous actors, such as Kalyk Akiev, Osmonkul Bolobalaev, Alymkul Usonbekov, Aibatyrov. For three months I was together with them. At that time I understood life. [She mentions Askar Akaev here.] One has to learn to live from good people. I was a spoiled girl. Osmonkul would say, "Sabike, don't sleep, stay awake. One has to watch movies awake." Or, they would criticize a woman: "Look at the food she gave us, she is a good woman," they would say. I wouldn't understand anything and try to figure everything out myself. That's how I learned from them. There was a good poet, Musa Baetov. One day our director said, "People are forgetting how to laugh, everybody is sad. We need to send you to the collective farms, and you will entertain them. Who is willing to go?" Musa Baetov said that he is willing to go. Seven of us decided to go with him. We went from one village to another. At that time we saw what starvation was. I am eighty eight years old now out of which I worked sixty eight years. We experienced lots of difficulties. We came to Bystrovka once with our group. There was a man in Bystrovka. He had two wives. After he went to war, his older wife became a village secretary and his younger wife was a head of the village. All of us went to her house, but she wasn't home. Once she came and saw us, she had her only sheep slaughtered for us. The next morning we had the leftovers and continued our trip. Raikan took all the bones saying that he would show us a trick, and put them in a bag. I am not making up these things. We came to a place with lots of reed. He told us to sit down and started his trick. "Each of you bring one long reed," he ordered. We gave him our reeds. He asked us to break them. He asked a dancer guy to bring two rocks. Then he broke the bones and gave one to

Musake. "Musake, you are the oldest one, take *joto jilik**," he said. The next one was mine. So, we took our reed and started scraping out the fat inside the bone and eating it. It was better than any dried corn; it gave us strength. At night we went to one house. Their son went to the war, they didn't have anything at home, but they kept inviting us in. An old woman seated us and left. She came very late with some dried corn in her handkerchief and some milk. She fried the corn and gave us milk. Raikan said, "Apa, please give me corn." He divided it between us, and gave an extra one to Musake, saying that he is the oldest among us. Even though those were war times, we didn't forget the respect for the old.

... We did take the bad and the good very well in the past. You ask where the culture is. Those old women saved us during the war giving us their corn, wheat, things that they saved for their sons. We traveled for five years.

8–2

A Chinese Student in the USSR

Huang Jian (A.K.A. Yura Huanpin, 1927–)
on What Sports Meant for His Life and for Socialism

H uang Jian (Yura Huanpin) was one of the Chinese students who studied at the Interdom (*Ivanovskii internatsional'nyi detskii dom*, or the International Children's Home of Ivanovo), a school founded in the USSR in 1933 for the children of foreign Communists from all over the world.[9] Located in Ivanovo, in an industrial region whose core city of the same name is approximately 190 miles northeast of Moscow, the school instructed, between 1933 and 1949,[10] several thousand children of Communists who were involved in risky activities, were in prison, or had passed away. Among the internationally renowned Communists whose children attended the Interdom were Mao Zedong, Joseph Broz Tito, Luigi Longo, Palmiro Togliatti, Dolores Ibárruri, and Enrique Lister.

From Huang Jian/Yura Huanpin, "The Pain and Happiness of an Old Trainer." Published with permission of the author. Translation: Elizabeth McGuire.

---

* *Jilik* is a sheep's bone that has meat on it. The *joto jilik* is a part of a sheep's leg (the knuckle bone, specifically) and is usually given to a male guest. Each of the sheep's twelve *jiliks* is given to an honorable guest, some to men, and some to women.

Yura's father, mentioned in the following excerpt from his son's memoir, was a significant figure in the history of the Chinese Communist Party. Born in Russia, Yura grew up, as he tells us, speaking Russian, not Chinese, and did not go to his "homeland" until the early 1950s, after he had graduated from the Lenin Institute of Physical Culture.

In the passage that follows, Yura proudly recounts his transformation from one of the Interdom's "bully troublemaker[s]" and "scallywag ringleader[s] of wild boys," into a "zealous P.E. assistant"[11] who came to understand the political significance of sport. Eventually, in fact, he became a renowned Olympic trainer. Crucial to his personal transformation, he claims, was the 1940 visit of Zhou Enlai to the Interdom, one in which Zhou emphasized that being a good revolutionary meant being physically fit.

FORWARD

In May of 1987 I turned exactly sixty years old.

It's time to look back and ask myself the question: "What did you do with your life? Can you take satisfaction in the fact that you were useful to people? Or will you be tortured until the end of your days by the idea that you could have done something good and useful, but somehow couldn't or wouldn't, and the train has already left the station, you won't catch it. . . . "

I'm a happy-go-lucky guy. Fate has beaten me often, but to make up for it has given me an unusual and interesting life:

My father was a professional revolutionary. He worked in the underground for a long time with comrade Zhou Enlai and was one of the leaders of the Canton Uprising, a prominent event in the history of the Chinese revolution. He lived for several years in Moscow, where he worked in the Comintern in the Chinese section. He met often with comrade Bukharin, of whom he had an extraordinarily high opinion, both as a person and as a politician.

During my school and student years—the 1930s and 1940s—I lived in the USSR and was a witness to the heroic labor and wartime victory of the Soviet people, during those difficult and tragic years of world history. Soviet people always treated me very warmly, helped me to grow up from a helpless little boy to a grown and independent person, graduating from the Lenin Institute of Physical Culture with honors.

In the beginning of the 1950s and up to the present I live and work in my homeland. I've seen it all: I have felt the "delights" of the so-called cultural revolution on my own skin, the betrayals, the envy and the slander of the "friends of the fellow travelers." Even so, the sunny joys of my life have been much larger than the dark patches. . . . I am also grateful to sport for the fact that it brought me so many happy moments, when my work as a trainer helped my students to set world, Asian, and national records. But I get no less moral satisfaction from knowing that many, many of my students in all parts of my country are working honestly for the good of my country and people. I have trained them for over thirty-seven years, but really, it is they who have taught and helped me. A huge thank you to you—my students! To you I dedicate this book....

CHAPTER ONE: A LITTLE BIT ABOUT MY CHILDHOOD AND YOUTH

Many people, especially young people, consider that in order to become a "great" trainer, you only need to have high-level professional knowledge and great practical experience in training work.... But, first, I never have considered and never consider myself a "great" trainer, and second, why isn't anybody interested in who I am as a person—good or evil, hot-tempered or even-keeled, fun or boring, or—hell—smart or dumb as a post. I am deeply convinced, that a real trainer above all else has to be a real person, with a rich life experience.... Therefore, I will try to recall some fragments from my own life, most of all to understand myself, how my own character was formed, my convictions, worldviews, and habits, that allowed me to achieve certain successes in work.

Moscow Region, Town of Vas'kino, Children's Home
It was the early 1930s. The country of Soviets still hadn't fully revived its economy, it was a difficult and hungry time....

"Granny! I'm hungry...."

"Ooh, my poor little ones! What to do? Lie down in your beds and listen carefully: 'Once upon a time there was an old man and an old woman by the deep blue sea....'"

That's how the kind old nanny from our children's home made us kids forget about our half-empty stomachs. I remember well how she felt sorry for us and gave us cheap village candies as treats; she taught us human kindness. But, I also remember clearly how we went to the village to see the first tractor. I remember the stories of old Red Army men, about their battles with the Whites. And I really remember my first introduction to "sport." The old carpenter made me, a little five-year-old boy, skis, out of planks from a barrel. They weren't exactly fancy, but what joy I got skiing on them with the other village ragamuffins. Even then I loved endless boyish games, the spirit of honest rivalry, of pure childhood friendship and loyalty. These little boys from so long ago played a big role in the formation of my character. Many years have passed, but I often had "childish lapses" in my work as a trainer with students: our training often took the form of games, friendly competition, fun and with lots of jokes. And in my teaching I always tried to foster directness, courage, boyish tendencies to fantasy, and indifference to all kinds of scratches and bruises.

City of Ivanovo, 1st International Children's Home
In 1933 I, along with many children—sons and daughters of revolutionaries of different countries of the world—arrived in the 1st ICH [International Children's Home], where I spent many years. This remarkable children's home was built on

the initiative of the Old Bolshevik E. Stasova, one of Lenin's real comrades-in-arms, with the hard-earned money of ordinary Soviet people. Many sons and daughters of leading revolutionaries from all different countries were raised in this home. I remember well the daughter of Dolores Ibárruri, the son of Broz Tito, the son of Togliatti. Amongst the Chinese students were the sons and daughters of Mao Zedong, the son and daughter of Liu Shaoqi, the adopted daughter of Zhou Enlai, the daughter of Zhu De and others. I have a sort of dual, mixed-up feeling about this time in my life: on the one hand, we were raised in the children's home from early on in a spirit of loyalty to the principles of Communism, internationalism, and patriotism. There were so many meetings with heroes of the October Revolution and the civil war, and also with famous pilots and shock-workers.... Even though I, living in the U.S.S.R., couldn't speak my own native language (like all the children in our ICH home), I decided without a second thought: "As soon as I grow up, I'll go to my Homeland, to my people!" The word Homeland was embodied for me then in fiery words like "Mao Zedong, Zhou Enlai, Liu Shaoqi, the 8th Route Army, the Long March, Jinggangshan!" I didn't hesitate for a second in my decision to return to my Homeland and to serve my people loyally.... But on the other hand, in my childhood and especially the years of my youth, I suffered from a sense of insult, of wounded pride, of great injustice to myself. It was a good thing that in that time long ago good people came to my assistance. Otherwise, it would have been very easy to break my childish spirit, and I would have been lost....

In 1940 Zhou Enlai paid an unexpected visit to us in the Children's home. He greeted each of us Chinese students warmly, was actively interested in our life and schoolwork, and was very satisfied that the Soviet people had created such excellent conditions for us. Then Uncle Zhou carried on a lively, spontaneous conversation with us. He asked all of us what we wanted to be when we grew up. Several answered things like doctor, pilot, engineer, etc. Finally, it was my turn. But I stood there, the cat had my tongue, I didn't know what to answer. Then everyone started yelling out, "Yura's our jock! He loves sports!" I blushed all over with shame, since I thought that sports wasn't a serious thing. But Uncle Zhou said approvingly, "Oh! That's really great. The Homeland needs strong and healthy revolutionaries. I'll tell you a really interesting story from my own life: When I was working in the underground, enemies happened upon me by chance and began to follow me. I ran for my life. The chase went on forever. Finally, the enemies gave up hope. Why did I beat them? Because I always practiced sports and had a lot more endurance and ran a lot faster than them." Then Uncle Zhou raise both hands in the air and said with a smile: "You must not only study well, but also do sports, so that our arms and legs are strong like steel...." That night I couldn't fall asleep for a long time. It was the first time I understood that sports isn't just for fun, but a really necessary and important thing for my people. And this is exactly why I signed up without hesitation at the physical education training college in Ivanovo.

The director of the children's home, T. Z. Makarov, gave me room and board at the home until I was finished with the training college, but made me work on a voluntary basis as a coach, in place of the regular employee who had gone off to the front. I was only fourteen years old then. The training college was a long ways from the children's home. I left early in the morning and got back late in the evening. Besides school and work, like everyone else, I participated in all kinds of patriotic events: We cleared out the deep snow on the landing strips at the military aerodrome, gathered empty bottles in yards for anti-tank defense (at the time the Red Army still didn't have enough anti-tank grenades and weapons), gathered metal, dug anti-tank ditches, worked as helpers to the workers at the artillery factory, helped in the collective farms to harvest potatoes, chopped down forests, etc. I, like all the other children from the home, earnestly passed through this first life test without dragging my feet or trying to get out of it. "All for the front! Everything for victory!"—this was how factory workers and collective farmers, children and old people worked heroically behind the lines. We lived though the most difficult years of the Fatherland's war against the brown Nazi plague, and I am happy, that during the years of the Second World War, I lived and worked in the Soviet Union, where the entire fate of humanity was decided....

In short, let's sum it all up:

Irrepressible mischief, endless spirited boyish battles, constant striving to be the lead instigator—that was the soil in which my deep and selfless love of sport flourished, because sport loves the desperate and the brave.... The children's home, of course, gave me a lot that was good and useful. But, I won't lie, I never experienced deep feelings of family loyalty to it. True, wherever I meet former students of the home, my heart starts beating quickly and happily—how could it not, meeting my very own brothers and sisters.

I lived and studied for many years in the U.S.S.R. This, without a doubt, this made a deep mark on my character and worldview. Exactly because of this I really caught hell from the Red Guards during the Cultural Revolution. After my return to my Homeland I repeatedly, and with pride, openly stated that I have two homelands—the Soviet Union, which raised me, and China—because I am a Chinese and from childhood dreamed of returning to my people. During the Cultural Revolution, my statements were judged on many "wall newspapers" as treason of my homeland, and they called me a lackey of the Soviet revisionists. They said a person can only have one homeland, and I answered them: "Not long ago we all read a big article published in *People's Daily* about the Chinese volunteers, who fought on the front of the civil war in Russia along with the Red Army, defending the victory of the Great October. Many of them, after returning to China, said that they had two homelands: Soviet Russia—the first socialist state in the world and China—the land of their ancestors. However, I am now the same as them, except I have learned to be reserved in the expression of my feelings.

In the beginning of my work in my homeland interacting with people was hard for me. To put it nicely, the straightforward "Russian" sides of my character came into conflict with Eastern etiquette of politeness. I often offended and even made enemies amongst my coworkers with my behavior, which reflected poor upbringing according to Eastern understandings. I even remember some funny incidents right from the time when I first started working. It was in the beginning of the 1950s. At the time China was carrying out a vigorous campaign of political education amongst the people. So almost every day there were some kind of political events: either political study, or lectures, or participation in all sorts of movements, and even the necessity of regularly reporting about the process of one's bourgeois re-education. Even today I don't like to sit a lot and for a long time, and in those young years, I simply rebelled. I made an official declaration that I wouldn't be participating in political education, listening to "marathon" lectures and doing reports on my own re-education. The reason: "I grew up and was educated in the U.S.S.R.—the first socialist state in the world. I studied Marx's *Das Kapital* for several years in college and passed all tests on this subject with distinction. In the Soviet Union, besides in the movies, I never once even saw a live capitalist, landowner, or kulak. So, in my consciousness there can't be any bourgeois remnants, and I don't need to re-forge myself." True, through long years of work I understood more and more and changed a lot. But right up to today I don't like how some people—even some young people!—work: you don't give them rice, but rather let them swim in an endless ocean of meetings. My friends have told me more than once: "With your great merit, honor, and position, it would have been possible long ago for you to have become a big boss and have a brilliant career. But you don't know how to relate to people, especially higher-ups." I remember a very curious incident that happened to me before the Cultural Revolution. In an ordinary political meeting they started working me over again for my willful pronouncements. One of the leading cadres of our organization started lecturing me face to face after the meeting: "In order to be in good standing, it requires very little: every day in front of everyone you must passionately dust the portraits of the great leaders. Be noticed more often in the halls of the dorm or the yard. Never openly disagree with the leadership, just listen to what others say and say the same thing." Unfortunately, I turned out to be a poor student, as the song goes: "However you were, is how you'll stay...." In short, I didn't want to change myself, and cannot adapt myself to circumstances in order to gain something for myself. So there it is, in a nutshell, about myself and my accomplishments and shortcomings.

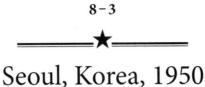

Seoul, Korea, 1950

Working as an Actress for the North Korean Communists

Ch'oe Ŭnhŭi* (born 1930), a passage from whose autobiography is published next, was a major star of the South Korean screen.[12] In 1978, she
and her husband, Shin Sang-ok, a film director from South Korea, were,
by command of Kim Jong Il (born 1941, the son of Kim Il Sung, the first leader of
Communist North Korea, and now the "Supreme Leader" of North Korea after his
father's death in 1994), abducted from Hong Kong on separate occasions and
transferred to North Korea.[13] This violent act was motivated by Kim Jong Il's bid
to improve the film industry in North Korea. Convinced, as head of Propaganda
and Agitation when he was in the Korean Worker's Party's Central Committee in
the 1960s and 1970s, that film was the key to revolutionary transformation of
North Korean arts and culture, Kim Jong Il supervised a number of film adapta-
tions from the early 1970s onwards, including works written by his father during
World War II. As Kim Jong Il put it in *On the Art of Cinema* (1973), "The task set
before the cinema today is one of contributing to people's development into
true Communists. This historic task requires, above all, a revolutionary transformation of the practice of directing."[14]

When Ch'oe* and her husband arrived in North Korea, they were subjected
to a five-year period of "reeducation"; upon its completion, they started producing movies. Among the movies made at the dictator-to-be's insistence was
Pulgasari, a North Korean version of *Godzilla*.[15] In 1986, while in Austria, they
"defected" to the West. Since their escape, the couple has been a source of what
is considered the "most extensive and reliable firsthand information on Kim."[16]

But the passage reprinted herein deals with a significantly earlier period
of Ch'oe Ŭnhŭi's life and artistic enlistment by North Korean Communists:
her experiences during the Korean War (1950–1953). In particular, she recalls
how it was that, during the three-month occupation of Seoul by the North
Koreans (late June to late September 1950), she was conscripted to work for

From Ch'oe, Ŭn-hŭi, *Ch'oe Ŭn-hŭi ŭi kobaek: Yŏnghwa poda tŏ yŏnghwa kat'ŭn sam* (*Ch'oe Ŭn-hŭi's Confessions: A Life More Movie-like than a Movie*). (Seoul: Random House Korea. 2007), 69–77. Published with permission of Random House Korea. Translated and partially annotated by Clark W. Sorensen.

---

* Ch'oe is her last name.

270

the "Security Police Auxiliary Troupe. "The passage attests to the importance that North Korean Communists ascribed to culture, even during wartime. But one of the most interesting aspects of the text reproduced herein concerns how Ch'oe Ŭnhŭi decided, when the North Korean forces were retreating as the Allied Armies approached Seoul, whether to "run away now" or "escape later." Such a momentous decision came down to "drawing lots." Essentially because of indecision, she, like many people, stayed in Seoul during the North Korean occupation. She would "escape later," and was forced to retreat North with the Security Police Auxiliary Troupe.

CHAPTER 4: AN ACTRESS'S SAD WAR

War Breaks Out

In 1950 we were on location in Mokp'o* shooting *A Man's Path*. At dawn on 25 June the North Korean People's Army crossed the 38th parallel, and descended on Ŭijŏngbu. We heard news that they would be pressing toward Seoul. My senior colleague Namgung Ryŏn was beside herself with joy saying, "Now a good world will come. A world like heaven is going to come."

"Huh? What kind of world is that?" I repeated, completely bewildered.

"I'm talking about a world in which the poor people will eat and live well."

Namgung Ryŏn later ended up crossing to the North. The production set began to get agitated, and the staff rushed around helter-skelter. The production team gathered up all the equipment, and the actors, too, hurried to pack their things.

"Since everybody is going to flee, let's us go to Pusan, too."

They urged everybody to go to Pusan, but I, as I often did, chose an inflexible path.

"I'm also worried about my family members, so I'm going to Seoul[†]."

Kim Haksŏng [her husband at the time] had been infirm and was suffering from tuberculosis, so if I went to shoot a picture my sister-in-law used to take care of him. But when I arrived in Seoul my sister-in-law Kim Yŏnsil had crossed north following Kang Haeil, the newspaper reporter she had been seeing, and was not there. They told me she had taken her younger daughter and Kim Haksŏng's son with her. They said she had left her older daughter with neighbors, and nobody knew where she had gone. Calling it a state of anarchy,[‡] nobody was in their proper mind.

---

[*] A port on on the southwest coast of Korea.

[†] Ch'oe Ŭnhŭi was nineteen years old during this period, so the influence of her family was very strong at that time.

[‡] The original text uses *nallit'ong* here, which might mean "expertise on rebellions," but it seems likely that the intended word is the more commonly used *nallip'an*, meaning "in a state of rebellion, or all in an uproar."

At sunrise the next day the People's Army entered Seoul with overwhelming force. In Seoul all Hell broke loose*. We could hear the sound of gunfire nearby, and the sound of tanks made a clamor. A little later an ashen soldier ran pell-mell into our house.

"Lady, please give me something to eat."

The soldier's manner was that of a young-looking kid.

"What on earth has happened?"

I was confused, and when I questioned him the soldier answered, breathing heavily.

"In the wake of the People's Army invasion we've done nothing but retreat overnight for three days. I've been pushed down here without let up, and I haven't slept at all."

I quickly served him some rice and wrapped up an egg for him. The soldier thanked me and quickly ran out the door. I hoped sincerely that the young man would just leave in health and without incident.

When those who had been imprisoned for leftist thought were freed due to entry of the People's Army into the city, they strictly played their role as agents of the Communist Party during the time that Seoul was occupied. They ferreted out families of policemen, families of soldiers, people who resisted by refusing to join leftist organizations, and reported them to the People's Security Bureau[†]. Among my cousins I had a younger one who was dragged into the mountains and shot for the reason that he was a policeman. The culture and art world was no exception to this. In order to live some of them even informed on the location of colleagues' houses. Young students for the most part were drawn into the People's Army.

I suggested that we flee together to Kwangju in Kyŏnggi Province, the home town of my parents' relatives. Though I kept pestering my husband that we should flee following my relatives, as a consequence of his resisting and always saying he didn't want to go, I had no choice but to remain in Seoul.

On 28 June 1950, Seoul after three days fell to the People's Army. Over the short time of three days frightful incidents swept past our life like a typhoon. People who would leave had mostly left, and the rest didn't go out and were hidden in their houses. The streets were exposed to danger, but the National Army had already retreated beforehand so fighting did not directly reach the streets. We merely heard the rumor that the bridge on the Han River[‡] had been blown up, but we didn't know what society was going to return to. On the radio they kept broadcasting that we should remain calm and not panic.

---

[*] The expression in the text Sŏul i abikyut'an ŭi hyŏnjang iyŏtta reads literally "Seoul was a scene of Avici and Raurava". Avici and Raurava are the Sanskrit names of two of the eight Buddhist hells.

[†] Inmin Powibu.

[‡] Seoul was originally built in a valley several miles north of the Han River, and in those days the built up areas were all north of the Han River. At Seoul the river is still a bit tidal and has deep swift sections that can be crossed only by boat or bridge, and in those days there was only one railway bridge and one car bridge across the river. The Han River, thus, became a significant barrier difficult to cross as a result of the destruction of the bridge.

We Entrust our Fate to Drawing Lots

We didn't have anything to eat at home. I emerged from the house determined to sell a watch in order to buy some rice or something. I came down a hilly lane in Namsan Precinct to city streets that were empty, though occasionally a People's Army soldier shouldering a machine gun was visible.

"Comrade! Comrade!"

I heard a voice calling me from behind, and then somebody firmly grasped my shoulder. I turned around startled out of my wits, and a man in the bluish uniform of a People's Army officer was standing smiling at me.

"Comrade. Aren't you Comrade Ch'oe Ŭnhŭi?"

"Yes . . . that's . . . right, but. . . . "

"I'm Sim Yŏng!"

As a famous actor who worked with Master Hwang Chŏl during the Japanese Colonial Period, I had heard the story that Sim Yŏng had crossed north after liberation. We had never worked in the theater together and we hadn't ever even met, but he said people in the north are broadly familiar with the performers of the south. At that time I had been rising as the bright hope of the Arang Theater, and having shot three pictures it seemed that my name had become known even in the north.

"Comrade. What are you doing right now?"

"Well . . . I'm just at home right now."

My heart went cold.

"Where are you going right now?"

"I'm on my way to the market to buy some rice."

He had been staring at me with sharp eyes for a while, and then he said, "Comrade, follow me," and started walking in front of me. I followed him up to a two-story house on a street corner, and he said that the place was the office of the Auxiliary Squad to the Security Police belonging to the North Korean Interior Ministry. While telling me that Mr. Sim Yŏng was gathering together artists, they encouraged me to join. They told me that already many artists were being lodged together at Myŏngdong Cathedral*.

"My husband is sick in bed, and I also have young children, so I can't work. If I go over there, there won't be anybody to look after the needs of the family."

"I also know Colleagues Kim Yŏnsil and Kim Haksŏng pretty well. We'll give you rations, so don't worry and go on home."

By that method I received rations of rice and cigarettes, so I went home to tell my family what had transpired, and left right away to join the Security Police Auxiliary Troupe. The Security Police Auxiliary Troupe was using the part of Myŏngdong Cathedral where the nuns had lived and eaten. There were the actors Kim Tongwŏn, Kim Sŭngho, Chu Chŭngnyŏ, Ha Okchu, the conductor Im Wŏnsik, the baritone O Hyŏnmyŏng, etc. about two hundred artists. North

---

* Myŏngdong Cathedral, a tall brick gothic edifice built by the French fathers, had been one of the tallest buildings in central Seoul since the 1890s.

Korea as a matter of policy had been pulling together artists of all genres without discrimination—theater, cinema, music, art, dance. Concentrated together like prisoners, during the day we rehearsed plays and did pacification activities* and so forth while at night we watched North Korean movies and received thought education. They said religion is opium, and even piled Bibles as high as a mountain in the courtyard and burnt them.

It was on an unusually bright moonlit night on my way back to the dormitory from watching a movie in the main sanctuary of the cathedral. Just then something somehow glinting in the moonlight caught my eye. I looked, worried that somebody might see me, and picking up the glinting object it turned out to be a crucifix. I wasn't a Christian at that time, but I quickly concealed in my breast the crucifix that had been walked on, and for a long time carried it around with me.

In the Security Police Auxiliary Troupe once a week, or every 10 days or so, they would give us our rations, and send us home on leave, but if one of us didn't come back by the permitted time they demanded that person do self criticism and ask forgiveness.

From 28 June until it was retaken three months later Seoul was governed by the Chosŏn People's Army. One day in the distance we could hear the sound of bombing, and through the 15 September Inchŏn landing campaign the allied army advanced, and it was said that Seoul was surrounded on three sides. The People's Army decided to retreat, and they sent the Security Police Auxiliary Troupe on a final leave. They threatened us that if we didn't come back at the appointed time, they would consider us reactionary elements, and even our families could not be secure. I went home carrying rice and cigarettes.

"If we don't run away now, we'll get dragged along with them. What should we do?"

"I'm not sure. What do you want to do?"

Kim Hak-sŏng asked me while smoking a cigarette.

"Can we go somewhere and hide out? Let's go to my home village."

"Perhaps, but how could we get there?"

"I suppose it's hard for you to move, but why don't you ride in a pushcart? I'll pull you along."

Time was pressing and we had to make a decision, but he just dillydallied. At my wit's end, I made up my mind to decide by drawing lots. On one piece of paper I wrote, "Run away now." On another piece of paper I wrote, "Escape later."

"OK. Pick one."

Carefully he selected one of the pieces of paper. It was, "Escape later." I had to go out of the house leaving word that I would return later. It was a tense moment alternating life and death for all I knew, but with no room for any other thought I ran panting back to the Security Police Auxiliary Troupe to meet the appointed hour.

---

* The Korean term *sŏnmu kongjak* (pacification activities) refers to propaganda activities designed to win over the populace, and implies spreading calming messages.

Northward, Northward

Left wing artists substituted for the People's Army in keeping watch on our fellow members. Because of talent, artists survived, and because of talent, artists met up with danger. It was a time when no matter how close your friendship you could not speak your inner mind. Park Min, who had risen from supporting actor origin in a theater troupe, now went around wearing a gun. He always emphasized ceremony, and used to criticize me fiercely saying, "Comrade, you've eaten wrong ideology. Do self criticism." If one suddenly was called a "reactionary," everything ended.

I had done performances of several works together with my senior colleague Kim Tongwŏn at Theater Guild, and we had even been co-stars in the film *Night Sun*, and so he was the only person to whom I could speak in confidence. He was a powerful performer, too, and yet he was an actor with a meticulous nature and his family life, too, was a model, so he was respected by everybody. Now that I had been dragged off together with senior colleague Kim Tongwŏn, we made plans together to escape taking the proper moment at the right time.

Our column being dragged north got divided into two. They told us that of the two hundred members of our unit one hundred would leave via Kaesŏng, and one hundred would leave via Ch'unch'ŏn. However there was the little trifle that senior colleague Kim Tongwŏn was paired off with Ms. Chu Chŭngnyŏ and left for Kaesŏng, while I was paired with Mr. Kim Sŭngho and made to leave for Ch'unch'ŏn. It was pitch dark in front of us. The only person I trusted was Kim Tongwŏn, and if even he were absent, how could I dare to escape?

The retreat of the People's Army began. It was in the middle of the night, and even I formed a line and left for the north wearing a People's Army uniform. The naval bombardment in Inch'ŏn lit up the sky. It was said that the National Army was going to return, and yet they were telling me I had to leave my beloved home-town behind, and go off on a road without a pledge of when I could return....

We all threw our rucksacks over our shoulders, and left forming a column along the side of the road. It was a scene different from a column of refugees. The musicians with their instruments fastened to their shoulders took up the rear. During the day, in order to avoid air raids we put up in people's houses putting on performances, and we only moved at night. Park Min and Ha Okchu of the Theater Alliance watched over us as foxes in tiger skins* so that we could only get it by observing their intentions. Doing a forced march following the People's Army was difficult even for the men.

"If you want to escape you can't tire now. Strengthening your legs has to come before anything else."

I walked until I didn't have any more strength. On either side I could hear the sound of labored, heavy breathing. My feet were a mass of blisters, and my toenails had begun to fall out. The few people who absolutely couldn't move any more got

---

* Foxes in tiger skins (*hogahowi*) is a metaphor for little people who borrow the authority of the powerful to throw their weight around.

picked up by People's Army trucks, but I grasped my walking stick, gritted my teeth, and walked stubbornly on.

An Opportunity for Escape

I heard the news that because of the success of the Inch'ŏn landing the [South] Korean government had returned and achieved the 28 September "recovery." I felt a sense of crisis that if I were carried off like this it would be the end. It would be hard to carry off an escape by myself, and so seeking a partner with whom I could discuss which day and how long, I furtively went up to Kim Sŭngho who was doing her make-up.

"What should we do? Do we just have to go north like this?"

When I whispered to her in a low voice, Kim Sŭngho stopped powdering her face and looked at me with a strange expression whose contents I couldn't understand.

"Hŭ-ŭng...."

She snorted and once again began getting absorbed in applying her makeup. I couldn't send another word her way. I was stung thinking that I had clearly made a mistake.

Ms. Kim Sŭngho was exceedingly clever as a natural born actor. When they did thought education she would be the first one to yell, "That's right!" and acted like an earnest element*, so she was able to be cooking squad leader. Because the cooking squad leader loaded rice and foodstuffs on a truck and had to go ahead to prepare meals in advance, she usually rode in the truck.

And so one day we had been sleeping, distributed three or four each in farm houses, and the People's Army banged on the doors, rushed in and indiscriminately shook awake male and female alike. We all gathered in the middle of the courtyard.

"Kim Sŭngho, that reactionary little bitch, has run away. I expect we'll drag that bitch back dead, so you comrades had better understand. Beware and be firm!"

Our hearts skipped a beat. To think she had run away alone without saying a word to anyone.... A vision of her in the make-up room floated up. She had been completely unfriendly. Just like me, too, she had plans from the very beginning to run away, and yet with lips as heavy as a lump of rock she hadn't betrayed the slightest emotion!

Later I heard that Ms. Kim Sŭngho had been riding in the truck, and on a mountain road she had acted as if her stomach hurt so much she could die. The People's Army officer, completely taken in by the performance of the famous actress, went to get a doctor, and in the meantime Kim Sŭngho calmly succeeded in escaping. While the surveillance of actors was becoming stricter due to the escape of Ms. Kim Sŭngho, Seoul was just getting farther and farther away. In

---

* "Earnest element" (yŏlsŏng punja) was a term applied to somebody enthusiastic about party activities.

Ch'unchŏn the baritone Mr. O Hyŏnmyŏng escaped, and the threats and intimidation of the People's Army got worse. As this went on more and more, I constantly looked toward the rear. The actors led the way, and behind them were the musicians and dancers. At the very end were the band, and I knew that I was glimpsing an opportunity for escape.

"Could you fit me in? I'm asking as a favor."

They accepted me without objection. The band were six persons in total, and among them was even the jazz perfomer Ŏm T'omi (uncle of the actor Ŏm Haengnan). They called each other by code names like First Gun, Second Gun, and Third Gun. Among the band members was a guy named Mr. Pak whose home town they said was Sŏngchŏn*. Their plan was that if they should get separated when escaping they would gather together at Sŏngchŏn and proceed to Seoul together. I became Seventh Gun.

8–4

East Germany, Late 1940s, Early 1950s

A Young Jazz Fan Trades on the Black Market to Dress in a "Decadent" Way

Jazz—and other kinds of music the Nazis had banned after they took power in 1933—enjoyed significant popularity, especially among young people, in the early post-war period in both East and West Germany.[17] In Leipzig, a major East German city located about an hour by train south of Berlin, one such young jazz aficionado was Reginald Rudorf (1929–2008). Rudorf, in fact, was one of the founders of the early post-war jazz scene in Leipzig, and would go on to become the "most outspoken promoter of jazz music in the GDR [German Democratic Republic, or East Germany]."[18]

From Reginald Rudorf, *Nie wieder links: Eine deutsche Reportage (Never Left Again: A German Narrative).* (Frankfurt-am-Main: Ullstein, 1990), 55–57. Published in English translation with the permission of Ullstein Publishers. Translation: Glennys Young.

* In the mountains northeast of P'yŏngyang.

Rudorf sought unsuccessfully to synthesize his love of music (jazz, boogie, etc.) with his commitment to socialism. He grew up in Leipzig, and studied Marxist aesthetics there and in Halle. In the early 1950s, he joined the East German Communist party, the SED; these were also the years in which he started teaching social sciences at the University of Leipzig. In 1954, he published two important articles in which he sought to argue that *some* forms of jazz (but *not* swing music and bebop) were compatible with East German socialism.[19] But in 1956, emboldened by Khrushchev's speech at the 20th Party Congress and the Hungarian uprising, Rudorf's promotion of jazz went beyond safe ideological and institutional boundaries: not only was he organizing jazz concerts in conjunction with the East German Protestant church, but he also called for freedom in modern artistic expression and fundamental political reform of the GDR regime.[20] Arrested in 1957 after being under surveillance by the Stasi, he was sentenced to two years of penal servitude. When his sentence ended, he fled to West Germany, where he worked for major newspapers and magazines, and, in 1977, now a staunch anti-Communist, he became the editor of "rundy," West Germany's first media information service.[21]

In the following passage, a brief excerpt from his 1990 autobiography, *Nie Wieder Links: Eine Deutsche Reportage* (*Never Left Again: A German Narrative*), Rudorf reflects upon his experiences in East Germany's early post-war music scene and youth culture, including young people's idolization of American culture. It is not just about the youth music scene, though. It also gives us fascinating glimpses into everyday life in early post-war East Germany, including how people turned to the black market for goods in short supply. And it illustrates the inventiveness and ingenuity of East Germans in getting around official rules even as they, under Soviet tutelage, built a socialist polity, economy, and society. This meant having people with the necessary skills and ideological commitment (or at least neutrality?), which, in the case of the author's neighbor, came out of a personal encounter when Hitler's *Wehrmacht* and the Soviet Red Army fought the battle of Stalingrad in 1942–1943 in Soviet Russia.

A SUIT MADE OF SUGAR

In the meantime I had a new black market business. I went by train for an hour to Köthen, where the Russians had dismantled a sugar factory. The sugar lay there in piles near the factory. A friend and I at that time filled a hundred-pound bag with sugar and rode back—not in the compartment but on the bumpers of overloaded trains. I don't know how often we went to Köthen. But at home on Güldengossaer Street we had filled at least two hundred empty air-raid protection sand bags with sugar. We ate sugar on all possible occasions, on bread, as dessert, thickened with coffee or by itself. I sold a pound of sugar for a hundred Marks.

With the money I went to the goods exchange on Hain Street and bought by myself some flashy checkered material used to make slipcovers. I needed a suit, because the latest fad in Leipzig was dancing. The old *Felsenkeller** was filled with

---

* *Felsenkeller:* A concert and dance hall from the nineteenth century. It is still in use today.

Woody Herman's Big Band hits. Kurt Henkels played in the *Haus Auensee*. There were six or seven big bands battling it out, playing the hot stuff that had been banned for sixteen years.

We had secret access to the zoo, and its large banquet hall, through Hanno Gebbing. What a time that was to experience the big bands of the first post-war years: Dobschinski, Widmann, RBT, Henkels, Ilya Glusgal on the drums, Macky Kasper, trumpet, Helmut Zacharias, fiddle, Rolf Kühn, the clarinet player.

During the week we went as often as we could to the RC-Tennis Club at the Holy Bridge*. I was a bit of a bigger deal than the other guys because I was dealing sugar. My suit, my big checkered suit with an extra long suit coat flapping around my knees, showing only a few inches of the shorts I wore underneath, ringed socks, and a huge cowboy hat my father got from West Berlin—all topped off with shoes made by Miss Pfaff.

Miss Pfaff was a nifty craftswoman who made shoes from fabric and leather scraps, adding a felt sole to the whole thing. These shoes were so cool and casual, they got you right in there with the girls. The Pfaff slippers showed you had dough. But those Pfaff things had one drawback: they would disintegrate after you'd put in a soft shoe at the Zoo dance floor. So the Pfaff-crowd—a pair of these slippers cost a couple of hundred Marks, a fortune—always had some tools on them: a needle, small pliers, and a little hammer. The "Pfaffen" among us would hang out together in the bathrooms at the Zoo and, in the breaks between dances, cobble our felty footwear back together again.

I had my crazy suits made at Günther's tailors on Springer Street. Günther never batted an eyelid—after all, these outfits, which he tailored for me as caricatures of fashion, were nice little earners for him. On the street I noticed that people thought I had gone off the deep end, strutting round like a rooster on Augustus Square† in shorts and a zoot coat and ringling socks and a giant hat. My father asked me not to greet him if we ran into each other, since it would be devastating for his business. A picture of me with the caption appeared in the *Leipziger Volkszeitung*‡: "Decadent Yankee type." Swell! American decadence. That's what I wanted. Awesome!

I was much talked about at the RC and at the Zoo. I had dug up a bicycle at the central exchange. A luxury. I was mobile.

In the RC Club the young wild things danced to Boogie and Traveller, songs like *Hello, Little Miss*. Night after night the Wolfgang-Günther Quartet heated up the hits. It was there that I first met Vera, my wife.

My girlfriend at the time was Hilde, a long-boned girl who moved shoes on the black market and who mastered the art of letting her breasts shake alarmingly by trickily trotting about in her red clogs. She was very knowledgeable in the arts

---

* The German name of the bridge is "Die Heiligenbrücke."
† In German, "Augustusplatz."
‡ *Leipziger Volkszeitung*: The name of the city's newspaper, run under the auspices of the Communist Party. English translation: *Leipzig People's Daily*.

of love, sophisticated, commanding. Then [there was] "Butter Inge," who moved oils and fats on the black market. In order to fire up the dancers in the RC-Club, I had concocted Schnaps in my laboratory on Güldengossaer Street, together with Ottomar, my bosom buddy after the war. He lived on Güldengossaer Street too, and had built himself a little booth with all electric modern conveniences on the sports field, where he got his electricity by tapping into the state-owned grid, which nobody noticed. By the way, no one ever found out. Ottomar's booth, which I later took over, was the perfect spot for our pubescent erotic encounters with the opposite sex.

I brewed the schnaps from carrots. I rode by bicycle to Merseburg. There were huge fields there. Here I got piles of carrots. I grated them at home and finally squeezed the gratings through a bed sheet. I let the juice ferment. One day I was running so late with my Schnaps-brewing that we took the still warm stuff with us to the RC, mixing it with sugar and peppermint flavor. Anybody who drank from this swill fell over. One lay in the pissoir of the club, another fell into the water from the Holy Bridge. I came with "Butter-Inge" to the taxi stand. She accompanied me to Güldengossaer Street, woke my mother up by ringing the bell and yelled up to the window: "Mompi is drunk." "Quiet," begged my Mother, who was horrified. My father had just been driven to Güldengossaer Street by a taxi driver who was even more drunk than he was. Both sang "The Flag On High*," which was, at that time, a stupid kind of protest. Our neighbor, Dr. Gerhard Dengler, heard this. He had been a First Lieutenant in the 6th Army. Soviet officers had found Dengler in Stalingrad, alive among all the dead, a Jewish doctor, whose entire family was murdered by the Nazis, nursed him back to health. Recovered from his wounds, Dengler asked the doctor how he could pay her back. She [replied]: "Become a Communist, go to the NKFD, to the National Committee for a Free Germany, where German officers retrain."

Dengler did it, became a Communist, came to Leipzig as the skilled Soviet top dog, took over as editor-in-chief of the *Leipziger Volkszeitung*, the mouthpiece of the SED in Leipzig.

---

* "The flag on high" ("Die Fahne hoch") is the first line of the "Horst-Wessel-Lied," ("Horst Wessel Song") which was the anthem of the Nazis, specifically the SA brownshirts. The SA or "storm troopers" (in German, *Sturmabteilung*) were a Nazi paramilitary organization that contributed to Hitler's rise to power.

———————★———————

Croatia/Yugoslavia, 1996, 1960s, 1950s

On Travel from a Land of Socialism to
One of Capitalism, and Back

Communist governments regarded their citizens' travels, whether domestically or internationally, with a mixture of hope and fear. In the case of domestic travel, or travel to other socialist countries, there was the hope, that people's socialist consciousness would be raised by, for example, traveling as part of a collective, or visiting places (including museums and statues) of significance to the history of Communism. Still, even domestic travel brought with it, for Communist officials and theorists, ideological challenges. For travel generally meant leisure, and leisure was at odds with Communist polities whose interpretation of history, and way of viewing the world, was based on labor.[22] When East Europeans and others living in Communist polities traveled to capitalist countries, they caused their leaders even more anxiety. For the danger, of course, was that when they saw the abundance of consumer goods available in the West, as well as the political freedom, they would question the socialist way of life. The danger was even greater when the post–World War II economic boom in Western Europe and the United States made cheap consumer goods, especially clothes, electronics, and household appliances, available to nearly everybody. Though aware of the risks, Communist governments did allow their citizens to travel to the "degenerate" capitalist West. Such travel was highly controlled, of course, and, before the late 1980s, consisted largely of diplomats on mission Party and Komsomol delegations, sports teams, visits to relatives, and organized tours.

In the following selections, the Croatian writer Lijerka Damjanov-Pintar reflects on her travels in the 1950s and 1960s from Yugoslavia to the capitalist West—particularly to London, England; Italy; Paris, France; and Norway, as well as to Hungary, another socialist country in the Eastern Bloc.[23] An implicit theme in all of these short accounts is what these journeys meant for her sense of herself, of both socialism and Communism, and of Yugoslavia's relationship to both the socialist and capitalist worlds. Another brief selection, "Taking a Hungarian

From Lijerka Damjanov-Pintar, *Putovanja i ogovaranja: Šest pasoša i jedna putovnica (Travels and Gossips: Six [Yugoslav] Passports and One [Croatian] Passport)*. (Zagreb: Znanje, 1996), pp. 16, 22, 47, 82–83, 114, 120–121, 156. Published with permission of Znanje publishers. Translation: Aleksandra Petrovic.

Language Tour Guide Exam," attests to the political significance that Yugoslav authorities ascribed to Hungarians' tourism in Yugoslavia.

"GOODIES FROM LONDON/UK"

I needed the money so I sold some of my things: a ring, a bracelet and two small pieces of Herendi porcelain. I bought a winter coat, a beautiful evening gown fabric at Harrods*, a purse, shoes, gloves and some other small items. When fall came, my nostalgia for home and family grew with every passing day. As the English did not yet discover double-pane windows or a normal heating system, I decided to go back. Close to a hundred days of stay was more than enough....

I crossed the border on the 8 December. In the train compartment I sat alone with seven coats and six suitcases. The customs officer in Jesenice glanced into one of my suitcases and that was all. Since I was out of the country for almost five months I could bring in as much clothing as I wanted. When I unpacked everything at home the whole family came and gaped at the quantity and marveled at the quality of things. Because of this, I decide to repeat my trip the next year.

CROSSING THE BORDER/ITALY

Those who travel abroad and have a foreign currency account in the bank or a Eurocard or an American Express card have no idea how stressful it was to cross the border in the '50s or '60s.

I had one, only one banknote, but in a foreign currency and I hid it so that even the most sly, the most cunning customs officer wouldn't find it.

In our compartment, besides my co-worker from school and her husband, there was a teacher from the countryside. But not for long. The customs officer felt her purse at the bottom of which she stitched a large wad of dinars†. She was taken off the train with two other co-workers.

IN OUR LITTLE FIAT/HUNGARY

In the next three years we repeated the trip to Gardony. In 1969 when Juju was three and a half, the trip was amusing once again. For the whole day before we left I was loading the car, mostly with folk ceramics that my mom used to buy by a ton. There were at least fifty pieces of cups, vases, plates, and ashtrays in all colors and sizes. All our acquaintances and friends in Zagreb and its surroundings used to get ceramics as presents. Every year. Our relatives gave us some fresh fruit, apricot brandy‡, and cherry wine that resembled Slovenian "Cviček" wine. In our "Muki" (that's how we affectionately called our car) we looked like headcheese.

---

* An upscale department store in London.
† This was, at the time, the Yugoslav currency. Only a certain amount of money was allowed out of the country.
‡ In Hungarian, *barack palinka*.

Juju got tons of toys, and I bought an old, hand-painted chest and some other knick-knacks. That year aunt Matilda, my late grandma's sister, turned a hundred and one, and she complained about her four daughters who were around eighty years old and completely senile. She wasn't senile at all. With a half a glass of red wine for lunch and another half a glass for dinner she still managed family affairs.

On the way back, the little Fiat looked as if it would break down under the pressure of all the baggage. Hungarian customs officer at the border asked us to open the suitcase that was lodged behind the back seat. We opened it. At the bottom of it he saw mom's strangely bulging bag and when he took it in his hands he heard a buzzing sound. You should have seen the frightened look on his face; he immediately threw away the bag. I laughed, opened the bag and showed him a toy submarine with the inscription "Lenin." It was a battery operated toy that Juju got to play in a bathtub. The customs officer, still pale, waived his hand signaling we can go. Poor guy, he thought it was a bomb.

TAKE WHAT YOU CAN/PARIS, NORWAY, CROATIA

I experienced some embarrassing moments when we got on the bus to go back home. The last one to get in was a young couple with two big bags. They took as souvenirs everything they could: brushes for clothes and shoes, ashtrays, three sets for vinegar, oil, salt and pepper, glasses, towels.... I was terribly ashamed. What will they think about us!

I read in the papers that the Norwegians would not let our national soccer team get on the plane until they returned the phones they took from the hotel rooms. A waiter in Mali Lošinj told me that, in a course of one year, the package deal groups from Bosnia took eight hundred spoons, serving trays, knives.... From the manager of "Amfora" on the island of Hvar I heard that guests send packages with coverlets and pillows to their home addresses and that at one event in Zagreb the gold-plated plaques that were supposed to be given to the two praiseworthy companies "Ledo" and "Kraš" went missing.

TAKING A HUNGARIAN-LANGUAGE TOUR GUIDE EXAM

When I was later telling people about the questions I was asked they didn't believe me.

Not to keep you guessing I'll tell you right away that I failed the exam. The tour guide, I knew this, has to talk to a group for three hours, taking them from Kaptol to Grič and the questions I was asked were:

"When and where was the Young Communist League of Yugoslavia founded?"

I knew the year and the place, but they wanted the street name and the house number.

"Tell us about Marjan Badel."

I said three to four sentences and finished with the information that he died in a battle nearby Zagreb, but the committee wanted to know the exact place of his death and the rank he held at the time, all of which I failed to answer.

"Where is the factory 'Marjan Badel'"?

I answered, but I didn't know the number.

"Which magazine celebrates its sixty-year anniversary this year?"

I fell silent.

"But comrade, it's *The Communist* of course. You had to know that!"

I came to the exam with a cold and a fever, but I felt my blood freezing in my veins.

"Tell us all you know about Sisak."

I talked about Siscium, an important Roman town, about the defense of Sisak from the Turks all the way to the steel mill and the city museum.

"And what other museum would you show to the foreigners?"

"But comrade, the museum with the wrought iron door, hand-made by comrade Tito."

Once again, I was speechless.

"When was the first tennis ball hit in Zagreb?"

I played tennis since I was little, and I took part in many competitions in the country as a member of first Spartak in Subotica and later of Dinamo in Zagreb—those were the names of tennis clubs of Šalata and Mladost na Savi then, but these people were obsessed with numbers and dates. My "but" . . . was rudely interrupted, and I knew that the last, deathly hit was soon to follow.

"Whose statue is found in front of the University of Moša Pijade?"

That was really an unexpected question, similar to "What river runs under the Sava Bridge*?"

Things in front of me got blurry, I didn't know if they were making fun of me, and I started to stutter.

"Thank you, the exam is finished."

As I heard later, the candidate that passed had never heard of Art Nouveau, but she was studying at the Department of Political Science. You don't believe me either?

The only certain thing is that beautiful Zagreb does not have a Hungarian-language tour guide to this day. Amen.

PANTYHOSE/ITALY

In Perugia I bought Elbeo pantyhose. With three pairs of such silk pantyhose mom went through the whole World War II and mine were still in good shape today—after twenty years. I could send them to the Elbeo factory, in Germany, as an exhibition piece.

---

* Over the river Sava.

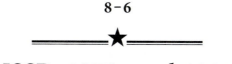

USSR, 1970s and 1980s

Inventing Soviet Rock 'N' Roll

I t might seem like a misnomer to speak of the "invention" of Soviet rock 'n' roll: after all, as conventional wisdom long had it, rock 'n' roll was, like Pepsi and blue jeans, a foreign import to the USSR. There is some truth to the cliché that Soviet rock 'n' roll was not home grown. In the 1960s, 1970s, and 1980s, many Soviet youth fell in love with Western rock stars and their music. Their love affair began in the 1960s with the Beatles (as the first selection, taken from an account by Vsevolod Gakkel', one of the original members of the popular Leningrad rock band Akvarium, attests). And it continued with other Western bands (Yes, Genesis, Pink Floyd, The Rolling Stones, among others.) But, as the three selections that follow indicate, Soviet rock musicians and their fans also created, even *before* Gorbachev's *glasnost'* would diminish limits on artistic expression, their own publications, ways of interacting with each other, and musical styles.

Focusing on the underground rock 'n' roll scene in Leningrad, the three selections reproduced herein demonstrate these home-grown aspects of Soviet rock. It was in Leningrad, for example, that the Soviet Union's first periodical for rock music, *Roksi*, was founded in 1977. The ideas that motivated *Roksi*'s founding are discussed in the last of three selections, excerpts from an interview of 1987 with Oleg Reshetnikov, who co-edited the journal from 1979 until 1983. *Roksi* was an example of *samizdat*, or underground, illegal, self-published literature, journals (and even pornography) that was passed from one trusted person to another. Another key figure in the production of *Roksi*'s first three issues was Boris Grebenshchikov, whose article in the first issue is excerpted in the second selection.

Grebenshchikov, along with such other major figures in the Leningrad underground rock scene such as Mikhail Naumenko (leader of the Leningrad group Zoopark) and Kolia Vasin (another editor of *Roksi* and an avid Beatles collector), drew upon mainstream customs in Soviet culture, such as "playing at dances in restaurants, giving private concerts in the apartments of sympathetic acquaintances, swamping records and sharing information about Western and local popular music and jazz,"[24] to create specifically Soviet patterns of interaction among rock musicians. As for home-grown music styles, Grebenshchikov combined, for example, American blues with Russian ballads.[25]

DISCOVERING THE BEATLES: VSEVOLOD GAKKEL' OF
THE SOVIET ROCK BAND AKVARIUM

Vsevolod Gakkel', the son of an aviation designer, was one of the original members of the Soviet rock band Aquarium (Akvarium), *founded in 1972. The band still exists. Gakkel' was a noted cellist.*

In 1981, Aquarium became part of an association of rock bands under state supervision created in that year. The official government sponsor, and overseer, of the Club was the Komsomol. But the KGB supervised from behind the scenes.[26] The Club was a place where Soviet rock bands were allowed to perform publically in exchange for submitting to surveillance by the Soviet authorities, especially the KGB.

When I started school, where Aleksei as well as Andrei went, it already had, fortunately, not been a boys' school for a long time. In first grade the whole class came to me on my birthday, and it was a grandiose holiday. But beginning with second grade they unexpectedly made the school an English one*, and almost the entire class changed....Foreigners often came to see us. They gave [us] chewing gum, and, if one was lucky, ballpoint pens. Once they brought a record, the Beatles' *Help!*. Somehow during the long recess, when I was the on-duty student in the class and remained behind to erase the blackboard, older classmates came in and put the record on the record-player [and] I, not having suspected anything, completely lost [my] sense of orientation upon hearing the first sounds. It was like nothing I had ever felt up until that moment or would feel for a long time afterwards. It was an incomparable feeling of joy, as if life suddenly took on meaning. The serenity of childhood was destroyed, even though I didn't remember anything except the word *Help*. The break ended, and the record was placed behind the glass in the office of the director of studies. I tried to share my joy with my friends and was pleasantly surprised when Andrei Kolesov wrote down the names of those who would mean for me more in this life than anything else I would encounter. It turned out that Andrei's cousin had owned *Beatles for Sale* for a long time. A little bit later, *Beatles: Oldies, but Goodies* and *Rolling Stones: Between the Buttons* joined the records in the school closet, and we found the plausible pretexts to go into the office and look at these records through the glass. A little bit later this music was invariably played at all school soirées, and the teachers were not in the least against it. There was yet, they said, the record *Hair*, but they never showed it to us, fearing for our morality. Once Finnish schoolboys came [to visit us], and instead of having class

---

From Vsevolod Gakkel', *Akvarium kak sposob ukhoda za tennisnym kortom* (*Aquarium as the Way of Tennis Court Maintenance**) (St. Petersburg: Amphora, 2007), 16–27. Published with the permission of Vsevolod Gakkel'. Translation: Glennys Young.

---

* In devising this title, Gakkel' drew upon Robert M. Pirsig's *Zen and the Art of Motorcycle Maintenance An Inquiry into Values (New York: William Morrow and Company, 1974)*. Personal communication by e-mail from Gakkel', 18 July 2010.

---

* Most likely, this means a school in which students studied the English language intensively.

they brought us into the assembly hall, and we danced to *Letka Enka**. It was very splendid, because it seemed to me absolutely modern and, even though it was only for a short time, it gave [us] the feeling, that somewhere there was another life. . . .

Andrei[†] and I lived in one room, and I got a little tired of such an amount of difficult music, which was constantly played at home. This was the period when he listened to Mahler, Berlioz[‡] and Stravinsky. And when Dvoržák's "Second Slavonic Dance" was playing, my mother began to cry. . . .

I hadn't listened to the *Beatles* for a long time, and there was nowhere to hear them. Really only when they showed figure skating [on TV], I always waited for the sports dances, because sometimes there it was possible to hear similar music. And when they broadcast the world championship in Davos[§], during the breaks, when they cleaned the ice, some group was playing. In school the next day everybody was arguing, was it the *Beatles* or someone else? Once, on the program *America Through the Lens*, there was a story about the *Beatles*, and their music was played, but they didn't show them. . . . And a little later, when we went to my mother's brother, uncle Seryezha, my cousin Marina, who was a big fashion queen and somewhere got a hold of Polish magazines, suddenly gave me a whole box (which had formerly contained chocolates) with clippings about the *Beatles*. When I brought them to school the next day, all the kids examined them and passed them around the entire class. I didn't have my own room at home, but I plastered the entire wall with these photographs at our dacha. . . .

None of my friends had a tape recorder, and, although everybody had record players of some sort, naturally, nobody had the latest records. A little latter, when pop music started to come into the circle of our passions, long-playing records and forty-fives began to appear in school among the kids from the older classes. I still clearly wasn't listening to anything seriously yet, but one girl in our class, Galia Muradova, suddenly gave me a book by Brian Epstein, *The Beatles—A Cellarful of Noise*[ʹ]. I tried to read it, but my knowledge of English was insufficient to read the entire book. I read with difficulty my school assignments. But on the other hand, there were a lot of real photographs. In ninth grade, when I had to go to [work on a] collective farm for a month, and I didn't have even a kopeck, I foolishly sold it [the book] to my friend from the dacha, Lesha Vetberg, for three rubles. By the way, he had a tape recorder, and in the summer I listened to the *White Album* and I could in no way reconcile what I heard with the understanding of the *Beatles* that I had formed after [hearing] *Help!* Someone intended to take a tape recorder to the collective farm. And Vova Ul'ev, whose mother taught in our school, was able

----

* The "Letkajenkka" was a dance craze that was popular in Europe in the 1960s. It was also known as Letkajenka, Letkiss, and Letka-Enka. It combined an adaptation of Madison, Conga, and Bunny Hop dances, and was played to a Finnish traditional folk dance song.

[†] The author's brother.

[‡] Hector Berlioz (1803–1869) was a French Romantic composer.

[§] In Switzerland.

[ʹ] Brian Epstein, *A Cellarful of Noise* (Garden City, NY: Doubleday, 1964).

to get a hold of the records we longed for and make a copy of them. Each day we began and ended with the *Beatles*....

At that time in school there was already a group in which kids from the upper classes played. From the eighth grade onwards we also became upper classmen, and we could already go to soirées, which were held at school every month. I was captivated by the sound of the electric guitar, which Repa played, and Grisha Asaturian at the same time sang the song *Beatles—Boys*, which I heard for the first time when he performed it. Unfortunately, I didn't have my own guitar, and did not even suspect that it would be easier for me than the others to learn to play it. When the kids in our class also decided to form a group, and it turned out there was no bassist, they suggested that I play, even though Lev Kapitansky, who played the guitar really superbly, was still in our class. I didn't have any skill, but I learned quickly, since the logic of how the base [instrument's] part was constructed made sense [to me] because of my experience playing cello in the orchestra of music school. We sewed double-breasted fustian* jackets and bell-bottomed trousers. But unfortunately I didn't have my own white polo neck sweater, and I had to borrow it from my friends for each performance. When we went to school, they forbade us to dress like that, and we were required to wear the uniform. Nikita Voeikov and Vova Ryzhkovsky played the guitar, and Vova Ul'ev played on small drum and cymbals. How electric guitars from Bulgaria appeared in the school, I don't know....

Everything was inserted into the amplifier *Kinap*. Also, out of the blue there appeared two yellow amps, on which we wrote "Vox"—just like on the Beatles' amps. We didn't have a name, and after the first performance they nicknamed us *Vox*, thinking that this was the name of the group. For our second performance Ul'ev already drew a poster with such a name. Unfortunately, no one [could] sing, and we played instruments. Gradually kids from the other school began to show up, among them a certain Valia, who sang the song *Every Night Before*.... Although each of us knew English better than this Valia, none of us knew even one English song, not to mention the fact that no one could clearly pick out even a single song. True, being on the kolkhoz, Andrei Kolesov, who was the main expert in the area of language, tried to make out the words to *It's Only Love*, which subsequently turned out to be a little different.

We unexpectedly received a gift in the form of a logo† in conjunction with a television show [broadcast] on Sundays. *Seven Days*‡ took *Can't Buy Me Love*, and now it was possible to hear it [the song] every week. By the way, the show itself was also interesting, in so far as there always remained the probability that they would

---

* A strong cotton and linen fabric.
† In other words, an image that was repeated each time a TV show began.
‡ This is a reference to the Soviet TV program, *Seven Days* (7 *dnei*), which appeared on Sunday nights. It gave an overview of the week's news.

show the forbidden fruit. The documentary film *Seven Notes in the Stillness*ˇ, in which one of the scenes was a story about the history of modern dance, ended with the twist and rock 'n' roll. They showed every dance for fifteen seconds, and of course everyone thought that they showed the *Beatles* there. Of course, it wasn't them, and [even] now I'd like to watch that film, in order to find out who, after all, in fact, they were. I think it was the *Animals* or some Americans. It was meager, but [it was] something.

CO-FOUNDING THE ROCK BAND AKVARIUM: BORIS GREBENSHCHIKOV

Boris Grebenshchikov, who was born in Leningrad on in 1953, was a major figure in the birth of Soviet rock 'n' roll. In 1972, he co-founded Aquarium (Akvarium)*, for which Vsevolod Gakkel', the author of the previous selection, played the cello and sometimes the bass. Grebenshchikov was also the group's main songwriter.*[27]

It is probable that what motivated him to write this essay was a failed concert by his band, a concert that took place in Leningrad. At this point, Grebenshchikov's band was not very popular. He was hoping that, with time, his band would attract additional attention at various gatherings.

...People differ in their relationship to rock music, one person appreciates it, others—do not, the rest—more. Up until now, it remains a mystery whether there is anything that unifies those who appreciate it, aside from the fact that they get it. It is pleasant to meet a person who is capable of valuing that unexpected fact that, in his last album, Jethro Tull turned out to be in direct collaboration with Cat Stevens. And who among such people did not experience joy upon discovering that his new acquaintance, who for some reason had never listened to anything, gets it and is beginning to ask questions and asks to listen to something else? And who did not experience [that sort of] incomprehension, bordering with dislike on disbelief, when an old acquaintance, who has been at your place a million times, asks, whether or not you have James Last? Isn't this person flawed? And isn't every-one, who doesn't appreciate [rock music], defective? This is something to ponder. It is less likely that having an affinity with rock music is such a primordial char-acteristic of human nature. However, it [meaning the relationship] is defined by something that lies quite deep in the situation. In any case, it is by all means the most distinct feeling of interaction among the most different people that is elicited precisely from the joint participation in listening to rock music, but not among those who don't possess this "something." What is it this "something"? Of what? And is this "something" so important? Was there no rock twenty years ago? And this "something," did it exist? And will it exist? These are enough questions.

From Boris Grebenshchikov, "O vrube," *Roksi*, no. 1, 1977. Translation: Glennys Young.

ˇ Sem' not v tishine.

"Rock-music did not emerge in Kaluga*," V. Feiertag[†] somehow once informed us. He's right. Therefore it is possible to look aside from Kaluga and its surroundings. Those who need to, know about where rock came from and when. That's not the thing. The thing is that already in 1972 a reviewer for the magazine *Rolling Stone* noticed, with regret, the presence in rock of clear signs of decline. And now?

Have a conversation with any eighteen-year-old rock extremist.

—Beatles? And what are the Beatles? No, listening is pleasant.... You can't say cool about Beatles. But rock lovers of the older generation remember what the Beatles were like in 1965–1967, and... echo what was happening around them there, [that's] where rock emerged. In such a way they could only come upon something awaited for a long time, even if unconsciously expected, to be sure.... And it changed. Everybody understood, except the completely hopeless and ill-intentioned. The explosion in rock that happened as a result proves that the basis for it had been created a long time ago. Rock was inevitable. Why?

...Who doesn't have an emotional or a behavioral problem? First, there are no such [people].... Second, children react in a significantly more natural way to many things, than adults [do], if they have still not been ruined by their upbringing. But the further [time goes on], the more the pressure of the environment makes itself felt, and some of the people turn out to be those who don't get it—those, who to a significant degree are susceptible to and inclined to take the form, corresponding especially to the pressure which is acting upon them. That is why rock did not become inevitable any earlier than it did. Each age that comes before the one that is underway appears methodical and unhurried in comparison with it. During Mozart's time, less happened during each fifty year period than now [happens] in a year. Traditions were strong. Music was harmonious and balanced. But "The Times, They Are Changing[‡]." A break happened right before our eyes. The older generation is living in one age, the younger generation in another[§]. The environment is changing before our eyes, and, like a sculptor, changing his perspective every minute, forms distortions—from this, anyone gives in. But time is needed in order to transform fundamentally a person once-and-for-all, for one person more [time is needed], for others—less.

The environment did not succeed in having an influence on John, Paul, George, and Ringo. Their songs were outside of traditions, and they were understood by

---

* Kaluga is a provincial city located about 188 km southwest of Moscow. During the 1970s, it was perceived as being—and actually was—much more culturally backwards than Moscow or Leningrad.

[†] Vladimir Feiertag was an important figure in Soviet jazz. He had a student jazz band in Leningrad.

[‡] A reference to Bob Dylan's 1964 album and song by that title. The actual title was "The Times, They Are A-Changin'."

[§] This is a rather transparent reference to Ivan Turgenev's *Fathers and Sons* (*Ottsy i deti*), and to the generational conflict in the nineteenth-century Russian intelligentsia and Russian society more generally that this novel of 1862 depicts.

those who were not swayed by generally received ideas to the point of losing a perception of that which fit in with them.

For those who sang, and for those who listened, music became a defense from the [Soviet] environment.... Rock became not simply music—it is a way of life. A youth subculture was born, to put it specifically, turning, in its extreme manifestations, into counterculture.... From escape from the environment it turned out to be the environment [status quo], with all the resulting consequences. And it turned out that the way a person goes about avoiding the pressure of the environment can itself put pressure and mould freaks, [can itself] turn out to be a [form of] pressure and moulds the distortions, if, even though one gets it, but not being consistent one does not resist the pressure.... It's possible that John Lennon was the first who observed the danger of turning out to be dependent upon the means of attaining independence, in any case, he was the first, who said about it:

I don't believe in Elvis
I don't believe in Zimmerman*
I don't believe in the Beatles
I just believe in Me.... The dream is over....

And let somebody try to say that John Lennon doesn't get it.

INTERVIEW WITH OLEG RESHETNIKOV

Aside from serving as the co-editor of Roksi, *Reshetnikov is a member of the band* Kaif (Pleasure), *which was founded in 1985 in then Sverdlovsk (now Ekaterinburg).*

> **RIO:** Oleg, why was this journal launched? Who created it and for what purpose, how did it come into being?
>
> **O.R.:** The magazine *Roksi* appeared in 1977. I suspect that the idea for *Roksi* was born at Grebenshchikov's wedding, at this grandiose drinking bout in August 1976. Perhaps [it was] exactly at that time that a number people felt a strong affinity towards one another—or at that moment the pretext of getting together and doing something together was vitally essential. Not getting together for a [music] session, not in [the café] "Saigon†," not just sitting around, but doing something concrete and at the same time interacting‡ with one another. I would call this natural desire a somewhat

---

From *RIO*, no. 13 (1987).

---

* Here Grebenshchikov alludes to the fact that Bob Dylan's original name was Bobby Zimmerman.

† "Saigon" was a café in Leningrad associated with dissidents and "countercultural" trends.

‡ I have translated the Russian verb "obshchatsia" as "interact." But as Alexei Yurchak has noted, there is really no complete equivalent in English to the Russian noun—*obshchenie*—connected to the verb *obshchatsia*. Translating *obshchenie* as "interaction" fails to convey that it means more than just "hanging out" with friends or family. It also involves "an intense and intimate commonality and intersubjectivity, not just spending time in the company of others." See Yurchak, *Everything Was Forever*, 148–151; here 148.

initial unifying function. That is, the magazine was born for the sake of unifying close friends in some sort of non-traditional way....Kolia Vasin, Natasha Vasil'eva, to some degree Gena Zitsev and Grebenshchikov did the first issue....Grebenshchikov did not play the most active part in the creation of the first issue*. The first issue was not even called "Roksi."...After that Vasin and Vasil'eva cooled off to the magazine, and in general Grebenshchikov produced the third issue.

...The first idea, with which the magazine *Roksi* was infused by the founders, is the idea of human interaction. To make a magazine together and to feel oneself of the same mind [with the others] was being in a state of pleasure†, therefore the most essential idea of the magazine became the idea of pure pleasure.

From the very beginning *Roksi* was infused with a second idea—the idea of information. At that time people really needed information, and from this point of view the third issue was especially interesting. Up until that point the information was limited to conversations of the type "who is doing what, who eats what, which boots is he/she wearing."

In the third issue they gave the opportunity to give an opinion to Makarevich‡....

With the fourth issue of *Roksi*, Misha Bruk, Shura Andreev and Vova Sorozhin began to get involved....

RIO: What to you think, for whom is this magazine being produced? Who is going to read it now, in 1987? What should *Roksi* be like now? And the rock press in general? Wouldn't it make sense to shift *Roksi* to a commercial foundation? Don't you have any interest in returning and working for *Roksi*?

O.R.: As for the commercial foundation, here the same old problem arises: what is better—a lot, but shit, or, a little, but good. As for the first, what I think is that its existence in the current state is senseless. Some new ideas

---

* Other versions exist. [This is in the original text.]

† The Russian word here—*kaif*—needs explanation. *Kaif* is derived from the Arabic word, *kayf*, which means pleasure. *Kaif*, which had been in the Russian language since the nineteenth century, enjoyed frequent usage in the post-Stalin period, especially in the 1960s. At that time, it meant to be, or aim to be, in a euphoric state. The verb form might be translated into colloquial English as "groove" or "catch a buzz."

‡ The reference here is to the quite popular Soviet musician, songwriter, writer, and visual artist, Andrei Makarevich (born 1953). He was the main figure of the well-known Russian rockband, *Time Machine* (*Mashina Vremeni*). For more on him, see Thomas Cushman, *Notes from Underground: Rock Music Counterculture in Russia* (Albany: SUNY Press, 1995); Yurchak, *Everything Was Forever*. Among Makarevich major publications are *Mashina Vremeni: Al'bom pesen i stikhov s risunkami Andreia Makarevicha* (*Time Machine: Album of Songs and Poems, with Drawings by Andrei Makarevich*)(Moscow: Kollektsiia, 1994); *Vse ochen' prosto* (*Everything is Very Simple*)) (Moscow: Lanterna Vita, 1994); and *"Sam ovtsa": Avtobiograficheskaia proza* (*"You Are a Sheep Yourself": Autobiographical Prose*) (Moscow: Zakharov, 2002).

are needed. Which ones in particular, I cannot exactly say right now. Those ideas, which Bruk and I were guided by, they have died.

What the rock press as well as *Roksi* should be like now in particular, is difficult to say. Here there are no unified recipes. Perhaps we have to transfer everything from a dilettantish to a professional level?...There is a lot of dilettantism in *Roksi*, it isn't going away as the years go by. And the worst thing is, this dilettantism is for [*Roksi*] not as a minus, but a plus. Professionalism is very dry and strict, [but] from dilettantism breathes more life into it. There is more life in dilettantism. It seems to me, that here we need a skilful, delicate union of professionalism and dilettantism.

Perhaps it is necessary to shift everything onto a monetary basis and do everything as it is done in the West. There [though] there aren't ideas, there is simply business, advertising....[What is] necessary without fail is its own musical criticism, good, thorough, argumentative. Without fail—varied, opposing opinions. Musicians need to know, what their listeners think about them, subconsciously essential. And here one must be careful, because each word that the musician reads about himself leaves a serious trace.

When the magazine came to us, it was based on two principles—association and information. We tried to add to them the idea of a certain philosophical meaning—for what purpose and why everything is happening—and reflect a bit about it. This idea was put into effect in two forms: first, some introductory articles, dedicated to the analysis of general problems, and, secondly, articles devoted to the analysis of textual structure....It was interesting to understand the phenomenon of the influence of the text and to juxtapose all these thoughts with those trends, in the direction of which Western music was developing at that time.

Everything was done with the help of translations from *Melody Maker*, *Rolling Stone*, *New Musical Express* and so forth. As an example let's take the translation of an article about "YES." For us, who had grown up with this band, the translation of the article from 1979 was extremely topical.

At that time "YES" found itself at the top, and suddenly the group goes to pieces and arrives at another understanding....In 1979 it seemed that rock was going to develop in the direction of a union of classical music—the synthesizer, symphony, something serious, big, and complex. Then everybody was living with the hope that "Pink Floyd," "YES," "Genesis" and others would move exactly in that direction. But this idea, as we know, died. Nevertheless, Ordanovsky said then, that precisely this article about "YES" significantly helped him in his creative work, and he complained about the insufficient availability of similar materials, helping to move [things] forward.

As a result the following picture developed. Those who were present at sessions and heard what the musicians said to them extracted their life principles, with the help of which they moved through life.

But someone should also say something to the musicians. The musicians were moving forward only with a look back at Western music, Western ideas, Western magazines and thanks to some personal thoughts. But there was absolutely no free exchange of these thoughts—each closed himself up among his own. Many groups, closing themselves off within themselves, reached a deadlock. And there you have it, *Roksi* took upon itself the function of the intermediary in the exchange of thoughts about everything that was happening.

At the same time in this same period the idea of humour and *stiob** gained force. I saw that it was very needed by and appreciated by musicians and all the readers of *Roksi*. As a result, at the moment that the forth issue of *Roksi* came out it was based on these four foundations, but nevertheless the possibility of interaction played the main role here. In general I think that the fourth issue—the most interesting, in terms of the richness of idea—was the most vital in the entire history of *Roksi*.

If up until this point *Roksi* was an informational–entertainment [magazine], then with the fourth issue it became theoretical–informational–entertainment. Besides, it came out in that period when it was more necessary than ever.

In comparison to the third issue material was collected on a principally new basis. To produce the new issue it was necessary to interact roughly with a half of a hundred completely different people who up until that point had not known each other. And it is as if this connection bonded them—not only the preparation of the issue, but the very reading about one another, the transmission from hand to hand. This process was a great unifying force. And it was evident how this force developed, not only among the members of the editorial staff, but also among everyone who had a connection to rock music in the city.

All of these events took place on the eve of the rock club's creation. This was a period of mass dissolution of sessions and the writing of a letter to the XXVI conference of the KPSS, signed by 500 people. The letter was written in December 1980, and in January its organizers were summoned to the Big House[†]. The letter sank into oblivion and disappeared who knows where, but the permission to create a rock club was granted all the same.

In this way, *Roksi* No. 4 came out on the eve of the club's opening, when everyone very much needed the journal. After the creation of the rock

---

* This Russian word is difficult to convey in English, but, as Aleksei Yurchak puts it, it can be thought of as an "ironic aesthetic practice," that is, a "peculiar form of irony that differed from sarcasm, cynicism, derision, or any of the more familiar genres of absurd humor." As such, it was characterized by "*overidentification* with the object, person, or idea" at which this practice was aimed. The result was that it was difficult for listeners to know whether those practicing *stiob* were engaing in "sincere support, subtle ridicule, or a peculiar mixture of the two." Yurchak, *Everything Was Forever*, 249–250.

† That is, summoned by the KGB.

club, when people began to get together on a daily basis, to chat, the need for the journal fell off sharply. Information was transmitted orally, and it was possible to interact even without *Roksi*. This certain superfluousness as a unifying and informational organ led to the fifth issue being held up. What remained was only the function of theory and humor—the fifth issue dragged out, dragged out and in the end came out in two parts with difficulty.

NOTES

1. These points are made in Robert Edelman's review of Anne E. Gorsuch and Diane P. Koenker, eds., *Turizm: The Russian and East European Tourist Under Capitalism and Socialism* (Ithaca, NY: Cornell University Press, 2006), published in the *Journal of Social History*, 42, no. 1 (2008): 230.
2. Recently, pioneering scholarship on leisure (entertainment, sports, travel) under Communism has emerged. On entertainment, see Uta Poiger, *Jazz, Rock, Rebels: Cold War Politics and Popular Culture in a Divided Germany* (Berkeley, CA: University of California Press, 2000); Richard Stites, *Culture and Entertainment in Wartime Russia* (Bloomington, IN: Indiana University Press, 1995) and *Russian Popular Culture: Entertainment and Society Since 1900* (New York: Cambridge University Press, 1992); Alexei Yurchak, *Everything Is Forever, Until It Was No More: The Last Soviet Generation* (Princeton, NJ: Princeton University Press, 2005); and Thomas Cushman, *Notes From Underground: Rock Music Counterculture in Russia* (Albany: State University of New York Press, 1995). On sports, see Molly Wilkinson Johnson, *Training Socialist Citizens: Sports and the State in East Germany* (Boston: Brill, 2008); Robert Edelman, *Serious Fun: A History of Spectator Sports in the USSR* (New York: Oxford University Press, 1993), and *Spartak: A History of the People's Team in the Workers' State* (Ithaca, NY: Cornell University Press, 2009), as well as the older but valuable study by James Riordan, *Sport in Soviet Society: Development of Sport and Physical Education in Russia and the USSR* (New York: Cambridge University Press, 1977). On travel, see the works by Wendy Bracewell, ed., *Orientations: An Anthology of East European Travel Writing on Europe* (New York: Central European University Press, 2009); Wendy Bracewell and Alex Drace-Francis, eds., *A Bibliography of East European Travel Writing on Europe* (New York: Central European University Press, 2008), as well as *Balkan Departures: Travel Writing from Southeastern Europe* (New York: Berghahn Books, 2009), and *Under Eastern Eyes: A Comparative Introduction to East European Travel Writing on Europe* (New York: Central European University Press, 2008), and the Gorsuch and Koenker cited in this chapter.
3. See Ol'ga Beborodova and Aleksandr Tuzov, "Koroleva ssteny" ("Queen of the Stage"), *Vechernyi Bishkek* (*The Bishkek Evening News*), 26 October 2001.
4. The four daughters were Kumushalieva, Saira Kiyizbaeva (1917–1998), Baken Kydykeeva (1923–1993), and Darkul Kuiukova (1919–1997). All four "daughters" were educated at School Number Five in Tököldösh, and they all sang in the village children's choir. Ali F. Igmen, "Four Daughters of Tököldösh," a chapter in of *Speaking Soviet with an Accent: Crafting Culture in Kyrgyzstan* (University of Pittsburgh Press, forthcoming). See also his PhD Dissertation, "Building Soviet Central Asia, 1920–1939: Kyrgyz Houses of Culture and Self-Fashioning Kyrgyzness," University of Washington, 2004.

5. The stamp can be viewed at http://home.nestor.minsk.by/fsunews/kirgizia/2008/kg535.html (accessed 19 February 2010). The (fairly) recently independent Kyrgyz Republic conferred the title of "National Hero" on Kumushialieva in 2000.

6. The director of this film, which took a prize at an All-Union Film Festival in the USSR, was Bolotbek Shamshiev, a celebrated figure in Kyrgyz cinema. Other Kyrgyz actors with roles in the film were Ayturgan Temirova, Orozbek Kutmanaliev, and Baydyla Kaltaev. The role that most propelled her to stardom, however, was that of the grandmother in *Ak Keme* (*Belyi parakhod* or *White Steamship*, 1976), another film by Shamshiev and based on one of Aitmatov's short stories. Kumushalieva's performance was even praised by Jennifer Dunning, a film reviewer for the *New York Times*, in December 1978. For more details, see Igmen, "Four Daughters."

7. On the nature of this resistance, see especially Benjamin H. Loring, "Rural Dynamics and Peasant Resistance in Southern Kyrgyzstan, 1929–1930," *Cahiers du monde russe et soviétique* 49, no. 1 (2008). Kazakhs often slaughtered their livestock rather than allow them to become part of the collective farm inventory. As a result, people went hungry and starved to death.

8. Igmen, "Four Daughters."

9. For the school's Russian language Web site, see www.interdom.info. Elizabeth McGuire, who generously provided me with a copy of the document being discussed here, has been working since 2003 on a project on the Interdom. It is entitled *Communist Neverland: The Russian International Children's Home in Ivanovo and the Global Family It Created, 1933–2013*. See also her paper, "Brothers, Friends, Sons, and Lovers: The Real-life History of Sino–Soviet Metaphors," given at the January 2008 meeting of the American Historical Association.

10. The school still exists.

11. He uses these terms of self-description in a passage I did not include in the excerpt.

12. Between 1954 and 1987, she appeared in ninety-two films. In the 1960s, she made a number of films with Shin Sang-ok, her second husband and a popular Korean film actor. She also directed three films in the 1980s. I thank Clark W. Sorensen for this information.

13. This summary of Ch'oe Ŭnhŭi's abduction to, and detention in, North Korea, is based on Kongdan Oh and Ralph C. Hassig, *North Korea Through the Looking Glass* (Washington, DC: Brookings Institution Press, 2000), 92.

14. Quoted in John Gorenfeld, "The Producer From Hell," *The Guardian*, 4 April 2003.

15. *Pulgasari*, a "monster of the people," is a "cautionary tale about what happens when the people leave their fate in the hands of the monster, a capitalist by dint of his insatiable consumption of iron. But it is also tempting to read the monster as a metaphor for Kim Il Sung, hijacking the 'people's revolution' to ultimately serve his purposes" (Gorenfeld, "The Producer from Hell"). While in captivity in North Korea, Shin also made what he considers to be one of his best films, *Runaway* (1984), which is the "tragic story of a wandering Korean family of 1920s Manchuria coping with Japanese oppression and the dishonesty of their neighbors." Ibid.

16. Oh and Hassig, *North Korea*, 92.

17. A major work on the implications of American popular culture, especially jazz and rock 'n' roll, for the construction of German identities in both East and West Germany from the late 1940s through the 1960s is Poiger, *Jazz, Rock, and Rebels* (cited in note 2).

18. Ibid., 150. He and his friend Heinz Lukasz succeeded in 1955 in getting the local chapter of the FDJ (*Freie Deutsche Jugend*) to give official recognition to their jazz group in Leipzig. (154.)
19. For details, see ibid., 151–154.
20. Ibid., 161.
21. For its German-language website, see http://www.rundy.de/rundy.html (accessed 22 February 2010).
22. See Edelman's review of Gorsuch and Koenker, cited in note 1.
23. Damjanov-Pintar's observations from her travels are discussed in Wendy Bracewell, "Adventures in the Marketplace: Yugoslav Travel Writing and Tourism in the 1950s and 1960s," in Gorsuch and. Koenker, *Turizm*, 248–265. The volume is an excellent introduction to original scholarship on travel within and beyond Eastern Europe and the USSR.
24. Polly McMichael, "'After all, you're a rock and roll star (at least, that's what they say)': *Roksi* and the Creation of the Soviet Rock Musician," *The Slavonic and East European Review*, 83, no. 4 (October 2005): 665.
25. Robert Service, *Russia: Experiment with a People* (Cambridge, MA: Harvard University Press, 2003).
26. Yurchak, *Everything Was Forever*, 192.
27. McMichael, "'After all, you're a rock and roll star,'" 665.

Everyday Life and Everyday Things Under Socialism, 1945–1989, and Beyond

Nationalizing a Factory Taken in 1949 in early postwar Romania, this photo depicts a worker who is covering up the former owner's name of the newly nationalized Tricorachĕ factory.

The establishment of communist regimes in early post-war Eastern Europe brought the creation of the foundations of a socialist economy. By design anti-capitalist, socialist states did away with private property and privately-held corporations. They also developed the bureaucracies and institutional infra-structure needed by a state that differed from capitalist states—including post-World War II welfare states—in fundamental ways. In socialist countries, the state was the origin of all mass-produced goods, including those for consumers. It also owned all retail establishments, and was the employer of all involved in the production process—of both industrial and consumer goods.

Socialist states also presumed to dictate the price, style, and display of goods. State-owned stores, it should be noted, developed their own forms of advertising and ways of displaying products, as is apparent below in the images on page 301. Ultimately, socialist states did not manage to control all aspects of consumer consumption, and "black" or "grey" markets emerged.

Courtesy of the Prints and Photographs Division, Library of Congress.

Rebuilding from War Depicted in this East German election poster of 1950 is the socialist built environment of the future. This was an urban landscape in which a specifically socialist modernist style would dominate from the 1960s onwards. This occurred throughout the Soviet bloc, as well as in other socialist societies, such as Communist China. The poster depicts images of large, modern buildings superimposed over the photo of a city destroyed by war. It is an indication of how the East German state tied its legitimacy to recovery from the ravages of World War II. By emphasizing the slogan "Risen Out of the Ruins" ("*Auferstanden aus Ruinen*"), the election poster sought to convince voters that candidates of the National Front (an alliance of East Germany's political parties, in turn under the control of the Socialist Unity Party or SED) were uniquely capable of helping East Germany rise, like a phoenix, out of the postwar ashes. The slogan at the bottom of the image says: "For reconstruction, vote for the candidates of the National Front on 15 October."

A major shift occurred in the USSR and the socialist states of Eastern Europe after Stalin died. The post-Stalinist 'thaw' coincided, as the introduction to chapter 8 emphasizes, with a period of dynamic growth in Western capitalism. One component of this was a new kind of consumer culture in which household appliances and electronics were an important element. Socialist states staked their own legitimacy on the quality of life that they could provide for their citizens, a trend that intensified over the decades of the Cold War (ca. 1945-1985). In the immediate post-World War II period, socialist states accorded their citizens the "right" to employment, housing, education, and medical care. But by the 1950s, and increasingly in the 1960s and beyond, socialist states sought to provide their citizens with the kinds of mass-produced consumer goods that Western, capitalist economies provided. Consumer goods, including household products, furniture, television sets, electronics, and the like, were "presented as signs of state munificence and caring for its subjects." (Quotes from Krisztina Fehérváry, "Goods and States: The Political Logic of State-Socialist Material Culture," *Comparative Studies in Society and History*, 51, no. 2 (2009): 431, on which this photoessay draws.)

Artist: Wittkugel. Published in Berlin. Issuing agent: Amt für Information. Courtesy of the Poster Collection, Hoover Institution on War, Revolution and Peace, Stanford University.

Inventing Socialist Housing Pictured here is the apartment complex at 362 Longchang road in Shanghai. Originally built by the British, the complex functioned in the 1920s as a police station. But in the 1950s, shortly after the Communist seizure of power in China, authorities turned the structure into an apartment complex by making the outdoor corridors open-air kitchens and places for hanging laundry.

Photo courtesy of Getty Images.

Waiting amidst Death This photograph depicts Budapest in late fall of 1956, after the Hungarian Revolution was crushed by the Soviets. People are standing in line for food and looking at the dusty corpse of one of the victims of state violence. Throughout the Soviet bloc in Eastern Europe, serious shortages of food and heating fuel contributed to uprisings through the 1950s. In Hungary, food short-ages only stopped being facts of everyday life in the 1960s. Even after such shortages ended, standing in line for particular goods at certain times (for example, a shipment of oranges that happened to hit a socialist city in the winter) was part of daily life in socialist societies.

Photo courtesy of akg-images/Erich Lessing.

Planning without Foresight Pictured here is a basic kitchen tool (*galuska deszka*) that was used in Hungary to make noodles. This is one of the many household goods that was unavailable in socialist polities. Such goods were unavailable not because there were no resources to make them, but, in general, because the bureaucrats who planned the socialist economy had not recognized that people needed them. In Hungary, for example, other household goods that were unavailable for this reason were plugs for bath tubs and metal boxes for the electrical wiring of newly built apartment buildings. (Fehérváry, "Goods and States," 434.) Photo courtesy of Jackie Sayet.

Exercising at Camp With good cheer, these young women do their morning exercises at Artek, the largest of the Soviet Union's youth camps. Founded in 1925, and located on the picturesque coast of the Crimean peninsula, Artek was the destination of approximately 30,000 children, who flocked to the complex to swim, hike, and learn to be good Soviet citizens. In the 1960s and 1970s, Artek also gave socialist vacations to children from all over the world, including Cuba, Asia, and even Western Europe.

In post-Soviet times, people still remember their vacations at Artek as some of the best times of their lives. These camps in socialist societies underscore an important point: while everyday life was often marked by a shortage of basic household and personal goods, lack of selection and diversity in consumer products, and the drabness of the built environment, life under socialism was not always about deprivation. Socialism provided some material goods and experiences in abundance. Among them, for example, were not only generous subsidies for vacations, including those enjoyed by youth at Artek, but low-cost cultural events and books.

Courtesy of Slavic and Baltic Division, The New York Public Library, Astor, Lenox and Tilden Foundations.

Standing in Line, Uzbekistan Taken in 1970, this photo evokes what it was like to be a shopper in socialist states. Here, people are standing in line in front of a street kiosk selling bread and other baked goods. The socialist shopper, unlike her capitalist counterpart, was not, according to the state's intention, to be subjected to advertising for unneeded products. In contrast to the deception and manipulation of capitalist advertising and display of products, socialist consumer culture was to be based on "transparency and truth." (Féhérvary, "Goods and States," 440.)

One example of such "transparency" was the standardization of the names of retail establishments, including those providing services. With few exceptions, the only differentiating element in the name of a retail establishment was its number. The smaller letters on the sign on the larger kiosk on the left say, "Hair Salon No. 36" in Russian underneath the larger Uzbek word, *sartaroshlik*, which also means barberhop or hairdresser. For some types of establishments, there was no differentiation whatsoever. The name given to the retail kiosk pictured here on the right—"Baked Goods"—would have been found everywhere throughout the USSR.

Photo by Peter H. Newman. Used by permission.

Buying Meat This photo was taken on 7 December 1991, not long before Soviet President Mikhail Gorbachev resigned on Christmas Day, 1991, and the Soviet Union's formal demise came on 31 December of that year. The transition from a socialist to a capitalist economy made food scarce. In fact, the day before the photo was taken, Gorbachev had pleaded with leaders of Soviet republics to

send food to Moscow. Here, Soviets are buying meat shipped from Germany. In general, shopping in socialist societies was a challenging and frustrating experience, even in the 1960s and 1970s, when socialist societies sought to provide more consumer goods to compete with Western capitalism. It was often the case that sales clerks were rude and deliberately unhelpful, often lording their power over the customers. In a symbolic display thereof, they were sometimes seated on a raised platform above the store floor. To be a consumer of everyday goods, then, meant experiencing one's vulnerability vis-à-vis the clerk.

AP Photo/Yuri Romanov. Used by permission.

Consuming Nostalgia Pictured here is a fascimile of athletic shoes made and worn by people in East Germany. These shoes are being produced for consumers who want to purchase—perhaps out of nostalgia—the kinds of goods made under socialism.

Despite the presumption that these facsimiles have fewer flaws than the shoes made in East Germany, consumers of socialist goods were often disappointed. The goods often fell short in the functions that they were supposed to perform, their durability, and basic design. In contrast, higher quality goods were available to Party elites or others having privileged status. Or, they were sold in Western capitalist economies.

Photo courtesy of ZEHA Berlin AG.

Manufacturing Toys East Germany was known for manufacturing high quality toys, such as the dolls pictured here. Produced around 1973, these "Sonni-Dolls" are made of porcelain and other materials. They exemplify that even as socialist shoppers often bought certain products that did not work or quickly fell apart, some socialist economies produced consumer goods of high quality and even exquisite design.

In fact, the favorable reputation of certain goods was known across the Eastern bloc. Toys made in East Germany, for example, were displayed in center city Budapest in the East German Cultural Center. (Fehérváry, "/Goods and States," 445.)

Photo by Klaus Morgenstern. Courtesy of akg/ddrbildarchive.de.

Designing Glassware Pictured here is another example of a high-quality consumer good produced in a socialist economy: glassware made in Czechoslovakia. In fact, Czechoslovakia, along with Italy and Scandinavia, comprised the "big three" of post–World War II glass design. All three countries were building on the strengths of the pre-war industry in glass design. Devastated by World War II, the Czechoslovak glass industry was rebuilt by the socialist state, which created its own educational system for training glass designers. While some of the more exquisite glass designs were exported to Western countries (bearing only the marking "Bohemian Glass"), everyday items such as plates, glasses, and cups were sold in state stores in Czechoslovakia and other Soviet bloc countries in Eastern Europe.

Hungarians would travel to Czechoslovakia to buy lingerie, linens, and glassware of higher quality than they could purchase at home. Travel in the socialist bloc was often about shopping!
Photograph by Carolyn Barber.

Vending, Socialist Style Depicted here is a Soviet-era vending machine that was still in use in Bishkek, Kyrgyzstan in 2005. Similar machines had been in use in Czechoslovakia and elsewhere in Eastern Europe. Among the ways in which this vending machine differed from those that dotted the capitalist West at the same time was that consumers were to drink the beverage (not Coke) from a common cup. The design of the vending machine privileged standardization of the consumption experience—perhaps down to the germs that one ingested in the drink!
AP Photo/Alexander Zemlianichenko.

Shopping in Special Stores   In late 1987, I purchased in Leningrad a coffee grinder very similar to the one pictured here. The store in which I bought it was a special one, where only Party elites and others having privileged status could shop for higher quality goods and products not for sale in regular stores. Because the special stores were not identified with a sign, and because the goods for sale were blocked from view by venetian blinds and/or curtains, people who lacked the status to shop in them walked by without knowing it. The privileged likely found out where the stores were when they obtained the coupons needed to shop in them. How one shopped in socialist societies depended on who one was.

Owing to the fact that I purchased the coffee grinder in this sort of store, and it worked so well, I and the other Westerners in the Soviet dorm thought that it was made in Hungary. We assumed it was an example of the higher quality Soviet goods from the Soviet bloc that were exported eastward to the USSR, for sale only to the privileged. But it turns out that it was made by the Soviet company Mikromashina, founded in 1935 and still in operation today! Reproduced by permission of Mikromashina.

Repairing a Car   Pictured here is a Volga sedan, model GAZ-M-21, in Leningrad in 1970. (The license plate, however, identifies the car as having been registered in the Tula region, or a little over a hundred miles south of Moscow.) Another way in which Party elites and others having privileged status in socialist societies differentiated themselves was by having a car. Ordinary people did own cars in the USSR and in other Soviet bloc countries, but in general it was the privileged who owned Volga sedans. The one pictured is likely an official car driven by a chauffeur, which was the case with most Volgas. People with lower status had, if they were lucky, a Lada. Non Party-elites in East Germany owned, if they were able to obtain one, Trabants or Wartburgs. And analogues existed throughout socialist societies around the world. (I am grateful to Lewis H. Siegelbaum for identifying the car and providing information about it.)
Photo by Peter H. Newman. Used by permission.

Living in Socialist Apartments Pictured here are two apartment buildings in Petržalka, a mass housing project built in the 1970s in Bratislava. Comprised of hundreds of blocks, this housing district was built south of the Danube River. The building on the left was recently renovated to meet the standards of the European Union, while the one on the right was not.

In the 1960s and 70s, socialist states around the world built mass housing in the form of high-rises often clustered on the outskirts of cities. The style was "socialist modern," and one of the purposes of such housing was to make socialist citizens modern. Standardization of such housing was, of course, a key feature. (It should be kept in mind that such standardized, mass housing was by no means unique to socialism.)

What was it like to live in this kind of housing? Although touted as an example of an alternative socialist "modernity," the experience had its downsides. Apartments were often small and construction was not of high quality. But perhaps most frustrating was the fact that the design and construction materials went against what people needed to make the apartments their home. The cement walls in many such buildings meant that it was impossible to hang a picture without a power drill, a tool that was often hard to come by.

There is also evidence that people living in such housing did not appreciate the "gift" that the state was giving them. Rather, they viewed such shoddy and uniform construction as an example of the socialist state's lack of care for its citizens, and of its "'intolerance for human diversity.'" (Fehérváry, "Goods and States," 447.) Put more directly, the people who lived in these housing complexes found them not to be examples of socialist collectivism and efficiency, but of socialist anomie and shoddiness. There is evidence to suggest that residents found them to be "authoritarian, dehumanizing, and atomizing." (ibid.)

Photo by Graeme Stewart. Used by permission.

Drying Clothes, Cuba Here, clothes-lines adorn a Havana street in the 1960s. Even though socialist states wanted their citizens to live in homogenized spaces, people found ways to use space creatively, thereby differentiating their living environ-ments from what the state intended.
Courtesy of the University of Miami Library, Cuban Heritage Collection.

"Carrying" Fruit and Produce Taken in Samarkand, Uzbekistan, in 1970, this photograph shows a woman using her "headgear" in a very creative way. For many social-ist citizens around the globe, the body was also a space to be per-sonalized, despite state-imposed socialist styles and the lack of prod-uct diversity with which one could create distinction from others.
Photo by Peter H. Newman. Used by permission.

Smoking "Western" Cigarettes Western goods, such as the Kent cigarette the man is holding in his hand in this photograph taken in Samarkand in 1970, were denounced by socialist states as decadent and corrupting. Yet, from the 1960s onwards, and with increasing frequency in the 1970s and 1980s, socialist citizens had increasing exposure to foreign goods. Though hard to come by, goods that could be purchased on the black market included such Western consumer products as blue jeans, cassette tapes, and electronics. In some cases, socialist citizens obtained Western goods by having contact with foreigners (such as foreign scholars, including myself, who provided gifts). In fact, the photographer's mother gave the man the Kent cigarettes as he shared his mid-morning treat of vodka and tomatoes.

As the underground market for foreign products attests, socialist citizens prized such goods, in part for their qualities, such as brightness and elegance of design. Another reason that people living in socialist societies craved Western goods was because they came to signify a "Western" style of life. This was a life to which they ascribed all kinds of imagined qualities—not just "freedom," but celebration of diversity and constant affirmation of human dignity. For this reason, they used Western goods, including castaway objects, such as empty Coke cans or plastic department store bags, to decorate their apartments.

Photo by Peter H. Newman. Used by permission.

Wearing Soviet Internationalism Taken in Leningrad in 1970, this photograph features a small but important detail: the peace sign adorning the uniform (for Aeroflot, the Soviet, and now Russian, airline) that this guide for foreign tourists was wearing. This symbol, which in the 1960s expressed opposition to the US government, or at least participation in the anti-Vietnamese war movement, was valorized in official socialist material culture because it fit with the Soviet regime's projected stance of pacifist internationalism.

Photo by Peter H. Newman. Used by permission.

CHAPTER 9

———————★———————

Search for the Self and the Fall of Communism

The year 1989 was one of dramatic events that shook the world. Before January was even half over, the Communist authorities in Hungary had permitted the formation of political parties and trade unions. In March, the first competitive elections in the USSR were held for the newly reestablished Congress of People's Deputies: multiple candidates vied for each seat, and they represented political views beyond that of the Communist Party. But early in June hope for political liberalization in China was squashed when the Chinese Communists cracked down on student protests on Tiananmen Square and in other cities. Just a day or two later, in Poland, following "Round Table" talks during February through April between the government, Solidarity, and other opposition groups, elections resulted in an overwhelming victory for Solidarity, which had been banned since 1982. And several months later, in September, the first independent political organizations on a nationwide scale appeared in East Germany. On 9 November, the Berlin Wall, the icon of the Cold War, came tumbling down. Later that month, on 19 November, Civic Forum, the Czech analogue to East Germany's New Forum and other independent political organizations, emerged in Prague, Czechoslovakia. On 25 December Romania's Communist dictator, Nicolae Ceauşescu, and his wife, Elena, were executed following a precipitous implosion of the Communist system. By the end of the year, the Communist Parties of Bulgaria, Hungary, Czechoslovakia, and East Germany had given up their monopolies on power and agreed to multi-party elections. Three months into 1990, the Communist Party of the USSR, the world's first socialist state, renounced its own monopoly on power. And these are but some of the political, social, and cultural milestones of 1989.

There is no shortage of interpretations of what transpired in the momentous year of 1989. Everybody, it seems, has a version of what happened, and why, not just in that year itself, but during what the year has come to stand for, namely the

Locator Map for Chapter 9.

fall of Communism. (And often answers to these questions are very much inter-twined.) For some, the global political tremors of 1989—which also entailed major political cataclysms in South Africa, the Philippines, Chile, and elsewhere—were the end result of economic, social, and cultural modernization. Such modernization generated "civil society," which in turn played a significant role in bringing down Communist systems.[1] Stressing the primacy of elite politics, others have attributed the massive, nearly synchronized political change to the discrediting of Communist political leaders themselves. Communist political elites—a self-enclosed world of corrupt, privileged, disenchanted leaders alienated from the people in whose names their Party claimed to rule—constituted an "uncivil society" whose leadership was undercut by massive economic debt to the West, failure to deliver consumer goods to their citizens, and the legacy of Stalinist violence.[2] As a result, many Communist establishments around the globe collapsed. And yet a third major line of interpre-tation has told 1989 as the story of dramatic popular resistance. The revolutions of 1989 were, first and foremost, people's revolutions, revolutions made by coura-geous people waking up from subjugation to claim their freedom. Having developed even before Gorbachev's *glasnost'* (openness) in mid-1985, grassroots movements in Eastern Europe and the USSR not only made these revolutions but were a major factor in their largely and surprisingly nonviolent character.[3]

Each of these three major interpretations grants people different attributes, capacities, and roles. When 1989 is told as a story of cataclysmic political change resulting from global modernization, Communist citizens fade from view, or become a more or less homogenous mass, one that benefits from structural processes they neither made nor controlled. When 1989 is written as a story of the self-implosion of Communist establishments, Communist citizens are pushed to the sidelines by political elites. The political competence of these citizens increases, to be sure, as and because the political competence of Communist elites declines. When 1989 is written as the story of people's revolutions against Communist tyranny, the people become a mass of a still different type: granted agency, they are cast as a heroic collective that naturally and inevitably rose up to restore democracy.

But when it comes to understanding how people subjectively experienced 1989—that is, the meanings it had for them in the context of their life histories, and in the history of their countries—that's where the shortage lies. The messy complexity of people's subjective experience of events is, on the whole, flattened in existing scholarship and other narratives. It is drained, that is, of its unremitting complexity by simplistic, one-dimensional characterizations of Communist citizens, characterizations that are either explicit or implicit. Heroic resisters. Seekers of democracy. Always fearless, confident, courageous. Desperate to do anything to escape from the way Communism had deprived them of things, of consumer goods people in the West took for granted. This is not to say that there is absolutely *no* recognition of complexity and variation among Communist citizens in histories of 1989.[4] To claim that would be a gross exaggeration. Nor have scholars and other analysts failed altogether to recognize that the people living in Communist polities often are, in these histories, those whom outside observers want them to be.[5] Yet for all that has been written about 1989, and the years of Communism's fall more generally, analysts, writers, and artists (including and especially filmmakers[6]) have not done justice to the different and changing meanings that people ascribed to their experiences.

The documents in this chapter can, of course, make but a small contribution to our efforts to understand the complexity and variation in how people experienced 1989, and the meanings they gave to that experience. But even though the number of documents and the number of countries represented is small, a deliberate effort has been made to choose documents that will encourage readers to question some of the omnipresent images of Communist citizens in 1989.

Some documents have been selected because they add complexity to dominant narratives of the origins and unfolding of 1989 in particular countries. Such is the case regarding the first document, which is a compilation of interviews with members of Poland's "Orange Alternative (Pomarańczowa Alternatywa)," which, beginning in the early 1980s and especially from 1986 to 1989, used street theater to create a social and cultural space for questioning the values, discourse, and aesthetics of Poland's Communist regime. Orange Alternative underscores that Polish politics and society in the 1980s were not just about the Communist government and opposition mounted by Solidarity. The second selection, a compilation of interviews related to the emergence in September 1989 of East Germany's first nationwide and independent political movement, New Forum (Neues Forum), reminds us that there were, in fact, East Germans who *opposed* the movement. And they remind us of how scared East Germans were in the fall of 1989 of a "Tiananmen outcome"—of the regime's brutal suppression of peaceful protests. The next selection, by the German writer Hans-Ulrich Treichel, underscores that West Germans experienced the Wall's fall in varied ways. Nor did it necessarily happen for them on 9 November.

Another way in which the documents are designed to add complexity is by giving attention to how gender influenced people's experiences in 1989, and the meaning they gave to those experiences. Too often, accounts of Communist opposition in 1989, and the roots thereof, do not pay enough attention to gender. For that reason, this chapter not only includes voices of women—in the Orange Alternative selections (Bogumila Tyszkiewicz), and in the New Forum selections (Sybille Freitag, then retired; Marie-Kristin, then thirteen years old; and Katrin Hattenhauer, then a twenty-one-year-old theology student who was detained and imprisoned for political activism). It also includes a selection that speaks to how one's gender—being a woman, in this case—influenced what one made of the new political opportunities of 1989. For the late Salomea Pavlychko, then an academic in Ukraine, the 1989–1990 conjuncture was in part about the discovery of feminism—to the dismay of her male colleagues.

This street plaque, which commemorates the events of 9 October 1989 in Leipzig, is located in the paved area next to St. Nikolai Church. The 75,000 to 150,000 people who took to the streets in Leipzig on 9 October feared a "Tiananmen outcome." That is, they faced the real possibility that they, too, would become victims of the state's repressive force, and that a "Leipzig massacre," with hundreds, or thousands, of dead and wounded, would come to pass. Instead, 9 October became the signature date of the "Peaceful Revolution" ("*Friedliche Revolution*"). Photograph by Glennys Young.

Finally, the selections are designed to remind readers that the "European revolution of 1989" was, from the very beginning, "an international event."[7] It is not just that dramatic political change happened in many countries. Rather, it is essential to bear in mind that cross-border dynamics between states, states and societies, societies, and individuals (and other combinations, too) created and shaped the political cataclysms of Communism's end.[8] To that end, the selection from the writings of Josip Šentija, a Croatian academic in the former Yugoslavia, underscores not only the influence that news of the fall of the Berlin Wall had in the former Yugoslavia. It also reminds us that there were people who, even as the events were unfolding, perceived, as Šentija put it, that a "world revolution [was] happening." The spread of information across borders in Eastern Europe influenced political change. This dynamic is suggested by the document from László Tőkés, the pastor whose resistance helped galvanize the fall of Communism in Romania. That the Romanian revolution of 1989 began in Timișoara, where Tőkés was a pastor, may well have been due to the city's location near the western border, allowing residents greater access to news from Hungary and Yugoslavia, than elsewhere in Romania. Eastern Europeans were also aware—though to an extent yet to be determined—of political cataclysms in the "Third World," such as in Chile. So, too, is it as yet unclear how such knowledge affected the political attitudes and strategies of Eastern European oppositions.[9]

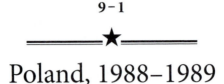

Poland, 1988–1989

The Orange Alternative and Revolution as Street Theater*

magine walking down the street in Wrocław, a city of about 600,000 people in southwestern Poland, in the fall of 1987, and coming upon a "happening" called the "Distribution of Toilet Paper," a basic consumer product that was, at the time, in short supply in Poland—and indeed throughout Eastern Europe and the USSR. Or, perhaps you can see yourself strolling along another of Wrocław's picturesque streets or squares on 8 March 1988 (International Women's Day), when you catch sight of a man in his mid-thirties handing out tampons—another product that was hard to come by. You might also indulge for a moment, and picture yourself in Wrocław in the spring of 1989, encountering several thousand people celebrating in carnival fashion, repeating the slogan "Socialism in Carnival, Carnival in Socialism!," and holding up small round tables, in a surreal gesture to the Round Table[†] talks between Solidarity and the Polish government that had begun the day before.[10] These are but a few of the actions on public streets staged by Poland's Orange Alternative, an underground movement launched in 1981 that was in deliberately playful opposition to Poland's Communist regime.[11]

From Padraic Kenney, ed., *Wrocławskie zadymy* (*Wrocław Demos*)(Wrocław: Oficyna Wydawnicza ATUT/Wrocławskie Wydawnictwo Oświatowe, 2007), 328–329, 333–334, 344–346, 354–358, 360. Published in English translation with the permission of the publisher, Oficyna Wydawnidza ATUT/ Wrocławskie Wydawnictwo Oświatowe. Translation: Christina Manetti.

---

* The Polish is "Pomarańczowa Alternatywa." See the multi-lingual Web site, http://www. pomaranczowa-alternatywa.org/

† Faced with strikes, economic stagnation, and high inflation, the Communist government in Poland launched talks with the trade union Solidarity, which had been banned, and other opposition groups (such as the United Peasant Party, the Democratic Party, the Christian Social Union, the Association of Polish Catholics, and the All-Polish Alliance of Trade Unions). The discussions took place in Warsaw from 6 February to 4 April 1989. The results were quite at odds with what the government had wanted, which was to legalize Solidarity but coopt it into the existing political system. Instead, the document of 4 April 1989, that concluded the talks, created the foundation for political pluralism. Analogous Round Table talks were held in 1989–1990 in Bulgaria, Hungary, Czechoslovakia, and the German Democratic Republic (East Germany).

Between 1986 and 1990, Orange Alternative held about sixty such "happenings," as well as smaller events, mainly in Wrocław but also in other Polish cities such as Warsaw, Nowa Huta (which readers will recall from Chapter 8), Łódź, and Lublin. It has been said that Orange Alternative was, most fundamentally, about creating a "politics of laughter"[12] that was an alternative to the Communist regime's monopoly on truth. Though that is an apt characterization, Orange Alternative is important for a serious understanding of Polish politics and society in the 1980s. For too often the latter is overly simplified as consisting of only the Communist authorities and its regime of truth, and Solidarity, industrial workers, and the culture of workplace resistance. But in fact, there was also room for "alternative social space," such as that taken up by Orange Alternative.[13]

The response of the Communist government to Orange Alternative varied. From 1986–1987, the Communist authorities wrote it off as the nonsense of youth. The year 1988 was the one in which the authorities began to take the movement seriously. They attempted to repress, through beatings and arrests, its leading members. One of them was the movement's founder, "Major" Waldemar Fydrych.

Born in 1953,[14] Fydrych studied, but did not earn a degree, in the Faculty of History and the History of Art at the University of Wrocław. Fydrych was born in Toruń, which, interestingly enough, had been in the 1970s the center of Poland's punk rock scene.[15] While the motivations and intellectual inspiration for his contributions to Orange Alternative are complex, there is no doubt that the movement had its origins in the early 1980s, in a student association, the "New Culture Movement," that gained legal status at the University of Wrocław in 1981, before the declaration of Martial Law in December of that year. The central figure behind this movement was Fydrych, whose "Manifesto of Socialist Surrealism" celebrated the capacity of imagination to make a "world without limits." Perhaps paradoxically, it attributed the reign of imagination to the oppressive politics of both the Communist regime and Solidarity. And it called for countering that oppression (including that of religion, deemed an "opiate of the daydream of the masses,") with "play."[16] From this intellectual point of departure, Fydrych led Orange Alternative in activities—whether full-fledged "happenings" that began in July 1987 or smaller scale "events" (such as, beginning in 1982, painting dwarves over the police's own painting over of anti-Communist grafitti[17])—that sought to create everyday street life that would involve people (including passersby) in play as protest. A central idea, too, was to mock the regime's values, practices, and ideologies through activities that displayed an ultra-serious (yet playful) *reverence* for them.[18] Such was the case, for example, in the Orange Alternative's staging of street celebrations for the anniversary of the Great October Revolution.[19] Especially during the years of martial law, Orange Alternative's activities contrasted sharply with protesters who were trying, illegally, to unfurl Solidarity's banners.

The passage that follows is a selection of interviews with Orange Alternative activists. The interviews were conducted mainly in 1996–1997 by Padraic Kenney, an American historian of Poland.[20] They give a sense of how the Orange Alternative's activities—including the happening that celebrated the October Revolution—came about, and what this and other events were designed to do.

The selection concludes with Fydrych's *claim* that the Orange Alternative played a significant role in causing the collapse of Communism in Poland.

KRZYSZTOF JAKUBCZAK*

Question: What kind of songs did you sing?

K.J.: Any kind, as long as people could sing along. Because everyone knew—if the little people were there, then there would be songs about little people, too. They didn't have to be about [beating Communism], as long as people were together and stopped being afraid.

Question: I read very positive things about those events in one of the Wrocław underground factory newspapers, something like this: "Listen, those people are nuts, but they are really great guys and it is worth going to." It looked a little strange in a factory newspaper.

K.J.: Actually, it didn't seem strange. All of Solidarity in general had [run out of ideas about why it existed]. There were no strikes, people didn't want to go to demonstrations, that is why our events made such a ruckus all over Poland. They were something that brought results.

Funny things, done by people who were nuts—but not completely nuts, because they were incredibly effective—and also made everyone excited—both workers and students, even those from outside Wrocław. All the underground newspapers were saying that in general it's a great thing.

Question: You mentioned Secret Police Day. Some people say this was one of the best happenings. Why do you think this wasn't the case?

K.J.: I was at the Secret Police Day—I was there, I walked around, but I didn't participate, I always went to take a look. By the way, I was always arrested first. Secret Police Day went like this: guests were standing there who had no idea what was going on. There was no main idea. Major wrote a great ideology—that we would be checking each other's IDs and search the secret police who did show up. But what was funny about this? How to gather people around you? So they were standing there and watching. The only one who got into an argument there was me: I got into a fight with a militiaman [policeman]. He was so upset that.... Well, because there was an action, that's all. You can describe that kind of action wonderfully and at the same time make up an ideology for yourself. But how to transfer this to real crowd control? When the October Revolution took place, something was happening: [there were parade floats], the Red Army is in caps, people were dressed in red, those people are stopped, these aren't. Something was

---

*This is a reference to Krzysztof "Jakub" Jakubczak. During the Orange Alternative's "happenings," he played a wide range of musical compositions—"children's songs, communist ditties, and nationalist hymns"—on the guitar. See Kenney, *Carnival of Revolution*, 24. This is an excerpt from an interview on 18 December 1996.

happening. And what was happening during the action titled Secret Police Day?

Question: It would seem that the October Revolution was one of the best happenings. Maybe you can recall for me how it began.

K.J.: The less planning, the better. Between ten and twenty of us met then. Someone tossed up the idea: let's do the October Revolution. It was a great idea, so we all said: geez, great, so we started getting ready—we'd make a [parade] float, and they'd make Red Army caps, and those guys would make something else, that we'd leave here, and that there we'd split up. Above all, the guys from MKO participated in this, Krzysiek Albin in his own way, and Major and I in ours. We sketched out the first outlines then, and then each of us prepared his task on his own.

Question: Do you see changes in the message of the Orange Alternative? Did it become more political, or less…?

K.J.: As I already have said, "adult" Solidarity had lost its raison d'être, didn't have any more ideas about its purpose. So they started gluing their own activists like Józef Pinior* onto the Orange Alternative, and some guys from RKS† or RKW‡. They used it for their own political activities. That explains that lousy event with Józef Pinior, who began making a speech about how someone should be released, that's not what it was supposed to be about. So it was that instrumental treatment that I hate, that I never had anything to do with.

Question: So that was in June 1988, when Pinior and Borowczyk were released from prison?

K.J.: That was one of the worst events. It wasn't funny, or serious. They were supposed to be happenings, so either you do a happening, and then it should be funny until the very end, or you do a serious demonstration to release Józef Pinior, but then you don't get dressed up like an idiot to go and yell "release Pinior." Then people don't even know what you're laughing about, or whether you aren't laughing. People came, because there was supposed to be something fun going on there. That fun was actually a serious value, and here suddenly it turns out that someone else is behind that fun. That was when a strong division emerged between the activists of RKS, RKW and Fighting Solidarity§.

Question: Thus for you the best would be an event with a political context, like everything then, but that its message would be clearly non-political?

---

*On Pinior, see the gloss on page 322.

†Regional Strike Committee of Solidarity.

‡Regional Executive Commission of Solidarity.

§"Fighting Solidarity" (Solidarność Walcząca) was created in 1982 by Kornel Morawiecki. From 1982 to 1990, it was, as one historian as put it, "Poland's premier underground unit." Its members conceived of themselves as carrying on the legacy of Poland's underground partisan forces during World War II. Kenney, *Carnival of Revolution*, 30.

K.J.: Not necessarily. Then we wanted the message to be political, too. Political in the simplest sense: we don't want Communism to be ruling here at all. That was the most important political message, because then everything was permeated with a political message. If the militia was there, it was good, because its presence emphasized that it didn't want to allow it [the event].

PAWEŁ KOCIĘBA-ŻABSKI*

Question: Was there any coherent idea behind the Orange Alternative?

P.K.: At first there was, but in my opinion, it became corrupted and misdirected.

Question: In what sense?

P.K.: What Major wrote in those declarations of his, all that surrealism, one could read and put aside *ad acta*. What was important was that we were attacking Communism, the system, though the society was also attacking it, and at its weakest point, ha ha ha...when it was totally on its way out. They didn't know what they were supposed to do, and people on the street had no idea at all of what to make of it, the militia was getting dumber and dumber, and the government went completely berserk, their [statements about] some kind of progress and new revolutionary strategy were eroding, it was just awful....The SB† told us many times: We know that your happenings serve to train the ranks and test the possibilities for revolution. Testing the possibilities for revolution, imagine. Our UB‡ at the University told us: You and Jakubczak will make a speech from the balcony, the crowd listens to you—this is testing, the crowd must become familiar with you, must listen to you, must be obedient, that is your method, and in half a year, you will tell them: away with Communism!

Question: And you know, maybe they were right?

P.K.: Well, they were absolutely right! Except that this hadn't occurred to us. There certainly might have been such a suggestion, but without any preconceived plan. For them, for such purebred, professional militia sociotechnicians, it was obvious; of course guys like that sense it...the idea, the crucial one, and not Major's not necessarily crazy and funny declarations—was that it is possible to contest reality, and particularly the government, laughing at it like mad, making fun of its props, of its ideology, of its sacred things, like Dzherzhinsky and the October Revolution. The same with the militia: after all, a wonderful happening, which is by the way not well known, was the Secret [Plain-clothes] Policeman Day. It was a real happening, because the real Security Service played its role without a miss, and people were acting marvelously. The real plain-clothes police started

---

*This is an excerpt from an interview on 16 December 1996.
†Secret Police.
‡Polish security apparatus.

checking the IDs of all the various secret police that took part in the happening (like Scotland Yard, the KGB and Mossad), and there were great situations. I remember Tomek Bolanowski, who was checking the ID of some guy on the street with a very serious look on his face, it was probably his friend he was checking, and then he started writing down his details with the guy's ID in his hand, but he didn't manage to write it all down because the plain-clothes policeman was mad, and some first lieutenant came up to him and said: "Kowalczyk," and he said: "Just a sec, let me finish, I have work to do, me first." And the guy ripped the ID out of his hand, to write down the details, and by accident wrote down the details of the guy that Bolanowski was checking.

The October Revolution was also wonderful—then the services were working terribly aggressively, because they felt that this was striking at their own foundations, making fun of them and the things that were sacred for them. Some of the people in the security services were secretly very anti-Russian, anti-Soviet, and I would say even pseudo-nationalist, so they probably thought, "geez, these young louts think we're Bolsheviks, so let's show them the Bolshevik fist!"

BOGUMIŁA TYSZKIEWICZ*

Question: I'd like to ask about a specific example: about the happening called Secret Policeman Day. What was the meaning of this happening, in your opinion?

B.T.: The problem of fear. Then a person's entire life story was organized on the basis of fear. People did various things because they were afraid of being repressed. During the period of martial law, this was very important to us. There were two problems: fear and alienation. In Poland, there were no intermediate structures between the citizen and the state, plus fear as the main factor organizing a person's life outside the home. I consider the idea of Secret Policeman Day to be one of the best. It was a little bit like a psychodrama, connected to the myth at that time about the omnipotence of the Secret Police. Moreover, as a result it was so effective that it was in Wrocław that the largest political demonstrations took place in 1988–1989. Here. Nowhere else in Poland had such demonstrations. At that time, Józef was the main organizer in an agreement with Fighting Solidarity, but the climate was created by the Orange Alternative, breaking the barrier of fear. Many people wound up under arrest, where they spent a day or two, and then they stopped being afraid of that [arrest]. In addition, they noticed that if three thousand people are doing it, then the militia doesn't know what to do about it, because there are too many people. Freedom begins with yourself.

---

* This is an excerpt from an interview on 22 May 1997.

Question: A kind of trap door. If you go through it, then...

B.T.: ...you are winning.

JAROSŁAW WARDĘGA*

J.W.: [About why he joined, his impression of Major] Because Major was interested in the opposition, which was at that time very hermetic, he wanted to create a chance for young people to fulfill themselves. In short, he realized that the opposition underground is too elite, that yes, it does mobilize people, but only garners about twenty to thirty percent support.

Question: Looking at it, I see three areas in which the Orange Alternative was active. First, to break the hermetic nature of the opposition; second, to tell the government something...

J.W.: ...to lay bare the authorities.

Question: Exactly. And third, to break the barrier of fear in society. Which of these was most important for you?

J.W.: The first element was to break the fear that stemmed from the hermetic nature of the opposition. The second element was specific to me, because I had always been attracted to artistic activities. Even within the framework of the Academic Ministry, and even earlier, before the ministry, I managed to found a theater group, which to a certain degree contested reality....

Another quality of the Orange Alternative, particularly for me, was based on the fact that for the first time an attempt was made to link activities where theater and politics meet in the sphere of opposition. Happenings as a theatrical event, on the street, illustrating the absurdity, laying bare and showing the surrealism of the situation, were precisely that—an event where theater and politics meet. The deathly serious opposition—deathly forbidding authorities. Young people from various places appeared in the framework of this phenomenon: Muslims, those ascribing to Hindu culture, young open Catholics, people who were not engaged in politics—for whom the convention of a battle between the bloody Communist regime and the deathly serious, but invisible hand of the underground was unacceptable. They accepted the need for change, but for young people, entering into either of the structures was impossible. Entering one of them was impossible because they did not agree with it, and besides, it had stopped being [viable]; the second structure was too hermetic. For these people, the chance to blow off steam, to go out in the streets, to protest in the form of a happening against that which was stifling the other reality, was the

---

* Wardega was born in 1964. This is an excerpt from an interview on 9 June 1997.

first form of activity in their life that broke through the barrier of fear. Of course, this was also determined by the opponent's behavior—the militia, that is to say the system, which, by arresting people who were, for example, participating in an event that laid bare their system, for participating in the surrealistic October Revolution event, was itself becoming involved in a surrealistic situation.

[The interviewer asks what the props were necessary for.]

J.W.: Yes, [the October Revolution event] was the first solidly prepared event. Of course, there were a couple of other events with props—for example, the one with handing out toilet paper. From that event, I remember a dog that was decorated with strips of toilet paper, and that dog also inspired us. So in the flyer about the anniversary of the October Revolution, there was a note about coming with suitably decorated dogs and information that the action would end in the "Barbara" luncheon bar with revolutionary dishes: red borshcht. Of course, we would be consuming the revolutionary dishes only after taking the Winter Palace, i.e., the "Barbara" restaurant. We wanted to inspire life, but life also inspired us. During the event with the toilet paper, the militia arrested a skin-diver who was going through the underpass on Świdnicka*, though he wasn't taking part in our event at all—he was going to his wedding, because it was a guy who belonged to the skin-diving club, and so he went to his own wedding dressed in his professional attire, just because he happened to have such an idea. So when the militia saw this skin-diver, they arrested him. Isn't that inspiring? Very inspiring. During the October Revolution event, the militia was running around and began arresting people who had anything red, or pink, or dark red in what they were wearing (it was getting dark, and so it was difficult to differentiate the shades of red). They just took everyone, one after another, just like when that other time they took everyone who had toilet paper, including those who had just managed to buy an armful of fresh toilet paper. And, suddenly, a black man appeared on the street wearing a red beret—it is a well-known story, famous—and suddenly both battling sides froze in anticipation of what would happen, because where did that black man come from? Out of nowhere—the militia in blue, the revolutionaries in red, and here suddenly a black guy appeared in a red beret. [...]

Question: And you wanted for this to spread to the whole world?

J.W.: I did. After all, I have already said why I was doing this. I wasn't interested in Wrocław, I wasn't interested in the first secretary of the voivodship committee of the PZPR, I wasn't even interested in General Jaruzelski. What's more—even the eastern bloc itself was too small for me.

---

* A major street in Wrocław.

JÓZEF PINIOR*

J.P.: I was tired of Solidarity, tired of the fact that Solidarity moved so easily into the parishes, by which I mean under the umbrella of the Church. It's not about criticizing the Church, but I simply believed that this shouldn't be done, that above all meant a loss of independence. The Orange Alternative allowed me to remove my mask. I was successful in doing so. After all, I could have become some kind of mindless combatant of Solidarity. In the Orange Alternative, there were people ten years younger than I was—young enough so that I hadn't had contact with them, but also young enough so that it was already a new generation. Workers were also in the Orange Alternative. It was wonderful, fantastic, that it actually had came to some rapprochement there. I saw that for the second time in my life. The first time was in 1980, and the second time was in the Orange Alternative—that there doesn't have to be the barrier that there usually is between the workers and the intelligentsia."

Question: Those barriers didn't exist in the joint happenings?

J.P.: Or during the preparation. It was because people were going to other people's apartments. Does a professor in the United States visit a worker's apartment? In Poland today this is also not so likely. But at that time we were at each other's houses. This was connected with the fact that it was necessary to work in secret, and some of the apartments were bugged, so it was necessary to find those that weren't. We were sleeping in workers' apartments and vice versa, workers were sleeping in the apartments of female intellectuals. During the preparation for a happening, these barriers didn't exist, and some professional skills were needed in order to get things done. It wasn't about having a high school diploma, but about openness, about being well read. If someone possesses certain professional skills, barriers disappear. The worker is better, because he can get something concrete done, and the intellectual woman is better, because she reads Kant for hours and knows what Kant was talking about. During the preparation for a happening or in political work, for example in working on a factory newspaper, it was fantastic.

---

* This is an excerpt from interviews on 20 December 1996 and 30 January 1997. Józef Pinior was a central figure in the leadership of Wrocław's Solidarity movement. He also co-founded, in 1987, the Polish Socialist Party (PPS). See Kenney, *Carnival of Revolution*, 30, 189. Pinior was arrested (along with Czesław Borowczyk, a "socialist worker activist") on charges of having beaten a police officer in a rally in May. On 27 June 1988—the very day that Pinior and Borowczyk were being tried in court—Orange Alternative staged a happening, "'The People of Wrocław Welcome Pinior and Borowczyk." Ambiguous was whether Pinior himself was being mocked. (He appeared at the Orange Alternative happening as a PPS politician, and gave a speech in that capacity.) (Ibid., 189.)

JOLANTA SKIBA*

Question: Many people from PPS[†] took part in the happenings. Was this thanks to Pinior?

J.S.: Thanks to Pinior and thanks to Major—Waldek Fydrych. Waldek knew all of us. Waldek, Ewa Kapała and I came up with one of the first happenings. It was the action called: "Away with heat waves[‡]." We sat in weird t-shirts: Józef Pinior, Ewa, Waldek and everyone thought it was good fun. Then, when it started to rain terribly hard, we demanded that the heat waves[§] return. Waldek, who was sitting next to me, had some weird crowns, incredible, I don't know, probably he thought that up himself.

Waldek was very direct, an incredible guy, he had some gift, maybe [even more a gift of] persuasion: when he would say something, everyone admitted he was right. It is hard to image that people would throw around toilet paper on the street, and then they did various very weird and very funny things. People somehow managed to relax. When I looked at Świdnicka Street, at those crowds, how some people who were [normally] very serious were behaving literally like children, were simply having a good time, I considered this to be incredible. Then a certain barrier of fear was unblocked. People knew that it was full of militia all around them, everyone knew that they were there, but people nevertheless kept doing their own thing. They were throwing that dumb toilet paper, running in some red jackets, in some vests, caps on their head and were honoring the October Revolution. The same with the referendum, I don't remember, was it about the economic reform? For the Day of Spring they got dressed as various beings from all over the world. I have the impression that they were overcoming their fear in this way.

WALDEMAR FYDRYCH[¶]

Question: During the 1980s, the group associated with the Orange Alternative changed very much. In the beginning it was a group of people from art schools; then, new people began to appear.

W.F.: It's normal that more and more people started coming. There was a rotation, but there were still people from the art school. And new people came also. It became increasingly rich.

Question: Rich in what sense?

---

[*] Skiba was born in 1965. This is an excerpt from an interview on 30 April 1997.

[†] The Polish Socialist Party, which was revived in 1987.

[‡] This was, in Polish, a play on words, because in the original it was *(u)pały*, and *upały* are heatwaves, and *pały* are just police batons.

[§] *Upały*. (See the preceding note.)

[¶] This is an excerpt from an interview on 17 June 2000.

W.F.: Rich in the sense of people's interests. Because if there had been only people who wanted to arrange some formal things in art, it would have just been waste of time. But if they were people who wanted to do something directly, then their art became increasingly richer. Its message wasn't vapid. People simply saw that there is a change for change—one that comes from inside people, which can have an impact on reality.

Question: So new people contributed a new view on art?

W.F.: It was above all something that hadn't been imported from the West. The Orange Alternative was perhaps the only movement that hadn't been imported from outside. That movement was based on socialist surrealism, it showed that socialism with its mechanisms has many surrealistic elements, while at the same time alluding (because every art movement alludes to something) to surrealism, which had developed in the world many years prior, and whose roots were definitely in France. It also alluded to socialist realism, whose roots lay in Soviet art in Russia. Except that our surrealism treated it differently: it wasn't imported Soviet art, or Western art of the 1930s—it was something completely new.

Question: And what were its Polish roots?

W.F.: It was the reality that surrounded us, and moreover...how should I say it...it spoke of that art's genetic code. It was art that we felt directly. Certain statements were close to surrealism, and through that surrealism close to the vision of socialist realist art in Poland, or in the Soviet Union—in general to revolutionary art. We had some extra chromosome, like it is in the genetic code. The next chromosome was definitely our knowledge on the subject of 1968 in America, France or Poland. Also that in Poland there was a party called the PZPR*, which expressed itself in its own way regarding socialism. These were all the new chromosomes within the genetic code, which somehow gave rise to that which followed. On the other hand, other activities couldn't have taken place in Poland, both in an artistic and social sense, because they alluded to Western art. That is why the Orange Alternative was such a phenomenon.

Question: Did the Orange Alternative take advantage of the right moment, couldn't it have existed earlier or later?

W.F.: No. Earlier I used to meditate and I didn't have time. Later, I found some time, because I didn't meditate as much, so I could work on it. I already had it encoded in my brain somewhere. Since I was painting the little people in 1982, if we had later continued doing all of that, it would have accelerated the reaction in Poland, because if we had made the revolution a year or two earlier, it is possible that the Round Table talks could've already happened then, too, since the West had stopped giving money, credits. It [the West] would have known that the political climate was suitable for staging events such as the Round Table talks, thanks to which it could discreetly dismantle the Soviet military bloc.

---

* Polish United Workers' Party, or the Polish Communist Party.

East Germany, September–October 1989

The Emergence of "New Forum" (Neues Forum)

In some popular and scholarly accounts of 1989, the dramatic appearance of political protests, demonstrations, and organizations is represented as spontaneous, natural, and inevitable, as the triumphant story of people destined to reclaim their freedom. But it was not so simple. There was nothing natural and inevitable about the size of these political protests and demonstrations, or the courage of the individuals who created and sustained these organizations. In fact, one of the lingering puzzles of 1989—one not likely to be solved for some time—is *how* and *why* these new socio-political organizations—whether Civic Forum during Czechoslovakia's "Velvet Revolution" or New Forum (as well as Demokratische Aufbruch, or Democratic Awakening, and Demokratie Jetzt, or Democracy Now) during East Germany's "Turn" (*Wende*)—developed so quickly,[21] against such seemingly great odds.

In the case of East Germany's New Forum, this speed was quite stunning. On 9 and 10 September, East German peace activists founded the organization, which was East Germany's first nationwide,[22] independent (and non-church) political movement. Its fundamental goals were democratic reform and popular participation from as much of East German society as possible in the political process. Ten days later, on 19 September, New Forum applied for official registration, an application that the East German Interior Ministry denied on 21 September (as the first of the following documents attests). Yet the denial did not prevent New Forum from playing a role in leading demonstrations in East Berlin, Leipzig, Dresden, Potsdam, Jena, Plauen, and elsewhere.[23] Popular pressure—the signing of New Forum's proclamation by an increasing number of East German citizens (200,000 had added their signatures to its founding document just four weeks after it "appeared in public"[24])—turned out to be a factor in the state's decision to grant legal status to the organization on 8 November. In effect, New Forum became the first independent political movement that would gain recognition by the East German state and its ruling political party, the SED. After the Berlin Wall fell, New Forum, together with other opposition groups, entered into negotiations

---

From *Neues Forum Leipzig: Jetzt oder nie—Demokratie Leipziger Herbst '89* (*Leipzig's New Forum: Now or Never—The Democratic Movement of the "Leipzig Autumn," 1989*) (Munich: C. Bertelsmann Verlag, 1990), 39–42, 85, 87, 296–301. Published with permission of C. Bertelsmann Verlag, a division of Random House. Translation: Glennys Young.

with the East German Communist Party (SED) about Germany's political future. On 18 March 1990, East Germany held its first elections, which resulted in power being transferred to a governing coalition from the Christian Democratic Party (CDU) and the Social Democratic Party (SPD). The reunification of Germany occurred on 3 October 1990—almost thirteen months after New Forum had been founded.

The following selections concerning New Forum cannot, of course, do justice to the movement's complexity, let alone answer the question of why and how it emerged so rapidly, and with so much power. But these selections *can* alert readers to some aspects of the East Germany *Wende,* and the events in Leipzig in particular, that are often forgotten. Among them are, as the first document attests, the challenges that New Forum's organizers faced in getting official registration, or recognition, of their association. Then there is the fact that *some* people in Leipzig actually *opposed* New Forum. The three other documents—one written by pensioners who joined the 75,000- to 150,000-person demonstration on 9 October, one by a teenage girl who had to forego her flute lesson because of that demonstration, and another by a young woman who was arrested during the demonstration on Monday, 11 September—remind us of the enormous risks that members of New Forum, and the demonstrators more generally, perceived they were taking at the time—and the real possibility, which miraculously did not come to pass, that they would become victims of state violence. After all, on 9 October, state authorities had on hand three thousand riot police, five hundred more militia members than usual, and three thousand regular army soldiers, who were armed with live ammunition.[25]

NEW FORUM (NEUES FORUM) LEIPZIG, FROM STATEMENT ON 26 SEPTEMBER

With this we make it known that the representatives of the leaders of the Council of Leipzig Region, Department of Internal Matters, and the director of the Department of Internal Affairs of the Council of the Leipzig Region have informed us that the application for registering the association New Forum [Neues Forum] was not approved. There is no social need in the GDR for the goals of this association. All the actions concerning New Forum are to be stopped at once. Nevertheless we want to insist further on laying claim to Article 29 of the Constitution of the GDR: "The citizens of the German Democratic Republic have the right to association, in order to realize through common activity in political parties, social organizations, associations and collectives their interests in accord with the principles of the constitution." It is not possible for us alone to demonstrate the social necessity of New Forum. Therefore, we ask each citizen who is convinced of the social necessity of the New Forum Association to contact by petition the Minister of the Interior,

Mauerstrasse* 29, Berlin 1086. We will gladly receive a carbon copy of their petition.

Michael Arnold

Edgar Dusdal

UNDERSTANDING IS LACKING[†]

We have been informed through our press about the incidents in the city center of Leipzig. We distance ourselves from them and we are in favor of these disturbers of the peace being punished with all the harshness of our laws. We want to go in quiet and peace to our jobs and build a secure future for us and for our children. We don't understand that a few church representatives allow such actions, where each citizen in our socialist state is assured of freedom of belief. Do people think, for example, that people can reach [their] goals through such riotous assemblies, which are directed against our state and its politics? To this we say a clear no!

Co-workers of the Industrial Generating
Plant of the VEB Leipziger Wollkämmerei[‡]
[State owned wool processing plant]

WOMEN'S VOICES: A PENSIONER AND A TEENAGER

My [female] friend and I, still inexperienced in demonstrations in which we were not ordered [to participate], made our way to the St. Nikolai Church[§]. It already became somewhat scary to us—we are, of course, pensioners—when we saw the truck convoys[¶] on Goethe Street, the policemen wearing helmets and the other special operations forces. Earlier a younger acquaintance had taken me for being crazy and had asked urgently that we call her when we got back!

After we went to the church we still stood there undecided, though fortified by the reading there the appeals of Kurt Masur's and other personalities, the demonstrators kept yelling again and again "join us"—until we spontaneously followed this invitation.

It briefly got precarious in front of the Stasi building as the command "Turn around, turn around" resounded. Frightened, we let ourselves be helped over the barrier to the left. At this moment I remembered the climbing of the fence at

---

* In German, this means "Wall Street," a reference to the wall, built in August 1961, that separated East and West Berlin.

[†] This is the title given this selection by C. Bertelsmann, the editor of *Neues Forum Leipzig*.

[‡] This letter appeared in the Leipzig newspaper *Leipziger Volkszeitung* on 30 September 1989, 2.

[§] As discussed in chapter 5, the St. Nikolai Church in Leipzig was the site of the weekly peace prayers, held on Monday nights there since 1981. For further information, see chapter 5.

[¶] In German, "*LKW Kolonnen.*"

the Prague Embassy that I had seen earlier on TV. But fortunately it was a false alarm, and with the call "No Violence," there were no clashes when we went past the Stasi.

Today we are still proud—after regular Monday marches—to have been there on 9 October.

Sybille Freitag, Pensioner

On Monday, 9 October, I left school. As always I hurried, because I had to go to my flute lesson. When I got home, my mother told me that I could not go to my flute lesson today. My flute teacher lives in the city [of Leipzig], and so I had to go home again by streetcar in the afternoon. At first I didn't understand at all why I shouldn't go, because I liked to go to flute lessons and was already looking forward to it. My Mom* explained to me that in the afternoon the whole city was closed, the streets were blocked and possibly none of the streetcars were running as well. I reconciled myself to it. Not until the evening, as the news came, did I first understand the actual reason: because the danger existed that the demonstrators would be fired upon.

Marie-Kristin, 13 Years Old

INTERVIEW BY NEW FORUM OF KATRIN HATTENHAUER[†], A YOUNG THEOLOGY STUDENT WHO WAS ARRESTED AND IMPRISONED FOR PARTICIPATING IN THE DEMONSTRATIONS AFTER THE LEIPZIG PEACE PRAYERS ON 11 SEPTEMBER[‡]

New Forum: The "arrest"[§] on 11 September was not the first for you. Would you describe how you live, what has motivated you in the last year, why you were repeatedly "arrested"?

Katrin Hattenhauer: At the moment I am taking a year off, that means, I've taken a break from my studies, and I am attending meetings of the theology seminar as an auditor. In winter I'm traveling around with my flute, in summer I want to set out again with the guitar. That I'm living this way at the moment has a lot to do with fun—a feeling for life. You stand in the passageway, play music, and something comes back from the people...and when I think over...why I ended up in the slammer—then the ultimate goal was nothing more than fun. This joy had let itself be transmitted onto

---

* In German, "Mutti," the diminutive or familiar term for "Mutter" ("Mother").

† As of January 1990, the interviewee, Katrin Hattenhauer, was a twenty-one year-old theology student. She was arrested on 11 September and spent five weeks in prison. See *Neues Forum Leipzig,* 296.

‡ It is said that fifty demonstrators, including Hattenhauer, were arrested following the 11 September peace prayer service at the St. Nikolai Church in Leipzig. They were given prison terms of four months. See Michael G. Huelshoff, Andrei S. Markovits, and Simeon Reich, *From Bundesrepublik to Deutschland: German Politics after Unification* (Ann Arbor: University of Michigan Press , 1993), 215

§ The German word here is "Zuführung." Quotation marks in the original text.

the street and to the people here. That is a feeling for life that a state like this one cannot tolerate.

New Forum: When were you "arrested" the first time?

Katrin Hattenhauer: That's already over a year ago. The reason was a poster campaign against the restriction of the church press. This is the way it usually went [during an arrest]: someone knocked on your door in the morning, and then you realized [that] you were going to have to spend the day with people who were out to get you. The authorities would stand there and ask you to come with them. Then [what] followed were endless conversations, a litany of questions. Sometime or other, after hours [had gone by], they would release you from custody.

Then we released air balloons in front of the "Capitol" during the 88th documentary film week festival, [balloons] on which the forbidden Soviet films were depicted. Another reason was that we called for a demonstration for human rights on the occasion of the memorial days for Luxemburg/Liebknecht. That was in January. Then there were the "arrests" during the street music festival in June. Those who played music consequently reached people on the street, brought upon [them] the joy of life—one was scared of that. We were under house arrest on certain occasions—Election Day, 13 August....

We could only endure this, because we have lived together, [because we] could cling to one another and because we had a big circle of friends domestically and abroad, who helped us again and again.

New Forum: What happened on 11 September?

Katrin Hattenhauer: On the previous Monday I had held up a poster with another woman: "For an open country with free people." That was probably the direct reason why I was taken away. On 11 September, after the peace prayer, things had really broken loose. I wanted to go home. However, someone provoked the demonstration, as only a narrow way was left for many more than a thousand people who were leaving the church. Everything else was blocked off. It was no longer possible to get out of the way to the side—force was used against people who tried that. Dogs were called out on the other side, you could hear cries of fear. And then naturally a panic broke out. And you became furious, you believe you have to put up something against that, and you just don't go as fast as you should go. The demonstration was then only a big cattle drive. People were driven back and forth. If you stood still, you were nabbed. I only noticed how two people next to me were dragged away. Then some person wound my hair three times around his wrist and I found myself in the truck again....

New Forum: How many people were on the truck? Where were you taken?

Katrin Hattenhauer: There were eight or nine people on the truck. They drove us to Dmitrov Street*. There were about fifty of us in a large room. We were taken away individually to be interrogated....

New Forum: How did it go for you? What did people ask you?

---

* In German, "die Dimitroffstrasse."

Katrin Hattenhauer: I just simply sat there and remained silent. I think that's the best thing to do, when you have to deal with people who don't want to do you any good. In this place that's the best defense. The interrogator asked questions to absolve himself, thus, he asked [questions], in order to justify [our] detainment. It was treated like a criminal act: When were you in the church? What time did you leave the church? Why were you there?...

New Forum: What happened after the interrogation?

Katrin Hattenhauer: At night we were driven to a gym in Paumsdorf. There we spent [the night] on mattresses, in considerable cold—the women in the equipment room, the men in the hall. In the early morning some-one called the first people—we thought that we would all be let go now. Most received monetary fines between one thousand and five thousand Marks. There were about a dozen remaining out of the 104 who had been "detained." Towards noon someone drove us to Dmitrov Street in the U-Haft and locked us in cells. I thought: this is shock therapy, in twenty-four hours you will be out there again. But it became 6 PM, then 8 PM. Then I demanded that either I be released or that I see the order to detain. At that point someone showed me the order to detain. I was being held temporar-ily on charges of being part of a riotous assembly, a judicial inquiry against me was underway, and it was being determined whether I was going to get a prison sentence—that's what was in there. Because from the beginning I refused to give a statement and had not signed anything, I had to go unfor-tunately into isolation....

New Forum: How did you feel then?

Katrin Hattenhauer: I had the real hope [that] it couldn't last for a long time. Something like this could really not last for a long time. They couldn't do that; for what you did, they can't lock you up. But such a concrete hope, this breaks you, this you have to set aside. There I understood that there are concrete hopes that can destroy you....

New Forum: How long were you in solitary confinement?

Katrin Hattenhauer: My solitary confinement ended after nearly two weeks. Then for a week I was in a cell with a woman, Ilona, whose face radiated with joy. We could make time go so easily for us that internally we left the slammer....

New Forum: Did you know what was going on "outside"?

Katrin Hattenhauer: Our lawyer, Wolfgang Schnur, told us what was going on. But he only came to see us once. He had demanded that we be released from punishment, had presented the case as unlawful....

New Forum: Were there other ways to hear about [what was going on] outside?

Katrin Hattenhauer: Yes, through the internal way of transmitting informa-tion, the alphabet made through knocking on prison walls*. [We got wind of

---

* In German, the "Klopfalphabet."

things] when someone who had been a prisoner had contact with the outer world—through a lawyer or through a visitation, which was allowed once a month. It is fascinating, how there, in oppression, one system works against another system. There you grasp that no system is so good that people cannot replace it through another. There are in fact sayings about this—for example, "Each condition stops causing fear with the passing of time...."

New Forum: At what point did you begin to hope you'd be set free?

Katrin Hattenhauer: I really didn't believe even up to the last moment that it would happen....

New Forum: What was said when they set you free?

Katrin Hattenhauer: Nothing. Only that the judicial inquiry was stopped. Nothing more.

New Forum: How did you feel?

Katrin Hattenhauer: I could not really grasp it as the big gate opened up. Then you're suddenly standing on the street, on which you didn't hope to stand at all....

New Forum: What do you think now about this time? Would you like the responsible authorities to be punished?

Katrin Hattenhauer: The worst thing that happens to a person there is that the hate of the guards is transferred onto you. There I learned: prison is never good, because it makes no one better. It also doesn't make the situation better. Therefore I wouldn't want people to go to jail.

They could make themselves useful, for example, by making children's toys—hopefully not so fanciless as they made their politics....

Grit Hartmann spoke with Katrin Hattenhauer on 5 January 1990.

9–3

West Germany

Hans-Ulrich Treichel (Born in 1952) Grapples with the Meaning of the Fall of the Berlin Wall

People from all walks of life played a crucial part in the "fall" of the Berlin Wall on 9 November 1989. The Wall did not so much "fall" as cease to have its prior meaning—a meaning that was ominous and, sometimes, deadly. And this collapse of meaning was, it seems, somewhat inadvertent. With the East

German regime in crisis, regulations on travel abroad were relaxed in response to popular pressure, though it was not the government's intent to open the border completely. But on the evening of 9 November, an East German Politburo member and Communist Party (SED) spokesperson, Günter Schabowski, gave a careless response on American TV to a question by reporter Tom Brokaw. Schabowski seemed to be saying that East Germans were free to exit the GDR if they wished. The program was broadcast on West German TV, which was in turn watched in East Germany. Emboldened by an announcement on West German TV that "the gates in the Berlin Wall stand wide open," tens of thousands of people arrived at the borders, including the Berlin Wall itself. Overwhelmed and under-instructed, the border guards made the choice to let them through. By 11:30 PM on 9 November, all regulatory oversight was gone. When Gorbachev heard what had happened the next day, he affirmed that the East Germans had "taken the proper action."

Pictures of the Wall's collapse have become icons of the fall of Communism. So much meaning was invested in a single day, then and now, we are told—for both East and West Berliners, for citizens of East and West Germany, for people around the world.

But the following selection by the German writer Hans-Ulrich Treichel (born in 1952 in Versmold, West Germany) reminds us how complex and varied West Berliners' (and no doubt East Berliners') experience of the Wall's collapse was. In November 1989, Treichel, then approximately twenty-seven years old and now a professor German creative writing at the University of Leipzig (a city in the former East Germany), was an instructor of contemporary German literature at the Free University of Berlin, and lived in West Berlin. For Treichel, the wall did not collapse on 9 November 1989, even though he saw the news reports on TV that night, on what was at the time the popular West German nightly news program, *Tagesschau (Daily Review)*. Rather, for him, at least in his retrospective assessment, it collapsed in the days and weeks thereafter, when, as he puts it in the following passage, "the GDR still existed and yet everything was already over." When he went to East Berlin to visit places he used to go, he realized that something was irretrievably gone.

What was it, exactly? Though the collapse of the wall suggests a fundamental change in the material environment, this is not what Treichel emphasizes. For him, everything looked and smelled the same! Rather, gone for him was the *feeling* he identified with East German socialism in the "capital of the GDR"—East Berlin. Though he does not say so, the reader also senses that he perceives he has lost a part of his past and, hence, of himself. His prose reminds us, too, of how the GDR figured in the identity of West Germans more generally. Not only did many West Germans have relatives in the East. The very identity of being *West* German hinged upon the existence of *East* Germans.

From Hans-Ulrich Treichel, "Zu spät," in *Die Nacht, in der die Mauer fiel: Schriftsteller erzählen vom 9. November 1989. Herausgegeben von Renatus Deckert* ("Too Late," in *The Night the Wall Came Down: Writers Talk About 9 November 1989. Published by Renatus Deckert*) (Frankfurt am Main: Suhrkamp Taschenbuch, 2009), 56–60. Published in English translation with the permission of Suhrkamp Taschenbuch. Translation: Glennys Young.

I really am not one of those people who keep their old calendars. Until, that is, a friend, appalled, once downright reproached [me]: "What? You throw your calendars away?" I have held onto my calendars ever since, provided they are in a condition to be archived. I kept the one from 1989, too. I did so even though the one from 1989 had become stuck onto two other calendars. The calendar from 1989 is stuck together, on the one side, to the one from 1988 and, on the other, to the one from 1990. Time, stuck together. I place the three calendars on the table and perform the operation. I am assisted in this by the big knife that I use as a bread knife, but which in reality is a so-called bakery knife and has an especially wide blade. In the end, three damaged and grubby, stuck-together calendars, which I'd rather dispose of right away, are lying in front of me. First of all, I carefully put the ones from 1988 and 1990 in a clear plastic folder. I leaf through the one from 1989, even though I am not especially curious about my old dentist appointments and meetings at the university.

I nevertheless open the calendar and read entries such as *Faculty Council, Barber, Basic Course,* and, as I presumed, *the Dentist.* On 3 March 1989 I went to the dentist at 1:30 PM....

The entries *Hans' arrival Hotel Esplanade** on 22 November [1989] and *Hans [at] Philarmonic* on 25 November [1989], followed by the 26 November entries *Hans 1 p.m.* and *Hans 7 p.m,* generate in me a certain subsequent biographical disquiet. Straightaway two meetings in a single day. Increased social activities, all things considered, some time after the Wall fell. The days around 9 November seem to have passed completely uneventfully. Bed deliveries is noted on 6 November, a basic course on Benn[†] on 8 November from 2–4 PM, and on 9 November only a single word appears: *Doctor.* On 9 November, I apparently went to the doctor, and, to be exact, at 10 AM. The rest of the day lies in the fog of the past. I believe that I can remember having seen the news about the opening of the Wall on *Tagesschau[‡].* But I didn't drive out to the Wall from Friedenau, either after *Tagesschau* or after the late news with the pictures about the checkpoint on Bornholm Street; rather I sat at my desk until late in the night.... The class on 10 November could actually have been cancelled because of a world-historical event. But it was not cancelled. Nor can I remember either having talked with students about the opening of the

<hr />

[*] Built in 1907–1908 in the Belle Epoque style, and located on the then thriving hub of Potsdamer Platz, the Esplanade was a famous luxury hotel where Kaiser Wilhelm II once held his famous "men's evenings." It was almost completely destroyed in 1944–1945 by bombing during World War II. Remnants of the hotel (including the Kaisersaal, or Emperor's Hall) remained and served as a popular gathering space until the Berlin Wall was constructed nearby in 1961.

[†] Gottfried Benn (1886–1956) was perhaps the most important poet of post–World War II Germany. He was noted for a pessimistic expressionism that evoked the decay and decadence in Germany after World War I. He died in West Berlin.

[‡] *Tagesschau,* which might be translated as *Daily Review,* was a popular West German TV news program. In was launched in 1952 by the Cooperative Association of the German Public Broadcasters (ARD, or Arbeitsgemeinschaft der öffentlich-rechtlichen Rundfunkanstalten Deutschlands), which was founded by the United States, Great, Britain, and France in the years immediately following World War II. At that point, the German mass media was under Allied control.

Wall. The Wall was of course pretty far away from Dahlem and from the Free University [of Berlin]*. Instead we were busy with Benn....

According to my recollections I first went on 11 November to the Wall, or, that is to say, to the Brandenburg Gate†, although there is no entry about it in my calendar. What was I supposed to have written down? "7–9 PM fall of the Wall?" It's possible that I spent the evening of 10 November at a pizzeria in the Dahlem [a section of Berlin], because it was too late to be a genuine witness to history anyhow. Even on 9 November I would have not been more of a witness to history. You certainly can't first watch an historical event in the news and afterwards still become a genuine witness of this historical event. As children we occasionally followed, on bicycle, the fire truck being put into action. Now I rode to the events afterwards, delayed by two days, and looked at, respectively, the Vopos‡ [and] the GDR border guards, who stood on the Wall and looked in the direction of the West. That was new. Border guards on the Wall. And we West Berliners in front of it. Nothing more than that happened. Actually, nothing was happening at all. There were no people from East Berlin to be seen. No embraces, no popping champagne corks, no Trabis§. Only West Berliners, who stared at the border guards, and border guards, who, with blank faces, tried to ignore the West Berliners.

My Wall did not fall on 9 November, but in the days or weeks afterwards. At a time when the DDR still existed and yet everything was already over. At some time or other I went to East Berlin, to follow my old routes. Yet they were not my old routes at all. Where else should they have been? Perhaps in Friedrichshagen¶, where I had relatives and where I can remember a picnic and a kind of beach where you can go by car on Lake Müggel**. We sat in the sand, leaning on the Wartburg††, and spooned fruit out of preserving jars. I certainly remember this only in black

---

* During the Cold War, Dahlem, a section of southwestern Berlin, belonged to the American sector of the city. The Free University of Berlin (Freie Universität zu Berlin) was established there in 1948. From 1945–1991, the seat of the Allied Command was located on Kaiserswerther Straße (Street) in Dahlem.

† The Brandenburg Gate (German: Brandenburger Tor), located in central Berlin, was incorporated into the Berlin Wall after its construction in 1961. Commissioned by King Friedrich Wilhelm II as a symbol of peace, and constructed between 1788 and 1791, it is the only remaining gate of a series of former entry points into the city. It is now a symbol of the reunification of the city and Germany as a whole.

‡ "Vopos" was the shorthand term used by West Germans for the East German national police or *Volkspolizei*. Police was something of a misnomer. In reality, the 100,000-strong *Volkspolizei* resembled more an army than a police force. *Volkspolizei* had armored personnel carriers, artillery, and lived in army barracks.

§ "Trabi" was short for Trabant, East Germany's signature car. Production of the two-cylinder car began in 1957 and ceased in 1991. The body was made of Duroplast, a sort of hardened plastic. Nonetheless, East Germans longed to own one, and the wait for one generally ranged between eleven and fifteen years.

¶ A locale in the Treptow-Köpenick area of Berlin, located on Lake Müggel.

** Lake Müggel, or, in German, the Müggelsee, is the largest of Berlin's lakes.

†† The Wartburg was a passenger car produced in East Germany.

and white, like images of film made by Defa*. I didn't go to Friedrichshagen in November 1989. I first went by way of Oranienburg Street and then I walked around in the area around Acker Street, perhaps because Acker Street is in Döblin's *Berlin Alexanderplatz*[†]. Everything looked like it always did, the eternal GDR, and it also smelled like it. November in East Berlin, damp and slightly chilly. Looking back, I wish I could have had my usual intense experience of November in East Berlin. My favorite would have been to walk barefoot over the fragile paving slabs, as I once, at the end of the seventies, went barefoot over a wooden footbridge in Alt-Ruppin on Lake Ruppin[‡],—where, admittedly, I had gotten a rusty nail in my foot.

Here was no wooden bridge, also no lake, but here was the autumn air saturated with the fumes of brown coal, a store of people's solidarity with faded brochures in the display window, and now and then the noise of a Trabi driving over the cobblestones. Yet the feeling that I desired nevertheless did not set in. Instead of that, a downright melancholy regret about the fact that the chance had passed, to go once more through East Berlin, or, that is to say, the *Capital of the GDR* and to experience, with all the senses, real, bad socialism, including the chilly fall air that belonged to it. That day everything looked like it always did on Acker Street. But at the same time everything was definitively over and past. Nothing was the same anymore—when looked at from the perspective of history. So that is good, too, my political intellect told me. But my life sense, which maintains only a very loose relationship to my intellect, told me something completely different: too late.

---

[*] DEFA (Deutsche Film-Aktiengesellschaft) was the publicly owned film studio of the German Democratic Republic, or East Germany.

[†] Alfred Döblin's *Berlin Alexanderplatz,* a montage novel about the Berlin underworld of the 1920s, was published in 1929. The *Alexanderplatz* is a large public square in what was once East Berlin.

[‡] A lake located eighty kilometers from Berlin.

★

Yugoslavia, 1989–1990

A Scholar (Josip Šentija) on Identity, Self, and the Croatian Nation

s Communist polities unraveled during the European Revolutions of
1989, so did the systems of meaning in which people constructed their
identities. This was because, as we have seen in previous chapters and in
the selections in this chapter, Communism offered, and even obliged, a language
of identity. And a central strand of Communism's language—or languages—of
identity concerned the relationship of the individual to the *nation*. This was the
case despite the fact that an essential element of Marxism, Marxism–Leninism,
and Maoist thought was the historical inevitability of the triumph of Communism
as an international project, and the historical lawfulness of world revolution.
Such was history's destiny. But the short-term reality was that the Communist
polities of the twentieth century (and beyond) were organized as nation-states,
"empires of nations"[26] (in the case of the USSR), and, in the important case of
Yugoslavia, a multinational, multi-ethnic federation.

That nationalism, ethnic conflict, and violence were an inextricable part of
Yugoslavia's disintegration had much to do with the specifics of Communism
in the Socialist Federal Republic of Yugoslavia (1945–1991/2).[27] The latter was a
multinational state comprised of six republics (Bosnia and Herzegovina, Croatia,
Macedonia, Montenegro, Serbia, and Slovenia) and two autonomous provinces
(Vojvodina and Kosovo) within the republic of Serbia. In all but one case (Bosnia
and Herzegovina), the title of the republic indicated the majority population
(that is, Croats were the majority in Croatia, Serbs the majority in Serbia). But all
of these republics also had significant minority populations—there were Serbs
in Croatia, for example. The centrifugal tendencies of the Yugoslav federation—
tendencies enhanced by the republics' cultural and linguistic autonomy, and,
eventually, the economic decentralization brought on by increased reliance
(by the late 1960s) on the market—were kept in check by Joseph Broz Tito and
by the structure of the Yugoslav Communist Party itself.[28] Up until his death in
1980, Tito kept the federation together, and checked the dominance of Serbia,
the largest republic territorially, by calling for unity, and also by playing off the

From Josip Šentija, *Ako Hrvatske bude. Zapisi iz onih godina* (*If Croatia Continues to Exist: Notes From Those Years*) (Zagreb: Školska knjiga, 2005), 39–41, 49–50, 101, 133–134. Published with the permission of Školska knjiga. Translation (and some annotations): Aleksandra Petrovic.

republics against each other—balancing privileges and complaints among them. Moreover, especially after Tito's death, the League of Communists of Yugoslavia[29] (LCY) functioned, as one scholar has put it, as a "state inside a state," as the supranational entity holding the power to resolve conflicts between the republics by imposing its disciplinary authority.[30] At the same time, the fact that the republic-level organizations of the Party (or League) amassed increasing power and prerogatives from the 1960s through the 1980s was among the factors that contributed to the rise of nationalisms within Yugoslavia prior to the Communist collapse.

In January 1990, the LCY crumbled at its 14th Congress, which was held in Belgrade. There, the Slovenes articulated their demands for more democratic practices in the LCY; Serbian delegates responded by saying that the Slovenes were asserting *their* kind of democracy—"democratic centralism." The Slovenian delegates then walked out, followed by the Croats. On 25 June 1991, Slovenia and Croatia declared independence. In 1992, the Federal Republic of Yugoslavia, which consisted of Serbia and Montenegro, was founded.

But even prior to these dramatic actions, and the deadly wars in the former Yugoslavia that ensued, nationalism was making heightened claims on people's identities and fueling political action for both Croats and Serbs. After the League of Communists of Yugoslavia fell apart, Serbian President Slobodan Milošević articulated his dream of a "Greater Serbia," a formulation of Serbian nationalism whose threat to Croats and other ethnic groups was heightened by Milošević's electoral fraud, his purges of ethnic Albanians from government, police, school, and hospital positions in Kosovo,[31] and his other anti-minority actions.[32] And well prior to Croatia's proclamation of independence, Serbs who lived in Croatia feared that *they* would be the victims of the nationalist violence committed by Croatians. Perceiving danger, and haunted by memories of the murder of 350,000 Serbs by fascist Croats during World War II, they began to arm themselves. Not all Croats and Serbs perceived one another as the dangerous enemy. But even when fear and hatred did not escalate to this point, what *had* increased was consciousness of national identities and of the uncertain future of one's *own* nation, whether Serbia, Slovenia, Bosnia and Herzegovina, Macedonia, Montenegro, or, in the case of the selection that follows, Croatia.

Among the Croats who lived through these events, and sought to make sense of them, was the scholar Josip Šentija, the author of the passages reproduced next. Šentija had already risen to scholarly prominence during the Tito years. Between 1977 and 1982, the General Encyclopedia of the Yugoslav Lexicographical Institute, of which Šentija was editor-in-chief, was published. During the intertwined unraveling of Yugoslav Communism and Yugoslav federalism, Šentija was a national figure.[33] On 28 July 1990—that is, a little more than six months after the collapse of the League of Communists of Yugoslvia—the Croatian News Agency (HINA, Hrvatska Izvještajna Novinska Agencija) was founded, and Šentija became its first director.[34] He had, indeed, played a decisive role in HINA's creation.[35]

The selections that follow are notes that Šentija kept in 1989 and 1990, during the demise of Yugoslav Communism and the breaking apart of Yugoslavia itself. Though brief, they speak to themes central to the European Revolutions of 1989 in general, and the Yugoslav case in particular. Regarding the former, Šentija perceives the fall of the Berlin Wall as an international event in the unfolding of the revolution, as an event with international origins (Gorbachev's influence) and international consequences (left unspecified, to be sure). Regarding Yugoslavia, Šentija's observations underscore how Croatians (and, by implication, Serbians, Slovenes, Macedonians, Albanian Kosovars, and so forth) were immersing themselves in the language of national identity—a language spoken, for example, on the T-shirts of the three Croatian teenagers whom the author talked with on 3 July 1990. Though the settings and content of his observations vary, they all speak to how people were grappling with decisions about who they were, and about what their relationship to the Croatian nation was.

5 AUGUST 1989

On the road to the South. Tisno. Tisno/Tijesno. Now the original is insisted upon: "Only Tisno. We are from Tisno, not from Tijesno*...." The frenzy of roots has begun.

Over at Višnja and Ivan P.'s for coffee, Zagreb's friendly deliberations about the Yugoslav crisis and its consequences continues. Ivan thinks the matter is simple: "One telephone call would be enough, one command over the phone and everything would be taken care of." His faith in the might of world powers is strong: "They could order a supra-Yugoslav solution."

"And what would that 'supra-Yugoslav solution' be?"

"European, integrated. In the spirit of broad agreements between Mitterrand and Gorbachev...."

Here, the things are quite simple: young J.P. in a conversation over lunch at his parents' house outlines the situation simply:

"We don't mingle with THEM anymore. We're avoiding each other. WE avoid THEM. WE learned how to steer clear of provoked troubles. And THE ONES that are here, they are coming to bars less often. They are isolating themselves because they feel they can't do with US whatever THEY want."

The polarization is complete: WE and THEY. Either–or. We are against the Wall. WE are and THEY are. A state before an all out fight.

---

*Tisno/Tijesno is the Ikavian/Ijekavian pronunciation distinction in Štokavian, one of the dialects of Croatian (also spoken in Bosnia and Serbia). This distinction is based on the pronunciation of Proto-Slavic vowel "jat". Ikavian is spoken mostly in Dalmatia and in parts of Slavonia. Ijekavian is spoken in Zagreb, and is the main dialect of Croatian. Ijekavian is spoken in parts of Slavonia, along the border with Bosnia and around Dubrovnik. Most of Bosnia and Montenegro also speaks Ijekavian.

9 NOVEMBER 1989

Around noon my brother Ivan calls from Berlin. He's reporting the exciting events around the Wall. Big groups of East Berliners rushed to the border crossings and they are making their way into the Western sector. The guards are not stopping them. East Germany's government, under huge internal and external pressures (Gorbachev!) announced that its citizens are allowed to cross into West Berlin without any problems or limitations.

Since that was announced the exodus is becoming more and more irresistible. As if the door of a large concentration camp opened up and the prisoners gushed out of it. Like a correspondent, Ivan is describing events that, he says, all German TV stations are covering. Everyone is glued to the TV screen. On both sides of the Wall, people are dancing with joy, shouting: "The Wall fell!," "Abschluss!," "Ende!," "It's finished, it's finished!" On the border crossings people are singing and dancing, drinking champagne, they are elatedly singing "Deutschland, Deutschland über alles!*" Thousands and thousands, tens of thousands are heading toward West Berlin and there they are welcomed with the same joy and happiness.

"It looks as if the nation exploded with happiness," Ivan says. "They are all beside themselves. TV is keeping us in suspense. We don't know whether there is anything equivalent to this...."

I feel that Ivan is excited, too. After all, for a long time now, he is also a Berliner, if not because of himself than because of his children, Teo and Stipe, who were born in Berlin and grew up in daycares, schools and parks of Charlottenburg and other Berlin neighborhoods just like so many other children of Croatian "guest-workers†" attracted by the prospect of better life in the years when the government in Bonn started supporting industrial and any other development of West Berlin, the Western oasis surrounded by Ulbricht's and Honecker's Soviet-influenced East Germany.

Last night our media was also reporting on dramatic events in Berlin. Until late last night I jumped from one frequency to another to find out what foreign stations are saying about these events. Everyone is in an extraordinary state. Everything seems unbelievable. As if there is a world uprising, a revolution happening. A bloodless revolution. Everybody is shouting, singing, dancing. They are like one. The Wall guards are all of a sudden participants in these events, just like

---

* This is the first line of the first stanza of the "Song of Germany" ("Das Deutschlandlied"), a song that, either in its entirety or in part (using one of its stanzas) has been the German national anthem since 1922, that is, during the Weimar Republic. The music was written by Joseph Haydn in 1797, and the lyrics in 1841 by August Heinrich Offmann von Fallersleben. The song was again selected as the *West* German national anthem in 1952. In 1990, the third stanza alone became the national anthem of the newly reunified Germany.

† The German word here would be *Gastarbeiter*. This refers to migrant workers who, in the 1960s, 1970s, and 1980s, came to Germany from Italy, Greece, Morocco, Portugal, Tunisia, Yugoslavia and, especially, Turkey. They took the humble jobs Germans did not want and also filled positions during the labor shortage of Germany's economic boom.

other citizens. They are befriending the excited crowd. The shattering of the camp is happening like in a fairytale.

31 JANUARY 1990*

Under the influence of what is going on in Kosovo—demonstrations, barricades, shootings, dead, wounded, feverish hourly reporting on domestic and foreign frequencies—we live in an atmosphere of tremendous tensions. People are demonstrating in Belgrade under the utterly nationalistic, vengeful, and threatening slogans. They are shouting the ultimatums for the country's Presidency and federal government: "If you don't solve this in the next forty-eight hours..." etc.

It seems to me that this could be an intro to some new "27th of March[†]" in Belgrade. Everything points to the extreme threats of that kind[‡]. A group of friends in D.B.'s home is envisioning what could happen next. For example, digging up of the famous coffin in the House of Flowers on Dedinje[§]. A friend of the host is unwaveringly calm, he's not getting excited at all: "So let it happen, even if it happens, so what?!" That would speed things up and in Serbia, the fall of the masks of "Titoism[¶]" would bring things to some final explanation.

---

[*] That is, after the LCY's collapse at the 14th Congress in Belgrade on 23 January 1990.

[†] On 27 March 1941, Yugoslavian Air Force officers toppled the pro-axis government in a bloodless coup. Šentija is probably referring here to the popular protests on 27 March. Thousands of protesters were on the streets, shouting the "Bolje grob nego rob," that is, "Better the grave than a slave," and demonstrating against the Royal Yugoslav's pact with Hitler. Subsequently, the Yugoslav Communists were to take credit for having organized this mass, "anti-fascist" demonstration. But it is likely that they were taking advantage of already existing anger about the alliance with Hitler. I thank Vjeran Pavlakovic for this point.

[‡] Some of the famous slogans of the 27th of March were "Bolje rat nego pakt"—Better war than the pact (with Axis powers)—and, as mentioned above, "Bolje grob nego rob"—Better the grave (death) than (to be) a slave.

[§] Tito, who was a half-Croat, half-Slovene born in Croatia, was buried in a mausoleum and museum complex in Belgrade's Dedinje neighborhood. It was in the 1980s that the backlash against Tito began in Serbia. There, he was viewed as responsible for "weakening" Serbia through the creation of the autonomous provinces, sacrificing Serbs during the Srijem battle (Sremski front), and federalizing the country with the 1974 constitution. These are the reasons why, in the 1980s and 1990s, many nationalist Serbs called for Tito's body to be removed from Belgrade. I thank Vjeran Pavlakovic for this point.

[¶] Incorporating the name of Yugsolavia's Communist leader from 1945 to 1980, Joseph Broz Tito (1892–1980), "Titoism" is conventionally used as a shorthand for the latter's formulation of a specifically Yugoslav philosophy and practice of socialism, after Yugoslavia's expulsion from the Cominform in 1948. On the split between Tito and Stalin, see Wayne S. Vucinich, *At the Brink of War and Peace: the Tito–Stalin Split in a Historic Perspective* (New York: Columbia University Press, 1982).

MARCH 1990 [IN SPLENDID—
A BAR/RESTAURANT IN THE
CENTER OF ZAGREB]

Today there are no regular drunks and drunkards from nearby offices who are spending their "breaks" here. Only the regular "Gradišćanci" and "Lepoglavci*." They are joyful. They have lived to see with their own eyes, in their lifetime, how the system in which they suffered is falling apart. But they are so experienced and wise that they know that even in times that are coming they will not get their own system. They are simply quiet with some sad satisfaction of miserable old men who already clearly see that "they" are finally leaving today. Although "they" of today are not directly responsible for their fate because, age-wise, they can be their sons, even grandsons, they still openly gloat: "they" are the descendants of "those" from around forty years ago, "they" are from the same nurseries and they should finally leave, they should leave as soon as possible. I too, am from this nursery but the "Gradišćanci" accepted me as a heretic, as a man who, in their eyes, has his papers stamped and so I can sometimes tell them what they might not like. Today I tell them: "Be careful, the boys from Mitrovica†, the Communists whose end you so eagerly hope for, can be saved only if they lose. But whoever wins is in trouble...."

They were puzzled. They wanted me to explain. I was in a hurry and I promised to continue our discussion tomorrow.

3 JULY 1990, MORNING

At the tram station in Frankopanska street there are three boys, fourteen to fifteen years old at the most. One is dressed in a white t-shirt that, at the front, has red, white and blue outline of Independent State of Croatia stretching to Zemun‡, including Istria and Sandžak§. A map from Ustaša's posters pressed into textile with that exact title—NDH¶. In the middle of the picture there is the Croatian coat of arms, positioned somewhere between Vakuf Gornji and Jajce** on the map, but in fact it looks like a target. That checkered red and white circle in the middle of this boy's chest is giving him a look of a live mannequin from a shooting range. I'm looking and wondering: "God, who is playing with these kids?! Who is getting them ready

---

* Former political prisoners from the prisons in Stara Gradiška and Lepoglava, respectively. There was a political prison in Stara Gradiška where individuals such as the former Croatian President, Stipe Mesić, were held. Thanks to Vjeran Pavlakovic for this point.

† This is a prison in Sremska Mitrovica, Serbia. It is for "ordinary" criminals, not political prisoners.

‡ This is a city in Serbia, across the Danube from Belgrade.

§ Sandžak is a region in southern Serbia on the border with Montenegro.

¶ Nezavisna Država Hrvatska (NDH): Independent State of Croatia.

** Both Vakuf Gornii and Jajce are towns in Bosnia.

Pictured is one of the victims of state violence in Timișoara, where the Romanian Revolution of 1989 began in December. By the 16th of the month, after six days of vigil designed to prevent the Romanian authorities from removing László Tőkés and resettling him elsewhere in Romania, about five thousand people had gathered in the streets of the city. Military forces arrived in the city on the morning of 17 December. Ceaușescu then vilified the demonstrators, and called for a state violence that followed the model of the Tiananmen Square massacre. As night fell, Romanian army forces began to fire into the crowd. According to official statistics, ninety-seven people were killed. Photo by Robert Maass.

for a shooting range?" I ask him to let me look closely at the picture on his shirt. He's flattered: "No problem, go ahead!" The other two are giggling with satisfaction, kids like attention. The advertisement works. "We got it from Canada.... You like it?" "No, I don't like it." "Why don't you like it, mister?" "Because it's a mirage." The boys are not Štokavian speakers,* so they ask: "Mirage, what's that?" "I can't tell

---

*The conversation is in Kajkavian, one of the dialects in Croatia; Štokavian and Čakavian are the other two dialects. The author uses "tlapnja," a word that boys, as Kajkavian speakers of Croatian, do not understand.

you exactly in Croatian but I can tell you in English, if you boys understand it...."
We understand English, go ahead, say it...." "So, mirage, that is, *an illusion, a false
show, a false impression, a phantom*...what's more a *hallucination*....Got it?"

"Got it, got it....An illusion...right? What are you, an English teacher? We
have one such bore in our school." And they got on onto tram number 13, pleased
that they made fun of the old bore. In five years these kids will be ready to carry a
gun. Maybe even sooner if we're to judge by the images from Vietnam's recent and
Palestine's always current reality.

9–5

Romania

*László Tőkés (1952–), The Pastor Whose Resistance
Helped to Galvanize the Fall of Romania's
Communist Regime, Reflects on the Events of
December 1989 in Timişoara*

László Tőkés, who became a major figure in the collapse of the Romanian
Communist regime in 1989, would seem to have been an unlikely candidate
to play such a part. Ethnically Hungarian, Tőkés was, at the time that the
sudden collapse of Communism in December in Romania capped the dramatic
events of 1989, an assistant pastor in Timişoara, a city (population at the time
about 355,000) in Western Romania. To be sure, Tőkés had for decades expressed
his opposition to the Ceauşescu regime. As far back as 1982, speaking out against
human rights violations in a Hungarian-language *samizdat* publication caused
him to be subject to the surveillance of the Securitate, the Romanian equivalent of East Germany's *Stasi* or the Soviet Union's KGB. He had also registered his
opposition to the regime's policies by giving courageous sermons in which he
assailed the Romanian governments' relocation of villagers to the cities, a policy
designed to spread out, and thereby dilute, the possible political resistance, of
Hungarians.[36] Because of these and other acts, the Romanian authorities had had
enough of Tőkés, and decided, in March 1989, that he was to be transferred from
Timişoara (in Hungarian, Temesvár) to a small parish in Mineu.

From László Tőkés (as told to David Porter), *With God, For the People* (London and Toronto: Hodder
nd Stoughton, 1990). Published by permission of Hodder and Stoughton.

Tőkés's decision to refuse to leave catalyzed what turned into a political revolution. Lacking any sort of equivalents to opposition movements, such as East Germany's New Forum and Czechoslovakia's Civic Forum, and governed by a veritable dictator (Ceauşescu) controlling the Securitate, Romania's Communist regime would seem to have been poised to withstand the European revolutionary winds of 1989. Yet it succumbed. Setting off the sudden implosion was Tőkés's call, made during a church service on 15 December 1989, for parishioners to resist his eviction and transfer. Street protests in Timişoara, Bucharest, and elsewhere followed, and were repressed by the Securitate. Yet large demonstrations nonetheless occurred. A week later, on 22 December, Ceauşescu and his wife Elena would take off in desperation by helicopter from the roof of the building of the Romanian Communist Party's Central Committee.[37] Ultimately, however, they were unable to elude their would-be captors, and faced detainment by the police and the military. As mentioned in the introduction to this chapter, they were executed, by a firing squad of eighty, on Christmas Day 1989, with the eighty having reportedly been chosen by a drawing of lots from all the volunteers in the garrison.[38]

In the interview excerpted next, László Tőkés reflects on the growing resistance to Communist power in Romania in December 1989. Even though he exhorted the resisters gathered outside his apartment to leave in order to avert "tragedy," they remained. It is possible that their resistance, as well as the growing defiance of many of Timişoara's residence, was fueled by knowledge of the fall of the Berlin Wall—knowledge that was perhaps easier to come by in Timoşoara, whose location near the western border allowed its population greater access to news from Budapest and Belgrade than other Romanians may have had. In any case, the Romanian Revolution of 1989[39] that began in Timişoara was marked by the paralysis of elites in the face of popular mobilization that had no organizational center.[40]

TEMESVAR [TIMIŞOARA]–DECEMBER 16

...Now there was no longer any pretence at negotiation. The mayor sent back a curt message that if the crowd had not dispersed by five o'clock, the fire brigade would be sent in to disperse them by water cannon. That was his ultimatum, and I knew then that the matter would end in tragedy.

The dominant obsession of the crowd outside the church that afternoon was that the Securitate were in our apartment, either holding us against our will or preparing to abduct us. It was a fear incited by provocateurs in the crowd, who could be seen clearly directing people's emotions. There was a core in the crowd composed of people who had come to join the vigil against the eviction, but most had come because they had seen the disturbance while out in the city or had heard about what was happening at the church. Some had no idea what had started the demonstration. All day people came and went; as some left to go to their homes or to queue for food, others arrived to take their place. Consequently I had to go to the windows frequently to assure new arrivals that I was still alive and had not been evicted.

My pleas to them no longer concerned the promises the mayor had made and apparently fulfilled. "Go home," I said. "They will use force, the Securitate will come back; the mayor has made it quite clear. What power have we against them? Only tragedy can come out of this."

But the crowd's resolve only hardened. "We want Tőkés! We love you, we won't let you be taken away!" Some forced their way into the hallway and almost broke down the door; we heard the fighting between my guards and the people who wanted to come in.

Our feelings were in turmoil. The pace of events was bewildering, and the cumulative effect of each new ultimatum was creating unbearable tension in Edit and myself. Every half-hour I had to go to the window and repeat the same explanations and make the same appeals. There was a rising hysteria in the crowd that was having its effect on me. I felt as if I had lost my bearings, that I had no way of orientating myself in the claustrophobia of the flat. Desperately worried about Edit, helpless to resolve the crisis developing outside, I thought I was going mad. Though the crowd looked to me as a figurehead, in truth I was a prisoner of their anger.

I was torn between two desires: as a Christian pastor I wanted to protect them from the violence which I was sure was inevitable, and at the same time I wanted to stand with them in their protests against the regime's illegality. Like Moses who accepted the role given him by God to stand up against an oppressive regime, I believed it was my duty to stand with the crowd.

I had spent the afternoon in that conflict. By six o'clock I had resigned myself to whatever might happen.

A few people in the crowd shouted up to me: "Come down into the street and lead us!" Others took up the idea, and soon there were dozens of people chanting appeals to me to lead them to the city centre for a mass demonstration. I refused. Partly it was because I wanted to be a pastor and not a political crusader, partly because I could see in the crowd people I knew to be Securitate officers, and I was alarmed at the obvious provocation from individuals in the crowd clearly intent on making the situation uncontrollable.

Later, thinking about the events of those two days, I realised that the authorities would have had a great deal to gain if the situation had become a riot. It would then have been possible to subdue it by force and put the entire blame on the Hungarian community. It would be a perfect excuse for even heavier oppression of Hungarians and all minorities.

By seven o'clock our friends reported that the crowd now stretched from the church down to the Opera Square several blocks away, where many people were gathered on the steps of the Orthodox church. Now there were two crowds in one.

Lajos Varga [a friend of Tőkés]: As on the previous night, the people had lit candles and some were singing hymns. There were Securitate officers in the crowd, observing, but they could do very little. Round the church, people joined hands in a human chain of symbolic defence.

László Tőkés appeared from time to time, and people begged him to conduct a service. He was too exhausted to do so, but he spoke briefly to us from the Bible, for only a few minutes at a time.

And then, about half past seven, among the shouting and the excitement, the unimaginable happened. From a number of places in the crowd the first notes of a prohibited Romanian song rose quietly into the night. "Awake, Romania," which had not been sung in public during Ceauşescu's reign, faltered bravely on the lips of people who could barely remember the words.

The song was an intensely nationalist one and unknown in the Hungarian community. I looked out of the window and was moved by the sight and sound of Romanians singing. It was a striking token that this was a demonstration not just by our minority church, but by the whole population of Temesvar.

I did not know the words of "Awake, Romania" and did not know how to respond. In the end I placed my hand over my heart as if a national anthem were being sung and listened quietly.

It would have been impossible to sing in any case. My throat was so sore that I could hardly speak. I had been calling down to the crowd every half-hour all day. But it was a solemn time of communion between us.

And then the crowd was shouting new and dangerous words; from the main road to the Opera Square, voices were crying, "Down with Ceauşescu! Down with the regime! Down with Communism!"

The situation changed irrevocably at that point. The crowd did not want to hear me any more. Nothing I had to say could shift the burning focus of their anger now. I closed the window and went to join Edit and our friends.

Arpad Gazda, member of the church and friend of László Tőkés: On the previous evening I had been one of those who had gone into László Tőkés's apartment with the Party secretary.

The next morning I went back to the apartment and was allowed to go in. I was with László and his wife all day. Other friends came as well. By the evening there were nine of us in the apartment: László, his wife Edit, her brother-in-law Pali, myself; a fifty-year old parishioner and four other friends of the Tőkés family.

We were very frightened. We had no idea how the matter was going to be resolved or how long the authorities would permit the demonstration to go on. But we knew we were in great danger.

"The crowd's moving!"

Our guards at the door came in with the news that the people had begun to move off. The demands for me to come to the window stopped. We looked out without being seen and watched the numbers in the side street diminishing as people moved over the bridge towards the centre. In the main road, the trams had long since stopped running. The stationary vehicles formed a natural barricade, creating a line of defence in front of the church building. After a short time, the side street was virtually empty. Only a core of church members and friends remained to keep their vigil.

One image from that night will stay with me forever. The Securitate and militia became increasingly active in the street as the number of people diminished. One young demonstrator was standing near the window. I did not know who he was. He was arguing with Securitate officers. Suddenly they began punching him and beating him with sticks. He fell to the ground. They kicked him, viciously and expertly. He was covered in blood, and unconscious long before they stopped their attack. His body remained motionless on the ground in front of our window for a long time before it was dragged away. He seemed to be dead.

Lajos Varga: The crowd divided. The largest part, including the students, headed for the city centre. They arrived at the Party headquarters in the mood for violence. They began by breaking all the windows.

Just before ten o'clock at night, police reinforcements arrived. They succeeded in breaking up that demonstration and forced the demonstrators back to László Tőkés's church where they turned water cannons on them. By then I had left the church demonstration to go home to my wife. I told her, "This isn't a demonstration any more. This is a revolution."

Later I was told what had happened next. The crowd seized the water cannon machine, broke it up and threw the pieces into the Bega River. This was an extraordinary achievement as the machine was supposedly virtually indestructible. More violence followed; they smashed shop windows; they broke into a bookshop, seized all of Ceauşescu's books and burned them.

9–6

Ukraine, 1990

Salomea Pavlychko (1958–1999) on a Self in Flux Amidst Political Uncertainty and Economic Hardship

F rom a certain vantage point, 1990 in Ukraine was a year of stunning political achievements that had profound implications for people there and throughout the Soviet Union—and throughout the world. The Chernobyl nuclear disaster in April 1986 catalyzed the formation of unofficial opposition

From Salomea Pavlychko, *Letters from Kiev* (New York: St. Martin's Press, 1992), trans. Myrna Kostash, with a preface and annotatations by Bohdan Kravchenko, 36–38, 98–105, 105–114, 120–124 (excerpts). Published with permission of St. Martin's Press.

groups, including those seeking Ukrainian sovereignty and independence. By September 1989, these groups had formed Rukh, Ukraine's popular front. 1990 was Rukh's year, so to speak. In the elections of March, Rukh gained a toehold in parliament. In July 1990, Ukraine declared sovereignty.

But 1990 was also a year of major *obstacles* to the forces pushing for democracy and national sovereignty. Conservatives sought to roll back these encroachments upon Communist institutions and legitimacy, and to maintain Ukraine's status within the USSR. By autumn of that year, Ukrainian politics had become sharply polarized.

Conservative forces were challenged by a remarkable student movement that, in early October, staged amazing and successful mass actions. As 1990 came to a close, Ukraine's conservative political elite was on the defensive and eventually a more moderate leadership would emerge under Leonid Kravchuk, Ukraine's future president. And on 24 August 1991, after the failed putsch by Communist hardliners in Moscow, Ukraine declared independence. Two days later, the parliament outlawed the Communist Party of Ukraine. A referendum on 1 December 1991, confirmed, with strong support, Ukrainian independence.

But at the time, Ukrainians had no idea of how things would turn out. As these opposing political forces clashed amid sharply deteriorating conditions, people felt tremendous uncertainty—and fear—about the future. This sense of uncertainty is clearly evoked by the late Solomea Pavlychko, whose observations in the following selection were delivered in letters she wrote between 12 May 1990 and 25 March 1991 from Kiev, Ukraine's capital, to a friend and colleague in Edmonton, Canada, where she had just returned from a stint as visiting professor from January to April 1990.

Pavlychko (1958–1999) was the daughter of the esteemed Ukrainian poet and former opposition member of parliament, Dmytro Pavlychko. Before her life was cut short by a tragic accident in her home, she made invaluable contributions to Ukrainian cultural and intellectual life as a writer, translator, and teacher. At the time she wrote the letters from Kiev, she held a position at the Institute of Literature of the Ukrainian Academy of Sciences, then a center of opposition to the Communist status quo in Ukraine.

The following excerpt from her letters offers a remarkable glimpse into the decisions—about politics, about her work, about life, and, perhaps most of all, about herself—that Pavlychko faced in 1990. She deems 1990 a year of immense inner change, one of "internal, personal transformation" when she became aware of "some new spirit or consciousness" that was "living inside the old body." A central element of this transformation was her discovery of feminism, and her decision to share her discovery with male colleagues—with deeply disappointing results. But she also lets us see how the generalized politicization of everyday life created liberating yet frightening choices for her and for her fellow Ukrainians.

June 28 [1990]

It's amazing how incredibly quickly the time goes. What yesterday was not even thought, let alone expressed, is today said out loud and becomes a subject of dispute. A year ago any discussion of a new Union treaty* was the height of revolution. Today we have the open proclamation by representatives of the Narodna Rada† that they are against the new treaty. And although there is no chance of success now, it seems that everything's been said. It's interesting to think about what will happen next....

October 29 [1990]

Fortunately, there were no such appeals as "Ukraine for the Ukrainians," although the Organization of Ukrainian Nationalists‡ activists could hardly contain themselves and much was said about relations between the nationalities, especially between Ukrainians and Jews. It's true that today Rukh encourages the Jews and promotes their culture, but they continue to leave Ukraine in droves. There are broad economic and political reasons for this.

Yesterday, I went home in a taxi that I caught near the Ukraine Palace. The driver asked me, "Are you from Rukh?" I answered that I was. And he bluntly replied, "I don't trust any of you. Rukh is a political prostitute. At first you said you support the Communist party and now you make speeches against it." We drove for ten minutes, during which I tried to find out from him just what he

---

* Gorbachev's "Union Treaty" was an attempt to save a modified version of the USSR's federal structure in the face of the "parade of sovereignties" that punctuated the summer of 1990 and followed Lithuania's declaration of independence in March 1990. (Quote at Martin Malia, *The Soviet Tragedy: A History of Socialism in Russia* [New York: Free Press, 1995], 482.) The revised version that Gorbachev agreed to, under pressure by Yeltsin, in late July 1991 allowed for quite a bit more decentralization, including the nine republics' right to collect taxes and turn in only part of the proceeds to the Center. (The Treaty was to be an agreement between the Russian Federation and the nine republics that had not seceded.) It was the specter of the Union Treaty's signing on 20 August 1991 that fueled the coup attempt on 19 August 1991, which failed.

† In English, "Narodna rada" means "People's Council." This was a democratic opposition organization.

‡ The Organization of Ukrainian Nationalists (OUN) was founded in 1929. Aptly characterized as an "underground army," it was a conspiratorial and authoritarian organization that used violence (for example, assassinations) in pursuit of its goal of integral nationalism and a "greater Ukraine." In the remaining interwar years, its conspiratorial activities were targeted against the Polish occupation of Western Ukraine. By the eve of World War II, it is said to have had twenty thousand members. In 1940–1941, the OUN split into to a more radical faction (OUN-B, which supported Stepan Bandera), and a less radical one (OUN-M, which supported Andriy Melnyk). The conflict, which resulted in factional fighting, was about strategies of independence and generational outlooks. During World War II, the OUN commanded the Ukrainian Insurgent Army (UPA), partisans who fought beginning in 1942 against both Nazi and Soviet occupiers. The leader of one of its more radical faction (OUP-B), Stepan Bandera, was assassinated by the KGB in Munich 1959. As Paylychko implies, the OUN was resurgent during the very late Soviet period, though the nationalist Inter-Party Assembly was not able to amass the 100,000 signatures required to register a candidate in the 1991 presidential elections. See Orest Subtelny, *Ukraine: A History,* 3rd ed. (Toronto: University of Toronto Press, 2000), quote at 443, consult also 444; Robert Zietek, "Organizacja Ukrainskich naçionalistów w okresie i wojny swiatowej (Organization of Ukrainian Nationalists during the Second World War)," *Rocznik humanistyczne* 42, no. 2 (2004): 81–106); Salomea Pavlychko, *Letters from Kiev* (New York: St. Martin's Press, 1992), 174, note 26.

does believe in, whether in the CPSU* or in Lenin, who were not merely prostitutes but quite simply murderers. But he did not even want to listen to me.

There isn't much ground for euphoria. Everything still lies ahead, and not even virtual famine, which we have now in Ukraine, has fully aroused the people. And the danger of an army coup or of martial law looms over us....

The congress concluded today on an unpleasant note. The Patriarch of Moscow, Aleksii the Second[†], arrived in Kiev, ostensibly to grant sovereignty to the Russian Orthodox church in Ukraine, now renamed the Ukrainian Orthodox church. This is the sovereignty of a daughter church, hence incomplete and ambiguous. Today he was to conduct a service in the Cathedral of St. Sophia[‡]. Rukh had sent the patriarch a telegram suggesting that the Moscow church decline the idea of conducting a service in this most important Ukrainian sanctuary. This, naturally, didn't go over. So, in the morning, pickets and commandos stood in the square, Mykhailo Horyn and Oles Shevchenko lay down on the pavement to obstruct the passage of the patriarch's automobile, and the police dragged them away by their feet. They took the patriarch around to the back door and, during the service, there were clashes on the square between believers of both confessions. Autocephalists[§], or perhaps provocateurs, beat up a monk from the Caves Monastery[¶].

---

[*] Communist Party of the Soviet Union.

[†] Alexei II (whose original name was Aleksei Mikahilovich Ridiger), was, from 1990 to his death in 2008, Russian Orthodox Patriarch of Moscow and all Russia. Born in Tallinn (Estonia) in 1929, he graduated from Leningrad Theological Seminar in 1953, and in July 1986 became Metropolitan of Leningrad. For more on his life, and for the reasons he was selected as Patriarch following Patriarch Pimen's death in 1990, see Nathaniel Davis, *A Long Walk to Church: A Contemporary History of Russian Orthodoxy,* 2nd ed. (Boulder, CO; Westview Press, 2003), 85–86. He was the first Patriarch during the Soviet period to be chosen without government pressure. Denis Janz, *World Christianity and Marxism* (New York: Oxford University Press, 1998), 45.

[‡] One of the most important religious and historical sites in Kiev, the St. Sophia Cathedral was built in 1037 by Prince Yaroslav the Wise. Its grandeur was meant to compete with the Saint Sophia Cathedral in Constantinople. As Christianity had only been adopted in 988 by Grand Prince Vladimir (about 958–1015), Kiev's St. Sophia Cathedral would serve as a center for Orthodoxy's development throughout the East Slavic world.

[§] Reference here is to the Ukrainian Autocephalous (or self-governing) Orthodox Church. In 1930, the Soviet government began massive repression against it. Bishops and priests were killed or sent to camps. Parishes were transferred to the Russian Orthodox Church. In February 1989, the Ukrainian Autocephalous Church, which had the support of *Rukh*, was re-launched. The "Autocephalists," as Pavlychko calls them here, had, by February 1990, seven bishops and at least two hundred priests. In June, Mystyslav, Metropolitan of the American Ukrainian Orthodox church, became autocephalous Patriarch of Kiev. Amended from *Letters from Kiev*, 175, n. 27.

[¶] The establishment of the Monastery of the Caves near Kiev (Kiev Pechersk Lavra) in 1015 was in part the work of the monks St. Antony (982–1073) and St. Theodosius (died 1074). This major center of Orthodox Christianity was transformed by the Soviet authorities into a museum (including for anti-religious propaganda) beginning in 1921. In 1961, the Soviet state allowed the opening of a small monastery with about one hundred monks. Restoration of the full function of the monastery began with the Soviet celebration in 1988 of the millennium of Christianity in *Rus.* See also David Prestel, "The Kievan Caves Monastery: What Do Monks Have to Do with the World?," *Russian History* 33, no. 3–4 (2006): 199–216.

I'm thinking about what Ukraine will be like by the third congress of Rukh and whether it will survive in its role as a coalition of democratic forces, whether independent workers' trade unions and strike committees will support it, whether it will fade into the shadows as new political forces appear on the scene from student or worker movements. And I cannot give any definitive answer. . . .

Everything still operates in the old way, in the sense of the unpredictability of each successive day, whether in political or personal life.

As for the sincere envy of our "very interesting" life—when "history is being made"—among numerous Ukrainians in the diaspora (they repeat this endlessly), this "interesting life" can be psychologically very difficult, even insupportable, because of its very unpredictability, and because the "better future" is cloaked in a thick fog of obscurity.

November 7 [1990]

Today is the "great" Communist holiday, October Revolution Day*. The 73rd anniversary. I'm one of those who consider this a day of mourning. But at this moment, the festival's military parade, the Communists' demonstration, and the funereal rally of the anti-Communists are all behind us. The sun is shining and everyone seems all right, even though my mood is not the best. But let's take things in order. There have been a great many events this past week that have shaken people, even stirred them up, and others which have touched only our family.

The end of last month, October 30, was marked in Kiev by a new panic. On Monday, rumors circulated that, as of November 1, according to a decision of the Council of Ministers, coupons for all goods more expensive than twenty kopecks would be introduced throughout Ukraine. . . . What is this supposed to accomplish? The idea is that only those who earn wages receive coupons, and that the coupons are based on 70% of their earnings. Anyone who doesn't have a steady income in Ukraine—e.g., visitors who buy everything up or locals, who likewise buy everything up wholesale and sell it on the black market—will be left out, hungry and naked. The problem is that millions of people don't have steady incomes or have only minimal earnings. All of us—formerly rather privileged and comfortable thanks to literary honoraria—now find ourselves partly among the poor. Thus, I've been given coupons according to my miserable academic salary, that is, one hundred rubles' worth of coupons per month. But I receive no coupons for my honoraria—and for one article I am often paid four times my monthly salary. Of course, I can survive as before, shopping only in the private sector, i.e., the market. But in one day, as of November 1, the

---

*7 November, the anniversary of the Bolshevik seizure of power in Petrograd (now St. Petersburg, and from 1924–1991, Leningrad), was one of the most important days of political celebration in the USSR and throughout the Communist world. Major military parades, for example, were held in Moscow, with Kremlin leaders presiding on Red Square.

prices there have risen astronomically. A kilo of meat costs twenty rubles, and everything else has gone up proportionately. Soon all this will be beyond my means....

November 22 [1990]

...Boris Yeltsin* arrived on Sunday and was very warmly received every-where. They say that Yeltsin was afraid he'd get the same reception as Patriarch Aleksii, but he was welcomed with enthusiasm and shouts of "Hurrah!" Immediately followed by cries of "Down with Kravchuk!†"...

On Monday Kravchuk and Yeltsin signed a co-operation agreement between Ukraine and Russia. In all his interviews, Yeltsin repeated that this was a completely new agreement between two sovereign states. This is proba-bly the most important element of the accord—the confirmation of each oth-er's sovereignty. Our television network prudently refrained from showing his speech before parliament, probably because it was too trenchant for Ukraine. Meantime, at the Paris meeting of European heads of state, Gorbachev said that the chief threat to European security may now be coming from separat-ists and nationalists within the borders of the USSR. For a moment there, he reminded me in his speech of the late Brezhnev. Something similar in the tone of voice or in his intonation. You can see, chalked up in a crooked hand on fences around Kiev, the graffiti, "Down with Gorbachev."...

Demonstrations with red Soviet flags continue to take place outside the Supreme Rada‡. Now the demonstrators are self-styled miners from Donetsk§ in snow-white miners' hard hats they're wearing for the first time, and collec-tive farm workers from the Chernihiv¶ region. Once more they are demanding: the immediate signing of the Union treaty, the text and terms of which they do not know, because they still haven't been published; and "the restoration of

---

* In June 1991, Yeltsin (1931–2007) was elected President of Russia, the first in Russia's history to be democratically elected to this post.

† Leonid Kravchuk (born in 1934 in Veliky Zhytyn, Ukraine) was, by a 61.6 percent majority, elected President of Ukraine in December 1991, and served as such until 1994. This followed his election in July 1990 as the head of the Ukrainian Parliament or *Rada*, discussed in the next note. From 1960 onwards, he held numerous posts in the Communist Party of Ukraine. Eventually, he became the Party's second secretary for ideology. Amended from *Letters from Kiev*, 179, n. 19.

‡ This is the parliament of Ukraine, a unicameral body with four hundred fifty deputies. It only began to play a significant role in Ukrainian politics in March 1990. "Rada" means "council" in English, and "Soviet" in Russian. Amended from *Letters from Kiev*, 170, n. 9.

§ In July 1989, coal miners from the city of Donetsk joined the waves of strikes by miners in the USSR. Strikers sought democratization and economic gains. The strikes, and the strike committees who led them, persisted after the collapse of the Soviet Union. For a revealing collection of interviews, see Lewis J. Siegelbaum and Daniel J. Walkowitz, *Workers of the Donbass Speak: Survival and Identity in the New Ukraine, 1989–1992* (Albany, NY: State University of New York Press, 1995).

¶ Chernihiv (also Chernigov, in Russian) is the major city in Ukraine's northern region. It is about eighty-nine miles north of the capital, Kyiv (Kiev).

order, at last." If the first seems rather unrealistic, the second appears all too real and sinister, in light of Khmara's* arrest.

Yesterday's *Radianska Ukraina* (the Communist party newspaper) came out under the slogan, "Faithful to the Red Banner."

The press and television enthusiastically publicize these demonstrations, which no one ever bothers to disperse. In the crowd are men of a certain type, whose average age is at least forty, in hats and caps, gray coats (the collective farm elite and regional party activists)....

This turn of events has once again left me feeling very disagreeable. I catch myself thinking that my soul is on the point of utter collapse. I remember how, in the days of Brezhnev, in the news reports about official Ukrainian congresses, when all the speakers gave their talks in Russian, I would jump up and turn off the t.v. I had the unbearable feeling that this system was strangling us, destroying and crushing us; that everything Ukrainian was doomed; that soon nothing would be left of it. We didn't want to know, to think, to see, out of a normal instinct of self-preservation in order not to go mad. What galling, unrelieved powerlessness!...

Another subject that throws me into the same state of stark terror is Chernobyl†. For a long time now, I've simply been switching channels at the first mention of it on the television, and I read almost nothing of the newspaper articles on the subject. Why? Because psychically I cannot bear to watch children who are breathing radiation, and the elderly evacuees who return to their villages in the zone where it is dangerous to live....The worst thing is that Chernobyl didn't teach us anything and the system which engendered it is still alive and people who defended it are still defending it. It terrifies me to think about what kind of world I live in....

December 31 [1990]

I've had a good year. I'm really proud of the collection of T. S. Eliot's poetry that I edited—his first appearance in the Ukrainian language....But the most

---

* Reference here is to the arrest of Stepan Khmara, a member of Rukh and a deputy from Western Ukraine in Ukraine's Supreme Soviet, on 13 November 1990. He was arrested for allegedly assaulting a plain-clothes police officer at the 7 November, 1990, celebration of the October Revolution. Sharon Wolchik, *Ukraine: The Search for a National Identity* (Lanham, MD: Rowman and Littlefield, 1999), 36. Following his arrest, he went on a hunger strike from 26 November to 12 December. Protests were made on his behalf by nationalist supporters in the Ukrainian Supreme Soviet. See http://hansard.millbanksystems.com/written_answers/1991/mar/05/mr-stepan-khmara. In July 1991 Khmara was arrested again because he did not recognize the "legality of the court trying his case." *Letters from Kiev*, 177, n. 44.

† Pavlychko refers here to the nuclear accident on 26 April 1986, in Chernobyl, Ukraine. The initial response of the Soviet government was to cover up the accident. It was the Swedes who first alerted the world about increased radiation coming from Ukraine to Western Europe. The Soviet government's lack of transparency about Chernobyl would ultimately prove to be a central catalyst for Gorbachev's development of *glasnost'* (openness), as well as for disenchantment with, and opposition to, late Soviet socialism.

important thing that happened to me last year was that internal, personal transformation which I have been feeling. It's almost as though some new spirit or consciousness were living inside the old body. I have discovered myself irreconcilable to the world around me. My view on life has become sharper. "View" is exactly it—I notice things I did not notice before. I react strongly to things that formerly left me indifferent. At times I find "my" society utterly intolerable. The degraded state of Soviet academic scholarship, in which I, alas, still formally participate, is more and more irritating. My feminist enthusiasms cause me a lot of trouble. Some innocent, thoroughly unremarkable statement—for example, that a woman is a person, just like a man—provokes a storm of indignation in my immediate professional milieu. A few days ago, a very decent and quite sensible young poet said to me, "I didn't know you were a feminist. I used to have more respect for you." I myself don't know to what extent I am a feminist and what I can distill for myself from the various ideological strands of Western feminism. What I'll retain and what I'll discard. But the young man, who has no real understanding of feminism, already has "no respect" for me.

For all of us in this country, politics has become a total obsession, a mania, a narcotic. From the janitor to the academician. Like true fanatics, we all put other business aside to rush to the television set and watch the first broadcasts from our first parliaments....

I experienced some extraordinary moments last year. Having become one with the demonstration of September 30, about which I wrote you, I felt for the first time the potential strength of thousands and thousands of people around me, felt the stirrings of this people, felt that the injustices of history may yet be repaired and its iron logic shattered—as in the victory of the students in October.

At the same time, as never before, in 1990 I succumbed to attacks of pessimism, thinking of our domestic woes—Chernobyl, our fearsome and mendacious system which turns people into cripples, the total brutalization and dehumanization of life. And, although I live in exceptionally good circumstances—as far as local conditions go—and mingle not with the "working people" but with intellectuals, poets, and theoreticians in various fields— from versification to management—nevertheless I see and understand it all quite well That is, I see how everything is bad and becoming worse, and harder. Thus, the end-of-the-year counters of Kiev force me to think of hunger (earlier, I would simply not have believed such a thing) and the endless, closely packed queues of wan, exhausted people in the suffocating grocery shops lined up for sausage (which turns blue when exposed to the air) or butter once more convinced me how terrible is the abyss of disrespect for each other at which we have arrived after these seventy-three, now seventy-four, malignant years.

So, a year has gone, flown by, and what an incredible number of things have happened in Ukraine, in Kiev, in the USSR....

We have moved forward at an unbelievable rate, and much of what seemed unimaginable even a year ago has come true: the blue-and-yellow flags fluttering over our cities, democratic councils in western Ukraine*, the declaration of sovereignty, the accords between Russia and Ukraine. Political prisoners have become members of parliament.

At the same time, all these triumphs have failed to satisfy us; on the contrary, they have brought us overwhelming, all-consuming disappointment: the more you have, the more you want. We have all understood how far we still have to go to attain democracy, freedom of expression, freedom in general. And well-being? Now there's something quite unimaginable! This disappointment has laid a shadow across our whole life, on every conversation; it's in people's gestures and pantomime; it is within me: I feel it almost biologically, as something which is always just *there* and cannot be shaken off.

NOTES

1. See especially Francis Fukuyama, "The Modernizing Imperative: The USSR as an Ordinary Country," in Nikolas K. Gvosdev, ed., *The Strange Death of Soviet Communism: A Postscript* (New Brunswick, NJ: Transaction Publishers, 2008).
2. See Stephen Kotkin (with a contribution by Jan T. Gross), *Uncivil Society: 1989 and the Implosion of the Communist Establishment* (New York: Random House, 2009) and *Armageddon Averted: The Soviet Collapse, 1970–2000* (New York: Oxford University Press, 2001, revised edition, 2008). For Kotkin, "uncivil society"—the "Communist establishment"—connotes "party bosses and propagandists, secret policemen and military brass," whom he characterizes as "incompetent, blinkered, and ultimately bankrupt" (xiv). On the decisive contribution of opposition elites, see Krishan Kumar, *1989: Revolutionary Ideas and Ideals* (Minneapolis, MN: University of Minnesota Press, 2001). On the GDR's debt, see Jeffrey Kopstein, *The Politics of Economic Decline in East Germany, 1945–1989* (Chapel Hill, NC: University of North Carolina Press, 1997). While not ignoring the role of opposition movements, James F. Brown's *Surge to Freedom: The End of Communist Rule in Eastern Europe* (Durham, NC: Duke University Press, 1991), places even more emphasis on how Communist elites discredited themselves through bad government and economic failure. Elements of this argument—that is, Communism's fall as a disintegration of an indebted and illegitimate Communist establishment—can also be found in Daniel Chirot, "What Happened in Eastern Europe in 1989?," and Katherine Verdery, "What Was Socialism, and Why Did It Fall?," in Vladimir Tismaneanu, ed., *The Revolutions of 1989* (New York: Routledge, 1999).

---

* These democratically controlled councils were among the entities that sought to create "separate security forces" for Ukrainians. They also put pressure on Ukrainian conscripts to "undertake their military service in Ukraine," and fostered antagonism to all-Union Soviet Armed Forces and Moscow's rule more generally. In Western Ukraine, the democratic councils created municipal police forces that included a good number of Afghan veterans. Bruce Parrott, *State Building and Military Power in Russia and the New States of Eurasia* (Armonk, NY: M. E. Sharpe, 1995), 160–161.

3. Padraic Kenney, *A Carnival of Revolution: Central Europe, 1989* (Princeton, NJ: Princeton University Press, 2002); Charles Maier: *Dissolution: The Crisis of Communism and the End of East Germany* (Princeton, NJ: Princeton University Press, 1997), which argues for the "decisive accommodations" from the regime that "collective action" brought (xiv); for the influence of opposition movements such as Czechoslovakia's Charter 77 and Poland's Solidarity, see Gail Stokes, *The Walls Came Tumbling Down: The Collapse of Communism in Eastern Europe* (New York: Oxford University Press, 1993).

4. See, for example, Padraic Kenney's book, *1989: Democratic Revolutions at the Cold War's End: A Brief History with Documents* (Boston: Bedford/St.Martin's, 2010).

5. Anna Krylova, "The Tenacious Liberal Subject in Soviet Studies," *Kritika: Explorations in Russian and Eurasian History,* Vol. 1, no. 1 (2000): 119–146.

6. For example, Florian Henckel von Donnersmarck , *The Lives of Others* (*Das Leben der Anderen*) (Munich: Wiedemann and Berg, 2005), the award-winning film, produced by Quirin Berg and Max Wiedemann, about the Stasi's surveillance of East German society in the 1980s, has been criticized for oversimplifying East German society by overemphasizing victims of Stasi repression and underrepresenting the large percentage of the population who found accommodation with the regime. By implication, then, 1989 becomes oversimplified, too: to the joyous moment when the film's protagonist, a Stasi agent who wrote reports that covered up the dissident activities of the human objects of his surveillance, learns that the Berlin Wall has fallen. See Mary Beth Stein, "*Stasi* with a Human Face? Ambiguity in *Das Leben der Anderen*," *German Studies Review* 31, no. 3 (2008): 569.

7. Timothy Garton Ash, "1989!," *The New York Review of Books*, 5 November 1989.

8. Ibid.

9. Poles were aware of the events of 1989 in Chile, for example. See Jarle Simensen, "The Global Context of 1989," in Gerd-Rainer Horn and Padraic Kenney, *Transnational Moments of Change: Europe 1945, 1968, 1989* (Lanham, MD: Rowman and Littlefield, 2004), 167. The year 1989 in Chile brought watershed events that ended, or heralded the end of, Pinochet's repressive military dictatorship. On 30 June Chileans voted on a referendum in a national plebiscite to amend the Constitution of 1989. In December, in Chile's first presidential election in nineteen years, voters elected the Christian Democratic candidate, Patricio Aylwin.

10. Kenney, *Carnival of Revolution*, 251.

11. For these and many other examples of the Orange Alternative's activities, see Kenney, *Carnival of Revolution*; Bronislaw Misztal, "Between the State and Solidarity: One Movement, Two Interpretations—the Orange Alternative Movement in Poland," *The British Journal of Sociology*, 43, no. 1 (March 1992): 55–78; Sabrina P. Ramet, *Social Currents in Eastern Europe: The Sources and Consequences of the Great Transformation* (Durham, NC: Duke University Press, 1991), among other sources. There is also an extensive body of Polish-language scholarship, too large to cite here.

12. George E. Marcus, *Cultural Producers in Perilous States: Editing Events, Documenting Change* (Chicago: University of Chicago Press, 1997), 128.

13. I draw here on an argument advanced by Bronislaw Misztal in "Between State and Soldarity." See especially 58.

14. This date of birth is significant in that it made him part of Poland's last socialist generation—those, born between roughly the late 1950s and the early 1970s, who

were the last cohort to come of age—between roughly the mid-1970s and the mid-1980s—before the collapse of Communism. I adapt here Yurchak's concept of the "last Soviet generation." See *Everything Was Forever*, 31–32. As far as I know, no researcher has yet investigated the "particular understandings, meanings, and processes" that Poland's "last socialist generation" had in common. (31.)

15. Michael M. J. Fischer, *Emergent Forms of Life and the Anthropological Voice* (Durham, NC: Duke University Press, 2003), 249. Other centers of punk rock were (likely) Warsaw, Gdańsk, and Wrocław.

16. Portions of Fydrych's "Manifesto of Socialist Surrealism" are reprinted in Misztal, "Between the State and Solidarity," 61.

17. The first such dwarves were painted on 30–31 August 1982, in the Wrocław district of Biskupin and Sępólno.

18. In this, there were similarities between the "socialist surrealism" of Poland's Orange Alternative and the *stiob* of late Soviet rock 'n' roll.

19. Mistzal, "Between the State and Solidarity," 64.

20. Dates of the interviews are given in notes below. Most of the interviews took place in Wrocław. I thank Padraic Kenney for comments on an earlier version of this introduction and the annotations.

21. This is a point emphasized by Garton Ash in his provocative review essay, "1989!," *New York Review of Books*, 5 November 2009.

22. It should be noted, however, that New Forum was created in East Berlin, and that half of New Forum's supporters lived in East Berlin and nine nearby counties. Steven Pfaff, *Exit-Voice Dynamics and the Collapse of East Germany: The Crisis of Leninism and the Revolution of 1989* (Durham, NC: Duke University Press, 2006), 217.

23. On these demonstrations, see "Telegram from the Romanian Embassy in Berlin to the Ministry of Foreign Affairs Regarding Protests in East Berlin on the Anniversary of the GDR Calling for Following the Model of the Soviet Union and Liberalizing," sent 9 October 1989, 2:30 PM, available in AMFA, Berlin/ 1989, vol. 2, pp. 286–288, and in translation on the Web at http://wilsoncenter.org/index. cfm?topic_id=1409&fuseaction=va2.document&identifier=5034D57E-96B6-175-C-90AB89CFFA21225D&sort=Subject&item=Erich%20Honecker (accessed on 23 February 2010).

24. Interview with Bärbel Bohley, an artist and one of the founders of New Forum, in Dirk Philipsen, ed., *We Were the People: Voices from East Germany's Revolutionary Autumn of 1989* (Durham, NC: Duke University Press, 1992), 295.

25. Kotkin, *Uncivil Society*, 58.

26. I invoke here the title of Francine Hirsch's *Empire of Nations: Ethnographic Knowledge and the Making of the Soviet Union* (Ithaca, NY: Cornell University Press, 2005).

27. On the origins of the Yugoslav collapse following the years since Tito's death in 1980, see, *inter alia*, Sabrina Ramet, *Balkan Babel: The Disintegration of Yugoslavia from the Death of Tito to the Fall of Milošević*(4th ed.) (Boulder, CO: Westview Press, 2002). Dejan Jović's *Yugoslavia: A State that Withered Away* (West Lafayette, IN: Purdue University Press, 2008) offers a very useful overview of the various theories of why Yugoslavia collapsed. Other useful studies are Ivo Goldstein, *Croatia: A History* (Montreal: McGill-Queen's University Press, 1999) and his more recent book in Croatian, *Hrvatska, 1918–2008* (Zagreb: Novi liber, 2008); and Sabrina P. Ramet, *The Three Yugoslavias: State-Building and Legitimation, 1918–2005* (Bloomington, IN: Indiana University Press, 2006).

28. On decentralizing tendencies in the economy following the establishment of central economic planning in Belgrade, the federation's capital, see Bogdan Denitch, "The Evolution of Yugoslav Federalism," *Publius: The Journal of Federalism* 7, no. 4 (1977): 113.

29. In 1952, in consequence of the split between Stalin and Tito, the Communist Party of Yugoslavia changed its name to the League of Communists of Yugoslavia.

30. Mark Thompson, *Forging War: The Media in Serbia, Croatia, Bosnia and Herzegovina* (revised and expanded edition) (Luton, UK: University of Luton Press, 1999), 223.

31. Milošević revoked the autonomy of Kosovo and Vojvodina.

32. These purges began in 1990. By 1993, more than 130,000 Albanians in Kosovo had been purged. See Christina V. Balis, "De-Mystifying the Serbian Horse," *SAIS Review* 20, no. 1 (2000): 181.

33. Prior to establishing the news agency HINA, Šentija had been approached to be Minister of Foreign Affairs, a position he turned down. See Stipe Mesić, *The Demise of Yugoslavia: A Political Memoir* (Budapest: Central European University Press, 2004), 7.

34. HINA's headquarters are in Zagreb, but it also operates bureaus in Rijeka, Split and Osijek, and maintains a correspondent in Ljubljana (Slovenia). Fifty-five percent of HINA's budget comes fromé the state. Thompson, *Forging War*, 148.

35. Thompson, *Forging* War, 148; Mesić, 7.

36. See http://20years.tol.org/2009/10/26/laszlo-tokes/; on Tőkés's dissident activities in the 1980s, including his contributing to the *samizdat* journal *Ellenpontok* (*Counterpoints*), see Peter Siani-Davies, *The Romanian Revolution of December 1989* (Ithaca, NY: Cornell University Press, 2005), 29.

37. On the events of this week, see chapter 2 of Siani-Davies, *The Romanian Revolution*. Tőkés's role is discussed on 56–59.

38. Details are from Kotkin, *Uncivil Society*, 70–71.

39. On whether "revolution" is, in fact, an appropriate concept for the 1989 upheaval in Romania, see Peter Siani-Davies, "Romanian Revolution or Coup d'état? A Theoretical View of the Events of December, 1989," *Communist and Post-Communist Studies* 29, No. 4 (December 1996); 453–465, as well as his *The Romanian Revolution*.

40. These points about the possible causes and nature of Romania's 1989 Revolution are taken from Kotkin, *Uncivil Society*, 71. For more extensive analysis of the causes of the 1989 upheaval in Romania, see Siani-Davies, *The Romanian Revolution*.

CHAPTER 10

━━━★━━━

Taking Stock: Reckoning with Communism's Pasts

I n the German film *Goodbye Lenin!* (X Filme Creative Pool, 2003), the immediate post-1989 German present meets the pre-1989 past of the GDR in an
especially evocative way. They collide in Alex Kerner, the grown-up son, in his
early twenties, of an ailing mother whose heart attack and subsequent coma causes
her to miss out on the fall of the Berlin Wall and the collapse of East German
Communism. Ostensibly to shield his mother from the traumatic shock (and fatal
heart attack) that would befall her were she to learn, upon her post-November
1989 emergence from her coma, that the *Wende* had indeed occurred, he creates
an East German sanctuary in the bedroom to which she is confined. Everything
from the drab (but homey) domestic interior of her bedroom, to the food she
eats (suddenly hard-to-find GDR *Spreewald* pickles, for example), and the news
broadcasts she watches (performed and taped by Kerner and his friend) serve a
double purpose. All this not only prevents her from learning the truth. It also
helps Kerner cope with the trauma *he* has experienced as he grapples with his *own*
nostalgia about life in the GDR. Yet their GDR sanctuary is one in which memory
and forgetting combine to create an East Germany that *might* have existed. He
acknowledges, for example, "The GDR I created for her increasingly became the
one I might have wished for." Paradoxically, or perhaps predictably, a movie about
coming to terms with the Communist collapse became a capitalist success. More
than 1.8 people million went to see it in the first two weeks after it was released in
Germany.[1] They saw a movie that was not only provocative but also funny.

But *Goodbye Lenin!* grapples with a serious question: What has it meant for
people to reckon with the fall of Communist polities around the world? This is
not a question that has a single answer. This is a simple point, but one that bears
emphasis and deserves elaboration. Indeed, one of the most striking aspects of
post-1989/1991 history has been how many different answers there have been to

Locator Map for Chapter 10.

this question. Everyone from scholars, to journalists, to artists, to people who did not live in Communist polities and people who did, have debated not just the answers, but the underlying meaning of the core elements (Communism, its "fall" or equivalent, to "reckon with," for instance) of the question itself.

Perhaps the most contested part of the question has been the most fundamental: "Communism." The post-Communist present has brought an inexorable interrogation of what, in fact, Communism was and what it meant to live through it. By no means is it the case, as should by now be clear to readers of this book, that it was only after the 1989 Revolutions, and the Soviet collapse itself, that people asked, discussed, and debated such questions. Those questions, and the controversy that surrounded them, were alive and well during the Cold War itself; indeed, they are an essential, and fascinating, part of the history of the Cold War. But in a largely post-Communist age (largely, but not completely, as the recent Maoist government in Nepal, for example, attests), people from all walks of life have raised such questions from the vantage point of how, for the time being, the Communist story turned out. This is a mixed blessing. For as archives have opened up (only, in the Russian case, to close up in part once more), as memoirs of the Communist era have multiplied, as interviews never thought possible with former high-ranking Communist officials have indeed been undertaken, students of Communism have had to balance the deluge of information against the temptation to impose the knowledge of how the story ended on interpretations of earlier periods. If the Communist past can only be seen "through a glass darkly," what its students do have is this: a wealth of subjective perceptions, from the vantage point of hindsight, of what Communism was and how it operated. Illustrating one such perception, and a common one at that, is a selection herein by a historian in the former East Germany (Hartmut Zwahr). He indicts Communism, at least in its GDR variant, as a system whose essence was its chief effect: the destruction of the self, a destruction that had psychological, cultural, physical, and environmental dimensions.

As people have disagreed, sometimes vehemently, on the essence of Communism and on interpretations of the Communist past, so, too, have they ascribed deeply polarized meanings to the *symbols* of that past. All political systems have their symbols, but the symbolic legacy of Communism is especially rich. This is because of Communism's politicization of space and everyday life, and its creation of counter-rituals and counter-symbols to those of the capitalist system with which it was in ideological (and moral) battle. For some, especially younger people who were either born after Communism's fall or were not very old when it collapsed, Communism's symbols are a source of playful connection (if that!) to a past they did not directly make. Communist *kitsch* has become a thriving (or at least viable) business in Eastern Europe and Soviet successor states. But Poland has recently changed its criminal code to ban, with some exceptions (such as for artists and educators), the wearing of Communist symbols.[2] Donning a T-shirt picturing Ché Guevara—or Lenin, or Rosa Luxemburg, or Castro—can mean jail or a fine.

As these opposing stances on Communism's symbols remind us, addressing the question of what Communism *was* means defining the relationship of the individuals who lived and made Communism to how Communist polities functioned, both on an everyday basis and over the long haul. Were people (sometimes "we," sometimes "they," sometimes a mixture of both, depending on who is posing the question) victims or perpetrators of Communist repression, depredations, and self-destruction? Are these even the right concepts? How do we (or they?) know? One thing is for sure: Since Communist polities have collapsed, it has become common for people who lived in them to portray themselves as having been in opposition to Communism, a portrayal that others have questioned. Exemplifying how contested the post-Communist past has become, a Polish woman who joined Solidarity during its underground days of martial law puts it: "Just ten years after the change of system, myths are developing that say that the whole country was doing nothing else but fighting that awful Communist regime. That is nonsense... it isn't true that there was some kind of 'Them' and 'Us'—I mean a hardworking society that was fighting 'Them' with gritted teeth. 'They' were simply us, all of us. We, people who were active in the opposition, also belonged to that system in a certain sense."[3]

"Reckoning" with Communism's end has also meant asking the following question: What exactly *was* the "fall of Communism," anyway? This question is not as simple as it seems. Its complexity lies not just in the difficulty of forging consensus about which scholarly concepts—revolution, *coup état*, implosion, or something else—best fit the history of a given case.[4] It is also complex because an essential element of post-Communist history is the *variety* of subjective meanings that people have given to the fall of Communism: 1989 as a conspiracy, as a form of treason from which they have suffered;[5] 1989 as Francis Fukuyama's much-celebrated "end of history;" 1989 as the triumph over what former President Ronald Reagan called the "evil empire"—to give but a few examples. Another element of complexity lies in the formidable task of writing histories of "1989" that take into account such subjective meanings yet do not remain trapped within them.

No less complicated—and no less productive of a dizzying array of answers—is the question that is *implied* in the original query about what it means to reckon with the end of Communism: what has *followed* Communism, and how do we explain (and live in) what has come next? To break this question into smaller parts, what should the organizing frameworks be that help us make sense of what people went through as they moved from living in Communist polities that many thought would "last forever"[6] to living in polities where Communism as a political party, ideology, and civilization was utterly discredited? Black had become white, and white, black. For the case of East Europeans emerging from Communism into the brave new post-1989 world, the Polish sociologist Piotr Sztompka has suggested "cultural trauma" to capture the psychological effects of sudden and massive change.[7]

Cultural trauma happens, it is claimed, when members of a collective group (whether a nation, a generation, or some other unit) undergo a "horrendous event" that forever marks their identities, memories, and attitudes towards the future.[8] Certainly the concept itself is not beyond reproach. It is questionable whether a collectivity of any sort can undergo trauma, or whether the latter is something that individuals go through in different ways.[9] And the concept begs the question of just how horrendous an event, or a series thereof, has to be in order to produce trauma. Yet despite these limitations, the concept is useful, I believe, because it alerts us to the disorientation, experienced by an individual as part of social interaction with others, that accompanies even change that is not only wanted but also celebrated—as the collapse of Communist polities was. And it reminds us that this disorientation—the loss of identity produced by positive change—was something that people experienced at the same time as they confronted the horrors of Communist repression, the suffering it had caused them and their loved ones, and their own complicity in repressive acts. Certainly, if one wants to find it, the legacy of such cultural trauma is palpable in some of the selections presented in this chapter, such as that of the East German historian (Hartmut Zwahr) for whom the essence of East German Communism was self-destruction, or even for his fellow East German *apparatchik* (Manfred Uschner), who writes his personal history for the needs of his political career in a reunified Germany. It can also be detected in the final selection of the book, from the Italian Communist Nichi Vendola, who writes eloquently of his simultaneous loss of bearings and continuing search for "another possible world" after Communism's fall.

Connected to the question of how we might think of what people living through Communism went through after it ended is that of what has come next. Several of the documents speak to this issue: that of a philosophy student at a university in Bratislava, Slovakia, who worries about a new "totalitarian ideology" that threatens freedom and democracy in the post-Communist age; the reflections of the renowned Estonian poet, novelist, and essayist, Jaan Kaplinski, for whom global capitalism entails a new kind of self-colonization and looms as a "USSR through the back door"; and even that of Vendola, whose continued search for social justice leads him to keep hope alive for a "soft revolution." As evocative (and no doubt controversial) as these selections are, they do not, of course, exhaust the

Banner at outdoor exhibit, "Das Jahr 1989: Bilder einer Zeitenwende." ("The Year 1989: Images of a Historical Turning Point.") The exhibit was held on Berlin's Alexanderplatz (in what was formerly East Berlin) from 29 May to 30 August 2009. The picture on the banner shows East and West Germans sitting and standing on the part of the Berlin Wall that was in front of the Brandenburg Gate. This image, along with others depicting the fall of the Berlin wall, have attained the status of what Vicki Goldberg in *The Power of Photography: How Photographs Changed Our Lives* (1991) has called "secular icons"—images that "almost instantly acquired symbolic overtones and larger frames of reference that endowed them with national or even worldwide significance." (135.)

    This exhibit was part of a series of events held in Berlin to commemorate the twentieth anniversary of the "fall" of the Berlin Wall and the collapse of the Communist regime in East Germany. Numerous exhibits and conferences were held throughout Europe (and elsewhere) to debate and discuss the meaning of "1989." Photo by Glennys Young.

range of answers to the question "What has come next?" But they are nonetheless valuable because they raise important questions such as the following: What should we do about what has come next? Celebrate it? Enjoy it? Improve it? Resist it? And regarding the latter, what is possible, given the legacy of Communism? That is, for those wishing to engage in resistance, does the history of resistance to Communism offer a toolkit, or are its tools irrelevant to what has come next?

Entailed here, too, is the following question: What has it meant, historically and culturally, to "reckon"—or, depending on one's preference, come to terms with, attain closure with, or work through—the fall of Communism and what has come next? Whatever one calls it, the question is what the process has entailed, and how this has varied nationally, culturally, and individually. Films, literature, and plays that simultaneously narrate Communism's repression, suffering, and difficult choices, yet reduce the trauma into manageable images and fictional stories with closure, have, arguably, played an important, even therapeutic, role, in this regard.[10] It can also be to acknowledge the *lack* of closure, the failure "to alter the mindset" that has persisted from Communist pasts even as they recede in time and people distance themselves from them.[11] And whichever words one uses, the question is also what the results of these processes have been, individually and culturally. To write the history of the post-Communist present is to take stock of how dealing with the Communist past has, in Sztompka's words, generated a "mobilizing force for human agency," and has "stimulated creative social becoming."[12] Or not. Or something, at times, in between.

Manfred Uschner (1937–2007), a Former Assistant of the East German Communist Party's Central Committee Secretary, Writes His Communist Past for a Post-Communist Political Career

After the fall of Communism in East Germany that began in 1989, East Germans of all walks of life had to wrestle with issues of complicity with, and guilt regarding, the operations of the East German Communist regime. This was especially true for informers for the Stasi, or German secret police,[13] and for those who worked in the East German government and belonged to the East German Communist party, the Socialist Unity Party (SED, or Sozialistische Einheitspartei Deutschlands). Issues of complicity and guilt, in turn, related to a central challenge faced by East Germans after Communism: how to construct one's post-1989 political identity in relationship to one's political past in the GDR. These issues are palpable in the following excerpt from the memoirs of a Manfred Uschner, who rose from a humble working-class background to the upper echelons of the SED apparatus.

Uschner's political and scholarly career spanned the 1989 "divide." In 1968, he began his stint as a researcher in the Department of International Relations of the SED's Central Committee, serving for twenty years as the personal assistant of the Central Committee secretary, Hermann Axen*. On 20 February 1989, less than nine months before the collapse of the Berlin wall, the SED General Secretary,

From Manfred Uschner, *Die zweite Etage: Funktionsweise eines Machtapparates* (*The Second Floor: The Operation of a Power Structure*)(Berlin: Dietz Verlag, 1993), 28–32. Reprinted by permission of Dietz Verlag. Translation: Glennys Young.

* Hermann Axen (1916–1992), a survivor of Auschwitz, was East German Communist Party General Secretary Erich Honecker's closest advisor on foreign affairs. He was the highest ranking East German official and Communist Party member to make an official visit to the United States, where he met with then Secretary of State George P. Shultz in April 1988.

Erich Honecker[*], removed Uschner from the Central Committee. Honecker cited Uschner's political unreliability as a result of his close contact with Egon Bahr[†].

Uschner's memoirs—especially his explanation for why he worked in the upper echelons of the SED—must be read in the context of his political ambitions after 1989. After the collapse of East German Communism, Uschner tried to make a political career in the Social Democratic Party of Germany (SPD), formed in 1875 as Germany's first political party, and still a major player in German politics today.

This was not as abrupt a change, of course, from his service to East German Communism as it might seem. Through his work in the foreign affairs department of the SED's Central Committee, he had by the time of the *Wende*, developed close contacts with the West SPD. The West SPD, in fact, welcomed him. But this accommodation alarmed the East SPD, which identified Uschner as Axen's long-standing personal assistant. His post-1989 SPD careerist desires seem to have motivated how he characterized his career in the SED center of power: as a product of coercion, or at least manipulation. In the following excerpt, for example, he claims that he faced the brutal choice of either working for the SED or heading to the coal mines. He *portrays* himself as having been in "inner opposition," as having tried to keep the SED at bay as long as possible. So, too, the passage can be read as a simultaneous attempt to enhance his SPD credentials and minimize his SED connections by stressing his parents' proletarian SPD background and how they had been victimized by the Nazis and the Communists.

"THE THOUGHTS HURRY BACK"[‡]

Oh yes, my life path—the thoughts hurried far back, while the conversation continued.

---

[*] Erich Honecker (1912–1994), first secretary of the East German Communist Party, or SED (Socialist Unity Party, or, in German, Sozialistische Einheitspartei Deutschlands), was the leader of East Germany from 1971 (when he succeeded Walter Ulbricht) until his fall from power in the collapse of East German Communism in 1989. Other noteworthy positions he held in East Germany include his founding of the East German Communist Youth Organization (FDJ, Freie Deutsche Jugend, or Free German Youth), which he chaired from 1946–1955. In 1961, he was in charge of the construction of the Berlin Wall. Aging, ill, and adverse to reform, he was forced to resign in October 1989 and died in 1994 in Chile.

[†] Egon Bahr, who was born in 1922 in Thuringia, made hugely influential contributions to West German foreign and domestic policy during the Cold War. From 1969 to 1972, he served as the chief advisor on foreign policy to Willy Brandt, West Germany's first Chancellor from the Social Democratic Party (SPD). He functioned as Brandt's personal secretary to East Germany and the Soviet Union. In that capacity, he formulated, with Brandt, the West German foreign policy toward East Germany and the Soviet Union known as *Ostpolitik* (Eastern policy), whose hallmark was West German initiative for greater interaction, dialogue, and negotiation with the East. Bahr was the chief negotiator in what became the Moscow Treaty (12 August 1970), in which West Germany and the USSR renounced force in future dealings with each other. He was also central in the conclusion of the German Basic Treaty, signed on 21 December 1972, in East Berlin, which addressed unanswered questions left by the post–World War II division of Germany.

[‡] This "interrupts" a conversation that is taken up again later.

I was born on Whitsunday 1937 as the first of three children to a poor working-class family in Magdeburg—"Little London." The environment of my first childhood years was gloomy, narrow courtyards.

On 16 January 1945, when I was seven years old, I experienced, along with my sister, Hannelore, who was three years younger than I was, the heavy bombing of Magdeburg by the Americans and the British. At about a quarter to nine in the evening, when we were awoken in great haste by our grandmother and grandfather, the ceilings and the exterior walls of the house caved in. We found ourselves in the middle of a flaming inferno. Our grandmother was hit by a phosphorous bomb while rushing outside into the narrow backyard. She burned [to death], right before our very eyes and ears, only ten to fifteen meters away from us, crying, her loyal German shepherd jumping around her till the last moment. Our grandfather could do nothing; he pulled us children through the passageways and onto the main street and hurried back [to her]. In the chaos of the collapsing walls of the house I also lost my sister. I finaly met her again in a bomb crater on the bank of the ice-covered Elbe River in the vicinity of the Magdeburg Finance Administration. On the next day we made our way through Magdeburg, which was still burning, over mountains of burnt corpses. Magdeburg had lost about fifteen thousand citizens during the night. The shock lifted only when we had reached the home of our maternal grandparents on the other end of the city. For hours on end, we cried and raised a racket as the adults held us tightly.

This horrible experience has burned itself into us forever. I have never gotten over it. And it was the key for my becoming political, for my becoming politically active. It made me become, already in 1947, a member of the children's union of the FDJ and to become, in 1948, a young pioneer. As a child, at antifascist demonstrations on Magdeburg's Cathedral Square and in the "Crystal Palace," I exhorted the grownups, with a trembling voice, not to permit a new war and a new catastrophe.

In addition, my father and mother, who had already become members of the SPD at age sixteen and had experienced the worst years of unemployment, played a leading role in establishing the SPD in Magdeburg's Old City. I was often with them in the smoky Party premises, when representatives of the SPD and the KPD argued ferociously with one another. If there was a lot I still didn't understand, this way I of course became aware of the mutual insults.

At some time at the beginning of 1946, my father was called to appear in the Magdeburg Soviet Headquarters on the Fürstenwall. He was full of fear. As he subsequently told my mother, the KPD* chairperson from Magdeburg's Old City already sat there. It had been made clear to both of them that it was necessary for the Workers' Party to unify in order to prevent a new fascist development. In particular, my father and mother and their political friends had big problems with

---

* KPD: Communist Party of Germany (*Kommunistische Partei Deutschlands*). The KPD was an important political party from 1918–1933, during Germany's Weimar Republic. It also existed in West Germany until it was banned in 1956.

that and heated discussions, because the proportion in strength between the SPD*
and KPD in Magdeburg was 5:1. But in the final analysis, wasn't the decisive factor
that Magdeburg had been occupied since the summer of 1945 by Soviet troops?
In addition, my mother and father had experienced before 1933 how Nazis and
Communists together had chased and beaten them in assembly hall riots.

There were also vehement conflicts early in 1946 in Magdeburg Province, yet
the SED[†] was founded in April. My father gave up his small construction firm and
became acting second country secretary of the SED. He of course came out of the
SPD. Therefore the post of the first secretary remained temporarily vacant. His
reputation was, however, used, indeed misused, because already at the Thirteenth
Meeting of the SED Central Committee of 14 May 1953, as people were drawing
"Lessons from the Trial against the Slánský Conspiracy Center[‡]," he was expelled
from the Party on specious grounds. He lost all Party posts. His seat as deputy
to the People's Chamber was simply eliminated. What I discovered only in 1992
[was this]: it was my subsequent boss, H. Axen, who on 15 May 1953 brought the
Magdeburg SPD in "line," that had experienced the social democracy of Uschner.

I have never gotten over what was done to my father. He was an honest Social
Democrat, full of energy and always in restless service to the people. He was not
to outlive for long his rehabilitation in 1956. The expulsion of my father from the
Party, and the way it had been done, caused me for the first time to make my own
decision that ran counter to the preceding developments[§]; contrary to my father's
advice, who believed one had to differentiate between the ideal and individual
degenerate KPD functionaries, I held back for two years all the completed forms
for admission to be a candidate member of the SED. I never wanted to become
a doctor or an electrical engineer. But after Stalin's death in 1953, a few well-
intentioned teachers at my international high wanted to make up for the study

---

* Established in 1875 as one of the world's first socialist political parties, the SPD
(*Sozialdemokratische Partei Deutschlands*), like the KPD, played an important role in Weimar politics
from 1918–1933, when it was banned by Hitler. Reference here is to the SPD's fate in the Soviet Zone
of Occupation, out of which the German Democratic Republic or "East Germany" was formed.
There, as noted later, the Soviets forced the SPD's merger with the KPD.

† The SED (Sozialistische Einheitspartei Deutschlands) was formed out of the forced merger of
the SPD and KPD in the Soviet zone of occupation.

‡ This is a reference to one of the major actions taken at the 13th SED Plenum of 14 May 1953,
when that body removed Frank Dahlem, who, at the time, was perceived to be the only formidable
rival of Walter Ulbricht within the Party. The Plenum characterized its action as demonstrating the
"lessons of Slánskýism." This phrase called to mind the fate of the Czechoslovak Communist leader
Rudolf Slánský, who had been purged from the Party and executed for being an "Anglo-American
spy" in December 1952. For more on the measures taken at the plenum—including the raising of
industrial work norms that contributed to the uprising of 17 June 1953—see Christian F. Ostermann,
Charles S. Maier, and Malcolm Byrne, *Uprising in East Germany, 1953: The Cold War, the German
Question, and the First Major Upheaval Behind the Iron Curtain* (New York: Central European
University Press, 2003), 5.

§ Here he seems to be implying that his earlier joining of the Young Pioneers was not a decision
made from conscious reflection, but he is now liberating himself from conformist thinking.

program abroad that had been rescinded from me under pretexts: they recommended to a "Cadrehunter" who had hurriedly arrived from Potsdam-Babelsberg that I be matriculated at the Academy for Politics and Law for the first four-year course in Foreign Policy.

So I was now to become a diplomat. After four and a half years of study at the Academy's Institute for International Relations, I assumed, on 2 December 1959, my job as special assistant in the Ministry for Foreign Affairs.

On 18 January 1961 I was sent to Budapest as a special attaché. Budapest—this pulsing metropolis was like a dream. Unforgettable impressions are, for me, associated with this city, this country and its people. Yet I was soon ordered back by Party instructions to my old Institute. One saw the international recognition of the DDR dawning on the horizon, and I was supposed to accompany, as seminar instructor, considerably older cadres in the subject "History of International Relations since 1961."

During my student days I had heard, no less than three times, a philosophy lecture series, in other words, "dialectical and historical materialism": before the 20th Party Congress of the Communist Party of the USSR*, shortly after that, and towards the end of my studies. Always in a very different interpretation, with newly selected quotations, but always by the same professors. For almost all of us, this had left deep doubts about the "universality," about the scientifically lawful predictability, and the reliability of the "collective wisdom" of the Party. From then on, one no longer accepted everything uncritically, and almost religiously.

Now, however, I was to work in an institution that felt itself to be solely responsible for the "care and management of universality" and which was called, in whispered conversations among intellectuals, the "Central Department of Eternal Truths." . . .

My thoughts returned to the round of conversation in which I just now found myself. Half unconsciously, I became aware that the "Party" had already decided to place me for a few years in the field of practice, Praxis, or, in other words, in the Department of International Relations of the ZK†. There was no alternative for me. The leadership of my Institute had already been "convinced." I would not be allowed to return to the Institute. Later, however, it would be possible. During the conversation I was threatened several times to be sent to the coal mines‡. I would still be able, of course, to learn a lot at my new job. Moreover, I would get around a lot in the world and would be able, finally, to apply once again in a practical way what I had learned during my studies.

---

*This was the Party Congress at which Nikita Khrushchev delivered his "secret speech" about Stalin's crimes, launching de-Stalinization in the USSR and sending shockwaves throughout the Eastern Bloc.

†In a conversation with a superior, his mind has wandered back to an earlier time of his life (as the title of this section of his memoirs indicates). But now he realizes, subconsciously, and at the same time, the seriousness of the words spoken to him. This is a realization that brings him back to the conversation in which he is engaged. I am grateful to Christoph Giebel for this point.

‡He is probably implying that the only alternative for him was "labor reform."

So I finally gave in, though reluctantly, yet also not without opportunism. The path of the coal mines would surely have been more sincere, but, as relatives and friends suggested to me, one likewise had to take into consideration that such a long education should not go to waste.

What happened to me, happened as well to innumerable people in the history of the GDR. We were children of the GDR, [we] were fostered by it.

10-2

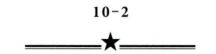

A Historian from the Former East Germany (Hartmut Zwahr, Born 1936) on Complicity, Responsibility, and Victimization

Manfred Uschner, the author of the previous passage, seeks to justify his service to the SED. But the author of the next passage, the East German historian Hartmut Zwahr, who until 2000 was Professor of Social and Economic History at the University of Leipzig, takes a different approach toward the East German past—and the big questions of guilt, complicity, and victimization. If Uschner paints himself as a victim of the DDR, and minimizes, to some extent, his own responsibility for the choices he made (such as to reject the more "sincere path" of working in the coal mines in favor of the easier way of serving the East German Communist Party), Zwahr goes in the other direction.

Not only does he emphasize his *own* complicity in the destruction of the self wrought by Communism in East Germany. He emphasizes the complicity of nearly everyone in East German society. Advancing a broad, indeed elastic, definition of complicity and responsibility, he insists that one could be complicit even if one was not in direct service of the Party (SED), working for the Stasi, or helping otherwise to perpetrate political repression. Being "complicit" entailed working at jobs that hurt the environment, sent cultural treasures to West Germany for precious West German currency, or helped to build substandard housing. He indicts not just how and where East Germans worked, but how and where they lived—that

From Hartmut Zwahr, *Ende einer Selbstzerstörung: Leipzig und die Revolution in der DDR (An End of a Self-Destruction: Leipzig and the East German Revolution)* Göttigen: Vandenhoeck and Ruprecht, 1993), 15–18. Published in English translation with the permission of Vandenhoeck and Ruprecht. Translation: Glennys Young.

they chose to reside in "Trabanten cities" (that is, bedroom communities with large apartment complexes, named for the flimsy East German car mentioned in a previous chapter) while historic city centers fell into disrepair. Hence, Zwahr expands the social, occupational, educational, and cultural identities of who was complicit. Having to earn a living, no matter how economically disadvantaged one was and no matter how restricted one's alternatives seemed to be, did not exempt one from the burdens of complicity. It should be noted that along with this expanded concept of complicity went an expanded concept of the political.

Zwahr's expansive concept of complicity bears a connection, if not necessarily a causal one, to the particulars of his scholarly career. He is an accomplished historian of East German labor; in fact, even the studies he had produced given the DDR's ideological constraints on historical interpretation were well-received in the West.[14] Since the *Wende*, Zwahr has continued his focus on labor and social history, contributing, for example, an important volume of his own diary notes on East Germans' (especially workers') response to Soviet suppression of the 1968 "Prague Spring" in Czechoslovakia.[15] He has also been a historian of the *Wende* itself, co-editing a volume (and producing a map) of the East German "peaceful revolution" in the region of Saxony.[16]

Given his scholarly achievements as a historian, it is not surprising that he offers, in the following passage, a historical perspective on East Germans' complicity in their own self-destruction, placing the East German past in relationship to the Nazi period against which the GDR defined itself. For Zwahr, what made this complicity possible was the creation of a certain personality type—diligent, intolerant, conformist, uncritical, and authoritarian—during the Nazi period of 1933–1945. Another point to be made about this passage, then, is that he refuses a simplistic, one dimensional characterization of East Germans. Though he goes further than Uschner in recognizing his and his fellow citizens' complicity in "self-destruction," he also, by emphasizing the historical and structural roots of this complicity, in effect acknowledges their lack of agency, and victimization. That is, East Germans produced a system that denied themselves, as he puts it, their own "free will." Hence, Zwahr emphasizes the hybrid identities of East Germans as *both* agents and victims of their own destructive choices.

We have all moved and established ourselves in the structures of the closed society. Not least there are those who have been accessory through nothing other than their work—a casualty of the Chain of Command*, which weighed on them,

---

* In German, "Die Weisungspyramide." Zwahr's original text cites the following as examples: Lutz Rathenow, "Symptome einer Krankheit. Das Post-DDR-Syndrom oder die verfaulte Vernunft," ("Symptoms of an Illness: The Post-East German Syndrome, or the Rottenness of Reason," *Die Tageszeitung*, 23 June 1990; Jens Reich, "Nation mit schlechtem Gewissen. Selbstreflexionen eines Mitschuldigen," ("A Nation with a Bad Conscience: Self-Reflections of an Accomplice,")) in *Die Tageszeitung*, 4 July 1990; Konrad Weiß, "Von 'Musterbürgern' und verpaßten Chancen. Inteview mit dem DDR-Bürgerrechtler und Regisseur Konrad Weiß ('Demokratie jetzt'),)" ("Concerning 'Model Citizens' and Missed Opportunities: An Interview with the East German Civil Liberties Activist and Director Konrad Weiß ['Democracy Now']) *Frankfurter Rundschau*, 6 June 1990.

[a pyramid] at whose top was the First Man* of the GDR. There were hundreds of thousands who were the last ones† to carry out the directives and orders. Many were stuck in the pressures of self-destruction, such as the tractor driver who regularly let the manure from a large livestock plant flow out of a tank truck into the Elbe [River]. For that he was paid. The worker, who participated in brown coal decomposition and dug out the pavement stones of historic streets, knew that they would be exchanged for West German Marks [D-Marks]. Many educated people let it happen that, right under their eyes, art treasures, valuable old books, and duplicates‡ from library collections were used to obtain foreign currency. Work under such pressures lost its meaning. City planners knew about the destructive effect of constructing buildings with prefabricated plates, about the summary power of huge construction firms that razed the historical quarters of cities in order to make the way free for an erection crane and a concrete plate. Usually the workers did not ask why, as long as their pay was right. Tens of thousands of people lived in the Trabanten cities§ and watched how the historic city centers, which they had left, became more and more uninhabitable and went to ruin. By 1989/1990, one out of ten apartments in buildings in the historic city centers in the GDR had such serious defects and damages that they should have been at least partly closed. About 20 percent of all old buildings were damaged; out of approximately forty-eight thousand free-standing buildings that were protected as historical monuments, a quarter were considered to be in extreme jeopardy. A part of them still are today. After the rent controls that were introduced in 1955, the rents still only covered 36 percent of the costs that would have had to be applied to their upkeep.

Holding onto power at any price also destroyed the natural environment on a catastrophic scale. Examples of this are the central German industrial districts. Places like Borna, Espenhain, and Bitterfeld, the "dirtiest city of Europe," lay as "smoking monsters" in an ecological disaster area. The painting by Wolfgang Mattheuer, "Friendly Visit to the Brown Coal District" (1974)¶ takes up this reality and combines it with the political staging of a delegation that grants honors to a symbol of the contradiction between existence and appearance in the GDR. Like no other did Mattheuer as a painter and graphic artist preserve in symbols the mental states of people in the GDR—for example, in the portrait "Behind the Seven Mountains" (1973)**—something of the westward-directed yearning for a

---

* I assume this is a reference to the leader of the SED, Walter Ulbricht, and, later, Erich Honecker.

† In the command pyramid, that is.

‡ Here, "duplicate" means that a library has two items of exactly the same book.

§ "Trabanten city," or, in German, "Trabantenstadt," is an expression for the outskirts of big cities, with high buildings that all look alike. These are places from which residents commute to work, and in which they do not form close social bonds. The term is used with respect to Germany as a whole, not just East Germany. An English equivalent would be the oxymoron "bedroom community."

¶ In German, the name of this photograph was "Freundlicher Besuch im Braunkohlenrevier."

** "Hinter den sieben Bergen" (1973).

better life, a yearning that had to be downright pushed away from the reality of the GDR. *"From Borna come heat and light,/however, what is in the air we do not see*** " (Banner at the "Monday demonstration[†]" on 30 October, 1989 in Leipzig). Billions will be sucked away in the decontamination of the uranium mining regions contaminated by radiation in the south of the GDR. A shepherd from the highly contaminated area south of Leipzig asks: "Who thinks even once about us? About our health, from which, everyday, [we lose a piece that we can never get back?" Industrial firms have allowed [water with] harmful chemical elements [to flow into] in the Elbe [River] or its tributaries. This environmental scandal has been known at least since Greenpeace detected "the dirtiest river of Europe" on a four week journey from the German-Czech border to Cuxhaven. The indescribable condition of public and technical scientific libraries in Saxony, a state with an old library tradition, has also attested to the loss of cultural valuables.

The "dismissal of reality[‡]"—both through the Politburo members and other members of the inner circle of power and also in the "Apparatus"—drove people to intolerance and political violence against those who thought differently, to lying and adaptation and shameless sharing in privileges, to a fractured consciousness and speechlessness behind the mask and the muzzle in which they function. A lone person, who stands for many, confesses that "the practices of the Stasi left deep wounds in him." A consequence of state self-destruction was also the intolerance, indeed hostility, against those who thought differently, which broke forth in the mass call and mass singing "Reds out of the Demo" [*Demonstration*] in Leipzig. In the GDR, the national educational system tried to form a new kind of person[§]—an authoritarian one—and went far towards actually forming [one]. The functionary of developed socialism was to be a combination of work diligence, [of] being uncritical, and [of] being easily satisfied. He rarely experienced tolerance towards himself. And he acted according to the law "An Eye for an Eye," about which Martin Luther King said that it makes both parties blind. Superintendent[¶] Magirius of the St. Nikolai Church in Leipzig first articulated the problem: "Broken houses can be repaired, [can be] looked after with paint and a new roof." It is a different thing with people "who are so narrowly brought up that they have never found their way to their own point of view because in school they only experienced schooling, but not their own thinking, their own decision making, [never] practiced their own responsibility. I think

---

* The German rhymes: "Von Borna kommen Wärme und Licht,/doch was in der Luft ist, sehen wir nicht."

† In German, "Montagsdemo." In other words, this was one of the demonstrations held after the Monday evening peace prayers in St. Nikolai Church. See also document 5 in chapter 5.

‡ In German, "Abschaffung" means that one is ignoring reality on purpose, thereby abolishing it.

§ This is a reference to socialism and Communism's attempt to form the "new person."

¶ This is a position in the Protestant Church.

This image is a still from the filming of "Journey Home" (Réka Pigniczky, 2006). One of the many films made in the post-socialist present about the socialist past, the film chronicles the emotional journey of two daughters whose father, they believe, was a Hungarian freedom fighter who had emigrated through Yugoslavia to the United States. They return to Hungary fifty years after the Hungarian Revolution of 1956 in order to fulfill László Pigniczky's dying wish to have his remains buried in his homeland. As they take their father's remains on his last journey home, they encounter surprises that change their understanding of him, and of themselves. Their dialogue with their father's past—and the past of a nation—takes them to archives, to offices of historians, and to the streets their father once walked.   Used with the permission of Réka Pigniczky.

that is the greatest damage that we have sustained." As a pastor he feared new bogeymen.

To live never again in a closed society, to never again have to be exposed to its pressures! In the GDR there was a Party administrative system with its own unique foundations. It humiliated almost everyone because it took away almost everyone's free will. This system originated in the first decade after the war. Men and women from the opposition stood next to Communist cadres and supported the system along with young people who were filled with the thinking of rectification and whom the change in ideology—which they carried out—motivated. Among them were many accomplices of National Socialism, people seduced by it, fellow travelers. Often they had already been brought up in an authoritarian way in the home of their parents. Then later they had behaved automatically in an authoritarian way with people as grammar school pupils, as Hitler youth or as girls in BDM*, in labor service† as soldiers. Those were the premises under which the black shadows of Stalin and Stalinism, which fell on anti-fascism, could be asserted to be a wealth of light. Perhaps the Party-administrative system could reach its size only with these "young people" of the postwar years, who had been shaped in this manner, and the youth they were in charge of for decades, often until the end of the GDR. It [the Party administrative system] supported itself through the HJ‡-Generation's—and everyone who was disciplined by it—readiness for obedience, which permitted the self-destruction of a country to last so long.

10–3

A Philosophy Student in Bratislava, Slovakia on the Spectre of a New "Totalitarian Ideology" in the Post-Communist Age

I n the following passage, a young Slovak, then (in 2007) a thirty-one-year-old philosophy student at Bratislava's Comenius University, offers an insightful meditation on the legacy of Communism's collapse. Though grounded in the

---

* BDM: Bund Deutscher Mädel, or German Girl's League. It was one of the two Hitler youth organizations for girls created in 1928. (Its original name was the "Schwesternschaften der Hitler Jugend," or "Nurse Teams of Hitler Youth"; it became the BDM in July 1930.) It was for girls between the ages of fourteen and eighteen. The other Hitler youth organization for girls, the JMB (*Jungmadelbund*, or Young Girl's League), was to enroll those between ten and fourteen years of age. Membership in the BDM was voluntary until 1 December 1936, when the Hitler Youth Law was ratified. Jean-Denis G. G. Lepage, *Hitler Youth, 1922–1945: An Illustrated History* (Jefferson, NC: McFarland & Company, 2008), 37; Volker Berghahn, *Modern Germany: Society, Economy and Politics in the Twentieth Century,* 2nd ed. (New York: Cambridge University Press, 1987), 134. An important English-language study, recently translated from German, that includes the BDM is Dagmar Reese, *Growing Up Female in Nazi Germany* (Ann Arbor: University of Michigan Press, 2008). There is also a recent German-language study of the BDM: Gisela Miller-Kipp, *"Der Führer braucht mich": der Bund Deutscher Mädel (BDM): Lebenserinnerungen und Erinnerungsdiskurs* ("*The leader needs me": The League of German Girls [BDM]: Memoirs and Memory Discourse*) (Weinheim: Juventa Verlag GmbH, 2007).

† The German word here is "Arbeitsdienst," which can also be translated as "labor battalion." "Labor service" (Arbeitsdienst) was obligatory for males in Hitler's Nazi Germany when they reached their eighteenth birthday.

‡ HJ: Hitler Jugend or, in English, Hitler Youth.

author's recollections of what was to be called in the Czech Republic the "Velvet Revolution," and what was in Slovakia called the "Gentle Revolution,"[17] the passage makes important points about Eastern European—and, indeed, world, history since the 1989 Revolutions.

He emphasizes, for example, that 1989 was not the *culmination* of the battle for freedom and democracy. This might seem obvious now, but at the time, that is how many people—not just the Francis Fukuyamas* of the world but people like this then thirteen-year-old Slovak—experienced 1989. He also makes the fundamental point that Communism is not the only source of what the author calls "totalitarian ideology." In the (largely) post-Communist age, threats of a new, non-Communist "totalitarian ideology" exist in the form of intolerance and conformist thinking that emanates from corporate control of the media. Loss of critical capacities—and one's psychological, intellectual, and spiritual bearings (because of the *abundance* of information)—-is a threat to democracy and freedom not only in formerly Communist polities but in the world as a whole.

This passage is not just a diagnosis of the ills of the post-modernist, post-Communist age, but a call to action. It is a summons not just to Slovaks, but also to world citizens more generally, to be vigilant about recognizing new threats to critical thinking. And it is a call to battle against those threats, lest they would imperil, beyond salvation, "freedom" and "democracy."

"17 NOVEMBER[†] OPENED THE WORLD TO US"
BY JAROMÍR SALAJ

I took notice of the Gentle Revolution and the events that followed it quite well for my age. I was thirteen. Like others, I enjoyed an uncertain atmosphere, but with a welcome relaxation. And I also got a good feeling that all of a sudden it was permissible to speak "out loud."

Originally published in *Pravda* (Bratislava), 16 November 2006, 17. Published in English translation with the permission of *Pravda* (Bratislava). Translation and some annotations: Scott Brown.

---

* In 1989, in a famous essay published in *The National Interest*, Fukuyama identified the "universalization of Western liberal democracy as the final form of human government" and as the "end point of mankind's ideological evolution." (*The National Interest* 16 [Summer 1989]: 4.) See also his 1992 book, *The End of History and the Last Man* (New York: Free Press, 1992).

† The author refers here to 17 November 1989, the date that is conventionally given as the beginning of what would in Czech be called the "Velvet Revolution" (*Sametová revoluce*) and in Slovak the "Gentle Revolution" (*nežná revolúcia*). That day, on which peaceful student demonstrators (observing "International Students Day") were beaten by riot police, marked the beginning of a growing wave of protests that, by 28 November, culminated in the Czechoslovak Communist Party's relinquishing of its monopoly on political power. By 19 December, President Gustáv Husák, the Communist leader, resigned and named Czechoslovakia's first non-Communist government since 1948. On 29 December 1989—four days after the televised execution of Ceaușescu and his wife Elena in Romania—Václav Havel became president of a non-Communist Czechoslovakia. The "Velvet" or "Gentle" Revolution ended when students called off their strike.

Many years later I've already digested the first fruits of the revolutionary changes. I enrolled in a college of my own choosing and on vacations during my studies I've traveled through almost all of Europe. The world opened to us and it seemed that no barriers existed except for those that we carry within ourselves.

For a long time the liquidation of borders became synonymous with the revolution for me. These changes seem more complicated to me today, but the slogans of the Gentle Revolution haven't lost any of their relevance. Quite the contrary. If it seemed at times that the battle for freedom and democracy culminated in 1989, I'm convinced now that it's only a convenient self-delusion. Totalitarian ideology has many forms and the battle against it demands unceasing effort.

Even today there are those who try to convince us that there is only one way, a universally applicable lifestyle and worldview. Perhaps they will want to erect new

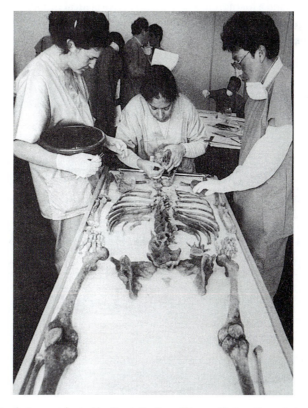

An exhumation being conducted by Peru's Truth and Reconciliation Commission, which was established by the Peruvian Congress on 28 August 2003. In its investigation of the violence that wracked Peru from 1980 to 2000, the Truth and Reconciliation Commission (CVR) conducted exhumations of 4,600 mass or common graves (*fosas comunes*) in sites where massacres had occurred. Photo by Gilmar Pérez.

borders and fences. And similarly sometimes they might be unable to resist label-
ing those with whom they disagree as public enemies.

Another thing that will hamper the situation for us is how much our life has
changed after seventeen years. We live in a closely monitored society of media,
regimented consumption, credit cards and mobile telephones. The word freedom
is gaining new meaning today and it will be necessary to grapple with this. The
same is true of democracy. At a time when public consent is manufactured just like
any other product, it is hard to prevent the creative confrontation of ideas from
being reduced to a contest between ad agencies.

Behind all these complications stands one important, even decisive post-
revolutionary change. A society that suffered for many years from a lack of information became, almost overnight, a society with an abundance of information.
It is practically impossible for most people to get their bearings in this deluge of
contradictory facts. Orwellian "doublespeak" (double thinking) is ubiquitous and
leads to a lack of clarity and resignation.

It will demand a lot of time and effort to revive critical thinking in such a situation. Perhaps more than anyone realizes. But it will be unavoidable if we still long
for the words freedom and democracy not to belong only to the world of myths.

(The author studies philosophy at Comenius University in Bratislava.)

10–4

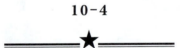

An Estonian Writer, Poet, and Politician*, Jaan Kaplinski (Born 1941), on Global Capitalism as a New "Soviet Union"

Jaan Kaplinski, the author of the passage that follows, is a major figure of
Estonian letters, a writer who has gained international acclaim for his
poems, novels, and essays. He grew up in Tartu, a city with one of the most

---

Reprinted from http://jaan.kaplinski.com/opinions/fromthebackdoor/html (accessed 24 August 2009).
Published with the permission of Jaan Kaplinski. Punctuation and spelling left as in the original text.

---

* From 1992 to 1995 he served as a member of the Estonian Parliament.

important universities in Estonia. In fact, Kaplinski graduated from the University of Tartu with a degree in French philology in 1966. Two years later, by the time he was twenty-seven years old, he had written three important collections of poems, and had been awarded the Juhan Liiv poetry prize. Already in the 1960s, Kaplinski was well-known in Estonian households, and his poetry was beginning to draw attention in the West. But it was not until the mid-1980s, with Gorbachev's reforms, that his poetry was actually translated into English, as well as thirteen other languages.[18]

Even when he was in his early twenties, Kaplinski wrote poetry that incorporated diverse philosophical, artistic, mystical, and spiritual approaches. Among the philosophical currents upon which he was drawing were the those of the Taoists, in particular Zhuangzi and Laozi, as well as Mayahana and Zen Buddhists, especially D. T. Suzuki and Alan Watts. Western philosophers who influenced him included Ludwig Wittgenstein and Bertrand Russell. He was also in dialogue with the work of Fritz Mauthner, Gunnar Ekelöf, T. S. Eliot, and Tomas Tranströmer, as well as with the values of American Indian culture and the non-Christian animism of early Estonian culture.[19]

Kaplinski's prolific literary production has also been shaped by his dual identity as an Estonian with a Polish-Jewish background, and by the tortured history of his country as it was refracted in his personal history. He has recognized his bond with "two cultures that were not given a chance to develop fully, strangled and destroyed by the Western and eastern imperialists [...] As the Jews are mourning over the destruction of their temple [...] the Estonians, Finns, Samis, Samoyeds, Maris and others can mourn over the destruction of their sacred groves, trees, and lakes." He calls these "two fatal identities."[20] Estonian identity indeed proved fatal for his father, whom the Soviets arrested and killed during the first Soviet occupation of Estonia in 1940–1941. Indeed, his literary work both before and after 1991 is concerned not only with the colonial experience of Estonia under Soviet occupation, but also with Estonia's future in relationship to a new global order.[21]

The nature of the global order (or disorder!) that has emerged since 1991, not only in Estonia but throughout the world, is the theme of this passage, taken from his essay, "USSR From the Back Door." Though writing in a post-colonialist Estonia, one that has attained national liberation from Soviet occupation, Kaplinski's anxiety is focused upon what he perceives as a new colonialism, one in which global capitalism, defined by the power of "mega-companies" that dominate global markets, involve the people of the world in their own self-colonization. This he calls a "USSR from the back door."

"USSR FROM THE BACK DOOR"

Our time seems to be the time of fusions of big companies. News of such fusions and megafusions reach us more or less once per week. The stock market reacts to these news with enthusiasm, the public opinion seems to be somehow confused and concerned. The situation is unprecedented in several aspects. The mega-companies are gaining more and more power, their economic potential nullifies the political power of small and medium-size states. It means that new power centres are emerging that are outside the control by democratic mechanisms. Instead of strengthening of the democracy in the world we are witnessing its downgrading. As there are less and less big firms, important changes are about to occur in the market regulation. The statistical rules of competition that allowed the consumer to control the producer to some degree are not effective any more. It becomes more and more difficult to avoid the rise of monopolies, cartels and dividing of the markets between the megacompanies.

Something has decisively changed in the psychological climate of the economy. The competition has become struggle where less and less attention is paid to the choice of means. It is a struggle for life and death: the aim is no more maximizing profits but getting rid of the enemy, either by liquidating it or swallowing it: for the loser it's nearly the same. The number of players in the big business is decreasing rapidly.

The victorious megacompanies as Microsoft, Coca-Cola, McDonalds or Boeing can often ignore both the market rules and laws. Their financial power is sufficient to kill any potential competitor. And the legislators are more dependent on them than they on the legislators. The competition between companies is being replaced by the competition between the nations for the favours of big companies, for their investment. A nation that takes steps against the interests of Microsoft, Coke or McDonalds sooner or later end[s] up in financial difficulties and sooner or later their government is replaced by one that pays more attention to the interests of the big business. The times when megacompanies toppled and installed governments, organizing coups with the help of armed groups, are over. Nowadays the capital has in its hands more powerful weapons that can bring even the governments of big nations to their knees. The aggressive takeover of Mannesmann by Vodafone against the will of the German government, and probably also of the German people shows us what are the forces who are now endangering the German democracy. These forces have a different origin than the Nazi-ism that once destroyed democracy, however, their impact can be similar.

We can find many similarities between the propaganda techniques worked out and used by the Nazis and the advertizing [sic] techniques used by the present rulers of the world. But these techniques have also parallels with the Soviet propaganda. A former Soviet citizen can easily notice how the Party agitprop that had such a central role in the mass media has now been replaced by an agitprop by big companies, their advertizing. In the place of Communism that was the name of our happy future, we now see the slogans, logos and flashes of cosmetics firms, whiskey sellers, sanitary towels makers, toothpaste manufacturers and travel agencies that display much more ingenuity and technical skill. Still the basic message of both the Communist Party and the big firms is the same: believe in us and do what we teach you to do, and you will be happy. This message is of course not an original one, both Communist propaganda and the Coca-Cola company have borrowed it from the Christian gospels. Communism and Consumerism are two secular sects, originating in Christianity. As the former one is now vanishing from the world scene, the latter is enjoying an unprecedented success, conquering one nation and one continent after another and subjecting even the religion itself to its interests.

What is the result of this globalization and concentration process? A former Soviet citizen already has a name for the coming New Brave World. He or she will call it Soviet Union, the second coming of the Soviet Union. Indeed, the world seems to be moving in the direction that was taken by the Soviet Union before its fall. In the USSR, the economy was run by some monopolies fused with the state and the Party and on whose production and its prices the people had no control. This amalgamated power dictated the people its way of life and consumption. Criticizing the power was a harshly punished crime. There was no middle class in the USSR, only executives of one huge corporation and the proletarian masses under their authority. In the USSR the main task of the press was to advertize the state, its monopolies and its ideology, there was no free press. How long will there be a free press in this new brave world?, thinks the former Soviet citizen. Probably until the megacompanies have gained control over main papers, TV channels and the Internet. But the process is going on, and the time when a group of magnates

1 May has been one of the major holidays in the Communist world. It is International Workers' Day, and celebrates the heroic struggle of laborers around the globe. In the successor states of the Soviet Union and Eastern Europe, Communist May Day is no more. But here, Maoists—hundreds of thousands of them, in fact—own the streets in Nepal's capital, Kathmandu. So proceeded May Day, in Nepal—2010. Source: On-line newsletter: "Revolution in South Asia: An International Project," available at http://southasiarev.files.wordpress.com/2010/05/kathman. Photo by Jed Brandt.

will have in their hands the finances, the industry, the communication and information, the time when a journalist will no more be able to publish critical materials about Microsoft, Coca-Cola, MacDonalds or the Rupert Murdoch empire, is approaching at a fast pace.

Is it inavoidable [*sic*]? Can't we do something to oppose such a development?, asks the former Soviet citizen. He or she sees that most people around him or her, especially in the former East dont ask such questions. It seems as if the people have become smaller, resigned, are doing what the new rulers of the world are expecting them to do. Where are the rebels, the dissidents?—asks the former Soviet citizen. Aren't there really any forces capable of stopping this second coming of the USSR from the back door?

10–5

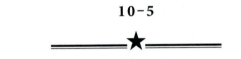

An Italian Communist (Nicola Vendola, Born 1958) on the Pre-1991 Communism of His Youth, and the Post-1991 Communism of His "Maturity"

His Continuing Search for "Another Possible World"

In the decades since 1991, as people have reckoned with the Communist past, a particular challenge has fallen on those who called themselves "Eurocommunists." Eurocommunism developed in the 1970s and 1980s as some Communist parties in Western Europe created an ideology and set of political strategies that were both crafted for parties operating within European democracies and distinguished by some independence from the Soviet Union.[22] Organizationally, a major landmark in Eurocommunism's emergence was a

---

Nichi Vendola, *Soggetti Smarriti: La sfida di un altro mondo possibile* (*Lost subjects: The challenge of another possible world*), 3rd ed.., rev. (Rome: Datanews Editrice, 2005). Published with the permission of DATANEWS Editrice, Rome. Translation and annotations: Mary R. O'Neil.

1977 meeting in Madrid between the Italian Communist Party's (PCI) Enrico Berlinger, the Communist Party of Spain's (PCE) Santiago Carrillo, and the French Communist Party's (PCF) Georges Marchais. Carillo's *Eurocommunism and the State* would turn out to be the manifesto of a movement whose commitment to democracy and independence was, in part, generated by disillusionment with Soviet repression of the Prague Spring. Eurocommunism's orgins, political strategies, and political results varied from country to country.

One Italian Eurocommunist was Nicola Vendola, the author of the passage that follows. Still an active politician on the Italian left, Vendola was the first openly gay member of the Italian Communist Party (PCI). As such, he exemplified Eurocommunism's shaping by, and commitment to, social issues such as feminism and the gay movement.

Vendola's personal practice of Eurocommunism bore the imprint of his southern Italian roots. He was born in 1958 in Bari, into a family that was both Catholic and Communist. The evolution of his first name reflects this synthesis: named for Saint Nicholas, the patron saint of Bari, his name was abbreviated early on to Nichi, after Nikita Khrushchev, then head of the USSR. In his childhood home "there were two large portraits that hung next to each other: Yuri Gagarin [the Soviet astronaut] and Pope John XXIII."[23] In this passage, Vendola evokes his experience of how Catholicism and leftist politics meshed in the communitarian values of the Italian south.

Vendola became active in the world of the Italian Communist Party at an early age. When he was fourteen, he joined the Italian Communist Youth Federation. He would belong to the Italian Communist Party until its dissolution in 1991, following the fall of the Soviet Union. As Vendola underscores, the intellectual exploration that began in his teenage years and would continue through his young adulthood (and no doubt beyond) was part of his personal construction of what being a Communist meant. He earned a literature degree from the University of Bari with a thesis on Pier Paolo Pasolini, a famous post-war Italian writer and filmmaker whose artistic work was marked both by his leftist politics and his homosexuality. Vendola then wrote for the Italian Communist newspaper, *L'Unità*. He also founded Arcigay, the first Italian organization for the rights of gay people. As a committed Communist, he opposed the breakup of the PCI and became a founding member of a new Party for Communist Refoundation in 1991. He was elected to the Italian Chamber of Deputies in 1992, where, as a member of the Anti-Mafia Commission, he battled the chronic problem of organized crime. In 2005 he was elected President of his native region of Puglia (the heel of the boot), a victory that came as a surprise to many because of his sexual orientation and the generally conservative nature of southern Italian society. In 2009, Vendola was defeated in an internal election for the leadership of the Communist Refoundation. Continuing his quest for social justice, he then founded a new party called the Movement for the Left, which stresses ecological together with other social and political issues.

The following passages, taken from Vendola's memoir, *Lost Subects: The Challenge of Another Possible World*, evoke the way he, as a committed Italian Eurocommunist, experienced the cultural trauma brought by the Soviet collapse. Even though the PCI had distanced itself from the Communist Party of the Soviet Union, the collapse of 1991 nonetheless brought serious soul search-ing for Eurocommunists such as Vendola. As Vendola puts it, he was "wounded." He lays out what the process of reckoning has meant for him, and what he thinks it must entail for others. For Vendola, the resolution of this reckoning has been a continued commitment to Communism, a "return to the journey," one in which its writing of its "new history" seems to entail, in its search for a "soft democracy that spreads from procedure to feeling," a return to the Communism of his youth in Terlizzi.

THE OLD AND THE YOUNG

I was born in Terlizzi, a land of flowers and olives, thirty kilometers from Bari, nine from the sea. The thousand year old Norman tower, in whose shadows I participated in scores of rallies, faces on the central piazza; crouched behind it is a tangle of narrow streets in the Arab style. It is a town that retains a certain bloody feudal charm, surrounded by the noble, well arranged palaces of the eighteenth and nineteenth centuries.

While still in short pants, I encountered Communism among the manual laborers and old comrades of Terlizzi. It was a poor, clean Communism, filled with a popular ethos and fed by legend. It was the simplicity (at times heroic) of calling each other comrade, not only to break bread together, but also to break down the ancient hierarchies of oppression. Communism was Giuseppe Di Vittorio*, who taught the landless not to remove their hats in the presence of a landlord. Certainly this is a topos of Communist rhetoric, but also an elementary and defiant gesture of "intellectual autonomy," the proud act of a critical distancing from those centu-ries old relationships of dominion founded both on paternalism and on the idea of the natural superiority of those who have and can act (while those who have not and cannot will never have or be able, or at most will be able to dream of having the same things and acting in the same manner as their masters [*padroni*]).

Communism was my father and my uncle Vito, representatives of that graft-ing between subaltern classes and an educated, committed *piccola borghesia*†. In particular my father freed himself from youthful fascist suggestions and drew closer to Communist ideals, reading novels by Jack London and A.J. Cronin, but also confronting the terrible disaster of World War II, whose vortex had swallowed his twenty year old brother. (Of Uncle Enzo, there is only a plaque on a cypress in the cemetery.)

---

* Giuseppe Di Vittorio (1892–1957) came from a family of agricultural day laborers in Puglia (the heel of the boot). He was active in trade union and socialist movements before joining the PCI (Italian Communist Party). Sentenced on political charges under Mussolini, he fled first to France, then to Russia, and fought in the Spanish Civil War. After World War II he was the head of both the CGIL (Italian General Confederation of Labor) and the World Federation of Trade Unions.

† *Petit-bourgeoisie* or lower middle class, especially small shopkeepers.

At eight years of age, I met Pietro Ingrao* for the first time. He came to my town to commemorate two of our own, the priest Don Pietro Pappagallo and the Communist philosopher Gioacchino Gesmundo, both assassinated in the massacre of Fosse Ardeatine†. The official version of that meeting, a true one I believe, says that Ingrao tenderly delivered the following exhortation to me: "Prepare yourself to become a good Communist." Who knows if I have ever succeeded in that?

My Communism was philanthropic, humanistic, literary; in its domestic political incarnation it followed the line of D'Amico‡. I read everything with a disorderly voracity. At thirteen, I mixed Erasmus of Rotterdam with Sigmund Freud, then discovered the poetry of Neruda and Garcia Lorca. All of this converged at a point where my intellectual progress was distilled through dialogue with the oldest comrades. How many faces! I have not forgotten a single one, with those romantically plebian nicknames, Ciccillo the Ragged (secretary of the Workers' Chamber), Marietta of the Old Cloth (a type of *pasionaria*, a woman rebel and an authentically popular leader) and those manual laborers who packed our section. They were not anonymous replicas of a line imposed from above, but impassioned and curious people, grateful to the Party because to that entity they owed their ability to discuss great events, but never so great that they could not be understood in some manner by the most ordinary person. In that place, in that encounter, a person like myself, madly in love with Alexandrine verse§, learned a sense of decorum. It was there I saved myself.

1991 first edition

ONE MORE LIFE: PREFACE TO THE 2005 EDITION

As the roaring eighties gave way to the depressing nineties, the entire world fell on our shoulders, all in the space of a few thunderstruck seasons. Not only the East,

---

* Pietro Ingrao (1915–) was involved in the Italian resistance during World War II, and then was a leader of the left wing of the PCI. He served as member of Parliament, editor of the party newspaper, *L'Unità*, and was the first Communist to become President of the Chamber of Deputies in 1976. After the breakup of the PCI in 1991, he briefly joined the *Partito Democratico della Sinistra* (Democratic Party of the Left). However, in 2004, he returned to the *Partito della Rifondazione Comunista* (Party of Communist Refoundation) of which Vendola was also a leading member until 2009.

† Fosse Ardeatine was the site of a German massacre in March 1944 in Rome; 335 Italian civilians were herded into a cave and shot in reprisal for a partisan attack in which thirty-two German police were killed by a bomb. The number of victims, based on ten Italians for every German, was personally ordered by Hitler.

‡ Michele D'Amico (1900–1980) was a member of the Constituent Assembly, which wrote a new Italian Constitution after World War II. Born in western Sicily, he was a member of the PCI and elected to the Chamber of Deputies in Rome. He is best known for having organized the occupation of uncultivated land in Sicily, with the goal of transferring ownership from large landowners to landless peasants and agricultural workers as part of a post-war agrarian reform.

§ Alexandrine verse is a line of poetic meter composed of twelve syllables and used in French and German poetry of the early modern period.

a cardinal point which represented the axis of our existence, whether as faith or as heresy. Not only a great secularized church, the PCI (Italian Communist Party), which had overseen our education, the discovery of the past and the search for the future. But more: the earth and the sky fell upon us. The tragic ruins of the mummified Communism of the party-state appeared to carry away in its wreckage the very idea of social transformation. Socialism was suddenly real, unreal, bruised and bestial, a promise devoured by the bureaucratic followers of the "dream of one thing*," a prophecy that vomited itself out into its opposite, the sun of the future snuffed out in the darkness of the gulag.

That was a terrible moment, not only having to account to others, but above all in the urgent weighing of one's own choices, in the bitter and agonizing confrontation with one's own conscience. I have been a Communist, and to identify myself, I have always struggled continuously against the barrier of Stalinism (ideological, architectonic, anthropological). But it was not enough; it didn't save me. This is what I told myself in those days and nights of 1991.

To be Communist now, today and tomorrow, to refound an identity and a direction†, it is not enough to define myself outside of the shadowy realm of error and horror. I must instead enter into the infernal geography, descend the circles of that omnipotent mysticism which transformed the Party into the great Thaumaturge of human history. I must weep with the victims of the demented paradise built by the camps of re-education. I must tell myself everything, not deny any of it to myself, and must find the principle of a "new beginning" in the prism of the truth of that continuing search.

Thirteen years ago I wrote this book because I had to confront my youth. Within me there was still so much ingenuousness, sorrows difficult to reduce to the measure of political reflection, and a sometimes eclectic anxiety to restore the thread of civil passion to the fabric of daily militancy. What saved me was the idea that a new history should be born from the absolute and prophetic repudiation of the paradigm of violence, whether violence of the state or cathartic violence, both indications of a primacy that sacrifices concrete humanity to the ferocious abstraction of Power. What saved me was my education in Communism as a "sentimental connection" with the multitudes: people, subjects, cultures, communities, individuals, the reconnections of rich personal ties—in short an affective and programmatic exchange that liberated me from the paranoid cult of the avant-gardes and their monumental but suffocating pedagogies.

---

* *Il Sogno di una Cosa* (*The Dream of One Thing*, 1962) is the title of the first novel written by Pier Paolo Pasolini (1922–1975), the famous Italian writer and filmmaker. It tells the story of rural farm workers who emigrate from Friuli after World War II.

† After the dissolution of the PCI in 1991, Vendola was a founder and leader of the *Partito della Rifondazione Comunista* (PRC) until 2009. As part of the continuing pattern of schisms and reorganizations in Italian politics of the last two decades, Vendola founded a new party in January 2009, now called *Movimento per la Sinistra* (Movement for the Left). The fact that this newest party has dropped the term "Communist" is striking in light of his strong identification as a communist in this memoir and throughout his career.

This was the Communism I then pursued, in this opening of a new millennium, in the dawning of the anti-global narrative, in the planet-wide rising of the
peace movement, challenging the governing system of "unending war" in thousands of untold stories of actions where the lower levels of society [*basso*] acted
as a protagonist against the higher [*alto*]. But also in the feverish, delicate and
sorrowful reweaving of the threads of religious reflection and of faith: a lay faith
in a "new order" that would eradicate the roots of war from the territory of collective life; an intimate faith (held as if in the flickering light of the angel killed by
the twentieth century) in the god "who dances life," who celebrates godliness by
incarnation in the most extreme and most lost of humans, who in the glory of this
radical dispossession announces the news of that resurrection which will restore
all the light and truth of the world.

I am republishing this small book which marked my entry into the passage between youth and maturity, in part to see if, beneath graying hair and
some impertinent wrinkles, the dream of "another possible world" has remained
intact and incandescent. Honestly I believe that it has, even now as my per-
sona threatens to supplant my person, even as I dance around the symbols and
representatives of power. Ever since my adolescent commitment to history, I
have been marked by its formative imprint as well as its pleasurable diversions
[*stimme e svagatezza*]. Even today the signs of power do not intrigue me as much
as I am intrigued and converted by the power of signs. Signs and dreams of a soft
revolution, of a democracy that spreads from procedure to feeling, of a vision
that flees from the violent coercion of consumerist insignificance, and from the
solitude of those who live here in Babel. I am wounded but alive; I return to the
journey.

February 2005

NOTES

1. Stephen Lagg, "Review Essay: Memory and Nostalgia," *Cultural Geographies* 11
(2004): 99. To put this figure in perspective, it should be noted that 1.7 million people
in Germany went to see the *Das Leben der Anderen* (*The Lives of Others*), the Oscar-
winning film (for best Foreign Language Picture) about the surveillance and other
methods of the East German Stasi. This is the figure given in Cheryl Dueck, "The
Humanization of the Stasi in *Das Leben der Anderen*," *German Studies Review* 31,
no. 3 (2008): 599.
2. Hilary Heuler, "Poland: Your Ché Guevara T-shirt Can Land You in Jail," *Christian
Science Monitor*, 20 January 2010.
3. Interview with Alina Cała in Ewa Kondratowicz, ed., *Szminka na sztandarze: kobiety
Solidarności 1980–1989: rozmowy* (*Lipstick on the Banner: The Women of Solidarity,
1980–1989: Conversations*) (Warsaw: Sci!, 2001), 343. Cała also asserted: "I grew up
in a working class neighborhood [housing estate for workers], and many of the residents there were workers from the Kasprzak Factory....And there was a quite widespread opinion that they actually have Communism to thank for everything. Even if
they weren't ideological Communists, they surely weren't against it. It surely wouldn't

have occurred to any of them to overthrow the system." Translation by Christina Manetti.

4. "Revolution," as the previous chapter has made clear, is the most popular scholarly conception of 1989: See, *inter alia*, Michael Zantovsky, "Resumption: The Gears of 1989," *World Affairs* 172, no. 3 (2010): 33–43, where he favors revolution for the events of November 1989 in Czechoslovakia but acknowledges that participants considered, as alternatives to the "Velvet Revolution," the Velvet "Collapse," "Overthrow," "Takeover," etc.; Padraic Kenney, *1989: Democratic Revolutions at the Cold War's End: A Brief History with Documents* (New York: Bedford/St. Martin's, 2010); Vladimir Tismaneanu, *The Revolutions of 1989* (New York:Routledge, 1999); Piotr Sztompka, "Looking Back: The Year 1989 as a Cultural and Civilizational Break," *Communist and Post-Communist Studies,* 29, no. 2 (1996): 115–129, especially the section "'Revolutions of 1989': the Name is Deserved," 115–116; Timothy Garton Ash, *The Magic Lantern: The Revolution of '89 Witnessed in Warsaw, Budapest, Berlin and Prague* (New York: Random House, 1990). Debates exist about the merit of the concept of "revolution" for particular cases. To give but one example, Peter Siani-Davies has argued forcefully that 1989 in Romania was a revolution, not a *coup d'état*, while asserting that 1989 in East Germany, Bulgaria, and Czechoslovakia were *coups d'état* and *not* revolutions! See Peter Siani-Davies, *The Romanian Revolution of December 1989* (Ithaca, NY: Cornell University Press, 2005), 268. For 1989/91, as an "implosion"—or a self-immolation of a corrupt Communist elite ("uncivil society")—see Stephen Kotkin (with a contribution by Jan T. Gross), *Uncivil Society: 1989 and the Implosion of the Communist Establishment* (New York: Random House, 2009). For 1989/1991 as "coup d'état," see, for the case of Romania, Nestor Ratesh, *Romania: The Entangled Revolution* (New York: Praeger, 1991).

5. This view tends to be more prevalent in some former Communist countries, such as the Czech Republic and Hungary, than in others, such as Poland. And it tends to be held by people who are between fifty and seventy years old. For discussion of conspiracy theory with respect to the Yugoslav case (Yugoslavia's collapse as engineered by a conspiracy of Western imperialism), see Sabrina P. Ramet, *Central and Southeast European Politics Since 1989* (New York: Cambridge University Press, 2010), 112.

6 As mentioned previously, it was common for Soviet citizens in what turned out to be "late Socialism" to believe that the Soviet system would last "forever," or nearly so. See Alexei Yurchak, *Everything Was Forever, Until It Was No More: The Last Soviet Generation* (Princeton: Princeton University Press, 2006), 1.

7. Piotr Szompka, "The Ambivalence of Social Change: Triumph or Trauma?" (Berlin, 2000), available at http://bibliothek.wzb.eu/pdf/2000/p00–001.pdf; see also the discussion (and summary of critiques) in Dueck, "The Humanization of the Stasi," 601–602.

8. See Jeffrey C. Alexander's introduction to Alexander, Ron Eyerman, Bernhard Giesen, Niel J. Smelser, Piotr Sztompka, *Cultural Trauma and Collective Identity* (Berkeley, CA: University of California Press, 2004), 1, as discussed also in Dueck, "The Humanization of the Stasi," 601–602.

9. Dueck mentions the critiques of cultural trauma, especially Sztompka's formulation thereof, made by Hans Joas: his challenging of the "subjectification of a collectivity, the tensions between the individual psychological and construction of cultural trauma," and the perhaps too elastic notion of trauma that the concept invokes. Dueck, "The Humanization of the Stasi," 601–602.

10. An example of how such closure might be provided by manageable, if perhaps too neat, too tidy, and too unrealistic images, comes from the conclusion of von Donnersmarck's *Das Leben der Anderen* (*The Lives of Others*): Two years after unification, the playwright who was the object of the Stasi's surveillance reads his Stasi file and discovers that the Stasi agent saved him by covering up his dissident activities. The writer (Dreyman) then dedicated his next novel, *Die Sonata vom Guten Menschen* (Sonata for a Good Man) to HGWXX, the code name of the Stasi operative (Wiesler). The film closes with a scene in which the Stasi agent finds the book in a store, reads the dedication, and purchases a copy. When the clerk asks him whether he wants the book gift-wrapped, he replies: "Nein. Es ist für mich." ("No. It is for me.") While acknowledging that the ending is perhaps "too neat and closed," Dueck notes the ending's positive service: "In trauma treatments, narrating traumatic events brings together the fragmented images of the trauma, helps to reduce patient dissociation, and results in fewer intrusive symptoms." "The Humanization of the Stasi," 607.

11. David Turashhvili, preface to "Flight from the USSR," in *The Jeans Generation*, translated by Maria Kiashvili. (Privately circulated manuscript; the Georgian original was published in Tblisi in 2009.) Takashvili refers in particular to what he calls the "Soviet past of Georgia," characterized, he says, by a scarcity of "benevolence."

12. Quoted in Dueck, "The Humanization of the Stasi," 602.

13. The Stasi (short from Ministry of State Security or, in German, Ministerium für Staatssicherheit, or MfS), was, from its founding in 1950 until its dissolution 1990, responsible for domestic political surveillance and foreign espionage. Its operations were overseen by the SED. Although recruiting informers is said to have become more difficult after 1986, by the time of the collapse of the East German regime in 1989, the Stasi had over 90,000 employees and over 173,000 informants. A 2007 article by the BBC claimed that there was an informer for every seven East German citizens.

14. See, for example, Hartmut Zwahr, *Proletarat und Bourgeoisie in Deutschland: Studien zur Klassendialektik* (*Proletariat and Bourgeoisie in Germany: Studies in Class Dialectics*) (Köln: Pahl-Rugenstein, 1980); and *Die Konstituierung der deutschen Arbeiterklasse von den dreissiger bis zu den siebziger Jahren des 19. Jahrhunderts* (*The Making of the German Working Class from the 1830s to the 1870s*)(Berlin:Akademie-Verlag, 1981).

15. Hartmut Zwahr, *Die erfrorenen Flügel der Schwalbe: DDR und "Prager Frühling": Tagebuch einer Krise, 1968–1970* (*The Frozen Wings of the Swallow: East Germany and the "Prague Spring": Diary of a Crisis, 1968–1970*) (Bonn: Dietz, 2007). See also Hartmut Kaelble, Jürgen Kocka, Hartmut Zwahr, eds., *Sozialgeschichte der DDR* (*A Social History of East Germany*) (Stuttgart: Klett-Cotta, 1994). In the 2007 publication of his diary notes (*Die erfrorenen Flügel*) that recounted his eyewitness experience of the "Prague Spring," (focusing on the period between March 1968 and April 1970), he emphasized the widespread opposition in East German society (including by workers, which is not often recognized) to the Soviet suppression of the Prague events. And he stressed that this suppression was, for some East Germans, the cause for giving up their belief in socialism.

16. Sigrid Meuschel, Michael Richter, Hartmut Zwahr, eds., *Friedliche Revolution in Sachsen: das Ende der DDR und die Wiedergründung des Freistaates* (*Saxony's Peaceful Revolution: The End of East Germany and the Refounding of the Free State of*

Saxony) (Dresden, 1999); Hartmut Zwahr, *Friedliche Revolution 1989/90 in Sachsen* (*A Peaceful Revolution: 1989/1990 in Saxony*) (Dresden: Hannah-Arendt-Institut für Totalitarismusforschung, 2009). (In the Series *Atlas zur Geschichte und Landeskunde von Sachsen; Kriege und soziale Bewegungen, Militärwesen; Zeitgeschichte (1945 bis 1952; 1952 bis 1990; 1991)* (*Atlas of History and Regional Studies in Saxony: Wars and Social Movements, Military Issues, Contemporary History (1945 to 1952; 1952 to 1990; 1991)*).

17. On 1989 in Czechoslovakia, see Vladimir Tismaneanu, ed., *The Revolutions of 1989* (New York: Routledge, 1999); and Bernard Wheaton and Zdenek Kavan, *The Velvet Revolution: Czechoslovakia, 1988–1991* (Boulder, CO: Westview Press, 1992).

18. The three collections of poetry he had written by age twenty-seven were the following: (*Footprints on the Wellspring*), 1965; *Kalad punuvad pesi (Fish weave their nests)*, 1966; and *Tolmost ja värvidest (Of dust and colors)*, 1967. The first translations into English were *The Same Sea in Us All* (1985/1990), *The Wandering Border* (1987/1992), *I Am the Spring in Tartu* (1993), and *Through the Forest* (1996). The year 1996 was also the year in which Czesław Miłosz nominated him for the Nobel Prize in literature. Thomas Salumets, "Conflicted Consciousness: Jaan Kaplinski and the Legacy of Intra-European Postcolonialism in Estonia," in Violeta Kelertas, ed., *Baltic Postcolonialism* (New York: Rodopi, 2006), 431–432.

19. This exposition of Kaaplinski's intellectual biography draws upon Thomas Salumets, "Conflicted Consciousness: Jaan Kaplinski and the Legacy of Intra-European Postcolonialism in Estonia," in Kelertas, *Baltic Postcolonialism*, 429–450.

20. Salumets, "Conflicted Consciousness," 431.

21. Ibid., 444.

22. An excellent, and fairly recent, introduction to Eurocommunism can be found in Geoff Eley, *Forging Democracy: The History of the Left in Europe, 1850–2000* (New York: Oxford University Press, 2002), 408–428.

23. http://www.nichivendola.it/

Chronology: World History and the History of Communism

WORLD HISTORY, 1840s TO THE PRESENT

1842:	Treaty of Nanking, after Opium War of 1839–1842 over British designs of forcing trade with China, stipulates concessions (opening of ports, cession of Hong Kong) by China to the British.
1848–1849:	Revolutions in Europe (France, Austria, Prussia, Italy)
1849:	Algerian Revolt against France
Ca. 1850–1914:	Era of land-based empires. Majority of world's population live in such land-based empires as the Ottoman, Habsburg, Russian, and Chinese, or in colonies of nation-states (such as Africa, the Middle East, and Southeast Asia), rather than in nation-states themselves.
1850(s):	Reform in Ottoman Empire
1852–1864:	Taiping Rebellion of peasants in the Qing empire. Qing dynasty prevails, but at cost of central authority's diminished power, agrarian devastation, financial ruin, refugee crisis, and increased power of local gentry.
1853:	U.S. Officer Commodore Matthew Perry enters Edo (Tokyo) Bay, beginning the "opening" of Japanese ports by the Americans, Russian, Dutch, and British.
1856–1860:	Second Opium Wars end with China's defeat by British and French forces. By treaty, sale of opium is legalized and freedom of religion in China is established.
1858:	Beginning of the "Raj" (British term for their system of administrative rule in India) following British suppression of Indian Rebellion of 1857
1859:	Charles Darwin's *Origin of the Species* is published.
1861:	Emancipation of the Serfs in the Russian Empire

1860s, early 1870s:	"Great Reforms" attempt state-led modernization of Russia.
1861:	Unification of Italy is completed.
1861–1865:	Civil War in the United States
1866:	Sun Yat-sen, anti-Qing Chinese nationalist and leader of China's Nationalist Party or *Guomindang*, is born in Canton, China.
1860s (through 1890):	Bureaucrats in the Chinese empire adopt reforms, including some Western learning and technology, in "Self-Strengthening Movement."
1860s-1890s:	French occupation of Southeast Asia (Vietnam, Cambodia, and Laos)
1867–1868:	The Indian Rebellion—popular insurrection against colonial rule—ends with violent suppression by British, but some concessions. Karl Marx, with hopes for revolution in Europe dashed, follows and writes about the events in India.
1868:	Meiji Restoration in Japan. Ruling power transferred from the Tokugawa shōgun to the Emperor of Japan (Emperor Mutsuhito). The Meiji government undertakes industrialization, expands railway networks, and implements educational reform. Constitution of 1889 creates the Diet, an elected parliamentary body.
1869:	Suez Canal opens.
1871:	German Unification following Franco-Prussian War of 1870–1871
1871:	Paris Commune
1870s:	Take-off of industrialization in Germany
1870s–1880s:	Decades of British imperialism in Southeast Asia
1877:	First railway track is laid in China; torn up shortly thereafter.
1880–1881:	First Anglo-Boer War
1882:	Occupation of Egypt by the British
1886:	Gold is discovered in the Transvaal.
1888:	Revolution in visual media is produced by invention of photographic film and the debut of the Eastman Kodak camera.
1888:	Abolition of slavery in Brazil
1890s:	Take-off of industrialization in the Russian Empire
1891–1903:	Construction of the Trans-Siberian Railroad
1892:	*Shenbao*, likely the Chinese newspaper with the largest circulation in the Empire, publishes news articles in China via a new telegraph line.
1894–1895:	Sino-Japanese War: Japan fights war with China over Korea. Japan wins.
1898:	In the Chinese Empire, the Qing dynasty launches first comprehensive reform, the "Hundred Days' Reform,"

in the aftermath of defeat in the Sino-Japanese War. Reforms later squashed by the Empress Dowager Cixi.

1898: Spanish-American War. Cuba gains independence from Spain.

1899–1900: Boxer Rebellion against foreign encroachment in China ends with defeat by Japanese, European, and American forces.

1899–1902: South African War. Two Afrikaner states (Transvaal and Orange Free State) unsuccessfully fight for political independence against the British.

1901: Invention of the radio by Guglielmo Marconi

1903: Henry Ford establishes the Ford Motor Company. Production of the Ford "Model T" begins in 1908.

1904–1905: Russo-Japanese War ends with Russia's defeat.

1906: Women vote in national elections in Finland.

1910: Korea annexed by Japan.

1910: Beginning of the Mexican Revolution, the first major peasant uprising of the twentieth century. Fighting lasts ten years, taking the lives of one million Mexicans. Constitution is issued in 1917.

1911: End of Qing Empire, beginning of Republican China: Abdication of the Chinese emperor, then a six-year-old child, in February, 1912.

1914–1918: World War I: The United States enters the war in 1917.

1917: Revolution in Russia. March: Russian autocracy collapses. Provisional (temporary) government is created.

1917: Collapse of the Russian Empire

1918: Collapse of the Austro-Hungarian Empire

1918: Collapse of the Ottoman Empire. Ottoman sultan is deposed in 1922; led by Mustafa Kemal, Turkey becomes a nation in 1924.

1919: Treaty of Versailles, ending World War I

1919: May Fourth Movement in China. The Treaty of Versailles awards former German concession rights to Japan, sparking student and worker protest.

1918–1933: Weimar Republic in Germany

1920: Covenant of League of Nations goes into effect.

1922: Establishment of Republic of Ireland

1922: Italy's fascist dictator, Benito Mussolini, marches on Rome.

1925: Universal manhood suffrage in Japan

1927: Philip Farnsworth makes the world's first functioning television.

1928: Chiang Kai-shek, leader of the Guomindang after Sun Yat-sen's death, emerges as leader of China.

1929: Beginning of the Great Depression. Stock market crashes on "Black Tuesday," 29 October 1929.

1930: Sigmund Freud's *Civilization and Its Discontents* is published.

1930: Gandhi's "March to the Sea," a campaign of civil disobedience for India's independence from British rule

1931: Japan completes invasion of Manchuria. 1932: Manchuria is annexed by Japan.

1931:	Second Spanish Republic begins.
1933–1941:	New Deal in United States expands, in an unprecedented way, the federal government's role in social welfare programs and in intervention in the national economy.
1933:	Hitler is dictator of Germany.
1933–1945:	Three stages of the Holocaust. First stage: Hitler's accession to power in 1933 brings steps in mass expulsion of the Jews from Germany and in territories controlled by its armed forces. Second stage, from summer of 1941 to January 1942: the murder of 1.4 million of the Soviet Union's 5 million Jews by Nazi *Einsatzgruppen*, the German paramilitary units on Nazis' eastern front. Third stage: 20 January 1942 (meeting of Nazi officials in Berlin Wannsee) to May 1945. Jews deported to death camps throughout Central and Eastern Europe for systematic extermination using modern technology.
1936–1939:	Spanish Civil War
1936–1939:	"Popular Front" government in France
1937:	Japan invades China. War continues for eight years.
1939:	Nazi-Soviet non-aggression pact
1939–1945:	World War II
1941 (7 December):	Japanese bombing of Pearl Harbor. United States enters World War II.
1944:	Creation of the World Bank and the International Monetary Fund (IMF)
1945 (April–June):	Formal establishment of the United Nations by delegates meeting in San Francisco
1945 (6 August):	United States drops first atomic bomb on Hiroshima, Japan. 9 August: United States drops atomic bomb on Nagasaki, Japan. Beginning of the "nuclear age."
1948 (May):	David Ben Gurion, the first Prime Minister of Israel, declares that state's independence.
1948:	Beginning of apartheid in South Africa
1948–52:	Marshall Plan provides economic aid to Europe.
1947:	India and Pakistan become independent.
1949:	Creation of NATO (Greece and Turkey join in 1952)
1950s–1960s:	Independence of African nations
1954–1962:	Algerian War of Independence
1950s–1960s:	Civil Rights Movement in the United States
1954:	CIA overthrows the government in Guatemala, ending agrarian reform.
1956:	October: Suez Crisis. Egypt's nationalization of Suez Canal Company results in Israeli, British, and French invasion of

	Egypt. Invaders forced to withdraw. Gamal Abdel Nasser attains diplomatic triumph.
1960:	Creation of OPEC (Organization of Petroleum Exporting Countries)
1961:	Invention of the Silicon Chip by Jack Kilby and Robert Noyce, two American electrical engineers
1973:	Oil embargo by Arab states
1970s:	Rise of an international movement to save the Amazon Rain Forest
1974:	Watergate scandal. 8 August 1974: President Richard M. Nixon resigns.
1975:	Death of Francisco Franco, Spanish dictator, begins transition to democracy in Spain.
1976:	Steve Jobs and Steve Wozniak invent the personal computer.
1979:	Iran: Shah Mohammed Pahlevi's dynasty is toppled. That regime is replaced by a government headed by Islamic cleric leader Ayatollah Ruhollah Khomeni.
1979–1980:	U.S. hostage crisis in Iran
1979:	Revolution in Nicaragua
1984–1989:	"State of emergency" in South Africa
1989:	Desegregation of public facilities in South Africa
1990–1998:	Rwanda's Civil War
1991:	Gulf War
1992:	Treaty of Maastricht on European Union is signed; goes into effect in 1993.
1992:	Negotiation of NAFTA (North American Free Trade Agreement)
1991:	Remaining apartheid laws are repealed in South Africa.
1994:	(January) Beginning of the Chiapas Revolt in Mexico.
1994:	ANC (African National Congress) wins South Africa's first free, non-racially based elections. Nelson Mandela becomes President. South Africa granted a seat in the United Nations' General Assembly, which it had been denied for twenty years.
2001 (11 September):	Attacks on the World Trade Center and the Pentagon by Al-Qaeda. Two thousand, nine hundred ninety-five civilians killed in New York, Washington DC, and Shanksville, Pennsylvania, where a fourth plane crashes.
2001 (7 October):	In response to attacks on 11 September, war in Afghanistan begins with U.S. military's "Operation Enduring Freedom," joined by British military forces.
2003 (March):	Iraq War (also known as Occupation of Iraq, Second Gulf War, and Operation Iraqi Freedom) begins.

2005 (Feburary):	Kyoto Treaty, adopted in Japan in December 1997, enters into force, setting targets for industrialized countries to reduce greenhouse gas emissions.
2007–2010:	Global financial crisis

HISTORY OF COMMUNISM

1840s:	Marx synthesizes the main elements of his philosophy of history.
1844:	Friedrich Engels publishes *The Condition of the Working Class in England.*
1848:	Marx's *Communist Manifesto* is published.
1875:	Founding of the German Socialist Labor Party (*Sozialdemokratische Partei Deutschlands*)
1883:	Karl Marx, born in 1818, dies in London.
1893:	Birth of Mao Zedong
1898:	Founding of the Russian Social Democratic Labor Party (RSDLP), Russia's first Marxist political party
1903:	Split within the Russian Social Democratic Labor Party (RSDLP), at the Party's Second Congrsess in London, between Lenin's Bolsheviks and the Julius Martov's Mensheviks, over the definition of a Party member
1905–1907:	Revolution in the Russian Empire, with semi-constitutionalism as outcome. Russian workers create 'soviets' (elected councils of workers' deputies) as strike committees during the October General Strike.
1912:	One million German workers belong to the SPD.
1914:	Founding of the Indonesian Communist Party
1917 (November):	Bolsheviks seize power in Russia.
1918–1921:	Civil War in Russia; Bolsheviks (Reds) defeat White forces.
1918–1921:	Georgia, formerly part of the Russian Empire, is a Menshevik Republic.
1919 (March 2–6):	First Congress of the Communist International (Comintern)
1920 (Late December, Early November):	End of the Democratic Republic of Armenia and the creation, under control of Armenia's Communist Party, of the Soviet Socialist Republic of Armenia
1920 (July–August):	Second Congress of the Communist International (Comintern)
1920 (October):	Communist Party of India founded in Tashkent, Turkestan Autonomous Soviet Socialist Republic, by Manabendra Nath Roy
1921 (February):	Georgia is invaded by the Soviet Red Army and becomes a Soviet Republic.

1921 (22 June–12 July):	Third Congress of the Communist International (Comintern)
1921:	Founding of the Chinese Communist Party
1921–1928:	"New Economic Policy" (limited capitalism in agriculture and in other parts of the economy) in the USSR
1922:	Founding of Japanese Communist Party
1922 (November):	Fourth Congress of the Communist International (Comintern)
1924 (21 January):	Lenin dies. Succession struggle for leadership of the Communist Party begins. Triumvirate of Josef Stalin, Grigory Zinoviev, and Lev Kamenev to discredit Leon Trotsky
1924 (June-July):	Fifth Congress of the Communist International (Comintern)
1924 (December):	Stalin and Nikolai Bukharin advance the concept of "Socialism in One Country"
1925:	Stalin-Bukharin "centrist" position on industrialization and collectivization wins out against the Opposition at the Fourteenth Congress of the RKP(b).
1926 (April):	Leon Trotsky, Lev Kamenev, and Grigory Zinoviev form the "United Opposition," which condemns Stalin's growing power and attacks the Stalin-Bukharin "centrist" position on industrialization.
1926 (23–26 October):	Expulsion of Leon Trotsky and Lev Kamenev from the Politburo of the Communist Party of the Soviet Union. Zinoviev is replaced by Bukharin as Chairman of the Comintern.
1927 (April):	In Shanghai, Chiang Kai-shek orders mass purges of Communists from the Guomindang (Nationalists). Execution and imprisonment of Chinese Communists in order to eliminate their influence within the Guomindang
1927 (November):	Expulsion of Leon Trotsky and Grigory Zinoviev from the Communist Party of the Soviet Union
1928 (January):	Exile of Trotsky to Alma Ata, Kazakhstan
1928 (July-August):	Sixth Congress of the Communist International (Comintern)
1929 (February):	Communist Party of the Soviet Union's Politburo strongly censures the "Rightists" Nikolai Bukharin, Aleksei Rykov, and Mikhail Tomsky.
1929 (February):	Deportation of Leon Trotsky to Turkey
1929 (November):	Nikolai Bukharin is removed from the Politburo of the Communist Party of the Soviet Union by a Plenum of the Party's Central Committee.

1929 (21 December):   Stalin turns 50. The "Stalin Cult" is launched.

1929–32:   Stalin's "great break" (*velikii perelom*). Major push in industrialization and forced collectivization, whose transformation of agriculture continues until 1938.

1931:   Kim Il Sung, future leader of North Korea, joins the Chinese Communist Party.

1934–1935:   Mao's "Long March" in China. To escape from Nationalist forces under Chiang Kai-shek, Mao and Chinese communists retreat to the far northwest in a 6,000 mile journey over course of a year. Only 10,000 of 80,000 survive.

1934 (1 December):   Assassination of Leningrad Communist Party Chief, Sergei M. Kirov, in Smolny, Party headquarters (Leningrad).

1936–1939:   Great Purges in the USSR. 1938: Execution of Nikolai Bukharin

1935 (August):   Seventh Congress of the Communist International (Comintern)

1938:   Lavrentii Beria replaces Nikolai Ezhov as head of the Soviet Union's NKVD (People's Commissariat of Internal Affairs), or the Soviet secret police. Beria continues Stalin's Purges.

1940 (20 August):   Leon Trotsky is assassinated by a Stalinist operative, the Spanish Communist Ramón Mercader, in Mexico.

1943:   Stalin dissolves the Comintern.

1945 (15 August):   Communist Revolution in Korea

1945–1985:   "Cold War," primarily between the two major superpowers, the United States and USSR

1946 (December):   First Indochina War Begins. Ho Chi Minh's Vietnamese forces commence attacks on the French in Hanoi. Guerilla warfare lasts until 1954, when Vietnamese defeat the French.

1949:   Establishment of the People's Republic of China following war between Communists and Nationalists (Guomindang) from 1945–1949, which ends in Communist victory

1949:   Communist Party of Japan is legalized.

1949:   Creation of German Democratic Republic (East Germany), following establishment of communist regimes elsewhere in Eastern Europe

1950–1953:   Korean War

1953 (5 March):   Stalin dies.

1953 (17 June):   First major anti-communist workers' uprising in East Germany is suppressed by Soviet intervention.

1953 (23 December):   Execution of Lavrentii Beria, the head of the Soviet state security apparatus. Earlier that year, he had been arrested on charges of "criminal anti-party and anti-state activities."

1954–1975:	Vietnam War. (Also called Second Indochina War.) Protracted conflict between South Vietnam (and allies, including the United States), and North Vietnam. War ends with the fall of Saigon.
1955:	May: West Germany's inclusion in NATO leads to creation of Warsaw Pact (Military) Alliance between the USSR and seven Communist satellites in East Europe: Albania, Bulgaria, Czechoslovakia, East Germany, Hungary, Poland, Romania
1956:	Sergei Khrushchev's "Secret Speech" at the 20th Party Congress of the CPSU launches de-Stalinization in the USSR and in Eastern Europe.
1957:	*Sputnik* launched by the Soviet Union.
1959 (January):	Castro's 26th of July Movement seizes power in Cuba following revolution that begins in 1958.
1956 (June):	Mass protests by Polish workers in Poznań. Violent suppression brings civilian deaths, among them thirteen-year-old Romek Strzałkowski.
1956:	Hungarian Revolution in October. 4 November: Soviet army's invasion of Budapest
1958–1961:	China's "Great Leap Forward" results in largest famine in world history.
Late 1960s:	Abimael Guzmán creates Peru's "Shining Path" (Sendero Luminoso), based on Maoist teachings.
1961 (17 April):	Cuba: Bay of Pigs Invasion: 1,400 Cuban exiles launch what became failed invasion of Cuba's south coast.
1961 (August):	Berlin Wall is constructed.
1962 (18–29 October):	Cuban Missile Crisis
1964 (October):	Khrushchev is ousted.
1966–76:	"Cultural Revolution" in China
1968:	Czechoslovakia's "Prague Spring"
1975:	Khmer Rouge seizes power in Cambodia.
1976:	Mao Zedong dies.
1978:	Deng Xiaoping assumes power in China.
1979–1989:	Soviet Union at war with Afghanistan
1980:	Formation of Poland's "Solidarity," the first independent trade union in a Communist polity
1980:	22 January: Andrei Sakharov exiled to Gorky (now Nizhnii Novgorod) after his "Open Letter on Afghanistan," which criticizes the Soviet invasion of that country, reaches the foreign press. He spends the next six years there with his wife, Elena Bonner.
1980s:	The "Shining Path" (Sendero Luminoso) launches guerilla warfare in Peru.

1980:	USSR: Film, *Moscow Doesn't Believe in Tears,* is released and becomes huge success. Seventy-five million tickets are sold. Film dramatizes the "double burden" faced by Soviet women (and women in socialist societies elsewhere), who have equal legal rights but assume more than their fair share of housework, childrearing, shopping.
1982:	(November). Leonid Brezhnev, General Secretary of the CPSU, dies. Yuri Andropov, former KGB head, leads the USSR as General Secretary of the CPSU from November 1982 until he dies fifteen months later. Konstantin Chernenko replaces him in February 1984 and dies in March 1985.
1983:	United States authorizes Strategic Defense initiative.
1984:	Deng Xiaoping launches the creation of China's socialist market economy, urging people to "build socialism with Chinese characteristics," and opening fourteen coastal cities to foreign investment.
1985:	Mikhail Gorbachev becomes General Secretary of the Communist Party of the Soviet Union.
1986:	Chernobyl nuclear accident becomes a catalyst for Gorbachev's reforms, especially *glasnost'* (openness).
1989:	May–June: Tiananmen Square demonstrations and student protest movement throughout China
1989:	Collapse of East European communist regimes
1989 (9 November):	"Fall" (really, breaching) of the Berlin Wall
1989–2001:	"Wars of succession" in the former Yugoslavia
1990 (February):	CPSU relinquishes its constitutional monopoly on power; beginning of a multi-party system in the USSR
1991 (19–21 August):	Failed coup attempt against Gorbachev in USSR
1992:	Shining Path (Sendero Luminoso) leader Abimael Guzmán is captured.
1994:	Death of Kim Il Sung
2008 (August):	Coalition government led by Communist Party of Nepal–Maoist is sworn in.

Suggestions for Further Reading

What follows is but a partial list, chiefly of secondary sources in English, of general studies and monographs relevant to the themes of each chapter.

Primary sources are indicated by an asterisk (*) at the beginning of the entry.

INTRODUCTION

Avineri, Shlomo, *The Social and Political Thought of Karl Marx* (1968)

Dickey, Laurence W., *Hegel: Religion, Economics, and the Politics of the Spirit, 1770–1807* (1989)

Halfin, Igal, *From Darkness to Light: Class, Consciousness, and Salvation in Revolutionary Russia* (1999) (Also relevant to chapter 4)

Halfin, Igal, *Red Autobiographies: Initiating the Bolshevik Self* (2011) (Also relevant to chapter 4)

Hellbeck, Jochen, *Revolution on My Mind: Writing a Diary under Stalin* (2006) (Also relevant to chapter 4)

Kolakowski, Leszek, *Main Currents of Marxism* (2008)

Lichtheim, George, *Marxism* (1961)

McClellan, David, *Marx after Marxism* (1979)

McClellan, David, *Marx before Marxism* (1972)

Toews, John Edward, *Hegelianism: The Path toward Dialectical Humanism, 1805–1841* (1985)

CHAPTER 1: BECOMING A COMMUNIST

Abrams, Bradley, *The Struggle for the Soul of the Nation: Czech Culture and the Rise of Communism* (2004)

Alba, Victor, *The Communist Party in Spain* (1983)

Armstrong, Charles, *The North Korean Revolution, 1945–1950* (2004)

Arnold, Anthony, *Afghanistan's Two-Party Communism: Parcham and Khalq* (1985)

Batatu, Hanna, *The Old Social Classes and the Revolutionary Movements of Iraq: A Study of Iraq's Old Landed and Commercial Classes and of its Communists, Ba'thists, and Free Officers* (1978)

Bernstein, Gail Lee, *Japanese Marxist: A Portrait of Kawakami Hajime, 1879–1946* (1990)

Bonnell, Victoria E., *Roots of Rebellion: Workers' Politics and Organizations in St. Petersburg* (1983)

Boswell, Laird, *Rural Communism in France, 1920–1939* (1998)

Botman, Selma, *The Rise of Egyptian Communism, 1939–1970* (1988)

Bradsher, Henry S., *Afghan Communism and Soviet Intervention* (1999)

Brass, Paul R., and Marcus F. Franda, eds., *Radical Politics in South Asia* (1973)

Brown, John Wilton, *The Communist Movement and Australia: A Historical Outline, 1890s to 1980s* (1986)

Chandler, David P., *The Tragedy of Cambodian History: Politics, War and Revolution since 1945* (1991)

Chandler, David P., and Ben Kiernan, eds., *Revolution and Its Aftermath in Kampuchea: Eight Essays* (1983)

*Chang, Chi-rak, and Nym Wales, *Song of Ariran: A Korean Communist in the Chinese Revolution* (1972)

Chen, Xiaoming, *From the May Fourth Movement to Communist Revolution: Guo Moruo and the Chinese Path to Communism* (2008)

Clapham, Christopher., ed., *African Guerrillas* (1998)

Clapham, Christopher, *Transformation and Continuity in Revolutionary Ethiopia* (1988)

Cohen, Robert, *When the Old Left Was Young: Student Radicals and America's First Mass Student Movement, 1929–1941* (1993)

Donham, Donald Lewis, *Marxist Modern: An Ethnographic History of the Ethiopian Revolution* (1999)

Draper, Theodore, *The Roots of American Communism* (1989)

Duiker, Wiliam J., *The Communist Road to Power in Vietnam*, 2nd ed. (1996)

Eley, Geoff, *Forging Democracy: The History of the Left in Europe, 1850–2000* (2002)

Evans, Grant, and Kelvin Rowley, *Red Brotherhood at War: Vietnam, Cambodia and Laos since 1975* (1990)

Farber, Samuel, *The Origins of the Cuban Revolution Reconsidered* (2006)

*Foner, Philip S., and Herbert Shapiro, eds., *American Communism and Black Americans: A Documentary History* (1991)

Fowler, Josephine, *Japanese and Chinese Immigrant Activists: Organizing in American and International Communist Movements, 1919–1933* (2007)

Ghosh, Sankar, *The Naxalite Movement: A Maoist Experiment* (1974)

Gilmartin, Christina K., *Engendering the Chinese Revolution: Radical Women, Communist Politics and Mass Movements in the 1920s* (1995)

Guiat, Cyrille, *The French and Italian Communist Parties: Comrades and Culture* (2002)

Heder, Stephen. R., *Kampuchean Occupation and Resistance* (1980)

Ismael, Tareq Y., *The Communist Movement in the Arab World* (2004)

Ismael, Tareq Y., *The Rise and Fall of the Communist Party of Iraq* (2008)

Ismael, Tareq Y., and Rif'at El-Sa'id, *The Communist Movement in Egypt, 1920–1988* (1990)

Kelley, Robin D. G., *Hammer and Hoe: Alabama Communists during the Great Depression* (1990)

Kerkvliet, Benedict J., *The Huk Rebellion: A Study of Peasant Revolt in the Philippines* (1977)

Kersten, Krystyna, *The Establishment of Communist Rule in Poland, 1943–1948* (1991)

Kertzer, David I., *Comrades and Christians: Religion and Political Struggle in Communist Italy* (1980)

Khánh, Huỳnh Kim, *Vietnamese Communism, 1925–1945* (1982)

Kiernan, Ben, *The Pol Pot Regime: Race, Power and Genocide in Cambodia under the Khmer Rouge, 1975–1979* (2008)

Koenker, Diane P., and William G. Rosenberg, *Strikes and Revolution in Russia, 1917* (1989)

Kovály, Heda Margolius, *Under a Cruel Star: A Life in Prague, 1941–1968* (1986)

McHale, Shawn Frederick, *Print and Power: Confucianism, Communism, and Buddhism in the Making of Modern Vietnam* (2004)

McKinley, Dale T., *The ANC and the Liberation Struggle* (1997)

McVey, Ruth T., *The Rise of Indonesian Communism* (2006)

*Mokgatle, Naboth, *The Autobiography of an Unknown South African* (1971)

Mortimer, Rex, *Indonesian Communism under Sukarno: Ideology and Politics, 1959–1965* (1974)

Mukherjee, Arun P., *Maoist "Spring Thunder": The Naxalite Movement, 1967–1972* (2007)

Myant, Martin R., *Socialism and Democracy in Czechoslovakia, 1945–1948* (1981)

Naimark, Norman, and Leonid Gibianskii, eds., *The Establishment of Communist Regimes in Eastern Europe, 1944–1949* (1997)

Nossiter, Thomas, *Communism in Kerala: A Study in Political Adaptation* (1982)

Ottanelli, Fraser M., *The Communist Party of the United States from the Depression to World War II* (1991)

Ottaway, David, and Marina Ottaway, *Afrocommunism* (1981)

Rafeek, Neil C., *Communist Women in Scotland: Red Clydeside from the Russian Revolution to the End of the Soviet Union* (2008)

Rubinstein, Sondra, *The Communist Movement in Palestine and Israel, 1919–1984* (1985)

Salucci, Ilario, *A People's History of Iraq: The Iraqi Communist Party, Workers' Movements, and the Left, 1924–2004 (2005)*

Sassoon, Donald, *One Hundred Years of Socialism: The West European Left in the Twentieth Century* (1997)

Saul, John S., ed., *A Difficult Road: The Transition to Socialism in Mozambique* (1985)

Scalapino, Robert A., *The Japanese Communist Movement, 1920–1966* (1967)

Senghor, Léopold Sédar, *On African Socialism* (1964)

Skrebnik, Henry Felix, *Jerusalem on the Amur: Birobidzhan and the Canadian-Jewish Movement, 1924–1951* (2008)

Smith, Stephen Anthony, *Red Petrograd: Revolution in the Factories, 1917–1918* (1983)

Smith, Stephen Anthony, *A Road Is Made: Communism in Shanghai, 1920–1927* (2000)

Solomon, Mark I., *The Cry Was Unity: Communists and African-Americans, 1917–1936 (1988)*

Solomon, Mark I., *Red and Black: Communism and Afro-Americans, 1929–1935* (1988)

Stavrakis, Peter J., *Moscow and Greek Communism, 1944–1949* (1989)

Steinberg, Mark D., *Moral Communities: The Culture of Class Relations in the Russian Printing Industry, 1867–1907* (1992)

*Steinberg, Mark D., *Voices of Revolution, 1917* (2003)

Stern, Steve J., ed., *Shining and Other Paths: War and Society in Peru, 1980–1995* (1998)

Storch, Randi, *Red Chicago: American Communism at Its Grassroots, 1928–1935* (2009)

Suh, Dae-Sook, *The Korean Communist Movement, 1918–1948* (1967)

Tiruneh, Andargachew, *The Ethiopian Revolution, 1974–1987: A Transformation from an Aristocratic to a Totalitarian Autocracy* (1993)

Van de Ven, Hans J., *From Friend to Comrade: The Founding of the Chinese Communist Party, 1920–1927* (1991)

Vickers, Miranda, *The Albanians: A Modern History* (2001)

Weitz, Eric D., *Creating German Communism, 1890–1990: From Popular Protest to Socialist State* (1997)

Wickham-Crowley, Timothy, *Guerrillas and Revolution in Latin America: A Comparative Study of Insurgents and Regimes since 1956* (1992)

Wildman, Allan K., *The Making of a Workers' Revolution: Russian Social Democracy, 1891–1903* (1967)

Young, John, *Revolution in Ethiopia: The Tigray People's Liberation Front, 1975–1991* (1997)

Yung-fa, Chen, *Making Revolution: The Communist Movement in East and Central China, 1937–1945* (1986)

CHAPTER 2: CHILDREN OF THE REVOLUTIONS

Ball, Alan, *And Now My Soul Is Hardened: Abandoned Children in Soviet Russia* (1996)

Frierson, Cathy, and Semen Samuilovich Vilenskii, *Children of the Gulag* (2010)

Georgeoff, Peter John, *The Social Education of Bulgarian Youth* (1968)

Holmes, Larry E., *The Kremlin and the Schoolhouse: Reforming Education in Soviet Russia, 1917–1931* (1991)

Mishler, Paul, *Raising Reds: The Young Pioneers, Radical Summer Camp and Communist Political Culture in the United States* (1999)

Kelly, Catriona, *Children's World: Growing Up in Russia, 1890–1991* (2007)

Kirschenbaum, Lisa A., *Small Comrades: Revolutionizing Childhood in Soviet Russia, 1917–1932* (2000)

Linehan, Thomas P., *Communism in Britain, 1920–1939: From the Cradle to the Grave* (2007)

Michaels, Paula A., *Curative Powers: Medicine and Empire in Stalin's Central Asia* (2003)

*Pran, Dith, and Kim De Paul, *Children of Cambodia's Killing Fields: Memoirs by Survivors* (1997)

*Zhu, Xiao Di, *Thirty Years in a Red House: A Memoir of Childhood and Youth in Communist China* (1998)

CHAPTER 3: VARIETIES OF COMMUNIST SUBJECTS: BEYOND THE ORDINARY

Davis, Deborah, *Long Lives: Chinese Elderly and the Communist Revolution* (1983)

Fitzpatrick, Sheila, *Political Tourists: Travellers from Australia to the Soviet Union in the 1920s–1940s* (2008)

Healey, Dan, *Homosexual Desire in Revolutionary Russia* (2001)

*Lemke, Jürgen, and John Borneman, *Gay Voices from East Germany* (1991)

Lumsden, Ian, *Machos, Maricones, and Gays: Cubans and Homosexuality* (1996)

McCagg, William O., and Lewis H. Siegelbaum, *The Disabled in the Soviet Union: Past and Present, Theory and Practice* (1989)

Sang, Tze-lan Deborah, *The Emerging Lesbian: Female Same-Sex Desire in Modern China* (2003)

Schluter, Daniel P., *Gay Life in the Former USSR: Fraternity without Community* (2002)

CHAPTER 4: IDEOLOGY AND SELF-FASHIONING

Deletant, Dennis, *Ceaușescu and the Securitate: Coercion and Dissent in Romania, 1965–1989* (1995)

Fulbrook, Mary, *Anatomy of a Dictatorship: Inside the GDR, 1949–1989* (1995) (Also relevant to chapters 5 and 6)

*Garros, Veronique, Natalia Korenevskaya, and Thomas Lahusen, eds., *Intimacy and Terror: Soviet Diaries of the 1930s* (1997)

Giebel, Chrstoph, *Imagined Ancestries of Vietnamese Communism: Ton Duc Thang and the Politics of History and Meaning* (2004)

Halfin, Igal, *Terror in My Soul: Communist Autobiographies on Trial* (2003)

Herrmann, Gina, *Written in Red: The Communist Memoir in Spain* (2009)

Jones, Polly, ed., *The Dilemmas of Destalinization: Negotiating Cultural and Social Change in the Khrushchev Era* (2006) (Also relevant to chapters 3, 5, 6, and 8)

Kharkhordin, Oleg, *The Collective and the Individual in Russia* (1999)

Kotkin, Stephen, *Magnetic Mountain: Stalinism as a Civilization* (1995) (Also relevant to chapters 5, 6, 7 and 8)

Lilly, Carol S., *Power and Persuasion: Ideology and Rhetoric in Communist Yugoslavia, 1944–1953* (2001)

Naiman, Eric, *Sex in Public: The Incarnation of Soviet Ideology* (1997)

*Siegelbaum, Lewis H., and Andrei Sokolov, eds., *Stalinism as a Way of Life* (2000) (Also relevant to chapters 5, 6, 7, and 8)

Yurchak, Alexei, *Everything Was Forever, Until It Was No More: The Last Soviet Generation* (2006)

CHAPTER 5: CONTESTING THE MEANING OF STATE VIOLENCE AND REPRESSION

Baron, Samuel, *Bloody Saturday in the Soviet Union: Novocherkassk, 1962* (2001)

Courtois, Stéphane, Mark Kramer et al., eds., *The Black Book of Communism: Crimes, Terror, Repression* (1999)

Getty, J. Arch, *The Origins of the Great Purges: The Soviet Communist Party Reconsidered* (1987)

Getty, J. Arch, Oleg V. Naumov, and Benjamin Sher, *Stalin and the Self-Destruction of the Bolsheviks* (1999)

Györkei, Jenő and Miklós Horváth, eds., *Soviet Military Intervention in Hungary, 1956* (1999)

Lendvai, Paul, *One Day That Shook the Communist World: The 1956 Hungarian Uprising and Its Legacy*, trans. Ann Major (2008)

Lenoe, Matthew E., *The Kirov Murder and Soviet History* (2010)

Litván, György, ed., *The Hungarian Revolution of 1956: Reform, Revolt and Repression, 1953–1963*, trans. János M. Bak and Lyman H. Legters (1996)

Kuromiya, Hiroaki, *The Voices of the Dead: Stalin's Great Terror in the 1930s* (2007)

Rosenhaft, Eve, *Beating the Fascists? The German Communists and Political Violence, 1929–1933* (1983)

White, Lynn T., III, *Policies of Chaos: The Organizational Causes of Violence in China's Cultural Revolution* (1989)

Williams, Kieran, *The Prague Spring and Its Aftermath: Czechoslovak Politics, 1968–1970* (1997)

CHAPTER 6: EVERYDAY LIFE, I: WORK

Andrle, Vladimir, *Workers in Stalin's Russia: Industrialization and Social Change in a Planned Economy* (1987)

Beinin, Joel, and Zachary Lockman, *Workers on the Nile: Nationalism, Communism, Islam and the Egyptian Working Class, 1882–1954* (1987)

Bloomfield, J., *Passive Revolution: Politics and the Czechoslovak Working Class, 1943–1948* (1979)

Bokovoy, Melissa K., *Peasants and Communists: Politics and Ideology in the Yugoslav Countryside, 1941–1953* (1998)

Bunk, Julie Marie, *Fidel Castro and the Quest for a Revolutionary Culture in Cuba* (1994) (Also relevant to chapters 7 and 8)

Burawoy, Michael, and János Lukács, *The Radiant Past: Ideology and Reality in Hungary's Road to Capitalism* (1992)

Chase, William J., *Workers, Society, and the Soviet State: Labor and Life in Moscow, 1918–1929* (1987)

Chávez, Lydia, ed., *Capitalism, God, and a Good Cigar: Cuba Enters the Twenty-First Century* (2005)

Chung, Joseph Sang-hoon, *The North Korean Economy: Structure and Development* (1974)

Creed, Gerald W., *Domesticating Revolution: From Socialist Reform to Ambivalent Transition in a Bulgarian Village* (1998)

Eckstein, Susan, ed., *Power and Popular Protest: Latin American Social Movements* (2001)

Feinberg, Melissa, *Elusive Equality: Gender, Citizenship, and the Limits of Democracy in Czechoslovakia, 1918–1950* (2006)

Filtzer, Donald, *Soviet Workers and De-Stalinization: The Consolidation of the Modern System of Soviet Production Relations, 1953–1964* (2002)

Fitzpatrick, Sheila, *Stalin's Peasants: Resistance and Survival in the Russian Village After Collectivization* (1994)

Frazier, Mark W., *The Making of the Chinese Industrial Workplace: State, Revolution, and Labor Management* (2002)

Friedman, Edward, Paul Pickowicz, and Mark Selden, *Chinese Village, Socialist State* (1991)

Garton Ash, Timothy, *The Polish Revolution: Solidarity* (2002)

Haraszti, Miklos, *A Worker in a Worker's State,* trans. Michael Wright (1978)

Hassig, Ralph, and Kongdan Oh, *The Hidden People of North Korea: Everyday Life in the Hermit Kingdom* (2009) (Also relevant to chapters 7 and 8)

Hessler, Julie, *A Social History of Soviet Trade* (2004)

Howard, Joshua H., *Workers at War: Labor in China's Arsenals, 1937–1953* (2004)

Hunter, Helen-Louise, *Kim Il-song's North Korea* (1999)

Jarausch, Konrad, ed., *Dictatorship as Experience: Towards a Socio-Cultural History of the GDR* (1999) (Also relevant to chapter 8)

Kenney, Padraic, *Rebuilding Poland: Workers and Communists, 1945–1950* (1997)

Kideckel, David A., *The Solitude of Collectivism: Romanian Villagers to the Revolution and Beyond* (1993)

Koenker, Diane P., *Republic of Labor: Russian Printers and Soviet Socialism* (2005)

Kolko, Gabriel, *Vietnam: Anatomy of a Peace* (2007)

Kopstein, Jeffrey, *The Politics of Economic Decline in East Germany, 1945–1989* (1997)

Kubik, Jan, *The Power of Symbols against the Symbols of Power: The Rise of Solidarity and the Fall of State Socialism in Poland* (1994)

Kürti, László, *Youth and the State in Hungary: Capitalism, Communism and Class* (2002)

Laba, Roman, *The Roots of Solidarity: A Political Sociology of Poland's Working-Class Democratization* (1991)

Lampland, Martha, *The Object of Labor: Commodification in Socialist Hungary* (1995)

Lane, David, *The Rise and Fall of State Socialism: Industrial Society and the Socialist State* (1996)

Lankov, Andrei, *North of the DMZ: Essays on Daily Life in North Korea* (2007) (Also relevant to chapters 7 and 8)

Lu, Xiaobo, and Elizabeth Perry, *Danwei: The Changing Chinese Workplace in Historical and Comparative Perspectives* (1997)

Millar, James R., *Politics, Work, and Daily Life in the USSR: A Survey of Former Citizens* (1987)

Myant, Martin, *The Czechoslovak Economy, 1948–1988: The Battle for Economic Reform* (1989)

Osa, Maryjane, *Solidarity and Contention: Networks of Polish Opposition* (2003)

Ost, David, *Solidarity and the Politics of Anti-Politics: Opposition and Reform in Poland since 1968* (1991)

Ostermann, Christian F., and Malcolm Byrne, *Uprising in East Germany, 1953: The Cold War, the German Question, and the First Major Upheaval behind the Iron Curtain* (2001)

Paczlowski, Andrzej, Malcolm Byrne and Gregory F. Domber, *From Solidarity to Martial Law: The Polish Crisis of 1980–1981; A Documentary History* (2007)

Pan, Yinhong, *Tempered in the Revolutionary Furnace: China's Youth in the Rustication Movement* (2003)

Perry, Elizabeth J., and Li Xun, *Proletarian Power: Shanghai in the Cultural Revolution* (1997)

Rossman, Jeffrey J., *Worker Resistance under Stalin: Class and Revolution on the Shop Floor* (2005)

Siegelbaum, Lewis H., and Ronald G. Suny, *Making Workers Soviet: Power, Class, and Identity* (1994)

Thaxton, Ralph, *Salt of the Earth: The Political Origins of Peasant Protest and Communist Revolution in China* (1995)

Tökés, Rudolf L., *Hungary's Negotiated Revolution: Economic Reform, Social Change, and Political Succession, 1957–1990* (1996)

Walder, Andrew, *Communist Neo-Traditionalism: Work and Authority in Chinese Industry* (1988)

Yang, Dali, *Calamity and Reform in China: State, Rural Society, and Institutional Change Since the Great Leap Famine* (1996)

CHAPTER 7: EVERYDAY LIFE, II: SPACE

Aulich, James, and Marta Sylvestrova, *Political Posters in Central and Eastern Europe, 1945–1995: Signs of the Times* (2000)

Bonnell, Victoria, *Iconography of Power: Soviet Political Posters under Lenin and Stalin* (1997)

Braun, Kazimierz, *A History of Polish Theater, 1939–1989: Spheres of Captivity and Freedom* (1996)

Crowley, David, and Susan E. Reid, *Socialist Spaces: Sites of Everyday Life in the Eastern Bloc* (2002)

Cushing, Lincoln, *Revolución! Cuban Poster Art* (1945)

Fitzpatrick, Sheila, *Everyday Stalinism: Ordinary Life in Extraordinary Times: Soviet Russia in the 1920s* (1999)

Heather, David, and Sherry Buchanan, *Vietnam Posters: The David Heather Collection* (2009)

Heather, David, and Koen de Ceuster, *North Korean Posters* (2008)

Portal, Jane, *Art Under Control in North Korea* (2005)

Qualls, Karl D., *From Ruins to Reconstruction: Urban Identity in Soviet Sevastopol after World War II* (2009)

Reid, Susan E., and David Crowley, *Style and Socialism: Modernity and Material Culture in Postwar Eastern Europe* (2000)

Ruble, Blair, *Leningrad: Shaping a Soviet City* (1990)

Siegelbaum, Lewis H., *Borders of Socialism: Private Spheres of Soviet Russia* (2006)

Smith, Mark B., *The Property of Communists: The Urban Housing Program from Stalin to Khrushchev* (2010)

Yan, Yunxiang, *Private Life Under Socialism: Love, Intimacy and Family Change in a Chinese Village, 1949–1999* (2003)

CHAPTER 8: EVERYDAY LIFE, III: ARE WE HAVING FUN YET? LEISURE, ENTERTAINMENT, SPORTS, AND TRAVEL

Barker, Adele Marie, *Consuming Russia: Popular Culture, Sex, and Society since Gorbachev* (1999)

*Bracewell, Wendy, ed., *Orientations: An Anthology of East European Travel Writing* (2009)

Bracewell, Wendy, and Alex Drace-Francis, *Balkan Departures: Travel Writing from Southeastern Europe* (2009)

Bracewell, Wendy, and Alex Drace-Francis, eds., *A Bibliography of East European Travel Writing on Europe* (2008)

Bracewell, Wendy, and Alex Drace-Francis, eds., *Under Eastern Eyes: A Comparative Introduction to East European Travel Writing on Europe* (2008)

Cushman, Thomas, *Notes from Underground: Rock Music Counterculture in Russia* (1995)

Edelman, Robert, *Serious Fun: A History of Spectator Sports in the USSR* (1993)

Edelman, Robert, *Spartak: A History of the People's Team in the Workers' State* (2009)

Feinstein, Joshua, *The Triumph of the Ordinary: Depictions of Daily Life in the East German Cinema, 1949–1989* (2002)

Gorsuch, Anne E., and Diane P. Koenker, *Turizm: The Russian and East European Tourist under Capitalism and Socialism* (2006)

Gundle, Stephen, *Between Hollywood and Moscow: The Italian Communists and the Challenge of Mass Culture, 1943–1991* (2000)

Johnson, Molly Wilkinson, *Training Socialist Citizens: Sports and the State in East Germany* (2008)

Poiger, Uta G., *Jazz, Rock, and Rebels: Cold War Politics and American Culture in a Divided Gernany* (2000)

Riordan, James, *Sports, Politics, and Communism* (1991)

Schweid, Richard, *Che's Chevrolet and Fidel's Oldsmobile: On the Road in Cuba* (2004)

Siegelbaum, Lewis H., *Cars for Comrades: The Life of the Soviet Automobile* (2008)

Stites, Richard, *Culture and Entertainment in Wartime Russia* (1995)

Stites, Richard, *Russian Popular Culture* (1992)

Urban, Michael, and Andrei Evdokimov, *Russia Gets the Blues: Music, Culture and Community in Unsettled Times* (2004)

Von Eschen, Penny M., *Satchmo Blows Up the World: Jazz Ambassadors Play the Cold War* (2004)

Vuic, Jason, *The Yugo: The Rise and Fall of the Worst Car in History* (2010)

Wang, Jing, *High Culture Fever: Politics, Aesthetics, and Ideology in Deng's China* (1996)

CHAPTER 9: SEARCH FOR THE SELF AND THE FALL OF COMMUNISM

Calhoun, Craig, *Neither Gods nor Emperors: Students and the Struggle for Democracy in China* (1997)

Garton-Ash, Timothy, *The Magic Lantern: The Revolution of '89 Witnessed in Warsaw, Budapest, Berlin, and Prague* (1990)

Kenney, Padraic, *A Carnival of Revolution: Central Europe, 1989* (2002)

*Kenney, Padraic, *1989: Democratic Revolutions at the Cold War's End: A Brief History with Documents* (2010)

Kotkin, Stephen, *Steeltown, USSR: Soviet Society in the Gorbachev Era* (1991)

Maier, Charles, *Dissolution: The Crisis of Communism and the End of East Germany* (1997)

McDermott, Kevin, and Matthew Stibbe, *Revolution and Resistance in East Europe: Challenges to Communist Rule* (2006)

Pfaff, Steven, *Exit-Voice Dynamics and the Collapse of East Germany: The Crisis of Leninism and the Revolution of 1989* (2006)

*Philipsen, Dirk, ed., *We Were the People: Voices from East Germany's Revolutionary Autumn of 1989* (1992)

Ramet, Sabrina P., *Balkan Babel: The Disintegration of Yugoslavia from the Death of Tito to the Fall of Milošević*, 4th ed. (2002)

Ramet, Sabrina P., *Social Currents in Eastern Europe: The Sources and Consequences of the Great Transformation*, 2nd ed. (1995)

Siani-Davies, Peter, *The Romanian Revolution of December 1989* (2006)

*Siegelbaum, Lewis H., and Daniel J. Walkowitz, *Workers of the Donbass Speak: Survival and Identity in the New Ukraine, 1989–1992* (1995)

Stokes, Gail, *The Walls Came Tumbling Down: The Collapse of Communism in East Europe* (1993)

Tismaneanu, Vladimir, *The Revolutions of 1989* (1999)

Wasserstrom, Jeffrey, and Elizabeth J. Perry, *Popular Protest and Political Culture in Modern China*, 2nd ed. (1994)

Weigel, George, *The Final Revolution: The Resistance Church and the Collapse of Communism* (2003)

Wheaton, Bernard, and Zdeněk Kavan, *The Velvet Revolution: Czechoslovakia, 1988–1991* (1992)

Zhao, Dingxin, *The Power of Tiananmen: State–Society Relations and the 1989 Beijing Student Movement* (2001)

CHAPTER 10: TAKING STOCK: RECKONING WITH COMMUNISM'S PASTS

Berdahl, Daphne, *Where the World Ended: Re-Unification and Identity in the German Borderland* (1999)

Berdahl, Daphne, Matti Bunzl, and Martha Lampland, eds., *Altering States: Ethnographies of Transitions in Eastern Europe and the Former Soviet Union* (2000)

Cooke, Paul, *Representing East Germany since Unification: From Colonization to Nostalgia* (2005)

Darnton, Robert, *Berlin Journal, 1989–1990* (1993)

Drakulić, Slavenka, *Café Europa: Life after Communism* (1989)

Drakulić, Slavenka, *How We Survived Communism and Even Laughed* (1993)

Forrester, Sibelan, Magdalena J. Zaborowska, and Elena Gapova, *Over the Wall after the Fall: Post-Communist Cultures through an East–West Gaze* (2004)

Garton-Ash, Timothy, *The File: A Personal History (1998)*

Goldberg, Vicki, *The Power of Photography: How Photographs Changed Our Lives* (1991)

Hochschild, Adam, *The Unquiet Ghost: Russians Remember Stalin* (2003)

Kelertas, Violeta, *Baltic Postcolonialism* (2006)

Kenney, Padraic, *The Burdens of Freedom: Eastern Europe since 1989* (2006)

Khald, Adeeb, *Islam after Communism: Religion and Politics in Central Asia* (2007)

Light, Duncan, and David Phinnemore, *Post-Communist Romania: Coming to Terms with Transition* (2001)

Ost, David, *The Defeat of Solidarity: Anger and Politics in Postcommunist Europe* (2006)

Paperno, Irina, *Stories of the Soviet Experience: Memoirs, Diaries, Dreams* (2009)

Roman, Denise, *Fragmented Identities: Popular Culture, Sex, and Everyday Life in Postcommunist Romania* (2007)

Steinberg, Mark D., and Catherine Wanner, *Religion, Morality and Community in Post-Soviet Societies* (2008)

Todorova, Maria Nikolaeva, ed., *Remembering Communism: Genres of Representation* (2010)

Verdery, Katherine, *What Was Socialism, and What Comes Next?* (1996)

Document List by Theme

EDUCATION

ETHNICITY, RACE, AND NATIONAL IDENTITY

FAMILY AND HOME LIFE

INTERNATIONALIZING THE REVOLUTION

LAW AND JUSTICE

RELIGION

RESISTANCE TO COMMUNIST STATES AND MOVEMENTS

SURVEILLANCE

WOMEN

Index